INDEPENDENT NATION

How Centrists Can Change American Politics

E PLURIBUS UNUM

JOHN P. AVLON

THREE RIVERS PRESS • NEW YORK

To Toula Carvelas Phillips and Alexander K. Phillips,
M.D. From Ellis Island to Ohio, my grandparents
have lived the American dream.

And to the New York City firefighters, police officers,
and emergency workers who gave their lives on
September 11, 2001, so that others might live.

Image of eagle on page iii from battle flag of Theodore Roosevelt's Rough
Rider Regiment; courtesy of Sagamore Hill National Historic Site.

Copyright © 2004 by John P. Avlon

All rights reserved.

Published in the United States by Three Rivers Press, an imprint
of the Crown Publishing Group, a division of Random House, Inc., New
York.

THREE RIVERS PRESS and the Tugboat design are registered trademarks
of Random House, Inc.

Originally published in hardcover by Harmony Books, a division of
Random House, Inc., in 2004.

Library of Congress Cataloging-in-Publication Data

Avlon, John P.
    Independent nation : how centrists can change American
politics / John P. Avlon.—1st ed.
Includes bibliographical references.
    1. United States—Politics and government—20th century.
2. Center parties—United States—History—20th century.
3. Politicians—United States—Biography.   4. Politicians—United
States—History—20th century.   I. Title.
    E743.A95 2004
    973.9—dc22   2003015543

Printed in the United States of America

www.crownpublishing.com

ISBN 1-4000-5024-3

10 9 8 7 6 5 4 3 2

First Paperback Edition

PRAISE FOR INDEPENDENT NATION

"A brave and compelling case for the past persistence and future dominance of American Centrism."

—Ed Kilgore, Policy Director of the
Democratic Leadership Council, in *Blueprint* magazine

"To Avlon Centrism is not a matter of compromise or reading polls; rather it's an antidote to the politics of divisiveness, providing principled opposition to political extremes."

—*Publishers Weekly*

"[John P. Avlon] writes brilliant . . . well-researched and wonderfully written stories about men of principle. . . . The stories are told with attention to detail, with wit and warm good humor, and they deserve to be read by anyone interested in the history of our country and the great ebbs and flows of political thought."

—*Poughkeepsie Journal*

"John Avlon has an encyclopedic knowledge of American politics past and present, and he is an intelligent, informed, and original thinker with views worth considering. His book is remarkably free of ideological rhetoric, partisanship, hatred for those with whom he disagrees, or condescension for the reader. *Independent Nation* may or may not change the way you think about politics, but it will make you think about what you believe."

—*Theodore Roosevelt Association Journal*

"Author John Avlon has made a significant contribution to the ranks of literature covering the middle of ideological thought."

—Gregsopinion.com

"In highly readable prose that is equal parts history, strategy, and manifesto, Avlon unites nearly two dozen profiles of politicians into a rewarding portrait of a political trend the established parties have tried to ignore. . . . The rise of this increasing militant majority of Centrists should scare the pants off the self-appointed kingmakers at the RNC and DNC."

—*Barron's*

BLESSED ARE THE PEACEMAKERS
FOR THEY SHALL CATCH HELL
FROM BOTH SIDES.

—Sign on the wall of the Justice Department office
of Burke Marshall, 1964

CONTENTS

Introduction
1

PART 1

THE INCUMBENT UNDER ATTACK
FROM BOTH SIDES
29

Theodore Roosevelt—1904
The Rough Rider Takes On the Robber Barons
33

Harry Truman—1948
The Man from Independence Fights a Three-Front War
56

The Rise and Fall of Jimmy Carter
Facing Ronald Reagan, John Anderson, and Ted Kennedy
in the Election of 1980
75

Governor Buddy Roemer—1991
A Reformer Falls to a Crook and the KKK in the Big Easy
96

PART 2

THE OPPOSITION CANDIDATE REACHES OUT

115

Woodrow Wilson—1912
A Progressive Beats the Party Bosses
119

John F. Kennedy—1960
An Idealist Without Illusions Charts a Cold-Warrior Course
137

Richard Nixon—1968
A Promise to "Bring Us Together"
162

Bill Clinton—1992
Leading the Democrats out of the Wilderness and into
the White House
187

PART 3

THE PRIMARY CHALLENGE:
REFORMERS VS. THE OLD GUARD

217

California Governor Earl Warren—1946
The Knight of Nonpartisanship Wins Both Primaries
222

Eisenhower vs. Taft—1952
The Internationalist vs. the Isolationist
241

Nelson Rockefeller vs. Barry Goldwater—1964
The Liberal Republican vs. an Advocate of "Extremism"
264

Daniel Patrick Moynihan vs. Bella Abzug—1976
The Neo-Con vs. the New Left
287

PART 4

DECLARATIONS OF INDEPENDENCE
311

Senator Margaret Chase Smith—1950
The Lady from Maine Stands Up to Joe McCarthy
315

Senator Edward W. Brooke—1973
Stuck in the Middle of the Civil Rights Movement
332

Radical Centrists
The Independent Governors of the 1990s
357
Governor Lowell Weicker of Connecticut
359
Governor Jesse Ventura of Minnesota
365
Governor Angus King of Maine
371

Rudy Giuliani—1997
An Independent Reformer Restores the Glory to Gotham
379

PART 5

ELECTION 2000
The Compassionate Conservative vs.
a Practical Idealist
and the Straight Talk Express
407

CONTENTS

Conclusion
432

Notes
451

Selected Centrist Bibliography
485

Acknowledgments
487

Index
490

INTRODUCTION

America is an independent nation. Born out of a war for independence, we instinctively distrust individuals who surrender their conscience and common sense to walk in lockstep with any ideological group or political party.

In his farewell address, George Washington warned future generations of Americans against "the baneful effects of the Spirit of Party," which "render alien to each other those who ought to be bound together by fraternal affection."[1] But over the past several decades, the Democratic and Republican parties have become increasingly identified with their most fundamentalist wings—the "religious right" and the "lifestyle left"—a relatively small number of extreme partisans who view their opponents as enemies and appear obsessed with imposing their beliefs on the rest of the American people.

At a time when political debate is too often dominated by the far left and the far right, Centrists cut an independent path between the extremes—putting patriotism before partisanship and the national interest before special interests.

Centrism is the rising political tide in modern American life: It wins elections, moves media cycles, and drives political realignments. In response to perceived extremism by the two parties, voters are increasingly rejecting rigid partisanship, embracing instead the political principles of independence and moderation. In 1980, just 36 percent of American voters defined themselves as moderates. By 2000, that number had risen to 50 percent—a moderate majority at a time when just 20 percent of voters describe themselves as liberal and 29 percent call themselves conservative.[2] In addition, Independents now outnumber Republicans or Democrats nationwide,[3] and 44 percent of Americans under thirty identify themselves as Independent.[4] Looking back on the past thirty years in American culture, sociologist Alan Wolfe was correct to say that "the right won the economic war, the left won the cultural war, and the center won the political war."[5] Now more than ever, the center of the political spectrum is the center of political gravity in the United States.

Centrism frees voters from the false dichotomies that dominate American politics by offering them a third choice between the rigid extremes of left and right, a commonsense path that acknowledges the inevitability of change while never straying far from fundamental American values or founding principles.

The *American Heritage Dictionary* defines Centrism as "the political philosophy of avoiding the extremes of right and left by taking a moderate position." But Centrism is far more than a collection of cautious gestures toward the middle ground. It is a principled political philosophy with a distinct set of political strategies and a distinguished history detailed throughout *Independent Nation*.

Centrism is the most effective means for achieving the classic mission of politics: the peaceful reconciliation of competing interests. Extremists and ideological purists on either side of the political aisle condemn compromise. But inflexibility either creates deadlock or dooms a cause to irrelevance.

Idealism without realism is impotent. Realism without idealism is empty. By effectively balancing idealism and realism, Centrism offers both a principled vision of governing and a successful strategy for winning elections.

Centrism is practical politics. With swing voters residing in the center of the electorate, appealing to the moderate majority of Americans is essential to winning an election. This underlying political logic of appealing to voters outside a party's traditional base was succinctly described by President Calvin Coolidge, who began his career as the Republican mayor of the dependably liberal Northampton, Massachusetts: "If a Democrat votes for me," Coolidge explained, "that's two votes, one less for my opponent and one more for me."[6]

Centrism can also provide a principled guide to governing. Centrist leaders are uniquely free to create new coalitions that bring overdue reforms into the mainstream, moving society forward instead of to the left or the right.

For example, the phrase "Nixon in China" has become shorthand for the strategic and substantive opportunities of Centrism. Only a lifelong anticommunist like Richard Nixon could have opened up relations with Communist China in the middle of the Cold War; if a liberal Democrat like George McGovern had tried the same thing, conservatives in Congress would have been screaming for his resignation. Likewise, only a Democrat like Bill Clinton could have signed fundamental welfare reform; if his Republican predecessors Ronald Reagan or George H. W. Bush had tried, there would have been widespread protests and the threat of riots in the streets of the inner city.

While liberals and conservatives perpetuate stereotypes by adopting shrill and predictable positions, Centrism undercuts assumptions rather than reinforcing them. This independence causes voters to reconsider their preconceptions, often resulting in broad popularity for Centrist leaders because they are seen as rising above the special interests of their own party, possessing the courage to act in the national interest.

Centrists represent the silent majority of the electorate, divided between two parties, and generally less organized than committed political activists. As a result, professional partisans have more than their share of influence over the selection of their party's candidates and platform. Consequently Centrist leaders have influential enemies within their own party as well as in the opposition.

This is just one of the constant threats that a Centrist leader must learn to navigate. *Independent Nation* offers insights from history on how some have succeeded where others failed.

Advocates of extremism on both sides of the American political aisle—the Al Sharptons and the David Dukes, the Henry Wallaces and the George Wallaces, or the Ralph Naders and the Pat Buchanans of any era—often argue that the rise of Centrism means the death of dissent.

That's missing the point. Centrism *is* dissent from the outdated political orthodoxies of the past. Centrists are constantly under attack from members of their own party for not predictably toeing the party line. In a political climate where compromise is criticized and rigid insistence on ideological purity is excused by some as a sign of individual courage, Centrism places a premium on finding solutions and reaching a common ground beyond partisan politics.

Centrists do not have to feel politically homeless; they have a history and a heritage. The Republicans have the elephant, the Democrats have the donkey, but the symbol for Centrism is the American eagle. Independent and patriotic, eagles don't fly in flocks; they soar over the American landscape, possessing, above all, a sense of perspective.

THE CENTRIST POLITICAL TRADITION

In the United States, as in all countries where the people reign, the majority rules in the name of the people. The Majority is chiefly composed of peaceful citizens who by taste or interest sincerely desire the well being of the country. They are surrounded by the constant agitation of parties seeking to draw them in and enlist their support.

—ALEXIS DE TOCQUEVILLE, *DEMOCRACY IN AMERICA*[7]

Determined to build an independent nation, our Founding Fathers distrusted the pull of extreme partisanship in domestic politics. George Washington wrote during the last year of his presidency, "I was no party man myself, and the first wish of my heart was, if parties did exist, to reconcile them."[8]

His successor, the second president of the United States, John Adams, frankly admitted: "There is nothing which I dread so much as a division of the republic into two great parties, each arranged under its leader, and concerting measures in opposition to each other. This, in my humble apprehension, is to be dreaded as the greatest political evil under our Constitution."[9]

During the debate on adopting the Constitution in 1788, Alexander Hamilton told the New York ratifying convention, "We are attempting by this Constitution to abolish factions, and to unite all parties for the general welfare."[10]

His fellow author of *The Federalist Papers* and future president, James Madison, also believed that one of the great benefits of a well-constructed union was "its tendency to break and control the violence of faction."* Madison blamed the failure of Pennsylvania's Council of Revision to the Constitution on the fact that the state was "violently heated and distracted by the rage of party."[11]

Thomas Jefferson also objected to the abandonment of reason and personal responsibility that comes with blind obedience to political parties, stating: "I never submitted the whole system of my opinions to the creed of any party of men whatever in religion, in philosophy, in politics, or in anything else where I was capable of thinking for myself. Such addiction is the last degradation of a free and moral agent. If I could not go to heaven but with a party, I would not go there at all."[12]

In Jefferson's first inaugural address as president, he aimed to heal the wounds inflicted during the campaign leading up to the nation's first peaceful transfer of power from the Federalists to the Democratic-Republicans: "Every difference of opinion is not a difference of principle. . . . We are all Republicans; we are all Federalists."[13]

It is significant that once political parties began to dominate every aspect of the political landscape, beginning with the rise of Vice President Martin Van Buren to the presidency in 1837, the party system ushered in an era of forgettable politicians serving as chief executive, and a devolution of national discourse into intraparty Machiavellian machinations. When the storms of civil war began to appear on the horizon, Daniel Webster declared, "The extremists of both parts of the country are violent."[14] The rise of faction proved as destructive and divisive as our Founding Fathers had feared.

Looking forward from his perch in the mid-nineteenth century, Ralph Waldo Emerson urged individuals to reject the limitations of the two-party system, saying that "each is a good half, but an impossible whole. Each exposes the abuses of the other, but in a true society, in a true man, both must combine."[15]

As Emerson anticipated, there has been a steady stream of leaders

---

*Madison helpfully explained that "by a faction, I understand a number of citizens, whether amounting to a majority or a minority of the whole, who are united and actuated by some common impulse of passion, or of interest, adverse to the rights of other citizens, or to the permanent and aggregate interests of the community." (*The Federalist Papers,* no. 10.)

who rose to prominence in large part because of their principled objections to extremism on the right and left.

There is a proud and distinct tradition of Centrism in American political life. Far from representing bland points of consensus, Centrism often represents significant acts of courage and integrity on the part of elected officials, who must go against their own party leadership if they are to follow their conscience. Because its advocates have sought to forge a new middle ground between the political orthodoxies of their day, the history of Centrism necessarily does not follow the path of any single political party. Instead, various pivotal figures throughout the twentieth century have appropriated this political ground to powerful effect. Its influence has grown as Centrism has proven to be the key to the White House for more than one occupant.

- In 1904, Theodore Roosevelt took on the Wall Street robber barons who considered themselves the backbone of the Republican Party and championed environmental conservation. As a result, he was rewarded with the greatest popular margin of victory since James Monroe's uncontested election in 1820.

- In 1912, Woodrow Wilson took advantage of deep divisions within the Republican Party to claim the progressive mantle for the Democrats, beginning an association that would continue through the New Deal.

- In 1948, the Man from Independence, Harry Truman, angered southern segregationist Democrats with his support of civil rights, as well as left-wing liberals who favored a policy of appeasement with Stalin's Soviet Union.

- In 1952, General Dwight D. Eisenhower rescued the Republican Party from irrelevance by rebuking isolationists and firmly committed the nation to a bipartisan foreign policy.

- In 1960, John F. Kennedy captured the White House by embracing a confident cold-warrior stance counter to the tweedy liberalism associated with Adlai Stevenson, cutting taxes and confidently asserting American values abroad.

- In 1968, with the nation divided and dispirited, Richard Nixon emerged from political exile to be elected president by campaigning on the message that "America needs to hear the voices of the broad and vital center."[16]

- In 1980, the election of Ronald Reagan over Jimmy Carter—who first campaigned on and then abandoned Centrism—was possible because of repeated calls for disaffected Democrats and Independents to cross party lines.

- In 1992, Bill Clinton's effort to disassociate the Democratic Party from its far left wing reclaimed the allegiance of moderate and middle-class voters, leading four years later to the first reelection of a Democratic president since FDR.

- In 2000, Clinton's political success spurred George W. Bush's drive toward the center, emphasizing inclusiveness in the 2000 election by offering a blend of Democratic and Republican policies packaged and sold under the Centrist slogan "Compassionate Conservatism."

Centrism is effective in large part because it appeals to the American ideal of a leader with an independent set of mind. These dynamic and galvanizing figures used their influence to preach common sense, accommodating change while remaining true to basic American values—and in turn they realigned American politics. As Eisenhower adviser Arthur Larson once wrote, "In politics—as in chess—the man who holds the center holds a position of unbeatable strength."[17]

American history demonstrates just as clearly that when either of the two parties becomes intoxicated by ideology and nominates a candidate associated with its most extreme wings, the result is defeat of epic proportions. For example, the candidacies of radical conservative Republican Barry Goldwater in 1964 and liberal Democrat George McGovern in 1972 each resulted in more than 60 percent of Americans voting against these apparent advocates of extremism.

The fundamental strength of the Centrist position remains much the same as it was in 1965—after LBJ's crushing defeat of Barry Goldwater—when the *New York Times* columnist James Reston wrote, "The decisive battleground of American politics lies in the center and cannot be captured from either of the extremes, and any party that defies this principle does not improve its chances of national power or even effective opposition, but precisely the opposite."[18]

THE REAL DANGER OF EXTREMISM

Ideology offers human beings the illusion of dignity and of morals while making it easier to part with them.

—VACLAV HAVEL, *THE POWER OF THE POWERLESS*[19]

Political parties are the servants of democracy, but too often they are treated like masters, as candidates contort their positions to ingratiate themselves with the powerful special interests. These extreme special interests still thrive on a tribal mentality excused by ideology that causes them to view society in terms of competing groups—black versus white, rich versus poor, "us" versus "them."

The religious right claims to love America but too often they sound like they hate Americans, rhetorically dividing the nation, demonizing groups who disagree with their agenda and attempting to impose their religious values on other people's lives through a combination of government action, court edict, and constitutional amendment.

Likewise, the lifestyle left is associated with moral relativism, an entitlement-based vision of society that "robs Peter to pay Paul," an obsessive search for signs of discrimination and victimization, and a blame-America-first approach to foreign policy.

These are not distant caricatures; the following are quotes from just two contemporary voices of the far left and the far right, each trying to find a partisan perspective on the attacks of September 11.

The Reverend Al Sharpton, who threw his hat in the ring for the 2004 Democratic presidential nomination, stated in a November 28, 2001, speech at the State of the Black World conference in Atlanta: "While the rest of the country waves the flag of Americana, we understand that we are not part of that. We don't owe America anything; America owes us."[20]

Likewise, televangelists Pat Robertson and Jerry Falwell offered their take on the meaning of September 11 on the Christian Broadcasting Network television show *The 700 Club,* taped on September 13, 2001, and broadcast on the Fox Family Channel.

JERRY FALWELL: ". . . what we saw on Tuesday, as terrible as it is, could be minuscule if, in fact—if, in fact—God continues to lift the curtain and allow the enemies of America to give us probably *what we deserve.*"

PAT ROBERTSON: "Jerry, that's my feeling. I think we've just seen the antechamber to terror. We haven't even begun to see what they can do to the major population."

JERRY FALWELL: "The ACLU's got to take a lot of blame for this."

PAT ROBERTSON: "Well, yes."

JERRY FALWELL: "And, I know that I'll hear from them for this. But, throwing God out successfully with the help of the federal court system, throwing God out of the public square, out of the schools. The abortionists have got to bear some burden for this because God will not be mocked. And when we destroy forty million little innocent babies, we make God mad. I really believe that the pagans, and the abortionists and the feminists, and the gays and the lesbians who are actively trying to make that an alternative lifestyle, the ACLU, People for the American Way—all of them who have tried to secularize America—I point the finger in their face and say, 'You helped this happen.' "[21]

These voices are alien to the vast majority of Americans, and yet they come from influential members of the Democratic and Republican parties—including two people who have run for their party's nomination to serve as president of the United States.

Pat Robertson* beat then–vice president George H. W. Bush and

---

*In case anyone is tempted to think that Robertson was a victim of Falwell's on-air enthusiasm in the above dialogue, it's worth looking at the following passage from his 1991 book *New World Order*, p. 227: "There will never be world peace until God's house and God's people are given their rightful place of leadership at the top of the world. How can there be peace when drunkards, drug dealers, communists, atheists, New Age worshipers of Satan, *secular humanists* [italics added], oppressive dictators, greedy money changers, revolutionary assassins, adulterers, and homosexuals are on top?"

Senate Republican leader Bob Dole in the 1988 Iowa straw poll of Republican presidential candidates, and four years later was given a prime-time speaking slot at the 1992 Republican Convention in Houston. Al Sharpton's 2004 presidential campaign was predicated upon urging the Democratic Party to move further to the left. Despite his inflammatory role in the racially charged Tawana Brawley hoax, his indictment for tax fraud, and the fact that he has never held elected office, Sharpton plays a self-appointed king-maker role in New York City that local Democrats—including the Clintons—feel obligated to indulge.

The center of the political spectrum holds these divisive voices at equal distance. Centrists have no patience with advocates of intolerance; neither do they give in to the demands of demagogues. As Senator John McCain bravely stated during the 2000 campaign, "Neither party should be defined by pandering to the outer reaches of American politics and the agents of intolerance, whether they be Louis Farrakhan or Al Sharpton on the left, or Pat Robertson and Jerry Falwell on the right."[22]

The most important reason to oppose the presence of extremism in politics is also the most obvious: Hate leads to violence. Extremists invariably preach hate because it's easy to blame others for problems; this solidifies support among the already insecure faithful, but it can be murder on the rest of society. As Eric Hoffer wrote in his book *The True Believer,* "Hatred is the most accessible and comprehensive of all unifying agents. . . . Mass movements can rise and spread without belief in a God, but never without belief in a devil."[23]

Extremists on opposite sides of the ideological spectrum feed off one another and provide justification for each others' existence. In this respect, politics follows the basic laws of physics: "For every action, there is an equal and opposite reaction." The presence of one political extreme encourages the creation of an equally rabid opposition.

For example, the rise of the Nazis in Germany was predicated upon the threat of the Communist Bolsheviks in Russia; Hitler was accepted by many middle-class Germans and wealthy Westerners as a check upon the violent social revolution that Lenin and Stalin planned to export. By the 1930s, there were an estimated 6 million

Communists in Germany, and the militant Union of Red Fighters was promising German supporters that they would make "every comrade a commander in the coming Red Army!"[24] The fear of an invading ideological force fueled Hitler's rise and provided the measure of public support needed for his power grab to succeed. He understood this; after the 1933 fire at the Reichstag, he turned to a reporter and said, "God grant that this is the work of the Communists. You are witnessing the beginning of a great new epoch in German history."[25] In turn as the Second World War escalated, the KGB recruited students to spy for the Soviet Union by inducing them to join the Anti-Fascist League, referred to coldly by KGB supervisors as the "Innocents' Clubs."[26] Anger toward the opposite extreme provided the best recruiting tool for both Nazis and Communists, although history has proven that there was ultimately no moral difference in the effects these ideologies had on the human race. As Arthur Schlesinger Jr. wrote a half century ago in *The Vital Center,* "The totalitarian left and the totalitarian right meet at last on the murky grounds of tyranny and terror."[27]

Likewise, on a thankfully far-smaller scale in the United States, the Nation of Islam and the American Nazi Party—while theoretically dedicated to each others' destruction—shared a belief in racial separatism and opposition to integration. Consequently, in June of 1961, twenty American Nazi storm troopers in uniform approvingly attended a Nation of Islam rally to hear Malcolm X give a speech titled "Separation or Death." The following year, Nazi leader George Lincoln Rockwell brought more followers to hear Nation of Islam founder Elijah Muhammad speak in front of twelve thousand supporters at the Chicago International Amphitheater. Rockwell liked what he heard so much that he put a $20 bill in the collection plate and gave a short speech assuring the assembled that "no American white desires to intermix with black people."[28] Later, Rockwell dreamed of expanding his affiliation with the Nation of Islam, writing party members, "Can you imagine a rally of American Nazis in Union Square protected from Jewish hecklers by a solid phalanx of Elijah Muhammad's stalwart black stormtroopers?"[29] How can this surprising solidarity between apparently opposite, although equally hateful, ideological factions be explained?

Imagine watching a walled city. At first glance, there appears to be a left and a right on either side of the city's main gate. But the walls circle back upon one another and the appearance of left and right is really an illusion. The far left and the far right end up blending into one another; they are ultimately the same thing. White separatist movements and black separatist movements are equally threatened by the vision of pluralism that American society represents. So, too, the geopolitical extremes of left and right ideologies—Communism and Fascism—ended up as mirror images of each other, murderous totalitarian dictatorships despite their heated claims that they represented opposite visions of humanity.

"There is more that binds us to Bolshevism," Hitler once admitted, "than separates us from it."[30] Each extreme preached the necessity of submerging the independent conscience to the larger ideological movement. "True Bolshevik courage," said Stalin, "does not consist in placing one's individual will above the will of the Comintern. True courage consists in being strong enough to master and overcome one's self and subordinate one's will to the will of the collective, the will of the higher Party body."[31] This was echoed by Hitler's chief propagandist, Joseph Goebbels, who darkly explained, "To be a [national] socialist, is to submit the I to the thou; socialism is sacrificing the individual to the whole."[32] These ideological extremes shared a telltale belief that the individual is not the essential building block of society, and that all independent actions are selfish if they defy the will of the party.

After the attacks of September 11, ideological extremism had a new face, and a new chapter began in the age-old conflict between freedom and fundamentalism. Fundamentalist extremists have been murdering moderates to derail the prospects of peace in the Middle East for decades, most starkly with the assassinations of Egypt's president Anwar Sadat by Islamic extremists and Israeli prime minister Yitzhak Rabin by a right-wing Israeli gunman. Now this extremist violence has come to our shores. But as essayist Paul Berman recounts in his book *Terror and Liberalism,* the rhetoric of Islamic extremists is strikingly similar to the exhortations of Hitler and Stalin. He quotes Algerian Islamic Salvation Front leader Ali

Benhadj telling his followers: "Principles are reinforced by sacrifices, suicide operations and martyrdom for Allah."[33] This is the language of extremism taken to its ultimate conclusion, the small but decisive step from being willing to die for an ideology and being willing to kill for it.

We have faced this enemy in other incarnations before: like Fascists and Communists, Islamic extremists believe that the essential diversity of American democracy makes us weak and can be exploited. Like the generations of patriots from both parties before us, we need to stand up to their challenge united. While other nations spent much of the twentieth century wrestling with the competing demons of ideological extremism, the United States remained largely committed to a Centrist path of steady progress: faithful to freedom, free markets, and democracy. In an age of murderous ideology, American democracy and individualism stood like a steady beacon between Communism and Fascism. The terrorists preaching Islamic extremism will fail for the same reason that Communism and Fascism failed so completely before it: The essential diversity of human life will not be crushed into a crude ideological cage. Centrism, like democracy itself, incorporates change—ultimately making society more stable and more just. By favoring unity over division and evolution to revolution, Centrism slows the swing of the pendulum between the extremes.

THE RISE OF INDEPENDENTS

The future lies with those wise political leaders who realize that the great public is interested more in Government than in politics. . . . The growing independence of voters, after all, has been proven by the votes in every Presidential election since my childhood—and the tendency, frankly, is on the increase.

—FRANKLIN D. ROOSEVELT, 1940[34]

In the more than sixty years since FDR predicted the rise of independence in the American electorate, analysis of congressional voting records shows that Washington has grown more polarized, driven by ideology and disdaining compromise, than at any time in the recent past.[35]

This trend has especially been on the increase since the election of Ronald Reagan in 1980, and continued to grow with the anti-Clinton fervor of the 1994 Newt Gingrich–led Republican Revolution. As columnist George Will has written: "Some ideologically intoxicated Republicans think Democrats are not merely mistaken but sinful. . . . Some Democrats, having lost their ideological confidence, substitute character assassination for political purpose."[36]

This polarization has been cemented by redistricting—creating safe congressional seats for incumbents to occupy without the built-in check and balance of a credible opposition candidate. Currently, 90 percent of congressional seats are considered "safe." Once upon a time in America, people chose their congressmen; now congressmen choose their people.

As Congress has grown more partisan, however, the electorate has grown steadily more Centrist, with the number of self-identified moderates rising from a bare plurality of 36 percent in 1980 to 50 percent in 1998 and 2000. At the same time, the number of Americans who are reluctant to identify themselves completely with either political party has been steadily rising.

In the mid-twentieth century, party identification was a badge of honor. According to the National Election Studies program at the University of Michigan, fifty years ago 47 percent of voters identified with the Democrats and 28 percent with the Republicans, while just 23 percent were independents. In the year 2000, however, those numbers were almost reversed, with 40 percent of American voters describing themselves as independents, 34 percent as Democrats, and 24 percent as Republicans.[37]

Only 23 percent of Americans agreed that "the two-party system works fairly well,"[38] while another study found that just 14 percent of the electorate said they always supported the candidates of a single party.[39] This willingness to vote for candidates from different parties is another indication of independence and the corresponding inclination toward Centrism. It amounts to a civil statement of discontent with the two dominant choices and their divisive approach to common problems. Centrism is civility.

Not coincidentally, as our professional politicians have become more partisan, Americans have reacted by voting in a new era of divided government, balancing the power of the president with a Congress from the opposite party for all but six years since 1980. The object of these voting patterns is not a wish for gridlock, but pursuit of the implicit assurance that extremists in one party will not be able to hijack the national legislative agenda. Likewise, there is a presumption that with a balanced government the best ideas from both parties will be the only legislation able to be passed. It is an instinctive extension of the constitutional principle of checks and balances, an attempt to moderate excesses in an excessively partisan era.

The steadily growing ranks of independent voters constitute a quiet revolution, and it is growing: This independent plurality becomes even more pronounced when you look at the politics of younger Americans. Again, fully 44 percent of those aged eighteen to twenty-nine identify themselves as Independents.[40] Demographics are destiny.

"This old left-right paradigm is not working anymore," remarks author Douglas Coupland, who coined the term "Generation X" with his 1992 novel of the same name. "Coming down the pipe are an extraordinarily large number of fiscal conservatives who are socially left."[41]

This independence from the traditional dogmas of left and right finds its political expression in Centrism. Centrism accommodates a healthy degree of skepticism about the predictable rhetoric and rigid policy solutions ideologues offer for every problem, while offering individuals the freedom to choose the best ideas from either of the two parties. Because Centrist leaders are not slaves to ideology or party policy, they have a higher degree of freedom to speak their mind and find the best solution to any given problem.

This commonsense perspective led to the election of Maine's popular and successful two-term Independent governor Angus King. He was one of a group of Independent governors—including Connecticut's Lowell Weicker and Minnesota's Jesse Ventura—who were elected in the last decade of the twentieth century. All were reformers who believed in fiscal responsibility and social inclusiveness, and they rode to office campaigning against the ideological straitjacket imposed by the two-party system.

"It's becoming more acceptable for voters to consider Independent candidates, and they're collecting more and more votes," admitted the National Republican Senatorial Committee's former political director David Carney. "People aren't sticking to just the two major party candidates as they once did."[42]

Whereas in the past Independent third-party candidacies were driven by individuals representing the far left or the far right—for example, Henry Wallace's Soviet-sympathizing Progressive Party campaign for the presidency in 1948, or George Wallace's segregationist American Independence Party campaign in 1968—there is an undeniable trend in the last several decades toward Independent candidates running as Centrists. They feel, as much of the public does, that the two political parties are increasingly controlled by their partisan extremes and special interests. They are compassionate but antibureaucratic, socially inclusive but fiscally responsible. They are fed up with politics as usual and determined to shake up the system. These Independent voices and Independent voters are on the rise as America moves increasingly toward the center.

THE MODERATE MAJORITY

It is only common sense to recognize that the great bulk of Americans, whether Republican or Democrat, face many common problems and agree on a number of basic objectives.

—DWIGHT D. EISENHOWER[43]

The majority of the American people believes broadly in the same political principles, but what Colin Powell has called "the sensible center" is still divided down the middle between the two parties. Former

Minnesota governor Jesse Ventura was not wrong when he estimated that "you have the far left at 15 percent, you have the far right at 15 percent, and there's 70 percent of us in the center."[44]

People who define themselves as liberal Republicans or conservative Democrats essentially support the same policy positions on major issues. But the will of the majority of the American public is divided, and thus diluted, as more partisan voices devote themselves to the maintenance of their party's apparatus. As a result, partisan political professionals have more than their share of influence over the selection of their party's candidates and platform despite the fact that they are out of touch with mainstream American opinion.

Centrism is not an abstract or academic concept. It is a common-sense balance between idealism and realism intuitively understood by most Americans. With 50 percent of the electorate defining itself as moderate, chances are you are a Centrist.

If, for example, you describe yourself as fiscally conservative but liberal on social issues, you are a Centrist. You are uncomfortable associating yourself with the extreme wings of either political party. You may consider the liberal left wing of the Democratic Party naive and irresponsible, supporting out-of-control entitlement programs, and diminishing personal responsibility by encouraging politically correct bureaucracies. On the other hand, the exclusionary attitudes, big-business bias, and rigid-right-wing social agenda advocated by some conservatives may make you reluctant to call yourself a Republican.

You are too liberal to be a conservative, but too conservative to be a liberal. You are a Centrist.

Centrists reject the "two-party, two-policy" straitjacket that is too frequently applied to every foreign and domestic problem. The third way between the two extremes is usually the most reasonable and practical course of action. It is certainly the most popular—66 percent of American voters "favor solutions that come from the political center," rather than the political right (13 percent) or left (8 percent).[45] Here are some examples of the Centrist position versus the political positions of the left and the right.[46]

LEFT POSITION	CENTRIST POSITION	RIGHT POSITION
We should not pass a tax cut because we have other, more important priorities, like expanding health-care coverage and reducing poverty.	**W**e should pass a tax cut, but only one that will let us maintain a balanced budget, secure Social Security and Medicare, and pay down the national debt.	**W**e should pass deep tax cuts in order to both provide tax relief and maintain a strong economy.
Government should remain neutral on values issues but protect individual rights such as the right to have an abortion and the right of gays to serve openly in the military.	**G**overnment should reinforce mainstream values and provide parents with the tools they need to reinforce their personal values, but government should also be tolerant of diversity and not impose a particular moral code on people.	**G**overnment should promote stronger values by allowing prayer in schools, opposing special rights for homosexuals, and banning abortion.
We need government to make a greater commitment to ensure strong public-education and health-care systems for all Americans and a strong safety net for those for those who need it, even if it means bigger government.	**G**overnment should create opportunity for all citizens, but those who receive benefits needs to live up to certain obligations and give something back to their country in return.	**T**he size of the government should be reduced by cutting taxes, and the free market should be allowed to work unencumbered by government interference.

    The traditional choice between "Brand A" and "Brand B" of partisan political positions in a two-party system is false. There is an alternative to rigid adherence to the scriptures of the left and right. Centrism is rooted in the individual conscience and bridged by common sense; it is free to borrow the best ideas from the two parties without being weighted down by obligations to the special interests that inevitably form the base of any partisan political organization.

There is in fact a growing consensus on supposedly controversial issues that frequently are used by extremists on either side of the political aisle to divide political parties and the American public.

PRO-CHOICE: Sixty-four percent of Americans agree that the decision to have an abortion should be between "a woman, her doctor, her family, her conscience and her God" (Luntz Research Companies, August 2003). As the Gallup Organization explains on their website, reflecting on decades of data: "In part because Americans support the idea of individual choice, they do not want to ban abortion." A *CBS News/New York Times* question asked in 1982 and again in 1998 shows even larger majorities (68 and 76 percent, respectively) opposed to an amendment to the Constitution that would make all abortions illegal. Moreover, only 19 percent of Americans think that abortions should be illegal in all circumstances, a number that has held steady since the passage of *Roe v. Wade* (Gallup/*Newsweek* Historical Poll available at gallup.com). This is an overwhelming popular rejection of the Republican Party platform's perpetual call for a constitutional ban on abortion.

PRO-ENVIRONMENT: Seventy-five percent of Americans favor stronger enforcement of environmental regulations, including higher emission and pollution standards for business and industry (Gallup Poll, March 2003), while only 10 percent believe that government is doing "too much" in terms of protecting the environment (Gallup Poll, April 2000). The vast majority of the American people believe that environmental protection is an important basic responsibility of government that should be reasonably built upon, not cut back.

BALANCED BUDGET: Sixty-seven percent of Americans believe that the fact that the United States will have federal budget deficits for the foreseeable future is either "a crisis" or "a major problem"

(Gallup/CNN/*USA Today* Poll, January 2003). Seventy percent of Americans prefer a balanced budget to more tax cuts (*CBS News* Poll, February 2002), and 53 percent would give up their tax cuts to balance the budget (*CBS News* Poll, February 2002). Sixty-three percent of Americans believe that we "should work to maintain a balanced budget consistent with our values" (Penn & Schoen, July 1998).

REASONABLE GUN CONTROL: Sixty-nine percent of Americans agreed with the statement "I believe in the right to bear arms, but I am willing to put up with a registration or waiting period" (*Newsweek* Poll/Princeton Survey Research, September 1995). In 2003, this same question was polled again with precisely the same results, showing that 69 percent of Americans continue to agree with this sensibly Centrist position (Luntz Research Companies, August 2003). In a Gallup Poll conducted in October 2000, 59 percent of respondents favored a law making it illegal to own semiautomatic weapons.

SCHOOL PRAYER: Sixty-nine percent of Americans agree with the statement "I have no problem with a quiet moment, but I'm against any stricture that says 'You will pray.' " (*Newsweek* Poll/Princeton Survey Research, September 1995). This poll was updated eight years later by the Luntz Research Companies (August 2003), again showing similar results: Sixty-three percent of Americans continue to agree that a quiet moment should be permissible, but reject the idea of mandatory prayer in public. In addition, an overwhelming 84 percent of Americans opposed the contested federal court ruling that the phrase "Under God" in the Pledge of Allegiance was unconstitutional (Gallup Poll, June 2002). Americans don't want religion imposed upon them *or* unreasonably forced out of the public realm by activist lawsuits.

CAMPAIGN FINANCE REFORM: Seventy-three percent of Americans support stricter laws controlling the way political campaigns can raise and spend money (*ABC News/Washington Post* Poll, March

2001). Seventy-two percent favor a ban on "soft money" (CNN/*USA Today*/Gallup Poll, October 2000). Most significant, even after the long-blocked passage of the McCain-Feingold campaign finance legislation, 72 percent favor passing additional campaign finance laws (Gallup/CNN/*USA Today* Poll, February 2002). The vast majority of Americans continue to want to limit the influence of big money on our democracy.

TAX SIMPLIFICATION: Sixty-six percent of Americans believe the federal tax system is too complicated (Associated Press Poll, March 1999). Seventy-eight percent of Americans believe that a maximum of 30 percent of a person's annual income should go to taxes (*Fox News*/Opinion Dynamics Poll, January 2003), while 60 percent of all Americans across party lines believe that everybody should pay income taxes on the same percentage of their income over a minimum level (Harris Poll, March, 1999).

BILINGUAL EDUCATION REFORM: Sixty-three percent of Americans support English-intensive immersion programs over bilingual education programs that teach students in their native language (Gallup Poll, May 1998). A Zogby poll conducted in October–November 2000 shows an overwhelming 77 percent support for immersion nationwide. Most significant, 76 percent of all Latinos and 79 percent of Spanish-speaking immigrants support immersion (Zogby International, May 2001). Immigrants and all Americans recognize the basic need for a common currency of communication.

TORT REFORM: Seventy-four percent of Americans think that the issue of medical malpractice insurance in health care today is a major problem or crisis (Gallup Poll, January 2003). Fifty-seven percent believe patients initiate too many lawsuits (Gallup Poll, January 2003). Spiraling insurance costs combined with a cumulative impact of decades of news stories about frivolous lawsuits and multimillion-dollar damage decisions and settlements make it likely that some reasonable cap on damages will become increasingly identified with the common good.

These are positions supported by a clear majority of the American public, but neither political party even attempts to bring this balance of policy positions together. As Harvard political scientist David C. King explains, "Both political parties have been growing more extreme . . . they are increasingly distant in their policies from what the average voter would like."[47] Neither party entirely represents the interests of these voters, in part because they still are influenced by the ideological relics of the Industrial Age. In contrast, Centrism is attuned to the realities of voters in the Information Age.

Centrism is not merely about finding a middle ground between any two opposing ideas or issues. Centrism is about cutting a decisive and consistent path through the partisan politics that artificially divide policies and the American public.

For example, it is far more philosophically consistent to support school choice* and be pro-choice on the issue of abortion if you believe in max-imizing individual freedom of choice. But neither political party attempts to bridge these policies; it is considered political heresy. What's stopping them is the influence of special interests that drives the parties off center. As the founder of the Democratic Leadership Council, Al From, once despairingly said, reflecting on the Democrats' inability to embrace education reform, "We had become the party of teachers, when we should have been the party of education."[48]

The center of the American electorate is fiscally responsible and socially inclusive. The center is pro-choice and pro-environment, and believes in being tough on crime and pursuing balanced budgets while reducing the influence of big money on politics. It opposes absolutist stands on school prayer and gun control, instead seeking a reasonable middle ground that addresses realistic concerns without unduly sacrificing individual freedom. This distrust of extremes is a codification of what George Will called "the most important four words in politics . . . 'up to a point.' "[49]

---

*School choice entails giving low-income families with children in chronically failing public schools a voucher equivalent to their allocation of public school tax dollars so they can choose whether to send their child to a private or parochial school. School choice programs have been declared constitutional by the Supreme Court and a 1999 poll by the Joint Center for Political and Economic Studies showed that 70 percent of African-Americans under the age of thirty-five support school choice.

"Moderation and tolerance—an appreciation of the modest virtues—are the bedrock moral principles of the American middle class," wrote sociologist Alan Wolfe in his study *One Nation, After All*. "On most controversial issues, Americans instinctively try to find the centrist position between two extremes *and* attempt to carve out private spaces in which people can do what they want so long as others do what they want."[50]

When we look for the original principles that support these positions, we find the faces of Thomas Jefferson and Abraham Lincoln staring back at us. The common ground of the Centrist consensus appears to be based on the oldest of American formulations: Thomas Jefferson's motto of "equal opportunity for all; special privilege for none." When considering what consensus can be formulated for the proper role of government, few articulations do better than Lincoln's famous dictum: "The legitimate object of government is to do for a community of people whatever they need to have done, but cannot do at all, or cannot so well do, for themselves—in their separate, and individual capacities. In all that the people can individually do as well for themselves, government ought not to interfere."[51]

In typical Centrist fashion, the American public wants to believe in a party of both Jefferson and Lincoln, one that is motivated above all by a sense of generational responsibility. Unless the two major parties are irretrievably hijacked by their most extreme elements and a stable Centrist third party emerges, we will have to depend on Centrist political leaders, who combine the best elements of both parties and, through their willingness to move free of special interests and apart from partisan politics, remind us that America is an independent nation.

A FEW WORDS ON THE FORM AND CONTENT OF *INDEPENDENT NATION*

Independent Nation is a collection of heroes' journeys and cautionary tales, politics as history in the present tense—an essentially human drama.

It is not intended to be a formal work of political science. I'm not convinced that politics is a science; at its best it is an art, and at its worst it is something like a war. But in all cases, success is its own proof, and history remains the best teacher. There are four classic contexts that Centrist leaders must learn to navigate, and the book is organized into four primary sections accordingly.

PART I, "THE INCUMBENT UNDER ATTACK FROM BOTH SIDES." Centrist political leaders in office—such as Theodore Roosevelt in 1904 and Harry Truman in 1948—often find themselves criticized by both the opposition party and members of their own party's extreme wing who accuse them of abandoning the interests of the party faithful.

PART 2, "THE OPPOSITION CANDIDATE REACHES OUT." Young Centrist leaders—such as JFK in 1960 and Bill Clinton in 1992—often face the challenge of leading their party back to the White House after years in the wilderness. They understand that the only way to do so is by expanding their party's appeal and directly addressing perceived weaknesses, but they meet resistance from the old guard as well as the opposition party in the process.

PART 3, "THE PRIMARY CHALLENGE: REFORMERS VS. THE OLD GUARD." In times of interparty turmoil, Centrist reformers frequently wrestle in a primary contest with ideological hard-liners, as was the case with Eisenhower versus Robert Taft in 1952, Nelson Rockefeller versus Barry Goldwater in 1964, and Daniel Patrick Moynihan versus Bella Abzug in 1976. Even when these contests result in failure for the insurgent, they permanently change the inner-party landscape and lay the seeds for future realignment.

PART 4, "DECLARATIONS OF INDEPENDENCE." Centrists often find themselves at odds with the dominant voices in their party, and many—such as Senator Margaret Chase Smith and Senator Edward Brooke—have spoken out at pivotal times in our nation's history. Rudy Giuliani challenged an entrenched partisan bureaucracy and showed a generation of mayors how to reduce crime and improve the quality of life in urban America. Other Centrist leaders find themselves stranded outside the two-party system altogether and increasingly run as Independents to preserve their integrity and freedom.

Some of these Centrist candidacies led to victory, others fell to the forces aligned against them. But in all cases, there is much to be learned from the mistakes that were made as well as from the successful strategies employed.

It may surprise some readers that this book includes the stories of people who failed in their attempt to run or govern as a moderate. But the study of losses can be as worthwhile as analyses of strategic successes. After all, unless we learn from the mistakes of history, we will be doomed to repeat them.

There are great stories to be told in political history, stories that illustrate the drama of our choices and their consequences, stories of individuals struggling against the group, and the comparative difficulty of uniting people instead of dividing them. Political history can also help shed light on the possibilities in our own lives. These are the stories of individuals doing their best against seemingly insurmountable odds. Their lives are our legacy.

Each biographical sketch attempts to communicate a sense of the character of the individual, the contours of his or her personality and the tone of the times in which he or she lived. It is impossible to comprehensively document the life of a political leader within the span of twenty pages. Therefore, I tried to stay with what is strictly relevant and let details flesh out an individual's character. Excessive ruminations on scandal and personal life have been left out, unless they directly impacted the individual's political effectiveness at the time in question.

This work is intended to popularize existing history that has languished in the shadows while ideologically driven analyses gain the most attention. Many academics make a good living avoiding the obvious, and the typical historian is usually interested in advancing broad theories, causing individual human experience to become subservient to academic theory. I've tried to understand the subjects as their contemporaries saw them and as they saw themselves. Happily for the subject of Centrism, few people proudly consider themselves ideologues or extremists—although these individuals certainly do exist. Most of all, it was my modest aim to write a book that is not only enjoyable and informative, but also inspiring and useful.

Centrism springs from the revolutionary idea that neither political party has a monopoly on good ideas. Accordingly, Centrism requires a healthy degree of skepticism that can stop ideologues and would-be dictators at the gates. It asks that we all—to paraphrase Benjamin Franklin—doubt a little bit in our own infallibility.

I should offer some definitions of the language used in *Independent Nation* to help the reader get a sense of the geography of Centrism. Professor Ted Lowi of Cornell University believes that the word "extreme" is too pejorative to be accurate. He prefers to use the word "radical." According to Professor Lowi's linguistic definitions, there are no extremists in American politics, just ideological purists who occasionally use extreme tactics—such as violence—to publicize their cause. While Professor Lowi's reasoning has its advocates, I firmly believe that language is our servant and not our master; to be useful, it has to be understood.

The word "radical" was happily appropriated by California surfers and skate punks beginning in the 1980s. I don't think there's much point in trying to academically reclaim it to describe ideological zealots. So as subjective as the term "extremist" may be, I'm going to use it to describe members of the far-right and far-left wings of the political spectrum, people who analyze life through the inflexible lens of ideology and romanticize extremes of order and disorder. These are the folks Winston Churchill was describing when he said that "a fanatic is one who can't change his mind and won't change the subject."[52]

Some readers will also note that I've chosen to use the word "Centrist" instead of "moderate" to describe those whose principled political philosophy causes them to stand between the extremes. This is, of course, not an accident. "Moderate" carries with it an unfortunate connotation of inactivity, a noncommittal defense of the status quo. "Centrist" is a decidedly more vigorous word, implying decisiveness and momentum. That is appropriate, because Centrists do not simply seek a safe middle ground between extreme political movements; they are problem solvers who combine the best ideas from both political parties to move society forward toward responsible reform—meeting the challenges of a changing world while remain true to fundamental American principles.

One of the great problems for Centrists in the past was that they felt politically homeless, adrift without a coherent sense of their political heritage. I hope that this collection of biographical sketches can serve as a hymn rooted in history to the spirit of reason, reconciliation, and balance that Centrism can bring to American politics, so that we do not lurch to the left or the right, but move forward as our Founding Fathers intended—as one independent nation.

PART 1

THE INCUMBENT UNDER
ATTACK FROM BOTH SIDES

Things fall apart; the centre cannot hold; . . .
The best lack all conviction, while the worst
Are full of passionate intensity.

—W. B. YEATS, "THE SECOND COMING," 1919[1]

*W*hen Centrists reach high elected office, they face a far wider array of opposition than conventional candidates who can always depend on the allegiance of the hard-core partisans in their own party. Liberals on the far left and conservatives on the far right each try to deny Centrist leaders legitimacy in office because their reforms represent a direct challenge to the special interests that make up the base of both parties.

As the Centrist incumbent reaches out to the center of the electorate, he or she runs the risk of losing touch with his or her party's base of supporters. As an old political saying warns, "Those who do not watch their base, better watch their back." The key to surviving this high-stakes, high-wire act is to proactively set the terms of the debate while being willing to work with moderates of both parties. The Centrist incumbent must define the special interests he or she is eager to take on in the name of the public interest. There will, of course, be challenges, but the bully pulpit of any public office has inherent advantages. A lack of defined direction, however, can be deadly.

In 1904, Theodore Roosevelt ran for election in his own right to an office he had inherited after the assassination of President William McKinley. Within months of assuming the presidency,

Roosevelt began to take action on what he regarded as one of the great threats of the age. The Industrial Revolution led to concentrations of great wealth in comparatively few hands, while poverty among the laborers grew deeper and more desperate. Roosevelt felt that this growing gap needed to be moderated for the long-term health of the nation. He took on the big-business base of the Republican Party, and while he earned the fury of many powerful people, in the process he won the admiration of the vast majority of Americans, who saw his willingness to fight beyond partisan conventions as a sign that he was an honorable and uncommon leader. To gain the support of the reasonable edge of the opposition, TR praised the essential contributions of entrepreneurs, making the case that the best way to save the integrity of capitalism was by moderating its excesses. In the process, he helped ensure that socialism never gained a foothold in the United States. This principled political stand was rewarded with the greatest popular mandate of any president up to that point. By reaching beyond the traditional base of the Republican Party, he gained the allegiance of moderates and independents, Democrats as well as Republicans, and helped realign American politics well into the future.

Likewise, Harry Truman found himself isolated in the White House after the death of Franklin Delano Roosevelt. The New Deal coalition forged by FDR fell apart as Truman's support for civil rights led to a revolt by southern segregationists, while his resolve to face down the expansionist ambitions of Stalin caused many on the left to desert him. Virtually no one believed that Harry Truman could be elected in his own right in 1948. But the benefits of incumbency are powerful. Harry Truman was able to call the Eightieth Congress into a special session to test the Republicans' commitment to their moderate political platform that ran counter to their conservative congressional record. Truman defined himself in opposition to his chosen opponents with the help of energetic campaigning, surprising everyone with the greatest come-from-behind political victory in American history.

Other incumbents caught in the middle have been less lucky. Jimmy Carter rode into the White House on a wave of popular discontent with politics as usual after Watergate weakened the Republican Party and faith in American political institutions in general. Carter was in many ways conservative, promising fiscal responsibility as well as a compassionate administration. But Carter's good intentions got lost in the transition from candidate to incumbent. He picked unnecessary fights with the Democratic-controlled Congress, and was forced to watch as his ambitious but unprioritized legislative agenda stalled on Capitol Hill and he became ill-defined in the public's mind. In 1980, while seeking re-election, he found himself challenged by the sole remaining brother of the Kennedy clan, while Ronald Reagan fought for the Republican nomination in the name of conservatives, and John Anderson offered an Independent's protest candidacy. Reagan was far more charming and optimistic than previous standard-bearers of the conservative cause. In addition, he was careful after receiving the nomination to surround himself with moderate leaders of the party, picking the moderate George H. W. Bush to serve as his running mate. While Carter floundered—neither fish nor fowl in the voters' eyes—Reagan reached out to disaffected Democrats and Independents, quoting FDR three times in his speech accepting the Republican nomination, creating the "Reagan Democrats" phenomenon that would persist throughout the 1980s. In contrast, it is not surprising that the term "Carter Republicans" never made it into the American vernacular.

Finally, in an absurd case that illustrates the dangers of cannibalistic culture politics, a young Democratic reform governor of Louisiana named Buddy Roemer lost momentum and lost touch with his populist base. Four years later, while running for reelection as a Republican, he found himself knocked off his perch by unlikely assailants that included a disgraced former governor, Edwin Edwards, and former Klu Klux Klan grand wizard David Duke. The center could not hold amid the high-water mark of voter dissatisfaction, and the entire nation then held its breath as

Louisianians were forced to choose between Edwin Edwards and David Duke for governor, spawning bumper stickers that memorably read "Vote for the crook. It's important."[2]

Centrist political leaders in office attempt to walk a road of integrity and reform that causes them to take on entrenched special interests. But the broad public interest is guarded less jealously than special interests—as Yeats warned, "The best lack all conviction, while the worst/Are full of passionate intensity"—and thorough bulwarks must be built to stop special interests from undermining the integrity of an incumbent reformer's administration. In politics, as in sports, a good offense is the best defense.

THEODORE ROOSEVELT — 1904

THE ROUGH RIDER TAKES ON THE ROBBER BARONS

NO MOLLY-CODDLING HERE

(This is the prevailing Wall Street notion of
President Roosevelt's attitude toward corporate interests.)

From the *Globe* (New York)

We Republicans [must] hold the just balance and set ourselves as resolutely against improper corporate influence on the one hand as against demagogy and mob rule on the other.

—THEODORE ROOSEVELT[1]

The former president began to speak with a bullet lodged in his chest.

Less than five minutes before, a deranged gunman had shot Theodore Roosevelt at close range as he walked to give a speech on behalf of his bid to recapture the White House in 1912 as a Progressive. Aides insisted that Roosevelt head straight to the hospital, but flush with a sense of destiny, the old lion refused. He would not retreat; he would give this speech if it killed him. With the bloodstain spreading against his white shirt, he began:

> I have altogether too important things to think of to feel any concern over my own death. . . . I am ahead of the game anyway. No man has had a happier life than I have led. . . .

This effort to assassinate me emphasizes to a peculiar degree the need for the Progressive movement . . . every good citizen ought to do everything in his or her power to prevent the coming of the day when we shall see in this country two recognized creeds fighting one another, when we shall see the creed of the "Have-nots" arraigned against the creed of the "Haves" . . .

My appeal for organized labor is two-fold; to the outsider and the capitalist I make my appeal to treat the laborer fairly . . . That is one-half of the appeal that I make. Now, the other half is to the labor man himself. My appeal to him is to remember that as he wants justice, so he must do justice.[2]

Theodore Roosevelt was publicly issuing his political last will and testament, standing his ground on the idea that societal division between special interests could mean suicide for the American experiment.

As president, TR had used the full weight of the White House to reign in the power of big business while also instituting reasonable reforms on behalf of organized labor. It was his belief that "constructive change offers the best method of avoiding destructive change . . . reform is the antidote to revolution."[3]

Extremists on either end of the spectrum detested him, but TR's studied independence—especially his defiance of the Wall Street robber barons who considered themselves the backbone of his Republican Party—led directly to his landslide victory of 1904 and made him one of the most popular presidents in American history.

Roosevelt was a man of action who preached the virtue of "the strenuous life"—"I believe in men who take the next step, not those who theorize about the two-hundredth step,"[4] he said—and his politics defied easy categorization. He sometimes described himself as a "conservative radical,"[5] who was devoted to keeping "the left of center together."[6] As one contemporary explained, "Neither reformers nor bosses were satisfied . . . but this fact only confirmed him in the notion that he was steering a course equally safe from the mercenary rocks on the one side and the doctrinaire shallows on the other."[7]

In happy times, Roosevelt found the fervor of his critics on the left and the right amusing. Energetically dismissing them, he coined the term "lunatic fringe."[8] Even after the presidency, Roosevelt joked that opponents regarded him as "a kind of modified anarchist . . . hesitating only whether to denounce my speeches as containing only platitudes, or being incitements to revolution. . . . They may fall into either category but they can't fall into both."[9]

In both his private and public lives, Theodore Roosevelt transcended all labels. His friend the nature writer John Burroughs said that "Roosevelt was a many-sided man and every side was like an electric battery."[10] TR was a Harvard-educated son of the aristocracy, but his character was forged by tragedy and the Badlands of North Dakota. Omnivorously intelligent, he was the first true Renaissance man in the White House since Thomas Jefferson: soldier, statesman, scholar, politician, police commissioner, preservationist, and prolific author of over thirty books. He made himself president by the age of forty-two.

His best-known personal motto—the West African proverb "Speak softly and carry a big stick"—reflected TR's belief in balancing the idealism of peaceful diplomacy with the realism of overwhelming military strength. He remains beloved by modern conservatives for his strong advocacy of American military expansion. Yet he did more than any previous president to implement a progressive domestic agenda. He was a devout believer in military might who won the Nobel Peace Prize, a proud hunter of wild game who helped found the modern conservation movement, a reformer among politicians, and a politician among reformers.

What his critics never understood is that those contradictory qualities—along with his exuberant personality—were the key to his love affair with the American public and the reason why he remains so admired on both sides of the political aisle today.

Before there was a name for it, Centrism was the source of his popular support and political strength. In the words of historian John Morton Blum, "Roosevelt defined for himself an imprecise line between the 'lunatic fringe' he detested and the 'selfish rich' he despised. Equally to each of these extremes he was anathema. To many of the wholly sane but more impatient reformers he seemed insincere. To the inert he seemed mad. Most of early-century America, however, agreed with or at least voted for his Square Deal."[11] As his biographer Edmund Morris stated, "In situations involving extremes, Roosevelt's instinct was to seek out the center."[12]

Theodore Roosevelt began life as a sickly boy born into privilege three years before the Civil War, son of a southern mother and a northern father. His father, Theodore Sr., taught him that to overcome the considerable challenges of ill health and chronic asthma, he would have to "get action" and embark upon a relentless process of self-improvement. Through sheer force of will, monotonous exercises dutifully performed over a period of months and years, Roosevelt slowly gained physical strength. He extended that spirit of self-improvement to every aspect of his life. TR later wrote, "There were all kinds of things I was afraid of at first, ranging from grizzly bears to 'mean' horses and gun-fighters, but by acting as if I was not afraid I gradually ceased to be afraid."[13]

The roots of TR's rugged brand of independent reform politics are apparent in his early life. Roosevelt idolized his father, and when his father was passed over for a prominent appointed post, Roosevelt Sr. wrote in a letter to his son, "The 'Machine politicians' have shown their colors. . . . I feel sorry for the country . . . as it shows the power of partisan politicians who think nothing higher than their own self-interests."[14] This contempt for party bosses would be handed down from father to son.

Beyond his father, the man Roosevelt most admired was Abraham Lincoln, who was president during his childhood. TR's later assessment of Lincoln provides a similar window to the political instincts that would define his career. "Lincoln," Roosevelt wrote, "was a great radical, but a wise and cautious radical. From all his record it is safe to say that if Lincoln had lived to deal with our complicated social and industrial problems, he would have furnished wisely conservative leadership; but he would have led in the radical direction."[15] As president and after, TR would attempt to be the restrained agent of the radical changes in society that he believed were inevitable.

After attending Harvard, sustaining the crushing blow of his father's death but falling in love with a beautiful Boston girl named

Alice Hathaway Lee, Theodore decided to embark upon a career in politics. At the time, many of his classmates viewed politics with distaste, as a lowly career for ambitious saloon keepers. But Roosevelt thought their objections soft and haughty; he was determined to be part of "the governing class."

He ran for the New York State Assembly from a wealthy district on the East Side of Manhattan. Impressed by his father's good name and the precocious energy of the young candidate, residents sent young TR to Albany in 1881. Like children of the Victorian era, first-term assemblymen were supposed to be seen and not heard, but Roosevelt immediately set about attacking not only the Democrats from New York's notoriously corrupt Tammany Hall but the political bosses from his own party as well. He heartily criticized the assembly's atmosphere of "narrow and bitter partisanship," writing his sister that "most of the members are positively corrupt, and the others are singularly incompetent."[16] Referring to a member of his own Republican Party's leadership, Roosevelt wrote that he had "the same idea of public life and civil service that a vulture has of a dead sheep."[17] From the outset, Roosevelt made it clear that he was a reformer before he was a Republican. In the process, he made himself into the leader of the young reformers of both parties in the assembly.

Republicans were widely seen to represent the interests of the rich. Roosevelt toured tenements with Samuel Gompers, and purposefully set about sponsoring bills that benefited the poor sweatshop workers and tenement dwellers in the rapidly expanding metropolis. It was his intention to bring the Republican Party away from the defense of special privilege and to the forefront of progressive reform. To that end, he brought impeachment charges against a prominent judge for colluding with the multimillionaire Jay Gould and tried in vain to reduce the influence of the Tammany Hall machine in electing aldermen in New York City. He was more successful in achieving civil service reform by crossing party lines to form a coalition with the Democratic governor—and future president—Grover Cleveland.*

---

*Like Roosevelt, Grover Cleveland had a reputation for determination and uncommon honesty in pursuit of reform. "A Democratic thief is as bad as a Republican thief," the fellow New York governor and future president would sensibly say. (Philip B. Kunhardt et al., *The American President* [New York: Riverhead Books, 1999, p. 361].)

Roosevelt's career as a crusading young Manhattan politician was proceeding smoothly. He was reelected to his seat with nearly twice the number of votes as in the previous election, despite a general Democratic sweep of the state. His outspoken independence helped him to stand out and gain widespread support beyond party labels. Despite being blocked in a precocious bid to serve as Speaker of the Assembly, he was getting action in the direction of his father's beloved social gospel of good works.

Then, on Valentine's Day 1884, the sun suddenly sank on Theodore Roosevelt's charmed life. His wife, Alice, and his mother, Martha, both passed away suddenly, Alice after giving birth to their first child. The baby girl, also named Alice, was baptized the day after her mother was buried. Grief-stricken, Roosevelt wrote in his diary that "for joy or sorrow, my life has now been lived out."[18] As newspapers recorded the tragedy in hushed tones, Theodore sought refuge in action—throwing himself into his work like a man possessed, writing, "I think I should go mad if I were not employed."[19] It was evidence of a personal philosophy of dealing with grief memorably expressed in his phrase "Black care rarely sits behind a rider whose pace is fast enough."[20]

Even in despair, his high-voltage personality shone through the surrounding gloom. Inspiring friends and followers alike, he was a natural leader who would not allow himself to be isolated on the fringes of political life. Typical was journalist William Allen White's breathless account of his first meeting with TR: "I went hurrying home from our first casual meeting . . . he poured into my heart such visions, such ideals, such hopes, such a new attitude towards life and patriotism and the meaning of things as I never dreamed men had . . . it was youth and the new order calling youth away from the old order."[21]

Roosevelt's determination to break free of the constraints of the old order almost led him to renounce the Republican Party while he was still a young man. At the 1884 presidential convention, the Republicans nominated Maine's James G. Blaine, who had been widely accused of accepting bribes from the railroad industry. Roosevelt aggressively opposed Blaine's nomination and put forward the name of the comparatively virtuous Vermont senator

George F. Edmunds. When Blaine and the Republican bosses proved victorious, Roosevelt impulsively threatened to leave the party while speaking to a reporter from the *New York Evening Post*. Positioning himself as leader of the independents, Roosevelt reportedly said that he was ready to leave the Republican Party, adding that "any proper Democratic nomination will have [the independents'] hearty support."[22]

But for all of Roosevelt's frustration with the old guard in the Republican Party, corruption in the Democratic Party—particularly within New York City—was worse. Roosevelt harbored a deep contempt for the corruption of Tammany Hall and would never consent to forming an alliance with Boss Tweed's machine. Roosevelt's friend Henry Cabot Lodge convinced him to campaign for the Republican ticket during the 1884 election, but TR spoke on behalf of the party, avoiding any mention of the name James G. Blaine.

Two-thirds of Roosevelt's fellow independent Republican objectors left the party in response to Blaine's nomination. TR's ultimate refusal to do so reflected the pragmatism that would make him president while earning him the enmity of many fellow reformers. He believed that the best way to be an effective reformer was to work within the imperfect bounds of the Republican Party organization. He later explained that "I am a loyal party man, but I believe very firmly that I can best render aid to my party by doing all that in me lies to make that party responsive to the needs of the state, responsive to the needs of the people, and just so far as I work along those lines I have the right to challenge the support of every decent man, no matter what his party may be."[23] Until he formed the Progressive Party, Roosevelt would remain a party man, equal parts realist and reformer.

Still healing a broken heart, Roosevelt went into self-imposed exile, living the life of a rancher in the Badlands of North Dakota. The barren earth seemed to reflect his interior landscape, while the long days of physical labor helped him exorcise his soul. In time, he gained enough perspective to begin to contemplate a return to public service. He was coaxed back to Manhattan in 1886 by the prospect of running for mayor.

A lengthy campaign letter was composed on Roosevelt's behalf by the good-government group Committee of One-Hundred, addressed to "The Independent Voters of New York." The letter proclaimed that "Theodore Roosevelt is our candidate for Mayor, nominated by us on the simple platform of an honest and energetic city administration, entirely disconnected from national and state politics. In response to the demand of his own party to stand as its representative, he declares that reform is impossible 'except through the unsparing use of the knife wielded by some man who could act unhampered by the political interests which sustain the present abuses.' "[24]

In his first major campaign, Roosevelt was running on his independence from special interests and the political bosses in both parties. In Tammany Hall–controlled New York City, Roosevelt lost by over thirty thousand votes, but his taste for political combat was revived. He soon found the heart to remarry—a childhood friend by the name of Edith Carrow—and in subsequent years, TR distinguished himself by serving as civil service commissioner in the Democratic administration of President Grover Cleveland, as New York City police commissioner, and as assistant secretary of the navy in the Republican administration of President William McKinley. He was willing to serve presidents of either party as long as he was given the freedom and authority to do his job honestly and effectively.

Always a believer in American military intervention, when war broke out with Spain over its control of Cuba, Roosevelt resigned from his administrative post and volunteered for active duty, stating that "if I am to be any use in politics, it is because I am supposed to be a man who does not preach what I fear to practice."[25] He created a handpicked regiment of cowboys and college friends, known as the Rough Riders, and led them during the victorious charge at the Battle of San Juan Hill.

His well-documented heroism led to his election as governor of New York in 1898 and, two years later, his nomination to be President William McKinley's vice presidential running mate. Establishment Republicans such as the influential Ohio senator Mark Hanna howled at the selection, asking all who would listen,

"Do you realize that there is but one life between that madman and the presidency?"[26]

Their worst fears were, of course, realized. Within seven months of the inauguration, President McKinley was assassinated and Theodore Roosevelt became the youngest man ever to serve as president of the United States. His first day in the White House fell on what would have been his father's sixty-seventh birthday. "It is a dreadful thing to come into the presidency this way," Roosevelt wrote, "but it would be a far worse thing to be morbid about it."[27]

From his first hours in office, he was urged to restrain his well-known independence. His brother-in-law Douglas Robinson wrote him a letter after a meeting with the panicked Republican State Committee chairman, a Mr. Dunn: "I feel I must be frank . . . [if] when you start you will give the feeling that things are not to be changed and that you are going to be conservative . . . it will take a weight off the public mind. Mr. Dunn told me today that either he or I must get to you to impress upon you the fact that you must, no matter how much you are pressed and badgered, be as close-mouth and conservative as before your nomination for governor."[28]

TR initially tried to calm conservatives' fears. But once the markets stabilized and the party was unified behind the young president, the man derided by critics as "His Accidency" set about implementing his ideals and recasting the party and the nation in his own image.

The first president to ride in a car, an airplane, and a submarine and to travel abroad, TR would also be the first to wrestle with the challenges of the twentieth century amid near-constant opposition from both Republicans and Democrats in Congress, as he looked toward 1904 and election in his own right. In the decades before Roosevelt reached the presidency, the nation had been transformed from a rural republic to an industrialized nation on the edge of becoming a world power. Now, struggles between labor and big business, smoldering racial tensions, and the problem of preserving the wilderness all demanded to be addressed.

The threats were real. An anarchist's bullet had claimed the life of his predecessor, and the winds of revolution that would culminate with the Russian Revolution of 1917 had begun to blow across the industrialized world. The unregulated trusts, and the "malefactors of great wealth"[29] who controlled them, were operating as monopolies that killed competition and assumed power at least equivalent to that of the federal government. But Wall Street barons continued to feel a sense of relative invulnerability as long as a Republican was in the White House. They were in for a rude awakening.

Roosevelt used the occasion of his first formal message to Congress in December of 1901 to sound an evenhanded but still unsettling call for a more equitable balance between free enterprise and corporate responsibility.

> The captains of industry . . . have on the whole done great good to our people. Without them the material development of which we are so justly proud could never have taken place. . . . Yet it is also true that there are real and great evils . . . there is a widespread conviction in the minds of the American people that the great corporations known as Trusts are in certain of their features and tendencies hurtful to the general welfare. This is based upon sincere conviction that combination and concentration should be, not prohibited, but supervised and within reasonable limits, controlled; and in my judgment, this conviction is right.[30]

Roosevelt was concerned that if industrialization's excesses were not moderated through democratic evolution, then socialist revolution would find a fertile ground to sprout in the United States. "The more we condemn unadulterated Marxian Socialism," he wrote, "the stouter should be our insistence on thoroughgoing social reforms."[31]

Roosevelt decided to take a shot across big business's bow and chose the biggest target available: J. P. Morgan, a legendary international investment banker who at the time controlled resources with greater value than the entire contents of the U.S. Treasury. Morgan and his partners had consolidated power over the railroads in the Pacific Northwest, forming a trust known as Northern Securities that was valued at more than $400 million, at a time when the average wage for working Americans was roughly $750 a year. Roosevelt quietly ordered his attorney general to proceed with a federal lawsuit prosecuting Northern Securities under the Sherman Anti-Trust Act. "Neither this nor any other free people will permanently tolerate the use of the vast power conferred by vast wealth without lodging somewhere in the government the still higher power that seeing that this power is used for and not against the interests of the people as a whole," Roosevelt reasoned.[32]

Now the plutocrats were under attack by the White House they had previously depended on to defend them from populist attacks. Republicans in Congress and in the cabinet were offended that they had not been consulted about Roosevelt's directive. No warning had been given. This was, by the standards of the day, an outrage—a violation of the unspoken agreement between wealthy gentlemen.

Morgan rushed to Washington to discuss the matter with the president personally, protesting that "if we had done anything wrong, send your man [meaning the attorney general] to my man [one of Morgan's army of lawyers] and they can fix it up."[33] But Roosevelt was resolute—there was a new sheriff in town; the era of special privileges for special interests was over.* One journalist dryly reported that "Wall Street is paralyzed at the thought that a President of the United States would sink so low as to try and enforce the law."[34]

The president's problems with conflicts between big business and labor were far from over. In the summer of 1902, blood was flowing in the hills of northeastern Pennsylvania, where 150,000 anthracite coal miners had walked off the job. At first few took notice, but eleven weeks into the strikes frustrations erupted into vio-

---

*After a lengthy legal battle, in March of 1904, the Supreme Court affirmed the president's action by a vote of 5–4 and declared the Northern Securities merger illegal. During the course of Roosevelt's term, he took on other trusts controlling beef, sugar, and tobacco. But he left other corporate consolidations—such as U.S. Steel and General Electric—alone. TR's intention was not to derail private industry, but to moderate the excesses of the age and direct entrepreneurial energies to the general benefit of society. "I believe in corporations," Roosevelt wrote. "They are indispensable instruments of our modern civilization. But I believe they should be so regulated that they shall act for the interest of the community as a whole."

lence; by October, the clashes between strikers and the proxies of management had claimed no less than seven lives amid sixty-seven violent assaults. The menace of mob rule loomed as mines were flooded and bridges blown up. Many people feared that this marked the first stirrings of a socialist revolution in America. Pennsylvania's governor gave his National Guard troops orders to shoot to kill at the first sign of violence.

Amid the first chills of winter, with the possibility of no coal to heat homes, calls for a settlement had a new urgency. In New York City, schools were closed because there was no coal. With elections looming, Republican politicians protested to the president that the public's anger would be felt in that fall's congressional elections. The governor of Massachusetts told Roosevelt in no uncertain terms that "unless you end this strike, the workers in the North will begin tearing down buildings for fuel."[35]

Roosevelt's conservative advisers argued that he had no constitutional responsibility to intervene. But TR believed that "the Constitution was made for the people, and not the people for the Constitution,"[36] and decided to act. Few held out hope that there would be a peaceful and speedy resolution. No president had ever mediated a strike personally, and the last person in whom labor leaders expected to find an ally was a Republican in the White House.

Nonetheless, on the morning of October 3, representatives of labor and the mine owners themselves pushed past swarms of reporters and were led into a second-floor conference room, where they were seated at a circular wooden table. Roosevelt greeted them warmly with a wave of his hand, and then the normally extemporaneous president began to read a carefully worded statement: "I wish to call your attention to the fact that there are three parties affected by the situation in the anthracite trade—the operators, the miners, and the general public. I speak neither for the operators nor the miners, but for the general public."[37]

TR instinctively sought a Centrist solution to the first great crisis of his presidency—urging the agents of special interests to act in the national interest. But despite his commitment to finding a middle path between extreme positions, the talks soon hit an impasse.

Roosevelt felt frustrated at the lack of progress his personal involvement had been able to achieve. In a letter to Henry Cabot Lodge, he wrote: "Unfortunately the strength of my public position before the country is also its weakness. I am genuinely independent of the big monied men in all matters where I think the interests of the public are concerned, and probably I am the first President of recent times of whom this could be truthfully said. . . . I am at my wits' end how to proceed."[38]

Again, TR's thoughts turned toward Lincoln's precedent in search of guidance. His language is telling of his Centrist political faith: "Just as Lincoln got contradictory advice from the extremists of both sides . . . so now I have to carefully guard myself against the extremists of both sides."[39]

Arbitration—a negotiated settlement by a neutral third party—proved the solution to navigating the rocky shoals between the competing interests on both sides. It had been proposed by labor representatives but rejected by the owners. Then Roosevelt forced the owners' hand by taking the unprecedented step of readying federal troops to nationalize and operate the coal mines in the absence of an agreement. News of this "big stick" was quietly leaked to the business leaders, who promptly decided that an arbitration commission was acceptable after all. But they cautioned that only individuals acceptable to them would be allowed to sit on the commission. Big business was attempting to stack the deck.

The coal mine owners proposed a five-member panel composed of government officials, businessmen, and one "eminent sociologist," but no representative of labor. Roosevelt countered by offering to expand the commission to seven people and took advantage of their insistence of a sociologist by proposing that Edgar Clark, chief of the Railway Conductors' Union, fill that slot—justifying the move by asserting that as a union executive, "Mr. Clark must have thought and studied deeply on social questions."

Roosevelt was amazed at the ease with which the executives accepted this compromise: "I found that they did not mind my appointing any man, whether he was a labor man or not, so long as he was not appointed as a labor man. . . . I shall never forget the mixture of relief and amusement I felt when I thoroughly grasped the fact that while they would heroically submit to anarchy rather than have Tweedledum, yet if I would call it Tweedledee they would accept it with rapture."[40]

In the end, the arbitration panel was formed, the coal miners went back to work, and the Republicans held on to control of Congress. In March, a settlement was reached that gave the workers a 10 percent raise and restricted their work to nine hours a day—but, for the time being, their union was not recognized. While Wall Street again grumbled that the young president's independence revealed an antibusiness bias, Roosevelt confided to a friend, "I wish the labor people absolutely to understand that I set my face like flint against violence and lawlessness of any kind on their part, just as much as against arrogant greed by the rich. . . ."[41]

Roosevelt's balanced but decisive action established him as a different kind of Republican, one who not only limited the power of the trusts but defended the legitimate rights of labor. No side received a perfect victory, but it was a definite step forward both for workers and for the activist model of the presidency. As Roosevelt later remarked, "The insistence upon having only the perfect outcome often results in securing no betterment whatever."[42]

Labor crises were evidence that the United States was no longer a frontier nation. The end of the frontier also meant that the presence of wild open land could no longer be taken for granted in America.

Then, as now, business interests and their representatives in Congress opposed setting aside valuable land beyond the reach of development. As a onetime rancher, Roosevelt understood the struggle of farmers to tame the land and the importance of giving them the assistance they needed to make a living. But he was also among the first men in high political office who understood that the remaining wilderness would need to be protected for future generations.

Even in the infancy of the environmental movement there was a contentious divide between the conservationists and the preservationists. Conservationists believed in the inevitability and desirability of planned *use,* whereas preservationists would settle for nothing less than maintaining the absolutely pristine state of nature as it was found. TR characteristically opted for a third way.

TR was a committed wise-use conservationist, someone who believed that the wilderness existed for man's benefit and enjoyment. "Conservation means development as much as it does protection," he said. "I recognize the right and duty of this generation to develop and use the natural resources of our land; but I do not recognize the right to waste them, or to rob, by wasteful use, the generations that come after us."[43]

Acting on his belief that "there is nothing more practical in the end than the preservation of beauty,"[44] Roosevelt used the bully pulpit of the presidency, issuing executive orders to set aside millions of acres, including the Grand Canyon, and establishing the U.S. Forest Service. During his first full year in office, Roosevelt increased the amount of federally protected land by a third.

Despite his willingness to go it alone, Roosevelt was also a practical politician who believed in working with Congress whenever possible. After much lobbying and personal persuasion, TR convinced Congress to pass the Reclamation Act of 1902, which ultimately added irrigation to 3 million acres of arid wilderness in the West. In a telling letter to the Republican chairman of the House Appropriations Committee and future Speaker of the House Joseph Cannon, the most powerful anticonservationist in Congress, TR pleaded its case in uncommonly personal terms:

My Dear Mr. Cannon:

I do not believe that I have ever before written to an individual legislator in favor of an individual bill, but I break through my rule to ask you as earnestly as I can not to oppose the [National Reclamation Bill]. Believe me this is something of which I have made a careful study, and great and real though my deference is for your knowledge of legislation and your attitude in stopping expense, yet I feel from my acquaintance with the Far West that it would be a genuine and rankling injustice for the Republican Party to kill this measure. . . . I cannot too strongly express my feeling on this matter.

Faithfully yours, Theodore Roosevelt.*

---

*This letter can be found in Edmund Morris, *Theodore Rex* (New York: Random House, 2001), p. 114.

Roosevelt prided himself on his independence from party bosses, but after spending a life in politics, he appreciated the strategy that went into achieving the power needed to bring about lasting good. As he scanned the map of the United States, his fondest political wish was to break the Democrats' stranglehold on the South.

The "Party of Lincoln" had not been welcome in the South since the Civil War, but Roosevelt's resolutely national perspective—combined with respect for his mother's southern roots—made him want to reduce sectional divisions by expanding his party's reach. Booker T. Washington, head of the Tuskegee Institute, was the most prominent African-American leader of the time, and shared with Roosevelt the belief that strengthening the Republican Party through patronage in the South could lead to improved conditions for blacks and an organized antilynching movement rooted in the federal government. But when Washington was invited to have dinner with Roosevelt in the White House, neither anticipated the outpouring of hatred it would provoke.

While some congratulatory telegrams trickled in, southern newspapers such as the *Memphis Scimitar* described it as "the most damnable outrage which has ever been perpetrated by any citizen of the United States." One-eyed South Carolina senator Benjamin "Pitchfork" Tillman declared that their meeting would only hasten the pace of lynchings, that "the action of President Roosevelt in entertaining that nigger will necessitate our killing a thousand niggers in the South before they will learn their place again."[45] (Tillman would later be banned from the White House by Roosevelt for having a fistfight on the floor of the Senate.)

When reporters asked the president whether he would have Booker T. Washington to dinner at the White House again, Roosevelt indignantly replied, "I shall have him to dinner just as often as I please." Three weeks later, he wrote a friend that "the only wise and honorable and Christian thing to do is treat each black man and each white man strictly on his merits as a man . . . while I am in public life, however short a time it may be, I am in honor bound to act up to my beliefs and convictions."[46]

Roosevelt subsequently appointed an African-American to serve as the collector for the Port of Charleston—the body of water where the Civil War had begun—over strenuous opposition in the Senate, but his dreams of realigning the South were dashed. Southern Democrats such as newspaper publisher and Mississippi governor James Vardaman began uniting the white vote—rich and poor—around populist racism and hatred of Roosevelt. As 1904 approached, the Democrats had a plan to keep the South in their column: Buttons were printed up showing Roosevelt and Booker T. Washington sitting down together at dinner. The button's printed slogan—"Social Equality"—was enough of a veiled threat to keep the Republican vote in the minority down in Dixie.[47]

Southern whites were not the only faction aligned against Roosevelt as the 1904 campaign began. A syndicate of Wall Street interests was offering a million dollars to establishment Republican leader Mark Hanna if he would run for president against the young reformer.[48]

Roosevelt anticipated this challenge: "As the time for the presidential election of 1904 drew near," he later wrote, "it became evident that I was strong with the rank and file of the party, but that there was much opposition to me among many of the big political leaders, especially among many of the Wall Street men."[49]

The buzz was that the president was "not safe," that he was an impulsive reformer and an unacceptable risk. Secretary of War Elihu Root, a McKinley holdover, addressed these concerns directly in a speech to a wealthy New York crowd, admitting freely: "He is 'not safe' for the men who wish to prosecute selfish schemes for the public's detriment. He is 'not safe' for the men who wish the government conducted with greater reference to campaign contributions than the public good." But because of his willingness to meet the public's desire for overdue reforms, Root continued, "I say that he has been, during the years since President McKinley's death, the greatest conservative force for the protection of property and our institutions."[50] The initially skeptical audience erupted into applause.

The "knockdown and drag-out fight with Hanna and the whole Wall Street crowd"[51] Roosevelt anticipated never fully materialized, as the aging Hanna resisted calls for a 1904 campaign and then fell ill with typhoid fever. Now standing alone in the Republican arena, and magnanimous in victory, TR visited the ailing senator's bedside and asked the old man's advice.

As the two men reconciled, their supporters were also forced to bury their deep distrust. But when Hanna passed away the Republican National Committee left no question as to who they considered their leader: Inside the Chicago auditorium where the nominating convention was being held, a seven-foot-wide and twenty-foot-tall portrait of Senator Mark Hanna dwarfed the speaker's platform. On the walls of the convention hall, there were no fewer than twenty-eight other pictures of Hanna gazing down on the proceedings. In contrast, pictures of President Roosevelt were virtually nowhere to be seen. But in all other evident respects, Republicans began to get in line behind their party's progressive nominee. The power of the presidency left them little choice. Even Wall Street, courted by Roosevelt's commerce secretary turned campaign manager, George Cortelyou, began to give contributions to the man they had caricatured as a devil just months before—in their eyes, a Republican president, however radical, was far preferable to a populist Democrat who wanted to take the United States off the gold standard.

Roosevelt's progressive reforms had also succeeded in stealing the thunder away from the Democratic Party's traditional populist claims. William Jennings Bryan complained bitterly that Roosevelt had stolen the best ideas Bryan had popularized during his campaigns in 1896 and 1900. TR swiftly replied: "So I have. That is quite true. I have taken every one of them except those suited for the inmates of lunatic asylums."[52]

By incorporating the Democrats' message in a more moderate and responsible manner, Roosevelt made the urgency of their calls for a change in government seem irrelevant—an unnecessary deeper leap into the unknown. After all, this Republican reformer did protect the legitimate rights of labor and reigned in the powers of the trusts, while championing environmental conservation. Roosevelt had acted on his belief that "this country would not be a permanently good place for any of us to live in unless we make it a reasonably good place for all of us to live in," and achieved what in the hands of another man would have been radical change, but he did so through determined conservative means.

Lacking any ability to define themselves in opposition to the president with Bryan, the Democrats nominated the conservative New York judge Alton Parker, a dour man with eyes resembling those of a suspicious walrus. The *New York Sun* described Parker as having all "the salient qualities of a sphere,"[53] while his eighty-two-year-old running mate, Henry G. Davis, was dismissed as "a reminiscence from West Virginia."

But Parker was able to generate enthusiasm for his candidacy when he abruptly announced that the Democratic platform would change the party's controversial, decades-long insistence on abandoning the gold standard. Roosevelt immediately recognized the political wisdom of Parker's shift to the right as "a bold and skillful move."[54] Conservative papers still searching for an alternative to the reform-minded Roosevelt, including the *New York Times,* the *New York Herald,* the *New York Evening Post,* and the *Springfield Republican* also applauded Parker's decision. Each of these papers had endorsed McKinley four years before; now they endorsed the stand-pat conservative Democrat over the independent Republican reformer.

Parker's unexpected step away from Bryan and the populists proved to be his campaign's high point. The judge was a candidate from another time, reluctant to travel, insisting on conducting a passive front-porch campaign more suited to the nineteenth century. Roosevelt was restrained by the tradition that said that sitting presidents must appear disinterested in their reelection, but he still found time to visit the Revolutionary War headquarters at Valley Forge, pay his respects to Stonewall Jackson's widow in Richmond, and speak at the Civil War cemetery where his hero Lincoln had offered up the Gettysburg Address.[55]

As summer turned to fall, TR's prodigious energy and established record overwhelmed the staid Judge Parker. The nation trusted a Republican reformer more than a conservative Democrat. Distant cousin Franklin Delano Roosevelt spoke for many young Democrats when he explained that he had crossed party lines to vote for TR because "he was a better Democrat than the Democratic candidates."[56] Likewise, even stalwart conservative Roosevelt critics, such as the Wall Street–friendly *New York Sun,* offered their reasoned, if reluctant, support. The *Sun*'s editorial endorsement—titled "Theodore, with All Thy Faults"—read in part: "We prefer the impulsive candidate of the party of conservatism than the conservative candidate of the party which the business interests regard as permanently and dangerously impulsive."[57]

Roosevelt's "strenuous moderation," his advancement of progressive causes through conservative means, left Republican Party leaders and radical Democratic reformers frustrated. Although he may have alienated Americans on the extreme ends of the political spectrum, he had gained the affection of the vast majority of Americans who believed that their president was an honest and independent man acting in their best interests.

On Election Day 1904, their approval was unprecedented. Theodore Roosevelt was elected president in his own right in a landslide. With thirty-three of the forty-five states in the Union supporting Roosevelt—including the southern border state of Missouri—it was the most votes any Republican candidate had received up to that point. The margin of victory was a direct measure of TR's ability to reach beyond the traditional Republican base of voters.

Roosevelt's inaugural address in the spring of 1905 eloquently expressed his intention to build on these gains, arguing that "justice and generosity in a nation, as in an individual, count most when shown not by the weak, but by the strong."[58] Despite a severe economic recession during Roosevelt's second term—and his impulsive public pledge to not seek a third term—the figure of TR dominated the 1908 election. Even the Democratic nominee, William Jennings Bryan, attempted to argue that his party would be best able to build upon Roosevelt's legacy by more aggressively reigning in the power of big business. But Roosevelt's handpicked successor, William Howard Taft, bounced to an easy victory thanks to TR's tireless campaigning on his behalf. Once again the voters overwhelmingly ratified the Roosevelt reforms.

But over the course of Taft's administration, relations between the two friends grew strained. Taft was by nature less aggressive and more of an ally to big business and the old eastern guard that had previously so comfortably controlled the Republican Party. Taft retreated considerably from Roosevelt's environmental activism and ordered the Justice Department to curtail its investigations of large corporations.

After returning from a big-game hunting trip in Africa and surveying the American political scene for several months, Roosevelt could not bring himself to stay silent, saying, "The Republican Party is now facing a great crisis. It is to decide whether it will be as in the days of Lincoln, the party of the plain people . . . or whether it will be party privilege and special interest, the heir to those who were Lincoln's most bitter opponents."[59]

By 1912, after much urging from party moderates and progressives, Roosevelt declared that he would challenge Taft for the Republican nomination. This election was the culmination of Roosevelt's lifelong quest for complete independence. It was an out-and-out battle between the establishment old guard and a former president who now allied himself squarely with progressive reformers in his party. TR won a majority of the state primaries—including Taft's own Ohio—but with a majority of delegates already committed to Taft, he was blocked at the convention by the machine politicians he had fought all his life. Roosevelt and his supporters marched off the convention floor in protest.

That evening of June 17, 1912, Roosevelt addressed a hastily convened meeting of his supporters in Chicago. He condemned Taft and the conservative Republicans for committing "a crime which represents treason to the people, and the usurpation of the sovereignty of the people by irresponsible political bosses, inspired by sinister influences of moneyed privilege . . . the corrupt alliance between crooked business and crooked politics. . . . The parting of the ways has come," he announced. The Republican Party must stand "for the rights of humanity or else it must stand for special privilege. . . . we will fight in an honorable fashion for the good of mankind; fearless of the future; unheeding of our individual fates; with unflinching hearts and undimmed eyes; we stand at Armageddon and we battle for the Lord."[60]

It was by some accounts the greatest speech of his career.

Roosevelt's progressive supporters let out a mighty cheer and marched out into the Chicago night, having at last broken free of the conservatives in the Republican Party they had so often fought. They would now form their own Progressive Party with TR running for president and tapping California's young Hiram Johnson for vice president.

But Roosevelt felt some concern about leaving the moderating influence of the established Republican party structure. Less than a year before he had confided to a group of fellow progressive leaders, "I am particularly anxious that in the progressive movement we shall not find ourselves landed where so many other movements have landed when they have allowed enthusiasm to conquer reason."[61]

The Democrats' nominee, New Jersey governor Woodrow Wilson, also attempted to paint himself as the progressive agent of responsible reform—taking pains to distance himself from the political bosses who controlled the Democratic Party, just as TR had throughout his career.

Wilson benefited tremendously from the split in the Republican ranks. Roosevelt carried 27 percent of the popular vote—still the highest percentage ever by a third-party candidate—and his 88 electoral votes dwarfed Taft's total of just 8. But despite his tremendous personal popularity, TR could not capture the White House without an established party organization to support him. The Progressive Party would fade with the absence of the bright star that TR provided, but its influence would endure, culminating in the New Deal legislation introduced by the administration of Franklin Delano Roosevelt.

By refusing to choose between the lesser of two evils, Theodore Roosevelt cut his own path through the political wilderness. He affirmed our nation's oldest ideals while challenging people to expand their sense of obligation to one another. TR was determined to see that our nation evolved progressively forward rather than swerving to the left or the right, and in the process he inspired all subsequent generations of Centrists. It is precisely because he had the courage of his convictions that TR realigned American politics during his lifetime and remains more widely loved than any president since. He is appropriately enshrined in the American memory not as a partisan, but as a patriot.

Theodore Roosevelt remained active in public life until his death, refusing to let ill health or the heartbreaking loss of a son in the First World War slow him down significantly, believing as he always had that "it is well to live bravely and joyously, and to face the inevitable end without flinching."[62] He died at home in his sleep on January 6, 1919. Centrist to the end, he left on his bedside table a note he had written concerning an upcoming trip to Washington: "prevent split on domestic policies."[63] The surviving children were telegraphed simply, "The Old Lion is dead." Americans everywhere mourned, among them the man who had tried to end TR's life with a bullet seven years before. "I am sorry to learn of his death," remarked his would-be assassin, John N. Schrank. "He was a great American. His loss will be a great one for the country."[64] But perhaps the most fitting tribute was offered by the Democratic vice president, Thomas Marshall: "Death had to take him while sleeping. If he had been awake there would have been a fight."[65]

THE MAN FROM INDEPENDENCE FIGHTS A THREE-FRONT WAR

The basic issue of this campaign is as simple as it can be; it's the special interests against the people.

—HARRY TRUMAN, 1948[1]

Philadelphia—July 15, 1948.

Harry Truman stood alone behind the podium, facing the weary delegates of a divided Democratic Party.

It was nearly two o'clock in the morning on the final night of what *Newsweek* called "the worst managed, most dispirited convention in American history."[2] The ballroom of the Ambassador Hotel was cramped and, without air-conditioning, had reached a sweltering ninety-three degrees. Not one of the previous speakers over the long evening had dared to even mention the word "victory."

Even Truman's wife, Bess, thought he would lose.

Not only was the Republican challenger, New York governor Tom Dewey, riding high in the polls, but the actions of Harry S. Truman—

this farmer and failed haberdasher from Independence, Missouri—
had already torn apart FDR's powerful electoral machine.

Liberal Democrats had left the party over Truman's strong anticommunist stand and thrown their weight behind Henry Wallace—
FDR's vice president before Truman—giving Wallace the nomination
of the newly revived (and now Communist-backed) Progressive
Party. Thirty-five conservative southern delegates had stormed off
the convention floor two nights before to protest Truman's support
of civil rights. They had announced the formation of the new States'
Rights Party—popularly known as the Dixiecrat party—and were
preparing to nominate forty-six-year-old South Carolina governor
Strom Thurmond to be the presidential candidate of the segregated
South.

Facing a united opposition with a divided party, President Harry
Truman needed to transform the aura of impotence that surrounded his reelection campaign into a powerful claim for four
more years in office.

Standing squarely behind the podium, cool in a white linen suit
while exhausted party regulars fanned themselves with leaflets,
Harry Truman leaned toward the microphones and growled, "I will
win this election and make these Republicans like it and don't you
forget it."[3]

With one speech, Truman began to turn the tide of the election,
generating a vigor and confidence that had been missing from the
Democratic Party since it lost control of Congress two years before.
Truman later explained that his aim was to "give them something
to cheer about and something to campaign for."[4] It worked. As one
delegate on the convention floor yelled within earshot of a *Time*
magazine reporter, "You can't stay cold about a man who sticks out
his chin and fights."[5]

The Man from Independence transformed the public's perception
of himself entirely—from that of a modest man out of his depth to
the hard-hitting, straight-talking "Give 'em Hell Harry" who now oc-
cupies a permanent place in American political history.

The strategy was deceptively simple: Throughout the campaign,
Truman took every opportunity to characterize the Republicans as

the party of the special interests. "The basic issue of this campaign is as simple as it can be," Truman said over and over; "it's the special interests against the people."[6] Truman tapped directly into a basic American theme that accounts for much of the instinctive appeal of Centrism: politics as a battle between special interests and the national interest. As he thundered on the night of his nomination speech in the convention hall, "The people know that the Democratic Party is the people's party and that the Republican Party is the party of special interests, and it always has been and it always will be."[7]

FDR had first used this special interests versus the common man formula to establish his unlikely coalition of farmers and industrial labor activists, African-Americans and prosegregationist southerners, academic liberals and uneducated immigrants into a solid voting bloc that had carried him to the White House an unprecedented four times.

Truman had been vice president for only eighty-two days when FDR died suddenly from a cerebral hemorrhage while vacationing in Warm Springs, Georgia. It fell to Truman not only to end the Second World War by using atomic bombs against Japan, but also to secure the postwar world as Stalin usurped political power in Eastern Europe. "Within the first few months," Truman later reflected, "I discovered that being a President was like riding a tiger. A man has to keep on riding or be swallowed. . . . I never felt that I could let up for a single moment."[8]

It was a time of fateful choices on many fronts, and Truman's decisive executive style—summed up by the famous sign on his desk that read "The Buck Stops Here"—gained him as many enemies as advocates.

Within his own party, Truman's willingness to meet the Communists with equal force in Eastern Europe had cost him the not inconsiderable support of liberals with socialist sympathies. His endorsement of pioneering civil rights legislation provoked the wrath of conservative southerners, and his tough-minded tactics with striking rail workers alienated the labor vote that had always been firmly in Roosevelt's corner.

In Truman's first year in office, a congressional coalition of

Republicans and conservative southern Democrats had denied his efforts to increase the minimum wage, aid housing construction, and institute the first prepaid medical insurance in American history. In 1948, that same coalition, joined by left-wing Democrats, was poised to deny him election to the presidency in his own right.

Truman appeared stranded in the political center. It was a classic Centrist catch-22: In attempting to act in the national interest, Truman had alienated the special interests that formed the foundation of his own Democratic Party. As Truman biographer David McCullough explained in his Pulitzer Prize–winning epic, Truman "disliked the terms 'progressive' and 'liberal.' What he wanted was a 'forward looking program.' "[9]

The postwar years had not been kind to incumbents running for reelection, in any case. Twentieth-century giants like England's Winston Churchill were being unceremoniously retired from office as voters sought to put the war years behind them; Harry Truman seemed likely to be next.

New York governor Thomas Dewey was a popular former prosecutor who had first gained national prominence at age thirty-five for his conviction of mob boss "Lucky" Luciano. But what should have been a dynamic gang-busting profile was undercut by Dewey's awkward formality, emphasized by his thin mustache and thin-lipped smile. When a photographer on the campaign trail called out, "Smile, Governor," Dewey curtly replied, "I thought I was."[10]

Still, Dewey had run a credible insurgent campaign against FDR in 1944, consciously moderating the Republican Party to incorporate many of the innovations of the New Deal. He was steadfast in his support of civil rights and refused to back conservative calls to ban the Communist Party in America. Now, with FDR, that political giant, dead and the war over, Dewey's election seemed inevitable. In the 1948 primaries, he had defeated Ohio senator Robert Taft, leader of the Republican Party's isolationist wing, and moderate Minnesota governor Harold Stassen.

Dewey's Centrist brand of Republican politics appealed to Independents and disaffected Democrats. Polls consistently showed him ten points ahead of the president. The *New York Daily News* summed up the nation's attitude, reporting that "President Truman appears to be the only American who doesn't think Thomas E. Dewey is going to be elected barring a political earthquake."[11] Tom Dewey's campaign strategy was to play it safe, attempting to avoid such a political earthquake at all costs.

As Tom Dewey tried not to lose, Harry Truman fought to win.

Truman was in many ways liberated by the fact that so many experts counted him out. In his memoirs, he would write, "In order to circumvent the gloom and pessimism being spread by the polls and by false propaganda in the press, I decided that I would go directly to the people."[12]

Truman used an acceptance of an honorary degree from the University of California at Berkeley as an excuse to make an "official" presidential cross-country train trip, stopping in big cities and small towns along the way. Discarding written texts, he spoke to the crowds in a new impromptu style, and his obvious sincerity was inspiring. Journalists assigned to the White House beat took immediate notice of the transformation, with one reporter writing that "a new Truman, a real Truman, has emerged from the cocoon of self-consciousness. This new Truman is folksy, hearty and humorous. He dares to come from church and use the word 'damnedest' on Sunday."[13]

Truman's new rhetoric reinforced the image of Republicans as being in the back pocket of big business. Though the nation was then blessed with relatively good economic times, in the post-Depression years anxiety about the power of big business was still widespread. As a result, Truman could excite crowds and appeal to their experience by asking, "Is the government of the United States going to run in the interest of the people as a whole, or in the interest of a small group of privileged big businessmen?"[14]

Ironically, it was accusations that the administration had grown too friendly with the eastern establishment represented by Wall Street and the military that had driven many Democrats to Truman's primary challengers: Strom Thurmond and Henry Wallace.

South Carolina governor Strom Thurmond was a war hero and self-proclaimed "progressive" within the context of the southern politics of that day. He had resigned his post as a county judge in 1941 to serve in the Eighty-second Airborne and had participated in the D-day landing at Normandy. Returning from the war, he ran for governor and succeeded in a field of eleven candidates by positioning himself as a New Deal liberal and a defender of the "common man." The New Deal coalition began to fray in the South when Truman's civil rights legislation began to conflict with the interests of the "common man" as southern politicians of the time understood him.

In response to repeated incidents of violence against black servicemen returning home after the war, Truman convened a Committee on Civil Rights in December 1946. In October of the following year, the committee released a report that proposed dozens of specific recommendations, including the passage of a federal antilynching law, and the establishment of a civil rights division at the Justice Department. Truman endorsed the committee's findings and submitted civil rights legislation to Congress.

Southern Democrats reacted predictably, with Mississippi senator James Eastland calling the administration's civil rights package an attempt "to secure favor from Red mongrels in the slums of the great cities of the East and Middle-West."[15] Moderate southern politicians claimed to oppose the legislation on the lofty grounds of states' rights. This struggle continued at the convention in Philadelphia, where, as the *Jackson Daily News* reported, "there was bitter disappointment when the Southern group failed to push through its States' Rights declaration. There was hot anger when the liberal Democrats rammed their Truman Civil Rights Platform down the South's throat."[16]

In response, all the delegates from Mississippi and half the delegates from Alabama walked off the convention floor. On July 17, the gavel rang out at the convention of the States' Rights Party in Birmingham, Alabama. Some northern correspondents were struck by the surprising absence of Confederate flags hanging from the rafters of the Birmingham Municipal Auditorium. After all, if Dixie was rising again on the grounds of the right of states to decide their own racial policies, where were the original symbols of the rebellious South?

Instead, the Stars and Stripes decorated the hall that Saturday night, in a deliberate attempt to show that the Dixiecrats were the patriotic inheritors of the Jeffersonian tradition of the Democratic Party. Dixiecrats asserted that their real purpose was to win enough votes in the South to throw the election to the House of Representatives, where they could have their delegates support whichever candidate would renounce the proposed civil rights legislation.

Strom Thurmond initially stated that he wasn't sure if he could attend the convention—after all, he had scheduled a tour of South Carolina National Guard facilities, and he hated to let down the troops. "I wish those in charge of the meeting had waited a week or so before calling it to give us folks a chance to make our plans," Strom said.[17] Like Robert E. Lee before him, Thurmond knew that he needed to look like a reluctant leader of the insurgent southern forces to appear credible.

Thurmond's show of reticence continued at the convention. After a number of speakers nominated the South Carolina governor as their candidate using the fiery language of racial segregation, Thurmond stepped up to the podium and gave an acceptance speech notable mostly for its lack of racial rhetoric. The real principle he was fighting for, as he would say time and again, was that the other candidates had caved in to the demands of special interests. "States' Rights Americans are ready to stand . . . for individual liberty and freedom and for the right of the people to govern themselves."[18]

Even as he evoked the political equivalent of apple pie, delegates circulated pamphlets around the convention floor with titles like *The Negroes' Place in the Call of Race* and *Jews Have Got the Atom Bomb,* while students from Birmingham Southern College enthusiastically waved pictures of Robert E. Lee.[19]

In an interview a day after the convention, Thurmond described himself as a "progressive Southerner,"[20] and he took care to say that he did not personally approve of either white supremacy or lynching.

Henry Wallace and the other members of the revived Progressive Party had a much different definition of "progressive" from the governor of South Carolina.

Henry Wallace was a straw-haired Iowan who had made an unlikely fortune developing hybrid corn seed before being appointed secretary of agriculture and then serving as Roosevelt's vice president. But FDR's steadily declining health had led some Democratic Party leaders to worry that the vice president might actually be called upon to serve as president. Wallace was widely regarded as brilliant, but he often seemed aloof, retreating from the Senate floor to study Russian and Spanish, and he was widely rumored to follow the teachings of an Eastern mystic named Guru Roerich, whom he briefly put on the federal payroll. He had a fondness for playing Russian Red Army folk songs on a record player in his office. This was not a presidential profile.* Wallace's increasingly outspoken liberalism, which was seen as an asset while he was vice president, was deemed dangerous in a president. Wallace was duly appointed commerce secretary in Truman's administration, but a controversial speech he gave led Truman to request his resignation.

In front of an enthusiastic New York labor audience in September of 1946, Wallace took the liberty of outlining his vision of international affairs, arguing that as a great power, the Soviet Union should be given the same amount of latitude to pursue its interests in Eastern Europe as the Monroe Doctrine gave the United States in Latin America. This notion of moral equivalency between the USSR and the United States angered many Americans, coming, as it did, on the heels of aggressive Soviet expansion throughout the Warsaw Pact nations.

News of Wallace's speech reached Secretary of State James Byrnes while he was negotiating with the Soviets in Paris. This ap-

---

*The contours of Wallace's personality are reflected in a troubling diary entry from November 20, 1943: "I put on some Red Russian army song records for Mrs. Roosevelt and also some Russian rural songs. She seemed to like both. Also I put on several Spanish records. Mrs. Roosevelt put in most of her time knitting a sweater, which was nearly completed and which was very well done. Apparently she has rather unusual facility as a knitter." (Murray Kempton, "The Trouble with Harry [and Henry]," in *Rebellions, Perversities, and Main Events* [New York: Random House, 1994], pp. 422–436.) It is not too hard to see why the chairman of the Democratic National Committee, Robert Hannegan—who insisted that an ailing FDR drop Wallace as vice president and tap Senator Harry Truman in 1944—asked only that "when I die, I would like to have only one thing on my headstone: that I was the man who kept Henry Wallace from becoming President of the United States." (Douglas Brinkley, "Harry S. Truman: The Accidental President," *Washington Post*, December 24, 1995.)

pearance of division within Truman's cabinet did not please either the secretary of state or the president, and on September 20, Truman called a press conference to announce that Wallace would no longer serve as commerce secretary.

Wallace was now out in the cold, but he stayed active to keep warm, writing columns for the *New Republic* and giving speeches throughout the nation. Wallace came to embody the hopes of left-wing Democrats who felt that the Truman administration's aggressive stance against their former allies in the Soviet Union was provoking Stalin to expand his area of influence as a purely defensive measure. They contended that FDR would never have led them down this Cold War path. Incurring the wrath of the Democratic Party's far-left wing did not bother Truman at all.* Surveying the anger his decision to fire Wallace had caused, the president wrote, "Well, now he's out, and the crackpots are having conniption fits. I'm glad they are. It convinces me I'm right."[21]

Many liberals also faulted Truman for his heavy-handed tactics with striking labor unions. After the war, union workers sought to gain a peacetime dividend of their own. In 1946, there were five thousand labor strikes across the nation. Under pressure from businesses, Truman removed price controls on many goods, resulting in escalating prices for all Americans. In May, the railroad workers went on strike—seventeen thousand passenger trains and twenty-four thousand freight trains sat stalled in their yards—and the nation ground to a halt. In response, Truman took the tough and unprecedented step of threatening to draft the striking workers into the army.

These positions seemed far more conservative than left-wing Democrats felt they had a right to expect from a Democrat in the White House. Turning from Truman, a collection of pacifists, Communist sympathizers, and labor activists found their candidate in the solitary figure of Henry Wallace.

---

*Truman later commented on Wallace: "You take a fella that carries on too much about the pee-pul—it's like what I told you about folks that pray too loud. You better get home and lock the smokehouse, and that's the way I always felt about Henry Wallace. I didn't trust him." (Quoted in Kempton, "Trouble with Harry [and Henry]," p. 425.)

As vice president, Wallace had been a nationally recognized symbol of Roosevelt's New Deal policies, but by 1948 he was the sole veteran of that administration who refused to condemn Communism and the Soviet Union. After declaring his candidacy in December 1947, Wallace appeared in auditoriums across the country, introduced by leftist luminaries like actor and opera singer Paul Robeson and folksinger Woody Guthrie. He roused crowds through condemnations of the anti-Soviet foreign policy embraced by both parties in Congress, and roundly criticized the Marshall Plan, saying that through its interference "America will become the most hated nation in the world."[22] His belief that "the communists are the closest things to early Christian martyrs" drew only slightly less applause.[23]

In an attempt to discourage support for Wallace's candidacy, Eleanor Roosevelt wrote in her nationally syndicated column that "the American Communists will be the nucleus of Mr. Wallace's third party." And when, in fact, the Communist Party of the United States formally endorsed Wallace's candidacy he did little to distance himself from their affections. Speaking in front of two thousand supporters in Columbus, Ohio, Wallace said that "the most frequent charge against the American Communists is that they advocate the violent overthrow of the Government of the United States. I have not seen evidence to substantiate the charge . . . any Communist who supports the independent ticket will be supporting our program, not the Communists' program."[24]

In front of a packed crowd in Madison Square Garden on May 11, Wallace accentuated these perceptions by unveiling his "Open Letter to Premier Stalin," in which he called for arms reductions and open trade between the two nations, and adding that "there is no American principle or public interest which would have to be sacrificed to end the Cold War and open up the Century of Peace."[25]

Stalin replied publicly to the letter in thankful and agreeable tones, saying that peaceful coexistence was of course desirable, and that negotiations along the lines Wallace proposed were acceptable to the Soviet Union. One month later, the Soviets began their brutal military blockade of West Berlin.

Truman's administration secured its bid for immortality through the successful conception and implementation of the Marshall Plan. This effort, famously described by Winston Churchill as "the least sordid act in history," shipped food and medicine to postwar Europe and helped stabilize those countries after years of bloody warfare had depleted their ability to provide for themselves. It was a brilliant bit of statecraft whose bipartisan presentation made its enormous price tag easier to bear and ensured its passage.

The first stroke of genius was choosing the new secretary of state, George C. Marshall, to embody the merits of the bill. General George Marshall was one of the most respected Americans alive, the architect of the war effort and the first career soldier ever sworn in as secretary of state. His character was beyond reproach, and his nomination sailed through the Republican-controlled Senate with unanimous support. When an aide suggested to Truman that the proposal carry his name instead of the general's, Truman wisely and bluntly refused, saying, "Anything that is sent up to the Senate and House with my name on it will quiver a couple of times and die."[26] Secretary of State Marshall was selected to announce the plan in a speech at Harvard, and it was Marshall who worked on the bill behind closed doors with Republican Senate majority leader Arthur Vandenberg. The result of this strategy was a broadly bipartisan foreign policy that served as a bulwark against the expansionist impulses of the Soviet Union and Joseph Stalin. The bill carried George Marshall's name, but it was a victory for Truman and the free world.

The unfolding of international events began to erode public support for Wallace's positions before the Progressive Party officially nominated him in July. The Progressive Party platform criticized the Marshall Plan as a way "to subjugate the economies of the European countries to American big business." In the face of the growing Soviet military expansion in Eastern Europe, it became clear that Wallace and his fellow Progressives were dangerously naive. In the words of Arthur Schlesinger Jr., "For the most chivalrous reasons, [Progressives] cannot believe that ugly facts underlie fair words. However [they look] at it, the USSR keeps coming through as a kind of enlarged Brook Farm community, complete with folk dancing in native costumes, joyous work in the fields and progressive kindergartens. Nothing in their system has prepared them for Stalin."[27]

Nonetheless, thousands of Americans attended Wallace's speeches across the country, and the *New York Times* estimated that the election would go to Dewey in no small part because Wallace's candidacy had made it virtually impossible for Truman to carry the crucial battleground states of New York, New Jersey, Illinois, and Pennsylvania.

Harry Truman seemed isolated and alone in the Oval Office, fighting a political war on three fronts that no one was giving him much of a chance to win. David Lilienthal, the chairman of the Tennessee Valley Authority, angrily wrote in his diary that "the Southern Extremists and the perfectionist 'liberals' together have created the impression (eagerly encouraged, of course, by the reactionaries and Republicans) that the people don't have confidence in him."[28] The Dixiecrats had the southern states locked up, Wallace was undercutting his support in the Northeast among liberals and labor activists, and the end result was that Thomas Dewey was marching toward what appeared to be a coronation.

It was in anticipation of this bleak scenario that in the fall of 1947 a small number of Truman's staff had written what would become one of the most famous political memos in American history: "The Clifford Memo."

White House special counsel Clark Clifford and aide James Rowe believed that reports of Truman's political death were greatly exaggerated. As bad as things were, there were still strategic opportunities to be found in Truman's situation, not least of which was the institutional power of the presidency itself. "The Independent and Progressive voter will hold the balance of power in 1948," Clifford wrote; "he will not actively support President Truman unless a great effort is made."[29]

The memo recommended that Truman concentrate his efforts on attracting the votes of the farmers of the West, making amends with labor, and reaching out to independent voters across the nation. The memo also advised Truman not to worry unduly about alienating southern conservatives, mistakenly believing that they would not bolt the party, but instead concentrate on keeping black

Americans in the Democratic fold. So many disparate groups of Americans had benefited from the New Deal policies, the memo reasoned, that Truman should directly appeal to their loyalty. Finally, Truman should get out on the campaign trail. There, he should concede nothing, unify the party as much as possible, and fight hard for every vote that could be gained.

On the podium in Philadelphia that hot night in July 1948, Truman set an aggressive tone, and then began bringing the party together. He directly addressed the divisions in the Democratic Party by frankly admitting, "There have been differences of opinion, and that is the democratic way. Those differences have been settled by a majority vote, as they should be. Now is the time for us to get together and beat the common enemy, and that is up to you."[30]

He reminded the base of the Democratic Party just why they had become Democrats in the first place. Farm income had increased from less than $2.5 billion in 1932 to more than $18 billion in 1947—American farmers were the most prosperous farmers in the history of the world, and if they didn't vote Democrat in this election then they would be "the most ungrateful people in the world." Likewise, wages in the country had increased from $29 billion in 1933 to $128 billion in 1947—"that's labor, and labor never had but one friend in politics, and that is the Democratic Party and Franklin D. Roosevelt."[31]

By speaking directly about the divisions that had absorbed so much energy and attention, he diffused their power by first acknowledging the differences that existed and then emphasizing what all Democrats shared—a common opponent in the Republican Party. And then he went on the attack, bringing his crusade against the Republicans directly to the American people.

Truman exploited an opportunity given by the scheduling of the conventions. Two weeks before, the Republicans had held their convention in the same Philadelphia auditorium, and in an attempt to expand their appeal they had passed a broad campaign platform that promised action on everything from housing, high prices, health care, and education to civil rights. As Truman described to the crowd and the television and radio audience, "They promised to do in that platform a lot of the things I have been asking them to do that they have refused to do when they had the power."[32]

And so, in a dramatic show of presidential power, Truman announced that he would call Congress back into session to pass legislation on the issues that the Republican platform claimed to be so concerned about. "If there is any reality behind that Republican platform, we ought to get some action from a short session of the Eightieth Congress," Truman said. "They can do this job in fifteen days, if they want to do it. They will still have time to go out and run for office." The results of the special session would be the test Americans would use to determine their vote, Truman predicted. "They will decide on the record, the record as it has been written. And in the record is the stark truth, that the battle lines of 1948 are the same as they were in 1932, when the nation lay prostrate and helpless as a result of Republican misrule and inaction."[33]

With one thunderous speech, Truman took a significant step toward changing the terms of the debate of the election. To Democratic voters, he was no longer the out-of-his-depth incumbent catapulted to office after FDR's death. Instead, he was the embodiment of the continued crusade that had been begun by Roosevelt in 1932 at the depths of the Great Depression. And to those independent voters who held the president responsible for the apparent drift of the nation, he had successfully placed the blame squarely on the Republicans for blocking legislation when they controlled Congress.

Had the special session of Congress resulted in new laws, Truman would have been vindicated as a man who could use the power of the bully pulpit to get things done. But when the Eightieth Congress emerged from its special session without accomplishing much—as Truman had predicted—he was able to run against the "do-nothing" Eightieth Congress.

The defection of the southern Democrats also presented Truman with an opportunity to assert the authority inherent in the office of the president. The day after the Dixiecrat Convention convened in Alabama, Truman took the unambiguous lead on civil rights by issuing Executive Order 9981, effectively desegregating the armed forces. Truman would not bother campaigning in the South. Instead, he would focus his energies west of Washington.

Truman made the decision not to attack Wallace personally, choosing to ignore him instead. The most effective way to nullify this liberal challenge was to move substantively to the left himself, in legislation and executive action. The attacks on Wallace would be left to liberals themselves.

There were reports that amid the enthusiasms of the campaign trail, Wallace's always eccentric personality had taken a decided turn toward the bizarre. Clifford confided in his memo to the president that "the most recent reports on Wallace's personality by the men who know him well are that while his mysticism increases, the humility that was once his dominant characteristic has decreased to the vanishing point; there is something almost messianic in his belief today that he is the indispensable man."[34]

Moreover, with the Cold War rapidly emerging as the defining issue of the era, anticommunist liberals had squared off against liberals like Wallace who favored accommodation with the Soviet Union by forming the Americans for Democratic Action. Initially, the ADA had courted General Dwight David Eisenhower to run against Truman as a Democrat, but when the general decided to serve as president of Columbia University instead, they reluctantly lined up behind Truman.

These anticommunist liberals felt that Wallace was ultimately serving as the Republicans' unwitting ally by dividing Democrats and justifying the increasingly hysterical voices of archconservatives, which would soon become embodied in the shadowy figure of Senator Joseph McCarthy. To help unite disaffected Democrats behind his candidacy, Truman argued that a vote for Wallace would amount to a vote for Dewey, saying that "a vote for the third party plays into the hands of the Republican forces of reaction whose aims are directly opposed to the aim of American liberalism"[35] at a campaign stop in Los Angeles while Hollywood Democrats like Humphrey Bogart, Lauren Bacall, and Ronald Reagan nodded in agreement.

While Strom Thurmond spoke to auditoriums and county fairs across the South, and Wallace's candidacy slowly imploded,

Truman took his case to the American people. Between September 6 and October 30, Truman crisscrossed the nation three times by train, visiting every part of the country except the South, making 275 speeches and covering nearly twenty-two thousand miles of American soil.

In front of twenty-five thousand people standing outside the Colorado state capitol in Denver, Truman was careful to draw the line between the Republican Party and Republican voters he was attempting to sway:

> Understand me, when I speak of what the Republicans have been doing, I'm not talking about the individual Republican voter. Nobody knows better than I that man for man, individually, most Republicans are fine people. But there's a big distinction between the individual Republican voter and the policies of the Republican Party. Something happens to Republican leaders when they get control of government. . . . Republicans in Washington have a habit of becoming curiously deaf to the voice of the people. They have a hard time hearing what the ordinary people of the country are saying. But they have no trouble at all hearing what Wall Street is saying. They are able to catch the slightest whisper from big business and the special interests.[36]

As Election Day grew closer, Truman intensified his attacks on the Republicans as representatives of a small group of rich private interests—attacks that Dewey notably failed to return in kind. Typical of Truman's campaign rhetoric was the following: "If you give the Republicans complete control of this government, you might just as well turn it over to the special interests, and we'll start on a boom and bust cycle just like we did in the twenties, and end up with a crash, which in the long run will do nobody any good but the Communists."[37] This was rhetoric that was designed to make people vote out of fear, rather than hope, but it was effective. In his attempt to hold on to the lead and appear "presidential," Dewey left these attacks unanswered.

With Election Day approaching, some polls showed Dewey's

margin shrinking slightly, but this was attributed to the contrast between Dewey's more reserved approach to campaigning and Truman's fevered campaign schedule. Reporters and pundits still did not give Truman a chance. On October 11, *Newsweek* offered the headline "Fifty Political Experts Unanimously Predict a Dewey Victory."[38] When Truman was shown the magazine, he defiantly replied: "I know every one of those 50 fellows. There isn't one of them who has enough sense to pound sand in a rathole."[39] The Gallup Poll was so confident of the outcome that it stopped polling before the end of October.

On Election Day, the head of the Secret Service left for New York to be by Governor Dewey's side as the widely expected outcome was made official. Dewey celebrated the end of the campaign at an Upper East Side apartment in Manhattan, dining with expectant advisers—some of whom had already bought houses in Washington—on a dish of roast duck with braised apples.

That same evening, Harry Truman checked into a hotel just outside of Independence, Missouri, had a glass of buttermilk and a ham sandwich, and then went to bed.

He woke up to the greatest upset in American political history.

The man who had every faction imaginable stacked against him had won through his direct appeal to the American people. Only 51 percent of the registered voters turned out that November 2, possibly because Dewey's election seemed like such a foregone conclusion. In contrast, labor had turned out for the Democratic ticket in large numbers, and the farm vote, which had deserted FDR four years before, rallied behind the Man from Independence. Truman won by a plurality of 2 million votes, carrying twenty-eight states to Dewey's sixteen. Strom Thurmond won Alabama, Mississippi, Louisiana, and South Carolina. Henry Wallace received barely over a million votes across the nation, and not a single electoral vote. Truman's victory was made even sweeter by the fact that the Democrats regained control of both the House of Representatives and the Senate. The *Chicago Tribune* famously printed the wrong headline in its early edition—"Dewey Defeats Truman"—and a delighted president held it aloft for cameras on his way back to the White House.

In some ways, Truman's challenges from the left and right wings of his own party proved to be blessings in disguise. While Truman's second term would be characterized by Republican accusations that his administration was "soft on Communism," the presence of Wallace's Progressive candidacy inoculated him from such attacks during the campaign. Truman couldn't be soft on Communism if the socialist sympathizers in his own party were so alienated by his foreign policy that they supported another candidate. Truman was the original anticommunist Democrat from the heartland.

Likewise, the Dixiecrat revolt also allowed Truman a great deal of flexibility that he would have been denied if the southern Democrats had uneasily agreed to remain in the fold. Truman was spared the accusations of hypocrisy that would have resulted from the incongruity of proposing civil rights legislation while courting segregationist support. Instead, he was free to claim the moral high ground on this issue, strongly advocating civil rights legislation and denying the Party of Lincoln the ability to make new inroads toward the African-American electorate. It marked the beginning of the re-alignment of the white South toward the Republican Party.

The angry desertions of the Progressives and the Dixiecrats made it clear that at least by comparison, President Harry S. Truman was squarely in the middle of the sensible center of the American electorate.

The election of 1948 has gone down in history as the prototype for the incumbent as underdog, fighting his way toward reelection. Most recently, Truman's example has been invoked by President George H. W. Bush in 1992 as he attempted to run against "the do-nothing 102nd Congress," and President Clinton in 1996 when he took a cross-country train trip to speak "directly to the American people." The 1948 election endures in the American memory primarily as the mythic triumph of the people over the pollsters—a memory that grows sweeter the deeper we enter the twenty-four-hour media cycle.

But the lessons of the 1948 election to its contemporaries reflect a considerably more complex reality than just the memory of Truman giving fiery speeches from the back of a train. Seen through the prism of Centrism, Truman's successful fight against the bewildering variety of factions organized against him seems to be one of the chief lessons of this famous campaign. One contemporary, moderate Massachusetts Republican senator Henry Cabot Lodge Jr., offered this assessment of what the public was saying to the Republican Party in 1948: "You have made some real progress in liberalizing yourselves"—in other words, moving toward the center of the electorate—"and making yourselves a forward-looking instrument of the popular will—but you have not progressed far enough. We are afraid that you might back-slide."[40] The 1948 election was about Centrism, after all.

Truman's position at the center of the political spectrum of 1948 was reinforced by the very factional defections that seemed to doom his candidacy at the start of the campaign. By repeatedly characterizing the Republican Party as the party of special interests, Truman carved out the political ground of common sense and the common man for himself. He was not only the safest candidate for people prospering in the postwar years to support, but he also came across as the most personally courageous. "You've got to give the little man credit," Republican Senate leader Arthur Vandenberg later admitted. "There he was, flat on his back. Everybody had counted him out but he came up fighting and won the battle. That's the kind of courage the American people admire."[41]

Truman's take on the 1948 election was characteristically direct and comprehensive. "The greatest achievement," he wrote in his memoirs, "was winning without the extreme radicals in the party and without the Solid South. It is customary for a politician to say that he wants all the votes he can get, but I was happy to be elected by a Democratic party that did not depend upon either the extreme left-wing or the southern bloc."[42]

THE RISE AND FALL OF JIMMY CARTER

FACING RONALD REAGAN, JOHN ANDERSON, AND TED KENNEDY IN THE ELECTION OF 1980

On human rights, civil rights, and environmental quality, I consider myself to be very liberal. On the management of government, on openness of government, on strengthening individual liberties and local levels of government, I consider myself a conservative. And I don't see that the two attitudes are incompatible.

—JIMMY CARTER, 1976[1]

As the election of 1980 approached, a joke was snaking its way across the nation:

The President was up working late one night when Teddy Roosevelt's ghost drifted into the Oval Office. Jimmy Carter jumped up and offered him his chair. "No," said TR. "You're the President now; I'm just haunting the place. How's it going?"

"Not too good," said Carter; "the Iranians have imprisoned fifty-two of our diplomatic personnel." "So you sent in the Marines, right?" said TR. "Uh, no," drawled Carter, "but Ah registered a strong protest at the United Nations."

"Anything else?" TR asked in a cold voice. "Well, the Russians just invaded Afghanistan," Jimmy said. "And of course you retaliated with every weapon in our arsenal," TR said confidently. "No," shrugged Jimmy, "but Ah've withdrawn our athletes from the Olympics."

At that, TR blew his top and shouted, "The next thing you're going to tell me is you've given back the Panama Canal."[2]

But the president caricatured in public memory as an ineffective liberal was actually considered "the most conservative Democratic President since Grover Cleveland"[3] by his contemporaries.

Jimmy Carter was constantly at war with liberals in his own party because of his commitment to cutting the federal budget, while conservatives mercilessly criticized his human rights–based foreign policy and unfocused leadership. After four years in office, Carter faced challenges from liberal Ted Kennedy, conservative Ronald Reagan, and Independent candidate John Anderson. Criticized on all sides, Carter lost control of his original Centrist message. His failed administration illustrates the danger of an incomplete transition from reformer running against Washington to incumbent commander in chief.

Four years before, in the bicentennial year of 1976, Jimmy Carter had been elected as an outsider, an earnest, born-again southern reformer promising not just an honest government, but a relentlessly efficient administration. He was described by *Time* magazine in its Man of the Year award issue as "a catalogue of contradictions: liberal, moderate, conservative, compassionate, ruthless, soft, tough, a charlatan, a true believer, a defender of the status quo, a populist Hamlet. . . . Carter is a Democrat who often talks and thinks like a Republican. The former Navy officer and nuclear engineer is an efficiency expert who values long-range planning and prides himself on his managerial ability ('I like to run things'). He also considers himself to be a fiscal conservative, a businessman who has had to meet a payroll, and he pledges to produce a balanced budget by the end of his first term."[4]

The incoherent idealism and ambition of the man collided harshly with the elevation to high office, leading to indecision and an inability to work with a Congress controlled by his own party. Blessed and burdened with high expectations, just a month before moving into the White House, 61 percent of the American public was sure Jimmy Carter would be a "good or excellent" president; but by the summer of 1980, he had only a 21 percent approval rating, the lowest in presidential history, lower than Richard Nixon during his death roll leading to resignation. Carter would be seen as a good man who tried to do the right things the wrong way.

The darkest of dark horses, it was amazing that Jimmy Carter had reached the Oval Office at all. One year before his election, the former one-term governor of Georgia had just a 3 percent national name recognition. No president had been elected from the Deep South since Zachary Taylor before the Civil War, and Carter's candidacy seemed so unlikely that when he announced his intentions, a local Atlanta newspaper prominently carried a column titled "Jimmy Carter's Running for What?"

He had been elected governor in 1970 by running to the right of all the other Democratic candidates. "I was never a liberal," Carter told Georgia voters that year. "I am and have always been a conservative."[5] The former state senator campaigned against school busing and derided his opponent as "Cufflinks Carl," wealthy and out of touch with the hardworking common man. When Carter was elected in an upset to succeed the segregationist governor Lester Maddox, Georgians were surprised to hear the supposedly conservative southerner announce in his inaugural address, "I say to you quite frankly that the time for racial discrimination is over."[6]

Counter to the political tide of the time, Carter sought to be a fiscal conservative but a liberal on most social issues. He equalized state school funding for rich and poor districts, appointed African-Americans to formerly all-white state boards and agencies, and opened the state capitol to portraits of notable black Georgians, beginning with a portrait of Martin Luther King Jr. He balanced these efforts with an unsentimental reorganization of state government, which he termed nothing less than "a revolution . . . that got rid of 278 of 300 state agencies and reduced administrative costs by 50 percent."[7]

Time magazine put Carter on its cover as leader of the New South with the headline "Dixie Whistles a Different Tune." But no one would mistake the Georgian governor for a liberal Democrat; only four months into office, this supporter of the Vietnam War declared "American Fighting Man's Day," in support of Lieutenant William Calley after his court-martial on charges of massacring civilians at My Lai. At the 1972 Democratic convention, Carter was a delegate for conservative senator Henry "Scoop" Jackson's campaign for the presidency. Barred by the Georgia state constitution from seeking a second consecutive term as governor, Carter stepped down in 1974. Few people could have guessed what he had in mind as a next step.

But Jimmy Carter had a clear vision of what the American public was looking for in a leader after Watergate. One of his earliest champions was Dr. Hunter S. Thompson, the *Rolling Stone* political correspondent and author of *Fear and Loathing in Las Vegas.* Thompson saw the inner logic of Carter's ascendancy, writing:

The electorate feels a need to be cleansed, reassured and revital-ized. The underdogs of yesteryear have had their day, and they blew it. The radicals and reformers of the Sixties promised peace, but they turned out to be nothing but incompetent trouble-makers. Their plans that had looked so fine on paper led to chaos and di-saster when hack politicians tried to implement them. The prom-ise of Civil Rights turned into the nightmare of busing. The call for law and order led straight to Watergate. And the long struggle be-tween the Hawks and the Doves caused violence in the streets and a military disaster in Vietnam. Nobody won, in the end, and when the dust finally settled, "extremists" at both ends of the political spectrum were thoroughly discredited. And by the time the 1976 presidential campaign got under way, the high ground was all in the middle of the road. Jimmy Carter understands this, and he has tailored his campaign image to fit the new mood almost perfectly.[8]

It was a measure of his contradictory appeal that in addition to the editorial staff of *Rolling Stone,* among his strongest supporters were evangelical preachers later associated with the religious right. The Reverend Lou Sheldon, leader of the Traditional Values Coalition, announced to the faithful that "God has his hand upon Jimmy Carter to run for President." The Reverend Pat Robertson also made a pilgrimage to Carter's peanut farm in Plains, Georgia, to tape a fawning profile for his fledgling television show, *The 700 Club.*[9]

On the campaign trail, Carter effortlessly combined high culture and counterculture, alternately describing himself as "basically a redneck" or "a very conservative Southern businessman by heritage," and then making a reference to the work of theologian Reinhold Niebuhr or the lyrics of Bob Dylan. It was just such a performance that drew Hunter S. Thompson to champion his candidacy.

The event was a Law Day speech late in his term, covered by only a few journalists including, by chance, Thompson. Carter was speaking off the cuff, typically earnest but relaxed in the assumption that no one would be covering the address. His staff did not even bother to tape the speech. Once the jaded and hungover journalist began to listen, Thompson began recording the sole known surviving tape.

"It was the anger in his voice that first caught my attention," Thompson recalled,

> but what sent me back out to the trunk to get my tape recorder instead of another drink was the spectacle of a Southern politician telling a crowd of Southern judges and lawyers that "I'm not qualified to talk to you about law, because in addition to being a peanut farmer, I'm an engineer and nuclear physicist, not a lawyer. . . . But I read a lot and I listen a lot. One of the sources for my understanding about the proper application of criminal justice and the system of equities is from Reinhold Niebuhr. The other source of my understanding about what's right and wrong in this society is from a friend of mine, a poet named Bob Dylan. Listening to his records

about 'The Lonesome Death of Hattie Carroll' and 'Like a Rolling Stone' and 'The Times They Are A Changing' I've learned to appreciate dynamism of change in a modern society."[10]

Typical politicians did not talk that way in 1974 and Hunter S. Thompson took notice, writing a column on the speech and the governor, creating a buzz for the ultimate underdog presidential campaign.

Carter ran as the last honest man in politics, declaring that "the people of the country feel they've been betrayed. . . . The competence of government is not an accepted characteristic anymore. No matter what a person hopes to do ultimately in life, no matter what his top hope or aspiration may be, he feels, generally, that Washington is an obstacle to the realization of that hope. . . . We know from bitter experience that we're not going to get the changes we need simply by shifting around the same group of Washington insiders. . . . Washington has become a huge, wasteful, unmanageable, insensitive, bloated bureaucratic mess."[11] At a time when the University of Michigan's annual survey of public attitudes found that trust in government had fallen from 64 percent in 1964 to just 22 percent in 1976,[12] this was a popular message, especially coming from a politician who could not be tainted by association with Richard Nixon.

Carter's faith also conveyed a comforting sense of humility, as when he famously said that "as you know, Christians don't have a monopoly on the truth, and when I go out of office, if I'm elected, at the end of four years or eight years, I hope people will say, 'You know, Jimmy Carter made a lot of mistakes, but he never told me a lie.'"[13]

Carter campaigned as a moderate amid a crowded field of liberals, sometimes describing his philosophy as "enlightened conservatism." No longer serving as governor, he could devote himself full-time to the campaign, becoming a familiar figure in the cornfields and convention halls of Iowa. When he came in first with a third of the vote in the Iowa caucus, Jimmy Carter became an overnight media star. He repeated his success in New Hampshire, again running to the right of the pack, straining to make sure that he could not be labeled. When Carter was asked about his ideology in a magazine article, he replied, "On human rights, civil rights, and environmental quality, I consider myself to be very liberal. On the management of government, on openness of government, on strengthening individual liberties and local levels of government, I consider myself a conservative. And I don't see that the two attitudes are incompatible."[14]

He sounded the themes of individualism and self-sufficiency that many people no longer associated with the Democrats, favoring work requirements for welfare reform and stating, "We should decentralize power. . . . When there is a choice between government responsibility and private responsibility, we should always go with private responsibility."[15]

When Carter won New York, he proved that a moderate southerner could win in a big industrial northeastern state; when he beat George Wallace in Florida, he eliminated the specter of southern segregationists that had haunted the Democratic Party for more than a century. Jimmy Carter's modest little campaign that could was transformed into a juggernaut, and as his nomination appeared increasingly inevitable, old-line Democratic power brokers panicked. Fearing a loss of control, party mandarins unleashed an anybody-but-Carter movement, questioning whether the relatively inexperienced governor could be trusted to win what was likely to be the best chance for a Democrat presidency since LBJ demolished Barry Goldwater. But the momentum behind this southern-accented *Mr. Smith Goes to Washington* candidacy could not be stopped.

In a speech in front of the AFL-CIO, the candidate showed a cold flash of temper as he directly addressed his opponents, saying: "My critics don't want to stop Carter. They want to stop the reforms I am committed to. They want to stop the people of this country from regaining control of their government. They want to preserve the status quo, to preserve politics as usual, to maintain at all costs their own entrenched, unresponsive, bankrupt, irresponsible political power. They know I do not believe in business as usual or politics as usual or a blind acceptance of the status quo."[16] Carter defanged criticism by depersonalizing the issue; when an opponent attacked Carter, they were disrespecting his supporters and, by extension, the democratic process.

In Boston, a week before the convention, he again turned the outsider accusation into an asset, saying: "There is a major and fundamental issue taking shape in this election year. That issue is the division between the 'insiders' and the 'outsiders.' I have been accused of being an outsider. I plead guilty. Unfortunately, the vast majority of Americans—like almost everyone in this room—are also outsiders."[17]

At the convention in New York City's Madison Square Garden, Carter selected liberal Minnesota senator Walter Mondale as his running mate to solidify liberal support within the party around his defiantly moderate candidacy. At the time, a *New York Times/CBS News* Poll showed that 52 percent of the public considered Jimmy Carter a conservative.[18]

President Gerald Ford had barely survived an unexpectedly strong challenge from former California governor Ronald Reagan. The onetime Hollywood actor had evolved from an anticommunist Harry Truman Democrat to an anticommunist conservative icon, famously explaining, "I didn't leave the Democratic Party, the Democratic Party left me."[19]

In the face of President Ford's perceived weakness, Carter surged ahead in the polls. During a presidential debate, when Ford grossly misspoke, asserting that "there is no Soviet domination of Eastern Europe," Carter went on the attack, saying, "I would like to see Mr. Ford convince the Polish-Americans and the Czech-Americans and the Hungarian-Americans in this country that those countries don't live under the domination and supervision of the Soviet Union behind the Iron Curtain."[20] The Democratic challenger was turning the tables, accusing the Republican president of being insufficiently anticommunist.

Carter's Centrist campaign won over many people who initially felt they could not vote for a Democrat after the liberal excesses of the late 1960s. Even former Spiro Agnew speechwriter John Coyne wrote in the pages of the *National Review* that "there are many things to recommend Carter. As a devout Christian, he is also a dedicated anticommunist. As a firm believer in the afterlife, he can be counted upon not to attempt to build the perfect society here on earth."[21]

Republican attempts to describe Carter as a "Southern-Fried McGovern" failed to resonate because of their surface lack of credibility, but it reminded many voters of their lingering doubts about the liberal wing of the Democratic Party, even in the aftermath of Watergate. Down the stretch, Carter remained something of a Rorschach test, with a Harris Poll in late September finding that Carter "comes across as more conservative to conservative voters, more middle-of-the-road to middle-of-the-roaders, and more liberal to liberals."[22]

On Election Day, Carter snuck past the sitting president, winning 50.1 percent of the popular vote. But in what should have been an ominous note amid the celebration, Carter's pollster Pat Caddell found that "fifty percent of the public still does not know where Carter stands on the issues."[23]

The bicentennial election brought a new, more moderate generation of Democratic politicians into office: Al Gore Jr. to the House of Representatives from Tennessee, Bill Clinton to the office of attorney general in Arkansas, and Pat Moynihan to the U.S. Senate from New York. These victories prompted conservative columnist Robert Novak to despondently predict that the election results marked "a continuation of the long descent of the Republican Party into irrelevance, defeat, and perhaps eventual disappearance."[24]

And so, for a few months in late 1976 and early 1977, America briefly fell in love with Jimmy Carter, with *Time* rhapsodizing that "by showing that a non-racist Southerner could win a major party nomination, Carter gave new pride to his region and went afar to heal ancient wounds."[25]

So how did Jimmy Carter squander all the goodwill given to him by his fellow citizens? He began by unintentionally starting a cold war with Democratic leaders of Congress while simultaneously overloading them with a lengthy, unprioritized legislative wish list.

In his first meeting on Capitol Hill with Speaker of the House Thomas P. "Tip" O'Neill, Carter dismissed O'Neill's offer of advice on how to get his ambitious agenda through Congress, breezily explaining that in Georgia he had bypassed the state legislature entirely, appealing directly to the public. O'Neill recalled replying, "Hey wait a minute. You have 289 guys up there [House Democrats] who know their districts pretty well. They ran against the [Ford] administration and they wouldn't hesitate to run against you." Carter frostily replied, "Oh really?" At subsequent inauguration festivities, O'Neill was furious to discover that his guests had been given the worst seats in the house.[26]

Carter unwittingly isolated himself in the White House, surrounding himself with the same group of Georgians who'd helped him get elected. He appointed an old friend with virtually no Washington experience to run the pivotal Congressional Relations Office, where relationships are the key to getting things done. Carter even declined to appoint a chief of staff, so that he might have a direct hand in all decisions. On his desk in the Oval Office, Carter placed Harry Truman's motto: "The Buck Stops Here."

Carter initially pushed for a tax cut to help stimulate the economy, spending precious political capital to get Democratic votes in line over the objections of liberals who wanted more government spending. But when the nation's economic numbers showed a slight improvement, Carter abruptly abandoned his call for a tax cut without notifying Congress. Just as abruptly, he canceled fifteen water projects important to Democratic congressmen, a move reversed by a two-thirds Senate vote.

In February, Carter sent a memo to all federal agencies requiring them to adopt zero-based budgeting as a means to control government spending. "The idea was simple," explained author Steven Hayward; "in fact, it sounded more like something Ronald Reagan might propose. At the beginning of the annual budget cycle, each agency and every program would start 'from the ground up,' justifying each item in its budget as if beginning from zero."[27] Jimmy Carter pledged that he would halt new spending to achieve a balanced budget by the end of his first term in office.

At a breakfast for the Democratic congressional leadership in the spring, Carter lectured the assembled legislators for nonetheless tacking on $61 billion in new spending to his budget, presciently driving home the point that "the Democratic Party needs to remove the stigma of unnecessary spending."[28]

In Carter's determination to cut pork barrel spending and petty patronage, he put himself at odds with Congress. "The president thought there was something tawdry—tawdry—about the idea of political appointments," Democratic House majority leader Jim Wright of Texas sputtered."[29] Another Democratic congressman was more direct, complaining that the holier-than-thou White House staff "thinks we're just a pack of crooked whores."[30]

Carter's reform-minded focus on fiscal conservatism and commitment to deliver a balanced budget drew applause from Americans: By June, half of all Ford voters supported the new president's job in office, and his national approval rating climbed past 70 percent. But his actions drew fury from liberal icons and interest groups within the Democratic Party. At the annual Americans for Democratic Action convention—which by the 1970s had come to define the liberal left wing of the party—1972 Democratic presidential candidate George McGovern attacked Carter for "trying to balance the budget on the backs of the poor and the jobless," while the ADA national director declared that if Carter continued to press for budget cuts, "the liberal movement will go into the opposition." Senator Ted Kennedy warned that "the party that tore itself apart over Vietnam in the 1960s can tear itself apart today over budget cuts in basic social programs."[31]

White House press secretary Jody Powell was apoplectic. In a May 1977 *Newsweek* article entitled "Jimmy vs. the Liberals," he asked, "How many times did Jimmy Carter say during the campaign he was a fiscal conservative—50,000 times? That's the mistake people have made all along—not believing he means what the hell he says."[32]

Carter's commitment to fiscal conservatism went even further than his most fervent supporters may have wanted to believe, with the new president billing each congressional and cabinet attendee to presidential breakfasts $1.75 for their morning meal at the White House. The sale of the presidential yacht *Sequoia* for $267,000 and the shutdown of the air-conditioning systems in the White House reduced morale far more than the federal budget, while the president's habit of monitoring the use of the White House tennis courts raised further concern that the notoriously hardworking Carter was not working intelligently.* When a Pentagon official subjected to a late-night presidential phone call regarding the accuracy of a chart on page 432 of a briefing book was later asked about Carter's tendency to miss the forest for the trees, he exclaimed, "My God, he was a leaf man!"[33]

Amid this micromanaging, lack of focus, and fostering of counterproductive congressional relationships, Carter sent a flood of proposals to Congress requesting support for a new conservation-based national energy policy, the transfer of the Panama Canal to local control, and industrial deregulation, as well as the reform of welfare, the civil service, and Social Security. He would later admit that those in Congress who encouraged him to prioritize his agenda were correct. "There is no doubt I gave Congress too heavy an agenda—12 to 15 important issues the first year I was in. I would've been better off in the public's estimation as well as with Congress if I had narrowed those down to one or two."[34]

Most of Carter's legislative programs stalled along with the economy, and the once-heroic problem solver saw his poll numbers drop as interest rates climbed to 20 percent. The perception was one of incompetence; as Democratic House whip John Brademas memorably put it, the White House appeared to have "all the finesse of an alcoholic hippopotamus."[35]

The corrosive Capitol Hill rumors about the possibility of Carter being dumped by his own party also took a toll on farsighted proposals put forward by the administration, most notably regarding health care. Noting that presidents since Harry Truman had tried and failed to enact comprehensive health insurance, Carter presented a national insurance program gradually phased in over four years to cover 18 million uninsured Americans and cover cata-

---

*Carter's puritan approach to fiscal policy extended to other matters as well, with the president finding time to offer a brief lecture to senior staff on their personal lives. "For those of you living in sin," Carter told his staff, "I hope you'll get married. For those of you who've left your spouses, go back home." (Steven F. Hayward, *The Age of Reagan* [Roseville, Calif.: Prima, 2001, p. 513].)

strophic illnesses for full-time workers in conjunction with private carriers. "It is time to rise above the differences that have created stalemate for the last thirty years,"[36] Carter said, flanked by Harlem congressman Charles Rangel and Louisiana senator Russell Long. "The idea of all or nothing has been pursued now for nearly three decades. No one has benefited from that."[37] But Senator Ted Kennedy had introduced a competing universal health-care proposal based on Canada's single-payer system and dismissed the president's phased-in approach as "too inequitable."[38] With the strong support of the labor unions and many liberals in Congress, Ted Kennedy felt sure he could hold out for something better. Consequently, no comprehensive health-care legislation was passed by the Democratic Congress during the Carter years.

In addition to their problems with the Democratic-controlled Congress, Carter and his aides complained bitterly that the press was out to make them appear ineffectual. Interestingly, a study of network news and newspaper coverage found that 85 percent of the criticism toward President Carter in the media had come from his fellow Democrats.[39]

Ten years before, Lyndon Johnson had ruefully warned, "The only difference between liberals and cannibals is that cannibals don't eat their friends and family members." Now Jimmy Carter was being cannibalized by his own party, and no matter how much Republicans appreciated his efforts at achieving a balanced budget, they were not about to come to his defense. Increasingly, people talked about the Carter administration as a failed presidency led by a well-meaning man who was in over his head. As Ronald Reagan and other Republicans readied a conservative challenge to the president in 1980, liberals were in open revolt against the president.

Ted Kennedy had been encouraged to run for president in 1972 and 1976, but a combination of an unsteady personal life compounded by highly publicized scandals and family obligations kept the brother of martyred American icons John F. Kennedy and Robert F. Kennedy from entering the presidential arena in his own right. Now polls showed Kennedy beating Carter handily among registered Democrats. Ted Kennedy saw 1980 as his time.

The long-awaited Kennedy restoration began on Labor Day 1979 with an announcement in Boston's Faneuil Hall. With the widows of his murdered brothers seated in the front row, Ted Kennedy approached the podium warily, stared into the crowd for what seemed like an eternal fifteen seconds, and then began his liberal insurgent campaign to unseat the sitting president with the words his brothers had used to begin their quests: "I announce today my candidacy for President of the United States . . ." He was far more liberal than his brothers, younger, more impulsive, and more inclined to adopt the left-wing attitudes that his brothers viewed with a degree of detachment. Ted Kennedy's candidacy proved more compelling in theory than in fact.

In a widely viewed television interview with Roger Mudd, Kennedy was asked why he wanted to be president and appeared to have no clear answer. This was seen as a further sign of his immaturity and sense of entitlement. Kennedy's relentless rhetorical focus on the inequities and injustice of American society also became the subject of jokes between reporters. One television anchorman reportedly returned from Washington without having completed his interview with Kennedy, feeling it was a waste of time. "If I had asked him any question, he would've replied the same way. If I asked him about weather, he would've said 'When I think about weather, I think first about the sick, the black, the old people, the underprivileged.' "[40] Ted Kennedy, like much of the liberal establishment, had come to be seen as pedantic and predictable—a caricature of himself.

While Kennedy's campaign gave every sign of flaming out, Carter's political operatives—returning to the campaign world they preferred to actual governing—did a masterful job of raising expectations for Kennedy's success. Reporters who trotted out to Iowa for the 1980 Democratic caucus were greeted by a grim-looking Carter press spokesman who told them in hushed tones that Ted Kennedy "had the best organization on the ground ever seen in Iowa."[41] The supposed "insider" rumor became reported as fact, shaping expectations for a resounding Kennedy victory. When Carter beat Kennedy by a three-to-one margin, the victory of the incumbent president in Iowa was viewed as a comeback rebuke of the Kennedy dynasty. From that point on, Kennedy's campaign—despite a stirring speech at the Democratic Convention—was treated as a romantic curiosity, the death knell of unreconstructed liberalism.

On Carter's right, Ronald Reagan was solidifying the front-runner status he achieved by almost getting the nomination for president four years before. The conservative movement was united behind him, with two Houston residents—former Texas governor (and former Democrat) John Connally and moderate former UN ambassador and CIA director George H. W. Bush—fighting for second place. Reagan's rock-ribbed conservatism was regarded as a barrier to success in the general election, but within the ideologically isolated atmosphere of the party primaries it was unquestionably an asset. His politics may have been largely in line with Pat Buchanan, but his photogenic familiarity and sunny disposition allowed him to appeal on a personal level to a far wider audience. His heartfelt patriotism won over many converts, as did his repeated attempts to counter the elitist associations of the Republican Party. "We're the party of Main Street," Ronald Reagan would tell audiences. "We're not the party of the corporation boardroom, the country club set. Let's tell the cop on the beat, the shopkeeper . . ."[42] But Reagan's emphasis on tax cuts disproportionately benefiting the wealthy as a way to stimulate the economy (famously derided as "voodoo economics" by then-candidate Bush) and well-courted support from the religious right alienated many moderates, who in turn invested their hopes in the lanky figure of Illinois congressman John Anderson and his quixotic Independent candidacy.

John Anderson was the frontier preacher in the race, an austere Republican from the heartland whose voting record drifted decidedly to the center after the assassination of Martin Luther King Jr. Devoutly religious, Anderson was annoyed when after eighteen years in Congress, he had to fight off a primary challenge from a local leader of the religious right. The increasing vitriol of the right wing frustrated him. When Anderson entered the race for the Republican nomination in 1980, he was initially a minor curiosity as a candidate, but he impressed many people with his steely passion and grasp of public policy. He characterized an election between Carter and Reagan as "not a choice but a dilemma," and he was positively evangelical about the need for moderates to rise up and take back the party apparatus. As polls showed deep dissatisfaction with Reagan and Carter, Anderson's announcement that he would pursue an Independent candidacy for president drew major attention. The purpose of the campaign, he said, was to bring about "a more centrist position in American politics."[43] Almost overnight, Anderson's poll numbers rose to over 20 percent. "He finds his own constituency in that other half he sometimes calls 'the alienateds,' " *Newsweek* wrote, "the disaffected, middle-class grandchildren of Teddy Roosevelt's Progressives."[44]

Built on a "national unity" platform, Anderson's insurgent candidacy was a wake-up call; political aides in both campaigns worried that he would take the swing votes in the center and tip the balance of the election to their opponent. But, tellingly, it was Carter who would suffer the greatest loss when moderates and progressives looked elsewhere for a candidate they could believe in.

President Jimmy Carter had an even more pressing problem than getting reelected—the seizure of the U.S. embassy in Iran and the taking of fifty-two of its personnel as hostages. In this tense atmosphere of American impotence, Carter's young pollster Pat Caddell drafted what is perhaps the most bluntly unflattering memo ever directly addressed to the president of the United States.

This memo is an attempt to give some early attention to the need for strategy/themes which we neglected to address until late in the 1976 campaign—much to our woe ... President Carter faces an extremely difficult re-election ... we face a united Republican party with a challenger posed to our right attempting to crowd our center. . . . The issue structures could not be worse. After a long period of runaway inflation ... we face what could be a worse political problem—unemployment. . . . The public is anxious, confused, hostile, and sour. . . . *More to the point, the American people do not want Jimmy Carter as their President. Not forced to choose a specific candidate, voters by almost 2 to 1 would reject Carter as President* . . . by and large the American people do not like Jimmy Carter. Indeed a large segment could be said to loathe the President. . . . The problem thus becomes, in this basic strategic memorandum, to construct a definition: People Must Be Given a Positive Reason to Vote for Jimmy Carter.[45]

This was a stunning statement from a long-standing and loyal member of Carter's team; the man in possession of the bully pulpit had failed over the course of more than three years in the job to define himself in the American mind. Carter's perceived failure in the White House was not only undermining U.S. prestige abroad, but also undercutting America's faith in the accessibility of the American dream. Carter's weakness was destabilizing America itself.

Carter retreated to Camp David in the Maryland mountains, indulging in a fit of self-analysis. Camp David had been the site of his administration's greatest triumph: the negotiation of a peace treaty between Israel and Egypt, where Carter's workaholic intensity and intrinsic desire to mediate conflicts between special interests had finally been rewarded. But down the mountain, across America, Jimmy Carter was under attack by a bewildering array of special interests: left, right, and center. The White House felt like it was under siege, the sense of drift and despondency leavened only by dark humor, as junior staffers passed a harshly self-deprecating Xerox from office to office.

Six Phases of a Project
1. Enthusiasm
2. Disillusionment
3. Panic
4. Search for the Guilty
5. Punishment of the Innocent
6. Praise and honor for the non-participants[46]

The lack of structure and well-defined support was dooming the administration from within and without. Few people knew that Carter had succeeded in deregulating huge swaths of American industry, including commercial and cargo airliners, oil and natural gas prices, banking, broadcasting, and the trucking industry. While Reagan called for increased spending on Cold War defense, few people knew that Carter had already successfully fought to significantly increase military spending for the first time since the Vietnam War, invested in the development of high-tech weaponry, and declared that the United States would be willing to go to war if the Middle East were further destabilized by expansionist dictatorships. The depth of dissatisfaction with Carter's leadership had an element of irrationality to it; as the *Economist* pointed out, "Mr. Carter's ratings in the Gallup poll have ranged from 61% to 21% in nine months, which surely says as much about the public as about the president. Everyone seems to want less government spending, less taxation, but more dollars for defense and for whatever federal shelter they like to run to in time of trouble."[47]

John Anderson's insurgent campaign—offering policy and philosophy, but lacking charisma or the infrastructure of an organized political party—lost ground as the gap between Carter and Reagan closed. As Gore Vidal archly quipped, "Compared to Carter and Reagan, Anderson looks like Lincoln. Compared to Lincoln, he looks like Anderson."[48]

Perceptions of the president's weakness were only reinforced at the Democratic convention, where instead of delivering a fiery address to unify his support and paint the Republicans as tools of the special interests—like Harry Truman did in 1948—Carter anemically apologized for his mistakes and promised to do better. Instead of reaching out to Independent voters with positive proposals, the president pandered to the special interests of the Democratic Party on national television, ending his speech with a litany of promises to disaffected groups: "teachers . . . women . . . farmers . . . workers . . . minority citizens."[49]

In contrast, Reagan's Republican convention the month before in Detroit was meticulously scripted. Without much personal enthusiasm, but with full appreciation of the political necessity, Reagan tapped Bush to be his vice president. Unlike Barry Goldwater—whose conservative campaign was widely rebuked in 1964—Ronald Reagan understood that the Republican Party needed to be unified, and that he would depend on moderate and independent support in the general election to gain the White House. Reagan's address accepting the nomination was a masterwork, putting the crusade that he—a self-styled citizen-politician—humbly led into historic perspective, reaching beyond mere partisan politics to the revival of national purpose.

> More than anything else, I want my candidacy to unify our country; to renew the American spirit and sense of purpose. I want to carry our message to every American, regardless of party affiliation, who is a member of this community of shared values. . . .
>
> Everywhere we have met thousands of Democrats, Independents and Republicans from all economic conditions and walks of life bound together in that community of shared values of family, work, neighborhood, peace and freedom.

Reagan then called upon disaffected Democrats to join the crusade, quoting Democratic icon Franklin Delano Roosevelt no less than three times in the course of his speech, most powerfully toward the end, when he placed himself in the role of the true inheritor of the Roosevelt legacy, saying:

> The time is now to redeem promises once made to the American people by another candidate, in another time and other place. He said, ". . . For three long years I have been going up and down this country preaching that government—federal, state and local—costs too much. I shall not stop that preaching. As an immediate program of action, we must abolish useless offices. We must eliminate unnecessary functions of government. . . . we must consolidate subdivisions of government and, like the private citizen, give up luxuries which we can no longer afford. . . . I propose to you, my friends, and through you that government of all kinds, big and little, be made solvent and that the example be set by the president of the United States and his Cabinet."
>
> So said Franklin Delano Roosevelt in his acceptance speech to the Democratic National Convention in July 1932.[50]

All that remained was the knockout punch, delivered in the first face-to-face debate between the president and his challenger, when Ronald Reagan looked into the camera lens and asked the American public, "Are you better off today than you were four years ago?"

The unambiguous answer on Election Day was "Hell, no." Jimmy Carter won only six states and 41 percent of the popular vote as Reagan triumphed in the electoral college with 489 votes and carried the Senate into Republican control. John Anderson's Independent candidacy captured 7 percent of the vote. There was a clear mandate for change: a rejection of Jimmy Carter's attempt at a reform presidency. Carter's concession came before the polls had closed in California—the earliest since Judge Alton Parker had been overwhelmed by Theodore Roosevelt in 1904.

The exploration for the cause of Carter's failure did not end when the votes were counted. After all, it seemed to violate the ancient principle that character is destiny: How could a man who even his opponents agreed was intelligent, hardworking, and moral fail to inspire the public and master the presidency? Perhaps no administration was treated to as exhaustive and remorseless a public autopsy.

One of the most thorough explanations came from the pen of Carter speechwriter James Fallows, who wrote an extended essay titled "The Passionless Presidency" detailing the rise and fall of the administration from an insider's eyes. It was not pretty. "I worked for him enthusiastically and was proud to join his Administration, for I felt that he, alone among candidates, might look past the tired formulas of left and right and offer something new," Fallows explained. But the transition from campaigning to governing had been disastrous for the candidate and his team.

I came to think that Carter believes fifty things, but no one thing. He holds explicit, thorough positions on every issue under the sun, but he has no large view of the relations between them. . . . Carter has not given us an idea to follow. The central idea of the Carter Administration is Jimmy Carter himself, his own mixture of traits, since the only thing that finally gives coherence to the items of his creed is that he happens to believe them all. Hubert Humphrey might have carried out Lyndon Johnson's domestic policies; Gerald Ford, the foreign policies of Richard Nixon. But no one could carry out the Carter program, because Carter has resisted providing the overall guidelines that might explain what his program is.[51]

In the end, armed with the best intentions, Jimmy Carter allowed his personality to gain primacy over his policies and eclipse any larger philosophic vision of what he wanted to accomplish in his time as leader of the free world. He never learned to wield the full power of the bully pulpit. The absence of managerial discipline and prioritization reflected the great danger a reform Centrist incumbent can face once in office. His support was broad but not deep, and burdened with the actual responsibilities of leadership—rather than the rhetorical posturing of campaigning—Jimmy Carter's instinctive attempts to balance warring dichotomies made him appear reactive, drifting down the middle of the road, beset on all sides, ultimately pleasing no one.

The Rorschach-like appeal of candidate Jimmy Carter to liberals, moderates, and conservatives evaporated once he encountered turbulence in the White House; conservatives no longer saw Carter as one of their own, while moderates and liberals felt similarly abandoned. It was a failure of management and communication, but it was also something more: The ultimate absence of animating leadership within the Carter administration descended directly from the absence of a unifying idea bigger than Jimmy Carter himself.

GOVERNOR
BUDDY ROEMER — 1991

A REFORMER FALLS TO A CROOK AND THE KKK IN THE BIG EASY

Edwin Edwards

Buddy Roemer

David Duke

I love Louisiana, but I hate Louisiana politics.

—GOVERNOR BUDDY ROEMER [1]

Louisiana politics can get pretty strange, and no election exposed the tensions of the electorate in the Big Easy better than the 1991 governor's race, where an incumbent baby-boom reformer faced a born-again KKK member and an openly corrupt, twice-indicted predecessor known as the Sun King—and lost.

Buddy Roemer was supposed to be the hope of the New South. The Harvard-educated heir to a Louisiana political fortune, he was a conservative Democratic congressman who rode into the governor's mansion at the age of forty-four on a wave of populist anger at widespread corruption. His campaign slogan, "I Love Louisiana, but I Hate Louisiana Politics,"[2] resonated with the middle class and the media. Roemer pledged to bring businesses back to the state, clean up the environment, and improve education. Soon he was being mentioned in the same breath as Bill Clinton as a possible future candidate for president. Initially, the boy governor enjoyed real success, passing campaign finance reform, workers' compensation, and cutting taxes on business. But something funny happened on the way to the coronation: Buddy Roemer lost his mojo. He fell out of touch with his political base and fell out of love with his wife. He switched over to the Republican Party, picked fights with the powerful Democratic-controlled state legislature, and seemed increasingly ineffective. Perhaps worst of all, he disappeared from the public eye and became known as the "no-show" governor. Rumors about his fascination with New Age self-help movements heightened his image as just another yuppie out of touch with good-ole-boy Louisiana.

But Buddy Roemer still looked good by comparison to Edwin Edwards, a polyester version of legendary Louisiana populist Huey Long. Like Long, Edwards depended on a coalition of poor Cajuns and blacks to return to office year after year. In exchange for enduring frequent scandals and brushes with the law, the voters received an extensive program of public works. Edwards' greatest curse or asset—depending on how you looked at it—was a colorful personality perfectly suited to the Big Easy: an "open disdain for middle-class morality,"[3] as journalist John Maginnis put it. Edwards was a legendary gambler and womanizer, suspected of paying off Las Vegas creditors with $500,000 stuffed in a suitcase and accused of using his long white state limousine to attract sorority girls at Louisiana State University, a charge he hotly denied. "That was my son in the limo," the governor said. "I always took my personal car."[4]

Edwards used his three terms as governor during the oil-fueled boom years of the late seventies and eighties to unleash a dirty-money free-for-all of government by graft. Louisianians were willing to ignore the Sun King's excesses as long as the good times rolled, but when the economy tanked the indictments came down like rain. Edwards used all his political brilliance to beat two counts of racketeering and was eventually acquitted. But the high-profile court case sent several key aides to jail, and Edwards left office in disgrace. Surveying the wreckage of the Sun King's reputation, *Shreveport Journal* political columnist Lanny Keller predicted that "the only way Edwards can ever be re-elected is to run against Adolf Hitler."[5]

As luck would have it . . .

David Duke was looking for a new job. The skinny, pimply kid who used to walk around LSU in a Nazi uniform with a swastika armband in the late 1960s (predictably bad family life: father away, mother drank, son threatened to set her on fire, etc.) had by the late 1970s worked his way up to the pinnacle of the hate industry as grand wizard and national director of the Knights of the Ku Klux Klan. Preternaturally publicity conscious, Duke preferred not to wear hoods or white sheets at Klan rallies, opting instead for a suit and tie. In return for his presentable professionalism—as well as books from his small white-supremacist press—Duke was already receiving money through the mail from across America and overseas, especially Germany. In 1980, he decided that membership in the KKK was limiting his potential and formed what he termed "a civil rights group"—inevitably called the NAAWP, or the National Association for the Advancement of White People. He discovered an entrepreneurial streak, raising more than $20,000 in donations to pay a $50 fine given to him during a Klan march in Forsyth County, Georgia. He developed an extensive mailing list for his cause and noticed the growth of the mainstream conservative movement with much satisfaction.

Nineteen eighty-eight was a transformative year: Duke declared himself a born-again Christian and went under the plastic surgeon's knife to reduce the size of his nose. Perhaps not coincidentally, that same year Duke decided to run for president of the United States on the Populist Party ticket. His stated goal was to gain more votes than Jesse Jackson, but he came up far short, with forty-four thousand votes scattered over twelve states. Still, Duke's popularity in the poor white parishes of Louisiana grew, and when a seat in the state legislature opened up, David Duke changed his registration to the Republican Party and announced his candidacy with a flurry of media coverage. He ran on a conservative anticrime, antiwelfare, anti–affirmative action, and antitax platform, renouncing his Klan past and causing the White House to cringe with his enthusiastic appropriation of President Bush's "Read My Lips, No New Taxes" slogan. But Duke's campaign failed to drum up any real voter support until a series of fights broke out during a Martin Luther King

Day parade in nearby New Orleans, and television cameras caught a group of black kids beating up some white kids. The special election was the following week, and when the dust cleared David Duke found himself in a runoff against John Treen, the brother of a former governor. Now the national media descended on Louisiana, and a chorus of Republicans and Democrats denounced the apparent rise of David Duke to respectability.

On Election Day, Treen supporters passing out campaign literature found themselves outnumbered while Duke volunteers yelled "Nigger lovers go home"[6] at them for hours. A young, beer-drinking crowd congregated at the local VFW hall that served as Duke's election night headquarters. Black journalists and cameramen on hand to cover the event reported being repeatedly called niggers by drunk Duke supporters; Jewish UPI reporter Steven Watsky was greeted with the chant "We missed one of you in the gas chambers."[7] But the crowd cheered when David Duke took the stage and announced that he'd been elected to the state senate. Smiling widely, feeding off the crowd, he declared that it was "a new day for America" and had a message for the governor: "Buddy Roemer, read my lips, no new taxes." David Duke had found a new tune and a new target to go along with his victory margin of 227 votes.

Fast-forward two years. David Duke has been serving in the Louisiana State Senate without much distinction but garnering a great deal of media attention due to his "freak factor" as the only known former neo-Nazi in elected office. But a distressingly better-than-expected run for the U.S. Senate the year before has made it clear that this was a freak to be reckoned with. Buddy Roemer had tried and failed to pass a massive fiscal reform package, big business was angry at him for enforcing environmental regulations, and Duke's presence was making the governor regret he ever joined the Republican Party. The old political wizard Edwin Edwards sensed opportunity in the air and took himself out of retirement, marching in local parades with his twenty-six-year-old girlfriend, nurse Candy Picou, on his arm ("At my age a man wants either a nurse or beautiful young girlfriend. I have combined the two," Edwards reasoned).[8]

With the winds of a strange political season at their back, these three men found themselves facing off in the open primary for governor of Louisiana. How did they get there?

In 1991, the storm clouds of the culture wars were gathering force. A recession had settled in; Clarence Thomas and Anita Hill were squaring off on Capitol Hill; Louisiana-based televangelist Jimmy Swaggart (cousin of rock-and-roll legend Jerry Lee Lewis) had been pulled over with a prostitute and pornography in his car— all while President George H. W. Bush presided uneasily in the White House, trying to understand why he'd dipped sharply in the polls so soon after the success of the Gulf War.

In theory, Louisiana should have been comfortable with the concept of multiculturalism by now. Its second governor was named Don Allejandro O'Reilly: An Irishman appointed by the Spanish king to deal with a threatened French uprising in 1768, he executed a group of French nobles after inviting them to dinner.[9] Alternately wealthy and extremely poor, blessed with great natural resources but a failing education system, Louisiana had a rich and contentious history that made politics a full-contact spectator sport. The ghost of Huey Long, a poor boy turned lawyer and democratically elected near-dictator, hovered over the state. Each of his successors as governor was inevitably compared to the man who set the standard for populism and public forgiveness. Corruption was not only tolerated in the Big Easy, it was enshrined, as long as it was abidingly wrapped in a good-ole-boy cloak.

That was part of Buddy Roemer's problem. He had run as a straight-arrow reformer, the anti–Huey Long, and Huey's ghost did not appreciate apostates. Buddy should have known this: Before arriving in Congress at the tender age of thirty-seven, Buddy had benefited from his father's local political career and connections with a thriving political consulting company. Louisiana politics was in his blood and his brain, and every candidate who'd hired him had won their race, including come-from-behind wins over three incumbents. But while Roemer's father was serving as commissioner of administration in Governor Edwards's first administration, he was indicted for giving government contracts in return for kickbacks to a local Mafia boss. Now seeking to build a political career for himself and redeem the family name, Buddy Roemer ran for Congress in 1978. He was ahead in the polls until two weeks to go, when he was faced with a decision whether to bribe a powerful African-American organization in return for its endorsement or risk falling in the polls overnight. Roemer refused the bribe and—as expected—fell to third place. But this principled stand proved to be a smart investment; local journalists respected Roemer for choosing integrity over political expediency. State representative Buddy Leach, who had won the seat in Congress, was soon indicted on vote-buying charges stemming from the contested election.

Two years later, Buddy ran for the congressional seat again and won easily. Arriving in Washington, Buddy immediately set about establishing his independence, joining the growing "boll weevil" movement of southern Democrats who voted Republican in the age of Reagan. This frustrated the Democratic leadership: Speaker Tip O'Neill called him "often wrong but never in doubt," and *Congressional Quarterly* described Roemer as an "unguided missile on the House floor."[10] But Buddy Roemer was nobody's fool; he recognized that "the best thing to be in Washington was a conservative Democrat because both parties had to come to you."[11]

Roemer proved so effective in office that after his tough-won victory in 1980 he faced no opposition in 1982, 1984, and 1986. By 1988, he was bored and ready for a new challenge. He would challenge the Sun King's corrupt regime and run for governor, but not in a traditional Louisiana way. "I want to run a revolutionary race, not the way things have been in the past. That would not be fun. That would not be interesting," Roemer told an aide.[12] And so the dragon-slaying campaign began.

Edwin Edwards was weak and widely unpopular, but in the open primary system he'd brought to the state, all the other candidates who wanted to be governor were stacked against him in a manner that usually guaranteed the incumbent at least a place in the runoff. Roemer's campaign suffered from having less money than its competitors, and made a strategic decision to stay off television during the early stages of the race, opting instead for a full advertising blitz when the election came down to the wire. While other candidates were beamed across the state, Roemer's campaign seemed to be slipping into obscurity, stuck in fifth place and single digits. That's when a desperate and angry Buddy Roemer unleashed his signature campaign ad, staring straight into the camera and saying, "I love Louisiana, but I hate Louisiana politics." He was running against the system, and his straightforward, unorthodox appeal tapped into the anger of many Louisiana voters. Buddy Roemer was offering a revolution of tax cuts and real reform. Suddenly luck started to strike the Roemer campaign, with an unexpected endorsement from the influential *New Orleans Times- Picayune,* which notably passed over hometown Republican congressman Bob Livingston. The endorsement expressed the belief that a reform-minded conservative Democrat could better unseat Democrat Edwin Edwards than a member of the still-disorganized right-wing-dominated Republican Party. This made other newspapers and voters take notice of Roemer's candidacy, and he eventually won the endorsement of virtually every newspaper in the state. Roemer's cash-strapped campaign began pulling in money, more than $200,000 in donations the week of the newspaper endorsement, $96,000 one happy Friday alone. Momentum was building for Buddy Roemer, and in an open debate with all five candidates he pulled ahead decisively when he declared that he would endorse anyone but Edwards. "We've got to slay the dragon," he said.[13]

The reformer's campaign rallies now took on the tone of earnest good-government revival meetings. The *New Republic* now called him "St. Buddy"[14]—the young man was running a crusade. "It's not my footsteps the other candidates are hearing, it's yours," Buddy Roemer told the cheering crowds.[15] The state swooned, bringing together an unlikely if powerful coalition of middle-class moderates and poor Louisiana voters who were fed up with the fat cats and bureaucrats in Baton Rouge. When Election Day came around, Buddy Roemer had gone from fifth to first in a matter of months. His margin of victory was so decisive that Edwin Edwards, sensing defeat, declined to take part in the runoff. Buddy Roemer would be the next governor of Louisiana. "We proved a Democrat could put together a wholesale campaign without catering to the special interests," gushed one young supporter.[16]

On Roemer's first night in the governor's mansion, Edwin Edwards had left the boy-governor a reality check as a present: an execution scheduled for the evening of Buddy Roemer's inauguration. "People were on the lawn, dancing, while I was upstairs deciding," Roemer later remembered, shaking his head. "It's something that Governors and Kings are unprepared for. I didn't want to do that the first night."[17] The execution was carried out.

That sense of frustration, responsibility, and foreboding would haunt much of Buddy Roemer's term in office, but as the sun rose the next day he still had reason to feel hopeful. Buddy Roemer's first year in office would prove to be a success. He started off strong, rejecting the previous president of the state senate and speaker of the Louisiana house—who were old Edwards allies—in favor of new leadership, in line with changes he meant to bring to the state. Roemer cut back on social programs, which allowed him to collect more money for antipollution and environmental protection measures. He successfully demanded that teacher pay raises be linked to a new teacher evaluation plan that would allow the state to rescind the certification of unqualified teachers. Roemer pumped more money into the state university system and prioritized economic development efforts designed to bring more businesses to Louisiana. His most decisive victory was the passage of wide-ranging campaign finance reforms that forbade cash donations to candidates—cutting off the lifeblood that had made corruption in Louisiana politics a way of life. Roemer's forceful reforms were bearing results, and at least one local businessman breathlessly confessed to reporters that "I get out of bed every morning and run out to get the paper to see what the Revolution is doing."[18]

But then Buddy Roemer's revolution lost momentum. "Buddy's a sprinter, not a marathoner," explained his campaign manager.[19] He could not keep up the frantic pace of reforms that defined his first year in office. When the state legislature convened for its second session, Roemer put all his chips on an ambitious fiscal-reform package that needed to be ratified by the voters in order for it to be included in the state constitution. It was a complicated proposal not easily distilled to the direct message or broad themes that revolutions depend upon to keep up their momentum. Roemer touted his fiscal-reform package as a way to make the state tax system more progressive while ending the state's chronic budget shortfalls.

Despite its professed importance, the governor did not hit the road and sell the reform with a comprehensive campaign. Without the urgency of a full-fledged campaign behind it, the reform seemed just like government tinkering around the edges of the bureaucracy. It was voted down by a 55 percent to 45 percent margin. Roemer threw up his hands, claiming that the voters wanted revolution but not change. The state legislature had a different interpretation: Buddy Roemer was vulnerable.

The old-school local Louisiana politicians who had been in power since Roemer was a child decided to take their revenge, deposing his handpicked president of the state senate and speaker of the Louisiana house. Ridiculous bills seeking to jail record store owners for selling obscene music to teens and forbidding any fine higher than $25 for beating up a flag-burner (colorfully known as the "beat-up-the-flag-burner" amendment) were passed by the legislature and sent to the governor. A bill banning abortions even in the case of rape or incest attracted national attention; Roemer received ten thousand letters on the subject alone. "It's springtime for demagogues," observed one state capital insider, a bit prematurely.[20]

Chaos and cronyism again reigned in the state capital of Baton Rouge, and Buddy Roemer lost his focus. "The legislature threw a party, and I get to clean it up," Buddy complained.[21] His wife left him, moving out of the governor's mansion with their son, Dakota. It was Roemer's second failed marriage, and it prompted a very public midlife crisis.

One of his childhood friends now ran a New Age seminar known as Adventures in Attitudes. Roemer was so taken by the program that he encouraged senior staff members to take the course alongside him. One of the outward manifestations of his flirtation with the New Age movement was that the governor began wearing a rubber band on his wrist, which he was instructed to repeatedly snap whenever a negative thought entered his mind, while muttering "Cancel, cancel" to reinforce its effect.[22] Needless to say, this stab at self-actualization did not fly too high in the Bayou State.

To make matters worse, Buddy dropped out of sight, becoming almost an absentee governor in a state where glad-handing at the local barbecue was expected by constituents. Louisianians began to joke that you were more likely to see Elvis than the governor. This behavior was unbecoming to a populist reformer. Buddy Roemer was losing touch with his base. But he had no idea how bad it would get.

In late 1990, Roemer began to speak with the Bush White House about changing his registration from Democrat to Republican. Roemer had voted with Ronald Reagan during much of his time in Congress, and he was getting no assistance from Democratic lawmakers who resented his efforts to cut spending in order to balance the budget. Since Louisiana adopted the open primary system in the 1970s, the Democrats' twenty-to-one registration advantage had shrunk dramatically. You no longer needed to be a member of the Democratic Party to be a player in Louisiana politics, and conservative southern Democrats were switching their registration to the Republican Party—GOP registration had doubled during the past four years. Increasingly, Roemer was too conservative to be fully accepted in the Democratic Party, and he felt his national ambitions would be better served as a moderate Republican than a conservative Democrat. The White House was predictably thrilled about this high-profile defection, but members of the Louisiana Republican establishment resented the fact that Roemer did not consult them. These were, by and large, true believers who had labored in the trenches when other Louisiana politicians were content to go along with the Democratic Party to get along. This was the far right, and to them Buddy Roemer's moderation was not an asset, it was a threat. Buddy Roemer was about to understand the profound wisdom of his glib response when asked in the past if he would switch parties: "There is only one thing," he'd said, "that's kept me from being a Republican—the Republicans."[23]

The governor and the White House had a right to think that Buddy Roemer's defection would be a source of celebration within the Louisiana Republican Party. After all, it would mark the first time in recent history that the Republicans controlled the governor's mansion, and Roemer was automatically higher in the polls than any other conceivable GOP candidate. In addition, he would presumably spare Republicans the embarrassment of potentially nominating David Duke for governor. Other Republicans were asked to sign a pledge swearing they would not run if not endorsed by the party. David Duke notably refused. Roemer was irritated that he had to jump through the hoop of the party convention to get his nomination. He'd hosted a lunch at the governor's mansion to smooth things over with party leaders; that should have been enough. But Clyde Holloway, an antiabortion activist and darling of the religious right, was refusing to get out of the race. And just when the party leadership seemed resigned to muscle Holloway out in favor of Governor Roemer, Edwin Edwards stepped in to stir up a bit more trouble.

"Did you know that Buddy Roemer voted for Michael Dukakis?" Edwards casually mentioned to Clyde Holloway on the way to a parade. Roemer had confessed to a reporter in 1988 that he reluctantly intended to vote for Dukakis: "Dan Quayle helped me make up my mind," he'd said.[24]

This little bit of opposition research went a long way, and soon conservative Republicans were bristling at the news that their prospective nominee had voted for a Massachusetts liberal in the last election and insulted the intellectual honor of Vice President J. Danforth Quayle. (This was somehow less shocking than the possibility that their party might nominate a former grand wizard of the KKK.) Conservatives would not let Buddy Roemer represent their party without a fight. When Roemer was told by party leaders that he would face a challenge at the convention, he exploded, banging on his desk and shouting at party chairman Billy Nungesser, "Goddammit, sonofabitch, I don't need you . . . or the Republicans or the Democrats. I won without any of you last time."[25] This was unhelpful in winning over the party faithful. As far as Republicans were concerned, Buddy Roemer was still a guest in their house. They would teach him who was boss: Clyde Holloway became the official Republican nominee for governor.

After all that effort, Buddy Roemer was still a man without a home. Somewhere in Louisiana, both Edwin Edwards and David Duke were smiling that night; they knew that Clyde Holloway's place in the race spelled the end for Buddy Roemer. Holloway would slice off just enough votes to leave the sitting governor pressed from all sides, adrift in the middle. As governor, Buddy

Roemer could no longer claim to be an outsider intent on reforming the government. In the minds of most Louisianians he *was* the government, and unlike Harry Truman he did not unleash a campaign blaming the public's dissatisfaction on the "do-nothing" state legislature. The angry conservative antigovernment base of support that had lobbed him into the governor's mansion now had Republican alternatives that came in two flavors: racist and nonracist. Moderate Democrats felt betrayed by Roemer's party switch, while business-as-usual Democrats rallied behind the Sun King. The wind was out of Buddy Roemer's sails, and the reluctant candidate was doing nothing to rebuild his momentum. The crowds that came out to hear Buddy speak were a shadow of what they had been during his insurgent campaign for governor.

In contrast, like a cross at a Klan rally, David Duke's supporters could not have been more fired up. "Duke—I'd vote for him 150 times if I could," said twenty-three-year-old Napoleonville resident Roy Torres. "He's the only one willing to stand up and tell the truth."[26] Duke rallies were packed with cheering crowds, mostly poor and all white. "We're going to be the first state in America to begin to turn it around, to bring this country back to the Christian values it was founded upon," shouted Duke to an approving chorus.[27] The audience roared again when Duke talked about "people on food stamps who buy hamburger while you're buying Hamburger Helper, and then use their welfare checks to buy alcohol or lottery tickets."[28] The targets of populism had shifted 180 degrees since the days of the Kingfish: anger at the lazy and undeserving rich on Wall Street had been replaced by anger at the lazy and undeserving poor on welfare; distrust of big business had been replaced by distrust of big government.

Duke now played the race card with more subtlety and skill than he had during his youthful days as a member of the KKK. His pledges to end affirmative action, welfare, and other entitlement programs resonated with working-class whites while stoking the fires of racial resentment. Seventy-six-year-old Duke supporter Lewis Otto explained his vote: "When the civil rights movement started they said, 'We just want to go to school with whites.' Now there's no stopping the demands. There's no end to it all. The morning paper said there's no black owners of baseball teams. What do they want? To give them a baseball team? That's why I tend to Duke."[29]

As Duke's support climbed well past 20 percent, fan clubs sprang up as far away as New York and California. Almost all of Duke's campaign staff was volunteer, and 40 percent of his campaign contributions came from out of state.[30] Some polls showed that Duke had higher name recognition among Americans than any of the declared presidential candidates. The question America was nervously asking itself was "How could this happen here?"

Vice President Dan Quayle, when pressed to explain Duke's popularity in an interview stated, "The message of David Duke is this, basically: anti–big government. Get out of my pocketbook, cut my taxes, put welfare people back to work. That's a very popular message." The vice president then quickly added, "The problem is the messenger: David Duke, neo-Nazi, ex-Klansman, basically a bad person."[31]

Despite the White House's discomfort with him, Duke felt increasingly comfortable within the Republican Party. He now described himself as "the Republican candidate that actually bridges the gap between fiscal conservatives and labor" at campaign rallies.[32] To a smaller group of skinheads and Klansmen after his election to the state senate, Duke confessed that "the Republican Party of Louisiana is in our camp, ladies and gentlemen. I had to run within that process, because, well, that's where our people are."[33]

In the language of political consultants, David Duke's base was highly motivated: It was going to vote come hell or high water. Weirdly, and perhaps due solely to his plastic surgery, Duke had even been transformed into something of a neo-Confederate sex symbol. At a Duke campaign rally outside an antebellum courthouse in Clinton, Louisiana, a middle-aged woman in a turquoise dress exclaimed to a reporter, "Well, he certainly is the most handsome candidate." When the candidate passed by, she batted her eyelashes and reached out her hand, saying "Why, yes, Captain Butler, I remember you"—an apparent reference to Clark Gable's character, Rhett Butler, in the Civil War epic *Gone with the Wind*. She offered Duke the ring from her finger as a campaign donation ("worth about $100"), but, flustered, he returned it after a second, explaining that while the gift violated campaign finance laws, he could take a check.[34]

In desperation, Governor Buddy Roemer again turned toward television ads to light a fire under his faltering candidacy. Four years before, his slogan had been "I Love Louisiana, but I Hate Louisiana Politics." Now, having failed to change the tone of Louisiana politics and faced with the surging candidacies of Duke and Edwards, he opted for a new tag line: "We Can't Turn Back the Clock." Apparently, he had forgotten William Faulkner's famous admonition that in the South "the past is never dead; it isn't even past."

The candidate most likely to benefit from the oncoming electoral car crash was Edwin Edwards, and he knew it. Whatever his faults and moral failings, even his enemies acknowledged the man was, in the most cynical sense, a political genius. One year before, when he announced his intention to run for governor a record fifth time, even his oldest friends thought he was crazy. But by now it was obvious that he had sensed something in the state that other people were missing. Beyond the crowds lining the parade routes, beyond the television polls and other signs of popular discontent, Edwin Edwards had seen opportunity in the numbers. A lifetime of Louisiana politics and twelve years as governor had taught him to break down the state into districts, calculating likely turnout among whites and blacks, distilling the map of his state into a complicated numbers game. Percentages, odds—this was the mind-set of a lifelong gambler. Edwards even extended it to his womanizing, telling a legislator that "2 out of 10 women will go to bed with you, but you've got to ask the other 8."[35]

Now the polls were coming in showing Edwards in the lead with his dependable base of blacks and Democratic Party regulars. Roemer was slightly ahead of Duke in most polls, but if you looked at the map it became clear they were splitting the same vote Roemer had won by a huge margin four years before. Two other factors seemed ominous and would prove important: Duke's numbers were deflated due to the fact that many of his voters were reluctant to tell a pollster their true intentions and, four weeks out from Election Day, more than 40 percent of all voters were still undecided. Edwards ran through the numbers, confidently giving a seminar to reporters with coffee cup in hand, and then made a prediction. There would be a 67 percent total turnout in the primary: 70 percent among whites and 60 percent among blacks. Edwards claimed he would be vindicated with 34.7 percent of the popular vote, followed by Duke at 30.0 and Roemer at 26.9. Clyde Holloway and the other minor candidates would split 8.4 percent of the vote.[36]

As the race tightened in the final weeks, Buddy Roemer briefly seemed to be pulling ahead. Then, eight days out, a local businessman named Jack Kent walked into each of the three major New Orleans television stations with a briefcase and a blank check. He wanted to buy every available thirty-second spot from then until Election Day. Kent was the president of a hazardous-waste recycling company called Marine Shale. Unhappily for Jack Kent, Governor Roemer's newly strengthened Department of Environmental Quality had fined Marine Shale over $4 million for illegal disposal of hazardous waste during the past four years. Now Kent saw his chance for revenge. "He's tried to put me out of business," Kent said, "I can do the same to him."[37] Kent spent over $500,000 to blanket the airwaves with vaguely humorous anti-Roemer ads that advanced no other candidate, but slammed the governor as a holier-than-thou hypocrite. Kent had been friends with Edwards, and Marine Shale had prospered under the former governor's lax enforcement of environmental regulations, but both men denied a conspiracy. In any case, it was Duke who gained the greatest benefit from this last-minute attack. Undecided voters who had been leaning toward Roemer were switching their allegiance to the man they saw as the real conservative outsider in the race. All Edwards needed to do was get out of the way.

Just as he'd predicted, the Sun King was vindicated on primary day. The center did not hold. It was a political resurrection complete with a miracle; the detailed predictions he'd given to reporters more than a month before were nearly right on the money: Edwards came in first with 33.7 percent; followed by David Duke with 490,000 votes statewide, totaling 31.7 percent of the vote. Governor Roemer followed with a distant 26.5 percent of the popular vote. The black anti-Duke protest vote that Roemer had been depending on never fully emerged; as one black politician put it, "Duke's not our problem. He's a joke to us. He embarrasses white people. He's their problem."[38] Roemer's aides were walking around in shock, but the governor seemed oddly relieved by his defeat. By eight o'clock on election night, he was watching the National League playoffs on TV. Even Roemer's own mother, Adeline, shrugged off her son's performance: "We had everything going for us but a candidate,"[39] she said. The Republican Party's official nominee, Clyde Holloway, claimed 5.34 percent of the vote, enough so that if Holloway had not received the Republican nomination, Roemer would have knocked Duke out of the race. Instead, the Republican Party standard-bearer played the spoiler, causing a runoff that redefined the phrase "the lesser of two evils."

On Wednesday morning, America woke up to what the hell had been going on in Louisiana. The impossible had occurred: a former neo-Nazi and Ku Klux Klan member had gained nearly half a million votes, and stood a chance of being elected governor. President Bush went on television to say that if he lived in Louisiana he would cast his vote for the Democrat Edwin Edwards. The Sun King had gone from pariah to messiah in four short years. His political instincts and insight took on near metaphysical proportions—when he'd left office after being indicted, Edwards declared that God was not finished with him. Now many people were muttering that he was right, that Edwards was the only thing standing between the Antichrist and the governor's mansion.

Bumper stickers began to appear that read "Vote for the crook. It's important."[40] Roemer called a press conference and said, "I cannot, will not, must not vote for David Duke. It would be suicidal for Louisiana. And since my choices are only two, Edwards gets my vote. He does not get my endorsement."[41] A broad national coalition arose to speak out against Duke, with local celebrities like Aaron Neville and the Saints' quarterback, Bobby Hebert, making televised pleas on behalf of Edwards. New Orleans fund-raiser Hippo Katz promised to mobilize the Jewish community: "David Duke thinks he hates Jews now. Wait till we're through with him."[42] Money poured in from across the country to the Edwards campaign as America held its breath. Edwards played up his experience while keeping a light touch on the campaign trail: "The only similarity between me and Duke is that we're both wizards under the sheets,"[43] he joked.

The Duke campaign ran ads featuring the candidate's two daughters, and extensive mea culpas for his hateful past, denounced now in the name of Christ. Bizarrely, one Duke ad even featured an endorsement from James Meredith, the student who single-handedly desegregated the University of Mississippi under the cover of federal troops in the 1960s, now an anti–affirmative action activist.[44] Edwin Edwards understood the dark corners in Louisiana politics better than anyone, and he chose to hit Duke not on racism but on content and confidence, questioning his failure to pay income taxes and exposing his effort to dodge the draft. The Duke campaign was rocked by several last-minute "scandals"—this being a relative term—including the resignation of a senior aide who claimed that Duke's religious conversion was phony. On a statewide radio call-in show, a caller asked which church Duke belonged to—the question was followed by a panicked twenty-second pause. But Duke was pushing the fundamentalist Christian connection harder than ever, trying to give supporters a graceful excuse to back his program by making the election seem like a contest between two sinners: one repentant; the other still profligate. It was not simply accusations of racism that derailed Duke's candidacy; it was a confrontation with the facts on NBC's *Meet the Press,* where commentator Tim Russert asked the self-appointed defender of poor working-class whites to name the three top manufacturing employers in Louisiana and how many people in the state lived below the poverty line. Again, awkward seconds ticked by on the clock, followed by a full fumble on national television: ". . . I don't carry an almanac around with me" was the best Duke could do.[45] Typically, Edwards knew right away: Avondale Industries, General Motors, and AT&T, with 24 percent of Louisianians living below the poverty line.

But the dark energy around Duke's campaign was still palpable, and everybody now knew that the polls lied when it came to white support for David Duke.

Duke's crowds were right-wing revival meetings, full of passionate intensity, with baser emotions masked behind political issues like welfare mothers, whom Duke described as "punching out illegitimate children faster than I don't know what," to hoots of approval.[46] This was the closest the KKK crowd had come to the mainstream in America since 1925, when forty thousand of their hooded brethren paraded down Pennsylvania Avenue. The Duke campaign was a cause, like Custer's Last Stand. At his final campaign rally, a thousand people were crammed into Brown Auditorium at the Northeast Louisiana University campus, while four hundred more of the faithful waited outside. Signs were waving "Duke for President," and the crowd shouted for their hero when the prerecorded strains of Randy Newman's epic "Louisiana 1927" began to play over a ten-minute video montage that combined pastoral images of the state with shots of Duke greeting supporters in slow motion and kneeling in prayer: The chorus of the song—"They're tryin' to wash us away"—rang out as the crowd chanted for Duke. Ads in local newspapers showed pictures of Adolf Hitler with the slogan "Vote Duke—Create a Fuehrer."[47]

On Election Day, stores were selling bags with eyeholes cut out for a buck apiece to voters who wanted to conceal their identities. Turnout of registered voters was 80 percent, at record levels, and for the first time black turnout was equal to white. By sundown, it was clear that the Crook had been elected to an unprecedented fourth term by a landslide margin, 61 percent to 39 percent. But seven hundred thousand citizens of Louisiana had cast their votes for David Duke. At Edwards's election night victory party in New Orleans, the crowd was as jubilant as if they had just avoided execution. It was standing room only when the once and future governor, Edwin Edwards, ascended the stage and extended his hands to calm the crowd. "Tonight, reason and compassion reign in Louisiana. . . . I will make our people proud of our state, proud of their Governor. I will heal our wounds and bring our people together." Applause rang out and the Sun King smiled. "I will not let you down," he said.[48]

Six years later, Edwin Edwards was indicted on charges of corruption relating to the sale of riverboat gambling licenses. After an extensive trial and yet another resignation in disgrace, the Sun King was sentenced to ten years in federal prison, a term he is currently serving out in Fort Worth, Texas.

David Duke declared his seven hundred thousand votes a "moral victory," adding that the cause must go on, then announced his intention to run for the Republican nomination for president against George H. W. Bush in 1992. Duke did not necessarily think he could win, but he wanted to make a point: "I'll just be the Jesse Jackson of the conservative cause for a while and we'll see what occurs."[49] In the spring of 2003, Duke was sent to jail for a year on charges of mail fraud and tax evasion.

In the summer of 2003, looking back at what had become of his opponents in the dozen years since their 1991 campaign for governor, Buddy Roemer laughed and said, "Ain't life wonderful?"[50]

Buddy Roemer was now running a bank in Baton Rouge, trying to bring about change in Louisiana by giving out loans instead of signing laws. Below the surface charm there is a touch of bitterness when Buddy recounted the reasons for the death of his reform administration: "You've got to understand that Louisiana is still in many ways a developing democracy,"[51] with powerful business interests, racial divisions, and a vulnerability to demagogues. But most of all, Roemer blamed the open all-party primary system Edwin Edwards pushed through the state legislature in the late 1970s for his loss, just as he did in an interview weeks after the election: "The polls showed that if I run as a Republican among Republicans, I win. If I run as a Democrat among Democrats, I win. The open primary elects the left and the right comes after me and I'm stuck in the middle. . . . I was hoping that there would be about 33 percent of the people in the middle and then we would win the election, but it didn't work out like that. . . . The trouble with an open primary is that it polarizes voters and the extremes win. Centrist ideas lose. Progress comes in the middle, not on the ends."[52]

Extremists encourage each other's candidacy, and they can effectively marginalize a demoralized and disorganized moderate majority. And as the Big Easy proved in 1991, when a state dances with demagogues, it wakes up with one hell of a hangover.

PART 2

THE OPPOSITION CANDIDATE REACHES OUT

When a political party has been locked out of power for consecutive elections, negative perceptions need to be counteracted aggressively. In time a new leader from a younger generation steps up to the plate, determined to moderate the old excesses and reach out beyond the party's traditional base. Their reforms balance perceptions, and claim the allegiance of moderates and Independents in the decisive center.

In times of party crisis, a transformative leader must take the reins, redefining the organization by expanding its ranks and creating new alliances. An inclusive style of leadership, in word and action, is essential. Professor Erwin Hargrove of Vanderbilt University places contemporary political leaders into two categories, Includers and Excluders, explaining: "Includers have open arms. They will criticize opponents and seek to form coalitions against them but they will also work with opponents when necessary and seek to form the broadest possible coalitions. Excluders preach the superior value of their camp, rule out the legitimacy of the opposition, and seek to create divisions among citizens in a diverse society."[1] In the process of bringing an opposition party in from the wilderness, inclusive leaders hand a revived and redefined organization over to the next generation.

Each of the presidents profiled in this section were transitional figures, elected by slim margins, most in three-way elections with the opposition divided. In each case, after a decade of one-party rule, the public was ready for change, but their reservations about the opposition party needed to be addressed and calmed. These candidacies countered existing stereotypes and inspired voters to reassess their perceptions, while solving long-standing problems. Their use of Centrist strategy and substance in governing allowed them to become pivotal chief executives who defined their times and realigned politics for decades in their wake.

When Woodrow Wilson ran for president in 1912, Democrats had been locked out of the White House for sixteen long years. In just two years as the governor of New Jersey, Wilson had built a fresh reputation by publicly turning on the big-city bosses who had initially championed his candidacy, passing an ambitious set of progressive reforms over their outraged objections. By reforming his own party first, he laid the groundwork for their return to power. Wilson's cool academic demeanor contrasted with the radical airs of many other progressives, while bitter divisions in the Republican Party between Progressives and big-business interests allowed Wilson and the Democrats to seize the Progressive mantle of reform. His success in effectively managing the passage of Progressive legislation through Congress removed the rationale for a separate Progressive Party and allowed the Democrats to reemerge into the majority when a Wilson administration alumnus, Franklin Delano Roosevelt, lorded over the New Deal.

In 1960, John F. Kennedy understood that the Democratic Party was increasingly seen as weak on military and economic issues after the popular moderate Republicanism of President Eisenhower. As a result, he chose an aggressive course of attack against the Republican vice president, Richard Nixon, on these very areas of Republican strength. His vigor and personal charisma also stood in sharp contrast with the Democrats' previous candidate, Adlai Stevenson. Once in office, Kennedy called for tax cuts and appointed moderate Republicans to head up the Department of Defense as well as the Treasury. His confident balance of cold-warrior anticommunism and New Deal domestic policy proved popular and effective, capturing America's imagination just as the baby-boom generation was hitting its impressionable adolescence. It was the perfect meeting of the man and the moment, and Kennedy played his opportunity for all it was worth.

After the assassination of President Kennedy and the disastrous conservative candidacy of Barry Goldwater in 1964, an unlikely figure ran again for the presidency in 1968: Richard Nixon. Mindful of the mistakes of his own past candidacy as well as those of his party, Nixon was determined to reach out to disaffected Democrats and Independents in an effort to make the Republicans the majority party for the first time in his life. Against a backdrop of increasing resentment toward the excesses of Lyndon Johnson's Great Society and the splintering of the Democrats over the war in Vietnam, Nixon portrayed himself as a mature, moderate conservative who could best be trusted to implement reasonable reforms during an unstable time. Once in office, he created the Environmental Protection Agency and strengthened affirmative action and the National Endowment for the Arts, while using his established anticommunist credentials to open relations with China. The best way to measure his success before Watergate was by the fact that he was reelected in a forty-nine-state landslide in 1972. Even after his resignation, the Republican Party was able to emerge as a majority party.

When Bill Clinton appeared out of Arkansas in 1992, the Democrats had been repudiated by the American electorate, losing five out of the last six elections, and more than forty states in 1980, 1984, and 1988. They were perceived as a party controlled by liberal special interests hostile to the vast majority of Americans. Bill Clinton used his political talents to realign his party in the public's mind with the concerns of the middle class while distancing himself from the far-left wing. His campaign proposals to put one hundred thousand more cops on the streets and to make "welfare a second chance, not a way of life" countered perceptions that Democrats were weak on crime and personal responsibility, while his campaign also effectively associated extremism with the increasing influence of the religious right on the Republican Party. As a result, the New Democrats seized the mantle of moderation and made the GOP seem out of touch with the concerns of average Americans. Bill Clinton's political consultant Dick Morris dubbed this strategy "triangulation," explaining that it was "a process of taking the best ideas from each party and combining then into a coherent policy. It is not just splitting the difference but molding a creative synthesis that rises above the doctrine of either party."[2]

Centrism is historically the best means for winning an election, and it opens the door to lasting political realignment. It allows a candidate the freedom to co-opt the best ideas from the opposition, and to solve pressing problems with the flexibility and innovation that is ironically available only to the opposition. All the pivotal political leaders profiled in this section used Centrism to reclaim relevance for a political party that had been marginalized for too long.

WOODROW WILSON—1912

A PROGRESSIVE BEATS THE PARTY BOSSES

HELPING THE PRESIDENT

We stand in the presence of an awakened nation, impatient of partisan make-believe.

—WOODROW WILSON, 1912[1]

The film projector begins to flicker and whir, casting its combination of light and shadow on to the canvas screen of the movie house. The title appears suddenly—*The Old Way and the New*—white letters unsteady against a black background. The audience is about to watch one of the earliest extended campaign commercials.[2]

Fade to the room of a captain of industry, wood paneled with framed portraits of Republican presidents Taft and Roosevelt in the background. The lord of the manor appears in top hat and tails, with exaggerated belly and a bulbous nose reminiscent of J. P. Morgan. He sits down at his ornate desk and tears up a charitable request from a local hospital in disgust. When two workers show up asking for a 5 percent raise, he replies that they are "lucky to be alive," and his white-wigged French butler throws them out into the street. But when a man with a black mustache the size of a snake barges past the butler, he is welcomed with a backslap and a cigar; a chance to buy off the state legislature is enthusiastically accepted as an eager henchman begins shoveling money into a burlap sack. The top-hatted man lets out a laugh and words appear across the bottom of the screen: "The Old Way."

Cut to a sunlit day outside a factory's walls; a whistle is shown blowing a pitch of steam as workers spill out at the end of their shift. One of the same workers who was kicked out of the boss's house walks down the street, lunch pail in hand, looking tired and dejected. He walks past a poster showing a Republican flanking a fat rich man across whose belly is written "privileged interests"; shaking his head in disappointment, he walks on. The worker then stops in front of a poster that reads "Wanted: 1,000,000 Earnest Citizens to Contribute Each One Honest Dollar to Elect a President of and for the People—No Trust Money Accepted." Smiling, he takes a single crisp dollar out of his wallet and places it in an envelope marked "Woodrow Wilson for President." The camera lingers on the address and then it is slipped into a mailbox. "The New Way" is proclaimed. And then the real show begins.

In the election of 1912, the unlikely figure of Woodrow Wilson re-aligned American politics by seizing the mantle of progressive reform from the bitterly divided Republican Party. The Democrats, associated with the Confederate South and corrupt party bosses who ruled cities like personal fiefdoms, had been out of favor since the Civil War and entirely locked out of the White House for the previous sixteen years.

Woodrow Wilson—prim, thin-lipped, academic, and idealistic—made a name for himself as governor of New Jersey by repudiating the power brokers who had first proposed his candidacy, passing an ambitious set of progressive reforms over their objections. By re-forming his party first, he laid the groundwork for its return to power.

Wilson set a progressive agenda that placed him squarely between President Taft's big-business-leaning Republican politics and Eugene Debs's million-person Social Democratic Party, and he battled for votes from the center of the electorate with Theodore Roosevelt's insurgent Progressive Party. He described himself as "a man with common opinions but uncommon ability,"[3] and privately compared himself to a volcano, superficially cold but fiery on the inside. His powerfully persuasive speeches sounded to at least one listener like "the collective wail of the middle class."[4]

Once elected president, Wilson worked with a Democratic Congress to enact the Progressive Party's platform almost entirely within his first term in office years, removing the rationale for a major third party and helping to ensure his reelection. In the wake of his presidency, Woodrow Wilson was considered by many contemporaries to rank just below Washington and Lincoln as among our most effective and influential presidents. As historian James Chance recounts, "The terms liberal and conservative have a peculiar accreditation when applied to Woodrow Wilson because he shied away from violence and radical action on both ends of the political spectrum . . . he distrusted the labor movement while also demonstrating antipathy towards big business. Although he wished to reform the abuses of capitalism, he advocated one goal above all others—social order—and one means of obtaining it—representative government. Anyone who threatened that goal, whether from the left or the right, was anathema to this introverted and strangely driven man."[5]

Woodrow Wilson was born before the Civil War and baptized in Thomas Jefferson's hometown of Charlottesville, Virginia. Through a child's eyes he saw the bitter conflict unfold from beginning to end: among his earliest memories were hearing of President Lincoln's election; watching General Robert E. Lee ride by on horseback; and witnessing Confederate president Jefferson Davis being led in chains by Union troops through the street of Augusta, Georgia, where his father was a Presbyterian minister.

Woodrow struggled in grade school with what might now be diagnosed as a learning disability, but with characteristic perseverance, he studied hard enough to attend Davidson College and then Princeton University. He admired the reform British prime minister William Gladstone, hanging his portrait over his desk and explaining that Gladstone's career represented "one continuous advance, not towards power only . . . but truth also."[6] Inspired, Wilson was determined to run for office himself, and had business cards printed up that prematurely proclaimed him the "Senator from Virginia."

But instead of pursuing a life in politics right out of college, Wilson pursued a law degree and then a Ph.D. in political science at Johns Hopkins University, where he published his thesis, *Congressional Government,* a critical success that analyzed the practical methods of effective governance and criticized the primacy of Congress over the president. At the age of twenty-eight, he married the precocious young painter Ellen Louise Axson, and taught political economy and public law at Bryn Mawr College. Five years later, settled into family and academic life, Wilson was granted a full professorship at his alma mater, Princeton. His youthful ambition to enter politics was redirected, but not forgotten, with Wilson privately admitting, "I want to make myself an *outside* force in politics . . . to write something that men delight to read."[7]

In 1889, he published his second major work, titled *The State: Elements of Historical and Practical Politics.* In it, Wilson asked, "What is the proper role of government?" His answer shed light on the essential Centrism that motivated much of his public career.

On the one hand there are extremists who cry constantly to government, "Hands off," *"laissez faire,"* . . . who look upon every act of government which is not merely an act of police with jealousy, who regard government as necessary, but as a necessary evil . . .

On the other hand, there are those who, with equal extremeness of view in the opposite direction, would have society lean only upon government for guidance and assistance in every affair of life, who, by some dream of co-operative endeavor cunningly imagined by the great fathers of Socialism, believe that the state can be made a wise foster-mother to every member of the family politic.

Between these two extremes . . . there is a middle ground . . . which gives wide freedom to the individual for his self-development and yet guards that freedom against the competition that kills, and reduces the antagonism between self-development and social development to a minimum.[8]

Wilson's instinctive search for the middle ground between the extremes would inform his decisions during the tumultuous years when the initial promise of the Industrial Age collided with the cold reality of life in the early twentieth century.

He was an unusually powerful speaker with a high, clear voice. Shy and retiring among small groups, Wilson came alive in front of crowds. A popular lecturer whose classes were frequently concluded with a standing ovation, Wilson was voted the students' favorite professor at Princeton seven out of eight years.

Unusual among college professors of the day, he was unafraid to address contemporary issues in the classroom. In his mind, the principles of the past needed to be adjusted and updated in order to remain relevant. The depression of 1893 and its ensuing 20 percent unemployment caused Wilson to reassess his political views. Like Theodore Roosevelt, he was stirred by the photographs of abject poverty amid the nation's wealthiest city in Jacob Riis's *How the Other Half Lives*. Also like Roosevelt, he was concerned that unless government took steps to reign in the excesses of big business, the specter of violent revolution might come to America. As Wilson later explained, "The country, as it moves forward in its great material progress, needs and will tolerate no party of discontent or radical experiment; but it does need a party of conservative reform, acting in the spirit of law and of ancient institutions."[9]

In 1902, Wilson was appointed the first non-clergymen to lead Princeton University. His prominent new post made him a public figure overnight, a reputation he cultivated by continuing to write articles for newspapers and magazines. *Harper's Weekly* placed his picture on its cover, stating that "Wilson is a man the nation would do well to listen to."

Wilson increasingly saw danger to democracy in both the unregulated influence of big business and the untrammeled partisanship so prevalent at the time. In a speech titled "The Ideals of Public Life" that he gave in Cleveland, Ohio, Wilson warned that "party leaders are obliged in a great degree to be opportunists. But the country cannot afford to be guided by opportunists alone.... Let us insist now ... on thinking outside party formulas and class interests, as the men of our creative period did when the action was in process of birth."[10]

His decision not to support populist icon William Jennings Bryan's third Democratic nomination for president in 1908 made news across the country. Wilson's reasons were not just about ideology; rather, they were based on a clear-eyed appreciation of practical politics: The Democratic Party had grown too dominated by radicals, turning Centrist voters toward the Republican Party and away from the Democrats.

> Since 1896 [the year of Bryan's first nomination] the Democratic Party has permitted its name to be used by men who ought never to have been admitted to its counsels ... populists and radical theorists, contemptuous alike of principle and of experience, these men could never have played any role in national politics but that of a noisy minority. Since they forced themselves into the councils of the party and got the use of its name, every doubtful State has been turned into an enthusiastic supporter of the Republican Party ... [People] who wish for reform without loss of stability should ... reassert the principles and return to the practices of the historic party which has always stood for thoughtful moderation in affairs and a careful use of the powers of the Federal Government in the interest of the whole people of whatever class or occupation."[11]

Practical and principled, Wilson was positioning himself in the center of the Democratic Party. He was appealing to both conservatives and progressives in contrast to Bryan's populism of the proletariat. Unlike Bryan, Wilson did not long for a return to the simpler agrarian past. He was increasingly fascinated by the progressive reforms that were taking place on local levels across the nation, and in 1909 was elected president of a local municipal reform organization. In 1910, Wilson would begin an unexpected political odyssey that would lead him to be elected president of the United States less than two years later.

"Sugar Jim" Smith, the heavy-set Irish-born political boss of New Jersey, made his way to the leafy Princeton campus to secure Wilson's commitment to run for governor. Wilson had what the Democratic machine could not buy or bribe—respectability and a connection with progressive voters. Smith hoped that Wilson would be malleable enough to accept the traditional behind-the-scenes direction. He badly underestimated Wilson's backbone. When Smith offered the nomination, Wilson accepted on the spot. Sugar Jim was about to get schooled by the professor in the art of politics.

Because of his recruitment by New Jersey Democratic power brokers, Progressives were skeptical about Wilson's commitment to their cause. But Wilson declared independence from party bosses by publicly pledging that "I shall not, either in the matter of appointments to office or assent to legislation . . . submit to the dictation of any person or persons, special interest or organization. . . . I regard myself as pledged to the regeneration of the Democratic Party."[12]

He campaigned energetically, determined to provide a contrast to his image as a stiff academic. At a campaign stop outside a theater in Paterson, Wilson spoke to a crowd of twenty-five hundred and explained the purpose of his campaign. "The cause upon which we are met, ladies and gentlemen, is the purification of politics . . . the freeing of politics from the management of machine organizations . . . We have to fear that kind of management, which does not rest upon public opinion, does not rest upon public discussion, does not rest upon anything except the will and agreement of party managers."[13]

Three weeks later, the college president who had never before held public office was elected governor of New Jersey in a landslide, defeating the state's Republican banking commissioner by fifty thousand votes. A week later, Wilson confided to a friend that "it was no Democratic victory. It was a victory of the progressives of both parties who are determined to live no longer under the political organizations that have controlled the two parties of the state."[14]

But when Sugar Jim Smith came calling on the governor-elect with a detailed plan of how to proceed with the administration, he was rebuffed. Wilson played hardball, refusing to support Smith's supposedly safe appointment to the U.S. Senate, choosing instead to successfully throw his weight behind a political unknown. When Smith's son-in-law drunkenly denounced Wilson as "an ingrate and a liar" at a popular seaside restaurant, he was promptly replaced from his post as head of the Democratic Party in New Jersey.

In his inaugural address, amid flags and evergreens and the conspicuous absence of Sugar Jim Smith, Woodrow Wilson proclaimed the possibilities of this new era, pointing out that

> [t]he whole world has changed within the lifetime of men not yet in their thirties; the world of business, and therefore the world of society and the world of politics . . .
>
> We are servants of the people, of the whole people. Their interest should be our constant study. We should pursue it without fear or favor. Our reward will be greater than that to be obtained in any other service: the satisfaction of furthering large ends, large purposes, of being an intimate part of that slow but constant and ever hopeful force of liberty and of enlightenment that is lifting mankind from age to age to new levels of progress and achievement, and of having been something greater than successful men. For we shall have been instruments of humanity, men whose thought was not for themselves, but for the true and lasting comfort and happiness of men everywhere.
>
> It is not the foolish ardor of too sanguine or too radical reform that I urge upon you, but merely the tasks that are evident and pressing, the things we have knowledge and guidance enough to do; and to do with confidence and energy. I merely point out the present business of progressive and serviceable government, the next stage on the journey of duty. The path is as inviting as it is plain. Shall we hesitate to tread it? I look forward with genuine pleasure to the prospect of being your comrade upon it.[15]

The message was inclusive, uplifting, and pragmatic. Wilson put the challenges of the era in context, called on higher purpose to motivate the legislature toward four specific reforms—campaign finance reform, an anticorruption bill, statewide antitrust legislation, and the state's first workers' compensation program—and pledged to work alongside the legislature to secure their mutual success.

In the past, governors kept their distance from the inner workings of the legislature, but Wilson would take an active role in guiding legislative reform. During the campaign, Wilson had reasoned: "Parties respond to other things than the whip. I have never known anything useful done under the whip, but I have known very many useful things done under the kindly warmth of a great principle."[16]

Shortly after he assumed office, an extended interview captured the new governor's reputation and Wilson's attempts to carefully define it:

> Governor Wilson has been many times spoken of as radical. With the conservatism of the true political economist, however, he qualifies this—as he is modest in admitting freely many of the plans he has made to make legislation in New Jersey approach the idea. "Don't use the word 'radical,' " he urged. "There are too many people who are afraid of it—who do not yet understand radicalism, and see in it only an approach to socialism." Above all other things, the "reform governor," as Governor Wilson has come to be called, is modest about the reform he intends to bring about. Insistently he calls himself merely a comrade of the people in bringing about a progressive and serviceable government. "I believe and hope I am a practical politician," he says.[17]

Wilson's remarks were revealing, displaying the mind of a man determined to bring about political change, but conscious of the dangers of overreaching. He was aware that the success of his desired reforms was dependent upon his ability to convince the public. Consequently, he wanted to avoid using the word "radical" because of its associations with socialists. Instead, he took pains to present his agenda as a series of "practical" reforms that merely met the needs of the times.

Angrily, Sugar Jim sought to reassert his power over the party, the legislature, and the state by using his remaining political muscle to block the new governor's progressive agenda. As a group of ma-chine-backed legislators met in conference in the state capital, dis-cussing plans to derail Wilson's bills, they were startled to see the governor himself striding into their meeting. One politico objected, claiming that Wilson's presence was in direct violation of the state constitution. Wilson replied by calmly pulling a copy of the state constitution from his jacket pocket and citing the exact paragraph that gave him power to attend such meetings. Then, switching from vinegar to honey, the governor appealed to "their better, unselfish natures."

Eventually, each of Wilson's reform bills passed, including a pio-neering ban on corporate contributions to political campaigns. The *New York American* editorialized, "The 'scholar in politics' in New Jersey is demonstrating that he is made of sterner stuff than either his friends or his enemies expected. He is meeting the bosses at every salient point with the bristling guns of argument and with the serenity of courage and confidence."[18]

Wilson's success spurred national interest. He was fresh and ef-fective, a dignified Democratic contrast to the status quo adminis-tration of President Taft and the heated pronouncements of Theodore Roosevelt. In a speech to the Kansas Society, Wilson's notes showed clearly how he continued to see himself and the pro-gressive movement in the center of the political spectrum.

> **RADICAL**—one who goes too far.
> **CONSERVATIVE**—one who does not go far enough.
> **REACTIONARY**—one who does not go at all.

> Hence we have invented the term, label, PROGRESSIVE, to mean one who (a) recognizes new facts and adjusts law to them, and who (b) attempts to think ahead, constructively. Progress must build, must be cohesive, must have a plan at its heart.[19]

At a time when the socialists were gaining support across the nation, Wilson's progressivism was rooted in Centrism, a belief in individualism and a respect for self-sufficiency, as when he acidly challenged a crowd by asking, "Do you want big business beneficently to take care of you, or do you want to take care of your-selves? Are you wards or are you men? Do you want the court to appoint guardians for you or are you old enough to take care of yourselves?"[20]

Wilson spoke directly about economic issues, but he did so in a way that defused the combustive issue of class struggle by focusing on common interests that cut across class lines: "Each class must also think of the interest of the rest; they must try to come to a common understanding, in a common sympathy, with a common thought and purpose. And then if we can get a spokesman, an honest man, to lead them, we will recover the prestige and hope and accomplishment of American politics."[21]

Increasingly, people were saying that the governor of New Jersey could be such a man. "Why is Governor Woodrow Wilson now frequently mentioned as a Democratic candidate for the presidency?" asked the *Rocky Mountain News*. "We think the answer is to be found in two words: progressiveness and courage."

With the election of 1912 fast approaching, the presidency did appeal to him. "There is no national party choice except that of President," Wilson had written in his 1885 thesis *Congressional Government*. "No one else represents the people as a whole, exercising a national choice. . . . He can dominate his party by being the spokesman for the real sentiment and purposes of the country, by giving direction to opinion."[22]

Most of the nation was buzzing about the apparent return of Theodore Roosevelt from self-appointed exile. The great man had personally selected his friend and cabinet member William Howard Taft to succeed him in the White House. But while Roosevelt enjoyed the first months of early retirement by going big-game hunting in Africa and traveling to Europe, he kept hearing from progressive Republicans that the eager-to-get-along Taft was abandoning them in struggles with the powerful business interests that had dominated the party before the onset of the Roosevelt reforms.

In conversations with progressive allies like pioneering environmentalist Gifford Pinchot, Roosevelt had warned against the influence of "over radicalism. Remember that the extreme men on the insurgent side are really working for defeat just as much as the

Cannon-Aldrich leaders [of the Republican party in Congress]."[23] Back in the United States, fortified by the conviction that the growing socialist movement in Europe might spread to the United States unless underlying social and economic issues were met and addressed—"I might be able to guide this movement, but I should be wholly unable to stop it, even if I were to try"[24]—TR decided to return to the arena of presidential politics by challenging the sitting president, declaring in February 1912: "My hat is in the ring! The fight is on and I am stripped to the buff!"

TR called Taft a tool of "the bosses and the great privileged interests" and, as the campaign wore on, "a fathead" with "the brains of a guinea pig." While the former president was arguably the most loved man in America, his increasingly combative tone alienated some supporters and stiffened his opponent's resolve to defeat him. The unpopular Taft had no illusions about his likelihood of winning the election, but he persisted out of determination to "keep that madman out of the White House," adding on the campaign trail that "even a rat will fight in a corner when it is trapped."

Wilson's appeal was based on the fact that while he and Roosevelt shared many of the same political goals, Wilson was a fresh but responsible voice who presented progressive reforms in reasonable tones. In a speaking trip out West to kick off his campaign, Wilson discussed his support of progressive reforms such as the referendum and the recall not as a way to revolutionize government, but as a means of restoring it to the people, whose power had been illegitimately usurped. "To Western ears accustomed to the heated rhetoric of insurgents in both parties," biographer August Heckscher reflected, "Wilson's speech sounded cool and moderate; it was reprinted many times and praised precisely because it was not demagogic."[25] Wilson was fresh when all the other candidates for president seemed overheated.

Roosevelt campaigned in the first-ever Republican primaries for a restoration of his leadership to the White House under the slogan of "New Nationalism." His great personal popularity translated to continued support from voters—in fact, Roosevelt won all but two Republican presidential primaries in 1912, including Taft's beloved home state of Ohio. But regardless of the results of the nonbinding primaries, President Taft and other conservative Republican leaders were determined to deny Roosevelt the nomination. By hook and by crook, they slid delegates toward Taft, prompting outraged reformers to march off the convention floor and form the Progressive Party.

As the Republican Party splintered in the summer heat, Democrats gathered in Baltimore to select their nominee for president. The favorite was the Speaker of the House, Champ Clark of Missouri. He was, above all else, a safe choice—neither a reformer nor a reactionary—and his uninspiring profile as a Democrat establishment insider made opponents hope that he would receive the nomination ("Pop is praying for the nomination of Champ Clark," Kermit Roosevelt reportedly said).[26] Three-time loser William Jennings Bryan was not running, but his support would be crucial for another candidate to gain the nomination. Wilson's devoted wife organized a private dinner with Bryan in Princeton, without Woodrow's knowledge, in order to help patch up the rift between the two men. Bryan apparently emerged believing, as Roosevelt privately admitted, that Wilson was "the strongest man the Democrats could nominate."[27] After intraparty machinations that lasted forty-six ballots, Woodrow Wilson finally received the Democratic nomination. There was now a fresh progressive alternative to Theodore Roosevelt running for president on a major party's ticket.* With the Republican Party divided down the middle, the pragmatic former professor became the front-runner overnight.

"We stand in the presence of an awakened nation, impatient of partisan make-believe," Wilson asserted in his speech accepting the nomination. "The nation has been unnecessarily, unreasonably at war within itself." Wilson preached a doctrine of common interests allied against special interests, an essentially moderate and conciliatory message of reform he called the "New Freedom." As historian

---

*For all Wilson's appearance of arch confidence on the campaign trail, he was beset by personal doubts about how he stood up against Roosevelt, confessing, "He appeals to their imagination. I do not. He is a real, vivid person who they have seen and shouted themselves hoarse for and voted for, millions strong. I am a vague, conjectural personality, more made up of opinions and academic prepossessions than of human traits and red corpuscles." (Letter to Mary Hulbert, August 25, 1912.)

John Milton Cooper remarked, "Some in his partisan audience might have wondered whether their nominee was a Republican in Democrat's clothing."[28]

With President Taft anchoring the right wing of the spectrum and socialist Eugene Debs on the far left, Wilson's New Freedom and Roosevelt's New Nationalism battled it out for center stage, their slogans consciously echoing one another. As Roosevelt's friend the progressive journalist William Allen White wrote, "Between the New Nationalism and the New Freedom was that fantastic imaginary gulf that always has existed between Tweedle-dum and Tweedle-dee."[29]

Wilson's vision for reining in the trusts—"regulated competition"—stood between President Taft's establishment embrace of big business and TR's call for the creation of the Federal Trade Commission. Far from being motivated by malice toward free markets or entrepreneurial individuals, Wilson believed that "every great man of business has got somewhere a touch of the idealist in him."[30] His respect for the entrepreneurial man rising out of the middle class was indivisible from his optimistic view of America.

The problem with monopolies for Wilson was that they perverted the free market, stifling competition. His primary adviser on the issue, Boston lawyer Louis Brandeis—who Wilson would later appoint to the Supreme Court—was famously described as having "so much respect for private property that he wishes it were more equitably distributed, so much respect for capital that he wishes it to flow freely instead of being concentrated in a money trust."[31] As Wilson saw it, "A Trust is an arrangement to get rid of competition, and a big business is a business that has survived competition by conquering in the field of intelligence and economy. I'm for big business, I'm against the Trusts." But even though Wilson proposed new laws to rein in the excesses of Trusts on behalf of the middle class, he was also wary of the reach of big government, stating that "the history of liberty is a history of the limitation of governmental power, not the increase of it."[32]

On the campaign trail, Wilson was careful to reach out by expressing respect for Republican voters and the Republican progressive tradition, describing himself as "one of those who entertain a very great respect for the history of the Republican Party . . . A great many men and women of noble character, of the most elevated purpose, have joined themselves to that party because . . . of the reforms . . . I take off my hat to those people. I sympathize with their impulses. I have not a word of criticism of them for allying themselves with any force, any honorable force, which they think can accomplish these things."[33]

Practical and not partisan, Wilson was presenting himself as a man primarily interested in finding solutions. This was in sharp contrast to the two squabbling Republicans, who spent so much time attacking each other that Wilson was left relatively unscathed. Wilson benefited tremendously from the split in the Republican ranks; by late October, bookmakers were offering six-to-one odds the Wilson would be the next president of the United States.

On election night in 1912, bells rang out across the campus of Princeton University, as a students led a torchlight procession to the home of their president, who came out to meet them with his family alongside, warmly shaking hands as a feeling of deep responsibility settled in his soul.

Although Wilson earned only 42 percent of the popular vote, he won forty states, translating to an electoral college landslide of 435 electoral votes, thus denying Republicans a fifth consecutive term in the White House. TR won six states outright and gained 27 percent of the total vote—to date the highest amount for an independent third-party candidate. Taft ran a distant third, with the socialist Debs even beating the sitting president in a few states. Indeed, Debs's socialist vote provided one of the few true surprises of the evening, more than doubling its vote total from the previous election to over nine hundred thousand—the highest amount achieved by the American socialists then or since. A minor item in the newspaper also proved a powerful harbinger of political shifts to come: Wilson's election marked the first time that Massachusetts elected a Democratic state ticket and a Democratic legislature.

In 1912, the United States was in transition, splintering along economic and ethnic lines with a general leftward political drift. Republican Party stalwarts could find some comfort in the argument that the combined Taft and Roosevelt total amounted to an overwhelming Republican victory. But the combined progressive vote behind Wilson and Roosevelt alone totaled almost 70 percent of the American electorate. The public was endorsing progressive reforms—preferring in the end to give the reins of reform to the established and indeed comparatively conservative Democrats. That was the glass-half-full analysis that Wilson chose to take heart in, telling reporters the next day that "the result fills me with hope that the thoughtful progressive forces of the Nation may now at last unite."[34]

Wilson lost no time in attempting to secure this sense of unification. Days after taking the oath of office, President Wilson informed Congress that he would become the first chief executive in 113 years to come to Capitol Hill and address the members directly. Wilson pounded out the speech himself on his portable typewriter: "I am very glad indeed to have this opportunity to address the two Houses directly and to verify for myself the impression that the President of the United States is a person, not a mere department of the Government hailing Congress from some isolated island of jealous power, sending messages, not speaking naturally and with his own voice—that he is a human being trying to cooperate with other human beings in a common service."[35]

The strategy was considered novel in hyperpartisan Washington. The president would descend from the mountaintop to work with Congress in passing his legislative agenda.

As governor, Wilson had criticized the Republican antitrust policies for having "too much talk and too few practicable suggestions." Now in the highest office, he would back up his assertion that "government is not a warfare of interests"[36] by stressing the common interests of the Congress respectfully across party lines. He would adopt a collegial rather than imperial air, conduct an open-door policy for good ideas, and freely give credit to others in public. He also took care to unify the Democratic Party, giving important appointments to party leaders he had disagreed with in the past, and tapping William Jennings Bryan to serve as secretary of state. In cabinet meetings, Wilson's secretary of the navy, Josephus Daniels, described the president's role as that of a moderator, encouraging open discussion designed to elicit "what he was fond of calling common counsel," finishing the meeting with a recap of the general sentiments, saying "it seems to me that the sense of the meetings is so and so . . ."[37] To the party at large, he presented the success of legislation as a test of the Democrat's relevance.

This strategy proved stunningly successful. Wilson's term in office was marked by a furious pace of legislative accomplishment that rivals any in American history. In fact, Wilson and his Democratic-controlled Congress succeeded in passing most of the Progressive Party's platform, including abolition of child labor, as well as the establishment of the eight-hour day as a contract standard, the Clayton Antitrust Act, the Federal Reserve banking system, the federal income tax, and the Federal Trade Commission to mediate conflicts between big and small business. He quickly resolved the contentious issue of tariff reform, which had destroyed the last Democrat in the White House, Grover Cleveland. Wilson also secured passage of the Seventeenth Amendment, which allowed direct election of U.S. senators by the public instead of the state legislatures; the Eighteenth Amendment, establishing Prohibition; and—after initial opposition from Wilson—the Nineteenth Amendment, giving women the right to vote.

After this coordinated and quite disciplined activism, Wilson could declare that the essential reforms of the progressive movement had been achieved. He was, as always, well aware of the dangers of overreaching. By wisely focusing his reform program and restricting its ability to sprawl far beyond its original intentions, Wilson reasserted the relevance of the existing system without inviting backlash.

Roosevelt, while frequently consumed by personal dislike for Wilson in later years, understood that Wilson's success probably meant the end of the Progressive Party. "If the Democratic Party acts on the whole wisely and sanely," he told a friend, "it may be the Progressive Party will be eliminated."[38] And so it was.

In 1916 Wilson became one of only three Democratic presidents reelected in the twentieth century. Wilson believed that "if you think too much about being reelected, it is very difficult to be worth re-electing." Teddy Roosevelt's Progressive Party would dissolve after he returned to the ranks of the Republican Party. He was the favorite to receive the party's nomination for president in 1920 when he died suddenly in his sleep in Oyster Bay, New York.

Wilson's second term in office would be dominated by the First World War and his idealistically interventionist view of America's obligation to help "make the world safe for democracy." In domestic and international affairs, the dominant theme that would emerge in his thinking was the need to emphasize common interests over selfish special interests. "The longer I occupy the office that I now occupy," he reflected, "the more I deplore any feeling that one set of men has one set of interests and another set of men another set. . . . We cannot, and must not, separate our interests from one another, but must pool our interests."[39]

Likewise, when he was faced with the epic struggle to establish the League of Nations in the aftermath of the First World War, he stated that the league's success would only occur "when men of good will, of whatever country, come to understand their true common interests."[40]

The league's defeat was a severe blow for Wilson personally and politically. Defiant in defeat, Wilson remarked: "Sometimes people call me an 'idealist.' Well, that is the way I know I am an American."[41]

Wilson had no doubt that the idea underlying the League of Nations would be vindicated in time. "I am not one of those that have the least anxiety about the triumph of the principles that I have stood for. I have seen fools resist Providence before, and I have seen their destruction. . . . That we shall prevail is as sure as that God reigns."[42]

The establishment of the United Nations after the Second World War represented the progression of Wilson's vision nearly a quarter of a century after his death. Significantly, the birth of the international body was begun by Franklin Delano Roosevelt—who worked as Wilson's assistant secretary of the navy—and completed by Harry Truman, who served as an infantry captain in the First World War. More than any other president, Wilson was their hero in the recent history of the Democratic Party, a practical and progressive commander in chief in times of war and peace.

JOHN F. KENNEDY — 1960

AN IDEALIST WITHOUT ILLUSIONS CHARTS
A COLD-WARRIOR COURSE

This is a time for courage and a time of challenge. Neither conformity nor complacency will do. Neither fanatics nor the faint-hearted are needed. And our duty as a Party is not to our Party alone, but to the Nation, and indeed, to all mankind. Our duty is not merely the preservation of political power but the preservation of peace and freedom.

—UNDELIVERED SPEECH, NOVEMBER 22, 1963[1]

Politics is perception, and no one understood that better than John F. Kennedy. From an early age, his father, Joe, repeated, "You must remember: It's not what you are that counts, but what people think you are."[2]

Kennedy effortlessly embraced the contradictions of his existence—Irish-Brahmin, patrician-populist, playboy-statesman, foreign policy hawk but domestic policy New Dealer—dichotomies all fitting a man who was racked by physical pain most of his adult life while consciously projecting an image of youthful vigor. He restored romance to politics through the elevation of image, using idealistic rhetoric to inspire audiences, but Jack Kennedy was at heart a pragmatist, "a realist cleverly disguised as a romantic."[3]

In death he became the patron saint of liberal causes—a blank slate on which to project what might have been. "Grief," as his friend and adviser Arthur Schlesinger Jr. noted, "nourishes myth."[4] So we should take care to see him as he was in life, to see him as he saw himself.

Weeks after he leaned across a plate of asparagus at a Georgetown dinner party and asked her out on a date, twenty-one-year-old Jacqueline Bouvier was walking hand in hand with the thirty-six-year-old Massachusetts senator when she asked him to describe himself. "An idealist without illusions," he said.[5] When Jack Kennedy first ran for Congress in 1946, only one year out of the Navy, he chose two slogans to describe himself to voters: "The New Generation Offers a Leader," and "The Fighting Conservative."

Kennedy faced a crowded field of nine candidates in the Democratic primary in 1946 and surprised the experts when he beat the machine candidate who was heavily favored to win. From that first election on, he operated outside the Massachusetts Democratic establishment, preferring to mobilize an independent network of friends and family motivated by personal loyalty and funded by his father's Wall Street fortune.

Despite the fact that his grandfather John F. "Honey Fitz" Fitzgerald led the Irish into the corridors of power when he was elected Boston's mayor in 1910, JFK had more in common with Harvard Yard and Hyannis Port than the smoke-filled backrooms of machine politics; he found the petty corruption and ethnic pandering distasteful and had no patience for demagogues. He was the only member of the state's congressional delegation who refused to sign his name to a petition requesting clemency for Boston's incarcerated mayor, James Curley, who was serving out his term in a federal prison for mail fraud.

Kennedy fought to bring federal dollars to his mostly poor Irish and Italian immigrant district and strongly supported liberal programs to build new housing, but he was an outspoken critic of the Truman administration for being "soft on communism." When congressional debate raged over Mao's Communist takeover of China,

Kennedy aligned himself with Republicans when he placed the blame "squarely on the White House and the State Department."[6]

In 1952, after three terms in Congress, he challenged popular moderate Republican senator Henry Cabot Lodge for his seat. Eisenhower was running for president, and it was widely considered to be a year for the GOP. Kennedy campaigned hard while his opponent was busy stumping for the national ticket. Kennedy released a forty-page document analyzing Lodge's record while in office, condemning the incumbent for "straddling the big issue of the guilt or innocence" of State Department employees accused of spying for the Soviet Union. Republican senator Joe McCarthy—for whom Kennedy's younger brother and campaign manager Bobby briefly worked as deputy counsel for McCarthy's Government Operations Committee—was then at the height of his popularity and crucially refused to campaign for Lodge as the election went down to the wire. Kennedy's combination of Cold War and New Deal credentials appealed to his constituents, and he became the only Democrat elected statewide that year.

The Eisenhower years brought political stability but also a palpable sense of drift. There was prosperity, but no sense of overarching purpose. When *Life* commissioned a series of national leaders' comments on the country's growing malaise, Kennedy's assessment was direct and unsentimental: "The harsh facts of the matter are that we have gone soft—physically, mentally, and spiritually soft."[7] He was talking not only about the state of the nation, but also about the state of the Democratic Party. Kennedy's political vision and instincts stood in sharp contrast to the tentative, tweedy liberalism favored by the party's standard-bearer, Adlai Stevenson.

While the nation liked Ike, liberal leaders like Eleanor Roosevelt loved Adlai. The two-term governor of Illinois was eloquent and eminently reasonable, a strong supporter of the United Nations. But as a matter of politics and personality, he was conflict-averse. He was an academic, frequently described as an "egg-head" in magazines of the day. His reputation for indecisiveness compared unfavorably to the military experience of General Eisenhower. In the eyes of Kennedy and many other Americans, Adlai Stevenson was not tough enough to lead the nation.

So Kennedy continued to distance himself from the ultraliberal wing of his own Democratic Party; while some congressmen spoke of Adlai Stevenson and Harry Truman in hallowed tones, Kennedy preferred to recall the party's more distant icons: Jefferson, Madison, Wilson, and FDR. As Democrats tried to regroup after their first loss of the White House in twenty years, Senator Kennedy went so far as to declare: "I'm not a liberal at all. I never joined the Americans for Democratic Action or the American Veterans Committee. I'm not comfortable with those people."[8]

What was it that led to Kennedy's consistent impulse to distance himself from the liberal wing of the Democratic Party? The answers might be found in a family built around the principle of individual competition, rough games of touch football, and praise of winners and condemnation of losers accompanied by the only half-joking admonition "Kennedys don't cry." Kennedy's natural sense of ironic detachment also prevented him from affiliating himself 100 percent with any organization. Two anecdotes in particular shed light upon the Kennedy family's attitude toward what they saw as liberals' weakness and abdication of responsibility.

In 1960, when Jack was beginning his campaign for the presidency, his father paid a quiet visit to Henry Luce—the influential and staunchly anticommunist founder of *Time*. Luce told Joseph Kennedy: "Tell Jack not to worry about the way Time Inc. will treat him. We know he has to go with the Liberals on domestic issues, and we'll argue with him politely. On foreign policy, we'll be fair to him—unless he listens to you and turns soft. Then we'll cut his throat." To which Joe replied, somewhat hurt, "Harry, how the hell could any son of mine be a goddamn liberal? Don't worry about Jack being a weak sister. He'll be tough."[9]

Likewise, his brother Bobby, who idolized his brother and became a liberal icon in the years leading up to his fateful 1968 race for the presidency, also expressed a reluctance to associate himself with liberals. In a speech given at Loyola University by Justice Department aide John W. Douglas five months after RFK's assassination entitled "Robert Kennedy and the Qualities of Personal Leadership," Douglas stated:

Senator Kennedy was allergic to the word "liberal." I remember that when he returned to Washington after his 1964 election to the Senate he told several of us at the airport, with evident relish, that he had gotten through the campaign without his having to claim that he was a liberal. He chuckled at this recollection and seemed genuinely pleased. Yet, of course, he supported measures which were generally believed to carry the liberal line. Why then did the word tend to put his teeth on edge? I think his dislike for it stemmed from several things. First, like many, he disliked being pigeonholed by others; he wanted to be judged by his works and the statements and not by some label applied by somebody else. Second, he had a genuine distaste for some of those who proclaimed themselves "liberal" yet did not live up to their professions. And he believed that some individuals in this category devoted too much time to talking about and approaching problems and not enough in doing something about them. He favored solutions and proposals. He was less impressed by discussions and abstract ideas which did not point towards some conclusion. He wanted analysis to lead to suggestions.[10]

The Kennedys were impatient with liberal ideologues' penchant for criticism over action. Their experience in government made them partial to solutions rather than suggestions.

In 1954, John F. Kennedy angered liberals again when he refused to endorse the Democratic candidate Foster Furcolo for Senate, in favor of his respected Republican coworker Leverett Saltonstall ("Sometimes party loyalty asks too much," he bitterly explained to a friend). He penned an article for the Hearst newspapers in which he criticized the Democratic-controlled Congress's tax-and-spend policies, urging greater fiscal discipline. In 1956, Kennedy published the book *Profiles in Courage,* written with the assistance of aide Ted Sorensen while Kennedy was laid up in the hospital recuperating from serious surgery on his chronically bad back. The book detailed the pressures on great U.S. senators who defied their party and constituents to do what they thought was right at difficult periods in the nation's history. Kennedy included in his book a profile of "Mr. Republican," Senator Robert Taft of Ohio, Congress's leading isolationist. Liberals were again aghast.

JFK was now among the youngest U.S. senators, a decorated war hero, and a Pulitzer Prize winner for *Profiles in Courage*—a figure of both action and reflection, a Democrat who was willing to talk about self-sacrifice and national greatness. In 1956, he decided to seek the party's nomination for vice president. Kennedy mobilized his troops across the convention floor, but fell in the third round of balloting due in part to opposition from fellow Massachusetts Democrat and future Speaker of the House John McCormack, who threw his considerable weight behind the celebrated Tennessee senator Estes Kefauver. Kennedy conceded and in a nationally televised speech called on Democrats to make Kefauver's nomination unanimous. The loss turned out to be a blessing in disguise—a Stevenson-Kennedy ticket would almost surely have been defeated by the Eisenhower-Nixon team that was running for reelection, and the loss would have likely been blamed on Kennedy's Catholicism. Still, the rejection hurt. Trying to transform anger into resolve, Kennedy promised himself that from then on he would be "a complete politician."

In March 1957, several months after President Eisenhower's second inauguration, John F. Kennedy's face was in newsstands and grocery stores across the nation as he graced the cover of the issue of *Life* magazine that contained his essay "Where Democrats Should Go From Here."[11] It was intended to be both a call to arms and a slap of recognition in the face of complacent Democrats who were inclined to deny the realities of their recent defeat. In fact, Kennedy wrote, the Democrats had "not won a clear majority in both houses of Congress since 1936," and under Eisenhower's leadership "the Republican Party was now sufficiently progressive and internationalist, at least in appearance, to blur the once distinctive position of the Democrats."

The Republicans had moved to the center while Democrats lost their focus by becoming embroiled in intraparty squabbles that held little interest for the average voter. Kennedy felt that if the Democratic ship did not right its course, the party ran the risk of fading into oblivion like the Federalist and Whig parties before it. "Faced with an administration obviously to the left of the traditional Republican position . . . the Democrats are caught on the horns of a dilemma. We cannot, on the one hand, move to the right to oppose (without more progressive alternatives) the President's more constructive measures—on school aid or immigration, for example—without appearing obstructionist or reactionary. . . . But neither, on the other hand, can we move too far to the left in order to distinguish the Democratic position without alienating those wayward moderate and independent Democrats whom we're trying to move back from the Republican column."

Kennedy recommended that Democrats stop running "against Herbert Hoover" and start embracing new ideas and new candidates, building a "responsible progressive record" in a Congress that "demonstrates leadership in the problems of prosperity." Kennedy recommended that the Democratic Party take a forthright stand on civil rights and focused on the importance of mobilizing the younger generation. The Kennedy prescription was vague in parts, but it had the intended effect of presenting him as a charismatic and thoughtful young leader of the Democratic Party.

Kennedy began traveling widely around the country giving speeches, while fawning press coverage presented him as a dynamic moderate—not your typical pushover liberal. "Senator Kennedy Is a Realist Who Fights Own Battles"[12] proclaimed a headline in the *Tulsa World;* while the *Louisville Courier Journal* announced "Kennedy Combines Tough Practicality and Egg-Headed Political Concepts."[13]

Kennedy's 1958 reelection campaign in Massachusetts was considered the ultimate litmus test for whether he was ready to run for the White House. The Kennedy team went all out, sending field operatives to 279 of the state's 312 towns by early October. Kennedy knew that he already had the support of Massachusetts' big cities sewn up, so now he was taking the fight to GOP strongholds. Jackie later remembered it as "the hardest campaign ever . . . just running, running." He was rewarded by what was then the greatest victory margin in the history of Massachusetts, gaining nearly eight hundred thousand votes more than he received six years before.

Predictions for a White House run were no longer premature. Newspapers and magazines looked into their crystal ball and saw the 1960 race shaping up. "Kennedy has been regarded by many as the Democratic counterpart of the GOP's Richard Nixon," wrote the *American Mercury.* "Nixon is basically a moderate conservative but with some liberal tendencies. Kennedy is basically a moderate liberal but with many conservative leanings. Neither is an extremist in any sense. A showdown battle between the two for the presidency of the United States is not at all impossible."[14]

Kennedy had played his career up to this point perfectly. With an orchestrated media campaign he established himself as an instant front-runner for the 1960 nomination, despite the fact that many Senate colleagues considered him relatively undistinguished, a playboy lightweight. But the nation was now talking about Jack Kennedy, and that was what mattered. He seemed like a breath of fresh air, tough but thoughtful, young and energetic—the anti–Adlai Stevenson. Three significant hurdles remained to Kennedy's getting the Democratic nomination for President: his religion, his youth, and lingering liberal resentment.

As Kennedy began his campaign, the United States had never elected a Catholic or a person that young to the presidency. On the issue of age, Kennedy could confidently point out that many of our nation's Founding Fathers were in their thirties when they drafted the Constitution and the Declaration of Independence. The issue of religion was a bit trickier. The Democrats' 1928 nominee, New York governor Al Smith, had been defeated soundly by Herbert Hoover, and conventional wisdom held that his Catholicism had been a powerful reason for his lack of support in traditionally Democratic areas. In the South, for example, the Ku Klux Klan was created to enforce discrimination upon blacks, Jews, and Catholics. The polite reason given for denying the presidency to a Catholic was the individual's presumed subservience to the pope in Rome. Kennedy did not flaunt his Catholicism—like his membership in the Democratic Party, it was more a matter of birthright than personal conviction— but neither did he run away from it. When asked, he always asserted his strong belief in the separation of church and state. When Catholic bishops took a position against the spread of birth-control information by the United States or the United Nations, Kennedy declined to endorse their decision. His independence added credibility to his pledge to always place the interests of the nation first. When the issue of his Catholicism was raised in political debates, Kennedy benefited from his opponent's appearance of discrimination.

Liberal resentment of Kennedy was not nearly so easy to deal with directly. Throughout his congressional career, he had made a conscious effort to define himself as a moderate with an independent voting record. But liberals and labor represented the extreme wing of the party that could exert a veto on the Democratic presidential nominee. It appeared likely that they would veto a Kennedy candidacy. Kennedy's friend and former Stevenson adviser Arthur Schlesinger Jr. characterized liberal suspicions of Kennedy by writing: "Kennedy seemed too cool and ambitious, too bored by the conditioned reflexes of stereotyped liberalism, too much a young man in a hurry. He did not respond in anticipated ways and phrases and wore no liberal heart on his sleeve."[15]

He would not win the nomination by simply lining up delegates through the traditional political establishment. He was not their preferred candidate. JFK needed to prove his ability to defeat a liberal candidate, and so he trudged into the snows of Wisconsin to do battle with the liberal's favorite candidate, Minnesota's Hubert Humphrey. The fact that he was the representative of the neighboring state in the most liberal region of the nation gave Humphrey an advantage in the Democratic primary. Kennedy scored an upset victory over the favorite son, but skeptical pundits wrote it off to heavy turnout among Wisconsin Catholics. And so the Kennedy operation headed toward the next primary in West Virginia, a poor and rural state with virtually no Catholics. Implicit in this formula was the presence of prejudice, and so West Virginia was considered the acid test for JFK's presidential aspirations. As one elderly woman interviewed in Sutton, West Virginia, said, "We've never had a Catholic president and I hope we never do. Our people built this country. If they had wanted a Catholic to be president, they would have said so in the Constitution."[16] The issue of religion appeared to be alive and well.

To change hearts and minds, the well-oiled Kennedy PR machine rolled into town, fueled by seemingly unlimited amounts of money. It was far-reaching, close to the ground, and effective. Omnipresent JFK buttons, posters, and radio commercials (with Frank Sinatra singing a swinging campaign version of "High Hopes") briefly became facts of life in West Virginia. When necessary, the palms of local elected and union officials were greased with $100 bills. Franklin Delano Roosevelt Jr., the son of the still-legendary FDR, campaigned for Kennedy, giving the impression that the great man himself approved of this transfer of the Democratic mantle. Against the odds, Kennedy won West Virginia convincingly. And then it was on to sunny Los Angeles for the 1960 Democratic convention.

He did not arrive to the warmest of welcomes. Establishment liberals were outraged that Kennedy had essentially self-selected himself as their presidential nominee, leapfrogging ahead of more qualified candidates with more distinguished track records in Congress and greater fidelity to liberal principles. There was a brief but impassioned movement to draft Adlai Stevenson for a third consecutive run at the White House, which Hubert Humphrey endorsed. The Kennedy operation was disciplined and businesslike, with Bobby Kennedy lining up all the delegates needed to put them over the top. Now the question was who JFK would tap to serve as his vice president. Key southern conservatives argued for Senate majority leader Lyndon Johnson's appointment. Kennedy had spoken publicly of his intention to pick a midwestern liberal due to his concern about the economy's impact on family-owned farms, but Humphrey's endorsement of Stevenson made the Minnesotan's appointment impossible. The usual two priorities needed to be reconciled: uniting the party's warring factions around the ticket and setting up a balance that would have national appeal.

When word leaked out that Kennedy had offered the vice presidency to Lyndon Johnson, party liberals again felt betrayed by Kennedy. Local chapters of the Americans for Democratic Action flooded party headquarters with telegrams threatening to withhold their endorsement. From the West Side of New York City came this message in the clipped syntax of telegraph: "Majority for position we don't trust Kennedy and don't like Johnson, but Nixon so bad we have to do something." The ADA chapter from Dallas—in Johnson's home state—telegrammed this perspective: "Think ADA has higher duty than endorsing lesser of two evils. Should endorse Democratic platform but no candidate."[17]

Even Arthur Schlesinger Jr. initially felt betrayed by Johnson's appointment. In the midst of a minor crisis of political faith, he contacted the theologian Reinhold Niebuhr, an old friend who happened to be vacationing in nearby Santa Barbara. To Schlesinger's surprise, he found Niebuhr "strongly in favor of Johnson's nomination. He pointed out that the Democratic Party pledged itself to the strongest civil rights plank in history. If, in addition, it had nominated a militant northern liberal for the vice presidency, this could only have confirmed the South in its sense of isolation and persecution. But the nomination of a southern candidate who accepted the platform, including the civil rights plank, restored the Democrats as a national party and associated the South with the pursuit of national goals."[18]

Niebuhr's dispassionate theological perspective captured the essence of Centrism. In balancing the ticket, and attempting to reconcile formerly opposing political faiths, Kennedy was using contradiction to cause people to question their assumptions about the Democratic Party. This inclusive ticket balanced the idealistic and the pragmatic, and, as a result, made the prospect of achieving progress far more likely. After speaking to his friend Niebuhr, Schlesinger scribbled in his notebook that he now believed Johnson's selection "may come to be seen as a masterstroke . . . I now think that on balance, from the viewpoint of both winning the election and of governing the country, the decision was brave and wise."[19]

The Boston-Austin axis proved effective: Kennedy and Johnson balanced each other not just in terms of geography and policy, but also in personal style. Johnson was all New Deal populism, a backslapping representative of the good-ole-boy South and West, while Kennedy possessed the more reserved air of the Northeast intellectual, earnest yet slightly detached and cerebral. Together, they were able to unify the mutually distrustful wings of the Democratic Party that coexisted so uneasily since they were bound together by FDR and bring Texas back into the Democratic column after it had twice voted for Eisenhower.

In time, liberal New Dealers began to line up in support of this nominee from the new generation. FDR biographer James MacGregor Burns did a series of interviews with Kennedy and, though initially skeptical, came away with something not far from admiration. "He is a different type of Liberal from any we have known," Burns explained in an article for the *New Republic* subtitled "Liberalism Without Tears." "He is in love not with lost causes, not passionate evocations, not with insuperable difficulties; he is in love with political effectiveness."[20]

Kennedy ran an aggressive campaign that, consistent with his personal beliefs, was considerably to the right of most Democratic candidates. His signature pledge to "get the country moving again" promised to bring a renewed vigor to government that highlighted his own youth and charisma while calling attention to the stale status quo of the Eisenhower administration without criticizing the great man by name. He capitalized on popular concerns following the Soviet's successful deployment of *Sputnik* and alleged that a missile gap existed between United States and the USSR. Kennedy was promising a more aggressive approach to the Cold War, turning Nixon's right flank and making it impossible for the Republicans to trot out their usual accusation that Democrats were soft on Communism. This was a major sea change in perceptions surrounding the two parties, which associated liberal left-wing Democrats with Communist sympathizers.

Kennedy also aggressively addressed the 7 percent unemployment rate and three recessions under Eisenhower with an economic plan that called for tax cuts to stimulate the economy. Just as he had with the issue of Cold War preparedness, Kennedy turned the tables on the Republicans, who previously owned the issue of tax cuts.

Kennedy's strident anticommunism and heroic vision of classically liberal individualism allowed him to appear all things to all people. The conservative *National Review* ran a profile of Kennedy titled "The Chameleon Image of John F. Kennedy" that pointedly asked, "How can Northern Liberals and Southern Democrats, Free Enterprisers and

Welfare Statists, all like Jack Kennedy?" The article read in part: "John Kennedy, junior Senator from Massachusetts, is the perfect candidate because he looks conservative, acts with a judicious air, respects what passes for academic expertise, is rich without seeming to care for money, defers to the hierarchy of his Catholic Church in spiritual matters without admitting the pope to his own realm of Caesar, draws an apparent line between good and bad labor that is reminiscent of Teddy Roosevelt's distinction between good and bad trusts, and always in a pinch votes radical."[21] Even the Ivy League conservatives who traced all things wrong in America to the Democratic reign of FDR and the New Deal could not quite bring themselves to hate JFK.

Vice President Richard Nixon faced a considerable charisma deficit. Running hard, almost desperately at times, on his experience ("Incidentally, I have talked with Khrushchev"), he came across as defensive. In return for Kennedy's repeated comments that America was falling behind in the arms race, Nixon accused him of "running America down and giving us an inferiority complex." Nixon also asserted that a Democrat in the White House would cause prices to go up at least 25 percent. Even Nixon's choice of a running mate, former Massachusetts senator Henry Cabot Lodge, had a defensive ring to it—he was the man Kennedy had defeated eight years before. Fundamentally, Nixon tried to run a moderate campaign, consistent with the course Eisenhower had set for his administration. In fact, he and Kennedy had many similarities throughout their career. They had entered Congress together in 1946 after serving in the navy during the Second World War, and were friends while serving as low men on the labor committee. During the 1950s, Nixon's fortunes had soared with his appointment on Eisenhower's ticket. Now Nixon and Kennedy, the two youngest men to run for the presidency in almost a century, faced each other for the highest prize: leadership of the free world. Polls showed them running neck and neck, and the nation waited for the first televised presidential debates in history. The debates would prove decisive.

The Kennedy-Nixon televised presidential debates remain the most famous in American history. To gain a sense of their importance, one needs to appreciate the fact that only ten years before—in

1950—just 11 percent of all Americans owned a television. By 1960, 88 percent of Americans owned a television. In the years of mass consumption, 1954–1956, Americans were buying TVs at a rate of ten thousand every day.[22] It was a communications revolution unlike any before in our history and it changed everything, including—and especially—political campaigns. Kennedy was a seducer—he had been one all his life—and intuitively understood the potential of this new medium. His campaign headquarters requested five televised debates; Nixon initially wanted just one, but they "compromised" on four. Kennedy's advisers were exultant. "Every time we get those two fellows on-screen side-by-side," said Kennedy television guru J. Leonard Reinsch, "we're going to gain and he's going to lose."[23]

The first debate was scheduled for September 26 in Chicago. Kennedy got into town early the day before, and spent his time resting, relaxing, and prepping with trusted aides Ted Sorensen and Dick Goodwin. On the day of the debate, he gave a quick speech to a friendly union audience, took an afternoon nap, and ate an early dinner. Nixon, in contrast, had been hospitalized for a knee injury the week before, and had been campaigning hard to make up for lost time. He arrived in Chicago late the night before the first debate, and spent much of the next day in seclusion, out of contact with even his closest aides, emerging only to give a speech to an unfriendly union audience. His staff worried that the union's negative reaction to Nixon "would psychologically disturb their contender."[24]

Nixon's advisers had been at the television studio since eight that morning, negotiating details about the stage layout and making special requests: for example, that no camera shots be taken of Nixon's left profile during the debate. Kennedy's people had no special requests. JFK, with a deep Palm Beach tan, did not require the facial makeup that was standard for television appearances. Nixon noted Kennedy's refusal and, apparently fearing that the application of makeup would make him look comparatively effeminate, chose only to apply a thin layer of an over-the-counter product known as Lazy Shave, used to powder over a five o'clock shadow. The effect was that Kennedy looked tan and rested, while Nixon gave off a ghostly gray pallor. Kennedy's casual confidence did not diminish his respect for the rules and subtleties of this new medium. When a television producer made a comment about the camera catching a sharp glow from Kennedy's white dress shirt, he immediately sent an aide back to his hotel to get a blue shirt, which he slipped into just before going on air before the critical gaze of more than 70 million fellow Americans.

Kennedy aimed high and set his tone clearly with his opening statement, which began with an historic parallel: "In the election of 1860, Abraham Lincoln said the question was whether this nation could exist half slave and half free. In this election, and with the world around us, the question is whether the world will exist half slave and half free." This was sharp, declarative, high-minded politics; Kennedy was comparing himself implicitly to Lincoln and elevating the viewers' sense of their own responsibility in this election. And even though the debate was slated to focus on domestic affairs, Kennedy's opening statement highlighted his strong anticommunist credentials and his confidence in the world of foreign policy. Kennedy also took care to distance himself from stereotypes of big-government liberalism, saying, "I don't believe in big government, but I believe in effective governmental action."[25]

In contrast, Nixon began his opening statement by defining himself in relation to Kennedy's earlier comments: "The things that Senator Kennedy said, many of us can agree with . . . I can subscribe completely to the spirit Senator Kennedy has expressed tonight, the spirit that the United States should move ahead." This was perhaps an overreaction to concerns that Nixon would reinforce stereotypes stemming from his attack-dog role in the Eisenhower administration. Toward the end of Nixon's opening remarks, he stated, "The final point that I would like to make is this: Senator Kennedy has suggested in his speeches that we lack compassion for the poor, for the old, and for others that are unfortunate. . . . I know what it means to be poor. . . . I know that Senator Kennedy feels as deeply about these problems as I do, but our disagreement is not about the goals for America but only about the means to reach those goals."

Nixon, a champion college debater, had misread the medium and the moment. He was indulging in a one-to-one debate with his opponent, answering him point by point. Kennedy, in contrast, spoke directly to the American people, ignoring the opponent to his left almost entirely. This, in turn, made Nixon seem desperate for recognition from the Democratic nominee.

A Gallup Poll taken after the first debate showed that Kennedy's support had grown—Nixon had been leading 47 percent to 46 percent, with 7 percent undecided before the debate, but now Kennedy edged ahead 49 percent to 46 percent, with only 5 percent undecided after the first debate.[26]

No less important was the Democratic support Kennedy solidified after the first debate. A dozen southern governors were gathered in Hot Springs, Arkansas, for an annual conference and decided to watch the first televised debate together. Previously their support for Kennedy had been lukewarm at best—journalist and campaign chronicler Theodore White described it as ranging "from resigned apathy to whispered hostility"—but when the debate was over, flush with enthusiasm, they collectively sent a telegram of congratulations to Kennedy.

As the campaign wound down to its final weeks, Kennedy had effectively distanced himself from the liberal wing of his own party to such an extent that campaign gears were now shifted toward an overall get-out-the-vote effort. Democrats still enjoyed a registration advantage over Republicans, and despite the nation's slightly rightward tilt since the election of Eisenhower eight years before, getting voters to fall back on old loyalties remained one of the most effective ways to go over the top. In his final, fiercely paced campaign events, Kennedy sought to associate Nixon with the long history of unpopular Republican presidents and nominees beginning with Herbert Hoover, but he notably excluded the name of Eisenhower. Kennedy placed himself squarely in the tradition of Woodrow Wilson, FDR, and Harry Truman, all staunch internationalists—foreign policy hawks, but domestic liberals.

On election night, ballots continued to be counted until 5 A.M. the following day. As the process dragged on, someone in the Kennedy compound yelled at Nixon's flickering visage on the television screen: "Why don't you give up?" Kennedy shot a glance in the voice's direction and coolly replied, "Why should he? I wouldn't in his place."[27] Illinois finally put Kennedy over the top in the closest election up to that time, with neither candidate getting 50 percent of the vote. It's important to note, however, that even if Kennedy had lost Illinois he still would have won the electoral college by 270 to 246[28]—and the White House—thanks in large part to Lyndon Johnson's Texas.

Throughout his presidency, Jack Kennedy often kept a scrap of paper in his jacket pocket on which was written the number 118,574. It was the popular-vote margin by which he'd won the White House. To the occasional frustration of liberal Democrats, Kennedy always sought to govern with that margin in mind, consciously reaching out to Independents and moderate Republicans with his policies and appointments.

As president-elect, Kennedy set about putting together a cabinet that brought together the best and brightest while also uniting his party and the nation. Notably, Kennedy appointed high-level Republicans to prominent cabinet posts: Ford CEO Robert McNamara as secretary of defense; Harvard dean McGeorge Bundy as national security adviser; and Wall Street veteran Douglas Dillon at the Treasury Department. He also chose to retain the services of Eisenhower CIA chief Allen Dulles. Not coincidentally, the areas of national security, military, and finance were areas traditionally associated with Republican strength. Kennedy adviser Kenny O'Donnell remembered the president's Centrist rationale: "Kennedy wanted a Secretary of the Treasury who would give Wall Street some assurance that the New Frontier's fiscal policy would stay reasonably close to the middle of the road."[29] All these appointments were very public evidence that Kennedy was determined to set an inclusive tone where merit and not party politics was the determining factor in public service. Likewise, Kennedy reached out to different factions of the Democratic Party, appointing Adlai Stevenson–supporter Dean Rusk as secretary of state, and Stevenson himself as ambassador to the United Nations.

Even Kennedy's celebrated inaugural address was decidedly different from traditional messages of Democratic Party largesse. Its signature line "Ask not what your country can do for you—ask what you can do for your country" was, among other things, a gentle rebuke of the welfare state. By forwarding the notion of individual responsibility and individual sacrifice, Kennedy reversed traditional liberal sentiments about the government's primary obligation to provide benefits for the individual. His ringing pledge on behalf of the nation to "pay any price, bear any burden, meet any hardship, support any friend, oppose any foe to ensure the survival and success of liberty" was a Cold War call to arms. Avoiding the traditional Democratic subject of domestic politics almost entirely, Kennedy's inaugural address was focused on foreign affairs, and a headline in the *New York Times* proclaimed "Republicans and Diplomats Hail Address."

In the months following his inauguration, the American people's introduction to the Kennedy presidency was extraordinarily successful. His second child, John Jr., was born just seventeen days after the election, and Americans fell in love with the attractive young family living in the White House. Kennedy's conscious attempts to reach out to moderate Republicans were bearing political fruit as well. By March, his approval rating had reached 78 percent, a stunning increase over the 49.7 percent of the electorate who had supported him in the election just five months before.

Faced with the residue of an Eisenhower recession, Kennedy was determined to pursue a low-inflation economic policy. He rejected some aides' calls for a tax increase, believing this would deepen the recession; instead, he would push forward a large tax cut in Congress. In the interests of keeping prices down and inflation low, Kennedy sought to secure guarantees from both business and labor. To the frustration of many union bosses, Secretary of Labor Arthur Goldberg prominently argued that government "must increasingly provide guidelines to the parties to ensure that settlements reached are right settlements, that are not only in interest of the parties themselves, but which also take into account the public interest." Organized labor had assumed the Kennedy administration would be an ally to their interests. Instead, Kennedy was positioning himself both between and beyond the traditional interests of labor and big business, a strategy that would later be called "triangulation."

The government would not choose sides in this fight; instead, it would fight in the public interest, for the larger good.

After intense White House negotiations, the Kennedy administration was able to secure guarantees from the United Steelworkers union that it would accept a modest 10 cents an hour—or 2.5 percent—wage increase, well within the rate of inflation. United States Steel, in turn, offered its assurance that it would not raise prices—keeping inflation down. Kennedy's system of voluntary price controls appeared to be working, until the CEO of United States Steel appeared in the Oval Office a month later to inform the president of his intention to raise prices by $6 a ton—an announcement that had been sent out to the press minutes before. The rest of the nation's steel companies would be following suit. Kennedy responded with cool fury, "What you are doing is in the best interest of your shareholders. My shareholders are every citizen of the United States. I'm going to do everything in the best interest of the shareholders, the people of this country. As the President of the United States, I have quite a bit of influence."[30]

Reacting to what he regarded as a betrayal of a good-faith agreement, Kennedy ordered his brother Bobby—now the attorney general—to publicly announce an investigation into whether such price increases were a violation of antitrust laws, and privately he asked that steel executives' taxes be audited.[31] The next day, Defense Secretary McNamara announced that the Pentagon would only buy steel from companies that had not raised prices. These hardball tactics worked. That evening, eight steel companies that had previously announced their intention to raise prices backed down. During the Kennedy years, inflation was held at 1.3 percent, unemployment fell to below 5 percent, and economic growth averaged a healthy 5.6 percent.[32]

Kennedy had campaigned on the most aggressive civil rights platform in presidential history, but once in office, he directed his attentions to other—as he saw it, more pressing—issues. But history would not wait for Jack Kennedy to get around to civil rights. James Meredith, a nine-year air force veteran, was attempting to single-handedly integrate the University of Mississippi. Despite federal court orders requiring that he be enrolled, Meredith was denied entrance three times. In his fourth attempt, at Kennedy's orders, Meredith was escorted by three hundred federal troops and met by a mob of twenty-five hundred students and segregationists chanting, "Two-four-one-three, we hate Kennedy." A riot erupted that claimed two lives, and federal agents remained at Meredith's side until graduation.* The South seethed: in Georgia, a movie house showing the film of Robert Donovan's *PT-109* reportedly inscribed on its marquee: "See how the Japs almost got Kennedy." The Secret Service began to investigate the first of thirty-four threats on the president's life from the state of Texas alone.[33]

While liberals in Congress grumbled and segregationists screamed, Kennedy's wealthy neighbors in Hyannis Port and Palm Beach regarded the president—like FDR before him—as a traitor to his class. Both communities had voted heavily against Kennedy and the Democrats in 1960, and when the president returned from brief vacations to Palm Beach he often joked that he was now against his own programs. But despite criticism from the left and the right, Kennedy stuck to his middle course.

In a speech at the University of Washington, Kennedy discussed the encroaching age of extremism at home and abroad during the Cold War: "It is a curious fact that each of these extreme opposites resembles the other. Each believes that we have only two choices: appeasement or war, suicide or surrender, humiliation or holocaust, to be either Red or dead." Kennedy's distrust of the radical voices on the right and the left would serve him well during the greatest crisis of his presidency.

In October 1962, seventeen months after the disastrous aborted invasion of Cuba at the Bay of Pigs, Kennedy was informed that aerial photos taken by a U-2 spy plane clearly showed Soviet-built nu-

---

*At the same time that the Kennedy administration was being protested by southern white segregationists, the Justice Department found itself protested by the left for not hiring more African-Americans. When Attorney General Bobby Kennedy angrily responded to the protesters' taunts by saying, "Individuals will be hired according to their ability, not their color," reporter and protester Jack Newfield thought it "exactly the sort of impersonal, legalistic protest, blind to the larger moral implications of our protest, that we felt made Kennedy such an inadequate Attorney General." (Arthur Schlesinger Jr., *Robert Kennedy and His Times* [New York: Ballantine Books, 1978], p. 371.)

clear missiles being installed in Cuba, ninety miles off the coast of Florida. This constituted a clear and present danger to national security, and Kennedy summoned a respected group of cabinet-level and military advisers to the White House to decide what steps the United States could take. Air Force chief of staff Curtis LeMay strenuously argued for an air strike followed by full-scale invasion. In contrast, National security adviser McGeorge Bundy urged the president to adopt a wait-and-see approach, confronting the Soviets only through diplomatic back channels. Defense secretary Robert McNamara and others advocated a third option: establishing a naval blockade of Cuba. President Kennedy had been reading Barbara Tuchman's *The Guns of August,* a history of the disintegration of Europe into the First World War, and as a result he was especially conscious of unintended consequences and rash actions leading inevitably to an otherwise avoidable war—this time, with nuclear weapons. Initially, a preemptive military air strike seemed the most popular option among his cabinet, but Robert Kennedy worried that this would place his brother in history books alongside Hideki Tojo, the Japanese leader who approved the attack on Pearl Harbor. As the tide shifted against preemptive air strikes and toward a combination of diplomacy and a blockade, with direct intervention only a last resort, Curtis LeMay latched on to another Second World War metaphor: "This is almost as bad as the appeasement at Munich," he argued. "I just don't see any other solution except direct military intervention right now."[34]

President Kennedy resisted the military's call to attack, preferring to impose the blockade and present the U.S. case to the world at the United Nations. Simultaneously, he attempted to strike a deal with Soviet premier Nikita Khrushchev, giving him room to save face through the secret agreement to remove outmoded Jupiter missiles from the USSR's neighboring state of Turkey.

Publicly, many liberals on the international stage condemned the president for confronting the Soviet Union and bringing the world to the brink of nuclear war. British newspapers criticized American actions and urged England to vote against the United States in the United Nations. Prominent British pacifist and Nobel Prize–winner Bertrand Russell—who in any case had already described Kennedy as "much more wicked than Hitler"—sent a cable to Kennedy, stating: "Your actions desperate . . . no conceivable justification. We will not have mass murder . . . end this madness."[35] To Khrushchev, Russell practically genuflected, cabling: "May I humbly appeal for further help in lowering the temperature. . . . Your continued forbearance is our great hope."[36]

After thirteen tense days, Khrushchev turned his ships around, ending the crisis. Kennedy's combination of determination and diplomacy drew accolades from around the world. He was concerned, however, that future leaders and historians might take the wrong lessons from the Cuban missile crisis, and called Arthur Schlesinger Jr. into the Oval Office to record his thoughts. Schlesinger's notes revealed the following: "Our policy had worked, [Kennedy] said, for three reasons. First, we had overwhelming local conventional superiority; second, no vital Soviet interests were at stake in Cuba, so that they could afford to back down if they had to; and third, they did not have a case that they could plausibly sustain before the world. It was because of these factors that our policy worked—not just because we were tough."[37]

Forty years after the Cuban missile crisis, *Guns of August* author Barbara Tuchman's daughter Jessica—now president of the Carnegie Endowment for International Peace—offered this assessment of its lessons: "There are never two choices in foreign policy, and the right answer is not to choose an unacceptable one, but to look for a third. I think it's fair to say, in the missile crisis doing nothing was unacceptable, and so was going to war with the risk of nuclear holocaust." She added: "The other key lesson was, give your opponent some room to maneuver. Don't back him against the wall."[38] The search for a third way between knee-jerk pacifism and militaristic extremes had gotten the United States out of the worst crisis of the Cold War.

Kennedy's steady hand and ultimate success in the Cuban missile crisis led to a Democratic victory in the usually punishing midterm elections of 1962. Democrats picked up a total of four seats in the Senate—including one won by the president's youngest brother, Teddy, who'd been elected in Massachusetts.

In his 1963 State of the Union address, President Kennedy turned his attentions back toward domestic politics and tax relief: "One step, above all, is essential, the enactment this year of a substantial reduction and revision in federal income taxes. It is increasingly clear . . . that our obsolete tax system exerts too heavy a drag on private purchasing power, profits, and employment. Designed to check inflation in earlier years, it now checks growth instead. It discourages extra effort and risk."[39] Kennedy proposed a permanent tax reduction of $13.5 billion—at that time, equivalent to 15 percent of the federal budget. In addition, he advocated lowering the top rate of taxation from 91 percent of an individual's income to 65 percent, and the bottom rate from 20 percent to 14 percent.

Liberal Democrats again felt betrayed. After almost two years in the White House, the Kennedy administration was still being called a disappointment by many liberals. An article in the *New Republic,* titled "Kennedy and the Liberals," alleged that "liberals complain of the unwillingness of the president to spend and incur adequate deficits," while "some able and articulate writers of liberal propensities even said we might just as well have had Eisenhower."[40] Exasperated, Kennedy asked, "What do these liberals want? Of course, I know. They want a deficit of seven billion dollars."[41]

Presidential historian Sidney Hyman blamed the "trouble on the new frontier" on the Kennedy administration's moderation. "There's much talk about the need to steer a middle course," Hyman wrote. "This implies the existence of a kind of center strip along the political road; a place where the pulls from the left balance the pulls from the right. But the middle course is easier to talk about than to follow. The route veers right because the left no longer exerts its counter-pull. There just isn't a left any longer."[42]

Kennedy may have been held in low regard by New Deal liberal Democrats, big business, southern segregationists, and rabidly anti-Castro Cuban Americans, but the president remained quite popular with Americans as a whole, with approval ratings hovering around 60 percent. He seemed to have a lock on reelection.

Kennedy hoped to run in 1964 against Barry Goldwater,* the con-

---

*In his memoirs, Barry Goldwater accurately characterized Kennedy as "a Democrat by accident of birth; he was more of a pragmatist than a Democrat." (Barry Goldwater and Jack Cassidy, *Goldwater* [New York: Doubleday, 1988], p. 139.)

servative U.S. senator from Arizona whom he was beating in the polls by 55 percent to 39 percent. He considered a contest against moderate Republican New York governor Nelson Rockefeller more challenging, but still winnable. Still, he hoped to subtly encourage the right-wing takeover of the Republican Party. "Don't waste any chance to praise Barry," he told aides. "Build him up a little." A contest against a right-wing conservative might even be fun. "Give me Barry," the president remarked. "I won't even have to leave the Oval Office."[43]

The right-wing enthusiasm behind Barry Goldwater's candidacy was indicative of a growing anger directed at Kennedy from the extremes of the political spectrum. In 1963, the Secret Service had identified six categories of persons who posed a threat to the President: right-wing extremists, left-wing extremists, Cubans, Puerto Ricans, black militants, and a miscellaneous category that included mental patients.[44]

In November 1963, the president visited Texas to patch up divisions within the state Democratic Party. Texas was crucial to Kennedy's 1964 reelection effort. The trip from Washington marked his eighty-third as president; Kennedy believed in selling his administration to people directly. Still, Dallas was seen as a hotbed of radical right-wing activity. Only one month before, UN ambassador Adlai Stevenson was jeered, hit with a placard, and spat upon as he attempted to give a speech. But Dallas—perhaps not coincidentally—was the center of Texas's business community, and Kennedy wanted to mend fences there. He got one hell of a welcome. In the days before the president's visit, flyers were passed out in the streets of Dallas, with a picture of Kennedy and a caption that read "Wanted for Treason: This Man Is Wanted for Treasonous Activities Against the United States." On the morning of November 22, a full-page ad appeared in the pages of the *Dallas Morning News,* sponsored by the America-thinking Citizens of Dallas. It accused Kennedy of ignoring the Constitution and scrapping the Monroe Doctrine in favor of the "Spirit of Moscow," and said that the president had been "soft on Communists, fellow-travelers, and ultra-leftists in America."

After a speech in Fort Worth on the morning of November 22, the president, Governor John Connally, their wives, and their respective entourages took off for Dallas at approximately 11:20 A.M. While Air Force One was airborne, the president looked out the window and remarked to the governor with a smile: "Our luck is holding. It looks as if we'll get sunshine."

Two hours later, he was dead.

In the chaos of that day, administration insiders did not know whether the assassin was from the far right or the far left; either could have been possible. In the solemn transition following such a tragedy, little attention was paid to a speech the president had planned to give that evening at a Democratic Party dinner in Texas. The text had been given out to the press in advance, but embargoed. The address condemned the extremists and dividers who so often seemed to dominate domestic and international politics. President Kennedy's final speech, written but not given, could have been composed as a coda to his political career and his search for a purpose larger than partisanship.

Today . . . voices are heard in the land—voices preaching doctrines wholly unrelated to reality, wholly unsuited to the sixties, doctrines which apparently assume that words will suffice without weapons, that vituperation is as good as victory and that peace is a sign of weakness.

This is a time for courage and a time of challenge. Neither conformity nor complacency will do. Neither fanatics nor the fainthearted are needed. And our duty as a Party is not to our Party alone, but to the Nation, and, indeed to all mankind. Our duty is not merely the preservation of political power but the preservation of peace and freedom.[45]

RICHARD NIXON — 1968

A PROMISE TO "BRING US TOGETHER"

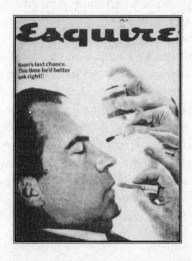

Run to the right in the primary election, and then run to the center in the general election.

—RICHARD NIXON[1]

Richard Nixon hated to lose. "Finishing second in the Olympics gets you silver," he'd say. "Finishing second in politics gets you oblivion."[2]

In January 1968, Richard Nixon was living in gilded oblivion, out of political office for eight long years—a wilderness of rejection made bearable only by the contentment of his family in their Fifth Avenue apartment. The big-money game of Wall Street did not satisfy the former senator from California and the youngest serving vice president in the twentieth century. Richard Nixon craved a return to the world stage. Since the election debacle of 1964, when the Republican Party had been hijacked by the extremism of Barry Goldwater and lost in a landslide, party regulars began looking for responsible leadership. Now Nixon had a plan; he would renew himself and renew the Republican Party at the same time. Humbled by the presence of loss and clearheaded without the arrogance of power, Nixon was determined to learn from his mistakes and redeem recent Republican defeats by running to the center during the bloody and divisive year of 1968.

He kicked off his campaign by saying, "The nation is in grave difficulty. . . . The choices we face are larger than any differences among Republicans or among Democrats, larger even than the differences between the parties."[3] Trusted aides such as Ray Price reinforced this message, explaining to reporters eager for a new angle that "Nixon is neither a conservative, nor a liberal. He is a centrist."[4]

Nine months later, speaking from the ballroom of New York's Pierre Hotel the morning after the election, finally victorious, Nixon discussed his hopes for the future by recalling a sign he'd seen on the campaign trail, which read "Bring Us Together." "And that will be the great objective of this administration at the outset," Nixon said, "to bring the American people together. This will be an open administration, open to new ideas, open to men and women of both parties, open to the critics as well as those who support us. We want to bridge the generation gap. We want to bridge the gap between races. We want to bring America together . . ."[5]

Over the next six years, Richard Nixon unapologetically took many unpopular steps but always sought to keep his critics off balance by reaching out and proposing Centrist policies that alternately antagonized and mollified the Democrats in Congress. It was this second Republican president in thirty-six years—a man who had first run for Congress in 1946 under the slogan "Practical Liberalism"—who strengthened affirmative action, created the Environmental Protection Agency, lowered the voting age, ended the draft, dramatically increased funding for cancer research and the arts, signed the Anti-Ballistic Missile Treaty and Chemical Weapons Ban, brought Communist China into the United Nations, and got the country out of Vietnam.

As a result, Richard Nixon was able to expand his base of support from the 43 percent of Americans who cast their ballots for him in 1968 to the 61 percent who voted for him in the 1972 forty-nine-state landslide over George McGovern, a total of 15 million more people who pulled the lever in favor of the job he'd done as president.

But for all his accomplishments, Richard Nixon was never loved so much as respected. Awkward, intense, and visionary, Nixon was difficult to understand. Close aides like H. R. Haldeman confessed that Nixon was an enigma, "a multi-faceted quartz crystal. Some faces bright and shiny, others dark and mysterious," while caustic conservative columnists like Emmett Tyrrell claimed that "everything about the man suggests palpable weirdness."[6] To relax during the summer months, Richard Nixon was known to turn the air-conditioning up in the White House, don a sweater, and sit in front of a roaring fireplace deep in thought. Once, when a motorcycle cop fell while accompanying Nixon's presidential motorcade, Nixon stopped everything to stay with him until the ambulance arrived; but being somewhat shy, the only thing Nixon could think to ask the police officer trapped beneath the bike was how he liked his job.[7] He was an introvert who propelled himself into the most extroverted of careers through sheer will, campaigning on five national tickets between 1952 and 1972, cumulatively receiving more votes than any twentieth-century politician, including FDR.

Richard Nixon prided himself on being a "political man" whose disciplined objectivity helped him see the broad outlines of history. Nixon read history books voraciously, looking for insights into leadership. A favorite biography of the great Jewish prime minister of Britain, Benjamin Disraeli, confirmed to Nixon that it was "Tory men with liberal principles who enlarged democracy."[8]

This master strategist and student of leadership believed that "unpredictability is the greatest asset or weapon that a leader can have, and unless he is unpredictable, he's going to find that he loses a great deal of his power." Accordingly, with almost clinical detachment but a deep sense of purpose, Nixon understood that his lifelong accumulation of anticommunist credentials made him the only president who could open relations with Red China without a revolt from the far right.

The success of his political strategy was often seen only as cynical opportunism, infuriating critics on the right and the left of the political spectrum, but as Nixon was careful to remind those around him: "Extremists on the left tend to be just as critical of pragmatism as extremists on the right."[9]

"The cold, hard facts are that Mr. Nixon is neither a Liberal, nor a Conservative, nor a 'pragmatist,' nor a 'centrist,' although at times he can pretend to be any of these. He is simply a man with all-consuming ambition," fumed Gary Allen, author of a right-wing rant against Nixon titled *Richard Nixon: The Man Behind the Mask*.[10] To the left-wing student radicals on college campuses, he was far worse: a warmonger, immoral, a contemporary vision of U.S. imperialism and evil incarnate.

Ironically, the "warmonger" Richard Nixon was raised as a pacifist in a poor Quaker community in rural California. His father was a grocer. At home, a high premium was placed on discipline: The Nixon boys worked in the family store after school and attended church four times on Sunday. Money was scarce, but Nixon remembered with pride that his father always refused offers of charity. Money did not prove the worst of their worries: two of his four brothers died of tuberculosis at a young age. The studious and serious Richard was accepted for college at Yale University but had to turn it down; he was needed at home, and they did not offer a full scholarship. He attended nearby Whittier College instead.

In college, Nixon classified himself as a liberal, recalled one classmate, "but not a 'flaming liberal.' "[11] He identified personally with the progressive concern for the poor, but his family's experience with poverty had taught him that hard work—not handouts—was the dignified way out of difficult times. The rugged individualism of progressives like Theodore Roosevelt and Woodrow Wilson appealed to him far more than the quasicollectivist solutions offered by their inheritors in the New Deal.

Nixon was elected class president while working his way through school. After four years, he was accepted at Duke Law School and headed east for the first time in his life. He graduated third in his class and should have been able to receive the job of his choice, but the Great Depression still dragged on and Nixon's applications to Wall Street law firms and the FBI were rejected. He returned to California to set up a local law practice, met a schoolteacher named Pat Ryan at tryouts for a community play, and told her that evening that they would someday marry. Two years later, they did. A largely anonymous domestic idyll seemed the most likely course for Richard Nixon's life. Then the Japanese bombed Pearl Harbor.

Nixon enlisted and eight months later was stationed in the South Pacific as a lieutenant. He was assigned to administrative duty and spent more time playing poker (with great success) than seeing actual combat. When the war was over, Richard Nixon returned to Whittier, receiving full recognition for his wartime service. A group of Republican businessmen approached the young naval officer about running against the five-term incumbent congressman, Jerry Voorhis, a liberal from a wealthy background. Nixon accepted the opportunity enthusiastically and impressed his patrons: "This young man is saleable goods," one remarked. The door of his destiny had swung wide open.

In the congressional race of 1946, Richard Nixon debuted the campaign tactics that would sustain him until 1968. The district was split evenly between Republicans and Democrats, a fact that Nixon recognized by offering assurances to voters on both sides of the aisle: ". . . I will be prepared to put on an aggressive and vigorous campaign on a platform of practical liberalism designed to return our district to the Republican Party."[12]

The implication, of course, was that incumbent Democrat congressman Jerry Voorhis's brand of liberalism was irresponsible and extreme. Nixon had used his limited campaign funds to hire a bow-tied Beverly Hills public relations man named Murray Chotiner who had one central piece of advice for his young candidate: "It is not a smear . . . if you point out the record of your opponent."[13] Nixon updated his tutor's advice with a bit of hardened realism of his own: "People react to fear, not love—they don't teach that in Sunday school, but it's true."[14]

It was a lesson Nixon never forgot and put into action right away: His campaign literature prominently asked, "Do you want a Congressman who voted only 3 times out of 46 against the Communist-dominated PAC?" Nixon tried to draw a connection between Voorhis's well-known liberalism and rising concern about Communism abroad and at home. Nixon made a point of appearing at campaign rallies wearing his U.S. Navy uniform to stress his military service to the nation while Voorhis was in Washington. By contrasting his modest upbringing with Voorhis's more privileged background, Nixon turned stereotypes about wealthy ivory-tower Republicans upside down.

The campaign was close, and as it came down to the wire, registered Democrats began receiving anonymous calls accusing Voorhis of being a Communist. This campaign of dirty tricks was never directly traced back to Nixon, but it was clearly the product of the implications he had established. Nineteen forty-six turned out to be a Republican year, and Richard Nixon was swept into office as part of the first Republican class to control the House of Representatives since before the Great Depression. Years later, Nixon would confess to a former Voorhis staffer: "Of course I knew that Voorhis wasn't a communist. But I had to win. That's the thing you don't understand. The important thing is to win."[15]

Nixon and his young family made an impression on official Washington. They seemed not only representative of California, but of an entire generation: servicemen who had returned home from the war and began families with their postwar brides. He was assigned to the House Education and Labor Committee with fellow freshman John F. Kennedy.* But it was as a member of the House Un-American Activities Committee that Congressman Nixon drew national attention, investigating accusations of spying against a young former State Department employee named Alger Hiss, one of the most influential stars of the New Deal State Department. The case was controversial, but Nixon eventually emerged vindicated and a household name. The previously unknown congressman ran unopposed for reelection in 1948.

Determined to ride the wave of political momentum, in 1950 he

---

*Perhaps Nixon's most intellectually influential experience as a young congressman is often ignored: He was unexpectedly appointed to the Herter Committee, responsible for touring postwar Europe, where he found "a continent teetering on the brink of starvation and chaos . . . without our aid, Europe would be plunged into anarchy, revolution, and ultimately, communism." Nixon joined the vast majority of the House of Representatives in voting for the Truman administration's Marshall Plan, and developed a devoted internationalist view of America's role in the world, at odds with many conservatives of the time. (Richard Nixon, *RN: The Memoirs of Richard Nixon* [New York: Grosset & Dunlap, 1978], p. 48.)

challenged Democrat Helen Gahagan Douglas for an open Senate seat. Following much the same strategy he used against Jerry Voorhis, he compared her voting record with the outspoken East Harlem Communist-sympathizer Vito Marcantonio (the subject of a 964-page FBI file). Nixon published the fact that she had voted with Congressman Marcantonio 347 times on a pink sheet of paper sent throughout the state, labeling her "the Pink Lady." He neglected to mention that the majority of these were party-line votes. By associating her with the most extreme wing of the Democratic Party, Nixon appeared comparatively moderate. On Election Day, Nixon won by 680,000 votes, the largest margin of any Senate candidate in the country.

That evening, sitting in front of a large chalkboard detailing his victory margin in different districts, Nixon spoke for the television cameras and newsreels: "A lot of people probably wonder how it is possible for a candidate to be elected into any office in California when he is a member of the Republican Party. I have just had that experience and I should like to point out the reason for our election victory. It's because in this particular election, the issues—rather than the partisan labels of the candidates—were what governed the electorate."[16]

At age thirty-seven, Nixon was the brightest Republican star rising in the West. At a time when newspapers were full of stories about the Communist menace and conversations about "Who lost China?" filled Washington-area cocktail parties, the time was right for Dick Nixon. California was the fastest-growing state in the Union, and from the perspective of demographics and political debate, Richard Nixon had a date with destiny.

Two years later, in 1952, General Dwight David Eisenhower agreed to pursue the Republican nomination for president, after Democrats—including FDR's son—had unsuccessfully tried to have him run for the White House on their ticket. Eisenhower was the most popular man in America, but many hard-line conservatives were suspicious of his internationalist politics. In their isolationist eyes, Eisenhower was a liberal. The young senator from California who had once been a Second World War officer identified with his former commander. On foreign policy, Nixon always considered himself "a liberal rather than a conservative because I have an international view rather than an isolationist view."[17]

Just as important, Nixon was a realist who wanted the Republicans to break their twenty-year losing streak. "The Republican Party is not strong enough to elect a President," he later remarked. "We have to have a presidential candidate strong enough to get the Republican Party elected."[18]

Nixon worked on the convention floor to swing California's delegates to Eisenhower's column, and in return the general surprised many by selecting Nixon to serve as vice president. While Eisenhower intended to remain "presidential" and above the partisan fray, Nixon would reprise his role as an anticommunist attack dog, adding the bonus of youth and geographic balance to the ticket.

During the next eight years as vice president, Nixon surprised his critics by generally behaving with dignified restraint and continuing to show courage under fire, whether it was debating Soviet premier Nikita Khrushchev on live television or undergoing a violent assault on his motorcade in South America. When Eisenhower had a heart attack, Nixon quietly assumed a high degree of day-to-day authority in the White House, without ever giving the impression that he thought the office was his.

In 1960, he was the party favorite to capture the White House. His former congressional colleague Jack Kennedy ran against him in an aggressive campaign that tagged Nixon as a defender of the sleepy status quo, falling behind economically and on national defense. Nixon was unable to counter this characterization effectively because campaigning for a new vision of America would have meant criticizing the administration he had been part of for eight years. As the nation saw in the first televised debate, there was an obvious charisma deficit as well—exacerbated by Nixon's refusal to wear full makeup on camera, making him look gray and weak in comparison to Kennedy's composure and Palm Beach tan. It was among the closest elections in American history, and Nixon suspected the victory margin was supplied by illegal ballot stuffing in Democratic mayor Richard Daley's Chicago. But he decided not to contest the election, out of concern it would destabilize the political process while making him look like a sore loser and thus doom his future political career.

Not everyone seemed as confident that Nixon had a political career ahead of him. He returned to California to run for governor in 1962, but was defeated by the popular Democratic incumbent, Pat Brown. The next morning, after the tallies had been made official, a bitter Nixon wandered downstairs to address the press corps: "For sixteen years, ever since the Hiss case, you've had a lot of fun . . . you had an opportunity to attack me and I think I've given as good as I've taken. But as I leave you . . . just think how much fun you're going to be missing. You won't have Nixon to kick around anymore, because gentlemen, this is my last press conference."[19]

It appeared Richard Nixon had burned his bridges and retired from politics for good. *Newsweek* called him "a has-been at age 49."[20] "Barring a miracle," *Time* wrote, "Nixon's public career is over."[21]

So began Richard Nixon's wilderness years. He moved to New York and set up shop in a prestigious Wall Street law firm and began making "real money" for the first time in his life. But politics was in his blood. "Once a man has been in politics," Nixon said, "once that's been in his life, he will always return, if the people want him."[22]

Nixon began his time in exile by cagily announcing that he would not under any circumstances be the candidate for the 1964 Republican nomination. This freed him up to serve as the party's youngest elder statesman, a role he encouraged by writing the best-selling book *Six Crises,* which analyzed his response to challenges on the world stage. The book had the intended effect of elevating Nixon in people's minds from a precocious politician to a mature thinker with an unusual degree of domestic and foreign experience for someone so relatively young.

Nixon backed Barry Goldwater in the 1964 elections, improving his reputation among conservatives and the party faithful. This new Nixon was a team player, making more than one hundred campaign stops and speeches on Goldwater's behalf. But Nixon the realist understood that the 1964 nomination was no prize; it was an uphill battle against Lyndon Johnson's position as the inheritor of John F.

Kennedy's office. Nixon also understood that while the rightward drift of the party may have been good for internal definition, it was disastrous in terms of expanding the Republican's national appeal.

One week after the forty-four-state defeat of Goldwater in the 1964 election, Nixon "confided" to a reporter that the Republican Party had "gone too far right, and now 'most of all needs some discipline . . . the Republican Party's national position must represent the responsible right and the responsible liberal.' The future position of the GOP, Nixon said, 'must be the center. . . . The formula [for victory] should be the Eisenhower-Nixon formula, not because it is more to the left, but because it is the right position. . . .' "[23] However quietly, his campaign for the presidency in 1968 had begun.

Sensing that conservatives in the party had begun to court southern voters who objected to Lyndon Johnson signing the Voting Rights Act, Nixon repudiated them in a monthly newspaper column: "Republicans must not go prospecting for the fool's gold of racist votes. Southern Republicans must not climb aboard the sinking ship of racial injustice. They should let Southern Democrats sink with it, as they have sailed with it."[24]

In private, Nixon was even more critical of the direction the Republican Party had taken, telling aide John C. Whitaker that the problem with right-wing conservatives like William F. Buckley Jr. was that "they really don't give a damn about people, and voters sense that."[25]

To his law partner, campaign manager, and future attorney general, John Mitchell, Nixon offered this admonishment: "Remember, John, far-right kooks are just like the nuts on the left; they're doorbell ringers and balloon blowers, but they turn out to vote. There is only one thing as bad as [a] far-left liberal, and that's a damn right-wing conservative."[26] Even though he was in exile, Nixon's instinctive Centrist compass caused him to seek a path between the extremes.

The Johnson administration's landslide of approval in 1964 had given way to disillusionment as the escalation of the Vietnam War and the excesses of the Great Society alienated many Americans. By late 1967, nearly 70 percent of the public thought the programs of the Great Society had gone "too far," and only 17 percent of whites thought the war on poverty was doing a good job.[27]

In this divided environment, Nixon's statesmanlike appeal was winning converts. A letter from a forty-year-old English teacher from Minnesota named William Gavin expressed the tenor of the times.

Dear Mr. Nixon:

Run. You can win. Nothing can happen to you, politically speaking, that is worse than what has happened to you. Ortega y Gassett in his *The Revolt of the Masses* says: "These ideas are the only genuine ideas; the ideas of the shipwrecked. All the rest is rhetoric, posturing, farce. He who does not really feel himself lost, is lost without remission . . ." You, in effect, are "lost"; that is why you are the only political figure with the vision to see things the way they are and not as Leftist or Rightist kooks would have them be. Run. You will win.[28]

When Nixon's bare-bones campaign staff was formed a year later, William Gavin was among the first hired. Surrounded by a comparatively young staff of true believers, the Nixon machine began to shift into gear. As they organized, Nixon cut down on public appearances and press conferences, announcing a six-month self-imposed moratorium from politics during which time he would presumably write and think and see the world. This made the former vice president seem above politics, and allowed his "reintroduction" to political life at the end of the six months to rise to the level of a news story.

In the meantime, photos of Nixon meeting with world leaders as a private citizen appeared in newspapers around the nation. In 1967, he published an article in *Foreign Affairs* titled "Asia After Vietnam," in which he openly discussed the inevitability of normalizing relations with China. The article infuriated anticommunist conservatives, but for these critics, Nixon had a ready answer: "As the facts change, any intelligent man does change his approaches to the problems. It does not mean that he is an opportunist. It means only that he is a pragmatist."[29]

As the war in Vietnam escalated, President Johnson increasingly found himself isolated in the White House, his policies protested by the increasingly radical students and their allies on the left while opposed on principle by Republicans on the right. Nixon realized the Vietnam was the unavoidable issue facing the nation, and he brilliantly maneuvered himself into the center of the debate while remaining above the fray. When Johnson returned from an overseas meeting in which he appeared to endorse the idea of putting more troops on the ground, Nixon prominently questioned the wisdom of this move: "How many more American troops—in addition to this latest 46,000—do we currently plan to send to fight in Vietnam in 1967?" Johnson reacted angrily to this criticism, which had the effect of elevating Richard Nixon's stature, and creating the appearance that Nixon was opposed to the war in Vietnam. As Nixon biographer Earl Mazo wrote, "Overnight Lyndon Johnson had transformed Nixon from *a* Republican leader into *the* Republican leader."[30]

In fact, Nixon had not come out against the war; he'd merely questioned the current administration's approach. This became something of a model for Nixon's 1968 campaign: People who were dissatisfied with the status quo could read what ever they wanted into Nixon's statements. By not siding with the Johnson administration or the Pentagon conservatives, Nixon seemed to offer a third way—"peace with honor"—but he refused to elaborate on his plans, arguing that showing his hand would compromise his ability to negotiate with the Vietnamese from a position of strength. The slogan itself was a clever Centrist appeal that had the intended effect: Liberals wanted peace; conservatives wanted honor; and moderates wanted both.

Consequently, moderates like New York's senator Jacob Javits could comfortably align themselves with the "new" Nixon, telling supporters: "I'm confident that Nixon will end the war. . . . if Humphrey would do what Nixon is going to do on Vietnam, Humphrey would be shot or impeached. Nixon will end the war."[31]

Likewise, he positioned himself at the center of the pack of Republican candidates running for president. The liberal wing of the party, led by New York governor Nelson Rockefeller, was supporting Governor George Romney of Michigan for the nomination. The recently elected governor of California, Ronald Reagan, had already established himself as a conservative icon and enjoyed strong support among southern delegates in particular. Nixon played the statesman in the center.

George Romney looked the part of president, tall and square-jawed, with private sector executive experience as a former president of American Motors, but he was prone to gaffes on the campaign trail and weak on foreign policy. Romney's campaign went down in flames when he was interviewed on a Detroit radio station and asked about his shift on Vietnam. He responded: "Well, you know when I came back from Vietnam, I just had the greatest brainwashing that anyone can get when you go to Vietnam . . . since returning from Vietnam I've gone into the history of Vietnam, all the way back into World War II and before, and as a result I've changed my mind."[32] It was a disastrous event from beginning to end. Governor Romney was followed on the program by a husband-and-wife team representing a spouse-swapping organization billed as the Swingers. The day after the broadcast, the *New York Times* ran the headline "Romney Asserts He Underwent 'Brainwashing' on Vietnam Trip." The full context of the rambling quote was lost and voter confidence in Romney evaporated. Political veteran James Rhodes, the governor of Ohio, weighed in on the aborted candidacy: "Watching George Romney run for the presidency was like watching a duck try to make love to a football."[33]

Faced with Romney's faltering candidacy, moderate icon Nelson Rockefeller flirted with entering the race. Polls showed him running decisively ahead of Nixon, and defeating Johnson or any Democratic candidate easily. Rockefeller could deliver the crucial battleground states of the Northeast, and repeatedly pointed out that only 27 percent of registered voters were Republicans: The party needed his broad popularity to bridge the gap. But Rockefeller played Hamlet on the Hudson, keeping supporters in the dark as he argued back and forth within himself as to whether he should run. In April 1968, after Johnson bowed out of the race, Rockefeller announced that he would compete for the nomination. But it was too late: Nixon already had delegates from the primary states safely committed to his corner. When Bobby Kennedy was assassinated after winning the California primary in early June, the Democrats lost their most compelling candidate, the only one who could rally the antiwar and civil rights movements while offering a message of law and order given credibility by RFK's experience as attorney general. Now Nelson Rockefeller's liberalism was no longer needed to compete with the Kennedy mystique. It seemed that for Richard Nixon—steady, experienced, and oddly self-assured in times of great uncertainty—his time had finally arrived.

At the Republican Party convention in Miami Beach, Rockefeller and Reagan supporters each tried to swing the nomination in favor of their man. But Rockefeller and Reagan delegates distrusted each other and found that their common ground lay in the unlikely figure of a resurrected Richard M. Nixon.

On the evening of August 8, 1968, Richard Nixon stood in front of the cheering mass of delegates that filled the auditorium and reintroduced himself to the American public. He began by offering his prayers for Dwight D. Eisenhower, who was recuperating from another heart attack in Walter Reed Hospital, thus reminding voters of Nixon's long association with the still-beloved former president who had been the lone Republican to reside in the White House during the past thirty-six years. Then the speech began in earnest.

"A party that can unite itself," Nixon said, "will unite America." He positioned himself as he had all his life, as a defender of

> the great majority of Americans, the forgotten Americans—the non-shouters; the non-demonstrators. They are not racists or sick; they are not guilty of the crime that plagues the land. They are black and they are white—they are native born and foreign born— they're young and they're old. They work in America's factories. They run America's businesses. They serve in government. They provide most of the soldiers who died to keep us free. They give drive to the spirit of America. They give lift to the American dream. They give steel to the backbone of America. They are good people, they are decent people; they work, and they save, and they pay their taxes, and they care. Like Theodore Roosevelt, they know that

this country will not be a good place for any of us to live in unless it is a good place for all of us to live in.[34]

Nixon's litany was strenuously inclusive—racially and ethnically, in terms of income and immigration—excluding extremists from the far left and, if only by implication, the far right. It was a vision of America as a place of quiet heroes and universal uplift.

Journalist Theodore White, author of *The Making of the President* series who had been covering the campaign from the start, remarked: "The speech was not new; those who followed him could transmit at the end of every tenth sentence the tested punch-line. What was new was context and frame. He was saying exactly what he thought; it was to be the campaign of a conservative, but not a radical conservatism of Barry Goldwater driving from the party all those who disagreed; it was a centrist conservatism, inviting both extremes to a unifying moderation."[35]

But Nixon's characteristic combination of political instinct and insecurity caused him to miss at least one crucial opportunity to redefine himself. Several prominent liberal members of the party had been discussed among the staff as possible vice presidents, including Oregon's Mark Hatfield, Massachusetts senator Ed Brooke, and New York City mayor John Lindsay. But in the end, Nixon played it safe by picking the obscure governor of Maryland, Spiro T. Agnew. Agnew had the benefit of being a conservative white ethnic—his father was Greek—and his safe Mid-Atlantic state was sure not to offend either the North or the South.* Instead of boldly reaching for

---

*Like Nixon in 1952, Agnew's role was to play ideological attack dog while the main candidate stayed above the fray. Also like Nixon, Agnew could be palpably weird at times, as is apparent during this exchange from a Nixon campaign meeting in which they watched unedited footage of Agnew being interviewed for upcoming commercials, recounted in Joe McGinniss's *The Selling of the President, 1968* (p. 55).

"It must have really been a thrill to have been picked for Vice President. Were you happy?"

"The ability to be happy is directly proportional to the ability to suffer," Agnew said. His tone indicated he might doze before finishing the sentence, "and as you grow older you feel everything less."

There was silence on the film. Then the voice of the interviewer: "I see."

"Jesus Christ," someone said out loud in the dark little theater.

balance, Nixon picked an introvert whose politics were motivated by a combination of patriotism and resentment, much like Nixon himself. The selection of Agnew proved to be a disaster. Agnew would resign from the vice presidency because of charges stemming from income tax evasion and accepting bribes less than a year before Nixon himself would leave office in disgrace after Watergate.

As summer turned to fall, Nixon kept a comfortable lead in the polls. In the vacuum of Robert F. Kennedy's death, the Democrats nominated Lyndon Johnson's vice president, Hubert Humphrey, at a Chicago convention that devolved into chaos as student protesters attempted to storm barricades and were attacked in retaliation by police.

Nixon managed to salvage an additional degree of political advantage from the Democrat's disaster by coming to Chicago just days later for a campaign rally and parade in his honor. News coverage reinforced the impression that Nixon's supporters were noticeably more peaceful than the young campus radicals who attempted to influence the Democratic convention.

On Nixon's right flank was the American Independent candidacy of arch-segregationist Alabama governor George Wallace—self-styled defender of "segregation now, segregation tomorrow, and segregation forever"—defiantly leading an insurgent coalition of white ethnics and southern segregationists who felt that the two parties had abandoned their small-town social conservatism.

Between the other two candidates, Nixon was, typically, the man in the middle.

Determined to avoid the mistakes of 1960, Nixon attempted to protect his lead by refusing to debate on television. Instead, he ran a campaign that was heavy on television advertisements, and because he often was awkward formally reading a speech, the campaign bought half-hour blocks of studio time to answer questions in front of a live audience. The campaign's young television consultant, Roger Ailes, took great pains to assure a racially and demographically diverse panel and audience.

Likewise, Nixon's ads stressed the fundamental law-and-order theme of his campaign, but always taking care to use the image of black children and families mixed in with the white. He worked with leaders from the Congress of Racial Equality to develop a distinctly Nixonian approach to civil rights and the needs of the inner city. Called "black capitalism," his plans stressed the role of the private sector in helping to revitalize inner-city neighborhoods and focusing on self-sufficiency instead of dependency on welfare ("They do not want to be recipients, they want to be participants"). In 1960, Jackie Robinson had stumped for Vice President Nixon; now the campaign turned to basketball star Wilt Chamberlain. Nixon knew that he would not get a large percentage of the black vote; these policies and gestures were designed in part to reassure moderate to liberal white voters that Nixon was no Wallace.

At the same time, the campaign tried to appeal to the millions of Wallace voters who knew that their candidate could never win but wanted their frustrations heard in Washington. Nixon's precocious strategist Kevin Phillips later explained, "The average American is fed up with the excesses of the liberal establishment. He is fed up with change for change's sake, with calculated erosion of middle-class values and standards, with fashionable liberal bigotry toward Irish, Italians, Poles, farmers, suburbanites and blue-collar workers."[36]

Nixon also made great use of radio, offering unusually thoughtful and well-written nationwide radio addresses that could be replayed and reprinted. Among the most revealing was an extended meditation on moderation titled "A New Alignment for American Unity."[37] In it, Nixon discussed the growing gap between classical liberalism and the far left in late 1960s America. It was an almost philosophic attempt to argue that the far left had gone too far and that Nixon's Centrist perspective—for the purposes of this address defined as "New Liberal"—was in fact the real defender of the values of classical liberalism.

A century ago, to be a "liberal" meant to be against the domination of governmental authority, to put personal liberty ahead of the dictates of the State. Only recently has the term "liberal" come to mean the dependence on federal action to meet people's needs. The future meaning of liberal is likely to return to the reliance on personal freedom. But it will have a difference: it will see that a key role of government is to provide incentives for the free enterprise system to accept more social responsibility.

In that context, liberals and conservatives will find themselves coming closer together, rather than splitting apart. Just as there is a difference between the New Deal Liberal and the New Liberal, there is a big difference between the New Liberal and the New Left. The New Liberal recognizes that progress and order go hand in hand. . . . The extremists of the New Left strongly—even violently—disagree. . . . The New Left has a passion, while the New Liberal has a program. . . . When it comes to a choice between getting something off your chest or getting something done, sooner or later most people choose to get something done.[38]

Nixon was appealing to the pragmatism of those who wanted to change the status quo rather than just criticize. In this same radio address, Nixon introduced an explicit appeal to the Americans he called the "silent center"—which in time he would famously refer to as "the silent majority."

The silent center, the millions of people in the middle of the American political spectrum who do not demonstrate, who do not picket or protest loudly . . . are no less committed to seeking out this new direction. They are willing to listen to new ideas, and they are willing to think them through. We must remember that all the center is not silent, and all who are silent are not center. But a great many "quiet Americans" have become committed to answers to social problems that preserve personal freedom. They have rejected the answers of the Thirties to the problems of today. As this silent center has become a part of the new alignment, it has transformed it from a minority into a majority. That is why we are witnessing a significant breakthrough toward what America needs: peaceful, orderly progress.[39]

Humphrey's campaign was crippled by its association with the hugely unpopular administration of Lyndon Johnson. The widespread antiwar protests had been so intensely directed at the government's escalation in Vietnam that many liberals were unable to feel enthusiasm for the Democratic candidate. Nixon, of course, emphasized this association, telling younger audiences "there is not a dime's worth of difference between the policies Hubert Humphrey offers America and the policies America has had for the last four years." To hard-hat crowds, Nixon reinforced his key message of law and order, saying that "Hubert Humphrey defends the policies under which we have seen crime rising ten times as fast as the population. If you want your President to continue with the do-nothing policy toward crime, vote for Humphrey. If you want to fight crime, vote for Nixon."[40]

Coming down the stretch, Nixon gave 178 speeches in the two months between Labor Day and Election Day. Newspaper endorsements also proved Nixon's unexpected ally, with 634 tabloids and broadsheets across the nation endorsing him, compared with 146 supporting Humphrey and 12 throwing their editorial voice behind Wallace.[41] But Humphrey's candidacy gained new momentum when Johnson suddenly ceased the bombing of Vietnam ten days before the election. Liberal ranks closed around the Democrats, almost entirely eclipsing Nixon's monthlong lead. Nixon, suspecting a dirty trick, worried that defeat might be snatched from the jaws of victory once again.

Election night 1968 dragged on almost as late as it did during the 1960 race, when Nixon lost so narrowly to Jack Kennedy. But now, finally, Richard Nixon was on the winning side—scraping by with 43.4 percent of the vote over Humphrey's 42.7 percent and George Wallace's 13.5 percent.

The next morning, President-elect Nixon remained on message, declaring that "America needs to hear the voices of the broad and vital center. The center is under savage attack. It must be held at all cost."[42]

With a calm sense of inner purpose, Nixon began assembling the government he had promised, one "open to new ideas, open to men and women of both parties, open to the critics as well as those who support us." As national security adviser, he brought in Harvard professor Henry Kissinger from Nelson Rockefeller's staff, a brilliant mind whose appointment sent a subtle but powerful signal about the end of anti-Semitism as a political issue. As chief domestic policy adviser, Nixon brought in Harvard professor Daniel Patrick Moynihan, who had served in the Kennedy and Johnson administrations as an undersecretary of labor before becoming disillusioned about whether the Great Society's welfare policy was having its intended effect. Tellingly, Nixon balanced Moynihan's counsel on domestic affairs with the more conservative views of economist and counselor to the president Arthur Burns, and balanced the two men's advice in his own mind.

Appointments such as these, combined with the self-consciously inclusive, thoughtful rhetoric of the president-elect, caused many skeptical former opponents to open their minds about the prospects of a Nixon administration. The most notable of these was the *Washington Post,* which wrote in December 1968: "The Nixon Cabinet, and that small part of the supporting cast which was unveiled earlier, has a look of careful practical-mindedness, a sense of purposefulness, and an air of competence, taken in the main . . . it is enough to say that Mr. Nixon has begun well, by collecting around him the sort of competent men that are the prerequisite to a competent Government."[43]

Nixon's inaugural address, perhaps the most underrated speech of the second half of the twentieth century, also eloquently addressed the practical and philosophic imperatives of its day within a framework of inclusiveness.

We have found ourselves rich in goods, but ragged in spirit; reaching with magnificent precision for the moon, but falling into raucous discord on Earth. . . . We are caught in war, wanting peace. We are torn by division, wanting unity. . . . We cannot learn from one another until we stop shouting at one another—until we speak quietly enough so that our words can be heard as well as our voices. . . .

Those who have been left out, we will try to bring in. Those left behind, we will help to catch up. For all of our people, we will set as our goal the decent order that makes progress possible and our lives secure. As we reach toward our hopes, our task is to build on what has gone before—not turning away from the old, but turning toward the new.[44]

As president, Nixon sought to combine conservative values with social activism, bringing together the realism of Eisenhower with the idealism of Woodrow Wilson—the two twentieth-century presidents he most admired.

In domestic and foreign affairs, his strategy was to keep his opponents off balance, driving first right and then left, like a football player dodging oncoming opponents in his attempts to get the ball down the field. That, after all, is how to score touchdowns. While too instinctively calculating and combative to be described as moderate, Nixon's inherent will to win caused him to pick the pragmatic Centrist path to achieve lasting impact. Recognizing that the nation—not to mention Congress—was considerably to the left of doctrinaire conservatives, Nixon pursued an agenda that was free from rigid adherence to right-wing ideology while avoiding the excesses of the New Deal.

Nixon's neoconservative agenda allowed him to propose conservative solutions to pressing social problems, ensuring a broad degree of support from the public even as he became the first president in 120 years to face an entirely opposition Congress. He founded the Environmental Protection Agency, ended the draft—creating an all-volunteer army—and lowered the voting age to eighteen. He increased the annual budget for the National Endowment for the Arts from $8 million to $150 million, gave Native American tribes more control over their land, and presided over a rise in Social Security payments while automatically tying future increases to the cost of living. Although he was criticized for pursuing the "southern strategy" of realigning the GOP, Nixon was ultimately successful in desegregating southern public schools: In 1968, 68 percent of African-American children attended all-black schools, but by the end of Nixon's term that number had fallen to 8 percent.[45] Legendary civil rights leader James Farmer called him the "strongest president on affirmative action up to that point."[46] In addition, he tried to overhaul the health-care system by requiring employers to pay workers' health insurance while allowing others to purchase limited coverage through private-sector regional insurance pools.

Nixon's most "progressive" legislative proposal was the Family Assistance Plan, in many ways a radical plan that was opposed by the far left and the far right. It was an attempt to create a national minimum income for the working poor through direct cash payments while requiring able-bodied recipients to take available jobs or work training. Championed by Moynihan as a way to fundamentally reform welfare while preserving the family, Nixon explained FAP as an effort to "cut down on red tape, and before long, to eliminate social services, social workers, and the stigma of welfare."[47] The proposal outraged conservatives who felt the cost was too great, and liberals who thought it was not generous enough. As *U.S. News & World Report* predicted, " 'Conservatives' will object. 'Liberals' will complain Mr. Nixon isn't moving fast enough. But the President will try to please the center majority."[48]

Indeed, while the far left burned Nixon in effigy and surrounded the White House with daily protests, it was conservatives who found the most substantive grounds to grouse about. Two years into office, Nixon's most conservative speechwriter, Pat Buchanan, would fire off the following memo to the president, speaking of their administration in the third person, and warning of the perils of a Centrist path.

Neither liberal nor conservative, neither fish nor fowl, the Nixon administration . . . is a hybrid, whose zigging and zagging has succeeded in winning the enthusiasm and loyalty of neither the left nor the right, but the suspicion and distrust of both. . . . Rather than draw up our own yardstick of success and failure, we have willingly invited judgment by the old measures of the old order. Thus, we proudly point out that we are spending more on "human resources" than for "defense resources." . . . We publicize statistics on how much "integration" has taken place. . . . The open embrace of an "expansionary deficit" . . . The President is no longer a credible custodian of the conservative political tradition of the GOP. . . .

Truly, the liberals went swimming and President Nixon stole their clothes—but in the process we left our old conservative suit lying by the swimming hole for someone else to pick up.[49]

But conservatives like Buchanan failed to fully appreciate the magnitude of the nation's outright repudiation of Barry Goldwater in 1964. Nixon's Centrism, his outright pursuit of a majority policy, was the cornerstone of his growing popularity.

Although Buchanan's memo was an internal document, *Look* published what amounted to a compelling rebuttal in a profile of the president, which praised his attempts to govern from the center in the national interest, free from the pressure of special interests of the right and the left.

[Nixon] has faced squarely the agonizing problem of minority domination and distortion of American policy. He is executing a majority policy. He does not wish to thwart minorities but to release them from their sole concern with their own interests. He wishes to make them a part of the whole of American life.

Vietnam. Race. Inflation. Israel. Russia. Protest. In each case, he has denied minority positions to find the common policy for the greatest number. This may mean his political ruin. He could be a one-term President. Or, he could create a new majority, proof against assault by any minority or combination thereof . . .

He has come to represent a majority point of view, an amalgam of prevailing opinion in an age of violent controversy. This is not a consensus, but the assertion of conventional, patriotic, devout American values, unshaken and in fact reinforced by the racing currents of revolt, anarchism, nihilism, and just plain kookiness in this troubled society. The Silent Majority. Forgotten Americans. Middle Americans . . .

Succeed or fail, [his] policies are consistently courageous, studiously moderate. . . . No representatives of organized labor can command him, or organized liberals or organized conservatives or organized racial or religious groups. Youth cannot find a political ground on which to terrorize him; he is impervious to war demonstrators; he is safe from intellectual scorn. And he knows it.[50]

Nixon pursued the same Centrist strategy in his favored arena of foreign policy, using his impeccable anticommunist credentials to bring about a thaw in the Cold War with the policy of détente, and to open relations with Communist China—a inevitable recognition of geopolitical reality that nonetheless would have caused calls for impeachment if a Democrat tried to do the same. As Nixon told Mao in their face-to-face meeting, "I think the most important thing to note is that in America, at least at this time, those on the right can do what those on the left can only talk about."[51]

Nixon's Centrism was successful in creating the broadest possible coalition of support, built on the appeal of policy, not personality. As one Democratic leader said when confronted with the Family Assistance Plan, "If this plan goes through, Richard Nixon will take over Hubert Humphrey's constituency and George Wallace's too."[52]

That was the idea. Throughout his first term, Nixon consciously set about transforming the Republican Party into a majority party with majority policies, leaving the appearance of culturally elite special interest group politics to the Democrats. As author Fred Siegel has written, "Nixon made a career of slicing off sections of the New Deal coalition by appealing to populist distrust of unconventional liberal elites. He mastered the wedge issues which separated Catholic Democrats in particular from upscale reformers convinced that Mao was an agrarian reformer or, later, that the destruction of small business by rioters was the price that had to be paid—by someone else of course—for progress in civil rights."[53]

He was not a naturally nurturing man, but it fell to him through history to play the role of healer to a society torn apart by domestic unrest second only to the Civil War and a world where divisions were highlighted by the unprecedented threats of proliferation of nuclear weapons. With his call for "peaceful, orderly progress," Nixon did achieve a great deal to help society's disadvantaged and instituted many substantive Centrist reforms that would have stalled or careened into excesses that invited backlash if they were proposed by an unchecked left-wing administration.

Despite his resignation in disgrace after Watergate, there is much to suggest his success as a political leader. Richard Nixon was only the second Republican president elected since Herbert Hoover. In the thirty-five years since Nixon was first elected, five different Republican presidents have lived in the White House. The Republican Party became a majority party based on the foundation that Richard Nixon so painstakingly built. The key to understanding Richard Nixon's strategic insights can be found in this coda, written for his memoir of life in politics, *In The Arena:* "Idealism without pragmatism is impotent. Pragmatism without idealism is meaningless. The key to effective leadership is pragmatic idealism."[54]

BILL CLINTON — 1992
LEADING THE DEMOCRATS OUT OF THE WILDERNESS
AND INTO THE WHITE HOUSE

We offer people a new choice based on old values. We offer opportunity. We demand responsibility. We will build an American community again. The choice we offer is not conservative or liberal. In many ways it's not even Republican or Democratic. It's different. It's new. And it will work.

—BILL CLINTON, 1992[1]

Bill Clinton put Centrism in the spotlight, delivering the Democrats from three consecutive landslide defeats by moderating their message and courting the "forgotten middle class."

But it was a rocky road from the wilderness to the White House. On the campaign trail, Clinton was fleshy and caffeinated, with a genius for empathy and a wandering eye. Propelled by a pure love of campaigning, his aides called him "Secretariat" after horse racing's legendary Triple Crown winner, a political thoroughbred whose natural talent, intelligence, and inner drive allowed him to emerge from obscurity to front-runner status. Through a stumble of scandals in New Hampshire to eventual victory over a once-popular incumbent president, watching Bill Clinton win was a full-contact spectator sport.

A year and a half before he was elected leader of the free world, Arkansas governor Bill Clinton was in Cleveland, Ohio, giving the keynote address at the Democratic Leadership Council's annual convention. The DLC had been formed to bring the party back into the mainstream of American politics, and Bill Clinton was now serving as its chairman. In the wings, a half-dozen other presidential hopefuls waited, while Jesse Jackson—deriding the group as "Democrats for the Leisure Class"—was down the street loudly staging a labor strike.

The forty-four-year-old Clinton calmly strode up to the podium, characteristically biting his lower lip, surveyed the crowd of several hundred, paused, and stared down at his notes. There was no written speech, just a list of twenty-one single words scribbled in a line down the center of a piece of paper to jog his memory.

Only two months before, President George H. W. Bush had received an 89 percent public approval rating—the highest ever recorded in the sixty-year history of the Gallup Poll. Inside the Beltway, conventional wisdom said that Bush was unbeatable, but the post–Gulf War euphoria glossed over a festering crisis of national confidence. The economy was in retreat, with escalating budget deficits and epidemic levels of violent crime on city streets. Only 36 percent of Americans felt that the future would be brighter for the next generation, and 77 percent felt that the country was being "run by a few big interests," while 75 percent blamed the state of the economy on the policies of Bush and Reagan.[2] While most leading Democrats chose to sit out this election against the seemingly invincible incumbent, there was a growing feeling that twelve consecutive years of Republican rule had left the White House out of touch with the concerns of average Americans.

"Why in the world haven't the Democrats been able to take advantage of these conditions?" Clinton asked the audience with a slight shrug and wide eyes. "I'll tell you why: because too many of the people who used to vote for us, the very burdened middle class we are talking about, have not trusted us in national elections to defend our national interests abroad, to put their values into our social policy at home, or to take their tax money and spend it with discipline."

He was bearing down now with a preacher's sense of momentum, and then, for the first time, he spoke the mantra that would help him win the 1992 election and four years later become the first Democrat reelected president since FDR: "Our burden is to give the people a new choice, rooted in old values, a new choice that is simple, that offers *opportunity,* demands *responsibility,* gives citizens more say, provides them with responsive government—all because we recognize that we are a *community.* We are all in this together, and we are going up and down together."[3]

It is difficult to remember how revolutionary those words sounded. Since the late 1960s, the national Democratic Party had stopped talking about individual responsibility almost entirely, preferring to focus on society's responsibility to the individual—usually in the form of ever-growing government entitlement programs and tax increases. The excesses of Lyndon Johnson's Great Society had begun to feel a little bit like extortion to the middle class, who increasingly wondered who was looking out for them. They responded by identifying the government outreach that had helped pay for their education at government expense with entitlements that required little personal responsibility.

As a result, between 1968 and 1988, the number of registered Republicans climbed from just 27 percent of the electorate to equal footing with the Democrats. After virtually owning the White House between 1932 and 1968—punctuated only by eight years of the moderate Eisenhower administration—the Democrats had run the executive branch for just four years under the presidency of Jimmy Carter.

Ronald Reagan explicitly encouraged the defection of disaffected Democrats, drawing upon his own evolution away from the party and encouraging others to do the same. Campaigning in middle-class Macomb County outside Detroit, Reagan told the crowd that "I was a Democrat once," and then condemned liberal Democratic leaders for "abandoning the good and decent Democrats of the JFK, and FDR, and Harry Truman tradition."[4]

His characterization of liberal Democrats as extreme and out of touch resonated deeply with voters. One former Democrat in Macomb County explained his disaffection with the party by saying: "I just have a feeling that the Democratic party is controlled by select, powerful minorities. I don't think maybe they reflect a broad spectrum, but they don't hit the middle. They are missing it."[5] This was the beginning of the "Reagan Democrats," moderate middle-class voters who grew up as Democrats but began voting Republican as liberals appeared to move their parents' party farther and farther to the left.

In 1984, after Reagan defeated liberal Carter vice president Walter Mondale in every state except his native Minnesota and the District of Columbia, a group of ninety moderates formed the Democratic Leadership Council. Their stated goal was to take on the "liberal fundamentalists" in the Democratic Party whose antibusiness and appeasement-based foreign policy had alienated so many Americans. According to founder Al From, the DLC would be dedicated to making "the mainstream movement the dominant political force in national politics. The first step towards that goal is to make it the dominant force in the Democratic Party."[6]

This transformation was still incomplete when the competent but colorless Massachusetts governor Michael Dukakis fell to Reagan vice president George H. W. Bush in 1988. Bush campaign manager Lee Atwater and media guru Roger Ailes used the word "liberal" like a weapon. After Gary Hart's campaign imploded in a sex scandal, Dukakis eclipsed the rest of the Democratic field—including Jesse Jackson, who preached the dangers of "economic violence," and thirty-eight-year-old Al Gore's precocious campaign as a "raging moderate"—by running on his record as a pragmatic, fiscally conservative executive. By early summer, the charisma-deficient technocrat was ahead of Bush in the polls. But the scales shifted when the Bush team successfully rebranded Dukakis through advertisements and innuendos as a "frost-belt, big spending, big taxing liberal who comes from the state that brings you Ted Kennedy and Tip O'Neill." Dukakis was unwilling to respond forcefully to the attacks, and the Republicans proved successful in associating him with the unpopular liberal wing of the Democratic Party.

Surveying the wreckage and facing the reality that the party of FDR and JFK had lost more than forty states in each of the last three presidential elections, Al From realized that the DLC needed a leader whose charisma and political skills were equal to Ronald Reagan's in order to pull the party out of its tailspin.

He looked to Bill Clinton, a longtime rising star whose future appeared briefly derailed after a disastrous keynote speech at the 1988 Democratic convention (delegates broke into a boisterous chorus of cheers when Clinton signaled the end of his thirty-eight-minute speech by saying, "In conclusion . . ."). What was most significant about this prime-time political face-plant was Clinton's characteristically buoyant response. Instead of going into nervous internal exile, Clinton pushed forward, using the negative notoriety of the event to get himself booked on the *Tonight* show with Johnny Carson a few nights later, playing the saxophone and charming the host in view of a larger national audience than had seen his speech.

Clinton was resilient, a natural talent; he had been a southern governor for eight years and had an established moderate record. Al From believed that "it would be very helpful if our next chairman be from outside Washington. A political movement needs to be built out in the country."[7] Acting on that principle, From flew down to Little Rock to convince Clinton to accept the chairmanship of the DLC. Clinton agreed. Together they set up a schedule of speeches across the country and began writing what would be known as the New Orleans Declaration—a revised statement of principles that set the agenda for the New Democrat movement. It was presented at Clinton's swearing in as chairman of the DLC in New Orleans in March of 1990 and included the following positions.

- "We believe the promise of America is equal opportunity, not equal outcomes."

- "We believe the Democratic Party's fundamental mission is to expand opportunity, not government."

- "We believe that economic growth is the prerequisite to expanding opportunity for everyone. The free market, regulated in the public interest, is the best engine of general prosperity."

- "We believe in preventing crime and punishing criminals, not in explaining away their behavior."

- "We believe that the U.S. must maintain a strong and capable defense, which reflects dramatic changes in the world, but which recognizes that the collapse of communism does not mean the end of danger."[8]

The New Orleans Declaration was crucial in establishing a new direction for the Democratic Party. It was a sharp rebuke of any lingering socialist sentiment on the left, as it applauded the entrepreneurial spirit while casting a skeptical eye toward the growth of government. While many liberals had been caricatured for their romanticization of criminals and comparative neglect of crime's victims, this declaration explicitly criticized the "root-cause" theory of crime, which stated that society rather than the individual was responsible for a life of crime. And while the post-Vietnam Democratic Party had lost the nation's confidence on foreign policy issues, the declaration addressed this by advocating a responsibly assertive role for America's military in the post–Cold War world.

In addition to staking out this new, Centrist ground in the vital issues of crime, bureaucracy, and foreign policy, the conference in New Orleans became the first event in modern Democratic history at which party members called for tax cuts—in this case, tax cuts for poor and middle-income Americans. The traditionally Democratic concern for the poor and the middle class was not abandoned, but approached in a different way.

Clinton presided over the event with typical good cheer punctuated with flashes of brilliant intensity, folksy wisdom, and clear vision. The gamble had paid off. Al From bragged to reporters: "This guy delivers our message better than any other politician."[9]

It was a role Bill Clinton had been preparing for his entire life.

He was a product of the southern middle class. He was born in 1946 in Hot Springs, Arkansas, three months after his traveling-salesman father died in a car accident on a rainy road. The resorts of Hot Springs were a host of contradictions in those days, part Bible Belt and part Sin City, dichotomies Bill Clinton would internalize all his adult life.

His mother was a nurse, and he was raised largely by grandparents who ran a grocery store in Hope, Arkansas. Clinton was outgoing and an excellent student. When he was twelve, his mother remarried and had another son with a man who sometimes drank to excess. Like many children of alcoholics, young Bill Clinton personally intervened when his parents would fight, standing up to his stepfather and placing himself in the role of peacemaker. Thirty years later, when Clinton was running for president, he would revealingly reflect: "I grew up with a much greater empathy for other people's problems than the average person has. It made me a lot more self-reliant and tougher than I might have been. And I learned some good skills about how to keep people together and try to work things out. On the negative side, if you grow up in an environment that causes you to want to avoid trouble, you tend to try to keep the peace at all costs. A leader can't do that. All my life, I've had to work to draw the line in the dirt, to make conflict my friend, not my enemy."[10] This accounted for much of his psychological attraction toward Centrism.

Clinton's hard work in the local public high school paid off: He was accepted at Georgetown University in Washington, D.C. Four years later, he was awarded a prestigious Rhodes scholarship, grew a beard, and applied to Yale Law School, where he met a fellow student named Hillary Rodham, whom he would marry in 1975. Together they volunteered on local Democratic political campaigns, and in 1972 Bill Clinton went to Texas to help run George McGovern's floundering statewide campaign. One of his friends and coworkers was the future Pulitzer Prize–winning civil rights historian Taylor Branch, who remembered that even then people were comparing Bill Clinton to a cross between LBJ and Elvis.[11]

When the losing McGovern campaign was over, Clinton surprised friends by announcing that he was going home to Arkansas to run for Congress in 1974. He had found a congressional district that no other Democrat wanted to run in. The great game was beginning for twenty-seven-year-old Bill Clinton.

His opponent was a three-term Republican incumbent named John Hammerschmidt, whose conservative congressional district had given liberal Democrat Hubert Humphrey only 27 percent of the presidential vote in 1968, splitting the rest between Richard Nixon and Alabama governor George Wallace. The per capita income in Arkansas averaged just over $2,000 a year.

Clinton's energetic grassroots campaign was based on reestablishing the Democratic Party's association with the common man. "Dropping in at hardware stores, barber shops, banks, second-hand stores and stopping people on the street," as the *Arkansas Gazette* reported, Bill Clinton hit the road in his 1970 Gremlin, young and hungry, shaking more than a hundred thousand hands. Years later, Clinton's recollection of his 1974 campaign still gave great insight into his pure love for the campaign trail. "I just got in my little car and drove and had a hell of a time," he recalled. "It's what I like about politics. You learn something. You hear another life story. It's like being able to peel another layer off an unlimited onion every day."[12]

In his campaign speeches, Clinton made Democratic populism palatable to the Republican district, declaring, "We need a congressman who's not afraid to say no to the unnecessary government spending that has been going on and has hurt the economy of the country,"[13] while criticizing the "feeling of general helplessness on the part of voters about the federal bureaucracy. It's unyielding, distant and not responsive. They want a strong Congress to stand up and do what it's supposed to do."[14]

But Clinton was unique among many southern populists in his outright rejection of racist appeals, a sentiment that was reinforced by Arkansas politics. While neighboring Mississippi had three hundred thousand members in White Citizens Councils at that time, Arkansas had no more than twenty thousand statewide.[15] The politics of the common man and the politics of racial inclusion would not be split apart in Arkansas.

Hammerschmidt was surprised by this stronger-than-expected challenge; he'd won each of his previous elections by increasing margins. Now he tried to slam Clinton by accusing him of harboring a "radical left-wing philosophy." But the reflexive conservative attack did not ring true with voters. Clinton lost the election, but he gained an impressive 48.5 percent of the vote and a reputation as a boy wonder. He used the new profile and lessons from his defeat as a stepping-stone to even higher statewide office. Two years later, he successfully ran for state attorney general. In 1978—at the age of thirty-two—he became the youngest governor in America.

It was a tough first term. Bill Clinton and his young staff stormed into the state capital in Little Rock with a determination to change the way things were done. Their longish-haired arrogance offended many of the state's political mandarins and middle-class citizens. When Clinton's troika of chief advisers (all under age thirty-five) spoke out against "corporate criminals," the effect was not populist cheers but disaffection in a state whose modest economy was based upon a few key employers like Wal-Mart and Tyson Foods. Like President Carter's administration, this team of self-identified outsiders pushed too ambitious a legislative agenda and lacked a clear sense of priorities. Their sometimes contentious relationship with the state legislature alienated potential political support. Clinton's decision to sharply raise license-renewal fees—by weight instead of by the expense of the car, which penalized poorer residents with older cars—frustrated many rank-and-file supporters. In 1980, Bill Clinton became the youngest ex-governor in the nation. Clinton, as biographer David Maraniss noted, seemed to have fulfilled the backhanded compliment bestowed on Rhodes scholars: "a young man with a bright future behind him."[16]

Out of office, Bill Clinton blamed those around him for the fall from the governor's mansion. He and Hillary blamed supporters for not understanding how close the race had become. They blamed President Carter for his lack of support and the landslide victory of Ronald Reagan that had swept across Arkansas as well. The Clintons called in an old friend, pollster Dick Morris, who told them in no uncertain terms that they needed first to blame themselves and then ask the voters for forgiveness if they wanted to return to a position of influence.

Clinton began the groundwork for a restoration, appearing at every event available, and solidifying his support among the black community. When asked point-blank if he was running for office, he always denied it—saying only that he was exploring his options. When Clinton did finally announce his second campaign for the governor's mansion, it was in an unorthodox manner devised by Morris and Hillary.

In a thirty-second television ad, Clinton announced his candidacy by apologizing for the mistakes of his first term, grinning slightly as he said that "my daddy never had to whip me twice for the same mistake." Using a touch of humor and down-home language, Clinton softened the discomfort of the moment without diluting its sincerity. "If you'll give me a chance to serve again," Clinton said, "you'll have a governor who has learned from defeat that you can't lead without listening."[17]

The ad was a masterstroke, inoculating him from the obvious criticisms by addressing them first, making the race about his vision for the future instead of the mistakes of his past. Faced with an honest apology, Arkansas voters were quick to forgive Bill Clinton. Opponents' attacks now bounced right off him, seeming like cheap shots and yesterday's news.

Clinton's new pragmatism came with a Dick Morris–penned playbook to help sell new programs to the voters and the legislature: "When you lead in an idealistic direction," Morris advised, "the most important thing to do is to be highly pragmatic about it. And when necessity forces upon you a problem of great pragmatism, you need to use idealism to find your way out of the thicket."[18]

Clinton's Centrist tack was vindicated in 1982, when he was re-elected to the job he would hold for the next ten years. From that point on, responsibility was a central theme of every campaign. Instead of putting forward a series of competing ideas, Clinton now focused on one single major initiative at a time and devoted all his energy and focus to selling it to the voters. This more-disciplined style bore incremental but important success in areas such as education reform. Clinton's package of smaller class sizes, competency tests for teachers, expanded course offerings, and the nation's first standardized test that eighth-graders had to pass to enter high school—financed by a one-cent increase in the sales tax—was a persuasive balance of carrot and stick, with more money but more accountability. The competency tests were opposed by the teachers' union and business resisted the sales tax increase, but the package received broad popular support and took Arkansas out of the cellar in national education. It was a textbook success.

In October of 1991, the Clintons summoned family and friends to Little Rock for an announcement that many had been expecting for a long time.

> Today I am declaring my candidacy for President of the United States. Together I believe we can provide leadership that will restore the American Dream, that will fight for the forgotten middle class, that will provide more opportunity, insist on more responsibility, and create a greater sense of community for this great country.
>
> The change we must make isn't liberal or conservative. It's both, and it's different. The small towns and main streets of America aren't like the corridors and back rooms of Washington. People out here don't care about the idle rhetoric of "left" and "right" and "liberal" and "conservative" and all the other words that have made our politics a substitute for action. These families are crying out desperately for someone who believes the promise of America is to help them with their struggle to get ahead, to offer them a green light instead of a pink slip.[19]

The themes that would lead him to the White House—refined over fifteen years in political life—were all in place: the New Democrat mantra of opportunity, responsibility, and community, the transcendence of political labels and condemnation of extreme partisanship, and the relentless focus on economic insecurity, all in the name of the forgotten middle class.

Clinton was staking out the ground on the right wing of the Democratic Party, using his Centrist rhetoric and credentials to establish his image as a different kind of Democrat, a New Democrat. Clinton understood that explicitly provoking fights between the left and right wings of the party was a losing proposition. Instead, Clinton decided to recast the choice as old versus new—a brilliant bit of positioning that reduced ideological conflict while stacking the deck in terms of which option most voters and journalists would choose.

Clinton's Centrism was not without critics from the right and the left. Republican consultant Karl Rove—who would later gain fame as the political genius behind the presidency of George W. Bush—offered this assessment of candidate Bill Clinton in 1992: "He has run a balancing act all his political career. The problem with a balancing act is that while you may look masterful on the high wire, you're not anchored to anything."[20]

New York governor and dean of modern liberalism Mario Cuomo echoed this frequent criticism of the New Democrats: "There comes a point where the eagerness to change can become an intent to pander—an intent not to lead, but simply to win."[21] The idea of the nobility of failure was still alive and well with liberal Democrats.

Bill Clinton had expected to run against Mario Cuomo, just as President Bush did. Both men looked forward to the opportunity. While Cuomo enjoyed passionate support among the Democratic Party establishment, his heavy-lidded embodiment of Northeast liberalism made him an attractive opponent in the eyes of the White House. For his part, Clinton sought to define his candidacy as a viable alternative to Cuomo. But like New York governor Nelson Rockefeller before him, Cuomo had developed a reputation as a "Hamlet of the Hudson," endlessly debating decisions from every angle, and much to everybody's surprise he left an airplane that was waiting on the tarmac in Albany to whisk him to New Hampshire in time to file campaign papers just under the deadline. The plane sat there with engines running in the cold night air until journalists and party officials received word that Cuomo would in fact not run—citing, somewhat suspiciously, his obligation to balance the New York State budget.

Literally overnight, Bill Clinton was transformed into the front-runner for the Democratic nomination. Tireless and uncomplaining through consecutive twenty-hour days, the smiling southern governor trudged through the snow of New Hampshire with one hand stuffed in his jacket pocket and the other hand outstretched. Battling an assortment of minor ailments—colds, allergies, ulcers, and laryngitis—instead of complaining, the candidate actually seemed to draw energy from the crowds. Clinton offered detailed policy specifics as well as charisma: His self-published economic plan—promoted in television ads—was a surprise draw for voters increasingly concerned about the economy.

Time magazine put his strong-jawed face on its cover, complete with the breathlessly qualified headline "Is Bill Clinton for Real? The Pundits and Politicians Have Made Him Front-Runner. Who Knows, They Might Be Right."[22] Their anointment proved premature.

One month away from the finish line of the crucial first New Hampshire primary, Clinton was hit with a series of sensational scandals that seemed to confirm suspicions about his character. An Arkansas lounge singer named Gennifer Flowers came forward with allegations of a twelve-year affair; a letter was released that suggested that Bill Clinton had evaded the draft; and a subsequent answer to a question about smoking marijuana in the past (which spawned the definitively wishy-washy punch line "I didn't inhale") all became shorthand for the candidate's penchant for accurate but misleading half-truths. His critics' characterization of Clinton as "Slick Willie" gained credibility. The generational appeal he'd tried so hard to cultivate as the baby boomers' first viable candidate for the White House now backfired. Clinton's narrative seemed to confirm many of the worst stereotypes about his generation: lack of discipline, drug use, and draft dodging.

As Clinton's brief lead in the polls evaporated, the candidacy of Paul Tsongas—mild-mannered, honest, thoughtful, and moderate—rose accordingly. Tsongas was the anti-Clinton, short on charisma but fortified by evident integrity. The former senator from neighboring Massachusetts was a cancer survivor, and his promise to fight for generational responsibility had a grave sincerity that no other candidate could match.

Pundits had dismissed Tsongas's candidacy because it seemed that the last thing the American public wanted—or the Democratic Party needed—was another serious-minded Greek American from Massachusetts in the mold of Michael Dukakis. But Paul Tsongas's message resonated with the voters. Like Clinton, he published a detailed plan of what he would do as president, titled "A Call to Economic Arms"; but unlike Clinton, his central message was the importance of balancing the budget to revive the economy. "What they did in the eighties is go from tax-and-spend to spend-and-borrow," Tsongas would say. "The difference is that the latter is generationally irresponsible."[23] As one of the leading Senate "Atari Democrats" in the 1980s, Tsongas had been an early advocate of the Democratic Party's need to moderate itself by working in partnership with the private sector. Tsongas's straight-talking crusade won converts, and he emerged as a briefly popular alternative to Bill Clinton, sharing much of the same message without any of the baggage.

But, characteristically, Bill Clinton pressed on. He took a page from Dick Morris's Arkansas playbook and used television to go directly to the voters, admitting to "causing pain in my marriage" without ever directly apologizing or acknowledging the charges. Believing that a good offense was the best defense, Clinton questioned his accusers' motives and criticized the media for devoting so much time to alleged scandals rather than issues of substance. The message was always that he had serious work to do on behalf of the American people.

With his back to the wall nine days before the New Hampshire primary, Bill Clinton stood on the stage of the crowded Elks Hall in Dover, New Hampshire. The room was wood-paneled, decorated with a single stuffed elk head and a lone mirror ball dangling cheerlessly from the ceiling. His voice was hoarse, the bags under his eyes heavier than usual. He knew that reporters standing in the audience were writing his political obituary, but Bill Clinton chose to fight on.

"This is the work of my life," he told the audience, his voice straining with passion as his hand gripped the microphone. "I'll never forget who gave me a second chance," he promised. "I'll fight like hell. . . . I'll be there for you until the last dog dies."[24]

On Election Day, New Hampshire Democrats gave the crucial vote of confidence to the man many were now calling "Robo-candidate" for his ability to take a direct hit and keep on moving. Paul Tsongas had actually won the primary with 35 percent of the vote, but he had been expected to do well in a state that bordered his native Massachusetts. Clinton, in contrast, had exceeded expectations. So many people had counted him out that Clinton's 26 percent of the vote felt like victory. Certainly, he did everything to spin it that way. "This has been a tough campaign," he admitted, "but at least that proved I can take a punch. I think tonight we can safely say that New Hampshire has made Bill Clinton the 'comeback kid.'"[25]

Clinton's optimism was more than just bravado. With the southern primaries all coming up in quick succession, culminating in the so-called Super Tuesday, the wind was now at Bill Clinton's back. Tsongas would briefly enjoy a bounce in the polls from his victory, but he could not hope to compete with the money, organization, and southern roots that Bill Clinton could bring to a national campaign. Two months later, Bill Clinton had the Democratic nomination sewn up. He should have been able to enjoy his accomplishment, but his problems were far from over.

Texas billionaire H. Ross Perot had been self-funding an exploratory Independent run for the presidency. His message amounted to a rejection of both parties: It was time for independent businessmen to take the reins in Washington to balance the budget, pay down the debt, and reform a corrupt partisan political system. This was an Independent message with Centrist appeal—bringing together fiscal conservatives, reformers, and secular libertarians disaffected by the Republican Party's drift toward the religious right.

Perot dangled his candidacy in front of the American people and then stated he would only run if there were a grassroots movement to put him on the ballot in all fifty states. The clever gamble paid off as a pragmatic "third-way" alternative between the Democrats and Republicans, and caught the public's imagination under Perot's adopted slogan "United We Stand."

Perot's popularity was in part a testament to voter dissatisfaction and increasing cynicism that the Republicans had given away the mantle of fiscal responsibility during twelve years of rule in Washington. But Perot's appeal to Independent voters also reflected how anemic the Democratic Party had become. Even voters who were fed up with the current party in power were reluctant to turn over the reins to the liberal Democrats.

By mid-June, a bipartisan poll found that Perot had become the first Independent candidate ever to lead the presidential polls. Perot led the way with 36 percent, President Bush was second with 32 percent, and Bill Clinton was a distant third, with only 24 percent of voters supporting his candidacy. This warning shot amounted to a real crisis within the Democratic National Committee: If the Democrats' candidate ended up with less than 25 percent of popular vote, their federal matching funds in 1996 could be lost, with disastrous repercussions for America's oldest political party. But over the course of the next month, Bill Clinton was able to turn the polls around and stay in the lead until Election Day.

While the traditional news media was busy following the Perot-phenomenon, the Clinton campaign made a decision to promote its candidate through nontraditional media sources like MTV, *Donahue,* and *The Arsenio Hall Show,* where he famously played "Heartbreak Hotel" on the saxophone while wearing dark Ray-Ban sunglasses. These conversational pop-culture formats appealed to a wide day-time audience, allowing voters to get to know the candidate over a half-hour conversation, instead of waiting for scarce eight-second sound bites on the evening news. As he had four years before, Clinton used late-night television talk shows to reach more voters and turn the tide.

Clinton overruled advisers who encouraged him to attack Perot, deciding instead to associate himself with the voters' desire for change. "What this country needs is dramatic change based on common-sense values, kind of a radical middle," Clinton would say. "I think this Perot boom, which I hope is a boomlet, reflects a desire for that."[26]

Now two candidates were forcefully running against the Reagan-Bush record. Polls showed that Perot's supporters included Independents and disaffected Democrats and Republicans, all of whom were cynical about the two parties' ability to solve Washington's problems. But the baggage of the far left of the Democratic Party continued to hold its candidate back. So, on June 13, Bill Clinton took on the left wing of his own party—specifically, the moral relativism and reverse racism that had alienated so many Americans.

Weeks before, a rapper known as Sister Souljah had given an interview to the *Washington Post* in which she'd expressed solidarity with the Los Angeles rioters who'd attacked white motorists following the police acquittals in the beating of Rodney King. Souljah was quoted as saying: "I mean if black people kill black people every day, why not have a week and kill white people? . . . If you're a gang member and you would normally be killing somebody, why not kill a white person?"[27]

At the time, her comments provoked only a minor controversy, but Clinton—noting that Souljah had spoken to Jackson's Rainbow Coalition the day before—singled her out for criticism in a speech on race, saying that her words were "filled with the kind of hatred that you do not honor."[28] He went on: "If you took the words black and white and you reversed them, you might think David Duke had given that speech. We can't get anywhere in this country pointing the finger at one another across racial lines. If we do that, we're dead."[29]

Jesse Jackson—who had invited both Clinton and Sister Souljah to the breakfast—now seemed to wish that it was his party's candidate who was dead. He furiously condemned Clinton's speech as a "Machiavellian maneuver" that was intended "purely to appeal to conservative whites by containing Jackson and isolating Jackson"[30]—speaking of himself in the third person. Jackson aide and Howard University professor Ronald Walters weighed in more tactfully, describing Clinton's remarks as "divisive . . . those are not messages designed to heal and to make people feel good."[31]* To critics who argued that the Rainbow Coalition breakfast was an inappropriate place to make such a statement, Clinton, who had such an impeccable record on civil rights that he did not need to pander, responded, "This was the best audience for that message. If not here, where would have been better?"[32]

---

*New York governor Mario Cuomo later chivalrously suggested hosting a Sister Souljah Summit, in which Clinton, Jackson, and the rapper would sit down and "reconcile the situation" for "the sake of the country." (Michael Kramer, "The Political Interest: The Green-Eyed Monsters," *Time*, June 29, 1992.)

The controversy became a seminal moment in the history of the campaign, with Sister Souljah's name still serving as shorthand for delivering a tough message to the extreme wing of your own party. Clinton's criticism of Souljah was largely seen as courageous. Political analyst Joe Scot wrote, "By going into the lion's den to attack reverse racism . . . Clinton has offered voters the first clue that he's got the moral fiber to lead—and won't pander to win."[33] These were important messages to send to the electorate, highlighting that Clinton was indeed a different kind of Democrat. Democratic adviser Stuart Eizenstat offered this assessment of the situation: "Clinton's strategy is not without risk, but we have no real choice. Our base is too small to win, even in a three-way race, so the old-time religion just won't work anymore."[34]

As the convention approached, Clinton took another calculated—if far less controversial—risk by selecting Tennessee senator Al Gore as his running mate. In the past, conventional wisdom had dictated that a nominee's selection was made on the basis of geographic and political balance—a southerner choosing a northerner, a conservative Democrat choosing a liberal. But Clinton's selection of Gore had its own subtle logic. The two men's many similarities—moderate baby-boom Democrats from neighboring southern states—highlighted the fact that this was a ticket of generational change. Moreover, Al Gore's Boy Scout image reassured voters who were concerned about the darker corners of Bill Clinton's personality. Likewise, on a policy basis, Gore's strong pro-environmental record, his vote in support for the Gulf War, and his service in Vietnam balanced doubts about Bill Clinton. Campaigning with their young families, the candidates were far stronger together than they were separately.

The Clinton-Gore team contrasted well against the odd-couple partnership of George Bush and Dan Quayle. In 1988, then–vice president Bush had surprised onlookers and insiders by selecting the junior senator from Indiana to serve as his running mate. Quayle had been regarded as an up-and-comer within the Republican Party, a conventional conservative with boyish looks. But once catapulted to the national stage, however, Quayle displayed an unfortunate aptitude for verbal gaffes—for example, "If we do not succeed, then we run the risk of failure"[35]—and his name became shorthand for over-your-head incompetence. One T-shirt of the time reproduced Edvard Munch's famous painting *The Scream* with the words "President Quayle" in block letters beneath it. Even Bush acknowledged he made a mistake in selecting Quayle, writing in his diary one week after the selection that "it was my decision, and I blew it, but I'm not about to say that I blew it."[36] But Bush was a man who deeply respected personal loyalty, and when he ran for reelection, he could not bring himself to drop Dan Quayle from the ticket. This was a lost opportunity to redefine his presidency and help convince the public that a second Bush administration would be different.

Bush also found himself boxed in by the influence of the far right. Bush had always been considered suspect by conservatives because of his roots as a genteel northeastern Republican who had run for president as a moderate in 1980. When the president decided to violate his own "no new taxes" pledge to begin to balance the budget, the right wing's simmering hostility exploded into outright defection. Bush beat back a surprisingly strong challenge from Nixon adviser turned populist conservative commentator Pat Buchanan, who won 40 percent of the Republican primary vote in New Hampshire. Quayle had played the role of conservative attack dog within the administration, and the president now desperately needed to shore up his support among conservatives. So despite the more than fifty-point erosion in President Bush's job approval rating over the previous year, the decision to keep Quayle was made, and the administration lost the opportunity to reposition itself. What the country had seen was what the country would get.

The Democrats came to New York that July for their presidential convention feeling the first glimmer of optimism, unified and finally focused on the larger goal of winning back the White House. The Democratic convention proceeded with unusual discipline: four days of on-message celebration, with the most divisive (Jesse Jackson) and discredited (Jimmy Carter) Democrats scheduled to speak at a time when most Americans would be watching baseball's All-Star game.

On the morning of July 16, Bill Clinton was putting the finishing touches on the acceptance speech he would give on the final night of the Democratic convention when he heard that Ross Perot had abruptly dropped out of the presidential race, citing "a revitalized Democratic Party."[37]

Clinton's aggressive full-court press toward the center, his embrace of fiscal responsibility, and his reluctance to personally attack Perot or his supporters helped create the logic of this withdrawal. Perot's withdrawal was the tipping point: The entire dynamic of the campaign changed that morning. Less than twelve hours later, Bill Clinton reintroduced himself to the American public as he accepted the Democratic nomination for president.

On prime time, Clinton opened his arms to Perot's abandoned supporters, saying, "I am well aware that all those millions of people who rallied to Ross Perot's cause wanted to be in an army of patriots for change. Tonight I say to them: join us and together we will revitalize America."[38]

His speech held closely to his successful message of moderating the Democratic Party's perceived excesses, promising "a government that offers more empowerment and less entitlement. . . . A government that expands opportunity, not bureaucracy—a government that understands that jobs must come from growth in a vibrant and vital system of free enterprise."[39] Attacking entitlements and bureaucracy while promoting private enterprise was not the message Americans were used to associating with Democrats.

Clinton called for a "new social contract based neither on callous, do-nothing Republican neglect nor on an outdated faith in programs as the solution to every problem, [but] a third way beyond the old approaches—to put government back on the side of citizens who play by the rules."[40]

Clinton promised specific results to back up his rhetoric, vowing to "cut 100,000 bureaucrats and put 100,000 new police officers on the streets of American cities"—a perfect balance of budget cuts and new spending—and held the line on his claim to make the Democrats the party of fiscal responsibility, saying that Bush "has never balanced a government budget. But I have, 11 times." Notably, the new leader of the party that was often perceived as being hostile to organized religion quoted the Bible ("Where there is no vision the people perish").[41] And in contrast to Democratic candidates in the recent past, Clinton also asserted a confident vision of America's role in the world, connecting the prestige of foreign policy with the state of the domestic economy, saying that "our country has fallen so far, so fast that just a few months ago the Japanese Prime Minister actually said he felt 'sympathy' for United States. Sympathy. When I am your President, the rest of the world will not look down on us with pity, but up to us with respect again." This was a bold attack on what was considered the incumbent's strongest area.

Finally, Clinton fired up the crowd with the resounding accusation that conservatives had been dividing the American public for political profit: "For too long, politicians have told the most of us that are doing all right that what's really wrong with America is the rest of us. *Them*. Them the minorities. Them the liberals. Them the poor. Them the homeless . . . Them the gays. We've gotten to where we've nearly them'd ourselves to death. But this is America. There is no them; there is only us. One nation, under God, indivisible, with liberty, and justice, for all."[42] This was an important reformulation of what constituted special interests in America. Clinton was pointing out that the religious right's resentment of difference amounted to a rejection of the essential diversity of the American family. The dividers and advocates of intolerance were the real minorities in an America on the cusp of the twenty-first century. And so the party that had so often been called "un-American" in the years after the Vietnam War was repositioned as the true defender of American unity in diversity.

As the obligatory red, white, and blue balloons fell down from the ceiling and the campaign's anthem, "Don't Stop Thinking About Tomorrow," thundered from the loudspeakers, Bill Clinton found his candidacy revived, and he roared to first from third place in the polls, up 27 points in the largest recorded post-convention "bounce" in American political history.[43] It turned out that the governor from Arkansas was ready for prime time after all.

In sharp contrast to the Democrats' convention, the Republicans compounded their problems by effectively turning over the reins to their convention in Houston two weeks later to the religious right. In theory, this decision was supposed to unite the Republican Party and affirm Ronald Reagan's "Big Tent" philosophy. But on opening night, coverage of Pat Buchanan's prime-time speech overwhelmed even the Gipper's swan song appearance with his announcement that "there is a religious war going on in our country for the soul of America."

Buchanan fired up the conservatives in the crowd by saying, "I watched that giant masquerade ball in Madison Square Garden—where 20,000 radicals and liberals came dressed up as moderates and Centrists—in the greatest single exhibition of cross-dressing in American political history." Buchanan accused Hillary Clinton of embracing "radical feminism" and described "the agenda Clinton & Clinton would impose on America—abortion on demand, a litmus test for the Supreme Court, homosexual rights, discrimination against religious schools, women in combat." Most inflammatory was Buchanan's vignette at the end of his speech in which he described members of the Eighteenth Cavalry turning back the rioters in Los Angeles after the police accused of beating Rodney King were acquitted: "When the troopers arrived, M-16s at the ready, the mob threatened and cursed, but the mob retreated. It met the one thing that could stop it: force, rooted in justice, backed by courage. . . . As they took back the streets of Los Angeles, block by block, so we must take back our cities, and take back our culture, and take back our country."[44]

Many in the conservative crowd inside the Houston Astrodome cheered at Buchanan's speech, but one Republican delegate confided to an ABC News correspondent, "I don't really feel welcome here tonight,"[45] while another said she was worried that "the extremist, far-right crazies seem to be taking over my party . . . I am offended, as a woman and a Republican, that Bush could let these fundamentalist Christian crazies become so prominent in our party." Even Republican senator John Danforth of Missouri—an ordained minister—described the convention as "a total disaster."[46]

The voices of disaffection were even louder among those watching at home. Sixty-nine-year-old retired executive Robert Brown—a lifelong Republican—exclaimed in frustration to a reporter that "the neo-fascists have taken over. Pat Buchanan, Pat Robertson and Jerry Falwell. If you disagree with them, you're un-American."[47]

Republicans for Clinton-Gore clubs began springing up in crucial swing states like New Jersey. Former Nixon adviser Kevin Phillips warned that "negative public reaction to the farthest-right GOP convention since 1964 . . . has dealt Bush almost as big a blow as continuing economic weakness. If the message of Houston lingers as an albatross, Bush may find that he made a fatal error in rallying the hard right at the expense of the center."[48]

Campaigning in the crucial moderate state of Michigan, Clinton calmly offered his own assessment: "It's interesting to me that the party of Abraham Lincoln and Theodore Roosevelt and Dwight Eisenhower is not very much in evidence in Houston this week."[49]

Despite expectations for a traditional postconvention surge, the Bush-Quayle ticket remained well behind its challengers. Furthermore, the Bush campaign had expected Perot supporters—many of whom were disaffected Libertarians and Independents—to come flocking back to the Republican Party. The opposite occurred: Perot voters threw their support two to one behind Clinton-Gore.[50] Although they were a combination of conservative and moderate, they were overwhelmingly secular and turned off by the Republican Party's courting of the religious right. Combined with their desire for reform and fiscal responsibility, the status quo of the Republicans held little appeal for them. Perot voters were attracted to the Clinton campaign's promise of reform and its central message of "change versus more of the same."

In fact, even after the conservative attacks, more than 40 percent of all voters still believed Clinton-Gore represented "a new kind of Democrat." The candidates' heavily publicized bus trip throughout the small towns in the South and the Midwest drew crowds not seen since the days of Harry Truman's cross-country train trips. Reporters were amazed at how many people they spoke to had driven long distances to hear the Democratic candidates speak. Mondale and Dukakis had never inspired this degree of enthusiasm.

On the stump and on the airwaves, Clinton focused on a limited number of policy issues that were well outside the spectrum of what voters had come to expect from traditional Democrats: crime, welfare reform, and the economy. Each of these issues had been associated with Republican strengths, but the Bush White House could not claim to have made obvious progress on any of them. The campaign published a detailed book of policy proposals titled *Putting People First* that offered prescriptions for an exhaustive list of societal ailments. This was consistent with Clinton's belief in practical policy solutions to public problems. "Politics is not about miracles," he'd say; "it's about direction. And the country's going in the wrong direction. Hire me."[51] Clinton's television ads stayed focused on content, pointedly reiterating his promise to "end welfare as we know it," making it a "second chance, not a way of life." This issue highlighted the New Democrats' reassertion of the relationship between rights and responsibilities.

Mindful of the Dukakis campaign's mistake in not forcefully answering the 1988 Bush team's critiques, the Clinton War Room ensured that no attack went unanswered—there was always an official response by the time the evening news went on air. "The purpose of the War Room," Clinton aide George Stephanopoulos explained, "was not just to respond to Republican attacks. It was to respond to them fast, even before they were broadcast or published, when the lead of the story was still rolling around in the reporter's mind. Our main goal was to ensure that no unanswered attack reached the people."[52]

The Bush campaign focused on Clinton's inexperience in foreign policy, characterizing Clinton as a "draft dodger," and insinuating that Clinton's student trip to Moscow while he was at Oxford raised credible questions about his patriotism and his loyalty to America. These accusations inspired a backlash when it came to light that Bush political appointees at the State Department pored over Clinton's passport files in an attempt to prove he'd considered renouncing his citizenship. But the Clinton campaign's most effective refutation of suspicions surrounding the candidate's patriotism and the party's competence on foreign affairs came in the form of a crucial September 21 endorsement from the Bush administration's former chairman of the Joint Chiefs of Staff, Admiral William J. Crowe Jr., who later explained, "I found myself increasingly disturbed by the Republican Party's tendency to exclude certain groups from the mainstream of American life and exploit antagonisms within the society."[53]

In October, Ross Perot did a U-turn and officially rejoined the campaign, buying half-hour blocks of television time to preach his economic plan for reducing the deficit. Three presidential debates took place in October, involving all three candidates. The second debate was the most memorable: an *Oprah Winfrey*–inspired talk-show format that Clinton had insisted upon, giving the candidates a chance to answer questions directly from a live studio audience. When a young woman asked the candidates, "How has the national debt personally affected each of your lives?" President Bush stumbled, saying, "I'm sure it has. I love my grandchildren. I'm not sure I get . . . help me with the question." Clinton saw his opportunity and he took it, walking three steps toward the young woman and asking her to tell him "how it's affected you." Clinton turned the question into an opportunity for a personal dialogue about the individual impact of economic problems, and with his body language and evident personal concern, the candidate's genius for empathy was on full display.*

In contrast, television cameras caught President Bush glancing at his wristwatch, waiting for the debate to be over—a moment that became a visual metaphor for all that was wrong with the administration: tired, impatient, and out of touch with the average American.

On the eve of Election Day in November, more newspapers across the country had endorsed a Democratic candidate than at any time since 1964, when Lyndon Johnson ran against self-proclaimed extremist Barry Goldwater, including the *New York Daily News,* which hadn't endorsed a Democrat for president since 1940, and Ohio's *Canton Repository,* President William McKinley's hometown paper, which had been dependably Republican for all of its 177 years.

The generally conservative British magazine *Economist* captured the tone of these unexpected endorsements when it wrote:

---

*Reflecting upon his reputation for Technicolor empathy, Clinton said, "I can feel people's pain a lot more than some people can. I think that's important for a politician. I think you literally have to be able to sit in the quiet of a room and accurately imagine what life might be like for people growing up on mean streets, people living their lives behind bars, people about to face death's door." (Peter Applebome, "Bill Clinton's Uncertain Journey," *The New York Times Magazine,* March 8, 1992.)

The Republicans, tired to distraction, out of ideas, have become prey to a far right whose economic nostrums run to demonizing taxes, and many of whose social ideas would rub salt in the country's wounds. . . . The Democratic Party, to be sure, has not yet proved that its new look goes beyond Mr. Clinton and his circle. But it has been working for 12 years on how to become a plausible modern party of government, and should be given a chance to try. During the campaign, Mr. Clinton has proved himself to be far more than a token candidate. He is intelligent; he is diligent; he is energetic; he has grasped most of the issues, and found persuasive solutions to some. He could mark an end to divided government and could, if he used the presidency well, begin to bring Americans, black and white, rich and poor, closer together. Despite the risks, the possibilities are worth pursuing. Our choice falls on him.[54]

To counter this flood of endorsements, the conservative Christian antiabortion group Operation Rescue took out full-page ads in *USA Today* and 157 other papers across the nation the weekend before the election that read, "The Bible warns us not to follow another man in his sin—lest God chasten us. How then can we vote for Bill Clinton?" A widely distributed leaflet by the same organization stated bluntly, "Christians beware, to vote for Bill Clinton is to sin against God."[55]

Turnout for the election was the highest it had been in more than thirty years. Bill Clinton received 370 electoral votes but only 43 percent of the popular vote—roughly equivalent to what Richard Nixon received in 1968. President Bush's 37 percent of the vote was the second lowest ever for a sitting president, while Ross Perot's Independent candidacy received 19 percent—the best a third-party candidate had done since Theodore Roosevelt, running as a Progressive, in 1912. Crucially, Clinton carried the highest amount of support from Independent voters of any of the three candidates. In his election night acceptance speech in Little Rock, Arkansas, Clinton accurately assessed the election not as a personal victory, but containing a clear "mandate for change."

Vice President Dan Quayle acknowledged Clinton's political skill in a gracious concession speech, stating, "If he runs the country as well as he ran his campaign, we'll be alright." But in the transition from campaigning to governing, Clinton forgot the Centrist source of his popular appeal and appeared to move to the left instead of further toward the middle of the American electorate. Throughout his two terms, every time Clinton stumbled on issues of policy it was a result of ignoring his Centrist script that the American people so strongly supported.

In his first press conference as president-elect, Clinton fell for a reporter's question that tried to make the issue of gays in the military the litmus test of Clinton's trustworthiness in filling campaign promises. Instead of sidestepping the issue, affirming that he would appoint a military panel to examine the issue at some point in the future and then moving forward to more pressing business, Clinton could not resist speaking at length on the issue, giving gays in the military the appearance of being of vital importance, positioning it at the top of the new president's agenda in the public's mind. "It sent precisely the wrong message," one of Clinton's advisers later reflected. "I'm not saying he shouldn't have taken that position. But as the first thing he did? It was exactly the sort of 'liberal elitist' issue that we'd been trying to submerge throughout the campaign. It sent the signal that he was going to govern differently from the way he campaigned—as an 'Old' Democrat."[56]

This perception gap between the New Democrat campaigning and the Old Democrat governing proved disastrous, an appearance that was highlighted by the president's decision to move forward with health-care reform—under his wife's direction—rather than first establishing his Centrist credentials with the Congress and the country on an issue like welfare reform. By retroactively raising taxes—albeit on the wealthiest 1 percent of the population—to reduce the $290 billion deficit in his 1993 budget, Clinton became vulnerable to accusations that he was just another "tax-and-spend liberal" even as he pursued the traditionally conservative goal of a balanced budget.

In the atmosphere of increased partisanship, even moderate Clinton initiatives were being opposed on all sides. For example, his omnibus crime bill was stalled by a procedural vote at the hands of an odd alliance of pro-gun Democrats, anti–death penalty liberals, and all Republicans. Eventually, with the help of moderate Republicans like New York mayor Rudy Giuliani lobbying Congress to get the funding for more police officers, the bill passed and crime rates began to go down across the nation. The generally acknowledged legislative high point of Clinton's first year in office was the passage of the North American Free Trade Agreement. Negotiated by his predecessor and opposed by labor unions, Clinton's support of NAFTA established a bipartisan position on free trade. But his popularity plummeted due in part to a hotly partisan atmosphere encouraged by Republicans, who smelled blood in the water after a 1,300-page health-care bill was submitted to Congress and characterized as a step toward socialized medicine.

Clinton was frustrated by the anemic support he was receiving from many liberal Democrats while Republicans attacked him relentlessly. In an extraordinarily revealing moment, he called a group of reporters into the Oval Office and read them a quote from Machiavelli's *The Prince:* "It must be considered that there is nothing more difficult to carry out or more doubtful of success, nor dangerous to handle, than to initiate a new order of things. For the reformer has enemies . . . and only lukewarm defenders."[57] Clinton's identification with the quote proved prophetic. In the 1994 midterm elections, amid heavy Republican turnout motivated by the administration's apparent turn to the left, Clinton's Democrats were resoundingly rejected, losing control of both the Senate and the House of Representatives for the first time in more than forty years.

Clinton responded to this defeat by once again righting his course and moving decisively toward the center. Declaring that "the era of big government is over" in his 1996 State of the Union address, Clinton set about co-opting Republican issues by driving down crime and reducing the deficit while serving as a check against Speaker of the House Newt Gingrich's perceived ideological excesses. This was evidence of Clinton's renewed contact with political adviser Dick Morris, who had helped him emerge from his defeat in Arkansas more than a decade before. Morris, who now worked for both Republicans and Democrats, saw himself as a Centrist and a "Clintonista" at war with the liberal advisers in the White House whose primary loyalties lay with the Democratic Party.

Brilliant but difficult, Morris sold the president on a strategy of triangulation, introducing the concept by bringing his fingers together in the shape of a triangle: "Triangulate, creating a third position, not just in-between the old positions of the two parties but above them as well. Identify a new course that accommodates the needs the Republicans' address but does it in a way that is uniquely yours. . . . if Democrats say 'no tax cuts,' the Republicans say 'tax cuts for everyone,' we say tax cuts if you're going to college or raising children or buying a first home or saving for retirement."[58]

"Triangulation" was a word for what Clinton had been doing instinctively throughout his career. This incremental approach toward forging a new middle ground was not emotionally satisfying for many Democrats, and it was deeply frustrating to many Republicans, but it was effective and it was successful.

Once Clinton tacked back toward the center, his popularity ratings rose. He was able to credibly sell himself as a responsible chief executive whose presence stopped Newt Gingrich's Republican Revolution from running away with the country. Clinton pursued a balanced budget but resisted a constitutional amendment requiring it, citing the need for financial flexibility in meeting future emergencies. He signed the 1995 Welfare Reform Act, angering many liberal supporters but delivering a reform discussed since Nixon and depriving the Republicans of an issue they had planned to build their 1996 campaign around. When White House liberals sometimes grew discouraged with the resolute moderation of the Clinton administration, the president would explain his vision of their historic mission: "Roosevelt saved capitalism from itself. Our mission is to save government from its own excesses so it can again be a progressive force."[59]

By the time Bill Clinton was ready to run for reelection, he was once again ahead in the polls and solidly identified with a Centrist style and substance of governing. In November 1996, he became the first Democrat to be reelected president since FDR, winning 49 percent of popular vote in the three-way race against former Republican Senate majority leader Bob Dole and Ross Perot.

In his first postelection press conference, Clinton reiterated what he felt was the central lesson of his presidency. "We have to build a vital center. The lesson of our history is clear," Clinton said. "When we put aside partisanship, embrace the best ideas regardless of where they come from and work for principled compromise, we can move America not left or right, but forward."[60]

PART 3

THE PRIMARY CHALLENGE: REFORMERS VS. THE OLD GUARD

*T*he catch-22 of Centrism is that it is often far easier for moderates to win a general election than to get past their own party's partisan primary.

Closed primaries are traditionally dominated by professional partisans who dedicate themselves to political activism. Although extremists make up a small percentage of the total population, they tend to operate the political apparatus of each party. Because they're more likely to see in the other party a pure opposite and a dangerous evil, they strongly support the far-right or left-wing partisans who they believe will carry their ideological banner into battle. The catch is that candidates associated with ideological extremism tend to go down to defeat in the general election. As columnist Jack Newfield memorably wrote, "Ignoring electability is the fingerprint of fanaticism."[1]

Ironically, while extremists control the party apparatus, political parties depend on moderate reformers to win general elections. The great question, then, is how moderate candidates can survive the primary process.

In 1946, California governor and future Supreme Court chief justice Earl Warren ran for reelection as a nonpartisan candidate in both the Republican and Democratic primaries. Warren's record as a fearless opponent of all special interests—whether Democratic or Republican—gave him the credibility to campaign as the candidate of all the people. After more than a decade of the New Deal, California Democrats far outnumbered Republicans, and while Earl Warren was a registered Republican, he understood that he needed

Democratic votes to win. When conservatives grew frustrated by his bipartisan approach to government, Warren had a ready reply: "There will be another election in four years and in the meantime I am governor of all the People of California, not just those who voted for me."[2] Such a clear-eyed approach angered the right wing, but gained the respect of many more voters. Attempts by the far right of the Republican Party to undermine his candidacy failed, and Warren's energetic campaign allowed him to do what few candidates have done before or since: win both the Democratic and the Republican primaries, effectively ending the election before it had begun. It was the most complete triumph imaginable for a Centrist candidate, but it was dependent upon an open party primary system that is now discouraged by partisans who have learned that it diminishes their control of the political system.

In the years immediately following the Second World War, the Republican Party was sharply divided between internationalists and isolationists. Senate minority leader Robert Taft of Ohio, "Mr. Republican," was the leader of the isolationist wing of the party, memorably characterized by *Fortune* magazine as "one of the vast groups of Americans to whom other countries seem merely odd places, full of uncertain plumbing, funny colored money, and people talking languages one can't understand."[3] Taft had opposed American intervention in the Second World War and the acceptance of responsibility in the Cold War. Defense of the isolationism, associated with the Republican Party since it opposed Woodrow Wilson's League of Nations, was to be the core of Taft's long-planned campaign for the White House in 1952.

The Republicans needed a candidate who could appeal beyond the isolationist base of the party, and they found such a candidate in General Dwight David Eisenhower, leader of the crusade to liberate Europe from Nazi tyranny and the most respected man in America.

Eisenhower had resisted previous calls to enter politics but, dismayed by the Republican Party's apparent acquiescence to the isolationism of Robert Taft and angered by the Democratic administration's issuance of yet another multibillion-dollar budget deficit, Eisenhower decided to enter the political fray he'd sworn to avoid so many times before. His fight for the party's nomination would prove far more difficult than winning the general election. To most Americans, Eisenhower's transcendence of traditional partisan politics was an asset; but within the ranks of the Republican Party, he was considered a pariah, attacked by ideologues who questioned his Republican credentials and were angered by his frontline support of the foreign policy of Franklin D. Roosevelt. Spreading vicious rumors about his wife and personal life, they tried to deny the nomination to General Eisenhower and almost succeeded, but Ike's extraordinary popularity helped him defeat Taft at the convention and win the general election, permanently committing the nation to a bipartisan foreign policy. All his life, however, Eisenhower would retain a barely concealed contempt for those who "go to the gutter on either the right or the left, and hurl rocks at those in the center."[4]

The divisions in the Republican Party continued to fester, but by 1964 they were focused on domestic affairs. The conservative movement gained momentum when the virulent anticommunism fostered by the late Joe McCarthy merged with Strom Thurmond's states' rights argument for less federal government intervention in the segregated South. Arizona senator Barry Goldwater's book *The Conscience of a Conservative* became an ideological badge of honor among the "crew-cut militants" who squared off against the presidential ambitions of the moderate governor of New York, Nelson Rockefeller. Despite the fact that moderates outnumbered conservatives in the Republican Party at the time, the tide was turning away from the historic capitals of the Northeast to the more conservative Sunbelt. Goldwater's conservative crusaders denounced Rockefeller as an "international socialist" and succeeded in blocking moderate planks on civil rights before sending the party down to overwhelming defeat in the general election, winning only Arizona and five states in the South. Future president George H. W. Bush described the consequences of Goldwater's militant conservative support: "an undecided voter would be pounced on by some hyper-tensioned type armed with an anti-LBJ book or an inflammatory pamphlet . . . Goldwater didn't want to repeal social security, but some of his more militant backers did. He didn't want to bomb the U.N. but these same backers did. They pushed their philosophy in Goldwater's name and scared the hell out of the plain average non-issue conscious man on the street."[5]

Of course, divisions between militants and Centrists occurred within the Democratic Party as well. In the mid-1970s, as liberalism was hitting its high-water mark in the streets of New York, a kid from Hell's Kitchen turned Harvard professor named Daniel Patrick Moynihan challenged militant feminist congresswoman Bella Abzug in a crowded field for the Democratic Senate nomination. The winner of that fight was scheduled to square off against Conservative Party candidate James Buckley, brother of *National Review* founder William F. Buckley Jr. Liberals had gone so far left by 1976 that the pendulum had begun to swing back among key middle-class voters in New York State. But the far left controlled the nominating process in the Democratic Party, and Daniel Patrick Moynihan had to fight for his political life.

His service as chief domestic policy adviser to Richard Nixon was the source of many liberal suspicions, while his strident defense of the United States in the face of third-world and Communist criticism as President Gerald Ford's ambassador to the United Nations was further evidence to some of his lack of loyalty to the Democratic Party. As the pitch of criticism increased, Moynihan referred to extreme voices of opposition as "those elements in our party that prefer to ruin if they cannot rule,"[6] and continued to offer up moderate aphorisms such as "liberals have been unable to acquire from birth what conservatives seem to have been endowed with at birth: namely, a healthy skepticism of the powers of government to do good."[7] But by associating himself with the older reform Democrat tradition of Harry Truman and the Kennedy brothers, Moynihan was able to narrowly win the primary and then go on to an overwhelming victory over Senator

Buckley in November. Interestingly, nearly half of the people who voted for Moynihan in the Democratic primary said they would have supported Buckley's reelection if Abzug had been the party's nominee.[8] The congresswoman's carefully cultivated association with the most liberal wing of the Democrats would almost certainly have led to the reelection of the Conservative Party's senator from New York.

Centrist reformers are essential to each party's long-term survival because they swing the parties back toward the moderate majority and allow them to remain relevant. But the extremist elements of the Democrat and Republican parties that prefer to "rule or ruin" remain a powerful influence; as the right-wing majority leader of the House Republicans, Tom DeLay, recently stated, "If you want to play in our revolution, you have to live by our rules."[9]

CALIFORNIA GOVERNOR
EARL WARREN — 1946

THE KNIGHT OF NONPARTISANSHIP WINS BOTH PRIMARIES

I am a Republican, but I shall seek the support of the people of both parties. I can do this honorably because I am an independent and therefore in a position to serve the people regardless of their politics or mine.

—EARL WARREN[1]

In the years during and after the Second World War, California was part paradise, part boomtown, with palm trees and developments scattered alongside desert highways. The Golden State was growing at a rate of ten thousand new residents each week, and as governor, Earl Warren oversaw its evolution with an efficient and honest administration that repudiated conventional partisan politics as it went to war against all special interests.

He was called "the knight of non-partisanship," a direct philosophical descendant and great admirer of the legendary California Progressive Hiram Johnson. Warren was described by author Irving Stone as "not partisan, prejudiced, one-sided; he can perceive many shades between black and white and he fears above all closed minds of the extreme right and the extreme left."[2] His determination to evenhandedly transcend typical political games eventually elevated him to chief justice of the Supreme Court—where his consensus-building skills enabled him to piece together unanimous support for the landmark desegregation case *Brown v. Board of Education*.

As governor in 1946, Warren's bipartisan approach to governing was so popular that he achieved one of the rarest feats in American politics: winning both the Republican and Democratic primaries, effectively ending the election before it began. Earl Warren showed how a Centrist could overwhelm his opponents on the far left and far right: not by forming a competing political machine, but by appealing directly to the people.

He was born in 1891, the son of Norwegian immigrants, and grew up outside Bakersfield, California. His father worked for the Southern Pacific Railroad and was active in the first attempt to form a rail union. When a strike was called in 1894, Matthias Warren put down his tools and walked off the job. In turn, he was fired and blacklisted, and the family struggled to survive.

Bakersfield was still a rough-and-tumble town, and as a boy Earl watched one turn-of-the-century union rally devolve into a near riot when a railroad manager was hung in effigy. The violence of the mob made an impression upon him about the importance of the rule of law, and after attending college, Earl Warren entered law school at University of California at Berkeley. He was not an especially strong student and failed to make the Law Review. But when it came time to apply the law in practical situations, Earl Warren excelled.

After graduating from law school, Warren briefly worked at the law department of the Associated Oil Company, and later at a San Francisco firm. After a year and a half at the firm, Warren, two classmates, and a prominent trial lawyer planned to open their own practice. As they were searching for office space on April 17, 1917, America declared war on Germany.

Warren enlisted and served as first sergeant of Company I of the 363rd Infantry. He was later promoted to first lieutenant, serving as bayonet instructor in the Central Officers Training Camp. After being discharged from the army, Warren began working at the Alameda County District Attorney's Office in Oakland, where he distinguished himself by his willingness to work long hours and master the details of arcane cases. He would remain there for the next fourteen years, rising steadily through the ranks until he was elected district attorney in 1927. "A man should never be in a hurry for a political job," Warren later reflected. "When he starts pushing he thinks and does things he would never do under normal circumstances."[3]

In Oakland, as in other cities across the United States, Prohibition-era corruption was often treated with a wink and a nod, but Warren made it clear that he would not play by the "go-along to get along" rules that dominated local politics. Without much enthusiasm, he gave up drinking, explaining that the appearance of hypocrisy in social circles would undercut his moral authority in all other areas: "How can I drink bootleg liquor at a party on Sunday night and then on Monday morning send my deputies to prosecute bootleggers?"[4]

Also uncharacteristic of elected officials in his day was Warren's commitment to running an office free of partisan politics. In 1928, Warren served as a county campaign chairman for Herbert Hoover's presidential campaign. When a fellow Republican committeeman complained that Warren's deputy, Frank Coakley, was taking a high-profile role in Democrat Al Smith's campaign, Earl replied, "The District Attorney's Office is nonpartisan. If Frank Coakley thinks that Al Smith should be elected, he has every right to devote his spare time to the Democratic candidate."[5]

All this constituted a near-revolution in mid-century California. Warren's independence and effectiveness led to his being named the nation's most effective district attorney. Warren was grateful for the honor, but he shrugged when the ethical standards he demanded in his office were applauded, pointing out that "government is a business and the integrity of those who carried it on is important. But for some reason keeping the business of local government up to the standard of private business is considered reform."[6]

In the spring of 1938, seventy-six-year-old California attorney general U. S. Webb announced he would retire from the office he had held for more than a quarter century. In deference to Attorney General Webb's lifetime of service, Earl Warren had declined to challenge him in the past, but he had told the older gentleman he intended to pursue his job whenever it was open. Now Warren was free to go after the office he had set his eye on a decade before.

Warren announced his candidacy for attorney general by putting his name forward on petitions for the Republican, Progressive, and Democratic parties' nominations—an unusual gift from the Progressive era known as "cross-filing." The normally circumspect Warren could grow passionate describing other progressive reforms, such as the "direct non-partisan primary for public office . . . reforms that made it possible for an impecunious young man like myself to launch on a public career that would last half a century. They sounded the death knell of the old-fashioned political boss."[7]

Despite the FDR-driven Democratic landslide of that year, Republican Earl Warren won the nomination of all three parties and ran uncontested in that fall's election.

Warren entered the office at 9 A.M. the first morning, and his coffee had not even gotten cold when he received an urgent telephone message. Retiring Republican governor Frank Merriam's personal secretary had spent the waning days of his bosses' term selling pardons to influential inmates at San Quentin. In an apparent payoff that would make the secretary virtually untouchable, one of Governor Merriam's final acts was to appoint his crooked personal secretary to the California bench.

By 10 A.M., Attorney General Warren was taking a deposition from the former governor's personal secretary, prohibiting him from assuming office as a judge and eventually leading to his conviction. Republican Party power bosses and editorial pages were surprised by Earl Warren's intensity in enforcing the law without regard to party label. "We knew the fur would fly when Warren took office, but we never expected it would be Republican fur," wrote one editorial page.[8] The publisher of the Democratic *Daily News* in southern California pronounced, "I believe that official California is in for a good scrubbing behind the ears."[9]

A string of high-profile cases and clashes with the Democratic governor Culbert Olson led some citizens to begin pushing for Warren to campaign for the statehouse. But Warren and his wife, Nina ("Best thing that ever happened to me"), now had six young children and, bizarrely, the governor's salary was less than the attorney general's. Warren publicly encouraged other candidates to run, but he privately agreed to consider a campaign if he were drafted by the public. This "play hard to get" strategy was earnest on Warren's part, but in his advisers' eyes it was also good politics. They began canvassing the state, lining up preliminary support. Most crucially, they secured the support of Joe Knowland, the conservative publisher of the influential *Oakland Tribune,* who had admired Warren's work as district attorney. This quiet endorsement solidified conservative support for Warren. In the spring of 1941, with the political groundwork all laid out, *Los Angeles Times* political editor Kyle Palmer wrote that "should Attorney General Earl Warren set aside personal preferences, he would be one of the strongest challengers the Republicans could put up against any Democrat."[10]

Then, on December 7, 1941, the Japanese attacked Pearl Harbor. Warren was one of the first Republican office seekers to fully appreciate how much this fundamentally altered the political landscape. "We are not Republicans now," he said. "We are not Democrats now. We are Americans. And we want the type of government in California that puts America first and all other things second."[11]

Suddenly at war, with California a potential target for attack or invasion, the nation rallied around incumbents and the administration of Franklin Delano Roosevelt. In Los Angeles, a group of sixty-five of the state's most powerful executives met at the California Club and decided that Olson was a lock for reelection. The "Smart Money" had spoken, and Warren was left without the traditional funding Republican candidates depended upon. He later stated that this was one of the great blessings of his campaign, because he would be inoculated from accusations that he was a tool of big business. He would be free to govern according to his conscience.

Polls showed that Olson had a ten-point lead on Warren, but with half of all voters undecided. This was where Warren saw opportunity. Pointing his finger at the poll of undecided voters, he told his campaign staff, "I'm going after them."[12]

In April of 1942, Warren officially filed petitions for the Republican, Democrat, and Progressive Party lines. In his memoirs, he recalled that "all that was necessary for me to qualify for the ballot was to have the endorsement of my notice of candidacy by sixty voters of my party—any sixty in the state—and to pay a filing fee of $250. This automatically placed my name on the ballot alongside that of the incumbent governor. And so it remained in the two succeeding campaigns when I was re-elected. By that simple process, all opponents could compete on technically equal terms."[13]

Warren decided he would campaign under the banner of the Warren for Governor Nonpartisan Campaign Committee, instead of the Republican label. He went so far as to refuse to endorse any other Republican candidate and chose as his slogan the decidedly nonpartisan "Leadership, Not Politics."

"My experience has been in the field of non-partisan government," Warren explained. "I believe in the party system, and have been identified with the Republican Party in matters of party concern, but I have never found that the broad questions of national party policy have application to the problems of state and local government in California."[14]

In sharp contrast, Governor Olson refused to cross-file in the primary. By pursuing only the Democratic nomination, he gave away many of the benefits of incumbency. He had an old-school politician's contempt for Warren's nonpartisan campaign. "Anyone who is so cowardly as to put on the cloak of nonpartisanship in an election like this, either . . . is a political eunuch and does not know what it is all about, or he is a political hypocrite," the elderly Olson shouted.[15] As the campaign dragged on and the governor found himself falling farther behind, Olson desperately compared Warren's slogan, "Leadership, Not Politics," to Hitler's *Führer-Prinzip*—Leadership Principle—adding, "Moreover, to profess nonpartisanship is to confess a lack of honest, firmly-held convictions, without which no man is fit or competent to be Governor."[16]

The Warren campaign formed subgroups such as the Loyal Democrats for Warren Committee to appeal to disaffected Democrats, who enjoyed a nine hundred thousand vote registration advantage in California. Democrats for Warren was publicized by his army buddy, movie star Leo Carrillo. Pamphlets passed out by the Men's Nonpartisan League for Warren emphasized the fact that "his father was a union man and was blacklisted for fighting for union rights."[17] What was intended by railroad operators to be a permanent mark of shame for the Warren family was now a powerful political asset—especially for a Republican candidate whose party was traditionally associated with big business.

Warren also aligned himself with the tremendously popular President Roosevelt, insisting that the California Republican Party platform include an explicit wartime endorsement of FDR: "In a critical situation such as now confronts us, party politics has no place and must be eliminated so that we may give President Roosevelt our unqualified support in prosecuting the war to a victorious conclusion no matter what the cost might be."[18] Largely as a result of this bipartisan expression of confidence, FDR declined to campaign in person for Olson.

On the day of the primary that August, Warren won the Republican nomination over two minor protest candidates, as expected. But the real news was that Warren received over 400,000 votes in the Democratic primary—just 110,000 less than Governor Olson. When all votes were taken into account, Earl Warren had received twice as much support across party lines as the governor.

Feeling the pressure, Olson moved further to the left, leaving Warren room to maneuver from the center-left to the right. With three months to go, Olson tried to demonize Warren as a "bitter end Republican partisan out of the most reactionary faction of his party." But his attempt to associate the attorney general with the unpopularity of the extreme isolationist wing of the Republican Party rang hollow with most Californians because Warren had already defined himself as moderate and progressive. As Election Day approached, Warren took other bold steps to advertise his independence. Speaking on a campaign broadcast, he claimed, "Just as I want no Democrat to vote for me who doubts the sincerity of my nonpartisan pledges, I want no Republican who doubts that pledge to mark his ballot in my favor."[19]

California voters resoundingly endorsed Warren's nonpartisan campaign on Election Day, giving him 57 percent of the vote. The people of California would get just what they had voted for: a nonpartisan chief executive for the fastest growing state in the Union.

In his first address to the state legislature in Sacramento, Warren thundered, "Let's cut out all the dry rot of petty politics, partisan jockeying, inaction, dictatorial stubbornness and opportunistic thinking. Let's do first things first."[20]

One of the first things Warren did was have a portrait of Hiram Johnson returned to the governor's office. It was the only portrait of a predecessor that Warren hung there. Once in office, Warren carried on Johnson's nonpartisan tradition, appointing roughly half Republicans and half Democrats to high-level positions. In a state with more Democrats than Republicans, Warren's appointment of Democrat William Sweigert as his chief of staff made good political sense—liberals would be sure they were getting a fair hearing from the governor's gatekeeper. "Some pretty good Democrats worked for him," aide Verne Scoggins remembered. "Republicans would bawl him out for appointing Democrats."[21]

To conservatives who were frustrated by the bipartisan nature of his appointments, Warren had an answer ready: "There will be another election in four years and in the meantime I am governor of all the People of California, not just those who voted for me."[22] Moreover, Warren wanted those with dissenting opinions on his staff to speak up so he could hear all sides of an issue before making his final decision.

Stories of Warren's disdain for politics as usual became legendary and helped bolster his image. After one eight-hour interview, Warren's choice for director of state welfare, Charles Schottland, said, "Governor, you've asked me every possible question except two. You haven't brought up the subject of my religion or my politics. I am a Jew and a Democrat," he volunteered. "I'm not interested in that," Warren retorted. "I am interested in one thing only, and that's whether you think you can do the job."[23]

Warren later explained the logic behind his open-minded but unorthodox approach to appointments: "I had to get Democratic votes to win. I conducted a nonpartisan campaign and I am determined to give the State a nonpartisan administration."[24]

But conservatives were gratified by Warren's fidelity to Republican principles such as balancing the budget and reducing taxes. Only months into office, Warren cut $55 million from Governor Olson's bloated last budget. He cut the sales tax and squirreled away the remaining surplus into a newly created "rainy-day" fund. He was balancing his obligations and expanding his political base of support, while rewarding core supporters with budgets that reflected the Republican principle of fiscal responsibility. He made sure that the public felt the new openness of government, bringing policy discussions to Californians across the state with daylong town hall meetings, widely publicized as being open to "concerned citizens without regard to political affiliation."

The scale of Warren's victory and demonstrated appeal to Democrats and Republicans made him a national figure almost overnight. Along with the newly elected Governor Tom Dewey of New York, Warren represented the new face and future of the Republican Party. Both men had law-and-order backgrounds, with Dewey first achieving notoriety as the high-profile special prosecutor against mob boss Lucky Luciano. While Dewey was regarded as the standard-bearer of New York's liberal Republicans, Warren was considered the hope of western conservatives. Within months of achieving office, the press began talking about how one of these men would one day live in the White House. Warren's twice-weekly press conferences gave the media plenty of opportunities to promote the new governor. Doris Fleeson, a reporter from the *Daily News,* published two articles detailing the governor's prospects for higher office. She noted that "unlike most Republican politicos, Warren displays no animus against the New Deal—probably good strategy in pro-Democratic California."[25]

Warren's first two years in office were primarily defined by the responsibilities of wartime leadership on the domestic front. The influx of war-related spending meant that employment was high and state coffers were overflowing. As a result, Warren was free to support targeted but generous increases in social spending, raising state pension benefits, increasing teachers' wages, and directing more funds to the poorest counties' school systems. This activist domestic concern for the wages of workingmen and -women was not traditionally associated with the Republican Party of Herbert Hoover and Calvin Coolidge, but at the same time Warren increasingly objected to "liberals who would . . . permit no change unless it was on their often unrealistic terms."[26]

In his memoirs, Warren repeatedly identified his governorship with a "progressive conception" of politics. "I did not care," he wrote, "to be categorized as either a liberal or a conservative. . . . I believed in the progressivism of Hiram Johnson." He did not approach issues "on the basis of an ideology," but "pragmatically as they arose"; he was not distressed because his administration "did not neatly fit, in all its actions, into some ready-made leftist ideology."[27] Later, Warren would elaborate on his political philosophy, echoing progressives like Woodrow Wilson from the generation before, writing:

If I had the choice of classification I would divide people politically into three groups—reactionary, progressive and radical . . . The reactionary, concerned only with his own position, and indifferent to the welfare of others, would resist progress regardless of changed conditions or human need . . . The radical does not want to see progress because he hopes that our democratic institutions will fail and that he will be able to take over with some form of alien tyranny.

The progressive, however, realizes that democracy is a growing institution and that, if it is to succeed, we must have steady advances from day to day to adapt it to human requirements on an ever-widening base. The progressive has faith in democracy. He is determined to work for its improvement and has the courage to develop it through trial and error, seeking to assure real freedom, not merely to a few, but for all, and to this end he is willing to subordinate his private interest to the common good.

I believe that the great body of American people, regardless of what party they are in, are progressive and liberal in this sense, and the finest thing that could happen to our political system would be to have such liberal thought and action dominate both parties.[28]

For all his nonpartisanship, when FDR declared his intention to seek an unprecedented fourth term in 1944, Warren felt a responsibility to the Republican Party. It became clear that Tom Dewey, New York's young governor, would be the GOP nominee, and party regulars pressured the California governor to give the keynote speech at their convention in Chicago.

The day before his address, Governor Warren received a draft of his speech written by Dewey's New York headquarters. It had already been released to the press, but its language was harshly partisan, attacking the president in personal terms and singling out California's largest labor union for criticism before a national audience. Warren rewrote the speech, and on the convention floor that night, he introduced himself to the American public on his own terms by saying:

> It is the purpose of this convention to put the public welfare above private self-interest; to put the nation above the party; to put the progress of the whole American community above special privilege for any part of it; to put indispensable principles—once and for all—above indispensable men.
>
> In those States which are already Republican you will find the record of public administration is progressive, enlightened and in the public interest. In those States you will find increased emphasis upon the public health, upon free education, upon care for orphaned and neglected children, upon support for the aged, for the victims of industrial accidents, for those handicapped by physical disabilities and for the victims of economic misfortune.
>
> This war cannot be fought and won as Republicans or Democrats. This is an all-American war. There is a place for every American in it. In or out of office, Republicans and Democrats share the responsibility of winning the war. We want to share it in the same spirit in which the sons of all of us fight from the same foxholes, through

the same jungles, across the same beaches in the same ships at sea and in the air. . . . Whether we win as a party is of less importance to us than whether we win as a people.[29]

Warren chose to paint himself as someone unwilling to stoke partisan fires for short-term political gain. He supported the president and the war effort, but he cautioned against the notion of the indispensable man (without ever mentioning Roosevelt by name), who he felt threatened our democracy. He made the case for a moderate, compassionate, and activist vision of the Republican Party that did not threaten to roll back the essential gains of the New Deal, but rather renew their promise with an efficient and honest administration already at work in the laboratories of the states.

This was a vision that could expand the appeal of the Republican Party, even during wartime. It was a speech that made Warren sound patriotic, sensible, and above all honest: Before he was a party man, he was an American.

Three days later, when Tom Dewey called Warren to offer him the vice presidency, Warren declined. After only two years in office, there was too much unfinished business left in California; moreover, according to the state constitution, a Democrat in the legislature would finish out his term. Again party loyalists accused Warren of being unfaithful and unpredictable—too much of a maverick California progressive and not enough of an old-line Republican.

On a windy Saturday in October 1944, Warren was busy campaigning in San Francisco with Dewey's vice presidential pick John Bricker when he came down with the flu. One week later, an infection had spread to his right kidney. It was nearly six weeks before he was able to return to work. The experience changed him. "One catastrophic illness can wipe out a man and his family," he remarked to his daughter-in-law Margaret. As governor, his salary continued throughout his illness, but he knew from bitter experience that other men were not so lucky. He recalled his father, Matthias, telling him about watching his own brother die slowly of tuberculosis because the family could not afford medical treatment and were too proud to beg. A quick study of California's medical costs in 1944 showed that Californians had taken out $11 million worth of private loans to pay for unbudgeted medical expenses in the prior year alone—only one in ten Californians had basic medical insurance.[30]

Warren reached back for inspiration to a voluntary health-care proposal put forward by Hiram Johnson's progressive administration. He developed a plan that allowed patients to choose their physicians, did not compel doctors to take part in any one program, and covered medical fees, medicine, and twenty-one days of hospitalization. It was compulsory only in the sense that the insurance would be paid for by a mandatory 3 percent payroll tax split between the worker and his or her employer. The insurance would cover the two-thirds of California working families earning $2,500 or less a year.

Warren called a small meeting of doctors in the California Medical Association to discuss the plan. Their response was guardedly positive, but when they brought the proposal forward to their members, all hell broke loose. It was derided as "communistic" and "socialized medicine." When Warren brought the legislation to the state assembly, opponents argued that a vote against the bill was "a vote against Stalin." Warren's personal physician opposed the bill so strongly that he opened the California Medical Association's lobbying office in Sacramento. A statewide campaign was inaugurated to fire up public outrage against the program, claiming that "doctors for all practical purposes will become state employees and the private practice of medicine will end."[31]

Warren was frustrated and fought back, saying, "I do not believe in socialized medicine. I do not believe in socialized anything . . . Neither do I believe in calling every proposal to bring good medical care within the economic reach of families of modest incomes socialized medicine."[32]

Warren's health-care proposal failed to get out of committee when nineteen out of twenty-nine Republicans voted against it. The governor could not keep his own party in line, and Warren blamed a combination of extremists and special interest group lobbyists for this very public defeat.

In fact, both political extremes were upset by Warren's health-insurance plan. The left maintained that it was insincere, intended as an expedient to get more votes; the right felt that Warren had deserted sound Republican principles for the same reason. Conservatives understood that he needed to appear nonpartisan to get into office, but the election was over. What neither extreme understood was that Warren's program was based on personal belief, not simple politics. "If I were a private citizen," Warren said, "I'd be pretty sore at my government if it were not concerned with my welfare. That's what government is for. That's what the preamble to the Constitution says our government is framed for—to promote the general welfare."[33]

The governor who just one year before had been asked to serve as vice president now seemed weak and isolated at home in California. After the disastrous legislative session ended, Warren sat down and wrote a letter to Tom Dewey, acknowledging the opposition he expected to face in the 1946 Republican primary: "It will come from those who believe I departed from orthodoxy in advocating the extension of social security and the solution of our race problems as proposed in our national platform and in following your campaign speech in Los Angeles on prepaid medical care. . . . I have no doubt that you also encounter some reaction from that group in our Party which believes in turning the clock back. In my opinion, these people do more harm to our Party than twice their number among our opponents."[34]

Just as Warren predicted, a conservative Republican soon announced his intention to run against him in the next primary election. Earl Lee Kelly was a banker who had served previous Republican administrations. In a speech kicking off his campaign, Kelly accused Warren of "vacillation," "opportunism," and "lack of courage and character." He then printed and sent out fifty thousand copies of his speech together with a cartoon that depicted Warren trying to ride the Republican elephant and the Democratic donkey simultaneously, with the animals running in opposite directions.

While Kelly succeeded in stirring anger among conservative extremists with his accusations that Warren represented "a creeping socialism" that amounted to "surrender to the New Deal," a vast majority of Californians still supported their governor's moderate course.

As the 1946 elections approached, polls showed that Warren would beat any opponent by a comfortable margin. With FDR dead and the war won, Harry Truman was in the White House and the Democratic Party was splintering apart. But despite positive portends for a Republican year, Earl Warren's campaign for reelection had history stacked against it. No incumbent governor of California had been elected to a second term since Hiram Johnson in 1914. Moreover, the Democrats still had nearly a million more voters registered in their party than the Republicans.

But Warren's Centrist attempt to give Californians a nonpartisan administration left him in an unexpectedly strong position to aim for reelection. The more conservative of the state's two labor unions, the American Federation of Labor, endorsed Warren's reelection before the Democrats had even settled on a candidate.

The left-wing Congress of Industrial Organizations was determined to find a candidate acceptable to its agenda. In no other state was the ultraleft wing better organized than California. Moderate Democrats were at a considerable disadvantage within the party structure and apparatus. The candidate they could most closely agree upon was the state's attorney general, Robert Kenny. The only problem was that Robert Kenny didn't want to take on Earl Warren.

Kenny was just forty-four, and felt he had plenty of time to aim for the governor's mansion. Moreover, he and Warren had been allies in many fights over the past four years and he respected the governor's politics and intellect. Years later he would reflect, "To my mind, Earl Warren was as good a politician as Roosevelt. He had the feel of the people because he was one of them. In addition, Warren was tough when he had to be, a quality every politician needs."[35] But Kenny was well liked among organized labor, liberals, and moderates within the party, and though he urged the Democrats to run Senator Sheridan Downey, Robert Kenny was the only man the divergent wings of the party could agree upon.

Kenny was colorful where Warren could appear dull. His wit made good newspaper copy, even as it sometimes got him in trouble, and he began the uphill battle with the personal affection of many reporters. As Kyle Palmer, the political editor of the *Los Angeles Times,* said, "If you were to look around this state for a man who can disarm you with a smile, who can turn suspicions aside with a friendly jeer or apt wisecrack, who can make you seem ridiculous even to yourself for suspecting he has ulterior motives, or, perhaps, too close sympathies with extreme leftists, you could begin and end your search with Smiling Bob Kenny."[36] But behind Kenny's amiable exterior was ambivalence. Days after declaring his candidacy, Kenny left the state for weeks to attend the trials of Nazi war criminals at Nuremberg.

Warren's announcement that he was pursuing a second term was squarely built on the nonpartisan tradition in which he had governed. "I am a Republican, but . . . I shall seek the support of the people of both parties. I can do this honorably because I am an independent and therefore in a position to serve the people regardless of their politics or mine. . . . I am not interested in political machines. I have not tried to build a political machine. No man should be permitted to be both governor and political boss."[37]

With the wind at Earl Warren's back in what was shaping up to be a Republican year, other Republican candidates—such as a young Richard Nixon—bristled at the governor's insistence that he once again campaign as a nonpartisan, refusing to even take a photograph with a fellow Republican office seeker. But the Democrats could not take advantage of this apparent division between the popular incumbent governor and other Republican candidates, because they were too busy fighting among themselves in a Senate primary. Moderates wanted to kick Congressman Will Rogers Jr.—son of the beloved American humorist—upstairs to the Senate, while the left-leaning machine politicians favored another congressmen named Ellis Patterson. The Democratic divisions caused a press secretary in the Warren campaign to later remember, "We kept feeling better all the time. It began to look as if we would take it all in the primaries. That didn't mean that we could relax. You never relaxed in a Warren campaign; the Governor wouldn't let you. But we were rolling in high gear long before the Democrats found out who was going to do the driving."[38]

As was his custom, Warren registered in the Republican, the Democratic, and the Progressive primaries. This time, his opponent joined him, as Kenny registered in the Republican primary as well.

In the face of the rising Warren juggernaut, conservative protest candidate Earl Lee Kelly formally dropped out of the race for the Republican nomination.

Things were looking good. Kyle Palmer of the *Los Angeles Times* predicted that "conservative democrats of the nonprofessional variety will be against Kenny from start to finish . . . Warren can polish off Kenny in the primaries if his advisers conduct their campaign wisely and aggressively."[39] This was, of course, what they intended to do—but no candidate for governor had ever won all three primaries in California history.

History was about to be made. On June 5, 1946, a record number of Californians turned out to vote in the Democratic, the Republican, and the Progressive primaries. Warren's victory eclipsed all expectations: He won the Democratic nomination by a comfortable margin, defeating Kenny on his home turf by several thousand votes. Despite right-wing Republican dissatisfaction with Warren's moderate record as governor, he won every district with margins as high as 100 to 1 in some cases. Kenny's attempt to appeal to Republican voters utterly failed; the total number of votes Warren received in both parties dwarfed Kenny's tally by almost 2 to 1.

Most impressive, perhaps, was the total Republican ticket's success. By following Warren's lead and cross-filing in the Democratic primary, every statewide Republican elected official had also been nominated by the Democratic Party.

Warren's controversial refusal to explicitly campaign with Republican candidates had not hurt his party's chances. In fact, exactly the opposite had occurred: Warren's strenuous nonpartisanship elevated all Republicans by making the Democrats seem narrow and partisan by comparison. By decidedly stepping outside politics as usual and embracing the progressive tradition, Earl Warren had taken an important step toward making the Republicans the majority party in California.

After accepting Attorney General Kenny's telegram of congratulation, Warren issued a statement saying that his triple nomination was "a clear indication that the people of California do not intend to be divided by narrow partisanship." This was echoed by the newspapers, which presented Warren's victory as "a triumph of public sanity."[40]

The California papers paid particular attention to Warren's endorsement by the American Federation of Labor and its split with the Communist-supported Congress of Industrial Organizations: "Not by the widest stretch of the most prejudiced or credulous imagination could Warren's reelection be taken as a setback for the legitimate objectives and rightful place of labor, organized and and unorganized. He was supported by the conservative leaders of labor, themselves under attack from those who sought to defeat him . . . Warren's re-election by such landslide proportions strikes a healthy blow at the entire band of left-wing radicals and communist schemers who, in hope of ultimate overthrow of our institutions, sought to establish and entrench themselves in California."[41] Warren's strenuous moderation had left his opponents on the left wing of the Democratic Party associated with Communists and the radical fringe, which even moderate Democrats abhorred.

Years later, Richard Nixon—who was first elected to Congress in California's Republican landslide of 1946—reflected on the lessons of Robert Kenny's loss to Earl Warren: "Kenny pointed out that each candidate in a campaign has a hard core of supporters—the Republicans on the right, the Democrats on the left. They aren't enough to win, but their enthusiastic support is essential if you are to survive as a candidate. The trick is for each to reach out to the center to get the total vote he needs to win. That was Warren's specialty. But in doing so, a candidate must not reach so far that he snaps the umbilical cord that provides him nourishment from his hard core. If he does that, he will be left twisting in the wind."[42]

In his inaugural address, Warren continued to resolutely stress the themes that led to his overwhelming reelection. He appealed to a joint session of the legislature to "cooperate for the common good without regard to party, faction or personality . . . We must recognize that a thorough consideration of human problems transcends partisanship."[43] Also, typically, Warren was willing to ask the tough practical questions: "How can we avoid Federal bureaucracy, which in the abstract we deplore, but which in everyday life we too often encourage?"[44]

In the words of biographer Leo Katcher, "Here was Warren, still stressing what both parties had in common, rather than what divided them. Instead of retreating to the past, he was pressing forward with suggestions for social and welfare legislation. He appeared to be a solitary swimmer, going against the tide. Instead of weakening under the strain, he seemed continually to gain strength."[45]

EISENHOWER VS. TAFT — 1952

THE INTERNATIONALIST VS. THE ISOLATIONIST

> The middle of the road is all of the usable surface. The extremes, right and left, are in the gutters.

> —DWIGHT D. EISENHOWER[1]

In 1952, the Republicans were staring down the barrel of what would have been their sixth consecutive presidential defeat. Locked out of the White House for the past twenty years, as the New Deal softened the blow of the Great Depression and the Second World War evolved into the Cold War, the Republicans' disdain for economic liberalism and foreign policy internationalism made them seem hopelessly out of step with history.

Many voters longed for a new administration that would moderate the inevitable excesses of a single party in power for two decades. But the Republicans seemed determined to nominate a candidate doomed to lose: conservative senator Robert Taft of Ohio. Known as "Mr. Republican," this son of the portly former president had risen to the position of Senate minority leader, bitterly opposing FDR's policies every step of the way, stating on the Senate floor that "if Mr. Roosevelt is not Communist today, he is bound to become one."[2]

Taft was also an avowed isolationist, declaring at the outset of the Second World War that "war is even worse than a German victory." In the postwar years, Taft offered support to Senator Joe McCarthy's anticommunist hearings, stating that "whether Senator McCarthy has legal evidence, whether he has overstated or understated his case is of lesser importance. The question is whether the Communist influence in the State Department still exists."[3] Taft was popular with Republican Party activists, drawing applause with his articulation of their old-time religion, but his strident partisanship alienated most moderates and independents. Despite broad dissatisfaction with the Truman administration, the Republicans once again seemed likely to lose the general election. Some people worried that a sixth consecutive GOP defeat in the presidential election might mean the end of the two-party system in America. Among these was General Dwight David Eisenhower.

Unknown before the war, with his military career apparently stalled at the rank of lieutenant colonel, Eisenhower was now known around the world as the five-star supreme commander of the Allied forces, the liberator of Western Europe and the warrior of democracy.

In vivid contrast to the narrowly partisan figure of Bob Taft, Eisenhower was a national hero, the only president to date named *Time*'s Man of the Year well before his election. As he was a product of the nonpartisan military establishment, Americans did not know what party Eisenhower belonged to, but they wanted him to run. In 1948, President Truman even offered to step down if Eisenhower would agree to accept the Democratic nomination, but Ike politely refused. In a press conference, he explained, "Ever since I have first heard my name connected with possible political office I have consistently declined to consider such a contingency. I am a soldier. I belong to the Army, and the Army is truly national. It lives to serve the nation and nobody else: no party; no special group."[4]

To this end, Ike avoided giving overtly political speeches, but occasionally glimpses of his Centrist philosophy slipped in, such as in a 1949 Labor Day speech in St. Louis in which he declared, "The path to America's future lies down the middle of the road between the unfettered power of concentrated wealth . . . and the unbridled power of statism or partisan interests."[5]

When he formally registered to vote in October 1949, he registered as an Independent, defiantly writing in his diary, "I stick to my determination not to appear with a definitely Republican or Democratic party."[6]

That same month the Gallup Poll asked the American people whether they viewed Eisenhower as a Democrat or Republican. Democrats were evenly divided in their opinion, while Republicans by four to one viewed Eisenhower as one of them. A plurality of voters said they didn't know Eisenhower's political affiliation. To them—as to himself—Eisenhower was a patriot, not a political partisan. Democratic senator Paul Douglas of Illinois took the step of formalizing this perception by suggesting that both parties draft Eisenhower for president. It certainly placed him in exalted company—only George Washington had been elected by acclamation.

New York governor Tom Dewey, loser of the previous two presidential elections and leader of the international wing of the Republican Party, made it his personal mission to convince the general to run for the White House as a Republican with consecutive visits to Columbia University, where Ike served as college president during the years immediately after the war. Dewey explained: "I felt that the Republican Party was weak with the electorate, and that a new style of candidate was the only sure way to win, and I was confident that General Eisenhower would win and I wasn't confident that anybody else would."[7]

The man who had most recently beaten Dewey for the presidency agreed with the governor's reasoning. Looking back, Harry Truman neatly laid out the political logic of the GOP's move toward the center: "The Republicans, being a minority party, knew they had to borrow strength from the Democratic and independent vote. Their only hope of gaining such strength was to find a candidate whose appeal to the voters would cut across party lines."[8]

Nonetheless, in 1951, Truman still held out hope that Eisenhower could be persuaded to take the reins of the Democratic Party and sail to an easy victory the following year. Truman dispatched aide Joseph Davies to Paris in June 1951, where Eisenhower was now serving as head of the newly created NATO. Eisenhower again expressed his reluctance to get involved with partisan politics, although he acknowledged that being nominated by both parties, while attractive, was a near impossibility. "There were things in both parties which appealed to him," Davies wrote in his diary that night. "Also in both, there were conditions and personalities which he could not tolerate. He named men in both parties he could not work with, and would not."[9]

That same evening, Eisenhower wrote in his diary about his feelings of frustration toward the rabid right wing of the Republican Party. "Taft, Wherry, et al. (and especially [Republican Senators] Kem and McCarthy) are disciples of hate—hate and curse anything that belongs to the administration," Ike wrote. "Heaven knows there is plenty for which to criticize the administration legitimately and decently and strongly, but what they are doing is apt to make HST [Harry S. Truman] an underdog and backfire on them."[10]

Equally distrustful of the extremes of both parties, Eisenhower was an instinctive political Centrist. Cases of civic corruption and escalating government spending from the Democrats bothered him, but the Republicans' call for withdrawal from NATO and the Marshall Plan seemed equally irresponsible and potentially more dangerous.

Ike had served on the front lines of foreign policy as Hitler's defeat had given way to the cold realities of Stalin and the potentially apocalyptic challenges of the nuclear age. In a speech shortly after the war, Eisenhower stated, "I hate war as only a soldier who has lived it can, only as one who has seen its brutality, its stupidity."[11] But he also understood as only a soldier could that peace came through strength and engaged involvement with the world. Robert Taft's isolationist calls for an end to NATO and the Marshall Plan seemed foolish in the extreme to the general, who was now living in Paris establishing NATO.

Nonpartisan Citizens for Eisenhower groups were springing up around the nation: grassroots groups of independent citizens attracted to the general's war-hero record and dismayed at the prospect of choosing between Taft and Truman. It was easy to imagine the general leading the nation from the oval office. Citizens for Eisenhower had the appearance of an entirely grassroots movement, but it was secretly bankrolled by wealthy moderate Republicans, channeling the general's tremendous personal popularity to do an end run around the old-guard Republican establishment's self-defeating insistence on Taft. Moderate Republicans led by Governor Dewey and Massachusetts senator Henry Cabot Lodge began meeting in quasi-secret to clear a path for Eisenhower's nomination. Joined by the publisher of the influential *New York Herald Tribune,* they secured that paper's endorsement before Eisenhower had even decided to consider a candidacy. The endorsement read, "By deed and by word General Eisenhower has shown himself a keeper of the great liberties to which Republicanism is dedicated."[12]

When President Truman was asked by reporters for his reaction to the endorsement, he stated, "They certainly picked a fine man for their candidate."[13] Truman was far from the only Democrat to appreciate General Eisenhower. A December 1951 Gallup Poll showed that while Eisenhower and Taft were locked in a dead heat among Republicans, as a potential Democratic nominee Eisenhower was favored over Taft by a fourth of Republican voters, more than two-thirds of Independents, and nine out of ten Democrats.[14] Democrats liked Ike even more than Republicans.

Faced with FDR's example of serving for more than the traditional two presidential terms, many people assumed that Harry Truman would run again. Despite his low standings in the approval ratings, it was generally perceived that he could beat Bob Taft. Truman was exhausted after seven years in the job, but he would have rather run than turn the White House over to an isolationist. On December 18, he wrote Eisenhower a letter inquiring about the general's chances of getting involved in politics. He indicated again that the Democratic nomination was open to him, should he decide to run, but that in the absence of an Eisenhower candidacy Truman would feel obligated to pursue a third term: "I must keep isolationists out of the White House."[15]

In a handwritten reply, Eisenhower told the president, as he did his

Republican supporters, that he was absorbed in his current NATO duties and not inclined to seek political office. But he left the door open to "extraordinary circumstances," stating that "any group of American citizens has a right to fight, politically, for any set of principles in which its members believe and to attempt to draft a leader to head that fight!"[16]

As the New Year came, with the election eleven months away, Eisenhower's supporters grew restless with the general's high-minded indecision. The "draft Eisenhower" movement would need to be mobilized in time for the presidential primaries if the general was to have a fighting chance at gaining the nomination. Senator Henry Cabot Lodge pressed him for permission to put his name forward in the New Hampshire Republican primary. Eisenhower stated that although he would not campaign, he could not stop such a movement. He gave Lodge permission to say that Eisenhower, while a registered Independent, had voted Republican in the recent past.

Three events within three weeks convinced Eisenhower that he had a responsibility to run for president. On January 21, Truman submitted a budget to Congress that produced a $14 billion deficit, prompting Eisenhower to angrily dictate eight pages of protest into his diary. On February 8, the last Republican president, Herbert Hoover—who had presided over the beginning of the Great Depression—joined Senator Taft and sixteen other conservative Republicans in signing a statement urging that all "American troops should be brought home" from Europe. America seemed to be facing a choice between creeping socialism and isolationism. Eisenhower, like much of the nation, wanted a third choice between the extremes. On February 11, fifteen thousand people showed up at Madison Square Garden after a boxing match at midnight to rally in support of Citizens for Eisenhower. A film of the event was flown over to Paris, where Eisenhower and his wife, Mamie, watched the displays of support and affection in stunned silence. That night, in his living room near NATO headquarters, Dwight David Eisenhower finally decided to run for president of the United States.

Running for president as a Democrat would have guaranteed Ike a landslide victory with comparatively little effort. But Eisenhower's decision about which party to join had little to do with political expediency or even ideology: He later reflected that he could have run as a conservative Democrat or moderate Republican in 1952. Eisenhower was motivated by something more practical and patriotic than partisanship: He simply believed that the Democrats had been in power too long. As Davies wrote after his June 1951 visit with Ike, the general "felt that where a party had been in control for a long time, a change in party control would be beneficial to clean out dead wood; get rid of some bad growths; and preserve the two-party system, which otherwise might be jeopardized."[17]

This line of reasoning closely paralleled one of Eisenhower's earliest-known political statements. In a 1909 address to the annual meeting of the Dickinson County Young Men's Democratic Club, made when he was just nineteen years old, Eisenhower declared his intention to support the Democratic Party as opposed to President William Howard Taft's Republicans, "because one party has been in power for fifty years, with only two brief interruptions." He reasoned that as a result of this stagnation, "many evils have sprung up in the machinery of the government, which a change in policy for a time would at least remedy if not blot them out."[18]

When President Taft's son, Robert, officially declared his candidacy in October of 1951, he declared defensively, but with some justification, that most Republicans "really desire me to be the candidate of their Party." A poll indicated that 70 percent of GOP county chairmen supported the conservative senator's candidacy. The *Chicago Tribune,* the semiofficial voice of the right wing of the Republican Party, was squarely in Bob Taft's corner. In editorials, the paper declared that "the Eisenhower organization ought to be called 'Republicans for Truman' " and criticized the general as the "candidate of effeminates."[19] Rumors began to be spread that Eisenhower was secretly Jewish (in fact, his parents were Protestant and of German descent) and that his wife, Mamie, was an alcoholic.

Taft tried to take advantage of Eisenhower's absence by campaigning hard in the Granite State, visiting twenty-eight towns and cities. But in March, when the votes were counted, Eisenhower had swept New Hampshire, winning every county and all fourteen delegates without ever having stepped foot in the state. A week later, in Minnesota, Eisenhower received 108,692 write-in votes, just 10,000 fewer votes than Minnesota's own Governor Harold Stassen. In March, convinced that Eisenhower would run for the presidency, Truman declared that he would not run for reelection at the annual Jefferson-Jackson Day Dinner: "I have served my country, long, and I think efficiently and honestly. I shall not accept a re-nomination. I do not feel that it is my duty to spend another four years in the White House."

In Paris, Ike responded to reporters' increasing pressure by saying that "the mounting numbers of my fellow citizens who are voting to make me the Republican nominee are forcing me to re-examine my personal position and past decisions." It was enough to give his supporters the encouragement they needed to feel that they were changing history without publicly committing him for candidacy. The general was wise enough to understand that—as he confided to friends—"the seeker is never so popular as the sought."[20]

Eisenhower approached his presidential campaign like a military campaign: laying the groundwork, securing crucial support, waiting for a weakness to open in his opponent's line of defense, and then marching forward with overwhelming force and lightning speed to seize the prize. As he prepared for a nationwide campaign, Eisenhower instinctively brought military metaphors to politics, as when he explained to supporters why he would not unleash a deluge of position papers at the start of his campaign: "A premature consumption of all the ammunition in a battle is certain to bring defeat—everything must be so calculated that the effort constantly increases in its intensity towards its ultimate maximum, which is the moment of victory."[21] Ike understood that his support was predicated upon being a well-known war hero, a blank slate upon which the public could project their hopes and dreams for the future.

Eisenhower finally returned to the United States in June 1952, a little more than five months before the presidential election. He formally announced his candidacy in his hometown, Abilene, Kansas, and watched a parade in his honor from the second-floor balcony of the tallest building in town, the Sunflower Hotel.

The subject of the speech announcing his campaign for the presidency was surprising. The man who was content to let others project upon his policy considerations offered a substantive speech about the importance of fiscal responsibility. Wearing a poncho in the driving rain, Eisenhower warned, "Today, staggering federal expenditures for civil and military purposes have soared to totals beyond the comprehension of ordinary individuals. In a world threatened by war, a great portion of these is inescapable . . . but because necessary expenditures are so great, our entire arms program must be under constant scrutiny that not one dollar be spent without full value received. . . . Heedless expense is an investment in bankruptcy."[22]

Everyone assumed that a Republican would campaign on fiscal responsibility, but few people imagined that the general would use as its primary example excessive military spending. It was a stroke of genius: in such a pro-military and anticommunist moment, only Eisenhower had the credibility to call for cuts in spending without being called a traitor. The speech was a stiff and uninspiring performance, but along the parade route—watching this hometown tribute of old high school teachers and classmates—Ike came alive, warmly nudging Mamie as each float passed. His life had come full circle, from common soldier to conquering general, back home to Abilene.

Ike was born in a tiny rented room beside the railroad tracks in Denison, Texas, on October 14, 1890. He had grown up the third of six children on the western edge of the Midwest in Abilene. His family was poor but hardworking, and each of the children would go on to worldly success. At the age of fourteen, Ike nearly died after refusing to let a local doctor amputate a badly infected leg; had he allowed the leg to be removed, it would have affected almost every aspect of his life forward, making sports and the pursuit of a traditional military career almost impossible. Eisenhower recuperated from the infection fully, and although his parents were pacifists, the promise of free education led him to apply for admission to West Point. He was an average student, graduating in the middle of his class, but Eisenhower distinguished himself on the football field and as a poker player. While most of his classmates were sent to Europe to fight in the First World War, Eisenhower's recognized talent for organization kept him on the domestic front, preparing tank squads for combat. He was frustrated and repeatedly requested transfers to Europe, finally receiving permission to ship out on November 18, 1918—but the war ended exactly one week earlier. Eisenhower thought he had lost his chance to fight in the Great War of his generation. While thousands of young officers left the army to join civilian life, Eisenhower decided to stay in the U.S. military. He was dispatched to the Philippines to serve as chief of staff and occasional speechwriter to General Douglas MacArthur, and later distinguished himself at the Command and General Staff College at Fort Leavenworth, Kansas, graduating first in his class. But when his only surviving son, John, inquired about pursuing a military career of his own in 1939, Eisenhower felt he needed to be honest about the limited career prospects that a life in the army offered.

The Second World War changed everything. When Pearl Harbor was attacked, Eisenhower anticipated his first career combat assignment. He was disappointed when he was called to Washington to serve as a planner for the army's chief of staff, General George Marshall. At the time, the military was divided internally between supporters of General MacArthur and General Pershing. Marshall had been one of Pershing's disciples, but within very little time he was impressed by Eisenhower's evident genius for organization and the fact that Ike was one of the few men who could work equally well with both the MacArthur and Pershing factions in the army. He was a born conciliator with backbone. After a few months, Marshall dispatched Ike to London to take command of the planned Allied invasion of North Africa, followed in time by the invasion of France. The soldier who had never commanded troops in combat took control of the most ambitious assault in modern military history. The lieutenant colonel whose career had seemed hopelessly stalled at the age of forty-five became a five-star general and the liberator of Europe less than a decade later.

While Eisenhower had been languishing in the middle of the military ranks, Robert Taft—son of the former president and chief justice of the Supreme Court—was serving on the White House staff of President Herbert Hoover. When the Second World War came, Taft argued against American involvement and intervention on behalf of Britain, saying that it would bring the United States into a war "to save the British Empire." He argued against assisting Russia on the grounds that "the victory of communism in the world would be far more dangerous to United States than the victory of fascism." While he developed a reputation for personal integrity among his colleagues, Taft displayed flashes of defeatism. In a letter to his wife in 1940, the Senate minority leader wrote, "I am very pessimistic about the future of the country. We are certainly being dragged towards war and bankruptcy and socialism all at once."[23]

Taft had run for his party's nomination as president twice and lost to moderates who were deemed to have more popular appeal by the East Coast establishment he distrusted. But 1952 was supposed to be Mr. Republican's year. Nevertheless, a relatively liberal figure had once again come out of nowhere and threatened to deny him the nomination and the White House. This time Taft and his supporters would not give in without a fight.

On Sunday, July 6, the first day of the 1952 Republican National Convention in Chicago, the ideological battle lines were drawn in what promised to be a fight for the soul of the Republican Party. The 532 delegates pledged to Senator Taft marched into the auditorium with arms linked, singing "Onward Christian Soldiers" in a show of their solidarity.[24] They were determined that this time the nomination would not be stolen from them.

Taft's years of toiling in the Republican vineyards and ten months of concerted campaigning—as opposed to Eisenhower's one month—seemed to have paid off. He was the heavy favorite going into Chicago, and by the second day of the convention, Taft had assurances from three more delegates than he needed to win the nomination. The conservatives were feeling confident that victory would be theirs. After all, what had Eisenhower done to deserve the Republican nomination? They felt that the general was just a tool of the discredited liberal Republicans from the East Coast.

Conservative Illinois senator Everett Dirksen, with a tobacco-soaked voice that sounded like "honey poured through gravel," pointed a bony finger in the direction of New York governor Tom Dewey and gravely intoned, "We followed you before and you took us down the path of defeat. Don't do it to us again."

With that, the Stockyards International Amphitheater exploded into a storm of boos and cheers; fistfights broke out between the moderates and the old guard; Eisenhower aides were spat on; and for twenty minutes the Republican convention devolved into chaos, beamed directly into 20 million American homes through televisions more accustomed to carrying *I Love Lucy*.

Despite Taft's strong position, divisions ran deep in the party. Many states found their delegations split down the middle between Taft and Eisenhower supporters, with the Taft delegates invariably more experienced in the arcane ways of political conventions. But Taft's supporters from Texas proved too clever by half; sensing a growing rebellion within their ranks, they formed a separate state convention and nominated the full slate of Taft delegates to go to Chicago. When two sets of Texas delegates showed up and demanded to be seated, a minor scandal blew up in their face. Bitter feelings were still fresh from the 1912 Republican National Convention in Chicago, where President Taft had outmaneuvered and essentially stolen the nomination from Theodore Roosevelt. As in 1912, moderates began carrying banners outside the auditorium that read "Thou Shalt Not Steal." The charge was personally resonant: No one alive was more sensitive to the division of the party in 1912 than Senator Robert Taft.

Eisenhower asked former Dewey campaign manager Herbert Brownell to investigate solutions to the divided Texas delegation. Over three days, Brownell sat in the New York Public Library reviewing the minutes of the 1912 convention. He emerged with a solution: the cleverly named Fair Play Amendment (after all, who could vote against "Fair Play"?), which kept delegates from unofficial state conventions from taking part in the nominating process. Crucially, the language of the parliamentary motion kept contested delegates from voting on the Fair Play Amendment themselves. This deft solution stopped Bob Taft's momentum dead in its tracks, dredging up old memories of stolen conventions in the past, and stacking the deck in favor of the amateur Eisenhower supporters. The tide turned, and when moderate Minnesota governor Harold Stassen threw his delegates to Ike, Eisenhower received the Republican nomination for president on the first ballot.

That evening, against the advice of his aides, an exhausted Eisenhower walked to Taft's hotel to extend an olive branch and try to unify the party. Passing weeping Taft supporters in the hallways,

Eisenhower surprised the senator with the uncustomary visit. "This is no time for conversation on matters of any substance," Ike said with his hand outstretched. "You're tired and so am I. I just want to say that I want to be your friend and hope you will be mine. I hope we can work together."[25] Taft swiftly acknowledged his opponents' broad popularity by saying, "You'll win the election all right."[26] The two men had a picture taken of them shaking hands in the hallway, and then as quickly as he'd arrived, Eisenhower walked back to his hotel.

In a meeting the next morning, Dewey advised Ike to take a vice president that would balance the general's well-known profile. He suggested Richard M. Nixon, a thirty-nine-year-old senator from California. Nixon was young, while the general was the oldest man at that point to ever campaign for the presidency. Nixon was from the fastest-growing state in the West, while Eisenhower hailed from the Midwest and kept a farm near Gettysburg, Pennsylvania. While many conservatives still groused that Eisenhower's tactics toward the end of the war allowed the Soviets to get to Berlin first, Nixon had impeccable anticommunist credentials due to his case against Alger Hiss, presented in dramatic fashion during a session of the House Un-American Activities Committee. Nixon's relative inexperience in the event of Eisenhower's premature death did not seem to be the subject of much conversation or concern.

That night in his acceptance speech, Eisenhower stated: "Ladies and Gentlemen. You have summoned me on behalf of millions of your fellow Americans to lead a great crusade for freedom in America and freedom in the world. I know something of the solemn responsibility of leading a crusade. I have led one. . . . I accept your summons. I will lead this crusade." Ike promised to bring an end to the "wastefulness, the arrogance and corruption in high places, the heavy burdens and the anxieties which are the bitter fruit of a party too long in power." He also vowed a "program of progressive policies, drawn from our finest Republican traditions."[27]

As he would in speeches throughout the campaign, Eisenhower condemned "the utter futility of any policy of isolation," while simultaneously blaming the Truman administration's lack of realism for the country's being sucked into the Korean War: "If we had been less trusting, if we had been less soft and weak, there would probably have been no war in Korea!" He also deftly bridged the gap between his authority on military matters with his newly articulated passion for fiscal discipline, arguing that "a bankrupt America is a defenseless America."[28]

New York Times columnist James Reston characterized the revolution at the 1952 Republican convention: "In opposition to most of the ideas by which American politics are supposed to be governed," he wrote, the nomination went "not to the pros but to the amateurs; not to those who shouted the most, but to those who said the least; not to those who sought the nomination the hardest, but those who shunned it almost to the end; not to the extremists of right or left, but to the moderates; not to the men who concentrated on the things that divide the American people; but to those who emphasized the things that unite them."[29]

Irving Berlin had been asked to write a campaign theme song and came up with the simplest and most memorable slogan in American political history: "I Like Ike." His song's lyrics emphasized Eisenhower's personal warmth (in contrast to Dewey) and bipartisan appeal (in contrast to Taft). The second verse read: "Courageous strong and human/Why even Harry Truman/Says I like Ike." The tune was catchy, reassuring, and sent the message that even lifelong Democrats could hold their heads up high and vote for Ike.

The Democratic nominee, Illinois governor Adlai Stevenson, derided the Republican Party by saying that GOP stood for "grouchy old pessimists." It was a quick and clever line with some justification; Republican standard-bearers like Senator Taft were always playing a negative role in debates of the day, standing against Roosevelt's policies instead of proposing new solutions themselves and predicting a darker future for America in their speeches and private correspondence.

In contrast, Eisenhower projected an optimism and confidence about the future of the country and the Republican Party. This reflected the key lesson he learned about leadership while preparing the Allied forces for the invasion. "Optimism and pessimism are infectious and they spread more rapidly from the head down than in any direction," he wrote in a discarded introduction to his Second

World War memoirs. "I firmly determined that my mannerisms and speech in public would always reflect the cheerful certainty of victory—that any pessimism and discouragement I might ever feel would be reserved for my pillow. To translate this conviction into tangible results . . . I did my best to meet everyone from General to private with a smile, a pat on the back and a definite interest in his problems."[30] Eisenhower extended this combat lesson in leadership to politics; the privately taciturn man was almost always seen in public with a broad smile across his face. Journalist Murray Kempton—an initial critic and later a grudging admirer—would write that "it was ten years before I looked at his picture and realized that the smile was always a grin."[31]

To defuse the issue of his age, Eisenhower purposely kept a vigorous schedule during his five-month sprint to the White House that kept reporters from articulating doubts that he was physically not up to the job, traveling fifty thousand miles and delivering 228 speeches—significantly more than Stevenson, who although nine years his junior, frequently showed signs of fatigue in press conferences.

Having committed himself wholeheartedly to the campaign, Eisenhower was in it to win, and he was not afraid to play political hardball when necessary. Ike was later memorably described by Nixon as "a far more complex and devious man than most people realized, and in the best sense of those words."[32] His chief of staff, Sherman Adams, remembered that "he was well aware that somebody had to do the hard-hitting infighting, and he had no objections to it as long as no one expected him to do it."[33] While Ike jealously guarded his nonpartisan reputation, Dick Nixon made a perfect attack dog. At every campaign stop, Nixon hammered at the alliterative themes the Republicans had decided to tar the Democrats with: Communism, corruption, and Korea.

Nixon's attacks were repaid when the then-liberal *New York Post* reported that wealthy California financial backers had set aside a secret slush fund for Nixon's personal benefit. With two months to go before the election, there were calls for Eisenhower to kick Nixon off the ticket. Nixon demanded a chance to tell his side of the story on national television. In an unprecedented and rambling, but awkwardly endearing, speech to the American public on live television, Nixon single-handedly revived his political career from a flat line. It became known as the "Checkers" speech, after the Nixon family's cocker spaniel, whom Nixon good-naturedly refused to count as a campaign contribution. At the end of the address, Nixon asked the American public to phone into Republican headquarters and offer their opinion as to whether he should resign or stay on the ticket. The calls that flooded the switchboard were overwhelmingly in favor of the young senator from California.

Eisenhower's greatest frustration during the campaign was running alongside the radical right wing and rabid anticommunists in the Republican Party. Senator Joe McCarthy of Wisconsin was then at the height of his popularity, while many senators who had opposed him found themselves voted out of office. Now McCarthy was running for reelection in Wisconsin, a state that the Republicans had lost during the presidential election of 1948. Wisconsin was considered a must-win state, and Eisenhower was convinced that he had to campaign there. But McCarthy had infuriated him with a new round of attacks on General George C. Marshall, architect of the Marshall Plan and Eisenhower's mentor during the war. Marshall's supposed "crime" was that he helped negotiate an end to the civil war in China, which Mao's Communist forces won, prompting McCarthy and other right-wing Republicans to accuse Marshall of being part of "a conspiracy so immense, an infamy so black, as to dwarf any in the history of man."[34]

Eisenhower had been defending Marshall and implicitly disavowing McCarthy on the campaign trail, but now it was time to go to Wisconsin. Eisenhower said he would support McCarthy "as a . . . Republican," but added forcefully, "I am not going to campaign for or give blanket endorsement to any man who does anything that I believe to be un-American in its methods and procedures. . . . There is nothing of disloyalty in General Marshall's soul . . . I have no patience with anyone who can find in his [Marshall's] record of service for this country anything to criticize."[35] Ike and McCarthy were scheduled to speak from the same platform in Milwaukee, and Eisenhower's speech contained an eloquent defense of his friend General George Marshall. But when the Republican governor of Wisconsin looked over the remarks on the Eisenhower campaign train, he told Ike that his defense of Marshall would be seen in Wisconsin as an attack on McCarthy, an advertisement for divisions within the Republican Party that could have devastating consequences for other GOP candidates in the state. The governor asked Ike to cut the lines from the speech and to give them in another state. Eisenhower reluctantly agreed, a concession to practical politics; but word of the tribute-never-given was leaked to the press, and it appeared that Eisenhower the politician had given in to petty tyrants in a way that Eisenhower the general never would.

In the end, it was Korea that finally put Ike over the top. The UN police action had been escalating for over two years. More than fifty thousand American lives had been lost, and a nation weary of war wanted to bring its boys home. Eisenhower, of course, had unique credibility on the field of battle; no one had to strain to imagine him as commander in chief. In contrast, Adlai Stevenson had spent the Second World War occupying high-level bureaucratic positions in Washington.

Ten days before the election, Ike gave what is regarded as one of the most effective campaign speeches in American history. A large number of undecided voters were still wavering as to whether they should vote Republican for the first time in twenty years, with the Korean War hanging over their decision. A speech was written and rewritten, designed to allow Eisenhower to make the case that the Korean War had been the Truman administration's fault by layering facts and assertions without ever accusing Truman by name. "We are not mute prisoners of history; that is a doctrine for totalitarians," Eisenhower said. "It is no creed for free men . . . There is a Korean War—and we are fighting it—for the simplest of reasons: because free leadership failed to check and turn back communist ambition. . . . Now where will a new administration begin? It will begin with its President taking a firm, simple resolution . . . to forego the diversions of politics and to concentrate on the job of ending the Korean War. . . . I shall go to Korea."[36]

"I shall go to Korea" was on the front page of every paper and the lips of nearly every citizen the next day; to the public it seemed that the great general had given his word that he would end the war. As a Democrat, Stevenson was forced to defend the Truman administration's actions. Ike's declaration effectively ended the Democrats' campaign and their two decades of control of the White House.

On Election Day 1952, amid a record voter turnout, General Dwight David Eisenhower was elected to his first political office, president of the United States, swamping the Democrats in the electoral college 442 to 89.

On his first day in the White House, Eisenhower remarked that being president felt like "a continuation of all I've been doing since July 1941."[37] Within six months, U.S. troops were withdrawing from Korea with honor while leaving an independent South Korea secure and intact. The American commitment to the North Atlantic Treaty Organization was now unquestioned. In the military, Eisenhower had distinguished himself as a master of mediating competing interests and directing them toward a larger goal. These skills proved useful when dealing with Congress. Eisenhower's victory in 1952 also led to narrow Republican majorities in the Senate and the House of Representatives. But the theoretical strength of the Republican coalition was undercut by the battles between the White House and right-wing senators. In his diary, Ike wrote, "Republican senators are having a hard time getting it through their heads that they now belong to a team that includes rather than opposes the White House."[38]

In his first State of the Union address to Congress, Eisenhower again articulated his intention to bring a principled moderation to the White House and modernity to the Republican Party: "There is, in our affairs at home, a middle way between untrammeled freedom of the individual and the demands for the welfare of the whole nation. This way must avoid government by bureaucracy as carefully as it avoids neglect of the helpless."[39]

Although Eisenhower achieved a good working relationship with Senator Taft before Taft's untimely death of stomach cancer in the spring of 1953, the new president found himself most frequently at odds with right-wing senators who remained skeptical of the administration's moderation and internationalism. They proved to be the primary opposition to Eisenhower's appointment of California's Republican governor Earl Warren to be chief justice of the Supreme Court. At one point early in his first term, exasperated by his constant battles with the conservatives in Congress, Eisenhower remarked to friends, "I can tell you one thing, if I ever do run again, it'll be as an Independent."[40]

Instead, Eisenhower moved to take control of the Republican Party, appointing forty-two new state chairmen loyal to his vision of "Modern Republicanism," which Eisenhower loosely defined as being conservative when it comes to money and liberal when it comes to human beings. Ike based Modern Republicanism's understanding of a limited but activist government on a quote by Lincoln: "The legitimate object of government is to do for a community of people whatever they need to have done, but cannot do at all, or cannot so well do, for themselves—in their separate, and individual capacities. In all that the people can individually do as well for themselves, government ought not to interfere."[41]

At a Republican Precinct Day rally in Denver before the 1954 midterm elections, he told the crowd that the Republicans' "goal is not political power for its own sake, but to advance the good of 163 million Americans. To that end, we are dedicated to the maximum of individual freedom, fostered by a government desiring not to dominate but only to serve—a government kept close to the hearthsides of America—a government liberal in dealing with the human concerns of the people, but conservative in spending their money. From Lincoln's day to this, these have been the fundamental aims of our historic Party."[42]

Eisenhower was fundamentally a practical man who prided himself on getting results and believed that "it is only common sense to recognize that the great bulk of Americans, whether Republican or Democrat, face many common problems and agree on a number of basic objectives." He quickly found that working with the Democratic minority leader Lyndon Johnson was a mutually beneficial arrangement. Eisenhower was the first Republican to win the electoral votes of Texas in a generation. Lyndon Johnson was up for reelection in 1954 and felt that he had to move to the right to secure his own position. The cooperation of the Democratic leadership allowed the president's legislation and nominations not to be held hostage by conservative Republicans in the Senate. The Democrats, in turn, were able to claim that they were being responsible and riding to the rescue, breaking gridlock and helping the White House reinforce the internationalist foreign policy of FDR and Truman that Eisenhower himself had helped create.

The president's moral authority and steely inner confidence ensured that Eisenhower's pragmatic instinct toward compromise did not diminish people's respect for him. As aide Emmet John Hughes recalled, "The man seemed in firm command of himself and of all around him. Nor—standing close to him—did one feel this command compromised or shaken on the few occasions when his own instinct did bow to another's urging."[43]

Despite Eisenhower's attempt at conciliation, the simmering feud between Eisenhower and the right wing came to a boil when Joe McCarthy turned his anticommunist attentions to the Eisenhower State Department, attempting to block key appointments. Among these was Eisenhower's friend and NATO colleague Charles Bohlen to serve as the ambassador to Russia. Eisenhower was furious to again have a friend who dedicated his life to American public service have his patriotism questioned by the senator from Wisconsin, but noting that President Truman's attempts to square off publicly with Joe McCarthy had only increased the senator's profile, Eisenhower chose to combat McCarthy quietly behind the scenes, depriving him of the oxygen of attention.

Eisenhower dispatched Vice President Nixon—whose conservative and anticommunist credentials were impeccable—to tell the right-wing senators to back off their opposition to Ambassador-designate Bohlen. He worked with Lyndon Johnson to secure the votes of moderate Democrats for nomination. Eisenhower also quietly began assembling a case against Senator McCarthy, investigating his actions in office and blocking his attempt to subpoena members of the administration. Eisenhower's behind-the-scenes actions against McCarthy initially publicly appeared to be acquiescence, but they resulted in McCarthy's censure by Senate colleagues in 1954. "There are some people you cannot afford to have as friends," Eisenhower pointedly remarked.[44] Eisenhower's strategy did not call attention to itself, but it was effective. McCarthy died alone and discredited in 1957. Eisenhower did not attend his funeral.

Eisenhower would later write, "I have no patience with the extreme rightists who call everyone who disagrees with them a Communist, nor with the leftists who shout that the rest of us are all heartless moneygrubbers."[45]

Ike was an unapologetic fiscal conservative, believing in the basic economic value of a balanced budget and skeptical of the self-interest inherent in bloated bureaucratic spending. As the first Republican president since Herbert Hoover, Eisenhower was well aware of widespread concern that the GOP was unable to manage the economy on behalf of the public good. In his memoirs, he wrote: "For more than twenty years economic depression had been the skeleton in the Republican closet, locked in by demagogues."[46]

Against the opposition of many anti–New Deal Republicans, Eisenhower not only supported popular entitlement programs such as Social Security, but expanded it to cover farm laborers and domestic laborers. Many times he succeeded where Truman had failed, creating the Department of Health, Education, and Welfare, and directing his administration to pioneer such public works programs as the construction of the interstate highway system—which from Eisenhower's perspective had national defense applications. Over the objections of many political aides, Eisenhower was committed to fulfilling all the campaign promises he'd made. In his memoirs, Ike wrote: "More than once I was to hear this view derided by 'practical politicians' who laughed off platforms as traps to catch voters. But whenever they expressed these cynical conclusions to me, they invariably encountered a rebuff that left them a bit embarrassed."[47]

To find the savings to fulfill his promises and balance the budget, Eisenhower looked to make cuts in existing bureaucracies. Significantly, the first place he started to look—just as he promised in the speech that kicked off his campaign in Kansas—was unnecessary spending in the U.S. military. He sought to achieve "security without paying the price of national bankruptcy,"[48] explaining the human costs of the arms race in terms that all Americans could understand: "The cost of one modern heavy bomber is this: a modern brick school house in more than 30 cities."

If any other president had discussed cutting the military budget in terms of lost investment in education, he would have been accused of not taking defense seriously. But no one could accuse

General Eisenhower of not taking defense seriously. This was Eisenhower's equivalent of Nixon going to China or Clinton reforming welfare; only he had the credibility to try to unify the country around reducing the military budget in favor of more social spending.

But even General Eisenhower was met with resistance from the army over his proposals to reduce peacetime defense spending during the escalation of the Cold War. When a military advocate warned him that further budget cuts might harm American security, Eisenhower testily replied, "If you go to any military installation in the world where the American flag is flying and tell the commander that Ike says he'll give him an extra star for his shoulder if he cuts his budget, there'll be such a rush to cut costs that you'll have to get out of the way."[49]

Ike relied on threats of nuclear retaliation and the expansion of covert operations through the CIA to keep the costs of defense down without sacrificing our strength or decisiveness. He also took an expansive vision of America's strength abroad, trying to persuade Congress to give him $5 million to spread America's culture through art, music, and drama around the world to give people abroad the true picture of America. Frustrated when Congress cut $200 million from a request for international civilian aid on the same day it had given the military $900 million it had never requested, Ike said somberly: "When will people learn that if you want peace, you have to fight for peace, you have to spend for peace, you can't have it any other way?"[50] At another time, he famously said, "God help the nation when it has a President who doesn't know as much about the military as I do."[51]

In his final speech to the nation from the Oval Office, Eisenhower warned that "only an alert and knowledgeable citizenry can compel the proper meshing of the huge industrial and military machinery of defense with our peaceful methods and goals, so that security and liberty may prosper together."

Eisenhower's administration does not receive the credit his record deserves: eight years at the height of the Cold War without a single American soldier's life lost in combat. The warrior was successful in securing peace, and the nonpartisan politician rescued the Republican Party from irrelevancy. He built what his attorney general, Herbert Brownell, called a "lasting bipartisan international approach to world affairs." Ike left office with a remarkable 64 percent approval rating and could claim with justifiable pride that "the United States never lost a soldier or a foot of ground in my administration. We kept the peace. People asked how it happened? By God, it didn't just happen. I'll tell you that."[52]

Historian Henry Steele Commager seemed to agree with Eisenhower's self-assessment when he wrote: "History will accord Eisenhower a major part of the credit for the generosity and maturity with which the United States accepted and discharged her obligations during the '50s; it will accord him credit for preventing the Republican Party—and perhaps the country—from going down the dusty road to a sterile isolationism at a crucial moment in history."[53]

NELSON ROCKEFELLER VS. BARRY GOLDWATER — 1964

THE LIBERAL REPUBLICAN VS. AN ADVOCATE OF "EXTREMISM"

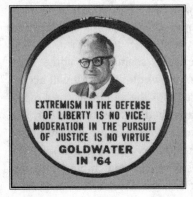

> I'm a hawk on foreign policy. I'm a hawk on national defense. I'm a dove on domestic issues. You've got two-thirds of me. What more do you want?
>
> —NELSON ROCKEFELLER[1]

Presidential primaries are always savage," wrote the legendary journalist Theodore White, "But the presidential primaries of 1964 were to exceed in savagery and significance any other in modern politics."[2]

It was the year that the Republican Party finally chose sides in a showdown between the last of the patrician reformers and the rising tide of rock-ribbed conservatives. It was an ideological blood feud between a high-flying East Coast Icarus, and the crusty leader of a western army of true believers who wanted to win a war of ideas even more than they wanted to win the White House. They got their wish. In the end, the conservatives seized the reins of the Republican Party but went down to a crushing defeat, with more Americans voting against their candidate than in any election up to that point in American history.

Nelson Rockefeller was the charismatic second son of what was regarded as the nation's wealthiest family—buoyant and brilliant, with an aura of seeming inevitability about him like a young Citizen Kane, Nelson was comfortable commanding attention wherever he went. He had worked in the Democratic administrations of FDR and Harry Truman, and then in 1958 ran for the first of four terms as the liberal Republican governor of New York State. But Nelson's eye was always on the White House, a prize he had dreamed of "ever since I was a kid," he confessed. "After all, if you think of what I had, what else is there to aspire to?"[3]

Rockefeller's moderate politics made him a perennial presidential favorite in national polls. Even John F. Kennedy said that if it had been Rockefeller rather than Nixon he faced in 1960, Rocky would have won.[4]

But in three successive attempts during the 1960s, conservatives blocked Rockefeller's Centrist efforts to gain the Republican nomination for president, most pivotally in the 1964 convention when he stood for a civil rights plank condemning the conservative John Birch Society as well as the KKK and was shouted down by the crowd and derided as an "international socialist." Toward the end of his life, when asked by a journalist why he had never been elected president, Rockefeller replied simply: "I was in the wrong party."[5]

Certainly conservatives like Barry Goldwater agreed. Goldwater was the unyielding junior senator from Arizona, square-jawed and hard-edged with admirably few pretensions. In 1960, he published *The Conscience of a Conservative,* a personal manifesto ghostwritten by William F. Buckley in-law Brent Bozell that became a surprising bestseller. The book presented conservatism as a rebellion from the existing New Deal "New Order" defended by moderates of both parties. Articulated as a defense of the Constitution, Goldwater's conservatism was essentially a negative proposition, arguing that "my aim is not to pass laws, but to repeal them. It is not to inaugurate new programs, but to cancel old ones that do violence to the Constitution, or that have failed in their purposes, or that impose on the people an unwarranted financial burden."[6]

Goldwater's rise from Phoenix city councilman to Republican presidential candidate took only twelve years. A prime example of the burgeoning upper middle class out West, Goldwater's grandfather—a Jewish immigrant from England—had developed a prosperous chain of department stores in towns throughout Arizona. Barry Goldwater was born on New Year's Day 1909 and raised in his mother's Episcopalian faith (prompting journalist Harry Golden to joke, "I always knew the first Jewish president would be Episcopalian"). Goldwater attended military school, but during his freshman year at the University of Arizona, his father's sudden death required that he return home to work in the family business. The stores were prosperous even in the depths of the Great Depression, and when the Second World War came, the nearly middle-aged Barry volunteered for active duty, flying transport planes and achieving the rank of lieutenant colonel. Goldwater returned to Arizona after the war and in quick succession ran for city council and served as campaign manager for the first successful Republican gubernatorial campaign in Arizona history. When he declared his intention to run for the Senate in 1952, Goldwater had the benefit of a name that was well known statewide and political connections. He proved popular, and his appeal was well articulated by the *New York Times*'s Tom Wicker: "Handsome, informal, friendly, a man without pomp, Barry Goldwater earned the instant liking—even adulation—of men already favorably disposed to his way of thinking. To the inhabitants of small-town America, he seemed like a man who was 'one of us.' "[7]

While personally likable, his political statements appeared extremist and irresponsible to many Americans. He was fond of asserting that the United States "is a Republic and not a Democracy,"[8] deriding the Eisenhower administration as a "dime-store New Deal," and stating, "I don't believe in federal aid to education, or aid to the aged, or any kind of medical assistance."[9] In a speech on the Senate floor, Goldwater alleged that former president "Truman was on the way to socialistic ideas"[10] and called Supreme Court justice Earl Warren "a socialist" at a Republican breakfast in Mississippi.[11]

Barry Goldwater's conservative rebellion coincided with the growth of the right-wing John Birch Society in suburban California and throughout the Sunbelt. The increasingly prosperous westerners, who populated climates uninhabitable before air-conditioning, resented the "little intellectual elite in a far-distant capital" telling them what to do, as Ronald Reagan said in a compelling televised speech on behalf of Goldwater at the outset of his own political career. They cheered when Goldwater said, "Sometimes I think this country would be better off if we could just saw off the Eastern seaboard and let it float out to sea."[12]

The John Birch Society had been founded in 1958 by a conspiracy-minded candy-manufacturing heir from Massachusetts named Robert Welch who believed that President Eisenhower and Secretary of State Dulles were secret agents of the Soviet Union. The John Birch Society's militant anticommunism found its most fertile ground amid the "wealthy businessmen, retired military officers and little old ladies in tennis shoes," of Orange County, outside of Los Angeles, according to a report issued by California attorney general Stanley Mosk in 1961.[13] That same year, the three-year-old organization drew fifteen thousand people to a five-day teach-in at the Los Angeles Sports Arena.

The right wing in America was becoming energized, combining the old supporters of Joe McCarthy's anticommunist crusade, Robert Taft's isolationist Republicans, and Strom Thurmond's states'-rights inspired segregationist Dixiecrats into a powerful new electoral force that would shape American politics and the Republican Party for decades to come.

This disparate group all rallied around Goldwater's *Conscience of a Conservative* and could quote from it chapter and verse. Goldwater returned their affection, stating: "These people who constitute the extreme right are good people. They are generally fairly well-to-do people. They are very sincere in their beliefs."[14] Now these good people had an ambitious plan: Get Barry Goldwater nominated for president in 1964. "We're going to force the Republicans to run Goldwater," conservative leader Kent Courtney explained in a keynote address to the Conservative Party of Kansas, "or they'll go out of business."[15]

It would not happen without a fight. Since President Kennedy's narrow election over Richard Nixon in 1960, New York governor Nelson Rockefeller appeared the clear favorite to gain the Republican nomination.

On the surface, Rockefeller was similar to President Kennedy in many ways: a charming and charismatic moderate millionaire who could cut into Kennedy's narrow base of support with promises to continue popular policies while reining in perceived liberal excesses with a return to Eisenhower's Centrist Republican style of administration. Although known for his East Coast liberalism—Rockefeller would double the size of the state university system, dramatically expand welfare, and sign pioneering legislation establishing a woman's right to choose—the governor had been assiduously courting conservatives since the 1960 election, wining and dining party leaders and preaching unity.* "I'm a hawk on foreign policy. I'm a hawk on national defense. I'm a dove on domestic issues," Rockefeller explained. "You've got two-thirds of me. What more do you want?"[16]

But the increasing inevitability of Rockefeller's nomination hit a self-inflicted snag in May of 1963, when the recently divorced governor announced that he had married a thirty-seven-year-old family friend over the weekend. His new wife—the former Margaretta "Happy" Murphy—had been just five years old when Nelson and his first wife, Mary Todhunter Clark, were married. While the announcement of Rockefeller's separation from his wife two years before created surprisingly little political fallout, news of his remarriage—accompanied by images of Happy's abandoned husband and children—would prove disastrous to Nelson Rockefeller's presidential ambitions. As journalist Theodore White would recount in his book *The Making of the President, 1964,* "One can no more discuss the Republican politics of 1964 without dealing with Nelson Rockefeller's divorce and remarriage than one can discuss English Constitutional development without touching on the stormy marriage of Henry II and Eleanor of Aquitaine."[17] Or, as one woman more succinctly explained: "I ain't going to vote a woman into the White House who left her children."[18]

---

*This was a tough line to walk. Aides were forced to contort themselves, as in the following note to journalists: "A number of you have requested some basic information on the Rockefeller Record which would show his 'Conservative' side. The items listed on the attached sheets do show this and is being sent to you for your use in talking to people who feel the Governor is strictly a liberal. It must be used cautiously and should not be published." (Robert D. Novak, *The Agony of the G.O.P., 1964* [New York: Macmillan, 1965], p. 72.)

On the morning of May 5, 1963, the *Washington Post* was full of news about Nelson Rockefeller. The *Congressional Quarterly* had released a poll, inspiring the headline "Poll of '60 Delegates Gives Rockefeller Nomination Edge." But another story detailed the governor's remarriage. Rockefeller must have known the possible fallout from his decision. Just hours after he said, "I do," he called Barry Goldwater at home to tell him the news before his potential rival heard it from the papers. Even on his wedding day, Rockefeller was keeping an eye out for his political aspirations, hoping to keep the party unified.

The unity would not last the through the weekend. The Chicago Chapter of Young Adults for Rockefeller abruptly disbanded at the news. The liberal Republican patriarch Senator Prescott Bush of Connecticut—long a Rockefeller family friend—released a terse statement calling Nelson a destroyer of American homes. When the happy couple jetted back from their sunny honeymoon on the Rockefeller family ranch in Venezuela, they landed in an entirely different political landscape. The last Gallup Poll taken before the marriage announcement showed Rockefeller beating Goldwater 43 percent to 26 percent among Republicans. In the days after the announcement, the numbers virtually reversed: Goldwater 40, Rockefeller 29.[19] The anvil-like intensity of this drop indicated that previous support for Rockefeller was broad, but it was not deep.

This reversal of fortune inspired rather than depressed the candidate. Rockefeller would not let a shift in public opinion—particularly one based in condemnation of his new marriage—derail his dreams of the presidency. Rockefeller looked for an issue to draw attention away from his new marital status, and the annual convention of the Young Republicans in San Francisco provided it.

The youthful ranks of Goldwater supporters heatedly expressed solidarity with the senator from Arizona's disapproval of the 1957 Civil Rights Bill. Their attitude seemed to follow the line of thinking expressed by an editorial in the *National Review* that same year, which said, in part: "The central question that emerges . . . is whether the white community in the South is entitled to take such measures as are necessary to prevail politically and culturally, in areas which it does not predominate numerically. The sobering answer is yes—the white community is entitled, because, for the time being, it is the advanced race."[20]

At the same time, long-simmering Democratic divisions between northern liberals and southern conservatives were being pushed toward rupture due to President Kennedy's televised commitment to pursue additional civil rights legislation. Rockefeller sensed an opportunity to make a statement, a declaration of principles that might turn attention away from his remarriage and toward his continued campaign for the presidency. On Sunday, July 14, he issued a stirring—if self-serving—statement on the virtues of political moderation from the Executive Office in Albany. It would be the hallmark of his candidacy and his political career.

It is now being seriously proposed to the Republican Party as a strategy for victory in 1964, that it write off the Negro and other minority groups, that it deliberately write off the great industrial States of the North. . . . The transparent purpose behind this plan is to erect political power on the outlawed and immoral base of segregation and to transform the Republican Party from a national party of all the people to a sectional party of some of the people.

The Republican Party is the party of Lincoln. It was founded to make men free and equal in opportunity . . . For that party to turn its back on its heritage and its birthright would be an act of political immorality rarely equaled in human history . . .

I am now convinced that the Republican Party . . . is in real danger of subversion by a radical, well-financed and highly disciplined minority. . . . The vociferous and well-drilled extremist elements within the party utterly reject these fundamental principles of our heritage. They are, in fact, embarked on a determined and ruthless effort to take over the party, its platform and its candidates on their own terms. . . . The leaders of the Birchers and others of the radical right lunatic fringe are every bit as dangerous to American principles and American institutions as the radical left. . . .

I have no doubt whatever that moderation and sound progress will continue to be the spiritual allegiance of the overwhelming majority of the Republicans in this country. But a complacent majority, or a fearful one, will surely be subverted by militant extremism as such majorities always have been throughout all history . . . The Republican Party stands today at the crossroads of its destiny. Its destiny is to save the nation by first saving itself.[21]

Some observers cracked that Nelson Rockefeller seemed to care more about saving his own political ambitions than saving the Republican Party or the nation. Conservatives were outraged by what they saw as an opportunistic sneak attack. The man who had expended such energy to unify the party when he was ahead in the polls now resorted to public criticism to change the debate. Columnist Stewart Alsop curtly wrote that Nelson "could have decided either to remarry or to run for president, but not both."[22] Predictably, the whiff of scandal proved more interesting to the public than a statement on political philosophy. Rockefeller's candidacy failed to rebound.*

But the assassination of John F. Kennedy on November 22 changed the dynamics of the 1964 presidential race yet again. Many believed that no one could defeat Lyndon Johnson in the fall, and other prominent potential Republican candidates chose to sit out the race in the face of a legislative powerhouse of a president defending the legacy of a martyred president. While moderates waited for marching orders from former president Eisenhower, who was reposing at his farm in Gettysburg, conservatives sensed a rare opportunity to take control of the Republican Party.

The right wing coalesced its efforts around the reluctant figure of Barry Goldwater. He did not necessarily think of himself as presidential material, and in that there was something refreshing; gen-

---

*Rockefeller would have been well served if he had heeded the advice of a former New York governor with successful presidential aspirations: "No man can lead a public career really worth living," Theodore Roosevelt wrote; "no man can act with rugged independence in serious crisis, nor strike out against great abuses, nor afford to make powerful and unscrupulous foes, if he himself is vulnerable in his private character." (Theodore Roosevelt, *An Autobiography* [New York: Charles Scribner's Sons, 1925, p. 84].)

uine and humble in an age of raw political ambitions. But his followers—led by a bow-tie-wearing New York City–based former liberal turned conservative named Clifton White—began lining up delegates and pushing him to declare his candidacy. More than fifty busloads of supporters from across the country responded to a call from the National Draft Goldwater Committee, descending upon the National Guard Armory in Washington, D.C., knowing full well that their hero would not be making an appearance. Self-conscious about dropping out of college, Goldwater confessed to a reporter, "I'm not even sure that I've got the brains to be President of the United States."[23] His apparent ambivalence hit a new low when he was asked whether he was intending to run for president: "I'm doing all right just poopin' around," the senator said.[24]

Supporters continued to beat the Barry-for-president drum precisely because their man seemed to care more about leading a cause than becoming president. As William F. Buckley observed, "He's a hero not merely to the members and followers of the National Association of Manufacturers but to all the Right-minded youth of the nation, for whom he seems to embody the Politician Unchained from the dreary, federalized, temporizing, circumlocutory, bureaucratized politics of the welfare state."[25]

Goldwater's credibility was ironically increased by the fact that he was willing to criticize moderate Republicans as well as Democrats; he was so driven by ideology that he was independent of the traditional partisan establishment. Barry Goldwater was the most prominent member of the conservative counterculture, what Pat Buchanan fondly remembered as "the crew-cut militants of the Goldwater era."[26]

In January 1964, Barry Goldwater accepted the call from conservatives and stepped into the void. At his announcement beneath the blue sky of Arizona, Goldwater was steely in his insistence that this would be a different type of campaign: "I won't change my beliefs to win votes. I will offer a choice, not an echo. This will not be an engagement of personalities. It will be an engagement of principles."[27]

The transition from the clear vistas of Arizona to the cold snows of the campaign trail in New Hampshire would prove difficult.

Before his announcement, Barry Goldwater was a peripheral figure, unknown—as most senators are—to the vast majority of Americans. But now he was running for the highest office in the land, and his statements received far greater scrutiny. The one-liners that received whoops of support at a Republican Party breakfast did not translate well in the morning newspaper. And Goldwater was particularly vulnerable on the two issues most on American minds in 1964: foreign policy and civil rights.

Memories of the Cuban missile crisis in October 1962 were still fresh, and the dangers of the Cold War escalating into nuclear war seemed to many more real than the dangers of an escalating jungle war in Vietnam. Against this backdrop, Goldwater's vote against the 1963 Nuclear Test Ban Treaty seemed outside the mainstream when seen alongside the senator's previous dismissive statements about disarmament. "We should, I believe, announce in no uncertain terms that we are against disarmament," Goldwater had written in his 1962 book *Why Not Victory?* "We are against it because we need our armaments—all of those we presently have, and more. We need weapons for both the limited and the unlimited war."[28] Even more troubling were Goldwater's repeated statements that as commander in chief he would leave decisions about whether to use nuclear weapons to generals in the field, including, if necessary, in Cuba.[29]

In addition, Goldwater had always been a vocal defender of Joe McCarthy, giving a strident speech in his defense during the 1954 decision to censure McCarthy.[30] Now attention was being given to how his anticommunist-at-any-cost beliefs translated in the wider world of foreign policy.

Likewise, at a time when America's civil rights movement was beginning to gain momentum, Goldwater drew his loudest applause among conservative groups for his attempts to draw a line between his personal opposition to segregation (he in fact had overseen the desegregation of his own family's department stores as well as the Arizona Air National Guard) and his opposition to civil rights legislation on constitutional grounds.

"It may be just or wise or expedient for Negro children to attend the same schools as white children," he said, "but they do not have a civil right to do so which is protected by the Federal Constitution or which is enforceable by the Federal Government."[31] Eight years after *Brown v. Board of Education,* Goldwater argued that "the Supreme Court decision is not necessarily the law of the land."[32] When television interviewer Eric Sevareid sought clarification by asking, "You have said, I believe, that we have no right to tell the southern states what they must do about school integration and segregation," Goldwater crisply answered, "That's right."[33]

Nelson Rockefeller was still keeping a frenetic pace flying between Albany and New Hampshire, campaigning as if his life was at stake. Rockefeller's outsized personality grew even larger when surrounded by crowds. Columnist David Broder described him as "an uninhibited master of backslapping, hand grabbing, straight campaign, and the spectacle of the Standard Oil heir wolfing hot dogs and plunging into Coney Island crowds was endlessly engaging to the photographers and television cameramen."[34]

In contrast, Barry Goldwater disdained the fake pleasantries of the campaign trail: "I'm not one of those baby-kissing, handshaking, blintz-eating candidates," he told his advisers.[35] When crowds of supporters would chant "We want Barry" at campaign rallies, the candidate would often respond, "If you shut up, you'll get him." His blunt edge was not without charm. At one campaign stop, Goldwater was presented with a soda developed by an enterprising young conservative, a yellow-colored carbonated beverage packaged and sold as "Gold-Water" ("The Right Drink for the Conservative Taste"). The candidate for whom the drink was named took one obliging sip of the stuff and unceremoniously spat it out on the ground. "This tastes like piss!" he exclaimed within earshot of the deflated young entrepreneur, "I wouldn't drink it with gin!"[36]

It was not the last of awkward unscripted moments: Goldwater's amateur campaign staff scheduled twenty-three straight days of events after their candidate had an operation on his right heel, causing the senator to hobble painfully from event to event, while Rockefeller was flown from state to state, and was escorted in a limousine with a cooler of beer tucked away in the backseat.

Oddly enough, the more locals saw of Goldwater and Rockefeller in New Hampshire, the less they liked them. Goldwater's statements about cutting off federal funding to the aged resonated badly in a state with the nation's fourth-oldest population, while Rockefeller's presence reminded voters of his scandalous second marriage. New Hampshire Republicans wanted a third choice, and they found it in the unexpected write-in candidacy of former Republican senator Henry Cabot Lodge, the moderate from nearby Massachusetts who had served as Richard Nixon's vice presidential candidate in 1960 and was then the Johnson administration's ambassador to South Vietnam.

Lodge's cause had been taken up by young group of Massachusetts Republicans who rented a storefront in the town of Concord for two months at a cost of $400. With their candidate ten thousand miles away and not even formally running, the Lodge campaign had an effortless atmosphere of fun about it, and was adopted as a local cause. Film footage of Lodge campaigning with Eisenhower in 1952 was salvaged and spliced together to associate the absent candidate with the popular modern Republicanism of Ike. Lodge offered the moderation of Rockefeller without the weight of his personal baggage.

When the primary votes were cast in March 1964, New Hampshire proved that absence makes the heart grow fonder. Lodge won, with Rockefeller running a close third behind Goldwater. At seven the next morning, the resilient Nelson Rockefeller boarded his six-passenger Saberliner jet and flew out to the West Coast to rally faithful supporters and tell them he would not give up this fight. The next primary was in Oregon, a state whose politics were in line with the Republican progressive tradition, embodied by its distinguished senator Mark Hatfield.

In posters, billboards, and campaign appearances across the state, Rockefeller contrasted his policy positions with Goldwater's public statements and positioned himself as "the responsible Republican," that is, a moderate in favor of federal aid to public schools, Medicare, and Social Security, while Goldwater was not. Rockefeller also raised the specter of nuclear war, asking whether an individual who once threatened to "lob a bomb into the men's room of the Kremlin"[37] might unwittingly set off a third world war. While Lodge was at work in Saigon, and Goldwater concentrated on delegate-rich California, there was Rockefeller at the shopping center or the University of

Portland, his campaign posters proclaiming "He Cares Enough to Come." In April, Oregon voters cast their votes for Rockefeller, giving him a decisive victory, with Lodge coming in second and Goldwater a distant third.

Now Goldwater was in the uncomfortable position of being the front-runner without having won a hotly contested Republican primary. It would all come down to California, where just Goldwater and Rockefeller would face off on the ballot. California had just catapulted past New York to become the nation's most populous state, although 60 percent of its residents had been born elsewhere. Republican politics in California had been dominated by a progressive tradition begun by Hiram Johnson and embodied in the governor turned Supreme Court chief justice Earl Warren. But by 1964, the Republican Party was split in the Golden State, with conservatives dominating the suburbs of Los Angeles and San Diego.

For conservatives, Barry Goldwater was more than a candidate—he was a cause. While Rockefeller paid his volunteers, Goldwater did not have to. For young conservatives, he was the political equivalent of first love. In Los Angeles, John Wayne and Ronald Reagan appeared at Goldwater fund-raisers, but outside of Hollywood the core of Barry Goldwater's support was very different. In Bakersfield, Goldwater supporters draped American and Confederate flags side by side on the podium for a press conference where the county leader of the Goldwater campaign denounced California's Republican senator Tom Kuchel—who was the state chairman of Rockefeller's campaign—as a "liberal extremist," while Goldwater winced beside him.[38]

The Rockefeller campaign compensated for Goldwater's ground support with a heavy barrage of television and mailed advertising. One week out from Election Day, polls in California showed Rockefeller with a comfortable ten-point lead. Goldwater strategist Clifton White was lowering expectations by pronouncing California "not a conservative state." But three days before the election, Happy Rockefeller gave birth to a seven-pound baby boy back in New York. Against the wishes of his political advisers, Nelson Rockefeller flew back in time to be there for the birth. Photos of the smiling mother and child were plastered on the front pages of newspapers across the nation, freshly reminding voters of the circumstances surrounding the governor's fall from front-runner status. Nelson and Happy Rockefeller's "blessed event" proved to be the California campaign's undoing.

On Election Day, Rockefeller received the newspaper endorsements, but Goldwater's troops, some forty thousand strong, came out in force, blanketing the state. They contacted three hundred thousand voters in Los Angeles County area alone over the weekend before the election.[39] Their effort, combined with the grinning image of Happy Rockefeller in the papers, motivated the conservative base to come out and vote in this local showdown. In contrast, the moderates in California were not nearly so motivated; as one local politician put it, "Moderates are the people who don't go to the polls on Election Day."[40]

Goldwater defeated Rockefeller by 68,000 votes out of more than 2 million cast in California primary. Polls showed that barely a third of all registered Republicans across the nation supported his candidacy, but by now it was all but decided—the conservatives had pulled off their coup. Barry Goldwater would be the Republican Party's nominee for president in 1964.[41]

There were six weeks between the California primary and Republican Convention in San Francisco. Squarely in the middle of that time, the U.S. Senate was scheduled to vote on the most closely watched legislation in a generation—the 1964 Civil Rights Act.

Barry Goldwater would vote against it.

The legislation first proposed by John F. Kennedy, supported by Martin Luther King Jr., and finally passed under the stage direction of Lyndon Johnson was controversial in its day. Under the cloak of states' rights, southern segregationists vehemently opposed its passage, while conservatives agreed on more lofty grounds that the legislation was unconstitutional. Goldwater reportedly agonized over his decision, knowing that this particular stand of principle could well serve as a political suicide note.

While Goldwater had supported the fight to desegregate Phoenix public schools, he also had established a long record of declaring all federal civil rights legislation unenforceable and unconstitutional. In 1957, he had offered South Carolina senator Strom Thurmond support in his record twenty-four-hour filibuster against the voting rights bill, taking the floor at 1:30 A.M. on unrelated business so that Thurmond could relieve himself and then go back to his filibuster.[42] In 1959, Goldwater solidified his support in the South with a speech in which he declared *Brown v. Board of Education* unenforceable "by arms" and because it was "not based in law."[43]

Now he consulted with an adviser and sometime speechwriter, a Phoenix-based lawyer named William Rehnquist—the future Republican-appointed chief justice of the Supreme Court—who assured him that the civil rights legislation was unconstitutional. For a second opinion, Goldwater went to Yale professor Robert Bork—later nominated to the Supreme Court by Ronald Reagan—who supplied a seventy-five-page legal brief in support of Rehnquist's opinion. Bolstered by the legal opinions of these two luminaries, Goldwater felt he had no choice but to vote against the civil rights act: "I don't like segregation," he had said, "but I don't like the Constitution kicked around, either."[44]

The country paid attention to the presumptive Republican nominee's actions; most of the other opposing senators were from the Deep South. A young soldier named Colin Powell noticed as well—he pasted a bumper sticker on his Volkswagen that read "All the Way with LBJ."[45]

Two days before the raucous 1964 Republican Convention began in San Francisco's Cow Palace, 525 people crowded into a motel conference room on a Saturday night to attend a right-wing rally sponsored by conservative leader Kent Courtney. The meeting featured the mayor of Salt Lake City, J. Bracken Lee (who would later advocate breaking up the United States). At the rally, Courtney called Rockefeller an "international socialist," while Lee accused Ike of having been too soft on the Soviets, saying, "I'm for drafting Dwight Eisenhower to do sentry duty at the Berlin Wall."[46] The heart of the meeting's message was that a Goldwater victory at the convention needed to be followed by—in Courtney's words—"a purge of liberals from the Republican Party."[47]

On Monday morning, as thousands streamed into the Cow Palace, moderates tried one final attempt to unite, this time behind the desperate last-minute candidacy of Pennsylvania's governor William

Scranton. Polls showed that Scranton had broad and deep support within the party, but inside the convention it was Goldwater's true believers from floor to ceiling. Tellingly, one hundred Goldwater delegates and alternates were self-identified members of the John Birch Society.[48]

To improve the odds of a stop-Goldwater movement, Rockefeller released all his delegates to Governor Scranton, and together they proposed three amendments to the party platform: one condemning the dangers of extremism; the second asserting the responsibility of commander in chief to make the ultimate decision on the use of nuclear weapons; and the third asserting the party's historic commitment to civil rights.

Nelson Rockefeller rose to speak on behalf of the amendments: "There's no place in this Republican Party for such hawkers of hate; such purveyors of prejudice; such fabricators of fear—whether Communist, Ku Klux Klan or Birchers." The jeers that had accompanied the beginning of Rockefeller's speech rose from a murmur to a roar when he reached the name of the John Birch Society. To accuse the Birchers of being morally equivalent to Communists was an outrage to conservatives. The chorus of "We want Barry," punctuated by shouts to "get off the stage," washed over Rockefeller, who stood patiently waiting for the disruption to subside with a smile plastered on his face.

The man with the gavel called out for calm and quiet. "This is still a free country, ladies and gentlemen," Rockefeller reminded them. "During this year I have crisscrossed this nation, fighting . . . to keep the Republican party the party of all the people . . . and warning of the extremist threat, its danger to the party, and danger to the nation. . . . These extremists feed on fear, hate and terror, [they have] no program for America and the Republican Party." Rockefeller's five-minute speech took more than fifteen minutes to deliver. He was interrupted by shouts twenty-two times. Afterward, Rockefeller reflected, with typical WASP understatement, "Taking a stand on the subject of extremism at the Republican Convention and being roundly booed for fifteen minutes was a really interesting and valuable experience."[49]

The antiextremist planks all went down to defeat, including then-congressman John Lindsay's motion to prohibit racial discrimination in the selection of delegates, which died an undignified death. Previously, Governor Scranton had confidently predicted that these planks would be successful, saying, "I can assure you that a Republican National Convention could never vote against a strong civil rights plank on a roll call vote, particularly not on television." But as conservative columnist Robert Novak smugly noted, "His time had passed. The Goldwater convention could and did."[50]

The next night, Barry Goldwater took the stage and asserted his control over the Republican Party. He had announced that his running mate would not be a moderate, but an obscure conservative congressman from upstate New York named William Miller, whose presence certainly balanced the ticket geographically, but definitely not ideologically. Likewise, it was not to be a normal acceptance speech; no effort would be made to unify the party. Crisp in a gray suit with his black-framed glasses and white hair contrasting brightly on the black-and-white televisions screens across the nation, Goldwater began by shooting a volley across the bow of Rockefeller's Republicans: "Anyone who joins us in all sincerity, we welcome. Those who do not care about our cause, we don't expect to enter our ranks in any case. And let our Republicanism, so focused and so dedicated, not be made fuzzy and futile by unthinking and stupid labels."

Then came the sentence he would become famous for, a sentence some aides had begged him not to deliver, but which Barry Goldwater liked so much he'd underlined it twice in his text: "I would remind you that extremism in the defense of liberty is no vice . . . and let me remind you also, moderation in pursuit of justice is no virtue."

The crowd of true believers in the Cow Palace went crazy, shouting themselves hoarse, hoisting eight-foot high banners with their hero's face emblazoned on them. Television cameras caught Richard Nixon in the audience, grinning broadly, but noticeably not applauding. In a private viewing room, Eisenhower—a man whose personal political mantra was "extremes to the right and left of any political dispute are always wrong"[51]—responded with barely contained outrage. This was the right-wing rhetoric that he had tried to moderate throughout his eight years as president. In public, Ike would tepidly support the party's nominee, but, in private, he remarked that Goldwater's speech was "giving the right wing kooks a pat on the back and everyone else a slap in the face."[52]

The next day, the *Charleston News and Courier* celebrated Goldwater's nomination by noting in its editorial that "no matter what happens in the November elections, the Republican Party and the nation turned the corner when the eastern forces in the GOP went down to defeat in the national convention. What emerges from the struggle is a realignment of political power in this country, with the South, Middle West and the Far West joined together in a new alliance."[53]

South Carolina's home-grown hero, Senator Strom Thurmond, was determined to play a central part in the creation of this new alliance, completing his revenge against the Democratic Party's pro–civil rights drift since 1948, when he'd stormed off the convention floor and formed the short lived Dixiecrat party. Now Strom barnstormed the South, being driven county to county in a hearse, reclining in the back to rest between speeches. At every stop, he would explain his decision in September 1964 to commit what had been considered southern heresy by leaving the Democrats for the Party of Lincoln. "My sole purpose in life until November 3rd is to do everything possible to elect Barry Goldwater President," he explained, because "a vote for Hubert Humphrey for Vice-President is a vote which could make him President, and he is the choice of the socialists and all left-wingers for that job." Strom painted himself as the defender of moderation against liberal extremism, arguing, "When it comes to extremism, the choice of Hubert Humphrey is the ultimate."[54]

The crowds went wild as the South began to swing toward the right. When Lady Bird Johnson was sent to campaign in the South for her husband—the first president from the South in one hundred years—she was met by hecklers from the local John Birch Society—some accompanied by their children—holding signs saying, "Black Bird Go Home," "Johnson Is a Communist," and "Johnson Is a Nigger-Lover."[55]

The Republican Party's realignment was not met with universal enthusiasm. The respected *New York Herald Tribune*, which had not endorsed a Democrat for president in its history, refused to support the Republican Party's nominee, writing in its editorial that "Senator Goldwater represents one wing of the Republican Party. He has made no attempt to reconcile the other wing, nor has he based his stand on those issues on which Republicans agree, and which would attract those Independents whose votes have been demonstrably necessary to Republican success."[56]

President Johnson's campaign deftly appealed to moderates and disaffected Republicans, while Goldwater ignored them. The Democratic campaign's legendary "Daisy Ad" exploited fears that Goldwater would be too quick to use nuclear weapons and thus plunge the world into Armageddon. It was considered so controversial it was only aired once—but it acquired a life beyond itself through constant repetition on news programs that discussed whether it was ethical. More effective was an innovative and largely forgotten television advertisement explicitly aimed at Rockefeller Republicans. If Goldwater would not reach out to the moderate wing of his party, Johnson's campaign would.

The set of the advertisement was a table with an anguished-looking young man wearing a white shirt, dark tie, and glasses. Looking directly at the camera, and speaking in a rambling, confessional tone, the character laid out his dilemma.

I certainly don't feel guilty about being a Republican. I've always been a Republican. My father is. His father was. My whole family is a Republican family. I voted for Dwight Eisenhower the first time I ever voted. I voted for Nixon the last time. But when we come to Senator Goldwater, now it seems to me we're up against a very different kind of a man.

This man scares me. Now maybe I'm wrong. A friend of mine has said to me: "Listen. Just because a man sounds a little irresponsible during a campaign doesn't mean he's going to act irresponsibly." You know the theory, the White House makes the man. I don't buy that.

You know what I think makes a president? Aside from his judgment, his experience, are the men behind him. His advisers, the cabinet. So many men with strange ideas are working for

Goldwater. You hear a lot about what these guys are against. They seem to be against just about everything; but what are they for?

I read now where he says a wave, a craven fear of death is sweeping across America. What is that supposed to mean? If he means that people don't want to fight a nuclear war, he's right, I don't . . . I wish I was sure that Goldwater is against war as I am that he's against some of these other things. I wish I could believe that he has the imagination to be able to just shut his eyes and picture what this country would look like after a nuclear war.

Sometimes I wish I'd been at the Convention in San Francisco. I mean I wish I'd been a delegate. I really do. Because I would have fought you know I wouldn't have worried so much about party unity because if you unite behind a man you don't believe in—a lie—I tell you those people who got a hold of that Convention— who are they?

I mean when the head of the Ku Klux Klan with all those weird groups comes out in favor of the candidate of my party either they're not Republicans or I'm not. I thought about just not voting in this election, just staying home but you can't do that because that's saying you don't care who wins and I do care. I think my party made a bad mistake in San Francisco and I'm going to have to vote against that mistake on the third of November.[57]

The ad was genius, articulating doubts about Goldwater from the voice of a "Republican"—not attacking him outright, but raising questions about his competence from a person who presumably cares about more than partisan politics. A disaffected moderate Republican had the moral authority to most effectively criticize his party's nominee.

Polls showed that less than one-fifth of voters supported Goldwater's extremist strategy. Sentiment was so heavily weighted in Johnson's favor that the president's primary concern was whether the people would feel it was necessary to vote on Election Day. The Goldwater campaign took the opposite approach to encouraging turnout despite the bleak prognosis. A palm-sized

Halloween handout, replete with grinning jack-o'-lantern, attempted to associate opposition to Goldwater with left-wing extremist groups.

Like the Goldwater campaign platform, its campaign literature was a negative proposition, attacking Johnson by association, asking voters whether they wanted to align themselves with these "extremist" groups—and then equating the NAACP and the Council on Foreign Relations with anarchists and Communists. The campaign had become a widespread object of ridicule. Billboards featuring his slogan 'In His Heart You Know He's Right" were sometimes defaced with the words "Yes . . . extreme right." An alternate version of Goldwater's campaign slogan was conjured up by comedians and encouraged by the opposition: "In Your Guts You Know He's Nuts."

A G A I N S T   G O L D W A T E R !

Bobby Baker and Billy Sol Estes are against Barry.

The communist Worker newspaper is against Barry.

Virtually every corrupt union boss is against Barry.

The black muslims, Harlem and big city rioters are against Barry.

Practically every misled Nego and White civil disobedience violator is against Barry.

Every communist, as well as as the communist and socialist press throughout the world are against Barry.

Most of the scores of foreign nations who are receiving billions of our foreign aid so they'll love us, are against Barry.

The NAACP, Council of Foreign Relations, the American Civil Liberties Union, CORE, ADA, and the anarchists are all against Barry.

The above groups are for Johnson and Humphrey. What a wonderful list of enemies against Goldwater and Miller! As a loyal American you can help:

KEEP U.S.A. FIRST
YOU VOTE FOR GOLDWATER
Our new U.S.A. President
★ ★ ★ ★ ★
It's Barry-Picking Time

On Election Day, the massive Johnson landslide became a referendum not so much on the president's own popularity, but on the widespread distrust of Barry Goldwater created by his self-described extremist label. Goldwater received only 38.5 percent of the popular vote, the lowest ever recorded for a major-party candidate in presidential campaigns up to that point. He won only his native state of Arizona and five states from the South, a first for the Republicans. In those few places it existed, support for Goldwater was not lukewarm; in Mississippi, he received 87 percent of the vote.

With Democratic sweeps in both houses of Congress and virtually all state governments, it was an unprecedented victory. President Johnson enthusiastically but accurately assessed the results as "a mandate for unity, for a Government that serves no special interest."[58] Despite the general gloom of Republican officeholders on election night, there was celebration in the offices of South Carolina senator Strom Thurmond. Thurmond's aide Harry Dent recounted the scene: "Great rejoicing went on within the Thurmond ranks . . . in the next two years, the seeds of the Republican Southern Strategy began to sprout and grow. The tree was bearing fruit."[59]

There was another way to measure this enthusiasm: while Eisenhower had received 40 percent of the African-American vote in 1956, Goldwater received only 6 percent. By the end of 1964, the disastrous effects of the extremist campaign could be assessed: 53 percent of Americans now considered themselves Democrats, and only 25 percent felt comfortable identifying themselves as Republicans. But the Goldwater campaign succeeded in coalescing the conservatives in the Republican Party. After the election, the man who would ultimately benefit from Goldwater's conservative movement, Ronald Reagan, denounced moderates who had voted against the Arizona senator, saying, "We will have no more of those candidates who are pledged to those same socialist goals of our opposition and seek our support."[60]

Columnist Robert Novak's election postmortem, *The Agony of the G.O.P.,* offered a reflection on the failure of the Republican moderates: "Rockefeller and Scranton lost because they had nothing to offer the people but themselves. Goldwater had a moral philosophy that stirred enough people to the heights of enthusiasm so that the nomination was his. Indeed, this attraction was so strong that the Goldwaterites could not see disaster looming ahead in November."[61]

But the ultimate lesson of the 1964 campaign was best expressed by *New York Times* columnist James Reston not long after the election: "The decisive battleground of American politics lies in the center and cannot be captured from either of the extremes, and any party that defies this principle does not improve its chances of national power or even effective opposition, but precisely the opposite."[62]

DANIEL PATRICK MOYNIHAN
VS. BELLA ABZUG — 1976

THE NEO-CON VS. THE NEW LEFT

> The central conservative truth is that it is culture, not politics, that determines the success of a society. The central liberal truth is that politics can change a culture and save it from itself.

> —DANIEL PATRICK MOYNIHAN

Daniel Patrick Moynihan, the kid from Hell's Kitchen turned Harvard professor, Kennedy, Johnson, and Nixon appointee, and now ambassador to the United Nations under President Ford, took a bite of his burger, a gulp from his beer, and gazed out the tavern window with a look of distaste.

"These god-damn elitist liberals almost succeeded in running the working man out of the Democratic Party."[1] He watched a bus wheeze by and began stabbing his finger in its general direction. "They made that bus driver out there feel illiberal; they turned him into a caricature. Liberals make sure to insulate themselves from all these drastic social changes, but they expect the masses to make them work. It's so intolerant. In their eyes, if you're not a cultural liberal, then you're not a political liberal."[2]

Seven months later he would be elected as the Democratic senator from New York.

It would not come easily. In the coming months, Pat Moynihan faced the divergent wings of the Democratic Party and was venomously attacked from all sides. Liberals condemned him for his work as Richard Nixon's domestic policy adviser, their contemporary devil himself. Black leaders branded him a racist due to government reports he'd written about the breakdown of the African-American family and his condemnation of Ugandan dictator Idi Amin in the United Nations. Clubhouse leaders said he was too independent, while reformers were suspicious of his success in the establishment. Republicans resentfully asked why Moynihan remained a Democrat at all. Only the neoconservatives called him their own: a relatively small group of intellectuals originally inspired by the idealism of the New Deal, who had shifted toward increased realism both in foreign and domestic policy as a result of the excesses of the late 1960s.

When the smoke cleared, the 1976 New York Democratic primary would become a pivotal standoff between the darling of the New Left—Congresswoman Bella Abzug—and the neoconservative Democratic hope, Daniel Patrick Moynihan. It was a down-to-the-wire fight with lasting implications for the ultimate strength of moderation and the marginalization of radical politics in America. Moynihan would remain in the Senate for the next twenty-four years; Abzug would never hold elected office again.

Daniel Patrick Moynihan entered the world without much ceremony the day before St. Patrick's Day, 1927. His father was a second-generation Irish American with a newspaperman's fondness for drink; his mother was trained as a nurse. When Pat was six, his father deserted the family, a devastating setback his mother gamely met by eventually opening a bar on the West Side of New York City's vibrant—and occasionally violent—Forty-second Street. Young Pat graduated from Benjamin Franklin High School in East Harlem, sold newspapers on street corners and in bars, and later worked as a longshoreman on the docks of New York before applying for admittance to City College. "I swaggered into the test room with my long-shoreman's loading hook sticking out of my back pocket," he remembered, "I wasn't going to be mistaken for any sissy college kid."[3] In serious study for the first time in his life, Moynihan enjoyed an intellectual epiphany. He wrote a friend that "a new life has come to me, and the glories of the capitalist system and the American way have burst into my life"; his new motto was "long live the American way of life—down with the reds and the labor unions."[4]

The Second World War was raging half a world away, and the resulting patriotism and full employment was formative in young Pat Moynihan's life. In March 1944, he enlisted in the U.S. Navy and was dispatched to Middlebury College in Vermont for officer training. It was there, and later at Tufts University, that Moynihan completed work for his college bachelor's and master's degrees. Again, Moynihan was frustrated by the lazy and undisciplined children of privilege, writing a friend that they "wallow in every kind of economic and social advantage our society has to offer and remain completely spiritually and mentally mediocre."[5] By the time he completed his training, the war was over, but Moynihan served in comparatively pleasant peacetime duties on ships bound for ports like Trinidad.

In 1947, he returned from his time at sea and began tending bar at his mother's Forty-second Street establishment, Moynihan's. He was commuting up to Massachusetts to finish his degree at Tufts and writing a political column for the campus newspaper. Significantly, Moynihan strongly took Harry Truman's side in the 1948 Democratic split leading up to the election. Truman's forthright anticommunism, combined with modest New Deal liberalism on the domestic front, seemed far more responsible than Progressive Party leader Henry Wallace's calls for accommodation with Stalin and a more socialist approach to the American economy. Moynihan's commitment to the anticommunist tradition of the Democratic Party would continue all of his life.

The luck of the Irish again smiled on Pat Moynihan when he received word that he'd been awarded a scholarship to study in England. He soon departed for a formative stint at the London

School of Economics, where he watched with interest as the British Labour Party fractured and fought internally, failing to lead the nation. On the boat back to America, now dressed in the tweeds and bow ties he would favor most of his life, Moynihan happened to meet a well-connected New York lawyer who thought the young man would fit in nicely with Robert Wagner's reform Democrat candidacy for mayor.

At that time, the Democrats were the only game in town in local New York politics, possessing an overwhelming registration advantage. Consequently, the real electoral contests were between competing wings of the Democratic Party, usually reformers versus the bosses. Tammany Hall had controlled New York's Democratic Party for the better part of a century, organizing labor leaders and new immigrants into a powerful voting bloc. But their bullying methods and uncompromising propensity to use politics as a way toward personal enrichment inevitably put them at odds with the party's liberal "good-government" reformers. New York City mayoral campaigns offer a crash course in urban politics, and Pat Moynihan was a quick study; although he worked only as a volunteer, he came to know the fault lines and power players in New York Democratic politics. The experience also inspired what would be the first of many essays in *Commentary* magazine, titled "Bosses and Reformers." Moynihan shared the reformers' goals and ideals, but he found himself put off by their upper-class disdain for the rough manners of the men who ran Tammany. Moynihan now had the education of an intellectual, but he continued to identify with the up-from-the-streets mentality of union members and immigrants, and he admired their determination to build a better life for their families. After Wagner won the Democratic primary and the campaign in 1953, Moynihan began work at the International Rescue Committee, a liberal anticommunist organization dedicated to helping refugees from Eastern Europe escape the descent of the Iron Curtain and move to America. But politics again came knocking with the 1954 Democratic candidacy of Averell Harriman for governor of New York.

Harriman was a legend of the New Deal. He was FDR's favorite diplomat, and a figure of such reputation that he had already made an unsuccessful run for the presidency. The governor's mansion in

Albany, where both Roosevelts had labored before him, seemed to Harriman an attractive backup plan. Through connections made on the Wagner campaign, Moynihan soon found himself "carrying the briefcase, literally, for one of the central world figures of the 20th Century," and crafting the candidate's speeches. Harriman was victorious and his administration was, for a short time, the most admired Democratic laboratory in the land during the Eisenhower administration. Moynihan enjoyed an insider's perspective on the administration, advising the governor on policy. But Harriman the successful statesman proved to be a luckless politician. Scandals in the state party and high-profile problems with the Mafia put him on the defensive, while liberals were dismayed by what they saw as his excessively moderate approach to wielding power in the state capital. Moynihan was dismayed by the disintegration of the administration around him. Harriman was defeated after only four years in office by liberal Republican Nelson Rockefeller, who proceeded to hold the post for the next sixteen years. Moynihan was again out of a job.

Politicians often head toward the hills of academia when voted out of office, and Pat Moynihan was no exception. Now married to a fellow Harriman staffer named Liz, with two young children, the apparent security of the university life seemed appealing. Moynihan took up residence at New York's Syracuse University, working on a history of the Harriman years (unpublished because it was deemed insufficiently congratulatory by Harriman himself) and completing his doctoral dissertation on the International Labor Organization, an indication of his deep-seated affection for the working-class labor movement. Moynihan published an influential critique of the automobile industry for its systemic avoidance of safety precautions—a cause he hired a young Ralph Nader to research. Moynihan kept token appointments in the state Democratic Party, and when 1960 rolled around, he accompanied Harriman to the Kennedy convention in Los Angeles. Again, Moynihan was infuriated by liberals' attempts to deny Kennedy the nomination on the first ballot in favor of a sentimental drive for liberal elder statesman Adlai Stevenson. Once Kennedy was elected, Moynihan joined the staff of Secretary of Labor Arthur Goldberg.

Moynihan, now thirty-four, identified with the charismatic balance of pragmatism and idealism advocated by the Kennedy administration. The New Frontier philosophy argued for economic and social intervention at home—a pragmatic extension and refinement of the New Deal—but balanced these altruistic impulses with a hawkish patriotism when viewing America's role in the world. The Communist bloc was challenged with an aggressive assertion of American values and promotion of freedom. Years later, Moynihan would still sentimentally describe himself as a Kennedy Democrat, a Cold War liberal seeking a synthesis of compassionate domestic policies and confident anticommunism abroad.

While Moynihan was never an insider in Kennedy circles, he viewed the president with an awe verging on hero worship. As an assistant secretary of labor, Moynihan was responsible for laying the groundwork for much of what would become the Great Society's War on Poverty and, on a more modest scale, beginning his lifelong crusade to beautify Pennsylvania Avenue. Moynihan's social and economic insights were recognized as incisive, and he was described by journalist Theodore White as "one of the most luminous and perceptive of the younger American officials in Washington."[6] It was a lively time with kids running around the Moynihan home and a fellow Irish Catholic Democrat living in the White House. On November 22, 1963, Moynihan had just completed testifying on Capitol Hill when he was told of the president's assassination in Dallas. Reporters and television cameras were clustering outside, looking for comment, when a somber and slightly dazed Pat Moynihan emerged and offered this enduring lament:* "I don't suppose there's any point in being Irish if you don't know that the world is going to break your heart one day."[7]

With President Johnson's nationally televised pledge that "we will continue," work went forward on the Kennedy agenda in a dramatically expanded fashion. The young assistant secretary of labor was devoted to helping the poor, but he began to question whether gov-

---

*There is another touching Moynihan moment to come out of the grief of Kennedy's assassination. His friend Mary McGrory, then a reporter for the *Washington Star,* called Moynihan up in a fit of melancholy and said, "We'll never laugh again." "Heavens, Mary," Moynihan replied. "Of course we'll laugh again. It's just that we'll never be young again."

ernment programs were having their intended effect. In contrast to many statist liberals of the day, Moynihan believed in the hand-up, not a hand-out individualistic approach to public assistance, going so far as to claim welfare was "rotting the poor" in a 1964 speech. That same year, he began compiling one of the most controversial, far-sighted, and influential government reports in twentieth-century America. Pouring over census data, Moynihan was shocked and disturbed to discover that the welfare provision known as Aid to Families with Dependent Children (AFDC), designed to give single-parent families extra government funding, appeared to be having an unexpected effect: providing a financial incentive for the breakup of two-parent families. Beginning in 1960, Moynihan saw the disturbing trend of unemployment decreasing, but new AFDC cases increasing. Sixty-nine percent of the children whose mothers were on AFDC in New York were nonwhite; the number shot up to 94 percent in Washington, D.C.

Moynihan called his 1965 report "The Negro Family—a Case for National Action" and argued that an aggressive course of affirmative action was needed to counteract the corrosive long-term effects of slavery on the African-American family structure. Describing the traditional two-parent family as "the key institution for socialization," Moynihan warned that "the children of our slums are being savagely cheated by society which thinks it is too sophisticated to care about whether children have fathers and mothers have husbands."[8]

Initially, the report was hailed by the *New York Times* as "a devastating indictment of what white Americans have done to Negro Americans." But when conservative syndicated columnists Rowland Evans and Robert Novak published an article that distilled the report to what was widely interpreted as "blaming the victim," Moynihan's name became shorthand for a realism bordering on racism almost overnight. The irony that Moynihan was himself the product of a broken home—and the report's obvious concern for children stuck in that same boat—was hardly noted.

The president and his assistant secretary of labor were having a philosophical and political falling out, hastened by Moynihan's active support for Bobby Kennedy's 1964 Senate campaign in New

York. In 1965, Moynihan himself left Washington to try his hand in New York politics. Mayor Wagner announced his intention not to run for a fourth term, and a reporter surprised Moynihan by asking him to comment on rumors of his candidacy for the top position in City Hall. Moynihan offered a hurried denial and then quickly began exploring his options, settling on an uphill candidacy for president of the City Council, with the stated goal of revitalizing urban America.

Reformers and radicals were now squaring off for control of the Democratic Party, and much to Moynihan's dismay, RFK refused to support him in the Democratic primary, preferring to play it safe within his newly adopted state. The chance to forge a New Frontier Democratic Party—both Centrist and progressive—in New York City was lost with Moynihan's resounding defeat in the primary for City Council president. In November's mayoral election, liberal Republican John Lindsay defeated Democrat Abe Beame and Conservative Party candidate William F. Buckley Jr.

So it was back to academia for Pat Moynihan, accompanied by a dark season of transition and reassessment. Heated critiques of "The Negro Family—a Case for National Action"—now and forever referred to as the Moynihan Report—circulated, accusing its author of ignorant manipulation of government statistics for personal gain and outright racism. But among a small cadre of disaffected liberal intellectuals, Moynihan's cutting-edge criticism of the entitlement's unintended consequences was gaining recognition among readers of the *Public Interest*, edited by Irving Kristol and Daniel Bell. Neoconservatives, memorably described by Kristol as "liberals who've been mugged by reality," had grown up identifying with liberal causes, but the increasingly anti-American and relativistic tone of the left wing in American politics alienated them entirely. Like Moynihan, they supported the safety net that a limited welfare state was supposed to supply, but they were concerned that individuals' dependence on welfare was making them less free to take personal responsibility for their own lives, with disastrous consequences for society. Moreover, they looked for a moral backbone in America's foreign policy, which led them to oppose appeasement with Communist nations on the grounds that "totalitarian states were fundamentally alike beneath their different ideological masks; whether of the left or the right, they constitute abhorrent menaces to democracy."[9]

Moynihan began publishing articles in the *Public Interest* on a regular basis and secured a position as director of the Joint Center for Urban Studies at Harvard and M.I.T. at a time when urban America was literally burning with periodic riots. He published a book called *Maximum Feasible Misunderstanding,* which attracted the attention of a New York lawyer named Richard M. Nixon.

Nixon was running for president again, this time attempting to moderate his image with an emphasis on national unity in a time of domestic crisis. While Moynihan spoke on behalf of Bobby Kennedy's brief but heroic presidential campaign, Nixon was reading widely and mobilizing new arguments in favor of his candidacy. He seized upon a September 1967 speech Moynihan had given to the National Board of Americans for Democratic Action, titled "The Politics of Stability." In his speech, Moynihan laid out three challenges for liberalism to remain relevant and help heal the nation in the late 1960s:

1. Liberals must see more clearly that their essential interest is in the stability of the social order; and that, given the present threats to that stability, they must seek out and make much more effective alliances with political Conservatives who share their interest and recognize that unyielding rigidity is just as great a threat to continuity of the social order as an anarchic desire for change.

2. Liberals must divest themselves of the notion that the nation—and especially the cities of the nation—can be run from agencies in Washington.

3. Liberals must somehow overcome the curious condescension that takes the form of defending and explaining away anything, however outrageous, which Negroes, individually or collectively, might do.[10]

In December 1967, Nixon spoke to the National Association of Manufacturers and quoted Moynihan approvingly and at length, saying that "Daniel Moynihan held out a hand that true Conservatives should be quick to grasp. . . . Let us not let that opportunity pass"[11]

After Bobby Kennedy's assassination, Moynihan campaigned halfheartedly for Hubert Humphrey. When Nixon won, however, it was only a matter of months before he asked Pat Moynihan to join his White House staff as chief domestic policy adviser. Many of Moynihan's liberal friends argued that he should not lend a hand to Richard Nixon's presidency, but Moynihan later described his logic: "I did it because there were machine gun placements on the White House steps facing north. What was being called the urban crisis was at its most intense. I was a director of the Joint Center for Urban Studies and thought I had at least as good idea of how to end it as anyone else who was likely to get the position. So when Nixon asked me, I accepted."[12] Privately, he also felt that Nixon was more likely to take on the welfare reform he thought essential to the nation's long-term stability.

Nixon and Moynihan were opposites in terms of temperament, but they had an abiding respect in each other's intellect. Nixon requested reading lists from Moynihan, which his adviser eagerly supplied. Among his most influential suggestions was Robert Blake's biography of British prime minister Benjamin Disraeli. Nixon quickly reported back that he had read the entire book cover to cover, and Disraeli references began cropping up in his speech, most notably in his widely circulated admonition to his cabinet that it was "Tory men with liberal principles who enlarged democracy."[13] This Centrist conception of political influence would drive Nixon's domestic policies during the course of his term.

Moynihan was instrumental in convincing Nixon to propose the administration's revolutionary Family Assistance Plan, which would have reformed welfare by reducing bureaucracy with limited direct cash payments to poor families, while requiring able-bodied recipients to accept jobs and job training. The bill was killed on Capitol Hill by a coalition of conservatives who felt the plan was too generous and liberals who thought it was not generous enough. More successful was his advocacy of the Basic Opportunity Grant program, which enacted direct grants to low-income college students. Moynihan noted with some despair, however, that Nixon chose to sign the Basic Opportunity Grant into law without any official ceremony. Lyndon Johnson, Moynihan was sure, would have staged a barbecue and gotten all the credit he could.[14]

For all his effectiveness and innovation as a policy adviser, Moynihan's time with Nixon became best known for a memo he wrote to the president about the increasing polarization of race relations at a time when the hateful rhetoric of Alabama governor George Wallace and the Black Panthers were feeding off each other in a frenzy of separatism. Arguing that "there is a silent black majority as well as a white one," Moynihan wrote:

> The time may have come when the issue of race could benefit from a period of benign neglect. The subject has been too much talked about. The forum has been too much taken over by hysterics, paranoids and boodlers on all sides. We may need a period in which Negro progress continues and racial rhetoric fades. The administration can help bring this about by playing close attention to such progress—as we are doing—while seeking to avoid situations in which extremists of either race are given opportunities for martyrdom, heroics, histrionics or whatever.[15]

Nixon loved the memo, underlining it extensively with enthusiastic comments in the margins, and finally ordered that it be copied and sent to his entire cabinet. Inevitably, it was leaked to the press.

Like the 1965 Moynihan Report, what came to be known as the "benign neglect" memo was a reasonable, essentially liberal document, but Moynihan's acerbic language invited out-of-context citations and general misinterpretation. Again, he was hurt and frustrated by accusations of racism, but the Nixon administration stood by him—a favor Moynihan returned with steadfast loyalty after Watergate.

Moynihan had been given a strict two-year sabbatical by Harvard to join the White House staff, and in 1970 he left Washington to return to Cambridge. But his heart was now in the action of government service rather than the theory of academia, and after Nixon's 1972 landslide reelection Daniel Patrick Moynihan was appointed ambassador to India. At the time, Prime Minister Indira Gandhi could dependably be found courting the Soviet Union. Accusations of American imperialism were hitting their high-water mark in the international community, and Moynihan was appalled by accusations of moral relativism between the USSR and the United States. After two years as ambassador, Moynihan wrote a defiant essay for the neoconservative journal *Commentary,* titled "The United States in Opposition."

> It is time that the American spokesman came to be feared in inter-national forums for the truths he might tell. It is past time we ceased to apologize for an imperfect democracy. Find its equal . . . it is time we asserted that inequalities in the world may not be so much a matter of condition as of performance . . . The Third World must feed itself, for example, and this will not be done by suggesting that Americans eat too much.[16]

The essay's effect was electric. The *New York Times* colorfully characterized its impact: "For thoughtful Americans, whose stomachs were paralyzed by guilt every time they bit into the inefficient proteins of sirloin steak or even the humble hamburger, and who suffered severe chest pains when they thought about Vietnam, Chile, the Congo and countless other examples of wickedness now coming to light, Moynihan's words soothed like a magical compound of aspirin, liniment, bicarbonate of soda and Valium."[17] Secretary of State Henry Kissinger was an immediate fan of its sentiments, and passed the essay along to President Ford. As it happened, there was an opening for the position of "American spokesman" and suddenly Pat Moynihan found himself serving as the U.S. ambassador to the United Nations. For once, he would depart a government post a hero.

Within months of his appointment, Moynihan found himself squaring off against the mindless radicalism he had decried in the international community. Criticizing the United States with impunity had become such a part of daily life at the United Nations that Moynihan was not informed when a subcommittee routinely condemned the presence of an American naval base on Guam by a vote of 108 to 1. "Do you think the Russians would forgive you for voting for them to get the hell out of their naval base in Somalia?"[18] Moynihan fumed. He bucked the standard State Department request that he ignore this condemnation, and criticized the UN's Committee on Decolonization for consisting of sixteen police states and only four democracies. "We are not about to be lectured by police states on the processes of electoral democracy," he said.[19]

Moynihan sparked a minor international uproar when he referred to the military dictator of Uganda, Idi Amin—who had recently called for "the extinction of Israel as a state" in a speech to the United Nations—as a "racist murderer." In that same speech, Moynihan asserted that "democracy has come increasingly under attack. I see it every day at the United Nations. Every day, on every side, we are assailed. There are those in this country whose pleasure, or profit, it is to believe that our assailants are motivated by what is wrong with us. They are wrong. We are assailed because of what is right about us. We are assailed because we are a democracy."[20]

But Moynihan's ultimate showdown at the United Nations came over a resolution equating Zionism with racism that was pushed forward on the thirty-seventh anniversary of Kristallnacht, when Nazi storm troopers had destroyed Jewish-owned stores in Berlin. The resolution passed by a vote of 72 to 35 with 32 nations abstaining. Moynihan waited until the vote was completed and then rose to tremulously thunder his anger in the language of a statesman. "The United States rises to declare before the General Assembly of the U.N., and before the world, that it does not acknowledge, it will not abide by, it will never acquiesce in this infamous act." Moynihan went on to explain in tense professorial tones that the very idea of Jews as a race could be traced not to Jews themselves but to nineteenth-century anti-Semites, and that a visit to Israel and the sight of Jews of different skin tones who had made their way to the state from countries around the world clearly exposed the alleged relationship between Zionism and racism as a lie. In fact, Moynihan concluded, by the very passage of this resolution, the United Nations removed meaning from the word "racism." After the vote, Moynihan hugged the Israeli ambassador and whispered, "Fuck 'em."[21]

Overnight, the speech gave Pat Moynihan an international reputation as an unflinching and articulate defender of American interests and values. Among Jews living in America and Israel, he was nothing less than a hero. Henry Kissinger and the Ford administration subtly began distancing themselves from their combative ambassador, but privately many were pleased by the decidedly undiplomatic stance Moynihan was taking at the United Nations. The kid from Hell's Kitchen, who had tended bar on the opposite end of Forty-second Street in college, left the United Nations in a blaze of glory.

Political figures whom people were willing to believe in were in short supply after Watergate, and a Draft Moynihan for Senate movement was begun. New York's incumbent senator was the Conservative James Buckley—brother of *National Review* founder William F. Buckley Jr.—considered vulnerable because of his unusual victory six years before as a Conservative Party protest candidate who came out ahead in a three-way race with a traditional Democrat and a liberal Republican, incumbent senator Charles Goodell.

Columnist Ben Wattenberg led the charge, applauding Moynihan's "charisma of common sense." Organized labor and moderate New Yorkers of all parties responded enthusiastically to the possibility of an eloquent advocate in the Senate. Perhaps most crucially, former Democratic state chairman and Erie County power broker Joseph Crangle offered his support, accompanied by this political logic: "Undoubtedly he's cut into an area of votes that Buckley might have thought was his own preserve. He's not only waved the flag at the U.N.; he's pretty much raised the flag. There's a freshness there."[22] With Moynihan, the Democratic Party could reclaim the issue of patriotism it had lost with the riots and antiwar protests of the New Left.

Moynihan chose to put off a final decision on his own candidacy, devoting himself to the presidential campaign of the closest candidate the Democratic Party still offered as a political and philosophical soulmate: Washington senator Henry "Scoop" Jackson's campaign for president.

Scoop Jackson was the leader—and at times it seemed, the sole remaining voice—of the Centrist Senate Democratic tradition that called for a balance of New Deal economics at home and an aggressive anticommunist foreign policy abroad. Moynihan became Jackson's principle advocate throughout New York State, traveling to virtually every county on his friend's behalf. He was also testing the waters for a senatorial campaign of his own.

Moynihan certainly acted like a born candidate, while protesting that he was not. Reporters watched, bemused and amazed, as "he discussed the respective merits of upstate beers; the religious revivals of the 1840's in the 'burned-over district'; the local roots of Mormonism; the origin of the name of Delhi, the seat of Delaware County; the importance of barges as carriers of inter-city freight; the excellence of upstate trout fishing; and a neighborhood in Syracuse so Irish that a traffic light has the green on top and the red below."[23]

In Syracuse, the mayor introduced Moynihan as "the natural enemy of dragons, sacred cows and demagogues,"[24] adding that he would make a fine Senate candidate. This sentiment was forcefully echoed by Robert Flavin, president of Local 1170 of the Communications Workers of America in Rochester, who promised an instant endorsement.

Moynihan was lining up the support of labor and party leaders without even asking for it—which was more than Scoop Jackson was achieving. The candidacy of the distinguished senator from Washington sadly went down in flames, leaving Pat Moynihan behind to pick up the mantle of responsible moderation within the Democratic Party. In discussions with a friend, *Commentary* editor Norman Podhoretz, about running for the Senate, Podhoretz pointed out that Moynihan had a unique opportunity to "define a winning centrist position, first by creaming the radicals within the party, and then the right wing outside the party."[25]

Moynihan had the political smarts to realize that he would need to win over Democratic insiders before he could get past the primary. He called on a favor from Scoop Jackson, who helped him to get a place on the subcommittee responsible for writing the Democratic platform. The party's convention in 1976 was scheduled, conveniently, in New York's Madison Square Garden. Newspapers noted that Moynihan was the only person on the fifteen-member Democratic subcommittee with expertise in foreign policy and speculated that the former ambassador's role at the convention would "help re-establish Mr. Moynihan's credentials as a Democrat."[26]

Despite his efforts, some liberal Democrats were unwilling to support—or even consider—a Moynihan candidacy. Manhattan borough president Percy Sutton, who was also serving on the platform committee, stated that he did not believe Mr. Moynihan could "represent my interests or the interests of black people generally in the area of foreign policy," raising the extraordinary possibility that African-Americans had fundamentally different foreign policy interests than their fellow Americans. City clerk and future mayor David Dinkins was a bit more grounded in his criticism, asserting that Moynihan was "unacceptable" because of his views on the Negro family reflected in the Family Assistance Plan that he developed for President Nixon.[27]

Resentment, anger, and divisions in the Democratic Party had been festering since the ascendance of the liberal wing of the party to power with the nomination of George McGovern in 1972. As with Barry Goldwater's disastrous 1964 Republican campaign, when extremists took hold of the Democratic Party, the result was overwhelming rejection by the American people. But strangely, in neither case did landslide defeats dampen the enthusiasm of these true believers. Moynihan referred to these extremist liberals as "those elements in our party that prefer to ruin if they cannot rule."[28]

These "rule-or-ruin" liberals were aligned against Moynihan on all fronts, determined to deny this Nixon-Ford alumnus the Democratic nomination, regardless of whether he stood the best chance of winning the general election against Conservative James Buckley in November. Moderate party leaders from across the state surveyed the divisions among liberal Manhattan Democrats and sighed. "The ultra-liberals seem to control the primary elections," said Representative Jerome Ambro Jr. of Long Island. "As a result, we wind up with kind of silly tickets."[29]

The liberals' leading contender for the nomination was Bella Abzug, the three-term congresswoman from one of the most liberal districts in the nation, Manhattan's West Side. She had cultivated an image of ultraliberal flamboyance, her trademark wide-brimmed hat bobbing above the crowd at nearly every protest rally. She was a graduate of Columbia Law School, Class of 1947, and legislative director of a liberal advocacy organization known as Women Strike for Peace. She was intelligent, hardworking, and proudly outspoken—a well-known symbol of the feminist movement. "I may not be what a Senator looks like," she would say repeatedly on the campaign trail, "but I am what a Senator should look like."[30] Because of her high profile and relatively prominent elected position for a self-described militant feminist and antiwar advocate, she was an automatic leader of the radical wing of the Democratic Party, known as the New Left.

"I am not a Centrist," Bella Abzug said.[31] But she was trying to moderate—some would say soften—her image; for example, by highlighting her thirty-two-year relationship with her husband, making the case that she was not hostile to middle-class values. "Instead of emphasizing anti-war and feminist militancy, Mrs. Abzug points up her congressional record and experience," opined the *New York Times*.[32] The crux of her attack on Moynihan was that he was not a "real" Democrat, but "the Republicans' favorite Democrat."[33] She was not alone in this criticism.

The other three candidates in the Democratic primary were all considerably to the left of Moynihan and attempted to use his tenure as U.S. ambassador and chief domestic policy adviser for Nixon against him.

Ramsey Clark was a former attorney general under Lyndon Johnson who had become a darling of the liberal left wing through his opposition to the Vietnam War and his near election to the U.S. Senate two years before. Paul O'Dwyer was the president of the City Council, holding the position Moynihan had tried and failed to win nine years before. The brother of a former mayor and a supporter of the Irish Republican Army, O'Dwyer was equally at home with the politics of Tammany Hall or the New Left. Abe Hirschfield was a millionaire owner of parking garages who would use his fortune to fund erratic races for public office in New York before being sent to prison for hiring a hit man to murder a business partner in the late 1990s.

From the sublime to the ridiculous, it was a crowded field reflecting the divisions within the emergent Democratic establishment in New York.

Moynihan announced his candidacy in the ballroom of the Roosevelt Hotel, motivated by his conviction that the Democratic Party had been hijacked by narrow special interests and pseudo-reformers who did not understand the real world of responsible governance or the real world of working-class New Yorkers.

In a campaign speech at the base of the Empire State Building, Moynihan attacked the hijackers of liberalism, saying, "Much lip service is given by persons of this political persuasion to the idea of improving and reforming things, but in practice, more often than not, they show no interest in the kind of incremental improvement that the traditional liberalism of the Democratic Party has always sought and always fought for."[34] In contrast, Moynihan explained, he believed in the "reformist liberalism" of the great Democratic leaders of the past. "It was a tradition based on the belief that the American political system is sound and healthy at its foundations and that the object of all reform is to improve the system, to make it work better, to make it truer to the ideals of individual liberty and equal opportunity which it helped establish in this nation."[35]

Moynihan was attempting to recast people's assumptions about what it meant to be a liberal in 1970s New York. He promised that he would be a check on the liberals' excesses, balancing liberal ideals with proven effectiveness and honest talk. Newspapers were fascinated by Moynihan's obvious identification with the essentially socially conservative working class. "Positioning himself in the Democratic center," the Wall Street Journal wrote, "former Professor Moynihan is sounding neo-conservative themes of anti-communism, defense of the family, ethnic pride and middle-class values. He argues, with some cogency, that the other candidates are too far to the left to build a Democratic coalition of working-class Catholics, Jews and upstate conservatives that's needed to beat Mr. Buckley. But Mr. Moynihan is much less confident about winning the primary than he is sure of his ability to defeat the incumbent Senator. That reflects the tricky political demographics of New York."[36]

It *was* a difficult assignment. The paradoxical reality was that it would be more difficult to win the Democratic nomination than to get elected to the Senate in the general election. But Moynihan was betting he could generate principled enthusiasm for his campaign while also benefiting from the left-wing extremism many upstate New Yorkers associated with Bella Abzug. Again and again he sounded the themes that had led to his success as UN ambassador. At a campaign rally outside the United Nations, wearing a suit and bow tie in the bright heat of August, he said: "I want to go on speaking up against the charge that we've exploited other countries or that our own prosperity rests on plunder. . . . I want to go on declaring that we are prosperous because we have been an energetic and productive people. I want to go on saying that we will not be bullied and that we will not be blackmailed."[37]

He backed up his rhetoric, and highlighted his foreign policy experience, by taking his opponents to task on the then-controversial issue of defense budgets. He called Ramsey Clark's call for a $30 billion cut in the defense budget "nothing less than sheer demagoguery. . . . Thirty-billion dollars is more than the entire cost of the United States Navy," he said, with some evident affection for his own days at sea. With Congresswoman Abzug, he had the advantage of a detailed voting record to compare her against. He contrasted her refusal to support any defense spending during her time in Congress with her strident calls for support of the state of Israel. Without defense dollars, he pointed out, "we would be unable to supply Israel with the weapons she needs to defend herself."[38]

In turn, Bella Abzug went on the attack, blanketing the city with ads. Her handbills featured a picture of Nixon and Moynihan standing side by side in the White House. A radio ad used an old tape of a White House ceremony, featuring the voices of Mr. Nixon and Mr. Moynihan. "In 1972," the announcer intones, "when Bella Abzug was calling for the impeachment of Richard Nixon, Pat Moynihan was still on his payroll."[39] Abzug's campaign manager, the cigar-chomping Doug Ireland, called Moynihan "the Tokyo Rose of the Nixon-Ford years," referring to a Japanese propagandist who broadcast to American troops in English during the Second World War.[40]

Abzug considered Moynihan a turncoat for working with Republican administrations. Neck and neck in the polls, Abzug was gaining virtually all the organized support from black and Hispanic elected officials, as well as national Democratic leaders like House Majority Leader Tip O'Neill, whose Beantown voice boomed from a radio ad, "She is some person! What a job she's done!" Moynihan's base was developing among moderates and swing voters, unions and party leaders, and conservative voters upstate. Abzug's frustration bubbled over three weeks before the primary, when a reporter asked if she would support Pat Moynihan if he pulled ahead of the Democratic pack on Election Day. "I don't see any reason for me to support anyone who continues Nixon-Ford policies," Abzug replied.[41]

Close campaigns are frequently determined by a pivotal mistake or pivotal success. This proved the big mistake of the 1976 New York Senate campaign. The next day, a newspaper headline stated simply, "Mrs. Abzug Says She Won't Back Moynihan If He Wins Primary." At first, Doug Ireland dismissed the importance of the political repercussions. "It's a one-day story, and that will be the end of it," he said.[42] This proved to be wishful thinking.

The apparent intolerance and abrasiveness of Abzug's comment reinforced negative perceptions about the "rule-or-ruin" wing of the party, and statewide Democratic leaders were displeased at the thought that another public rupture would cause them to lose the Senate seat yet again. Moynihan's team, led by Erie County Democratic leader Joseph Crangle, skillfully took advantage of the mistake. Within twenty-four hours, thirty-three upstate Democratic county leaders had signed a petition calling on Abzug to renounce her vow not to support Moynihan if he should win the primary. The headlines now read, "Mrs. Abzug Urged to Retract Repudiation of Moynihan," and as the story was extended to a second and then a third day, Bella Abzug was on the defensive.

With the final televised debate between the candidates still ahead, Bella Abzug hoped that it would be her shot at redemption. Previously, all the candidates were united in attacking Moynihan, the relatively conservative outsider and Nixon apologist. But now the issue became Bella's lack of party loyalty. Moynihan built on the rupture by adding a bit of political logic to the debate. Who, in fact, would have the best chance at unseating Senator Buckley? It was difficult for the Democratic machine to answer with a straight face that Mrs. Abzug would persuade many middle-of-the-road voters to swing over to the Democratic column.

Moynihan pointed out that

Senator Buckley ran six years ago with a slogan which was evidently effective. It simply said: "Isn't it time we had a Senator?" And it clearly was addressed to that very large body of working-class New Yorkers who have traditionally been Democratic and who, in the main, still enroll Democratic, but have felt more and more excluded from the councils of the Democratic Party . . . what I would hope to represent in the party is that older tradition—you can speak of myself as a Kennedy Democrat, which certainly I am, and people who go back before that—which was a party of coalitions and a party in particular which had a place in it for the working masses of the state, and their moral concerns and their patriotism, their feeling that this is not a country which is somehow a disease the rest of the world might catch and have to be isolated from.[43]

Moynihan's ads reinforced his toughness and national—as opposed to factional—perspective with the slogan "He spoke up for America. He'll speak up for New York" plastered across the state. His radio ads emphasized his balance and distinctive moderation in a primary against professional liberals, with Moynihan describing himself as "conservative, about a lot of things"—like the importance of family—but a "liberal economically."[44] Interestingly, he equated fear of rising crime in New York City streets with a kind of terrorism, pointing out that during the 1960s crime went up as state prison populations went down, and reiterated his support for "stiffer prison terms for habitual criminals and adequate prisons to hold them."[45]

Pat Moynihan was beginning to pull ahead, but many credit the endorsement of the *New York Times* four days before the primary with solidifying his lead and putting him over the top. This endorsement had been by no means assured. Moynihan and the paper's editorial page editor, John Oakes, had a falling-out during his tenure at the United Nations. While Oakes was on vacation, the paper's publisher, "Punch" Sulzberger, took the unusual step of intervening on Moynihan's behalf. Oakes, furious, demanded space to publish a terse three-line dissent alongside the paper's endorsement. It did not matter.

"We choose Daniel P. Moynihan," the editorial read in part, "that rambunctious child of the sidewalks of New York, profound student and teacher of social affairs, aggressive debater, outrageous flatterer, shrewd adviser—indeed manipulator—of Presidents, accomplished diplomat and heartfelt friend of the poor."[46]

The editorial went on to state: "Mrs. Abzug has had to moderate her flamboyant political style to appeal to constituencies on her right and to work so well with more conservative legislators in the Congress. Perhaps she could demonstrate her centrist credentials to a broad majority in the fall, but she would have the more difficult race. Mr. Moynihan should be able to sweep all the votes west of Mr. Buckley's left pinkie, were it not for his unfortunate—and undeserved—unpopularity among black citizens."[47]

Moynihan's moderation had made all the difference to the publisher of the usually liberal *New York Times*. When primary day rolled around, there was a heavy turnout throughout the state. Moynihan ran ahead of Abzug in the city, suburbs, and upstate—but with narrower-than-expected margins. To the surprise of some, the Irish-Catholic former United Nations ambassador ran ahead of the most prominent Jewish woman in Congress among Jewish voters (who made up 40 percent of the primary electorate), but lost the Protestant primary vote. Self-described "moderate" Democrats were overwhelmingly in Moynihan's corner, and—most interestingly—nearly half of Moynihan voters said they would have supported Buckley's re-

election if Abzug had been the party's nominee.[48] Her carefully cultivated association with the New Left would almost certainly have led
to the reelection of the Conservative Party's senator from New York.

Buckley immediately tried to tar Moynihan with the "liberal" label
he had hoped to use against Bella, kicking off his campaign with the
accusation that Moynihan was "to the left of the majority of New
Yorkers on such basic issues as inflation and the economy and the
extent of the Federal meddling in our lives."[49] But these charges
couldn't stick because of Moynihan's already well-defined credentials as a Centrist John F. Kennedy Democrat. Moynihan in turn focused attention on Buckley's rigid conservative philosophy, which
had led New York's senator to side with President Ford's refusal of a
federal bailout of New York during the city's fiscal crisis, memorably
captured by the *Daily News* headline "Ford to New York: Drop Dead."
Senator Buckley, Moynihan charged, had chosen ideological purity
over helping the people of New York. The working-class conservative
Daily News seemed to agree: "Buckley let New York down badly. . . .
Buckley acted on principle, but the unyielding defense of rigid views
often produces more practical harm than good. Whatever the de-
fects of the present federal system, it exists."[50] A memorable Moynihan campaign ad cut to the heart of the matter: "Mr. Buckley doesn't
fight for us. Sometimes he acts like he doesn't even like us."[51]

By promising to be both tougher and more thoughtful, more
moderate and more effective than their current senator, Pat
Moynihan won by a landslide on election day, running one hundred
thousand votes ahead of Jimmy Carter's victorious presidential
ticket.

Moynihan would settle into what had been Bobby Kennedy's old
Senate seat with ease. He grew more liberal with age, arguing as
early as 1979 that the Soviet Union would collapse under the
weight of its own inefficiencies and injustice, making—in his judgment—Reagan-style rhetoric and the accompanying arms race unnecessary. After the fall of the Soviet Union, Moynihan's old boss
Henry Kissinger wrote him a note that said: "I stand corrected. Your
crystal ball was better than mine." Pat Moynihan retained his skepticism about ideologues of every stripe, and while he sometimes
seemed content to serve as a social gadfly, he was proven right on

the big things time and again throughout his twenty-four years in the Senate: right on the fall of Communism; right on the importance of standing up to the closely linked anti-Semitism and anti-Americanism in the developing world; right on the necessity of welfare reform; right on the importance of responsible fathers to the structure of a civil society; and right on respecting the immigrant heritage of our nation. He took pride in never being politically pigeonholed and believed, with much evidence, that it increased his effectiveness. In 1998 he was reelected to the Senate for a third term by an unprecedented margin, winning sixty of New York State's sixty-two counties. In his Senate office, Moynihan kept two magazine covers framed, side by side. One bore the headline "Pat Moynihan, Neo-Liberal" and the other "Moynihan: The Conscience of a Neoconservative."

PART 4

DECLARATIONS OF INDEPENDENCE

*C*entrism means freedom from the extremes—for both the voter and the political leader. Principled independence, the willingness to take courageous stands at odds with the powerful and the partisan, is what we hope for in our political leaders. But the everyday life of an elected official in the United States is infused with a business-as-usual bureaucratic inertia that encourages individuals to think alike and vote the party line. Individual stands of courage that are at odds with the party line are strongly discouraged and frequently dismissed as evidence of selfishness or egotism. Declarations of independence from this corrosion of conformity are worth recognizing and respecting.

Senator Margaret Chase Smith was the first woman elected to the Senate in her own right at a time when Joe McCarthy was becoming the best-known voice of the Republican Party with his charges that Communist agents had infiltrated the Truman State Department. McCarthy's hearings struck terror into the heart and soul of official Washington, causing many members of Congress to abdicate their responsibility to question accusations and seek answers in the intellectually honest pursuit of truth and justice. Though she was a junior member of the Senate, and a Republican as well, on June 1, 1950, Margaret Chase Smith became the first senator to stand up to McCarthy's witch-hunt. Her "Declaration of Conscience" was a landmark American event that deserves to be remembered as a profile in courage. Her criticism of the far right's reach into the Senate and its control of the Republican Party was mirrored twenty years later by her issuance of a second declaration of conscience in which she warned that the irresponsible excesses of the far left threatened justice, peace, and order within the United States. Her twin declarations of conscience expressed the voice of those who are frequently drowned out by demagogues in American history. She also took care to point out the symbiotic relationship between the far left and the far right: how inevitably the rise of one feeds on the perceived threat of another.

In 1966, Edward Brooke became the first African-American popularly elected to the Senate. His achievement was all the more remarkable because his home state, Massachusetts, had at the time less than a 3 percent African-American population. Ed Brooke was determined to serve as a senator on behalf of all of his constituents. This difficult balancing act was widely misunderstood during the turbulent late 1960s, when the civil rights movement lost its self-evident moral clarity with its destructive drift toward black power. Ed Brooke did his best to expand the reach of the Republican Party by setting an example for openness and tolerance. But his good faith was undercut by the party's courtship of southern segregationist supporters of George Wallace, and one year after being overwhelmingly reelected to the Senate, Ed Brooke became the first Republican senator to call for Richard Nixon's resignation from the presidency. This stand was one of many during his career that demonstrated his allegiance to his office and his country ran deeper than party politics or the color of his skin.

Reform movements take the shape of a third party in America when large groups of people feel that their voices are not being heard in Washington. In the past, Independent and third-party candidacies were dominated by fringe movements of the far left and far right; Henry Wallace's Soviet-sympathizing campaign in 1948 and George Wallace's segregationist campaigns in the late 1960s and early 1970s come to mind. But in recent decades, reform movements in the United States have come from the center of the electorate. Increasingly, Independent candidacies offer a way for concerned individuals to run for office without compromising their principles. Against the odds, three Independent governors were elected in the last decade of the twentieth century: Angus King in Maine, Lowell Weicker in Connecticut, and Jesse Ventura in Minnesota. Unlike the leaders of third-party movements in the past, these individuals did not claim to represent specific disaffected groups, such as farmers in the dust bowl or poor whites in the South. They did not claim that the far left was not being represented in the Democratic Party or that the far right was not getting its due within the Republican Party's apparatus. Instead, one of the common threads between all their candidacies was a commitment to fiscal responsibility and a belief that government should offer individuals more freedom while respecting the separation of church and state. Their popularity is consistent with the rising tide of Americans who not only identify themselves as Independent—more than those who identify themselves as Democrat or Republican—but have a growing recognition that the moderate majority in America is fiscally responsible and socially inclusive.

But perhaps the most significant political movement in the last decade of the twentieth century was the return of urban America from the brink of oblivion. As a consequence of spiraling crime rates and swelling welfare rolls, there began to be movement away from the old paradigms and toward a new pragmatism that focused on improving the quality of life. A generation of "third-way" mayors, led by New York's Mayor Rudy Giuliani, found uncommon success with an emphasis on local innovation and individual accountability. The members of this new urban coalition were sometimes called the "new progressives" or "common sense conservatives," but they combined a focus on law and order with an understanding of the diversity that makes cities thrive. The resurgence of urban America after decades of decline was a hopeful narrative about the ability of determined public servants to make a difference by operating outside the narrow ideological limits of partisan politics. Mayor Giuliani's courageous and compassionate response to the terrorist attacks of September 11, 2001, highlighted his already considerable accomplishments in turning around America's largest city.

The last thing the nation needs is another typical politician who increases cynicism with his or her immediate sellout to special interests, someone whose lack of character allows him or her to be told how to vote by party bosses and power brokers in exchange for personal security, someone who encourages the worst in humanity by profiting from divisions in society. What Americans want are courageous, independent statesmen, determined to do the right thing, to represent both their constituents and their conscience, incorporating change while remaining true to core principles. There is a heritage of these heroes in American politics; a tradition of principled but maverick politicians who cut their own path between the extremes.

SENATOR MARGARET CHASE SMITH — 1950

THE LADY FROM MAINE STANDS UP TO JOE McCARTHY

It is time that the great center of our people, who reject the violence and unreasonableness of both the extreme right and the extreme left, searched their consciences, mustered their moral and physical courage, shed their intimidated silence, and declared their consciences.

—SENATOR MARGARET CHASE SMITH[1]

On June 1, 1950, Margaret Chase Smith—the first woman ever popularly elected to the U.S. Senate—prepared to give the speech of her life.

For the past six months, her fellow Republican senator Joseph McCarthy had been traveling around the country, drawing crowds with accusations that he had a list of "205 Communist agents in the Truman Administration." Sometimes the number was 57, sometimes just "a lot"—but McCarthy's message was always the same, hammered home with indignant patriotism and passionate intensity. Operating with legal immunity in the Senate, McCarthy transfixed and divided the United States, coercing witnesses to testify in front of his senatorial committee. An atmosphere of fear had paralyzed the nation and officials in Washington. Up to that day, not a single senator from either party had dared to speak out against Joe McCarthy.

That was about to change.

Margaret Chase Smith had been working on the speech she called her "Declaration of Conscience" during the Memorial Day weekend at her home in Skowhegan, Maine. She showed it to six liberal Republican colleagues and received their endorsement. Now, on her way to the Senate chamber in the antiseptic and cavernous subway that connects the office building with the Capitol dome, her nervousness and sense of purpose was compounded when she found herself sitting next to Joe McCarthy. "You look intent on something," he growled. "Yes," Smith replied. "I'm going to make a speech about you and you are not going to like it."[2]

Standing on the Senate floor, with Joe McCarthy sitting with arms folded three desks behind her, Senator Margaret Chase Smith began reading her prepared remarks in a clear and steady voice.

I speak as a Republican. I speak as a woman. I speak as a United States Senator. I speak as an American. . . .

I think that it is high time for the United States Senate and its Members to do some real soul-searching and to weigh our consciences. . . . I think it is high time that we remembered that we have sworn to uphold and defend the Constitution. I think it is high time that we remembered that the Constitution, as amended, speaks not only of the freedom of speech but also of trial by jury instead of trial by accusation.

Whether it be a criminal prosecution in court or a character prosecution in the Senate, there is little practical distinction when the life of a person has been ruined.

Those of us who shout the loudest about Americanism in making character assassinations are all too frequently those who, by our own words and acts, ignore some of the basic principles of Americanism:

The right to criticize;

The right to hold unpopular beliefs;

The right to protest;

The right of independent thought.

The exercise of these rights should not cost one single American citizen his reputation or his right to a livelihood, nor should he be in danger of losing his reputation or livelihood merely because he happens to know someone who holds unpopular beliefs. Who of us does not? Otherwise none of us could call our souls our own. Otherwise thought control would have set in . . .

The American people are sick and tired of being afraid to speak their minds lest they be politically smeared as Communists or Fascists by their opponents. Freedom of speech is not what it used to be in America. It has been so abused by some that it is not exercised by others . . .

The record of the present Democratic Administration has provided us with sufficient campaign issues without the necessity to resorting to political smears. America is rapidly losing its position as leader of the world simply because the Democratic Administration has pitifully failed to provide effective leadership. . . .

Yet to displace it with a Republican regime embracing a philosophy that lacks political integrity or intellectual honesty would prove equally disastrous to the Nation. The Nation sorely needs a Republican victory. But I do not want to see the Republican Party ride to political victory on the Four Horsemen of Calumny—Fear, Ignorance, Bigotry, and Smear.

As a United States Senator, I am not proud of the way in which the Senate has been made a publicity platform for irresponsible sensationalism. . . . I do not like the way the Senate has been made a rendezvous for vilification, for selfish political gain at the sacrifice of individual reputations and national unity. I am not proud of the way we smear outsiders from the floor of the Senate and hide behind the cloak of congressional immunity and still place ourselves beyond criticism on the floor of the Senate.

As an American, I am shocked at the way Republicans and

Democrats alike are playing directly into the Communist design of "confuse, divide, and conquer." As an American, I do not want a Democratic Administration whitewash or cover-up any more than I want a Republican smear or witch hunt.

As an American, I condemn a Republican Fascist just as much as I condemn a Democrat Communist. I condemn a Democrat Fascist just as much as I condemn a Republican Communist. They are equally dangerous to you and me and to our country. As an American, I want to see our Nation recapture the strength and unity it once had when we fought the enemy instead of ourselves.[3]

Senator Smith sat down to stunned silence from her colleagues, while isolated applause echoed from the visitors' gallery above. She braced herself for what she assumed would be Senator McCarthy's angry defense of his position. But none came. With his face white and drawn, McCarthy pulled his bulky frame out of his seat and walked quietly out the door. The bully had been stood down.

It would be four years until the rest of the Senate would finally censure Joe McCarthy, but Senator Margaret Chase Smith's independent Declaration of Conscience was the first action to cast forward the tiny ripples of hope that would lead to this American demagogue's undoing. She received both criticism and praise at the time, with conservative newspapers such as the *Chicago Tribune* mercilessly attacking her as unpatriotic. She was derided as "the Red Witch of the Senate," but her office was flooded with letters from the public that were 8 to 1 in support of her stand.[4]

Ten days later, the papers were still discussing the impact and ramifications of her speech. In an article titled "G.O.P. Progressives Want 'Dynamic Conservatism,' " the *New York Times* wrote:

Senator Margaret Chase Smith's recent speech on the Senate floor did more than castigate Senator Joseph R. McCarthy for his methods in charging Communist infiltration in government. What Mrs. Smith did was to thrust a warning finger under the noses of the Republican leaders and demand—again—that they readjust their thinking to the realities of present-day political life. She re-emphasized, in peculiarly dramatic and effective fashion, the mounting impatience and rebelliousness of many Republicans against the implacable conservatism that has become the party's symbol. . . . They want it to become a party of constructive opposition as long as it is in the minority, and a party of dynamic conservatism when and if it gains the majority. What, above all, they do not want is that the Republican Party shall deteriorate into angry, impotent obstructionism."[5]

As she would during all of her thirty-three-year congressional career, Margaret Chase Smith had defied her critics and defenders of the status quo. She was a rebel, a maverick who famously said, "When people tell you that you can't do something, you kind of want to try it."

Overcoming adversity came naturally to her. Born in 1897, Margaret Chase was the eldest of six children born to the local barber in Skowhegan, Maine, who ran his shop out of the back of their house. While in high school, she worked as a telephone operator: After graduation, she worked as a teacher in a one-room schoolhouse with a woodstove for $8.50 a week, and later as a circulation manager for the *Independent Reporter* newspaper. In 1930, at the age of thirty-two, she married the newspaper's publisher, Clyde W. Smith, who was fifty-five years old. Three years later, Clyde Smith was elected to Congress and brought his young wife along to serve as his executive secretary, where she researched policy and reached out to constituents. In 1940, Clyde Smith suffered a massive heart attack and hovered in and out of consciousness for three days. In a moment of lucidity, he announced to those clustered around his deathbed that it was his wish that voters elect his "partner in public life" as his successor. Margaret Chase Smith won the special election by a 2 to 1 ratio.

In Congress, the bright-eyed, silver-haired "Lady from Maine" with the signature single red rose in her lapel focused on defense issues, served on the House Naval Affairs Committee during the Second World War, and was pivotal in securing a permanent role for women in the military, including equal pay for equal rank. She decided to run for the Senate after a lunch in which a friend, television journalist May Craig, offered this bit of unsolicited advice: "Margaret, you have reached your peak—you can go no further—so you must adjust yourself to going downhill from now on." Margaret later recalled that "instead of resigning myself to going downhill, I determined to go up."[6]

Her decision was met with derision. Massachusetts senator Leverett Saltonstall, a fellow liberal Republican from a neighboring state, publicly predicted that she would go down to defeat.

Facing a crowded field—which included a popular incumbent governor, Horace Hildreth; former governor Sumner Sewall; and a prominent local minister, the Reverend Albion Beverage—she defeated all of them, winning the general election by over 70 percent. More than a decade later, she would replace Senator Saltonstall of Massachusetts as chairman of the Senate Republican Conference and become the ranking Republican on the Senate Armed Services Committee.

Margaret's decisive victory in a year when Harry Truman snuck past Tom Dewey made her an instant Republican celebrity. Her sense of humor also made good newspaper copy; when asked what she would do if she woke up one day in the White House, she reportedly replied, "I'd go straight to Mrs. Truman and apologize; then I'd go home."[7]

Her charm and evident intelligence drew the attention of another junior GOP senator with a reputation as a giant killer—Wisconsin's Joe McCarthy. He had also worked his way up from poverty, been educated in a one-room schoolhouse, and beaten the odds with bold choices about who he would run against. In 1939, at the age of thirty—just four years out of law school—McCarthy had successfully challenged a twenty-four-year judicial incumbent on the Tenth Circuit. He was censured by the Wisconsin Supreme Court for destroying court documents, then took a leave of absence from his post to become a first lieutenant in the U.S. Marines. Stationed in the Pacific, McCarthy served in several combat bombing missions, although he was never wounded as he later claimed. In 1946, campaigning on his war record as "Tail-Gunner Joe," he challenged the incumbent Robert M. La Follette Jr. for the Republican Senate nomination. La Follette had served as a senator for twenty-one years, enjoying high name recognition and real affection as the son of the legendary "Fighting Bob" La Follette. But La Follette Jr. had alienated many rank-and-file Republicans by recently switching back to the GOP after serving as a leader in the Progressive Party for many years. Conservatives backed McCarthy, and their young candidate threw himself into a typically energetic and vitriolic campaign. McCarthy beat La Follette by a narrow margin, and then easily defeated the Democratic candidate in the general election. At age thirty-eight, he was the youngest new member of the Senate, and his gregarious if slightly overbearing personality—fueled by increasing amounts of hard liquor—made him popular among many colleagues. When Margaret Chase Smith arrived in the Senate two years later in 1949, he tried to befriend her and publicly stated that she would make an excellent candidate for vice president in 1952.

As the 1940s turned into the 1950s, it was becoming apparent that Communism had replaced Fascism as the greatest threat to freedom. Stalin had brought his Iron Curtain down over the countries in Eastern Europe. Mao was triumphant—prompting calls of "Who lost China?" directed at the State Department—while Communist North Korea was on the verge of invading its democratic neighbor to the south. The Soviets' development of the H-bomb, and the subsequent revelation that they had received vital information from spies in America, created a fertile field for concern about Communist infiltration into a democratic society. Joe McCarthy thought of himself as a patriot, but he also saw a political opportunity, and he took it.

On February 9, 1950, before the Ohio County Republican Women in Wheeling, West Virginia, McCarthy announced in front of the whirr of television cameras: "I have here in my hand a list of 205 Communist agents in the Truman Administration . . . known to the Secretary of State and who nevertheless are still working and shaping the policy of the State Department."[8] At a speech less than a week later in Reno, Nevada, McCarthy sent a telegram to President

Truman demanding that the State Department's loyalty files be re-opened or he would label the Democratic Party as "the bedfellow of international Communism."[9]

This was big news, and—at the time—effective politics. When Joe McCarthy returned to Washington, D.C., his name was on everybody's lips and a new term was born—"McCarthyism," defined by the senator as "Americanism with its sleeves rolled up." He began giving inflammatory and highly publicized speeches on the floor of the Senate while brandishing a "photostatic copy" of the names of the Communist agents in the State Department. He would not, however, turn over those names, preferring to hold them as moral and psychological collateral over his detractors.

Margaret Chase Smith began attending his speeches on the Senate floor. The two senators had a good relationship on the Executive Expenditures Committee and the Senate investigations subcommittee. When McCarthy first began giving his anticommunist speeches on the floor of the Senate, Smith felt that they had the ring of authenticity and was inclined to believe him. But as the charges increased in ferocity, even though evidence was still not forthcoming, Smith began to think that Joe McCarthy posed a great danger to American democracy. "McCarthy had created an atmosphere of such political fear that people were not only afraid to talk but they were afraid of whom they might be seen with," she later wrote.[10] "Distrust became so widespread that many dared not accept dinner invitations, lest at some future date McCarthy might level unproved charges against someone invited to the same dinner party . . . but I was reluctant to respond to requests that I speak out and challenge McCarthy. In the first place, I was a freshman senator—and in those days, freshman senators were to be seen and not heard, like good children. In the second place, it was clear that he should be challenged by Democratic senators speaking in defense of the Democratic Administration, the Democratic president, the Democratic Secretary of State."[11] Margaret Chase Smith waited, but no such challenge came. In the end, she concluded, "Someone had to do it."[12]

She began working on her speech in secret, soliciting advice from a small group of liberal Republican senators and respected columnists such as Walter Lippmann, but she swore secrecy from all of them, and kept news of her speech secret from conservative Republican senators, lest they tell Republican Senate majority leader Robert Taft, who might try to use his power to intervene on McCarthy's behalf.

On June 1, on the way to the Senate floor with her speech in hand, she asked her press secretary not to release her remarks to journalists until she had been speaking for two minutes, just in case nervousness got the best of her. After she told McCarthy of her intention to speak out against him minutes before her speech, his previously friendly demeanor grew cold quickly. "Just remember," he threatened, "I control Wisconsin's delegation to the convention and I'll see to it you don't get any votes for Vice President."[13]

Her fifteen-minute speech, which was later considered one of the finest speeches given on the floor of the Senate during the twentieth century, was not appreciated by many of her colleagues. Few tried to intervene when McCarthy removed her—in violation of decades of Senate protocol—from the investigations subcommittee, replacing her with a more compliant junior senator from California named Richard M. Nixon. Smith and her six cosignatories on the declaration were derided by McCarthy as "Snow White and the Six Dwarves." And while it took four years for the rest of the Senate to take action against Joe McCarthy, her stand was a shot across the bow of the anticommunist movement's drift toward totalitarianism here at home. The fact that she was a Republican made her criticism of McCarthy more credible than if a Democrat had done so in defense of the Truman administration.

Many conservative Republicans never forgave her for publicly dividing the party against their most prominent voice at a moment when they still controlled the Senate. Facing the subtle rebuke of conservative colleagues, Smith increased her profile and independence by recording news reports for Edward R. Murrow's *See It Now* television program during her self-financed trip to meet leaders from twenty-three countries around the world. She returned to Washington to offer an affirmative voice on the Senate vote to formally censure Joe McCarthy. The senator from Wisconsin would die of alcohol and ulcer-fueled illness three years later.

Nineteen fifty-four brought another sweet victory to Margaret Chase Smith. Conservative Republicans led by McCarthy selected, financed, endorsed, and campaigned for a right-wing candidate named Robert L. Jones to challenge her in the Republican primary. She defeated Jones overwhelmingly, receiving five times as many votes, winning 623 of 626 precincts. *Time* magazine weighed in on the magnitude of her victory, saying that "Maggie Smith is one of the most formidable vote getters Maine ever saw, as well as one of the most valuable senators now in Washington."[14]

She was now on her way to setting a new record with 2,941 consecutive Senate roll call votes—a record that would stand until 1981. When asked about her stamina, Smith joked: "There are morning people and there are night people. I'm both."[15] She was establishing herself as a leader of the dozen progressive Republicans in the Senate. Denounced by both conservatives and liberals, she angered unions by voting for the Taft-Hartley Labor Relations Act, then upset right-wingers by voting against the creation of a permanent Un-American Activities Committee. Smith supported Democratic measures such as increasing the minimum wage and increasing federal aid to education, but during election time the self-described "moderate" and "independent" voted like a GOP regular.

Her philosophy of the proper role of the opposition party was well expressed by the 1950 *New York Times* article "G.O.P. Progressives Want 'Dynamic Conservatism' ": "Their view is to accept the inevitability of political evolution and to move forward intelligently to meet it. This is as possible for a party in the minority as it is for one in the majority. In many respects, the minority position has certain tangible advantages. The majority can do the wrong thing; its plans and its calculations can misfire. A constructive opposition is then in a position to move in with a workable alternative and reap the credit. Simply to criticize and gloat over the majority's failures is, they contend, to waste a golden opportunity."[16] Vermont senator George Aiken, a fellow progressive Republican and cosignatory of the Declaration of Conscience, memorably expressed this outlook by explaining: "If a Democrat says we need better health, I'm not going to come out for poorer health just to disagree with him."[17]

In 1956, Margaret Chase Smith supported Eisenhower for reelection, but took the then-unthinkable step of suggesting that some of Democratic nominee Adlai Stevenson's policies were worth examining, saying that "giving credit to the political opposition may be heresy, but it's honest, and in the long run, honesty is good politics."[18] In 1960, Smith won reelection by the largest percentage of any Republican senatorial candidate in the nation.

She had served in Congress with distinction for twenty years, and now she began to take the revolutionary step of running for the highest office herself. After all, when financier Bernard Baruch read her speech against McCarthy he declared, "If a man had made the Declaration of Conscience, he would be the next President of the United States." While she supported many of the Kennedy administration's domestic policies, she was a critic of the new president's foreign policy. A lifelong defender of peace through strength, she warned that the White House would have to take a harder line against Khrushchev—by staying ahead of the Soviets in the nuclear arms race—or risk being run over by the USSR. When Khrushchev heard about her comments, he called her "the devil in disguise of a woman." Margaret Chase Smith took it in stride. "Mr. Khrushchev really isn't angry at me," she explained. "I am not that important. He is angry because American officials have grown more firm since my speech."[19]

From her position on the Senate Armed Services Committee, she was quick enough and wise enough to question whether Secretary of Defense Robert McNamara was being forthcoming about the administration's steady expansion of troops in Vietnam, stating: "I fear that the American people are ahead of their leaders in realism and courage—but behind them in knowledge of the facts because the facts have not been given to them."[20]

But perhaps her finest moment on the Armed Services Committee occurred in May of 1961, when she learned that an air force missile base on Presque Isle in Maine would be closed as part of long-anticipated military cutbacks.

"The far easier course for me to pursue politically would be to vigorously protest this action and, as a Republican Senator, to point out that the decision was made by a Democratic president, and to make a political attack on the decision of President Kennedy," she stated. "The far safer course for me to pursue politically would be to demand the outmoded [missile] program be continued, so that the Presque Isle Air Force Base be kept operating, to aid the economy of the area and to avoid the impact and dislocation its closing is bound to have on the economy of the area. But in all good conscience I cannot do this, for this would simply be playing politics with our national security, our national defense, and our taxpayers' dollars. It would be submitting to the economic philosophy that our national defense establishment and our national security program must be operated primarily for the local economy."[21] It was a rare senatorial stand against self-interest and pork-barrel politics that benefited one's own district.

The courage and content of Margaret Chase Smith's time in office was drawing attention and respect from both sides of the aisle. "You know," said Georgia's Democratic senator Richard Russell, "she's just ornery enough that if she were a man she would make a hell of a good president." One week before his death, President Kennedy assessed the prospects of running against her for reelection, described her as "a very formidable political figure," and said he would not look forward to campaigning against her.[22] On November 22, 1963, when his assassination in Dallas was announced, Margaret Chase Smith left a single red rose on the wooden desk Kennedy had used during his eight years as a senator.

With Arizona's conservative senator Barry Goldwater the leading candidate for the Republican nomination, Margaret Chase Smith decided that moderates needed a voice more than ever, and it might as well be her. The Gallup Poll found that in a presidential race, only 57 percent of the public said they would vote for a woman, compared to 84 percent for a Catholic and 77 percent for a Jewish candidate.[23] Movie actress Sandra Dee offered this assessment of Smith's candidacy: "I wouldn't respect a woman's opinion on world affairs as much as a man's. It's the man's right to make the major decisions."[24] Sexism—both petty and overt—had always been a hurdle Margaret Chase Smith had to clear while running for office. In her first campaign for Congress in 1940, she'd been frustrated by the newspapers' constant attention to the dresses she was wearing and how her hair was styled. "Isn't a woman a human being?" she would ask. "Why can't she be just a person?"[25] When she first ran for the Senate in 1948, syndicated columnist Leonora Ross attributed her broad popularity to the fact that "she is lacking in the usual feminine faults of evasion, little deceptions and petty personality."[26] On June 1, 1950, when Margaret Chase Smith was taking on Joe McCarthy in the Senate, the newspapers of that day were running an ad that featured Kate Smith advising housewives that Cain's mayonnaise would most definitely give their potato salad "Man Appeal."[27] Smith always subscribed to a matter-of-fact approach to her pioneering role in the Senate, characteristically disdaining the limitations that others would place upon her. "I never went into something as a woman, but as a person," she said.[28] "I was treated fairly in the Senate not because of equal rights but because of seniority."[29] Toward the end of her life, she summed up her feelings on the matter by saying simply, "I have a different feeling from others. I think women are people. Women have come a long way in 40 years, and it's time to look upon them for their achievements, not their sex."[30]

On January 27, 1964, Margaret Chase Smith—then sixty-six years old—called a press conference at the Mayflower Hotel in Washington and announced her intention to run for the presidency. She described to the attending press her reasons for finally deciding to run. Chief among these were "an opportunity to break the barrier against women being seriously considered for the Presidency of the United States." Noting that she had accumulated more national political experience than any other candidate, she said that she hoped her candidacy would "destroy any political bigotry against women . . . just as the late John F. Kennedy had broken the political barrier on religion." Almost as important was her conviction that her candidacy would give "voters a wider range of choice—specifically a choice other than that of conservative or liberal—to give those who consider themselves to be moderates or middle-of-the-road advocates a chance to cast an unqualified vote instead of having to vote conservative or liberal."[31] Finally, she contended that "because I do not have unlimited financial resources or a tremendous political machine or backing from power bosses," she would benefit from the "political independence for not having such resources."[32]

She set out campaigning in the snows of New Hampshire and the cold plains of Illinois, sticking to her characteristic refusal of all donations and carrying her message of liberal domestic policies and a strong national defense. She spent just $250 of her own money to compete in the New Hampshire primary, and only $85 in Illinois, where she gained a respectable third-place showing. At the Republican convention at San Francisco's Cow Palace, Senator George Aiken of Vermont nominated her for the presidency, stressing her independence, achievement, and integrity. Aiken pointed out that only candidates not beholden to campaign contributors could be counted on to do entirely what they thought was right. "She took every big check—every little check—every $10 bill, every $1 bill and every penny and sent them straight back to where they came from," he said. "My candidate wants the nomination solely on her record and her qualifications for the job." Senator Margaret Chase Smith received the support of twenty-seven delegates for the presidency. She refused to release her delegates to Senator Goldwater, to avoid giving him the party's unanimous support, and became the first woman ever nominated for president by a major political party in America. Of course, as Smith had warned, Goldwater's hard-line conservatism went down to a crushing defeat that November.

The Republican Party was turning away from the liberal tradition of Abraham Lincoln that Margaret Chase Smith so strongly identified with. In 1966, she was the only Republican to win statewide office in Maine, securing over 70 percent of the votes cast for the third consecutive election. Her independence made her far more popular than her party.

But as riots over the war in Vietnam tore the country's social fabric apart, Margaret Chase Smith watched on with a sense of disillusion and despair. She had never liked Richard Nixon personally, never trusted him, but she supported the expansion of the war into Cambodia in the hopes of ending it through decisive military action. While her fellow senator from Maine, Democrat Ed Muskie, was gaining praise for his criticisms of the war and Nixon, Margaret

Chase Smith was persona non grata on many college campuses, despite the rise of feminism. The shooting of rioting students at Kent State by the National Guard in May 1970 increased the pressure surrounding the protests, which had been escalating since the Democratic convention in Chicago in 1968. The Nixon administration's apparent callousness to the deaths of the protesters (Nixon had been caught on tape referring to the students as "bums") heightened tensions further.

Smith had been urged to give another Declaration of Conscience many times over the course of her career, but she had always declined, concerned that the requests were self-serving and partisan. But as May headed toward June, Margaret Chase Smith decided that time was right for a follow-up to her landmark 1950 speech. On June 1—the twentieth anniversary of the first Declaration of Conscience—the silver-haired lady from Maine rose to give her second and final Declaration of Conscience.

. . . I spoke as I did 20 years ago because of what I considered to be the great threat from the radical right—the threat of a government of repression.

I speak today because of what I considered to be the great threat from the radical left that advocates and practices violence and defiance of the law . . .

Extremism bent upon polarization of our people is increasingly forcing upon the American people the narrow choice between anarchy and repression.

And make no mistake about it, if that narrow choice has to be made, the American people, even if with reluctance and misgiving, will choose repression.

Ironically, the excesses of dissent on the extreme left can result in repression of dissent. For repression is preferable to anarchy and nihilism to most Americans. Yet, excesses on the extreme right, such as those 20 years ago, can mute our national conscience.

As was the case 20 years ago when the Senate was silenced and politically intimidated by one of its Members, so today many Americans are intimidated and made mute by the emotional violence of the extreme left . . .

It is time that the great center of our people, those who reject the violence and unreasonableness of both the extreme right and the extreme left, searched their consciences, mustered their moral and physical courage, shed their intimidated silence, and declared their consciences.

It is time that with dignity, firmness and friendliness, they reason with, rather than capitulate to, the extremists on both sides—at all levels—and caution that their patience ends at the border of violence and anarchy that threatens our American democracy."[33]

The pendulum of American politics had swung from the hard right of McCarthyism to the far left of street violence and campus riots. Free from ideological blinders, Margaret Chase Smith was able to see clearly the apparently separate, but ultimately symbiotic, threats that both extremes represented to the integrity of our democracy.

Once again, the *New York Times* was outspoken in its support of her speech.

As she did twenty years ago in her "declaration of conscience" against the right-wing excesses of Senator Joseph R. McCarthy, Senator Margaret Chase Smith is attempting to rally the country to moderation and good sense. One can only hope profoundly that it will not take four years this time for her counsel to be heeded. The basic message of the Senator from Maine is that the deep pool of centrist opinion in the country, that essential guarantee against violent political upheavals, is being dangerously shaken. Primarily the threat this time is from the "radical left that advocates and practices violence and defiance of the law." But beyond that present danger lurks the threat of repression, just beginning to show itself in a governmental defense that is "too extreme and unfair and too repetitive." One feeds on the other.[34]

The two Declarations of Conscience bookended her distinguished senatorial career, providing parallel criticisms of excesses in different eras in American culture. In 1972, Margaret Chase Smith was narrowly retired from office in her attempt to secure a fifth term at the age of seventy-five. She returned to her hometown of Skowhegan, Maine—beautifully described by the *Boston Globe* as a place "where the sky is clear and the stars are crisp and on a windless night, from the paper mill at the edge of town, plumes of smoke rise vertically into an ivory moon."[35] There, in her modest white shingle home, she held court before journalists and politicians who came to listen to her perspective. "America has not been made great from Pennsylvania Avenue," she would say, "but from main streets and country-sides, and the more I serve in Washington and the more I see of the world the dearer my small hometown is to me."[36]

She lived in Skowhegan until she died in 1995 at the age of ninety-seven. She left behind an adoring state, an admiring nation, and an enduring legacy that embodied her belief that "public service must be more than doing a job efficiently and honestly. It must be a complete dedication to the people and to the nation with full recognition that every human being is entitled to courtesy and consideration, that constructive criticism is not only to be expected but sought, that smears are not only to be expected but fought, that honor is to be earned but not bought."[37]

Perhaps the best measure of Margaret Chase Smith's influence is the fact that thirty years after she left office, Maine's senators are both liberal Republican women, both outstanding moderates: Olympia Snowe and Susan Collins. They got to the Senate on their own, but they stand on the shoulders of a giant. About her distinguished predecessor, Senator Collins reflected: "She recognized that it is only through civil discourse and a spirit of cooperation that the people's business gets done."

SENATOR
EDWARD W. BROOKE — 1973
STUCK IN THE MIDDLE OF THE CIVIL RIGHTS MOVEMENT

We must reject separatism from whatever source. We must reject white separatism. We must reject black separatism. We must hold true to the course on which we have embarked—the course which leads to an integrated society of magnificent pluralism.

—SENATOR EDWARD W. BROOKE[1]

On a bright June day in 1969, Republican Senator Edward Brooke—the first African-American to be elected by popular vote to the U.S. Senate and the first to be seated since Reconstruction—gave the commencement address at Wellesley College. Future first lady and U.S. senator Hillary Rodham was sitting among the graduating class, waiting to give the student speech after Senator Brooke completed his remarks.

Three years before, this former "Goldwater Girl" and president of the Wellesley Young Republicans Club had volunteered for Massachusetts attorney general Ed Brooke's underdog campaign for the Senate. Now, as he spoke, she seethed. In the aftermath of the assassinations of Martin Luther King and Robert F. Kennedy the year before, campus politics had become radicalized, while Senator Brooke remained committed to the principle of moderation.

Wearing the honorary cap and gown, Brooke surveyed the Class of 1969 and spoke of the social discord occurring throughout the nation, stating:

> Protest movements reflect and stimulate the healthy self-criticism taking place throughout the nation . . . racial and social injustice is being seen in concrete terms, as a root cause of human misery and as a principal obstacle to the further development of this nation. Poverty, hunger, unemployment, inferior education, inadequate health care—these grave inequities are now being recognized for what they are—the responsibility of society as a whole as well as the individual . . . It behooves the disciples of politics as protest to reconsider the alleged merits of coercive tactics. By now they should be able to see that, apart from being morally unsupportable, such methods are politically ineffective.[2]

But young Hillary Rodham felt that Senator Brooke's commencement address did not deal directly with the issues affecting her generation. After he spoke, she strode to the podium, put aside her prepared text, and launched an attack against the man she had helped put into office three years before. "Part of the problem with empathy for professed goals is that empathy doesn't do anything," she explained. "We've had lots of empathy; we've had lots of sympathy, but we feel that for too long our leaders have used politics as the art of the possible. And the challenge now is to practice politics as the art of making what appears to be impossible, possible. . . . We're not interested in social reconstruction; it's human reconstruction."[3]

Student response to the senator had been polite; but the Class of 1969 jumped to its feet to applaud Hillary Rodham. Afterward, several guests approached Senator Brooke and apologized for the student's rudeness. He downplayed the incident and later reflected, "It didn't hurt me that she said those things. She was speaking as a student and I was speaking as a United States senator. We were coming from different perspectives."[4]

Understanding different perspectives was Ed Brooke's forte—he'd been elected to the Senate from a state with less than a 3 percent African-American population, where only one out of every ten voters was a Republican. This political miracle should have been a hero to the generation raised during the civil rights revolution. But some saw him as an enemy, insufficiently radical and thus part of the larger problem. Black militants called him an Uncle Tom, while to establishment racists and segregationists he was just a "pushy nigger." He was decried as "too white to be black and too black to be white."[5] Instead of screaming back, Brooke let his actions and accomplishments lead the sometimes wearying fight against what he saw as "extremists of black power and white power."[6] A quiet profile in courage, Senator Edward Brooke was stuck squarely in the middle of the civil rights struggle.

Race remains an American obsession, and Ed Brooke is an underappreciated pioneer in African-American electoral politics. But he refused to conform to anyone's idea of how a black politician should behave: He was an outspoken moderate Republican who sought to return his party to its roots, an innovative policy reformer, and a uniter—a believer in reconciliation and mutual respect—at a time when dividers dominated America's uneasy dialogue on race. Consequently, this classic American success story—Second World War combat veteran, Massachusetts state attorney general, and U.S. senator who reportedly twice turned down a spot on the Supreme Court—has been too quickly forgotten.

Tragically ahead of his time, Ed Brooke knew who he was, took America at its word, and never doubted that there was a place at the table for him: "I was an American before I was a Republican, and I believe I'm an American before I'm a black man. I love this country—I don't want to see this country torn asunder."[7]

Brooke grew up in segregated Washington, D.C., the son of a middle-class government lawyer. He attended Howard University, joined the ROTC, and when the Japanese attacked Pearl Harbor he was called into the army as a second lieutenant in the all-black 366th Combat Infantry Regiment. On the front lines in Italy, Brooke was decorated for leading a daring daylight attack on a hilltop artillery outpost and was later promoted to captain. Under fire and amid high casualties, some of the men under Brooke's command began to question why they were fighting this war for freedom in a segregated unit: "It's supposed to be a war against Nazis—and against racism and for democracy." In his 1966 book *The Challenge of Change,* Brooke recalled some of the men asking, " 'Why are black men fighting a white man's war? What's all this double talk about democracy?' They were not easy questions to answer. I tried to explain that the first task was to defeat the common enemy. And I asked them to bear with America's racial injustice until the war was won. But I knew that this was no more than rationalization."

Because he had studied Latin in school, Brooke was able to pick up the Italian language quickly and served as an army liaison to the Italian resistance. In his free time, he used his language skills to meet Remigia Ferrari-Scacco, the daughter of a wealthy Genovese paper merchant. After VE-Day, during the three months that Brooke waited to ship back to the United States, they began to see each other seriously, and they continued the romance through the mail after he left Italy. He went home and joined some friends studying at Boston University Law School and ascended to editor of the law review. He was later joined by Remigia and they were married in Boston in 1947.

Ed Brooke was twenty-six before he began studying law and nearly thirty before he ever cast a vote—which residents of the District of Columbia were denied. Now an attorney, he set up a law practice in the rapidly evolving neighborhood of Roxbury, Massachusetts, comprised of Irish, Jews, and African-Americans. In 1950, some friends encouraged him to stand for election in their local Ward 12. Because he had never voted before, Brooke debated which party to join. "My father and my mother both voted Republican because it was the party of Lincoln . . . because it was the party of African-Americans and minorities and the party of hope,"[8] Brooke reflected. But Boston was effectively a one-party town. Taking advantage of the last year in which cross-filing was possible, Ed Brooke registered to run for both the Republican and Democratic nominations. He won the Republican nomination but lost the general election; from then on, Ed Brooke was a Republican.

He ran again the next year, but Brooke was discouraged by disapproval from both the white and black communities in Roxbury at his interracial marriage. Although he continued to be active in the local chapters of the NAACP, the Crispus Attucks Club—named for the Revolutionary-era free black man who was murdered by British troops in Boston, becoming among the first casualties in the War for Independence—and the American Veterans of World War II (in which he was elected state commander and later national judge advocate), Brooke swore off direct involvement in electoral politics. Nonetheless, the presence of a black Republican running for office in Boston was not quickly forgotten, and the notorious former mayor and governor James Michael Curley sent Brooke an autographed copy of his biography, *The Purple Shamrock,* with the following inscription: "Don't get discouraged. You are destined for a successful career in politics."[9]

Brooke's opportunity came eight years later, when the Massachusetts Republican Party realized that it would have to adapt or die. Their traditional base of wealthy WASP voters had dwindled to influential minority status as the ranks of Catholics and recent immigrants overwhelmed these patricians, resulting in the Republicans' resounding defeats in recent elections. To remain relevant, they would have to expand the franchise. In 1960, they nominated a Roman Catholic Italian American, John Volpe, for governor and Ed Brooke for secretary of state. At the nominating convention, Brooke made the case for his membership in the Republican Party: "We will show the people of Massachusetts that we are an united party and that we will destroy the myths of class, race, creed, wealth, anti-labor, suburbia, which the Democratic Party has attempted to shackle us with. It is not the Democratic Party—it is the Republican Party which is truly the party of the people, the party of Lincoln."[10]

For many people, Ed Brooke's candidacy placed him in the role of spokesman for his race; but Ed Brooke felt more comfortable speaking for all of the people, not just his 20 million fellow African-Americans. Still, he felt compelled to speak out about the amount of time both parties spent debating their stance on civil rights. "It is unfortunate in 1960 that so much time must be spent on the fight for a strong Civil Rights plank, when Civil Rights are guaranteed by the Constitution . . . and the platform is merely a reaffirmation of our principle 'with liberty and justice for all . . . no platform can be acceptable to the American people which does not give meaning to those words.'"[11] In classic Centrist fashion, Brooke brought perspective to a contentious issue by connecting it directly with the nation's founding principles.

His opponent, Democrat Kevin White, caused a minor stir when his campaign slogan "Vote White" drew predictable accusations of race baiting (at the candidate's request, these signs were quickly changed to read "Vote Kevin White"). Brooke was unable to come up with enough votes to go over the top in the Massachusetts landslide for John F. Kennedy. Republican governor John Volpe offered Brooke his choice of state appointments, and Brooke surprised many people by requesting that he be placed at the head of the Boston Finance Commission, a moribund watchdog group directed to fight local corruption. Ed Brooke reinvigorated the commission with a series of aggressive high-profile investigations that made government officials nervous and reporters take notice. Two years later, he was ready to try for statewide office again.

In 1962, Ed Brooke declared his candidacy for Massachusetts state attorney general when the incumbent, Edward McCormick, decided to challenge Ted Kennedy for JFK's old Senate seat. But all was not smooth sailing for Ed Brooke: Eisenhower administration alumnus and Boston Brahmin Elliot Richardson was heavily favored by party power brokers to be the Republican nominee for attorney general. They urged Brooke to accept a judgeship or even the less powerful position of lieutenant governor, but he refused and unleashed an aggressive campaign, narrowly defeating Richardson on the second ballot at the nominating convention, and by a far wider margin when Richardson challenged him in the primary.

The next battle was in the general election. Brooke now faced Democrat Frank Kelly and, armed with a cross-party endorsement from the liberal Americans for Democratic Action, was pulling ahead in the polls when Kelly supporters began playing the race card crudely, sending a car plastered with Brooke stickers and "filled with flamboyantly dressed, half drunk, cursing blacks into fashionable suburbs, boisterously inquiring about houses for sale. They loudly and obscenely told realtors that they'd been sent to find a suitable house for Ed Brooke, the next Attorney General."[12] Anonymous notes began appearing under voters' front doors that read: "Do you want a nigger as your next Governor?"[13]

These desperate and despicable ploys backfired; money began pouring into the Brooke campaign headquarters as wealthy Bostonians sought to distance themselves from a dirty campaign. Local newspapers unaccustomed to endorsing Republicans endorsed Brooke, describing Kelly as "a discredited political hack with a record and platform so bad that his embarrassed colleagues on the Democratic ticket are trying to pretend he doesn't exist."[14] Brooke did not rest on the momentum created by the high-profile endorsements; he campaigned hard—"like a Democrat," *Time* noted approvingly, "at the factory gates by 5:30 A.M. waiting to shake hands."[15] With Jack Kennedy in the White House and Ted Kennedy running for Senate, it was another Democratic landslide year in Massachusetts, but this time Brooke was victorious. When President Kennedy, watching electoral returns in the White House, was notified of Brooke's impending victory, he said, "My God, that's the biggest news in the country."[16]

At the age of forty-two, after losing his three previous elections, Ed Brooke became the highest elected African-American official in the United States. At the time, virtually no African-Americans were running for statewide office anywhere in the country; considered a losing proposition and probably dangerous, it was just not done. But Ed Brooke's success—particularly in a state with a less than 3 percent black population—sent forth ripples of possibility that were felt far and wide. Soon Ed Brooke was receiving calls from African-Americans thinking of running for office from states across the country.[17] Eventually this trend would change the face of elected officials in America, but Ed Brooke was first.

With Bobby Kennedy as attorney general of the United States and Ed Brooke as attorney general of Massachusetts, the civil rights movement began gaining momentum, kicked into high gear with President Kennedy's televised address to the nation after the assassination of Medgar Evers. In Boston, school segregation came to the forefront with protests, sit-ins, and organized days when thousands of students skipped school. All eyes turned to Ed Brooke to see what he would do.

One cold afternoon he stared out his office window at a parade of protesters marching toward the statehouse across the snow-covered Boston Common. "You know I sympathize with them," he said while a reporter was in the room, "but I'm convinced that nothing I could do would harm the cause more than to conduct myself as a civil rights leader while I hold this office. I'm the lawyer for the 5 million citizens of Massachusetts, not only for its 50,000 Negroes."[18] His aide, Roger Woodworth, affirmed his boss's position: "The Attorney General isn't supposed to make decisions on the basis of pro-white or pro-negro, pro-Republican or pro-Democrat, pro–civil rights or anti–civil rights. If the law is on the books, he has to read it the way it's written."[19]

This was an emotionally unsatisfying position for many Boston area blacks. Brooke clashed with local civil rights leaders when he ruled against their request to place picket lines of truant students outside the local Board of Education. Brooke explained that state law required all children aged five to sixteen to stay in school unless they suffered mental or physical impairment, and he approved the school committee's plans to bring truant officers to the site and retrieve the absent students. This decision made local black militants like Cornell Eaton, chairman of the Boston Action Group, furious. "Brooke ain't nothing but an Uncle Tom," Eaton said. "He's too involved with the white power structure."[20]

This controversy drew attention from across the nation, prompting a black member of Illinois state legislature to weigh in: "Now, just by making a sober, honest judgment on how civil rights should be won, you can be called an Uncle Tom by anyone who disagrees. What does this do to Negro leadership? It demolishes it."[21]

Ed Brooke's style was to focus on results—not rhetoric. He quietly pressed ahead for equal justice and equal opportunity with an important set of legal victories. One of his first acts as attorney general was to file a brief in support of the Fair Housing Law, which banned discrimination in rental agreements statewide. He helped negotiate the integration of public housing in Boston, drafting an agreement that all the squabbling parties could sign. Eighteen other states added their signature to his brief supporting the constitutionality of the Voting Rights Act. He continued his crusade against government corruption and sent more than one hundred state and city employees to jail. But it was perhaps his judgment in the contentious issue of school prayer that best showed Ed Brooke's Centrist style.

When confronted with the Supreme Court's decision forbidding public classroom prayers, Brooke found a middle ground for Massachusetts that allowed teachers to begin the day with a moment of "reverent silence," but forbade prayer sessions to occur at any time during school itself. Vocal prayers were deemed permissible at graduation ceremonies, because attendance was optional and outside the educational process, and—against the wishes of the ACLU—Brooke determined that the observance of holy days such as Christmas, Easter, and Passover would continue in public schools if no single faith or orthodoxy was stressed. The powerful Roman Catholic periodical, the *Boston Pilot,* declared its support for Attorney General Ed Brooke's compromise, stating that "his opinion respects the U.S. Supreme Court decision, but carefully exempts those areas not included in it."[22]

Ed Brooke was developing a personal political philosophy that was as consistent as it was iconoclastic: a commitment to using power judiciously to forge compromise that allowed progress without prejudice.

As the conservative movement began to gain momentum with the nomination of Barry Goldwater in 1964, many people questioned why Ed Brooke would take the trouble to call himself a Republican when Massachusetts was so overwhelmingly Democratic and the civil rights movement had finally found its legislative champion in the presidency of Lyndon Johnson.

But Brooke preferred to look beyond the short-term currents and instead associated himself with the history of the Republican Party and its emphasis on the individual as the essential building block of society. He imagined that if Lincoln were alive today "he would lead a determined Republican attack on the problems of racial inequality, urban deterioration, and poverty here and abroad."[23] Brooke was also fond of quoting political journalist Theodore White, who observed that "it is forgotten how much of the architecture of America's liberal society was drafted by the Republicans . . . this is the party that abolished slavery, wrote the first laws of civil service, passed the first antitrust railway control, consumer-protection and conservation legislation, and then led America, with enormous diplomatic skill, out into that posture of global leadership and responsibility we now so desperately try to maintain . . . down through the first decade [of the twentieth century] the natural home of the American intellectual, writer, savant and artist was the Republican Party."[24] But Brooke's vision of an inclusive Republican Party received little support from party leaders.

Brooke publicly refused to endorse Barry Goldwater and ran for reelection that same year. While America rejected Goldwater's self-described extremism, Attorney General Edward Brooke was reelected overwhelmingly with the highest margin of any Republican candidate in the nation.

The lessons—both moral and practical—should have been clear. Goldwater had embraced states' rights in a thinly veiled attempt to attract southern segregationists and won only his native Arizona and five states in the Deep South—a near electoral shutout. In contrast, Brooke articulated an inclusive vision of the Republican Party, with liberal social aims achieved with a conservative emphasis on helping individuals help themselves. While voters around the nation overwhelmingly rejected Goldwater and the conservative movement, Ed Brooke was triumphant.

Almost immediately, Brooke began planning for a campaign that would have seemed impossible a decade earlier. Twenty-year Senate incumbent Leverett Saltonstall—the archetypal WASP statesman—was giving up his seat and Brooke decided he would throw his hat in the ring. In preparation for this challenge and in recognition of his unique ideological role within the Republican Party, Brooke had been busy writing *The Challenge of Change,* a political statement of purpose and a direct rebuke of the direction in which the Republican Party had been heading under Barry Goldwater.

In surveying the post-1964 political landscape, Brooke wrote, "Republicans have little cause for self-satisfaction now. We are weakened and wobbly—in a state of political exhaustion."[25] He decried a campaign that "made loyalty to ideology the supreme virtue, regardless of the damage inflicted upon the party. Moderates were excluded from high party councils . . . and the spirit of intra-party compromise was not so much violated as repudiated. Extremism was not only defended as a principle of good government; it was also practiced as a tactic of intra-party politics. Portraits of Presidents Lincoln and Eisenhower were removed from the offices of the Republican National Committee. This gesture symbolized the tone of the entire 1964 campaign."[26]

Brooke argued that the failed 1964 campaign was based on two Goldwater strategies, which Brooke termed Operations "Dixie" and "Backlash."

> [They] were developed in the hope that large numbers of Southerners motivated by anti civil rights (or anti Negro) sentiment would flock to the "new" Republican Party, and a huge backlash movement in normally Democratic cities containing heavy concentrations of Negroes would top off the electoral bonanza. These gambles reflected shamefully on the party's moral stature. Here was the party of Abraham Lincoln, as we are proud to call it, fighting for wrong on an absolutely clear-cut ethical issue—the issue of human dignity on which the Republican Party was founded. At best, Operations "Dixie" and "Backlash" were repudiations of the Lincoln tradition. At worst, they were appeals to naked racism. But the gambles also reflected a sophomoric approach to practical politics. They were based on wild miscalculation of the fundamental attitudes of the American people."[27]

Brooke cited polls taken by the liberal Republican Ripon Society in its report, *Election 1964,* which showed that "Senator Goldwater's position on Civil Rights alienated more voters than his position on any other domestic issue." With almost eerie prescience, Brooke took on the argument that the South represented a gold mine of potential support for the Republican Party, arguing that "our gains in the South not only should not, but cannot, be achieved on the basis of racism and segregation. For us, such votes are fool's gold."[28]

While repudiating extremists, Brooke was positioning himself as the most loyal of all Republicans—loyal to the party's original ideals—and he would campaign for the Senate in 1966 as a reformer, someone who would return the Republican Party from its recent radicalism back toward its concern for equal opportunity for all individuals. He backed up his historical analysis and contemporary commentary with a series of forward-looking policy proposals, including a negative income tax credit to help the working poor. He championed the need to build more affordable housing, advocated increases in the minimum wage and massive public expenditures to improve the quality of inner-city public education, argued against suburban "sprawl" before there was a name for it, and offered a vision of welfare reform that would take decades to be accepted and implemented.

Brooke was concerned that the Great Society's promotion of welfare diminished individual initiative and created an intergenerational cycle of dependence. This was far from conventional wisdom at the time. Brooke argued, "If you give a man a handout you establish a chain of dependence and lack of self-respect that won't be broken easily. If that is the situation of the grandfather, then the son, then the grandson, the great-grandson will probably be in the same desperate, dreary situation. But when a man wins self-respect, then everything else falls in place."[29] Regarding government programs, he wrote: "Unless a program is specifically designed to encourage the outcasts to engage in individual competition, it cannot be successful. But the Democrats have always been suspicious of individual enterprise. They are ill-equipped to reach the heart of our current problems—they prefer to deal with categories, groups, 'general welfare' programs rather than with the individual."[30] It would be several decades until the tragic effects of intergenerational dependence on welfare were established and led to the welfare reform act that Bill Clinton signed into law in 1996.

The Challenge of Change was published five weeks before the initial Republican primary. Brooke won easily and faced Democratic

Massachusetts governor Endicott "Chubb" Peabody in the general election. Few people gave him a serious chance to make history.

Brooke campaigned with an eye toward expanding his popularity. He announced that he would start his campaign in the towns of Blackstone and Millville, the only two towns he'd lost in his 1964 bid for reelection as attorney general. One morning while campaigning he met some opposition. "I don't want to meet Brooke," grumbled one man on the way to work. "But I want to meet you," said Brooke, and reached out his hand—which the other man took with something like grudging respect.

In the pivotal fall of 1966, the civil rights movement was shifting away from the self-evident moral clarity of integration as black separatism gained new prominence with the debut of Stokely Carmichael's "black power" speech, given at campuses from Berkeley to Boston. In this topsy-turvy environment, Governor Peabody argued that he would be a more staunch supporter of civil rights than Ed Brooke in the Senate. One Harvard professor confessed that his wife, a devoted white member of the NAACP, would be voting for "Chubb Peabody" because "Brooke's not Negro enough for her."[31]

Brooke consistently undercut stereotypes, speaking out against the war in Vietnam while his Democratic opponent supported the escalation implemented by President Johnson and encouraged by most Republicans. This brought many liberal Democrats and clergy over to Ed Brooke's side: The sixty-seven-member Committee of Religious Concern about Vietnam, representing congregations throughout the greater Boston area, endorsed Brooke "on the basis of religious conscience and moral conviction."[32]

But while liberals were flocking to Brooke's candidacy, conservatives were deserting him. Brooke appeared on national television, advocated an end to the Vietnam War, called for more money on social spending, and supported an increase in the minimum wage. In turn, a conservative youth group called the Massachusetts Committee to Preserve the Two-Party System began picketing during Brooke's speeches. Some conservatives called for supporting an independent candidate or even the Democratic nominee to block Brooke's election. But for every conservative who threatened to cross party lines as a protest of Brooke's alleged liberalism, many black and white Democrats were announcing their intention to vote for the moderate Republican attorney general. Eventually, a leader of the Committee to Preserve the Two-Party System, Daniel J. Carmen, changed his tune about Brooke, saying, "I'm very tired of hollow and wasteful efforts within the party that can only lead to self-defeat. There comes a time when we have to be absolutely realistic. If the party is going to work effectively, the two percent of extremists on either wing should either quit or come aboard."[33]

Brooke unified the Republican Party around his candidacy while continuing to make inroads against Peabody's traditional base through his qualified support of liberal policies and opposition to the Vietnam War. Like many candidates who find their territory taken by moderates, Chubb Peabody protested in vain: "He is trying to run my platform. He should resign from his own party."[34] In November, Ed Brooke beat Peabody with 61 percent of the vote.

Shortly after midnight on Election Day, Ed Brooke waded through the crowd of well-wishers, including Governor Volpe, and addressed the assembled fifteen hundred campaign workers, as well as the rest of the nation, while the television cameras rolled. He thanked Peabody; then, noting this was the first time that an African-American had been popularly elected to the Senate, he placed the day in historical context, saying:

The people . . . have answered all of the George Rockwells [president of the American Nazi Party], have answered all of the people who would divide us and who would keep men from being brothers; and I intend to merit their confidence and their support and their faith in me as a man . . . I am mindful of my pledge to Democrats and Independents as well as Republicans who have supported me, and I say to you that I go to Washington to do all that I can to give equal opportunity to all Americans; decent housing, a quality education, and equal justice under law; and I go to Washington to unite men who've never been united before and bring across this nation and across this world the brotherhood of man.[35]

Hopes and expectations could not have been higher; Brooke was considered the star of a new class of five moderate Republican senators—including Mark Hatfield of Oregon and Charles Percy of Illinois—whose election was interpreted as a repudiation of Goldwater's conservative wing of the party. Three months later, in January 1967, all eyes were on Ed Brooke as Senator Edward Kennedy walked him down the grand Senate aisle to present him to the vice president for his official swearing in. One reporter recalled that just four years before, Ted Kennedy had been presented by his senior senator, Leverett Saltonstall: the Irishman presented by the blue-blooded Yankee. Now the Irishman was introducing a black man to the highest corridors of power: "It is a sociopolitical progression that may have further presidential overtones."[36]

But perhaps the real sociopolitical progression going on that day was taking place between the warmth of the Senate chamber and the steps of Capitol Hill, which hung in a damp, cold fog. Harlem congressman Adam Clayton Powell had just been censured by his colleagues for corruption and forced to resign in disgrace. While Brooke was applauded by enthusiastic crowds of both whites and blacks ("I'm very proud today, God bless you"), Powell was surrounded by an angry mob, pushing reporters away and threatening to burn down the Capitol building, while Powell told his supporters they no longer had to pay taxes because Harlem no longer had a leader.[37]

Powell had served in Congress since 1944, allegedly enriching himself and taking extended vacations with secretaries on the island of Bimini, where he was fishing when he missed his chance to vote on the civil rights bill. Powell always argued against accommodation with white America, condemning advocates of integration, referring to Martin Luther King by the name Martin "Loser" King, and encouraging his supporters to throw eggs at King's limousine when the minister visited Harlem.

Extremists and cynics in the civil rights community harshly criticized Brooke because of his refusal to define himself primarily as a black leader. But Brooke's reply to these critics resonated with the vast majority of Americans: "If I did confine myself to Negro problems alone, there would hardly ever be another Negro elected to public office except from the ghetto—and understandably so."[38] Brooke was doing more than a thousand racial demagogues could in terms of moving civil rights forward in America by single-handedly desegregating the U.S. Senate.

Brooke approached the Senate with his characteristic combination of understatement and confidence. He was placed on the influential Banking Committee and served on the Aeronautical and Space Sciences Committee and later on the powerful Appropriations Committee as well, but he notably refused to join the Congressional Black Caucus in a widely misinterpreted refusal to label or limit himself.

Likewise, Brooke told the Republican leadership that he would not be voting in lockstep with the party line. "I will not have my vote taken for granted," he said. "I can be a team man, with the reservation that I can leave the team when I want to."[39] When reporters pressed Brooke to define his politics, he described himself as "a creative moderate," and "a liberal with a conservative bent."[40]

Brooke immediately became one of the most requested speakers in the nation, receiving more than 1,400 speaking invitations in his first two months in office, as well as more than 350 letters a day. In a high-profile speech before California Republicans, Brooke urged the Republican Party to become "broader and more creative," cautioning the party not to rely solely upon attacking big government and Communists for definition. "There is an obligation to propose rather than primarily to oppose," said Brooke.[41]

Propose he did, becoming known as "Mr. Housing" because of his tireless efforts to expand both public housing and home ownership. His Brooke Amendment successfully capped low-income subsidized rents at 25 percent of an individual's take-home pay. He was outspoken in his support for the need to expand access to abortions for poor women, and unrelenting in his efforts to end segregation in the nation's public schools, which included supporting school busing—a hot-button issue in Massachusetts that would devolve into riots during the 1970s. His combination of independence and activism put him in a unique position; as a contemporary biography of Brooke described, "Unlike many black leaders, Brooke has a power base in every state in the union because he's a temperate spokesman for both blacks and whites. Intent on winning allies rather than conquering enemies, he warns against violence while demanding constitutional rights through legislative and judicial process."[42]

In the summer of 1967, inner cities erupted in violence. Brooke felt that while the increasingly violent protests came out of "justifiable frustrations, they were playing into the hands of white racists, galvanizing the opposition and alienating allies."[43] In the middle of the worst riots, Brooke secretly met with militant black power leader H. Rap Brown, who was in hiding at the time and had requested that Brooke come alone to the meeting, which was held in a basement in Harlem. Unreported until Brooke recounted the scene in his still-unpublished memoirs, it was to be one of the most interesting meetings of opposites in the civil rights era.

Brooke wore his usual blue suit; H. Rap Brown and his self-styled revolutionary supporters were dressed in jeans and fatigues. Brown lost no time in lighting into Brooke: "You're not black. You are not one of us. You are part of the White establishment. You are what's wrong with America."[44]

Brooke calmly responded, "I am what I think is right for America and for all of us. I think what we want and what we need is to be part of the system, and change it for the betterment of our people. What's wrong with being in the U.S Senate at the seat of power? That's where the action is. That's where the power is. That's where we can get housing, jobs, education, and protection. That's where we can bring an end to police brutality. We need more of us there."[45]

Brooke told them that while he had experienced bigotry and hatred and corruption in America, "most Americans are good, decent, hardworking people, compassionate and concerned and we need reach out to them, not alienate them." As for black power, he asked, "What is power but the ability to change the basic conditions of life? Protest should aim to persuade not paralyze. Intemperance and intolerance serve no one, and hatred guarantees failure. It seems to me that black power is really self-defeating."[46]

Brooke and Brown debated for hours, disagreeing on every point, unable to come to a common ground. But that the discussion happened at all was significant.

In August, H. Rap Brown would join with Stokely Carmichael to call for an armed black revolution in the United States: Between 1967 and 1974, more than thirty police officers and civilians would be murdered by black militant groups.[47]

Ed Brooke returned to the Senate and continued his work the next year in developing the Fair Housing bill of 1968, a landmark federal law against housing discrimination.

In the 1968 presidential election, Brooke campaigned for Richard Nixon after moderate Michigan governor George Romney dropped out, declaring the Republican nominee to be "fundamentally a moderate" who would be an "aggressive, forceful and compassionate president," but advising him to add the word "justice" to his campaign litany of "law and order."

Nixon briefly considered Brooke for the vice presidency, but he was ultimately tapped to serve as chairman of the Republican National Convention in Miami Beach and given a prime-time spot in which to address the nation. Brooke's speech, "To Forge a New Unity," was reprinted in the periodical *Vital Speeches of the Day*.

"The Democratic Party," Brooke thundered in the Miami night,

has shown that it is at once feeble in inspiration and overbearing in application, intrusive in operation and incompetent in administration. . . . Americans have learned that the age of affluence is also the age of paradox. In a society of immense wealth, millions remain trapped in poverty. In a society where personal mobility has been a major factor of personal success, millions remain frozen in urban ghettos and rural backwaters. In a society dedicated to individual freedom, millions remain depressed by a social order in which personal liberty can perish through collective indifference . . . if people's lives are to be better they themselves must be directly engaged in planning and shaping their lives. The phrase "a hand-up not a handout" must be more than a slogan; it must be the governing maximum for public action in breaking the endless

cycle of poverty. This is the essence of Republican philosophy. . . .
We must reject separatism from whatever source. We must reject
white separatism. We must reject black separatism. We must hold
true to the course on which we have embarked—the course which
leads to an integrated society of magnificent pluralism.[48]

Ed Brooke's star was continuing its meteoric rise as the face of
black Republicans, a hopeful and quietly heroic figure. But when
Richard Nixon's administration took office in January 1969, Ed
Brooke quickly found himself fighting their "southern strategy."
Boston Globe reporter Matthew Storin wrote, "Brooke was wearing
the Republican colors with ease until the southern strategy began
to emerge."[49]

Against Brooke's urging, Nixon had begun to use the levers of
government to appropriate George Wallace's blue-collar southern
segregationist support in an attempt to expand the base of the
Republican Party. During the campaign, Nixon had pledged to appoint a southern "strict constructionist" in favor of states' rights to
the Supreme Court, and eight months into his term Nixon made
good on his promise. He nominated conservative South Carolina
judge Clement F. Haynsworth to take the Supreme Court seat of
Justice Abe Fortas, who had been forced to resign under threat of
impeachment after he'd been found to have concealed receiving a
$20,000 check from a financier who was later imprisoned. This had
traditionally been "the Jewish seat" on the Supreme Court ever
since Woodrow Wilson appointed Justice Louis Brandeis in 1916.
Nixon's decidedly non-Jewish and nonliberal appointment led to
opposition from the 13-million-member AFL-CIO. Questions were
raised about Haynsworth's commitment to civil rights and the quality of his legal decisions to date. Brooke initially declined to speak
out in public against Nixon's nomination, preferring instead to
write the president a letter: "My review of Judge Haynsworth's
record convinces me his treatment of civil rights issues is not in
keeping with the historic movement toward equal justice for every
American citizen." Brooke recommended that Nixon withdraw
Haynsworth's nomination from the Senate to avoid a defeat that
would "be extremely embarrassing for those of us who face a great

conflict between our principles and our sense of obligation to you." Brooke was choosing not to grandstand on this issue; instead, he was trying a conciliatory approach with the president he'd supported. But Nixon continued to push the nomination and Brooke, along with Senator Birch Bayh of Indiana, led the fight against confirmation. As Brooke predicted, Nixon was handed defeat by a vote of 55 to 44, with 17 Republicans voting against Haynsworth, including Ed Brooke.

Nixon was furious, blaming the liberal media and liberal Republicans, shattering the peace his aides had grown accustomed to during his first ten months in the Oval Office. Instead of backing down or moderating his course, Richard Nixon pushed harder, nominating the spectacularly unqualified federal judge Harrold Carswell of Georgia. South Carolina senator Fritz Hollings, who had been one of Haynsworth's strongest supporters, declared Carswell "not qualified to carry Judge Haynsworth's law books."[50] Conservative senator Roman Hruska of Nebraska memorably rose to Carswell's defense by readily acknowledging his intellectual limitations, then arguing that "there are a lot of mediocre judges and people and lawyers, and they are entitled to a little representation [on the Supreme Court], aren't they? We can't have all Brandeises, Frankfurters, and Cardozos and stuff like that."[51]

Two days after Carswell's nomination was put forward by the White House, rudimentary background investigations revealed that negative first impressions about the nominee's intellect and commitment to civil rights were firmly based in fact. In 1948, when Carswell was campaigning for a seat in the Georgia state legislature, he gave a speech to the American Legion in which he said, "I am a Southerner by ancestry, birth, training, inclination, belief and practice. I believe that segregation of the races is proper and the only practical and correct way of life in our states. I have always so believed and I shall always so act."[52]

Even after these words became public, the Nixon administration stood squarely behind Carswell: "You know," a White House aide confided, "the President really believes in that southern strategy more than he believes in anything else."[53] Brooke was angry with the administration he had helped put in office, especially in light of its recent dismissal of the Health, Education, and Welfare Department's civil rights chief, Leon Panetta.* Brooke had interviewed Panetta for his own staff and was impressed by the quality of his intellect and his commitment to integration. But Panetta's enthusiasm for desegregating southern schools ran counter to the Nixon administration's intentionally slow timetable for desegregation. The White House announced his resignation before Panetta submitted it. Brooke was furious, and in an interview he was uncharacteristically blunt. "Let's use the right word," Brooke said. "He was fired."[54]

In February, Brooke took the Senate floor and spoke for an hour without notes in strong opposition to Nixon's nomination of Carswell. "I cannot in good conscience support confirmation of a man who has created such fundamental doubts about his dedication to human rights . . . it is a most inappropriate time in history that this man should be appointed to the Supreme Court, a man who at one time in his life spoke out for white supremacy. I have fought black separatism every step along the way. I do not believe they are right. I do not believe there is any master race, black or white."

Senator Charles Mathias of Maryland accurately praised Brooke's speech as being "both eloquent and dispassionate at the same time." Brooke now threw himself into securing further Republican opposition to Carswell's nomination. He used his role as cofounder of the informal Wednesday Club—a collection of liberal to moderate Republican senators who met each Wednesday for lunch—to encourage senators who were straddling the fence to come out against Carswell. He went to the White House to speak to the president about another matter, but used the opportunity to tell Nixon to his face: "I want you to know that I am working day and night to defeat your nomination to the Supreme Court."[55] Nixon just smiled broadly and went on speaking about the previous conversation.

---

*After Leon Panetta left the Nixon administration, he left the Republican Party as well, returning to his native Monterey Peninsula in California, and successfully running for Congress as a Democrat. In Congress, he was widely respected on both sides of the aisle. With Bill Clinton's election in 1992, Panetta was tapped to run the Office of Management and Budget and later served as the president's chief of staff during what is generally acknowledged to be the Clinton administration's strongest period, between 1995 and 1997.

A rumor surfaced that Nixon was considering nominating Brooke to the Supreme Court to defuse this criticism, but when Brooke reiterated his opposition to Carswell in a second speech on the Senate floor, speculation of Brooke's possible nomination to the Supreme Court ended. The president had the power, but Brooke and his allies had the votes, and Carswell's nomination was rejected by the Senate by a vote of 51 to 45.

Nixon called a White House press conference and denounced Carswell's failure as "malicious character assassination" and an act of regional discrimination. "I have reluctantly concluded," the president said, "with the Senate presently constituted, I cannot successfully nominate to the Supreme Court any federal appellate judge from the South who believes as I do in the strict construction of the Constitution." Brooke responded almost immediately, calling Nixon's statement "incredible, mistaken and unfortunate." He asserted that the Senate would confirm "a Southerner and a strict constructionist who is qualified. I regret the President's statement deeply. I hope that after his anger has cooled, he will reconsider his remarks. It would be an act of great injustice to overlook competent nominees from the South on the utterly false assumption that the Senate will not confirm them."[56]

The senator and the president's relationship never entirely healed. Both men felt betrayed, but in the end it was Nixon who betrayed the Republican Party's historic commitment to civil rights in the name of political strategy.

Nonetheless, the popularity of both Brooke and Nixon increased over the next few years. Brooke was reelected by a record margin despite opposition from Massachusetts's conservatives, and some onlookers whispered that Brooke would make an ideal replacement for Vice President Spiro Agnew in Nixon's 1972 reelection campaign—"a President who goes to Peking and to Moscow can go to Brooke,"[57] opined one Republican adviser. Democratic strategist Frank Mankiewicz believed that Brooke's selection would be an unlikely stroke of genius; "Given just reasonable foreign policy success and economic improvement," he said, "I would say that ticket would end the campaign. It would be a shoo-in."[58]

Had Richard Nixon taken that bold step, Ed Brooke would have become our nation's first black president in 1974, after Nixon's resignation over Watergate. History, however, took another course, and Senator Ed Brooke would once again secure a small but important part in nudging that history forward.

Richard Nixon seemed briefly invincible after his landslide victory over liberal Democrat George McGovern in 1972, winning every state but Massachusetts. But as evidence of Nixon's approval of the cover-up after the burglary at the Democratic National Committee headquarters in the Watergate Hotel began to emerge, the president's popularity and hold on power began to slip. At first, many Republican senators stonewalled the investigation, preferring not to overturn rocks and reduce their president's—and their party's—hold on power.

But in November of 1973, Ed Brooke took the momentous step of becoming the first Republican senator to call for the President's resignation. "I do not think that the country can stand the trauma that it has been going through for the past months," he said. "It has been like a nightmare and I know that he doesn't want to hurt the country, and I certainly don't want to prejudice the case. He might not be guilty of any impeachable offense. On the other hand, there is no question that President Nixon has lost his effectiveness as the leader of this country, primarily because he's lost the confidence of the people, and I think, therefore, that in the interests of this nation that he loves that he should step down."[59]

It would be seven long months until other Republican senators joined him. To conservatives, Brooke's call for Nixon's resignation was just another example of insufficient partisan loyalty. But Brooke was acting out of a larger loyalty to the nation he had sworn to serve.

After President Ford took the oath of office in August 1974, there were once again calls to appoint Brooke to the vice presidency, but liberal Republican and longtime New York governor Nelson Rockefeller was given the nod instead.

Brooke remained at the forefront of many policy discussions, and was startlingly prescient at times. In 1974, he took up the mantle of citizen privacy, anticipating societal evolutions more than a decade away, pointing out that "for computer-caused invasions of privacy there are no laws. Here we must enact legislation to safeguard the constitutional rights of our citizens from cybernetic invasions."[60]

But as the Ford administration dragged on, Brooke's name began to appear more regularly in the social column than on the front page. His prodigious charm and intellect had made him the favorite in Washington political and social circles. Star-studded parties at the Iranian embassy with the likes of Liz Taylor became a Brooke favorite. The *Boston Globe* debated internally and finally decided to publish an investigative piece titled "Where Is Ed Brooke?" A separation from his wife was announced, and their divorce proved to be both painful and public, with Brooke's daughters speaking to the press about their father's neglect of their mother since coming to Washington. With bad news descending in quick succession and his decision not to fight back and not to criticize his wife and daughters, Ed Brooke's political star was fading fast.

In 1978, Massachusetts's conservatives again ran a candidate against Brooke in the Republican primary, taking advantage of his personal problems and charging that he was too liberal. Faced with the constant irritant of opposition from within his own party, Brooke was again asked by reporters why he remained a Republican, when he could presumably switch parties and run uncontested for the rest of his political life. Brooke explained that he felt a responsibility both to diversify the Republican Party and diversify African-Americans' base of political power. If this caused people to question long-held assumptions in the process, so much the better. "For a long time," Brooke explained, "Blacks have rallied to the Democratic Party. Before that, they all rallied to the Republican Party. But we cannot afford the luxury of supporting just one political party."[61]

Brooke won the Republican primary but lost the 1978 election to moderate Democratic congressman Paul Tsongas. Brooke remarried a few months later, and then went into seclusion—working in a profitable local law firm, but feeling a bit betrayed by all sides. His position of influence in the Republican Party diminished with the Reagan revolution as conservatives once again took hold of the party platform and apparatus. White southerners increasingly formed the backbone of the Republican Party, while blacks continued to vote overwhelmingly for the Democratic Party. Ed Brooke had become something of a phantom of history, a man whose enormous achievements are not adequately celebrated by what can only be described as an ungrateful state and nation. While significant streets have been renamed in major American cities to honor Malcolm X and Adam Clayton Powell, to date no streets have been named for Senator Ed Brooke.

Twenty-five years later, at the turn of a new millennium, Ed Brooke was living in splendid isolation on a horse farm in northern Virginia. While the left had willfully forgotten him, Ed Brooke felt most disillusioned about the drift of his own Republican Party away from civil rights and its historic position as the Party of Lincoln. Indeed, only two black Republicans—Connecticut's Gary Franks and Oklahoma's J. C. Watts—have been elected to Congress in the quarter century since Ed Brooke left the Senate. But, as Brooke explained, "you don't leave the church just because you don't like the minister; you keep the faith and stay and try to change things for the better."[62]

The slumbering scandal of the Republican right's embrace of old southern segregationists was reawakened in December 2002 when Republican Senate majority leader Trent Lott, after praising Strom Thurmond's 1948 campaign, was criticized and subsequently resigned. Brooke was contacted by *Washington Post* columnist E. J. Dionne for comment. Brooke expressed no surprise, offering just a sigh of dismay commensurate to his eighty-three years of struggle and experience. "I've never met Senator Lott, I don't know him personally," Brooke said diplomatically, "but this is a statement that is not only offensive to African-Americans but also to white people who want equal justice in this country."[63] Some digging through Ed Brooke's 1966 book *The Challenge of Change* gave E. J. Dionne the perfect coda to his newspaper column. More than thirty years before, Ed Brooke had distinguished himself not just as a pioneer, but as something of a prophet as well, when he wrote: "Our gains in the South not only should not, but cannot, be achieved on the basis of racism and segregation. For us, such votes are fool's gold."[64]

RADICAL CENTRISTS

THE INDEPENDENT GOVERNORS OF THE 1990S

I WANT YOU
TO JOIN
THE REFORM PARTY

Lowell Weicker   Jesse Ventura   Angus King

I'm too fiscally conservative for the Democrats and too socially liberal for the Republicans, like seventy-five percent of the American people.

—ANGUS KING[1]

What do a former senator, a professional wrestler, and a talk-show host have in common?

Each was elected governor as an Independent during the last decade of the twentieth century—impressive not just because they won without the support of the local political establishment, but because they ran explicitly in opposition to it.

Seen side by side, Connecticut's Lowell Weicker, Minnesota's Jesse Ventura, and Maine's Angus King make a motley crew. Each was a proudly unorthodox politician whose willingness to speak his mind was a primary source of his popularity. Their potent combination of common sense and maverick appeal was well expressed by one young woman working at a convenience store in Maine: "If you're a

Democrat, you're supposed to think like the Democrats, and if you're Republican, you're supposed to think like the Republicans," said twenty-one-year-old Stephanie Black, a Republican who voted for Bill Clinton. "But if you're an Independent, you can do what you think is right."[2]

Unlike the past third-party candidacies of Henry Wallace on the left and George Wallace on the right, these Independent campaigns were explicitly Centrist, seeking to give a voice to the moderate majority of fiscally conservative but socially liberal voters. They appealed to disenfranchised Republicans because of their emphasis on fiscal responsibility and personal freedom, specifically the bellwether issues of balancing the budget—which the economic policies of Ronald Reagan had first promoted and then ignored—and support of a pro-choice position on abortion that was starkly at odds with the GOP platform's call for a constitutional ban even in cases of rape or incest. They also appealed to moderate Democrats, who—frustrated by the endemic corruption and inaction of Democratic mayors in urban areas—were attracted to these Independents' central message of reform. These were the inheritors of the Perot vote, secular middle-class fiscal conservatives who were fed up with politics as usual and determined to shake up the system.

Significantly, each was a well-known personality within his state before setting out on his independent campaign. Weicker had been a maverick liberal Republican senator from Connecticut for eighteen years; Minnesota's Jesse Ventura had been a nationally televised wrestling star and a local radio talk-show host; and Angus King had hosted a popular public television program about Maine for nearly two decades and was independently wealthy enough to self-fund the initial stages of his campaign. An unknown Independent candidate would have a difficult, if not impossible, time of being taken seriously by the media and their fellow citizens, but the power of celebrity allowed them each to stand apart from the party apparatus without being ignored.

Providing effective leadership once in office proved even more difficult than getting elected. The Independent governors found they had no natural allies in office, but if they were determined to play the role of the honest broker, they could work with moderates in both parties and achieve gains for the common good. Their ability to use their independence to work with their legislatures was the ultimate indicator of their effectiveness, determining whether their states would be more likely to trust executive leadership to someone from outside the rigid two-party system.

Each of these Independent governors enjoyed differing degrees of success while in office, but they instinctively followed similar paths. While often criticized by the political establishment, they were regarded as colorful, courageous, and effective in the eyes of the general public, who respected their difficult, but principled, walk down the center of the aisle.

GOVERNOR LOWELL WEICKER
OF CONNECTICUT

He was called "the gutsiest governor in America" by *Time* and titled his autobiography *Maverick*—which described him on its cover as "an independent individual who does not go along with a group or party." But Connecticut's Lowell Weicker was also among the most vilified moderates of his generation.

He was always biting the hand that fed him: a genteel son of Greenwich combining a belief in fiscal responsibility with a commitment to social progressivism. In his eighteen-year Senate career, he continuously infuriated conservatives: by leading the charge against Richard Nixon's White House cover-up of Watergate; by getting arrested for protesting apartheid outside the South African embassy; by filibustering a Reagan-era bill on school prayer; by opposing the death penalty; by voting to raise taxes to balance the federal budget; and by constantly supporting abortion rights. As the religious right was gaining influence in Republican politics, Weicker called the separation of church and state "this country's greatest contribution to world civilization."[3]

Not coincidentally, in 1988 he lost his bid for a fourth term in the Senate to the conservative Democratic attorney general Joe Lieberman, who benefited from the support of *National Review* founder and Connecticut resident William F. Buckley Jr. In addition to running nationally syndicated columns promoting Lieberman's comparative merits, Buckley circulated unsubtle bumper stickers around the leafy state that asked this indelicate question: "Does Lowell Weicker Make You Sick?"

After being unceremoniously retired from office, the gregarious Weicker was described as "the loneliest man in Washington" because he had made so many enemies among the members of his own party. He considered dropping out of politics for good. But as recession enveloped Connecticut, creating the most serious budget crisis in its history, Weicker decided to take a journey of purpose and entered the arena one more time. As an independent with no future ambitions, he could take the unpopular stands necessary to solve the underlying problems in his state once and for all—and then go home beholden to no one, at peace with himself.

The Republican Party made it clear that it would not support him, but this was not the end of the world. "For a long time, opponents in the [Republican] party and I wrestled to a frustrating standoff," Weicker wrote. "Their problem was that I had become the strongest Republican candidate for statewide office . . . the only one to win statewide after 1970. My dilemma was that, while popular with voters, I was vulnerable to the whims of extreme, unprincipled partisans in my own party."[4] Weicker's victories had always been ensured by his support from a loose but dependable coalition of liberal Republicans, Independents, and moderate Democrats. He considered shifting his allegiance to the Democratic Party, but that party's chronic fiscal irresponsibility and petty corruption on a local level made joining its ranks feel like an impossible betrayal of the principles on which he built his career.

Weicker's solution was to codify his existing independent support in a new party built around his candidacy. It would be called "A Connecticut Party"—with the capitalized article up front ensuring it would be placed on the top ballot line.

Initially, leaders of the Republican and Democratic parties dismissed this effort as an essentially vain campaign. Weicker understood that it was an uphill battle, but he also understood the voters dissatisfaction with the two major parties. Moreover, he reasoned, "I was much better known than my opponents, so running as an independent was not proving to be the drawback it might have been for a newcomer."[5]

The heart of the deepening budget crisis, as Weicker saw it, was the collusion between the two parties to support economically unsupportable, unquestioning fidelity to the unofficial state religion of Connecticut politics: no income tax.

Popular former governor Ella Grasso and two-term incumbent William O'Neill had both signed "the pledge" to never institute a state income tax, making Connecticut one of only nine states not to have a state income tax. The cost of the pledge was passed on in the form of burdensome property taxes and one of the highest sales taxes in the nation. These more regressive taxes deepened Connecticut's stark social divisions between rural purity and inner-city squalor.

At the time, Connecticut had the wealthiest residents of any state in the nation per capita, but also three of the nation's fifteen poorest cities: Bridgeport, New Haven, and the state capital of Hartford. This was life in Connecticut: leafy enclaves where country clubs were a way of life, bordering inner cities of abject poverty and vivid hopelessness. Tensions and resentment on both sides were building to a boiling point. Now the state was billions of dollars in debt, but nobody wanted to pay up or cut services.

Weicker blamed the situation on a "decade of spend-it-but-don't-pay-for-it policies espoused by [Republican] Presidents of the United States." He also felt the state's reluctance to honestly face the income gap was in part due to political partisans protecting the status quo. "There is so much anger in elections now because both parties are refusing to realistically debate painful issues in their proper forum. So it all gets played out in polarized rhetoric a few weeks before election, or on talk radio."[6]

Announcing his campaign, Weicker emphasized broadening the tax base to get more revenue, recommended providing greater incentives to the private sector to grow and expand, and advocated cuts in spending. In his words, "Everything is on the table." And "if people asked does that mean increased taxes, the answer was yes. Everything meant everything."[7] It was not a popular stand, but it was serious and honest.

Weicker's victory over the Democratic and Republican candidates in November 1990 on a message of Independent reform and fiscal responsibility presaged the popular support for Ross Perot's candidacy two years later. The public was feeling taken advantage of and angry. They were about to transfer their frustrations to the new incumbent.

As governor-elect, Weicker was finally able, for the first time, to look at the state budget books in detail, and what he found exceeded his darkest suspicions. The budget gap was $2.5 billion out of a total $8 billion annual budget. "I ran for governor in one of the wealthiest states in the country and was elected in one of the most insolvent," he said.[8] He would not be able to worm his way out of this trouble by spending cuts alone.

Privately, some state legislators told him they supported creating a state income tax, but they could not say so publicly. "As an Independent," he recalled, "I could afford to be a lightning rod."[9] He could not have known exactly how much heat he would face.

Once in the governor's office, Weicker acted quickly, pushing through Connecticut's first income tax and vetoing four subsequent attempts by state legislators to overturn the levy. In response, forty thousand people turned out to an antitax rally in front of the state capital and the governor was burned in effigy. When Weicker attempted to speak to the crowd, he was spat on and police hustled him away. Death threats were not uncommon. The new governor was the least popular man in Connecticut.

Weicker balanced tax hikes with budget cuts that were similarly drastic, spreading the pain evenly, provoking outcries from all sides. But when conservatives argued that more savings could be found by cutting social programs, Weicker erupted. "I've long said that if you want to cut through all the bullshit of politicians, take a look at the budget. It tells you exactly what your priorities are," he said.[10] "In Connecticut, do you know what our number one budget item is? Not welfare, not food stamps. Nursing homes. Middle-class families, wealthy families, spend down their parent's money, then get nursing home support from the state. That's a subsidy. I went to law school on the G.I. Bill. That's a subsidy. Nearly everyone gets a handout at one time or another and that is how it should be. We've got to see it as a matter of common interest in making government work."[11]

Weicker saw the state budget as a matter of structural philosophy. He cut funding to prisons, eliminated state aid to private and parochial schools, angered labor by winning steep concessions on contracts, but managed to fund universal immunization for infants, community policing initiatives, and school-based health clinics.

Whenever his administration was faced with a tough battle with the state legislature—as it often was—Weicker tried to persuade legislators to do the right thing by offering to take the heat himself. "We just said to people that since we weren't concerned about re-election, the Governor's party can be blamed for any pain that's inflicted," recalled one aide. At a speech at New Haven's Yale University during his difficult first year in office, Weicker said, "Respect—if not reelection—comes from speaking the truth, standing up for what you believe in, and taking some licks."[12]

His subsequent work did not go unnoticed. Within two years the state government was running a surplus and the howls of outrage had subsided, replaced by admiring commentaries. In 1992, Weicker was awarded the John F. Kennedy Library's Profile in Courage award, which stated: "Governor Weicker demonstrated tremendous political courage and risked his career by challenging the status quo and the popular bipartisan no-income-tax tradition. Despite intense political and public criticism, threats to his safety, and large-scale bitter protests, he persevered and finally prevailed in this fight."

The left-wing magazine the *Nation* even found room to praise the former Republican, opining that "while he is a deeply committed civil libertarian and opponent of racial discrimination, he is not much of a critic of corporate power. Yet if his record suggests inconsistency, it also suggests a pragmatic compassion; if he is a liberal, he is a fighting liberal." It even went as far to consider a Weicker candidacy for president: "As a candidate he would certainly be the polar opposite of Bill Clinton's perpetual waffling, winning voters respect with tenacity rather than trying to buy it with compromise. A blunt talking ex-Republican ex-Governor who managed social justice and a balanced budget may be a winning combination."[13]

Dismissing immediate talk of a presidential campaign, Weicker instead became deeply involved with an informal group of Centrist leaders from across the nation. Sometimes known as the Gang of 8, the group was comprised of Weicker; former presidential candidates Paul Tsongas, Gary Hart, and John Anderson; Congressman Tim Penny; Senator Bill Bradley; Governor Richard Lamm of Colorado; and, in time, fellow Independent governor Angus King of Maine. Beginning with informal Sunday morning telephone conversations, the group coalesced in Minneapolis in December 1995 at a conference called "Locating the New Political Center in America," and released an influential report titled "The Road to Generational Equity." It read like a blueprint of the burgeoning independent Centrist movement.

> Too many Democrats do not recognize the limitations of government, and too many Republicans do not see the value of government. The Democrats are often fiscally irresponsible and the Republicans are often socially irresponsible. The Democrats cannot add and the Republicans cannot compassionately subtract. The Republican center of gravity is noticeably right of center, reinforcing the party's worst instincts of societal exclusion, environmental exploitation and a devil-take-the-hindmost social policy. The Democratic center of gravity, particularly among its congressional leaders, is now noticeably left of center, reinforcing the party's worst instincts of fiscal irresponsibility, interest group politics and incumbent protection. This bizarre scenario would be quite frightening if it were not for the fact that while the two major political parties are edging to the fringes, the majority of Americans are returning home to the political center.[14]

Ultimately, Weicker decided against running for president, with fellow Gang of 8 member Richard Lamm squaring off unsuccessfully with Ross Perot for the 1996 Reform Party nomination.

As his term of governor came to a close, Weicker respected his self-imposed one-term limit. Even the frequently critical *Hartford Courant* waxed nostalgic about his departure from the political stage, admitting that "Mr. Weicker has made life interesting—in Connecticut and in Washington—throughout his 31 years in the political fast lane. There's no denying that he and his family have earned a respite. He's lifted politics out of the banal. He gets things done, whether straightening out the state's fiscal crisis or battling right-wing ideologues in the U.S. Senate or helping to pass federal legislation to aid the disabled. He's been a talker and a doer—and that's uncommon in politics."[15]

Weicker's lieutenant governor failed in her attempt to run on the A Connecticut Party line for the top spot, coming in third. Weicker's success was personal and political, but it did not extend to the creation of a third party in Connecticut politics.

Nonetheless, Weicker's achievement was significant. The *New York Times* spoke for many when it wrote: "Mr. Weicker . . . has proved that a governor can govern without a major party behind him. He has accustomed the state to hearing its chief executive say what many people think: partisan politics does not make good government."[16]

GOVERNOR JESSE VENTURA
OF MINNESOTA

In 1998, a professional wrestler, actor, motorcycle club member, U.S. Navy Seal, and radio talk-show host ran for governor of Minnesota and won.

A self-proclaimed "radical centrist," Jesse Ventura commanded people's attention not just because of his chrome-domed six-foot-five-inch, 250-pound frame or distinctive voice described as "the low growl of a hundred bulldogs fed a steady diet of 60-grit sandpaper." His defiantly unorthodox candidacy caught fire because of his charismatic rejection of the far right and the far left.

He called himself a "working man with commonsense ideas and goals," and "fiscally conservative and socially moderate to liberal."

Campaigning across the state, Ventura spread his message, that "neither of the two parties is truly representing the people anymore. They are on opposite extremes with about seventy percent of us in the middle. That needs to change, and that's why I am a member of the Reform Party."

Dissatisfaction and distrust of partisan extremes that took form in 1992 with the Reform Party candidacy of Ross Perot and Bill Clinton's New Democrat movement reached a kind of generational apex in the 1998 Minnesota election.

It was a race he never should have won. Ventura was running against the best-known name in Minnesota politics—Hubert Humphrey III, son of the legendary senator and vice president. Humphrey had served with distinction as Minnesota's attorney general and received the Democratic endorsement easily. The Republican candidate was popular St. Paul mayor Norm Coleman. In a normal election year, either of these two candidates would have been considered well qualified. But 1998 was not a normal election year.

Partisan wrangling over Bill Clinton's impeachment created a new level of disgust for political party regulars on the local, state, and national level. In Minnesota, popular participation in the Republican and Democratic parties had been falling steadily for several years, giving extremists virtual control over the nominating process and resulting in a disconnect with the average voter.

Minnesota's Republican Party had become controlled by the anti-abortion activism of the religious right, while left-wing activists dominated the Democratic Party to such an extent that they were able to pass a motion requiring a "fragrance-free" political convention so that those with allergies toward perfumes would not suffer. There was a thirst for a candidate who would cut through the petty partisanship, stand up to special interests, and promote personal freedom. On cue, in walked Jesse Ventura.

Hearing Jesse talk about his dissatisfaction with the two major parties inspired people who'd long ago stopped caring about politics. He was speaking for himself from the gut, but in the sincerity of his statements many Minnesotans found their own political voice.

We need to keep a permanently tight rein on government spending. I believe working people should keep as much of their money as possible, and I believe they should have a more direct say in how it's spent.

But I don't believe we need the government's help as much as some think we do. That belief sets me apart from the Democrats, since their way of dealing with everything is to tax and spend.

I also believe that government has no business telling us how we should live our lives. I think our lifestyle choices should be left up to us. What we do in our private lives is none of the government's business. That position rules out the Republican Party for me. As the cliché says, "I don't want Democrats in the boardroom, and I don't want Republicans in the bedroom."

So I stand before you as an advocate of minimal government interference and of minimal public reliance on government which in anybody's book ought to spell lower taxes. And that pretty much keeps me out of both parties.[17]

Ventura was a native Minnesotan born by the name of James Janos. His father worked for the Minnesota Street Department; his mother was a nurse. Out of high school Ventura enlisted and served four years as an elite U.S. Navy Seal in Southeast Asia. His experiences in the military and later as a professional wrestler of some renown (legally changing his name to Jesse Ventura, playing the role of the California-inspired bad guy replete with wraparound neon sunglasses and a feather boa) made it impossible for him to be anything but refreshingly honest about his own imperfections. "I'm not going to sit here and tell you I haven't done some morally bad things in my life," Ventura stated. "I have. I'm an ex-frogman in the Navy. We're not exactly known for our great morality."[18]

He certainly hadn't expected to get involved with the disreputable crowd that runs in politics. Ventura had retired from professional wrestling in 1986, going on to play support roles in several movies with Arnold Schwarzenegger. But offscreen, he was also a devoted husband and father living in the suburb of Brooklyn Park, Minnesota, coaching high school football and honing his opinions by hosting a radio talk-show program for three hours every day. In 1991, the mayor of his small town passed a zoning law that infuriated Ventura and his neighbors. Playing off his name recognition and reputation for straight talk, Ventura ran for mayor and defeated an eighteen-year incumbent by a 2 to 1 margin. "They called me the most dangerous man in the city because I wasn't part of the status quo, part of the good ol' boy system," he recalled. After he won, Democrats and Republicans tried to convince the self-described Independent to join their party. He refused. "You know what that shows me?" he said. "It showed me they have no integrity. . . . I never at all felt I'd be involved in politics," he said. "But you can't change government from the outside. You have to change it from the inside."[19]

On Election Day 1998, Jesse Ventura got his chance to change the state. Amid a record turnout, his candidacy energized an entirely new segment of the voting population. A stunning 46 percent of all voters under thirty cast a ballot for the former professional wrestler. Republican strategist Frank Luntz attributed this phenomenon to energized apathy and the draw of celebrity: "They get their entertainment from Jerry Springer, not CNN. Ventura, because of his personality, was able to wake them up."[20]

But the conditions that allowed Jesse Ventura's electoral success were also unusual and are worth recounting because it was Minnesota's liberal campaign laws made a credible third-party candidacy possible.

First among these is a generous campaign finance law that entitled Ventura to $330,000 in matching public funds due to a previous Senate campaign in which the Reform Party candidate, Dean Barkley, gained just over 5 percent of the overall vote. This qualified the Reform Party for state funding and enabled Ventura to take out bank loans equivalent to 5 percent of the Republican and Democrat parties' funding.

He did not spend this money on high-paid consultants but on inexpensive yet memorable television ads: one showing a Jesse Ventura "Action Figure" beating up "evil special-interests man"; another demonstrating the evolution of Jesse "the Body" Ventura into Jesse "the Mind." These ads used humor to cast the emotional issues of the campaign into sharp relief, and as a result stood out from the usual pack of election season ads that voters typically tune out.

He was also aided by a unique political format that allowed eleven debates between the gubernatorial candidates. Democrats insisted that Ventura be allowed to participate, believing that he would draw voters away from the Republican Party. Instead Ventura's nothing-to-lose honesty, charisma, and common sense distinguished him dramatically from the two comparatively gray professional politicians. "He speaks from the heart, never from a script," said one supporter. "With Ventura, we've got oomph and energy, a regular guy who says it like it is."[21]

But the most critical element in Jesse Ventura's election was the fact that Minnesota is one of only seven states that allows voters to register on Election Day. In the 1998 midterm election, the average national turnout rate was 36 percent. In Minnesota it was 60 percent, and a remarkable one out of every six voters registered on Election Day. This is directly attributable to enthusiasm for Ventura's campaign among young voters who might not otherwise have gotten to vote at all. But exit polls also showed that Jesse Ventura gained significant crossover support from disaffected Democrats and Republicans. In fact, 33 percent of Democrats pulled the lever for the wrestler turned gubernatorial candidate, as well as 29 percent of Republicans.

Once elected, Ventura became an immediate object of popular fascination. T-shirts and signs in malls proclaimed, "My governor can kick your governor's ass."[22] Although just 37 percent of voters had cast a ballot for him on Election Day, around the time of his inauguration the governor-elect-by-plurality had gained 70 percent public support, surprising skeptics with his energy, integrity, and intelligence.

His campaign slogan had been "Retaliate in '98," and he meant to shake up the political system, but he found that working with the state legislature was more Byzantine than he'd expected. While the economy continued to grow, Ventura was able to return most of the $2 billion surplus back to Minnesotans in the forms of tax rebates—or "Jesse Checks," as people began calling them—but once the economy went sour, Ventura was forced to go back on a campaign pledge not to raise taxes, refusing to cut government spending with the sharp ax he had promised. Activists on the far left and the far right decried his time in office, with the conservative magazine *Weekly Standard* carping, "On social issues, it's downright impossible to get to the left of the abortion-on-demand, pro–assisted suicide Governor."[23]

A series of minor scandals and badly chosen battles, such as Ventura's refusal to sign a National Day of Prayer proclamation on the grounds that organized religion should have no part in the life of the state, caused Ventura's public support to fall slightly. More important, he grew tired of the fishbowl public service forced his family to live in, and at times seemed to miss the role of celebrity— he moonlighted as a television commentator for the short-lived XFL football league. But the governor continued to be a popular figure with people who felt disenfranchised from politics as usual, average Americans who liked Ventura's blunt common sense and lack of moralistic preaching. In an extensive article in *Atlantic Monthly,* political analyst Ted Halstead saw the figure of Jesse Ventura as the shape of things to come: "Much of Ventura's support came from young adults, who took advantage of Minnesota's same-day registration law and stormed the polls, helping to create a record turnout. This suggests that if a political candidate can somehow capture the passion of young adults, they will do their part. Ventura offered young Minnesotans something refreshing: a clear alternative to Democrats and Republicans, and a willingness to take on the status quo. But Jesse Ventura is no figurehead for Xers; he is just an early beneficiary of their pent-up political frustration."[24]

As Ventura prepared to leave office at the end of his four-year term, it was clear that he had not been an effective leader in the legislative sense. But he had been effective in terms of energizing the electorate, getting more people involved in the political process, and lending his gravelly voice to the radical moderates who increasingly make up the majority.

After the death of liberal senator Paul Wellstone in a plane crash during a close campaign against Ventura's old antagonist Norm Coleman, it suddenly fell to Jesse Ventura to name his successor. Although the individual would only serve in the Senate for several weeks, there was a great deal of partisan jockeying about whom he would name. With the Senate evenly divided, Democrats and Republicans put an enormous amount of pressure on Ventura to cede to their side, promising big things if he would help them gain control of the Senate for just a few weeks. But Ventura named his chief of staff, Dean Barkley, who had run for the Senate on the Reform ticket years before, whose quixotic candidacy had allowed Ventura to qualify for matching funds: "I'm the first former car wash operator to be a U.S. Senator," Barkley joked, while describing his politics as "a little Paul Wellstone and a little Rudy Boshwitz,"[25] referring to the conservative Republican senator Wellstone had replaced twelve years before.

In making the announcement, Ventura once again lashed out at the viselike grip the two parties had on political participation in the United States. "Today three very powerful institutions, the Democratic Farm Labor Party, the Republican Party, and the media, are conspiring to limit the hard-earned rights of ordinary citizens to rise up and compete for elected office without having to be a Democrat or a Republican,"[26] Ventura said. In contrast, he promised that Dean Barkley would fulfill during his brief time in the Senate what Ventura had tried to do during his brief term as governor: "He will put the people's interests before the party's interest." Then, as sort of a coda to his career, Ventura added, "If these two parties don't wake up from their bipartisan bickering in everything that they do, there will be more Jesse Venturas on the horizon."[27] Even coming from the gargantuan governor, it sounded like less a threat than a promise.

GOVERNOR ANGUS KING OF MAINE

"The public has an acute sense of when they're being bullshitted," reflected Maine governor Angus King. "They know when they're being conned. So I decided I'd level with them and see how it went."[28]

By all accounts, it went pretty well. Angus King was the only Independent governor in recent memory to win a second term in office. And he didn't just squeak by; he built a broad coalition based on his balanced commonsense approach. When King was first elected in 1994, his margin of victory was only 1.5 percent. In 1998, he received 59 percent of the vote in a five-person race, beating his closest opponent by 40 percentage points. It was the perfect marriage of the man, the moment, and the State of Maine.

In 1992, Ross Perot had received 30 percent of the vote in Maine, his highest in the nation, beating President Bush in his own lifelong summer vacation state. Maine's tradition of independence was deeply engrained; when FDR scored his landslide second-term victory in 1936, Maine had been one of only two states in the union to vote against him (inspiring the slogan "As goes Maine, so goes Vermont").

Some people wondered whether this insistence on independence was rooted in the state's historic industries of fishing and farming, both solitary pursuits that aimed toward self-sufficiency. But whatever the source, Maine's groundswell of support for Independent political reformers was reaching a high-water mark as the 1994 election approached.

For eighteen years, King had appeared in the living rooms of people across the state as host of the local PBS program *Maine Watch*. Consequently, he had an uncommon ease in front of the television camera, a way of expressing a pithy wisdom with a sound bite. But his once-a-week television appearances were just a sideline to the Senate aide turned entrepreneur. King had just sold his start-up energy conservation business for a healthy amount, and now—suddenly financially independent in middle age—decided to set his sights on an independent campaign for governor.

"I'm too fiscally conservative for the Democrats and too socially liberal for the Republicans, like seventy-five percent of the American people," he reasoned. "The two parties are largely controlled by the interest groups on the extremes. . . . Really passionate partisans usually have a stake in the deal, public employees unions or businesses that are wrapped up in legislation. The people don't give a damn whose idea it is or who gets credit. They just want the problem solved."[29]

As a young man, King described himself as a liberal Democrat, but over time he'd gotten increasingly fed up with liberal bureaucratic excesses. After growing up in Virginia (he listened to Martin Luther King's "I Have a Dream" speech while sitting in a tree by the reflecting pool at the base of the Lincoln Memorial), King went to law school. While training for a job at the Legal Service Corps he had his first Centrist epiphany when a professor leading a class on how to keep low-income people in their homes without paying rent asked, "'What if we are successful in representing our clients and the people who own the houses they live in say 'there's no profit in this' and walk away? There are no more apartments. Have we served our clients well?" This was "an important moment," King recalled. "It led me to focus on results. The rest of my career is in large measure asking that question—about the environment, social issues, everything. I want to know what works. What really helps people."[30]

King went to work for Maine senator William Hathaway, who served on the Labor and Public Affairs Committee. The committee took on issues like the creation of bilingual education ("The liberal orthodoxy was 'Don't make them speak English,'" King remembered) and safety at summer camp ("Walter Mondale sponsored an OSHA for campers"), both of which King found "perfect examples of the liberal penchant for wanting to fix everything and screwing things up in the progress."[31]

King rallied around the 1992 Democratic presidential campaign of Paul Tsongas, and his message of fiscal responsibility and social inclusion. It was on the issue of welfare reform that he grew most animated, believing as Tsongas did that "that the best social program is a good job." Too many Democrats, King felt, had been a little slow to learn that "you can't love employees but hate employers." When Tsongas lost the campaign, King felt that there was no longer any place for him within the organized Democratic Party, while intolerant Republican stands such as a constitutional ban on abortion made joining the Republican Party an equally uncomfortable fit. "There is an underlying dissatisfaction with the old parties—both here and across the country," King said at the time. "If they keep putting up the same kind of candidates and playing the insider game, I think you will see an independent movement that will be more significant than what Perot had in 1992."[32]

The first challenge was getting people to take his independent candidacy seriously. He began buying television advertising time in the spring of 1994, even though his name would not appear on the ballot until November. "If we weren't in the mix over the primary season, we would have fallen off the media radar screens, fallen in the polls, and never gotten back," explains King campaign media adviser Dan Payne. "Our credibility would have dried up." Even more important in establishing the candidate's credibility as a man with a plan for Maine was King's book *Making a Difference*—which he both wrote and self-published. The book proposed $50 million dollars in specific budget cuts, promised not to raise taxes, and set out a vision of targeted investment in education and high tech. The book was sent out to county libraries, newspapers, and television stations, and in all King advertisements voters were urged to write the campaign for their own copy. The book allowed King's volunteers to answer questions about the candidate's stands on policy without paraphrasing; all they had to do was to hold a copy of the book and say, "You can look it up!" Consultants had warned King to not write the book. "I was concerned that he might present his opponents with a shooting gallery—that's the conventional wisdom about such things," explained Dan Payne. "But Democrats and Republicans praised it. It really won over the media. They liked Angus anyway . . . but the book made them take us seriously."[33]

At first, establishment Democratic and Republican candidates dismissed him. Former governor Joe Brennan, a career politician who pulled the strings of the state Democratic organization, described King as a nice guy who didn't know anything about governing. When Brennan offhandedly charged that a person who didn't know the inner workings of the state legislature was unqualified to serve as governor, King politely went on the attack. "I want you all to realize what Joe Brennan just said . . . he said, in effect, that normal people don't count."[34]

King's directness and insight even won over people who disagreed with him. During a campaign event at a college in Waterville, Maine, King received a question about his stand on abortion. An older man asked King whether he supported the "termination of unborn children." Knowing full well by the way the question was asked that the individual was a antiabortion activist, King nevertheless did not hedge or frame his answer to suit the audience. Instead, he said directly that he supported the right of a woman to choose whether to have an abortion in consultation with her doctor. After the event was over, the older man walked up to King and asked to volunteer for his campaign, because in fifty years of following local politics, he had never seen a candidate speak so honestly to a crowd.

The buzz surrounding Angus King's Independent candidacy was growing, and his odds for election were significantly helped when the Republican Party splintered. The incumbent governor refused to endorse any candidate, focusing instead on getting his wife, Representative Olympia Snowe, successfully elected to the U.S. Senate.

Conservative Republicans were infuriated when a relative unknown named Susan Collins had won their primary. She had worked on the Senate staff of liberal Republican William Cohen before becoming an assistant to Massachusetts treasurer Joe Malone. Collins was pro-choice, and right-to-life activists began picketing her political appearances. When her brother was busted for buying half a ton of marijuana from an undercover DEA agent, the furious conservatives erupted, and they went to court to have her removed from the ballot for living in Massachusetts during the past two years. Moderate Republicans were turned off by the in-party fighting and began to look to the tough-sounding Angus King.

To build on this momentum, King's newspaper advertisements began prominently displaying the names of well-known individuals who had endorsed his candidacy; the lists were equally divided between Republicans and Democrats. He described his opponents as "consummate political insiders," cleverly breaking down the growth of government during Brennan's previous term in office by stating that the former governor had hired a new employee for every day he was in office. Likewise, King played up his rebel-entrepreneur image with almost humorous attacks on the frustrating inefficiencies of government regulation, saying, "I am the only candidate who has ever had to fill out an environmental impact statement." His campaign slogan crystallized his appeal: "Maine people have a strong independent streak. Now we've got a strong independent for Governor." On Election Day 1994, Angus King edged past his opponents. Now would come the hard part.

Maine had elected an Independent governor before, James Longley, who won in 1974 on a mad-as-hell, antitax, cut-the-size-of-government platform. But Longley was regarded as a practical disaster, having spent most of his time in office fighting with the state legislature—even going so far as calling them "pimps and whores" in public. When the economy went sour, voters lost their taste for their ineffective Independent governor. Angus King was determined to learn from Longley's mistakes.

In contrast to the standoffish Longley, King went out of his way to be accessible to state legislators and citizens. Informal press conferences were held every day at 11 A.M. On Tuesday mornings, King had breakfast with the leadership of the legislature. On Thursdays, rank-and-file legislators were welcomed to the governor's mansion for breakfast. It was all part of a conscious and commonsense effort to reach out, but its effect was near revolutionary to the political culture of the capital. In the past, members of the opposition party were frozen out of any formal functions at the mansion, but as an Independent, King was able to transcend the partisan two-party mind-set: "I started from the assumption that I had no automatic enemies and no automatic friends in the state legislature—just 186 skeptics."[35] He proceeded to try and win them over, in part by placing a higher priority on bipartisan relationship building. "I realized as an independent governor I would have to work three times as hard," King said, so he elevated the level of staff hires at the Governor's Office of Legislative Affairs. Instead of hiring overachieving twenty-nine-year olds, King brought in experienced former members of the legislature's appropriations committee to help negotiate and navigate the system. King was a reformer, but he was not naive. "An independent governor is an asset," explained chief operations officer Chuck Hewett. "He can work with both sides. He can be an honest broker."[36]

Angus King's approachable, informal style became one of his most powerful political weapons and the key to much of his popularity. On weekends, the governor wore blue jeans and rode his

Harley around town. Citizens who always thought of their governor as a remote figure suddenly wanted their pictures taken with Angus King. Working together with moderate members of both parties, King's administration was able to rack up an impressive array of victories: It enacted tax cuts; passed an education bill; instituted welfare reform (one year before the federal government); undertook prison reform; and mandated land conservation and river cleanup. But King was most proud of the achievements that didn't require legislation, just "running the place better," as he would say, by increasing government responsiveness and administrative accountability—resulting, for instance, in child support payments being mailed out within forty-eight hours instead of 3½ weeks—and getting all of Maine's state government online by July 1, 2001. "The bad news is I don't know the rules. The good news is I don't know the rules. It's a fresh-eyed approach. I can look at things and say: 'Why are we doing it this way?' "[37]

What many Maine citizens most remember about his administration was a trip he took on a snowplow during a heavy snowstorm early in his administration. The snow had been coming down for days, and the new governor decided he wanted to take a ride on one of the massive snowplows that were clearing Maine's highways 24/7. It was an impulsive decision, and no press release was issued. That's precisely why it received so much press when the word somehow got out. Reporters tracked down the snowplow's location and interviewed its driver, asking him if he was surprised. The driver replied that he never even had a supervisor in his snowplow, let alone the governor. The incident made big news and provided an anecdote that showed Angus King as an unpretentious bipartisan governor who did things differently than most politicians.

He *was* different. While King was cruising to an easy reelection victory in 1998, the chairman of the Maine Democratic Party virtually admitted the inevitability of defeat, saying that "the truth is that many Democrats admire independent Governor Angus King despite the fact that he has consistently promoted a big-business agenda. He has offset his pro-business track record with an image of liberalism and concern for Civil Rights."[38] His counterpart, the executive director of the Maine Republican Party, sighed, "He's like

Clinton without the intern."[39] Few Independent governors are able to win reelection, but Angus King again proved to be the exception, receiving an overwhelming 59 percent endorsement in a field of five candidates. In word and action, Governor King was articulating a principled, honest, open-minded style of government that proved very popular. "A true leader instinctively voices the aspirations and beliefs of the people, not by taking a poll," King said. "Can you imagine Margaret Chase Smith taking a poll to determine how she should stand on a particular issue? Absolutely not."[40]

At the end of his second term in 2002, blocked from reelection by term limits, King left Maine's state capital for home. Truthful to the end, he had always said that "the idea of our democracy was that ordinary people would go and serve some time in public service—and then go home."[41]

RUDY GIULIANI — 1997

To be locked in to partisan politics doesn't permit you to think clearly.

—RUDY GIULIANI, 1997[1]

The mayor of America's largest city stood in the spotlight of the Broadway stage in drag. Wearing a blond wig, a pink dress, and high heels, with his face covered in makeup, he announced to the assembled crowd in a falsetto voice that his name was now "Rudia."

It was the night of the Inner Circle—an annual charity event in which the mayor parodied a current Broadway hit for an audience of two thousand prominent citizens and journalists paying $400 a ticket. When actress Julie Andrews asked him onstage if he now better understood the challenge she faced every night in *Victor/Victoria*—playing "a woman pretending to be a man pretending to be a woman"—Mayor Rudolph W. Giuliani replied that she obviously hadn't seen his act: "a Democrat pretending to be a Republican pretending to be a Democrat."[2]

Long before he emerged from the dust and rubble of the World

Trade Center transformed into a national hero, Rudy Giuliani transformed New York City from the crime capital of the country to the safest large city in America. He cut the crime rate and welfare rolls in half, reforming welfare ahead of federal legislation by requiring longtime recipients to work in return for public assistance. He cut taxes more than any of his predecessors and brought businesses back to the heart of the city. His pre-9/11 appeal was expressed by a 1999 *Daily News* profile titled, simply, "Quality of Life: The Mayor Who Understood."[3]

In a city with an overwhelming 5 to 1 Democratic registration advantage, Giuliani's independent Republican politics proved surprisingly popular. New Yorkers were impressed by his ability to get results after decades of politicians shrugging their shoulders helplessly in the face of rising crime, welfare rolls, and social decay—in 1993, the year he was first elected, the city was averaging six murders a day, and according to a *Time*/CNN poll 59 percent of New Yorkers believed that "things had gotten so bad, they'd leave the City the next day if they could." But Giuliani's road to City Hall was hard won. He had to overcome reluctance on the part of many liberal New Yorkers to admit that a Republican in the post-Reagan era could be representative of their values and interests. Though controversial, his focus on results over rhetoric succeeded, and in 1997 Giuliani won the votes of 45 percent of Democrats and 65 percent of independents to become the first Republican reelected mayor of New York since his hero Fiorello La Guardia, more than sixty years before.

La Guardia and Giuliani were both first elected as fusion candidates—reformers catapulted to office by a diverse alliance of the Republican Party, small local parties, and good government groups fed up with cyclical scandals and chronic inefficiencies of the Democratic machine. Fusion campaigns unified these disparate groups behind a charismatic independent reformer—usually a Republican—who could credibly challenge the local political establishment.

Congressman Fiorello La Guardia unsuccessfully ran as a Fusion Republican-Socialist candidate for mayor two times against the popular Tammany-backed Jimmy Walker. As the Great Depression wore on, the public grew impatient with corruption investigations and Walker abruptly resigned. La Guardia stepped into City Hall soon after and proceeded to occupy it as no one before. Within months he'd won over former critics like the *New York Daily News,* which wrote: "We did not support LaGuardia for Mayor, but we are glad he won. What a fire he is building under the chair-warmers and the parasites!"[4] La Guardia's reputation for personal incorruptibility, obsession with streamlining government, and effective partnership with President Franklin Roosevelt during the New Deal allowed him to embody the energy of the city that never sleeps. Even after the last of his three terms crawled to an end in 1945, La Guardia was remembered with great affection and respect as the model New York mayor. La Guardia was famous for saying, "There is no Democrat or Republican or Socialist way to clean the streets"; Giuliani updated this idea by saying, "There isn't a Democrat or Republican way to run New York. When cities have such complex problems, they need the freedom to select the best solutions."[5]

Giuliani might best be described as a "law and order progressive"—in the original Theodore Roosevelt sense of the word "progressive"—a relentless reformer with contempt for corrupt special interests. Believing that public safety is the most fundamental civil right of all, Giuliani extended his prosecutorial insistence on personal accountability to every aspect of his executive leadership. His service in the Reagan administration was reflected by his belief in cutting taxes and reducing the size of government. But while these principles led to Republican accolades across the nation (columnist George Will called him "America's most successful conservative"), he consistently stood apart from the extreme right wing of his party on social issues. Rudy Giuliani is pro-choice, pro–gay rights, pro–gun control, and pro-immigration.

He accepted fights with the religious right while being thoughtlessly called a fascist by liberal activists. Refreshing among politicians, he refused to pander to colleagues or constituents, explaining that he follows "a very strict rule. I'll tell the people of the City what I believe is in the best interest in the City, what I think is the truth, rather than what I think people would like to hear."[6] He's a quintessential New Yorker—blunt, urban, and unafraid. Freedom from fear is the basic philosophic principle behind all his crusades.

The grandson of immigrants, Rudolph W. Giuliani was born in Brooklyn in 1944, just a few blocks from Ebbets Field, where the legendary Brooklyn Dodgers played. Nonetheless, his father raised him to be a New York Yankees fan and sent him out into the streets of Flatbush in a Yankees uniform. Predictably, he had to fight his way out of more than one sandlot, defying neighborhood bullies with the help of boxing lessons his father insisted he take from an early age. From childhood, Rudy Giuliani learned the value of fighting for his beliefs.

Just as young Hillary Clinton was a Goldwater Girl in suburban Illinois, young Rudy Giuliani volunteered with great enthusiasm for Bobby Kennedy's 1964 race for the Senate in New York. He was a self-described "liberal" columnist for his college newspaper who portrayed the pamphlets of the right-wing John Birch Society as the "disgusting neurotic fantasy of a mind warped by fear and bigotry."[7] He had idolized John F. Kennedy and led a group of friends to pray at their school chapel when the president was assassinated. At the age of twenty-one, Rudy Giuliani won his first elected office—Democratic district leader in Nassau County.[8]

Giuliani considered joining the priesthood during high school, and signed up to enter the Montfort Fathers—a religious order dedicated to serving people in the poorest countries. But increasingly distracted by the charms of the opposite sex, he soon reconsidered. He channeled his deep belief in the presence of good and evil and his rejection of moral relativism to a more worldly outlet—the law. He graduated from New York University Law School and held on to his Democratic politics despite his straitlaced perspective on the tumult of the late 1960s going on all around him in Greenwich Village. He even cast a vote for the quixotic liberal candidacy of George McGovern, overwhelmed by President Richard Nixon 1972's landslide.

But something was changing in young Rudy Giuliani's perception of the world. When he reflected upon why he had cast his ballot for McGovern he realized that it "was not an intelligent, but a reflexive, vote because I'd always been a Democrat."[9] He worried that McGovern "had a very naïve approach to America in the world," which was reflected in the general shift of the Democrats "away from the [John F.] Kennedy–[Scoop] Jackson approach, a strong foreign policy, an adequate and strong military defense of this country so we [could] negotiate from strength with the Soviet Union."[10] After some soul-searching, Giuliani went down to the Board of Elections to change his registration, but initially he could not quite bring himself to check off the Republican box—after all, "Republicans weren't perceived as sensitive to the poor and working class, whereas I strongly identified with the working people with whom I'd grown up"—so he checked off Independent.[11]

Giuliani joined the U.S. Attorney's Office in the newly formed Department to Combat Government Corruption and then rose to head the narcotics division (this, in the era of free dope rallies in his law school's front yard of Washington Square Park). Giuliani was clearly more a fan of the *French Connection* and *Godfather* films than *Woodstock* down at the local movie theater. After Watergate, Giuliani joined the Ford administration's Justice Department as associate deputy attorney general. During the Carter administration, Giuliani moved to private practice in New York. His growing commitment to the Republican Party was solidified when he watched President Carter exclaim that he was "shocked" by the Soviet invasion of Afghanistan. "I literally fell out of my chair," Giuliani later remembered, "Of course Carter shouldn't have been shocked by it. It was predictable behavior."[12] In 1981, Giuliani rode the Reagan revolution back into the Justice Department, where he was appointed associate attorney general—the third most powerful position in the Justice Department. At the age of thirty-six years old, he was in charge of all the U.S attorneys across the nation. His mother worried he was being demoted when after three years he chose to leave Washington to take the preeminent U.S. attorney job in the country: the Southern District of New York.

Free from the ivory tower of high administration, Giuliani was free to make a name for himself in the streets and tabloids of New York, targeting white-collar criminals and Mafia bosses alike. When the Republican appointee dragged scheming stockbrokers out of their offices in shackles, wealthy New Yorkers protested that he was being unduly harsh—after all, this was the go-go 1980s, the age of Wall Street. But Giuliani's high-publicity actions let the word go forth that no man was above the law, and made it difficult to categorize his political affiliations. Likewise, this Italian American's forceful prosecutions of mob bosses made it difficult for the Mafia to claim, as it had so often in the past, that it was the victim of discrimination. Giuliani's pioneering use of the RICO (Racketeer Influenced and Corrupt Organization) statutes proved the decisive legal weapon needed to break the back of the mob in the Northeast.

Like his youthful hero, Bobby Kennedy, Giuliani also moved against corruption in the Teamsters union—the only major labor group to support his boss Ronald Reagan. The 1988 elections were approaching and four candidates for president—Democrats Jesse Jackson and Paul Simon and Republicans Jack Kemp and Alexander Haig—formally called for an end to the investigation. To increase the pile-on of political pressure, 240 members of Congress signed a letter asking President Reagan to request that he instruct U.S. Attorney Giuliani not pursue the case. Giuliani—with the support of President Reagan and Vice President Bush—stood his ground.

The cases that Giuliani would become most famous for had to do with rooting out corruption from New York City government; it was a return to Giuliani's first responsibilities as a young lawyer in the U.S. Attorney's Office and he pursued it with single-minded devotion. He convicted leading members of the Bronx Democratic machine and senior members of Mayor Ed Koch's staff. Deputy Mayor Donald Manes, the self-styled "King of Queens," stabbed himself to death with a pair of scissors after being indicted. This wasn't just business; it was personal. "I don't think that there is anybody worse than a public official who sells his office and corrupts others," Giuliani said, "except maybe a murderer."[13]

After six years spent uncovering the most extensive corruption to afflict City Hall in a generation, Rudy Giuliani declared his 1989 campaign for mayor by invoking the memory of his hero, Mayor La Guardia—right down to the location chosen for the announcement, New York City's Metropolitan Republican Club: "In 1933, Fiorello La Guardia stood in this room and asked the people of New York to embrace a candidacy based not on political name tags, but on integrity, leadership and vision. He reached out to those excluded from the governing of the City, to those who wanted to reject a government that was negligent and corrupt. Now, fifty-six years later, in that spirit of La Guardia, I announce my candidacy for mayor of the City of New York. . . . Now more than ever before, the Mayor of New York must be both an idealist and a pragmatist."

It was a rough campaign, and while Giuliani's initial polling numbers were high, his campaign strategy was built around the assumption that he would be running against Mayor Koch, then campaigning for an unprecedented fourth term. But weighed down by the corruption scandals that Giuliani helped bring to light, Koch was defeated in the Democratic primary by Manhattan Borough president David Dinkins. Amid rising crime, racial tensions came to a boil with the murder of Yusef Hawkins at the hands of a group of white thugs in Brooklyn. Poised to serve as the city's first African-American mayor, Dinkins now received stronger support than the incumbent Democrat, at least partially along the lines that a vote against Dinkins was evidence of racism. "Reject New York's first serious black candidate for Mayor and risk producing more black haters," warned New Yorker columnist Ken Auletta.[14]

Giuliani's tough-on-crime stance suddenly seemed like it might incite further instability rather than solve it, and the new Democratic Party standard-bearer could credibly claim to be an agent of change. On election night 1989, amid accusations of voter fraud that some thought credible in light of a weak ballot security effort by the Republicans, Giuliani lost by less than 2 percent.

After his narrow loss, Giuliani went back into private practice. But as the city slid further into decline—averaging two thousand murders a year and losing more than 330,000 jobs between 1990 and 1993—Giuliani set his sights on City Hall once more. He now tried to balance his image as a hard-nosed former prosecutor by having his young family appear in campaign commercials and highlighting a diverse array of supporters that included high-profile moderate Democrats such as Ed Koch and the president of the Board of Education, Bobby Wagner Jr. Giuliani ran on the slogan "One City, One Standard," a response to Mayor Dinkins's memorable characterization of New York City as "a gorgeous mosaic," which seemed to contradict the "melting pot" assimilation metaphor the city had identified with in the past. Giuliani later said, "I think Dinkins' paradigm of the mosaic in some ways made things worse by playing on the divisions of society rather than bringing people together. A mosaic is made up of separate tiles. . . . Instead of having a city, we were beginning to have something as complicated as the Balkans."

Buoyed by widespread dissatisfaction about the direction of the city and a unusually high turnout from dependably Republican Staten Island (which was voting on a symbolic ballot item on whether to secede from the City of New York), Giuliani scraped by with a 2.5 percent margin of victory. Even in the worst of times, overwhelmingly Democratic New York was reluctant to turn the reigns of government over to a Republican. After winning the election, Giuliani's first trip as mayor-elect was to Harlem.

Giuliani immediately set out creating an administration that was conspicuously—defiantly—bipartisan in nature. At his inauguration, he would trumpet this achievement as the first note of his mayoralty: "Our city has never had as bipartisan a government as we have put together. Democrats and Republicans are working as one at the highest levels of government, as are people who voted for and against me, and people of all different backgrounds. They were chosen in our belief that they can best carry out the necessary changes."[15]

Giuliani retained two commissioners appointed by his Democratic predecessor, David Dinkins. He appointed half a dozen African-American commissioners, despite the fact that only 5 percent of the black community had voted for him over the city's first African-American mayor. He appointed more women to senior positions than had previously been seen in City Hall—including his press secretary and two out of four deputy mayors (one a registered Liberal Party member and the other a Hispanic Democrat). Soon the city's first openly gay, and HIV-positive, commissioner—Christopher Lynn—would take control of the city's fractious Taxi and Limousine Commission and institute a broad range of innovations and customer-service reforms.

These appointments challenged negative perceptions about what a Republican might do in City Hall and broadened Giuliani's narrow base of support—it was inclusive without giving into politically correct pandering. "If you look honestly at this administration, it truly is a representative cross section of the people of New York City," Giuliani stated. "And we didn't use symbolism to achieve that representation. We used merit. And for me, 'merit' means fresh approaches and fresh ideas, and no party, no race, no religion has a corner on that market."[16]

It was no time for business as usual. With a $2.3-billion-dollar deficit looming, the city was on the brink of bankruptcy; there was work to be done. Five weeks later, in his first State of the City address, Giuliani drove the point home by saying, "Smart people, dedicated people working together in the spirit of 'let's get this done' can outperform any ideological clique, any day of the week."[17]

This would also be the first administration in recent memory empowered to take responsibility for solving its own problems rather than endlessly crawling to Washington or Albany for more money. "God did not create City government," Giuliani thundered to the usual collection of local politicians seated inside the City Council chamber. "We did, and we can change it . . . It won't be easy, but it is necessary. We have to act, decisively and boldly."[18] In the tradition of a fellow New York Republican, Theodore Roosevelt—whose photo hung in his corner office in City Hall alongside a portrait of Fiorello La Guardia—Giuliani was determined to "Get Action."

Giuliani was introducing himself to New Yorkers as an independent, less interested in ideology than in results, not a partisan but a problem solver. And with the relentless determination of the mayor, long-standing problems began to be solved. Despite a chorus of protests from Municipal Union workers, sweeping budget cuts were enacted and the world did not come to an end. He strongly lobbied Congress to pass President Clinton's crime bill, which was being held up by an odd alliance of liberals and conservatives. Giuliani played conciliator on Capitol Hill, supporting Democrats' calls for a ban on assault weapons while also agreeing with Republicans demands for tougher sentencing. Many Beltway observers credited the mayor's display of bipartisanship with providing the momentum needed to narrowly pass the bill.

Giuliani used the additional funding from the crime bill to boost the number of police officers on New York City streets to forty thousand—the highest ever. He deployed these officers strategically, developing a comprehensive system known as "CompStat"—for computerized statistics—which identified crimes by location in real time. This allowed police to send in specially trained teams when crime began to surge. For example, five car thefts over two days in a Brooklyn neighborhood would immediately result in officers from the anti–auto theft squad being sent to the area. As a result, a relatively small surge in crime was stopped before it could become a crime wave and noticeably impact the quality of life in the community.

In the past, police commissioners received crime tallies every two weeks. Now the previous evening's crimes could be available the next morning, broken down by neighborhood and street corner. As a result, the police could be a proactive instead of reactive force. And despite a decade's worth of bad news about the inevitability of high crime, crime rates began to fall precipitously.

In August 1995, *New York* magazine carried the cover story "The End of Crime as We Know It: How Giuliani and Bratton Cut the Murder Rate 37% and Overturned 30 Years of Thinking About Law and Order." Murder would fall much further in time, but the revolution was under way. The article quoted a thief and drug dealer named Dread from the Bed-Stuy section of Brooklyn. He'd been forced into selling trinkets emblazoned with Africana to make ends meet. "I'm telling you, the police is out there now, know what I'm saying," wheezed Dread. "They don't slap you around anymore just to fuck with you. They want to make arrests."[19] Word was out on the street that there was a new sheriff in town.

Successfully reducing crime was the first front on a larger quality-of-life revolution that Giuliani was bringing to New York City. In the past, improving the quality of life in New York had been dismissed as too minor an issue for mayors to worry about with rising crime, homelessness, and crack epidemics escalating. Quality of life was for people who wanted to live in the suburbs and Sunbelt cities—not coincidentally, these were the places that disaffected New Yorkers were moving to in droves.

Giuliani was determined to bring the "Broken Windows theory" of policing to New York. First described in a 1982 *Atlantic Monthly* article written by Professors James Q. Wilson and George Kelling, the Broken Windows theory stated that the little things mattered in establishing the lawful environment of a civil society. They used the example of an abandoned building on a busy street: If the first window was broken and not repaired quickly, soon all the windows in the building would be shattered. Allowing vandalism and other quality-of-life crimes such as prostitution, graffiti, aggressive panhandling, or public urination to go unanswered sent a subtle but unmistakable signal that unlawful behavior was tolerated. Criminals would flock that neighborhood and law-abiding citizens—feeling unsafe—would move out. Soon more serious crimes would emerge.

But getting tough on these quality-of-life crimes was unheard of in New York. Giuliani started by expanding an initiative to drive the squeegee men from the city's streets. Long considered an annoying but inevitable fact of New York City life, squeegee men positioned themselves on the entry and exit ramps of Manhattan's tunnels and bridges, where they would essentially ambush passing motorists by spraying dirty water on the windshield, wiping it in quick strokes with a squeegee, and then demanding cash. Giuliani found that only 180 individuals accounted for the city's squeegee men—a relatively small number of people having a broad destructive effect on the quality of life. He ordered the police department to start issuing summonses for the illegal behavior; within weeks of Giuliani's inauguration, the squeegee men were gone. It was an example of how achieving a small definable goal could adjust the perceptions of millions of motorists each month.

And something interesting began to happen: As the police began arresting individuals for low-level quality-of-life crimes and running their records through the computers, they found many of these folks had warrants out for their arrest. One of these was a man named John Royster Jr., who had gone on a weeklong assault and murder spree, smashing the heads of his victims—three women—against the pavement and leaving them for dead. His rampage was stopped because Royster had jumped a turnstile in the subway some months before. His fingerprints were on file, and matching prints were found on the scene of the crime. Police arrested Royster the next day.

More than 180 languages and dialects are spoken on New York City's streets, and despite many worries that a Republican could not be "sensitive" to the needs and competing identities of David Dinkins's "gorgeous mosaic," Giuliani's instinctive defense of immigrants made him an effective—if unexpected—spokesman for tolerance who was also able to draw lines and take stands. Three months into his term at City Hall, Giuliani faced his first act of racial violence: A van carrying a group of young Hasidic scholars was riddled with machine-gun fire on the entrance ramp to the Brooklyn Bridge. Sixteen-year-old Ari Halberstam was killed in the attack by a Lebanese taxicab driver who admitted targeting the van in retaliation for the massacre of sixty-four people in a mosque by a Brooklyn-born man living in Israel. In a hastily called press conference at City Hall, less than a mile from where the shooting had taken place, Rudy Giuliani met the first crisis of his administration head on and surprised critics with his sensitivity and calm sense of control. "This act of evil is not the act of people," Giuliani said; "it's the act of a person or persons. Let's show America and the world that we can make that distinction, that we're not only the best of cities, but the wisest of cities."[20]

In his first year in office, Giuliani balanced his relentless emphasis on accountability with conscious bridge building. In the fall of 1994, he perhaps went a bridge too far with his endorsement of three-term Democratic governor Mario Cuomo for reelection. This seemed like a safe bet: Cuomo was heavily favored to win, and although he was something of a liberal icon, the Queens-born governor and Giuliani worked well together. Moreover, the governor's opponent was an upstate legislator and former mayor of Peekskill named George Pataki who'd been plucked from obscurity by Senator Alfonse D'Amato, the subject of frequent ethics investigations and consequently a Giuliani foe.

This early and obvious show of nonpartisan independence was popular with New Yorkers—and solidified perceptions that they had a man who'd make up his own mind on endorsements based on what was best for the city. Rudy was rewarded with a 70 percent approval rating among New York City Democrats. But his endorsement made Giuliani persona non grata among upstate Republicans and the national GOP establishment. In their eyes, he wasn't independent; he was a traitor. When Pataki pulled off an unexpected upset carried by the momentum of the 1994 Republican Revolution, Giuliani's political life became considerably more difficult overnight. Once and future supporter Staten Island Borough president Guy Molinari declared that "there is no place for Giuliani in the Republican Party."[21] Rudy Giuliani was, one Republican operative suggested, "a walking dead man."[22]

Giuliani was now in the awkward position of being the Democrats' favorite Republican. His predecessor John Lindsay had been in a similar position and ultimately defected to the Democratic Party. Would Rudy Giuliani do the same? As the nation watched Newt Gingrich and the Republican Class of '94 assume power with their Contract for America, many worried the radical right was now in the driver's seat. Within the first twelve months of Republican control of Congress, Giuliani would lead the fight against his party's attack on immigrants.

The right wing of the Republican Party, led by Pat Buchanan, had been campaigning against the legions of illegal immigrants who were crossing into the United States from Mexico—influencing the Republican platform to call for renouncing birthright citizenship for their children. This had increased Republican support among many whites in the border battleground states of California, Arizona, and Texas. But it had alienated suburban swing voters and other moderates across the nation. Now folded into the landmark 1995 welfare reform bill, passed by Congress and signed into law by President Clinton, was a provision that would deny legal immigrants food stamps and access to supplemental security income, which provided benefits for the elderly and disabled poor. Giuliani had long urged Congress to pass federal welfare reform legislation and—impatient for its action—proceeded with far-reaching welfare reform on a local level. But now this bill included provisions that attacked immigration, in Giuliani's eyes a sacred vehicle for American renewal. Another mayor could have gone along with the bill, not spoken out, and waited for the law to be amended—as it was eventually by an apologetic President Clinton—but that was not Giuliani's style.

"Giuliani Sues Government over Benefits for Immigrants," newspaper headlines proclaimed. At a press conference flanked by frequent liberal adversaries such as the Legal Aid Society, Giuliani criticized the aspects of the new law that cut off benefits to legal immigrants as "unconstitutional" and "un-American."

"It is inherently unfair to let people into this country and ask of them what you ask of anyone else"—paying taxes and obeying the law—"and then when they become disabled, cut them off," Giuliani declared.[23] The lawsuit charged that the withdrawal of benefits violated the Fifth Amendment's protection of the right to due process and equal protection. About 110,000 elderly and disabled legal immigrants in New York City alone stood to lose benefits beginning that August, while 70,000 immigrants lost their food stamps at the same time.

Giuliani revered the courage it took for men like his grandfather Rodolfo to cross the ocean with little money in their pockets and begin a new life in America. Unlike American opponents of immigration, Giuliani recognized his own family's past in new immigrants' future. "The people who came through Ellis Island had the same look in their eyes as the people that now come in through Kennedy airport. They did the same wonderful things for us that the new people are going to do for us. We can't be afraid of people. If we're afraid of people then we become a nation and a city in decline."[24]

Typically, there was a practical as well as idealistic element to Giuliani's lawsuit: The federal government's withdrawal of funds would stick the city and state with the $450 million bill. When it became apparent that a federal judge might uphold the constitutionality of this provision, Giuliani took action, creating the Mayor's Office of Immigrant Affairs, a permanent city agency whose sole purpose was to offer services to recent immigrants and make their transition to American life easier.

California Republican congressman Elton Galleghy—sponsor of a failed bill to allow states to exclude children of illegal immigrants from public schools—suggested that Giuliani "check his party registration to see if he's being honest." Giuliani replied, "This isn't a religion, it's a political party. So there are times I agree and times I disagree . . . I don't think you sacrifice your integrity and ability to do your job to a political party."[25]

Giuliani criticized leaders of both parties for backing away from their defense of immigrants and immigration: "Political leaders with few exceptions will not speak up on this. They just look at public opinion polls, which are very anti-immigrant, and then they just play into it. This is not an area where either political party has decided to carve for itself a chapter in 'Profiles in Courage.' "[26]

A Republican's strong support for immigrants had more of an effect than one hundred liberals who were already assumed to have such a position. By causing people to question their assumptions, Giuliani was a pivotal figure in turning the tide against the then-fashionable immigrant bashing. A year later, President Clinton rescinded the provision depriving legal immigrants of benefits, and the 1996 Democratic platform hailed Giuliani's "wisdom" in standing up to anti-immigrant forces. "People are now saying it's good politics," said Frank Sherry of the National Immigration Forum, "but when he first started speaking out, he seemed like the only Republican willing to do it."[27]

Increasingly, Giuliani indicated that he was committed to remaining a Republican, while the same time determining to use his profile to encourage a more inclusive vision for the Republican Party. To party faithful, he explained this as an extension of Ronald Reagan's "Big Tent" philosophy. The prominence of right-wing zealots like Pat Buchanan was "a terrible mistake for the Republicans and for the country," Giuliani said, because they "tried to narrow rather than broaden the Republican Party."[28]

Giuliani consciously set out to do the opposite—partly out of electoral necessity in diverse New York City, but also out of a stubborn sense of political principle. For example, "there is no reason why the party shouldn't appeal to gays and lesbians in the same way that it does to all Americans," he said. A cover story published in the gay weekly the *Advocate,* titled "The Tolerant Bully," stated: "Giuliani is likely to surprise even his staunchest gay and lesbian critics—and his anti-gay supporters—with a cautious and thoughtful support for gay rights that is at odds with his reputation as a political bully whose chief attribute is blind support for the police and fire departments. And for conservatives, Giuliani's Catholicism, background as a prosecutor, and law and order rhetoric add weight to the pro-gay public pronouncements he makes."[29]

Giuliani called on the state legislature to pass a hate crime bill—one of the few Republicans at that time to support the effort, which later passed in 2002. He drew some criticism by abolishing the office set aside for a liaison to the gay community, but set an inclusive tone through appointments of gays and lesbians to nontoken positions. In 1995, Giuliani proposed legislation that led to landmark domestic partnership benefits for city workers—highlighting his commitment to progressive and often controversial measures that avoided calls for special rights while promoting equal rights.

On the most important bellwether issue for whether women in the Northeast were likely to vote Republican—abortion—Giuliani was a consistent defender of a woman's right to choose. He explained that choice was, in his view, "more consistent with the philosophy of the Republican Party . . . because the Republican Party stands for the idea that you have to restore more freedom of choice . . . more opportunity for people to make their own choices rather than the government dictating those choices. . . . So it is consistent with that philosophy to believe that in the most personal and difficult choices that a woman has to make with regard to a pregnancy, those choices should be made based on that person's conscience and that person's way of thinking and feeling. The government shouldn't dictate that choice by making it a crime or making it illegal."[30] Despite the fact that being pro-choice was considered near heretical by the religious right of the Republican Party, polls showed that 65 percent of Republicans supported changing the plank in the Republican platform that called for a constitutional ban on abortion, and over 80 percent of Republicans believed that the decision with regard to an abortion should be made by a woman, her doctor, and her family rather than dictated by the government.[31] Pro-choice Republicans like Giuliani were able to clear one of the most fundamental hurdles to support from Independents and Democrats by remaining steadfast in their support of choice.

Giuliani's political independence proved popular with voters, but it infuriated party regulars. At a speech before the Kennedy School of Government in the summer of 1997, Giuliani described the road he'd taken to reach his style of governance.

> It always appeared to me that the City of New York traditionally did better when the Mayor was somewhat unpredictable, when the Mayor was not a complete captive of one political party or the other . . . Political power in America is apportioned between Democrats and Republicans, and correspondingly, you are going to have Republicans and Democrats in important positions. As the Mayor of New York City, I have to deal with a Republican governor, a Senate with a Republican majority, but an Assembly with a Democratic majority. Of course, the President is a Democrat and the two Houses of Congress are Republican controlled. It makes sense then to be unpredictable. To be locked into partisan politics doesn't permit you to think clearly.

Giuliani's independence and principled contempt for the extremes of right and left was put on display when he chose to give an address on tolerance that criticized both Pat Buchanan and the Reverend Al Sharpton.

Sharpton had been a mainstay in race-related New York politics since the late 1980s, when he injected himself into the case of a fourteen-year-old African-American girl named Tawana Brawley in upstate New York who accused police officers of raping her. Sharpton managed the press and inflamed the situation, refusing to cooperate with authorities even after a grand jury concluded that Tawana Brawley had lied. In the fall of 1995, Sharpton had been supporting calls for a boycott of a Jewish-owned store on 125th Street named Freddy's Fashion Mart. On the radio, Sharpton dismissed the business owner as a "white interloper"—despite the fact he'd been operating in that location for thirty years—and said, "I'm gonna go down there and do what is necessary to let them know that we are not turning 125th Street back over to outsiders."[32] Three months later, a man named Roland James Smith walked into

Freddy's Fashion Mart, pulled out a gun, and asked all the black customers to step out of harm's way. He then poured paint thinner on the clothing in the store, lit it on fire, and began shooting, murdering seven people, then killing himself.

In response to this combined rise of intolerance in his city and in his party, Giuliani prepared a typically hard-edged address on the importance of tolerance.

> From time to time a figure arises on the American political landscape, whose message is one of division . . . of intolerance . . . of fear. This year we have seen the rise and the apparent fall of Patrick Buchanan, who appeals to a fear of "foreigners," of people who look, speak and act differently than ourselves. . . . Patrick Buchanan represents precisely the opposite direction from the one New York City needs to follow. . . . We are interested in moving beyond the politics of race, the politics of division, to concentrate on the politics of unity . . . of common goals and common aspirations. It's time we recognized that prejudice and stereotyping can emanate from any direction . . . from any community . . . from any neighborhood.
>
> Most recently, it was the Harlem community that faced this dilemma following the burning of Freddy's on 125th Street. The mere possibility that race was a motivator in that terrible crime prompted some in the Harlem community to close ranks with the haters in their midst. It's time we recognized that anti-social, criminal elements exist in every group . . . and these people—the haters—are the ones we must oppose. . . . When we have broken this barrier we will have reached closer to the ideal of unity as human beings."[33]

Instead of being content to single out either the Republican Buchanan or the Democratic Sharpton for their promotion of intolerance—as many typical partisan politicians would—Giuliani unapologetically held them in equal contempt.

As Giuliani neared reelection, his unorthodox leadership style was getting unambiguous results: murder down 60 percent, with the lowest overall crime rate in three decades; 300,000 people moved off the welfare rolls, from a high of 1.1 million; 250,000 new private sector jobs; and a $2.3 billion deficit turned to a $1.2 billion surplus. At least by the numbers, the worst of times had been turned to the best of times. The resurgent spirit of the city could not be as easily quantified, but it was captured by the birth of a new dynasty for Giuliani's beloved New York Yankees, who in 1996 won the first of four World Series championships in the next five years—a feat the fans had not been treated to since the days of Casey Stengel, Mickey Mantle, Whitey Ford, and Yogi Berra. New York was back on top. And when the rising numbers of tourists visited the city, the change was most evident—the cesspool that had been Times Square, full of pornographic theaters and drug dealers, was transformed back into the crossroads of the world. When those visitors returned home, they told friends how the city had changed. Giuliani became a nationally known figure.

Rudy Giuliani was placed at the head of a class of new "third-way" mayors, christened "The New Progressives" in a cover story by the *New Republic*. These mayors—L.A.'s Republican Richard Riordan, Cleveland's Democratic Michael White, Indianapolis's Republican Steve Goldsmith, and Milwaukee's Democratic John Norquist among them—"represent a radical break with their predecessors . . . managing city government efficiently in the public interest rather than using it as a mechanism for arbitrating competing group interests. These new mayors are hugely popular . . . but they are outsiders in their own parties, viewed with suspicion and even contempt by their parties' most powerful constituencies."[34]

Pundits may have been falling over themselves in praise of these New Progressives, but there was angry opposition to many of their reforms. Before welfare reform was signed into law by President Clinton, protests were daily and characterizations vicious. When the city required fingerprinting individuals on public assistance to cut down on fraud, Councilwoman Una Clarke referred to it as "Branding the Slaves"[35]—a characterization that carried some weight in local newspapers until it was pointed out that city managers and commissioners were already fingerprinted as part of their contract.[36] When the "workfare" initiative was implemented, requiring longtime welfare recipients to work for the city cleaning parks in exchange for their benefits, Norman Siegel of the New York Civil Liberties Union said, "We believe that individuals should not be coerced into employment."[37] Despite the criticism, Giuliani did not turn back. He asserted the essential dignity of all work and was fond of quoting Martin Luther King: "If a man is called to be a street sweeper, he should sweep streets even as Michelangelo painted, or Beethoven composed music, or Shakespeare wrote poetry. He should sweep streets so well that all the hosts of heaven and earth will pause to say, here lived a great street sweeper who did his job well."

Welfare offices were turned into job centers and the entire organizational purpose of the agency shifted from a handout to a hand-up, success judged not by how many people were put on the roles, but how many were placed into jobs. Cutting welfare dependency in half had been thought as impossible as cutting crime in half—but now it was being done. Still, not everyone was pleased and protests continued; future state senator Liz Krueger argued that "welfare is a revenue producer for the city,"[38] while activist Maureen Lane claimed that "work is not a substitute for welfare because it either pays too little or takes jobs from union members."[39]

It was 1997 and New York City's liberal establishment—used to controlling City Hall, as it had for all but twelve of the past fifty-two years—now prepared to take back what it considered its birthright. They were on the ropes but fighting back. Rudy Giuliani was popular, but could his popularity outweigh the Democrats' 5 to 1 registration advantage? Ruth Messinger, the Manhattan Borough president and a twenty-year fixture on the liberal Upper West Side, was the conventional wisdom's front-runner for the nomination—but like Bob Dole, it was simply her turn. Bronx Borough president Fernando Ferrer was a much-hyped possible challenger: a moderate-sounding rising star and the city's highest-ranking elected Hispanic. But after months of flirting with a run for City Hall, Ferrer backed off, claiming the time was not right—perhaps intimidated by Giuliani's $6 million war chest. And so Ferrer endorsed Messinger, who waddled off into battle with the Reverend Al Sharpton, her most serious competitor for the nomination.

Giuliani paid little attention to his presumptive opponents, and used the bully pulpit of incumbency to dominate the airwaves without cutting into his campaign funds until midsummer. Messinger's campaign, meanwhile, provided a virtual seminar in what not to do if you wanted to get elected mayor of New York.

She announced the beginning of her campaign several times, the last of which was outside a public school on the Lower East Side. Giuliani puckishly decided to schedule a lavish welcome for the Yankees' much-hyped new powerhouse pitcher Hideki Irabu, complete with privately paid for sushi on the steps of City Hall at the same time. Predictably, most of the City Hall press corps decided to stay close to home that day.

For reasons beyond rational explanation, the Messinger campaign decided that the "formal announcement" of her candidacy was not worth renting a sound system for, and so the modest crowd of assembled reporters and supporters strained to hear the candidate over the wind, which whipped her prepared remarks to the ground, scattering them as she began to speak. "If you live high up in the sky, send your kids to private boarding schools, go to work in big black cars, eat at the finest restaurants, go to private doctors and need a team of accountants to figure out how much you really made last year, then Rudy is your guy," she shouted into the Lower East Side wind.

While Messinger decried the New York of private schools, private doctors, and hired accountants, the usually friendly *New York Times* pointed out that she had attended the exclusive Brearley School on the Upper East Side, went to a private doctor, had an accountant, and lived in a three-bedroom apartment overlooking Central Park. Messinger finished her speech with a final salvo against the entrenched and privileged by attacking those "who go to work in big black cars"—referring to the autos used by high-level city officials. Reporters could not resist noting that "the candidate then climbed into her chauffeured city-owned standard-issue big black car and drove off."

The string of avoidable campaign disasters continued when Ms. Messinger—at age fifty-six—tried to make the fifty-three-year-old mayor's health an issue. This line of attack took on tragicomic proportions as Ms. Messinger decided to circle around the City Hall parking lot on a bike, calling for Mr. Giuliani to "come outside and race," while wearing a large white bicycle helmet perched atop her head. Some enterprising staffer had apparently warned the candidate that she would be accused of flouting the city's bicycle safety laws if her head was not adequately protected, and sent Ms. Messinger in front of the cameras, producing an image that was reminiscent of the 1988 campaign-killing photo of Michael Dukakis riding around in a tank. One local television station played the footage over and over at high speeds with music from *The Wizard of Oz* playing in the background.

Prominent Democrats began clustering around Giuliani's candidacy, requiring two separate Democrats for Giuliani rallies in City Hall Park. These ranged from congressmen and state senators to council members and union leaders. Antonio Pagan, a gay Puerto Rican councilman for the Lower East Side district where Ms. Messinger had announced her candidacy, explained his support for Rudy Giuliani this way: When Giuliani was first elected "the city was falling apart. Giuliani gave voters a glimpse of hope that someone ballsy, aggressive, and tough could have an effect. Gays voted for him to have the streets cleaned up. Women are going to vote for him because he makes the streets safer for women." When pressed on the political logic of his apparent defection, Pagan replied, "What is the reaction of Democrats? What are the Democratic values to be upheld against Giuliani? Hypodermic needles? Crumbling schools? Violence?"[40]

Giuliani's demonstrable success on the basic issues had not only silenced many of his critics—he had so convincingly won the battle of ideas that some Democrats questioned the whole point of opposing him. The most impressive example of this philosophical victory was little noticed: The supposed dream candidate of unreconstructed liberals, Ruth Messinger, was quietly promising that no taxes would be raised to pay for more social programs if she were to be elected mayor. This was a sea change from the tax-and-spend policies of liberal Democrats in the past. In fact, stealing a page from Giuliani's playbook, Messinger proposed privatizing some city services to come up with greater savings. This gesture toward fiscal austerity did nothing to endear the remaining unions to her candidacy. When she remedied this fiscal conservatism with talk of achieving parity with the higher salaries of suburban teachers and police officers, the *Times* again took a shot across her bow: "The talk about parity with the suburbs may just be Ms. Messinger's attempt to mend her bridges with a little old-fashioned Democratic pandering. If so, she is playing right into conservative claims that liberals can no longer govern New York City."[41]

But Giuliani's smooth ride to reelection took a serious stumble when a Haitian immigrant named Abner Louima was assaulted by police officers in Brooklyn and sodomized with a plunger inside the Seventieth Precinct. Newspapers reported that the officers had yelled "It's Giuliani time" after the attack. Despite the fact that six months later Louima retracted the statement, saying that it had been suggested to him by a family friend as a way to attract media attention, the damage was done.[42] This grotesque degree of police brutality, combined with the widely reported statement, seemed to validate the worst fears about the cost of crime reduction under Rudy Giuliani.

The morning after the attack, Giuliani called a press conference to announce his firing of the Seventieth Precinct commander, the prosecution of the officers allegedly involved, and the reassignment of most of the other officers stationed there. He was flanked by unusual company—longtime civil rights advocates like Norman Seigel and other community leaders. He announced their appointment to a special citizens commission to analyze police brutality and come up with a series of proposals to end the problem. The commission's recommendations—civilian oversight of the NYPD—proved far more radical than Rudy Giuliani was willing to accept, but the swift reaching-out was effective. It was textbook: In a time of crisis co-opt the reasonable edge of the opposition.

In the wake of the Louima attack, Al Sharpton's candidacy suddenly caught fire. On September 9, he came in second in the Democratic primary with 32 percent of the vote in a four-person race with extremely low turnout. In the hours and days after the polls closed, he appeared to deny Ruth Messinger the 40 percent of the vote needed to declare victory. Sharpton celebrated by flapping his arms in broad birdlike motions as he shouted the lyrics to the song "I Believe I Can Fly," cheered on by a jubilant crowd at his National Action Network offices in Harlem.

The mood at Messinger headquarters was decidedly more somber. She had declined the advice of Democratic Party mandarins like former mayor Ed Koch, who had called on her to loudly denounce Sharpton's candidacy, preferring instead not to split the Democratic vote she seemed predestined to win. Now she was faced with the possibility of running against Sharpton in a head-to-head contest. After extensive recounts, it was determined that Messinger had, in fact, squeaked by with barely 40 percent of the vote. But even this victory felt like a loss—she was the technical victor, but the "news" in the election had been Sharpton's stronger-than-expected turnout. And without a runoff, Messinger was denied the ability to distinguish herself by delivering a knockout punch to her adversary, who could not have won the runoff because his harshly partisan profile made appealing to crossover votes impossible.

Messinger's luckless campaign trudged along toward November's general election, but enthusiasm even among Democrats was low. Giuliani campaigned aggressively, sending campaign staff to all her events with tape recorders and notepads at the ready. But as the final weeks of the campaign closed in, he was so far ahead in the polls that his team chose not to publicize a 1970s-era leaflet showing a young Ruth Messinger as a founding member of a grassroots socialist organization, whose slogan was "We're Democrats . . . and Socialists—for the same reason." Ruth Messinger was already on the ropes and in the margins—there was no need to play hardball, lest they create sympathy for their opponent and reinforce perceptions that the mayor was given to "bullying" behavior, as Messinger alleged.

Still, Giuliani ran with the energy and determination of a candidate who was trailing in the polls. He capped the campaign with a marathon forty-eight-hour bus tour throughout the city, stopping at Gracie Mansion only to change clothes. Messinger responded with a pledge to ride the subway throughout the city during the last twenty-four hours of the race.

On Tuesday, November 7, 1997, Rudy Giuliani was returned to City Hall with a stunning mandate. He had won four out of the city's five boroughs—all except the Bronx. In fact, he had trounced the

Manhattan Borough president in the borough she had represented for almost a quarter century, winning 60 percent of the vote in her home district of the Upper West Side.

Rudy had won a higher percentage of women's votes than the first serious female candidate for mayor, as well as 72 percent of the Jewish vote against Ms. Messinger. Nearly 40 percent of New York City's gays and lesbians voted for him, as had nearly 50 percent of Hispanic males. Forty-three percent of self-described liberals, 61 percent of moderates, and 72 percent of conservatives had pulled the lever for Giuliani, as well as 92 percent of registered Republicans, 65 percent of independents, and 45 percent of Democrats. All across the ideological aisle, New Yorkers cast their vote for Rudy Giuliani. Sixty-four percent of all voters said that the quality of life in New York had improved over the past four years.

"To get 60% in an 80% Democratic city isn't anything the Republicans—who have finally realized they need the Northeast—can ignore,[43] opined Mitchell Moss, director of NYU's Taub Urban Research Center. That afternoon, a new issue of *New York* magazine appeared on newsstands. The editors had been so sure of Rudy's victory that they'd risked "Dewey Defeats Truman" infamy to display a broadstroke caricature of Giuliani dressed as George Washington, with the headline "How Far Can Rudy Go?" That evening, with his voice hoarse but victory assured, Giuliani walked to the podium of the midtown Hilton Hotel, where he had celebrated his first election victory four years before. Then he had been a Republican pariah, daring to take on the first African-American to serve in City Hall. Now he was surrounded by as many Democrats as Republicans. He began by thanking supporters and sending his intended message for the second term in City Hall—that no New Yorker would be left behind.

The most important part of our new business is to have the spirit of pride in New York City—and the spirit of success and opportunity that has reached so many New Yorkers—to make certain that it reaches all New Yorkers. We want for all New Yorkers . . . freedom from welfare, freedom from dependence on government. We want them to be able to take control of their own lives and help their neighbors. That's the direction we're moving in now. Freedom. And that's the direction that we will move toward even more aggressively.[44]

Giuliani's next four years in City Hall would be marked by controversy surrounding the dissolution of his marriage and an aborted Senate campaign against Hillary Clinton abandoned when Giuliani was diagnosed with prostate cancer, the same disease that had claimed his father's life. But through it all, crime and murder rates kept declining, the local economy kept expanding with new private-sector jobs, and welfare rolls fell to their lowest levels in more than thirty years. Giuliani's successful fight against cancer inspired the creation of a new initiative known as HealthStat, which used the crime-fighting CompStat technology to pinpoint the areas of the city most in need of health insurance. As a result of Giuliani's concerted effort, more than 150,000 low-income children and families were enrolled with health insurance in the last fifteen months of his administration.

The successes far outweighed the scandals, but many pundits felt that Giuliani's career was over as he approached the end of his second term in office. He was prohibited from running for a third time under a new term-limits law he had supported, and no New York mayor in recent history had ever achieved higher office after serving in City Hall.

On the blue-sky morning of September 11, 2001, voters were lining up at polling places across the city to vote in the mayoral primary, and Rudy Giuliani seemed just hours away from being a lame duck. Then, at 8:46 A.M., Muhammad Atta shattered that morning's peace by ramming American Airlines Flight 11 into the North Tower of the World Trade Center, followed by fellow members of al-Qaeda slamming United Airlines Flight 175 into the South Tower. Giuliani raced to the scene to survey the damage and help orchestrate the rescue effort, as he would have in the event of any fire. He was taken to a landline one block away from the Twin Towers to speak to the White House, and while there, the first tower collapsed. Initially trapped, Giuliani emerged from the devastation covered in ash from the fallen towers, and television cameras captured him directing the evacuation of Lower Manhattan north to safety.

Two hours later—as the president was being shuttled from secure location to secure location on Air Force One—Giuliani gave the first full briefing on the attacks on America. He set a tone of resolve and indignation, balancing compassion for those many thousands of lives that had been lost with words of caution not to blame members of one ethnic or religious group. The mayor's unscripted remarks echoed the perfect pitch he had struck when Ari Halberstam had been murdered eight years before. The controversial mayor was rewarded for his grace under pressure with something like love; instead of being booed, he was spontaneously applauded wherever he walked. "Until now, New Yorkers didn't realize what it takes to be Mayor of this great city," the *New York Observer* editorialized one week after the attacks.

> Through his words and actions since the terrible morning of Sept. 11, Rudy Giuliani will go down in history as New York's greatest mayor of the past 100 years, easily surpassing previous favorites like Ed Koch and Fiorello LaGuardia. Mr. Giuliani has robustly steered the city through the worst crisis any city can face, and he has done so not by resorting to sentimentality or bravado, but by relying on bracing honesty, clear-eyed compassion and a core belief in the city's ability to renew itself. He has helped save New Yorkers from what could have been a citywide collapse into bitterness and despair, and across the country he is being hailed as a statesman. Not only has Mr. Giuliani reassured the city, he has comforted a nation.[45]

Two months later, the ultimate endorsement of Rudy Giuliani's independence and effectiveness occurred: Against all odds, and against the expectations of the city's political establishment, a reform Republican was succeeded by a reform Republican in City Hall. This had never happened before in all of New York City history. The shift from entitlement to accountability would not be rolled back by the resurgence of the old liberal Democratic machine. Rudy Giuliani had changed the rules of the game.

PART 5

ELECTION 2000

THE COMPASSIONATE CONSERVATIVE VS. A PRACTICAL IDEALIST AND THE STRAIGHT TALK EXPRESS

I'm a uniter, not a divider.

—GEORGE W. BUSH

In the summer of 1998, amid whispers that he was aiming for the presidency, George W. Bush ran for reelection as governor of Texas. As the campaign bus dubbed "Asphalt One" rolled along the highways of Texas, the people it passed could not miss the two words written on its side: Opportunity and Responsibility.

These were the same words that Bill Clinton and Al Gore had turned into a near mantra for the New Democrat movement that had led them into the White House, forcing the elder George Bush into early retirement just six years before. When a journalist pointed out the ironic similarity, George W. Bush seemed surprised. "You're kidding me," he said. "I was focused on 'four more years.'"[1]

The election of 2000, the closest presidential election in modern American history, was a millennial race between two Centrists from the South. It was slated to be a contest between the "compassionate conservative" and the "practical idealist"; but while George W. Bush reinforced his central message through carefully scripted sound bites and photo ops throughout the campaign, Al Gore overreacted to a lack of enthusiasm on the part of liberals by lurching to the left in his rhetoric, speaking in heated tones about the "people versus the powerful" at a time of record economic prosperity, recalling the class-based polarization of the old Democratic Party. Bush embraced the style of Centrism while taking care never to alienate the party's right wing in matters of substance, while Gore hid a lifetime of Centrist policies under a hastily fashioned cloak of old Democrat populism. As a result, Gore appeared the more narrowly partisan of the two candidates, and Bush—blessed with near-genius levels of emotional intelligence—was able to make significant inroads toward the center of the American electorate.

In the world according to Vice President Al Gore, the campaign was happening twelve years too late. In 1988, when George W. Bush was a footnote in his father's presidential campaign—two years sober and on the rebound from a failed oil venture—thirty-nine-year-old overachiever Al Gore was running for president in his own right.

A first-term senator who had been elected to his father's old seat from Tennessee, Gore was the first baby boomer to campaign for the nation's highest office, a self-described "raging moderate," and a foreign policy hawk. His wife, Tipper, burnished her conservative credentials by leading a parents' crusade to restrict the sale of obscene music to minors. Other Democrats accused Gore of pandering to the right wing of the party, but his precocious candidacy gained some traction in the primaries as a result of his association with the Centrist Democratic Leadership Council. The nomination went to Michael Dukakis, who lost to Vice President George Bush. Gore spent the following four years working on nuclear proliferation issues and writing a well-regarded book on environmentalism titled *Earth in the Balance.* In 1992, DLC chairman and Arkansas governor Bill Clinton tapped Al Gore to be his running mate. As vice president, Gore oversaw efforts to reduce bureaucracy and reinvent government, and his success was striking: Under his watch, the government payroll fell to its lowest level in nearly forty years.

As the millennium approached, and after two terms as vice president, Al Gore could again feel the Oval Office calling. After much deliberation, he decided on the slogan Practical Idealism, a reminder that he stood apart from his party's stereotypical penchant for pursuing idealistic ends without regard to practical consequences. Gore had turned somewhat new-aged and circumspect in his middle age, but his message remained the same.

On the night of November 3, 1998, Al Gore was watching the midterm election returns in the vice president's residence at the Naval Observatory. Contrary to all expectations, it was turning out to be a good night for Democrats. ABC News proclaimed it a "move to moderation." Despite President Clinton's impeachment, exit polls showed that 50 percent of voters were self-described moderates who were abandoning the GOP. The most notable exception, however, was in the nation's second largest state: Texas.

When George W. Bush had first been swept into the governor's mansion—in his first successful attempt at elected office—this son of the former president seemed like a minor figure in the Republican Revolution of 1994. Now, on the evening of his overwhelming reelection, he stood with his wife, Laura, as a powerful and popular political figure in his own right, becoming the first Texas governor in twenty-five years to be reelected and, as the newspapers noted, "setting the stage for a presidential bid in the year 2000."

"Tonight's resounding victory says my compassionate, conservative philosophy is making Texas a better place," Bush said. "But today's election says something more. It says that a leader who is compassionate and conservative can erase the gender gap, can open the doors of the Republican Party to new faces and new voices."[2]

In a year when overzealous Republicans were being cast out of office around the country, George W. Bush had been rewarded with an overwhelming mandate: 69 percent of Texans cast their ballot for Bush; nearly 40 percent of Hispanics had supported his reelection; and his margin among African-Americans in Texas increased from less than 10 percent to nearly a quarter of that population. Perhaps most persuasive were the high-level Texas Democrats who crossed party lines to support his candidacy. Even the legendary Democratic lieutenant governor Bob Bullock, then dying of cancer, had refused to support his own party's nominee—despite the fact that he was godfather to the candidate's child—choosing instead to support the young governor for reelection.

George W. Bush had built a reputation as a "compassionate conservative," the competent, easygoing executive of the nation's second-largest state, a man who could moderate the excesses of his own party. This was "it takes a village" conservatism, modern and inclusive, yet rooted in the family values of church and community.

First as governor, and then as a presidential candidate, George W. Bush consciously set about appropriating the middle ground on policy issues. This left Gore as the representative of the incumbent administration, unable—and at times, it appeared, unwilling—to respond. Members of the Democratic Leadership Council were frustrated by this role reversal.

"George Bush is trying to steal the mantle of reform and innovation from the New Democrats, and we can't let him get away with it," said Will Marshall, director of the Progressive Policy Institute, the academic wing of the DLC.[3] The Bush camp was forthright in its response to this charge. "I'd argue that we're retrieving Republican territory the DLC had encroached," replied Bush policy director Josh Bolton.[4]

This was by design. Throughout 1998 and 1999, Bush political strategists Karl Rove and Stuart Stevens had met countless times at coffee shops around Austin to develop the campaign plan that could lead them to victory. As they talked, they grew increasingly convinced that Compassionate Conservatism was the key to 1600 Pennsylvania Avenue. As Stevens explained in his campaign biography, *The Big Enchilada:*

We had to face reality. The Democrats had been successful in painting the Republican Party as a natural home for right wing lunatics and nutballs of all stripes. And the party hadn't helped itself with antics like shutting down the government or failing to denounce the wackos who were busy circulating pictures of Clinton behind the grassy knoll in Dallas. "Compassionate Conservative" was the shorthand to the world that Bush was different. We wanted people to hear it and think that yes, Bush was a conservative, but he cared about education, cared about the poor and lower middle-class, cared about finding new solutions to vexing problems of inequality. . . . Compassionate Conservatism would be the way to cut the Gordian knot that was holding back the Republican Party. Like the Democrats in the 1980s, the Republican Party's growth was bounded by the extremes. It wasn't that everybody didn't know it, it's just that nobody had come up with a way to get out of the box.[5]

The Bush team studied the Clinton-Gore administration's strengths in order to unseat them. Karl Rove, a strategic genius with a love for political history, admired one kingmaker most of all: Ohio senator Mark Hanna, who elevated Republican William McKinley to the presidency in 1896, and who famously said, "Politics are one form of business, and must be treated as a business." With money already pouring into Austin, the team could hire high-priced campaign consultants to plan for the restoration.

Senator John McCain of Arizona would have been Mark Hanna's worst nightmare. A maverick Republican reformer, a war hero with national appeal and an eagerness to take on the big money interests of his own party with his personal crusade for campaign finance reform, John McCain was also an outspoken admirer of Mark Hanna's nemesis—"that damned cowboy," Theodore Roosevelt.

As a man who had spent five and a half years as a North Vietnamese prisoner of war in the notorious "Hanoi Hilton"—and despite being tortured, refused early release—John McCain had a personal narrative that was widely admired in Washington. His record in the Senate received more mixed reviews: McCain's rugged independence made him a headache for the party leadership. He was conservative on many issues, but he kept taking on reform crusades against big businesses like tobacco and the pharmaceutical industry. He'd been in a running feud with Kentucky Republican Mitch McConnell for several years over McCain's dogged cosponsorship of an annually blocked campaign finance reform bill with Wisconsin Democrat Russ Feingold.* McCain was tenacious—once he gave his word that he would support a cause there was no surrender—but some Senate colleagues found his bluntness impolitic. McCain shrugged; his loyalties to the Republican Party ran deeper than his loyalties to the Republican leadership, and besides, he said, "I'm never going to win the Miss Congeniality Award in the Senate." His disarming honesty and dark humor caused reporters to fawn over him—one article in *Esquire* was titled simply "John McCain Walks on Water."

In 1998, Bill Clinton's spectacular failure of judgment and personal integrity dominated the headlines, and as people desperately looked to the next presidential election for relief, one thing seemed clear: America needed a hero in the White House. Al Gore's reputation for squeaky-clean behavior had taken a hit with his attendance at a campaign fund-raiser in a Buddhist temple. On this front, too, McCain seemed like the logical candidate for 2000. Finally, Americans were reacting in disgust to the toxic atmosphere of bitter partisanship that seemed to dominate Washington.

McCain was beyond bipartisan; he was an equal-opportunity offender, as when talking about the need for HMO reform: "The problem is, the Democrats are in the pocket of the trial lawyers and we Republicans are in the pocket of the insurance companies. And so there is gridlock, and there will continue to be, until we get the special-interest influence out of politics."[6] No voter was going to mistake him for Slick Willie; big-business conservatives may have been concerned, but moderates and Independents loved him. Everything seemed to point to the fact that the time was right for the uphill reform candidacy of John McCain.

---

*This split between the moderates and extremists of both parties occasionally resulted in darkly comic headlines, such as the following: "The campaign-finance debate resumes this week, and GOP leaders are again expected to try to kill reform legislation while appearing to back it." (*Wall Street Journal*, June 2, 1998.)

In January 1999, McCain became the first candidate to officially form an exploratory committee. Amid the celebration and high expectations, the skeptical *Arizona Republic* sounded a typically sobering note, asking whether "a stubborn non-conformist who delights in bucking trends [can] win enough support to lead the right-leaning Republican Party closer to the center."[7]

Normally, a candidate's first stop on the campaign trail was Iowa, but McCain decided to bypass it altogether, rationalizing that "the Iowa Republican caucuses weren't open to Independents and Democrats, as is the New Hampshire primary. They have very low turnout and are dominated by religious conservatives, whose leaders have decided for various reasons that campaign finance reform is a sin. As a vocal opponent of government subsidies to ethanol producers, I wasn't going to be the first choice of farmers in 'the land where the tall corn grows,' either."[8] John McCain headed straight to New Hampshire.

Buoyed by high name recognition courtesy of his birth certificate and the Centrist success of his compassionate conservative philosophy in Texas, George W. Bush was already considered the front-runner for the nomination. In June, after months of Rose Garden–style interviews surrounded by hoards of reporters in Austin, Bush made his way to Iowa. His announcement speech was relatively informal, but it captured the tone of the man and the campaign he intended to run.

I'm running because our country must be prosperous. But prosperity must have a purpose. The purpose of prosperity is to make sure the American Dream touches every willing heart. . . . It is conservative to reform welfare by insisting on work. It is compassionate to take the side of charities and churches. . . . It is conservative to confront illegitimacy. It is compassionate to offer practical help to women and children in crisis. . . . It is conservative to insist on education standards, basics, and local control. It is compassionate to make sure that not one single child gets left behind. . . . I'm running because my party must match a conservative mind with a compassionate heart. And I'm running to win."[9]

This was politics with a spiritual dimension, carefully worded, with the discipline of a born competitor evident behind every sentence. Bush acknowledged the nation's prosperity but questioned the values undergirding it without ever mentioning Bill Clinton by name. He illustrated exactly what the implicit promise of Compassionate Conservatism was—the social sentiments expressed made it a speech a Democrat might have given, but the content and audience were 100 percent Republican. This contradiction increased attention on the former president's son, who was now a serious candidate in his own right.

Al Gore had unveiled his slogan, "Practical Idealism," the previous December in a speech at the DLC annual conference in Washington, D.C. Like the slogan itself, Gore was trying too hard, quoting Gandhi, the Bible, and Steve Martin in a twenty-five-minute address weighted down with phrases such as "beyond the old polarities of individual choice and national government lie the subtle connections that are the matrix of community." By spring, the Gore campaign was falling like a lead balloon. With polls showing the vice president trailing his presumptive challenger from Texas by as much as fifteen points, his long-planned campaign hemorrhaging money on high-paid consultants, Gore's wife abruptly suggested that they move the headquarters out of K Street in Washington, D.C., and back to his native Nashville, Tennessee. After an empty mortuary was rejected as a possible campaign headquarters for obvious public relations reasons, a former medical rehabilitation center called Sundance Rehab was found. It was a fitting bit of synchronicity: Gore's Secret Service code name was Sundance.[10]

Gore designed the campaign logo himself after being dissatisfied with the options presented to him, drawing a shooting star in orbit around his name on a cocktail napkin. On the questionable advice of *Beauty Myth* author Naomi Wolf, he began wearing tight-fitting, earth-toned clothing. At his announcement in the town square of his hometown of Carthage, Tennessee, in June, Gore was pumped up and woodenly aggressive. But the carefully scripted event was disrupted early by a dozen AIDS protesters blowing whistles (which Gore handled deftly by grinning and saying, "I love free speech") and by a nightmare for the restless perfectionist—the television audience couldn't see him for minutes at a time because the signs the candidate had designed were waving in front of the cameras and blocking their view of the stage.

With the campaign now under way, Bush focused on proposals in a limited number of areas and stayed on message with admirable discipline, just as he had in his Texas gubernatorial elections. It was no accident that the majority of these policy issues were traditionally identified with Democrats: education, Social Security reform, and health care. Only the promise of tax cuts and a stronger military were identified with the traditional Republican agenda.

Bush was most passionate and articulate on the subject of education. The campaign adopted the slogan "Leave No Child Behind" from the Children's Defense Fund, a liberal advocacy organization chaired by Marian Wright Edelman—a former friend of President Clinton's who had broken ranks with him because of his support of welfare reform. Virtually every poll showed that education was the issue voters cared most about in the election, and it was an area in which Bush could credibly seize the mantle of innovation and responsible reform. Bush deftly claimed the high ground by championing education reforms such as higher school standards with elegantly crafted sound bites that denounced "the soft bigotry of low expectations."

Because Democratic candidates depended upon support from the teachers' union, Al Gore was effectively forced to defend the state of the school system as it existed, while Bush and the Republicans were free to support cutting-edge policies, such as school choice. This should have been a logical policy for New Democrats to embrace because it reinforced their central tenets of giving more choice and greater opportunity to disadvantaged individuals in society. But Gore and the Democrats could not support vouchers because the United Federation of Teachers had emerged as their party's largest financial backers. This was especially ironic because one of the most eloquent arguments for creation of the Democratic Leadership Council after the election of 1984 was that Democrats "had become the party of teachers, when we should have been the party of education."

Resistance to special interests and openness to new ideas had been the hallmark of Al Gore and his generation of New Democrats, but this had been softened by the political realities of incumbency. As the de facto defender of the administration he'd been part of for eight years, Gore was left with few options other than to tinker around the edges of education reform, and give platitude-laden speeches to union halls full of teachers who had a personal stake in the status quo.

Likewise, when it came to health care, Gore was saddled by memories of Bill and Hillary Clinton's failed first-term health-care plan, which was frequently characterized by conservatives as an attempt to socialize one-seventh of the nation's economy. Bush took advantage of this opportunity to endorse the conclusions of the National Bipartisan Commission on the Future of Medicare. Their legislation, cosponsored by Democratic senator John Breaux and Republican senator Bill Frist, had recently been rejected by the Clinton administration. By supporting this rejected bipartisan proposal, Bush seemed open to ideas from both sides of the aisle, while Gore was left to defend an action that appeared narrowly partisan.

The ads the Bush team ran painted Gore convincingly into this corner. An offscreen announcer intoned, "Gore opposed bipartisan reform. He's pushing a big-government plan that lets Washington bureaucrats interfere with what your doctors prescribe. The Gore prescription plan: Bureaucrats decide. The Bush prescription plan: Seniors choose."[11]

Single-issue candidates in the Republican primary, such as Gary Bauer, criticized Bush for his unwillingness to speak forcefully on abortion, and conservative senator Bob Smith from New Hampshire briefly flirted with an Independent protest candidacy. Pat Buchanan was so incensed by Bush's moderate message that he eventually bolted the party altogether. But far from harming his candidacy, this criticism actually helped Bush. Because he appeared far from a zealot on abortion, women voters were essentially free to read whatever they wanted to into his silence. Bush appeased the far right by promising to appoint a pro-life vice presidential candidate, but when pressed in debates he refused to say whether he would make *Roe v. Wade* a litmus test for judicial appointments.

Despite this emotionally unsatisfying stance, the right wing remained unified behind Bush's candidacy because they had no realistic alternative—eight years outside the White House had forced them to discipline their fractious impulses. Ralph Read, the former executive director of the Christian Coalition, remarked with the zeal of the converted that "the whole world has changed. As was the case with liberal Democrats in '92, religious conservative Republicans in 2000 are willing to give their candidates a little more rope to maintain their viability in the general election."[12]

Bush surrounded himself with an exceptional policy team that shared his vision of Republican politics free of outright fidelity to the party's past. In fact, several of his top advisers were former Democrats who found themselves inspired by his unassuming charm and relaxed confidence. To a large extent, Bush was willing to listen to these advisers on matters of policy. Beyond the broad statements of intent—such as enacting a $1.6 trillion dollar tax cut—his was a campaign in which the details of policy took a backseat to the importance of perception.

Politics is perception. Bill Clinton inherently understood this; his opponents—Newt Gingrich in particular—never did. George W. Bush's campaign would not make the same mistakes that led to the end of Gingrich's short-lived Republican Revolution. Photo ops were the cornerstone of the campaign, and though African-Americans made up only 12.9 percent of the population, they seemed to make up a significantly larger percentage of the staged crowds George W. Bush appeared with, beginning at the announcement of his exploratory committee when J. C. Watts and Condoleezza Rice were the two people positioned closest to him.[13] The welcome message these photographs sent was clear: This was an inclusive Republican Party, and a candidate who was not only comfortable with, but passionate about, our nation's diversity.

This conscious but not pandering appearance of multiculturalism did a great deal to calm people's lingering doubts about the Republican Party's commitment to civil rights and minority citizens. These suspicions were rooted in reality. After all, the most senior Republican in the Senate was Strom Thurmond, who ran for president in 1948 as the pro-segregationist Dixiecrat and who started the trend of the white South turning toward the Republicans shortly before

Democratic president Lyndon Johnson signed the Voting Rights Act. To win the presidency, George W. Bush understood that he had to disassociate himself from the well-justified suspicions that still hung around the Republican Party's right wing.

George W. Bush would have to pull a Sister Souljah.

Sister Souljah was the sometime rap star whom Bill Clinton had criticized during his 1992 campaign for saying that "if black people kill black people every day, why not have a week and kill white people?"[14] Clinton's condemnation of her statement in front of an audience of prominent liberal Democrats such as Jesse Jackson was seen as a declaration of independence from the culture wars of the day and liberated him from the albatross of association with the extreme left wing of his party.

And so, in early October of 1999, George W. Bush made his pilgrimage to the halls of Congress. While Republicans still retained control of the legislative body, they did not enjoy broad-based popularity in the eyes of the American public. Because Bush seemed so eminently electable, more than 150 House Republicans had taken the unusual step of endorsing Bush's candidacy before a single primary had taken place. In that expectant atmosphere of near coronation, the Republican leadership could be forgiven for thinking that they were being visited by a grateful candidate.

They were in for a rude awakening.

The political news of that week was a proposal to delay the payment of the current income tax credit to the working poor, in order to make money available to balance the budget. When asked by reporters at Capitol Hill what he thought of the proposal, Bush's response was quick and to the point: "I don't think it's right to balance the budget on the backs of the poor."[15] This was a attack more reminiscent in tone of a liberal Democrat,* not the presumptive Republican nominee for president.

A week later, in a speech on education in Manhattan, Bush seemed to be taking issue with the cultural legacy of the Republican

---

*In fact, Bush's comment unconsciously echoed George McGovern's attack on Jimmy Carter's fiscal discipline ("He's trying to balance the budget on the backs of the poor") more than two decades before.

Party as well, saying, "Too often, on social issues, my party has painted an image of America slouching toward Gomorrah."[16] Afterward, the candidate made his way to a charter school in Harlem for added emphasis. Soon Bush was speaking in front of the NAACP, admitting "there's no escaping the reality that the Party of Lincoln has not always carried the mantle of Lincoln."[17]

This charm offensive had the intended effect of providing proof points to the Bush team's constant message that their man was a "different kind of Republican." Whether these were carefully scripted sentences or confessions based in personal principle, these statements signaled to the rest of America that this was a Republican candidate not beholden to insiders or extremists. This was indeed a conservative who placed a primary value on compassion, contrasting with the sometimes hard-hearted members of his own party.

Some Republican pundits were outraged. But one Bush insider was overheard saying at this time, "Rush Limbaugh doesn't like us this week, so what does that really mean?"[18] To which *Newsweek* correspondent Howard Fineman approvingly replied, "If Bill Clinton's playbook is right, probably everything."[19]

As fall turned to winter, the Bush campaign had raised $70 million, and been endorsed by 38 Republican senators, 26 Republican governors, and 175 Republican congressmen. McCain's campaign coffers were considerably more modest, but he was still connecting with the crowds.

While the other candidates were making their faces known in Iowa and raising money on the rubber-chicken circuit across the country, John McCain was immersed in New Hampshire, in a bus called the Straight Talk Express, driving around with reporters to what would be more than one hundred town hall meetings in the Granite State. Shooting from the hip, entirely unscripted, McCain's gruff and sardonic wit played well there, as did his endorsement by the favorite son, former senator Warren Rudman—a fiscal conservative who was critical of the influence of the religious right on the Republican Party. McCain's memoir of life as a fighter pilot and POW—*Faith of Our Fathers*—became a surprise bestseller. Bush was outspending McCain two to one, but once again John McCain's biography was doing a lot of heavy lifting for him. Book publicity photos showing McCain as a young fighter pilot were doubling as campaign advertising, raising his profile and the issue of military service: Bush had been flying jets in the Texas Air National Guard and Gore was working as a Vietnam war correspondent for *Stars and Stripes* when McCain was a POW. McCain used dark humor to downplay the experience ("It doesn't take a war hero to get shot down") but when he started talking about the heroism of other men in the Hanoi Hilton he opened up and the crowds fell silent. He told the story of men like Mike Christian, who used a bamboo needle and scraps of cloth to sew a tiny American flag with which to recite the Pledge of Allegiance. The guards eventually found the flag and beat Mike to the edge of his life; when they threw him back in his cell, Mike tried to sew another flag. Duty, Honor, Country—a devotion to something greater than yourself—these were not just words to John McCain. And in a time of cynicism about politics and politicians, people were listening.

McCain's boots-on-the-ground approach was translating to broad popularity, buoyed by the fact that Independents and Democrats are allowed to vote in the New Hampshire Republican primary. The candidate had become a cause. Journalist Joe Klein described McCain's supporters as "the continuation of the intermittent, decade-long rebellion of the moderate, middle-class voters against a political system that has been hijacked by a variety of extremists, corporate and cause-afflicted special interests."[20]

In December 1999, with the Republican candidates assembled in New Hampshire for a televised debate, moderator Tom Brokaw asked them to name a favorite philosopher. Without missing a beat, Bush said Christ. Gary Bauer took the hint and added, "Christ taught us about our obligations to the unborn child." McCain, next in line, resisted the pious pile-on and named Teddy Roosevelt.

On election night, benefiting from high turnout from Democrats and Independents, John McCain won the New Hampshire primary by nearly twenty points. That night, victorious at the podium and surrounded by his family, McCain sounded the call that had gotten him that far: "I asked the people of New Hampshire to make room in this election and in our party for the forces of reform. I asked you to help me break the Washington iron triangle of big money, lobbyists, and legislation that for too long has put special interests above the national interests. Well, thanks to you, my dear friends, today we made room. We made room, and we have sent a powerful message to Washington that change is coming."[21]

The message was already being heard in South Carolina, home of the next do-or-die primary, where at 3 A.M. a rally for George W. Bush was held on the campus of Bob Jones University.

This fundamentalist college had long been a regular stop on the Republican lecture circuit. Both Ronald Reagan and George Bush Senior had given speeches there. In 1981, then-congressman and later Senate majority leader Trent Lott wrote an amicus brief on behalf of Bob Jones University to the U.S. Supreme Court, in which he argued that "racial discrimination does not always violate public policy."[22] But increased media scrutiny and cultural evolution had brought attention to the untidy fact that Bob Jones was one of the few remaining campuses in America to formally ban interracial dating. An official posting on the University website that compared Catholicism to a "satanic cult" also fell far short of the inclusive message Bush was trying to send.

But this was a stop-McCain movement led by the religious right. Evangelist Pat Robertson let it be known that a vote for McCain would be disastrous for the Republican Party. Bush, knowing that he was in a fight for his political life, ran to the center and the far right simultaneously, retooling his image as that of a "reformer with results"—explicitly building off McCain's appeal in New Hampshire and nationwide—while also assiduously courting the religious right. At a speech at Bob Jones University, gone were the obligatory black faces that had normally flanked him throughout the campaign, as former governor David Beasley introduced him as a man who "deeply loves the Lord." The Bush campaign began blanketing the airwaves with ads attacking McCain, spending an estimated $50 million, with the understanding that if they did not win here, McCain would be unstoppable. Soon South Carolina residents began getting anonymous phone calls slandering McCain and his family. "I've never seen anything like it," said Michael Graham, a self-described "screeching, wild-eyed conservative" radio talk show host in Charleston. "It was a hundred percent negative from the start. Every last Bush ad was negative. There was organized phone-calling to my show: McCain had collaborated with the North Vietnamese, fathered illegitimate children, his wife was a drug addict."[23]

The Reverend Pat Robertson announced on CNN that not only was he endorsing George W. Bush, but that the Christian Coalition would refuse to support McCain if he received the nomination. Robertson claimed that McCain's campaign-finance platform would be a "nightmare for the Republican Party," adding that "there wouldn't be so many Al Gore supporters in South Carolina urging Democrats to vote for McCain if they truly thought he was the strongest candidate." On the same program, conservative commentator Tucker Carlson reflected on the deep-seated opposition to McCain, saying, "Every Republican establishment hack in the world is on cable this weekend barking about what an evil guy John McCain is. I think the fear is real. Part of it is that the Republican establishment backed Bush early and they're desperate, of course, to sort of see good on their investment."[24]

With the South Carolina primary coming down to the wire, the candidates met for another televised debate. Before it began, Bush walked up to McCain with his hand outstretched, an apologetic look on his face. "John," he said by way of explanation, "it's politics." "George," McCain replied, shaking his head, "everything isn't politics."[25]

On Election Day, South Carolina evangelicals and conservatives turned out in record numbers, comprising one-third of the total votes cast. McCain had lost and the Bush team was back on top. Thoughtfully munching on a doughnut a few days later, reflecting on the loss in South Carolina, McCain looked up and said, "It reminds me of an old bumper sticker—'The Christian Right is neither.' "[26]

McCain's Straight Talk Express rolled on to victory in the pivotal Michigan primary, but still stinging from the velocity and viciousness of the attacks against him, McCain decided to go on the attack himself, rebuking the religious right in Pat Robertson and Jerry Falwell's backyard of Virginia Beach. In a speech at the Cox High School, McCain thundered:

The tactics of division and slander are not our values. They are corrupting influences on religion and politics, and those who practice them in the name of religion or in the name of the Republican Party or in the name of America shame our faith, our party, and our country. Neither party should be defined by pandering to the outer reaches of American politics and the agents of intolerance, whether they be Louis Farrakhan or Al Sharpton on the left, or Pat Robertson and Jerry Falwell on the right. . . . We are the party of Ronald Reagan, not Pat Robertson. We are the party of Theodore Roosevelt, not the party of special interests. We are the party of Abraham Lincoln, not Bob Jones.[27]

While newspapers praised the speech as a "rebirth of American oratory," it backfired in Virginia, again motivating local conservative turnout against McCain, effectively turning his declaration of conscience into the last stand of his 2000 campaign. Under the pressure of the Republican establishment, the wheels had come off the Straight Talk Express.

With the only real rival for the nomination out of the way, the Bush juggernaut continued to march forward, and by the time of the convention, George W. Bush was back on message. He declined to pick a pro-choice running mate, such as Pennsylvania governor Tom Ridge or New Jersey governor Christie Todd Whitman, influenced by threats that the religious right would not support the ticket, picking instead the respected defense secretary from his father's administration, Dick Cheney. But beyond that, the style, content, and tone of the convention was flawlessly inclusive. A twenty-six-year-old single mother from Arkansas spoke of her need for tax relief, a community leader from Kansas City spoke about making neighborhoods safer, and a fourth-grade teacher—a registered Democrat—spoke about the promise of charter schools. The only gay and African-American members of the Republican Congress were given prominent speaking roles, as were General Colin Powell and the candidate's half-Mexican nephew, George P. Bush, who gave a third of his address in Spanish.

George W. Bush's acceptance speech was crisp and Kennedyesque, stressing many New Democratic themes, and when it was through there was a mini-multicultural reunion on stage as the balloons dropped and the room hummed to the bilingual lyrics and Latin rhythms of Puerto Rican pop sensation Ricky Martin. The intended message was unmistakable: This was not his father's Republican Party.

After the 1992 election of Clinton-Gore, sociologist Alan Wolfe prematurely wrote about the apparent decline of the Reagan coalition: "In retrospect, it is surprising that white working-class males, cowboy libertarians, southern bourbon elites, religious fundamentalists, Yankee WASPs, Midwestern farmers, and Orange County nouveaux riches ever got along at all."[28] George W. Bush's success in uniting the Republican Party was predicated to a large extent upon his unexpected embodiment of virtually all these different aspects of American life. He was a Texas rancher, a product of Yale and Harvard who summered in Maine, a former frat boy, a born-again Christian, an entrepreneur who struck it rich with an investment in the Texas Rangers after repeated failures in the energy business. Without design, this son of the former president brought together in his rambling life experience virtually all the disparate elements and experiences of the national Republican Party.

Even the stubborn rumors and minor scandals having to do with Bush's checkered past seemed to have the effect of balancing his political profile. Rumblings about Bush's misspent youth worked to his favor to the extent that it made him seem like a changed man—the prodigal son returning home—rather than a stuffy Republican moralist. Despite his avoidance of baby-boomer rites of passage such as inner conflict over the Vietnam War, the exaggerated rumors of his hard-partying days gave him a certain generational credibility. He might not have joined AA, but he knew enough trouble from drinking to compel him to stop. It made his narrative one of redemption, instead of a rich kid born to perfection.

By his own admission, Bush was proudly not a policy wonk: "Reading a 500 page briefing book on policy is not something I'm good at,"[29] he breezily confessed to reporters. In contrast, Gore seemed at times determined to convince voters that he *was* a five-hundred-page briefing book, offering unsolicited lectures on policy minutiae in professorial tones. But what Bush often missed in detail he made up for in an intuitive sense of where he stood in the big picture. Like Ronald Reagan, and more so than his father, Bush understood the larger themes that tug at Americans' heartstrings. And while he was no great communicator, he had a self-confidence that allowed him to capitalize on the contradictory impulses in American politics and appeal to Main Street as well as Wall Street.

As Bush seemed to borrow page after page of Clinton's playbook to great effect throughout the 2000 campaign, Clinton's protégé appeared equally busy disregarding the lessons that had led to their election in 1992. Gore seemed determined to cast himself as an old school, labor lunch-pail Democrat in the tradition of Hubert Humphrey and Walter Mondale. This strategy was problematic in a number of ways, not least because it wasn't particularly convincing.

As a founding member of the DLC, Gore had devoted most of his political career toward crafting a conservative, New Democrat image for himself. As the incumbent vice president, Gore's call to protect the downtrodden from powerful corporate special interests did not have the resonance it would were he campaigning as a genuine outsider. Like it or not, Gore could not distance himself from the record of the Clinton administration. It was, in many ways, a record worth being proud of. After all, the Clinton-Gore administration had presided over the greatest period of economic expansion and technological development in the nation's history. Most Americans felt strongly that they were far better off than they had been eight years before, when Bush's father had been in office. But sex scandals had tarnished what would have otherwise been a sterling reputation for success. While Clinton continued to enjoy high job-approval ratings based on his Centrist policies, low regard for his personal conduct left an aura of disrepute around Gore's Boy Scout image. This proved enough to swing some Centrist voters away from Gore and toward the fresh promises of his opponent. While this was a millstone, Gore could not credibly blame Bill Clinton for the political strategy he employed to capture the White House in his own right during this time of prosperity. He seemed at times caught in the headlights, so concerned about opening himself up to attack that he was unable to act. Campaign staffers recalled:

"We would go into meetings with Gore urging him to speak out about the environment, but he would always make clear that he was afraid of being accused of supporting higher taxes as a result of what he had advocated in his book." "He didn't talk about tobacco because he was worried about being called a tobacco farmer." "He wouldn't discuss Internet taxation because he didn't want to be reminded that he had claimed to be the father of the Internet. And he wouldn't talk too much about the environment because he was afraid his book would be used against him."[30]

Tellingly, the biggest bounce of Gore's campaign coincided with his most Centrist strategic decision. The selection of a vice president can be either important or workaday and gray. Bush's selection of White House veteran Dick Cheney, while undeniably responsible, inspired few people and added few new dimensions to the ticket. Gore's selection of Joe Lieberman, on the other hand, was a home run, balancing the candidate's baggage and causing even critics to reassess what a Gore administration would look like. To begin with, it was the one intelligently bold decision of the campaign: Tapping the first Jewish vice presidential candidate gave the ticket a deeper sense of purpose while recalling the pivotal nomination of Catholic John F. Kennedy a generation earlier. In addition, Lieberman protected Gore from sticky associations with Bill Clinton. Lieberman had been the first Democratic senator to condemn the president publicly for his affair with intern Monica Lewinsky, calling it "not just inappropriate but immoral." He was a man of obvious dignity, integrity, and intelligence as well as a Centrist;* he was the current president of the DLC. Republicans and Democrats alike fell over themselves in praise of the selection.

---

*In his memoir *In Praise of Public Life*, Lieberman gently articulated his Centrist vision of politics, saying, "The past two decades have seen a sharp rise in enmity between the two major national parties, and this has severely damaged our perspective and purpose as a united government. The intensity of this 'us versus them' mentality has caused a decline in the nobler qualities of political leadership (statesmanship, civility, truthfulness, courage, wisdom, the capacity for compromise) and a rise in baser aspects of politics (deception, rigidity, meanness, mediocrity, conformity and irrelevance)." (Joe Lieberman, *In Praise of Public Life* [New York: Simon & Schuster, 2000, page 112].)

"It's a brilliant choice," said a government scholar at the conservative Heritage Foundation. "By choosing Lieberman, Gore chose to undermine the strongest argument that Bush is making—the need to restore integrity to the White House."[31] "A terrific choice," echoed Democratic senator John Breaux of Louisiana; "the Vice President is to be congratulated for recognizing that the race will be won by those who can capture the moderate middle out there."[32] Even Hillary Clinton, running for senate from New York, tried to align herself with Lieberman, describing them both as "mainstream, centrist New Democrats," prompting her Republican opponent's campaign to complain, "She's trying to hitch her rickety campaign wagon to Senator Lieberman's fine reputation."[33]

Most important was the reaction outside the Beltway in the American electorate. A *USA Today*/Gallup Poll taken the Friday before the announcement found Gore trailing Bush by nineteen points among registered voters. The same survey, taken Monday with Lieberman on the ticket, found Bush's lead essentially erased—down to a statistically irrelevant two-point advantage—over a single weekend. By balancing his ticket with substantive and strategic Centrism, Gore momentarily erased lingering doubts about his candidacy.

It should have been smooth sailing for Al Gore from that point on. After all, unlike George H. W. Bush in 1988, Gore did not have to face a crowded field of candidates in the Democratic primaries. Only former New Jersey senator and New York Knicks star Bill Bradley had dared to challenge Clinton's anointed successor. A widely respected senator with a largely Centrist voting record, and a member of the independent Gang of 8, Bradley positioned himself to the left of Gore. The strategy backfired. Despite initial enthusiasm among liberal constituencies, Bradley won no primaries. Disaffected liberals who were offended by the Clinton administration's moderate record in governing began to advocate support for the Green Party's candidate, Ralph Nader.

Nader himself harbored no illusions about winning the White House. His stated purpose was to gain enough popular votes—5 percent of the final total—to gain the Green Party a place on the ballot in all fifty states for the next election. He argued that Bill Clinton and the New Democrats had sold out to corporate interests and that his candidacy would show them that they could not afford to take the liberal wing of their party for granted. Centrism itself was at the heart of Nader's objections: In 1996, he had memorably declared that "President Clinton is too unprincipled to ever lose to Senator Dole. He will never let Dole turn his right flank."[34] Likewise, Nader's army of true believers in the Green Party were not swayed by the fact that Al Gore was the only presidential nominee in history to have written an entire book on environmental policy, or that he had been declared an "Environmental Paul Revere" by the League of Conservation Voters. This wasn't about the issues, it was about ideology.

In the end, Ralph Nader would get well under the 5 percent of the vote he was aiming for nationally, but he did manage to get 97,000 votes in Florida. But at this point it was still early in the campaign, and conventional wisdom was that Nader would have the same effect on Gore as Buchanan would on Bush: a single-digit drain of ideological extremists that would, in effect, cancel each other out.

In theory, Nader should have protected Gore from Republican attacks that he was an extremist on environmental issues, just as Buchanan spared Bush from accusations that he was extremist on abortion and intolerant of new immigrants. But while the Bush camp effectively ignored Buchanan, Gore's advisers appeared concerned about the implications of defections toward Nader in key states such as Michigan, Oregon, and Washington. The voters they were most concerned about losing in those pivotal swing states were not moderates, but labor unions within the auto industry and environmentalists. As a result, the Gore campaign chose to shift its candidate's rhetoric and overall strategy toward the left. The vice president adopted an aggressive "people versus the powerful" strategy, in which he attacked corporate special interests. This populist rhetoric worked for Harry Truman in 1948 partly because memories of Wall Street's association with the Great Depression were still fresh, and in part because Americans had developed an affection for his "Give 'em hell, Harry" persona. This was not true of Gore. While described as somewhat casual and self-confident in private, Gore stiffened up in front of cameras. He lacked the charismatic touch Clinton had so effortlessly exhibited on the campaign trail. Instead of seeming eager to be loved, he seemed eager to please, and as a result came across forced, disingenuous, and, in his worst moments—such as the dissonant sighs during the first presidential debate—condescending.

Moreover, as a majority of Americans began investing their savings in the stock market during the boom of the mid-1990s, the United States had become a shareholders' society in which many people identified with corporations and rooted for their success, instead of eyeing them with suspicion and identifying them as a special interest.

The irony is that as Bush was embracing the style and rhetoric of Centrism while keeping much of his policy content conservative, Gore was doing precisely the opposite. For example, while Bush's call for direct federal funding to faith-based charities was criticized as conservative, Gore had endorsed a similar plan. Likewise, at Gore's direction, the Democratic Party platform was a self-consciously Centrist document, backing free trade, a strong defense, and fiscal discipline. Through a curious twist in the evolution of the political parties, it was the Democratic Party that offered the more traditionally conservative fiscal policy of paying down the debt, while the Bush proposal squandered much of the surplus on a tax cut.

But then again, politics is perception. And voters' perceptions in the 2000 election were influenced much more by style than substance. A study done by Clinton administration pollster Mark Penn showed that Americans saw Al Gore to the left of the mainstream Democratic Party, while they identified Bush as closer to the center than the Republican Party as a whole.[35] The man who sat behind President Clinton* as he famously proclaimed that "the era of big government is over" was identified overwhelmingly as the candidate of big government.

On November 7, election returns demonstrated the effects of those perceptions. According to exit polls taken by ABC News, fully

---

*Astonishingly, Clinton's job approval immediately prior to Election Day was among the highest of any president in the last twenty years—higher even than before his reelection in 1996. (*Blueprint,* January 2001, p. 36.)

50 percent of voters described themselves as political moderates, and Bush claimed nearly half of these voters. While Bob Dole captured only 33 percent of self-described moderates in the 1996, Bush increased that number to 44 percent. Likewise, while Dole was supported by only 35 percent of Independents, Bush was supported by 47 percent of Independents. He had successfully encroached on Clinton's Centrist political ground and expanded the appeal of the Republican Party among moderates.

This Centrist swing vote provided the margin that turned the campaign into a ballot-counting frenzy in Florida that would ultimately be determined by the Supreme Court. With the economy in great shape and high job approval—if not personal approval—ratings for the incumbent president, political scientists agreed that Gore should have won the election in a walk. "This backsliding from reform-minded centrism to interest group liberalism was a key factor in turning a race Gore should have won handily into a virtual tie," editorialized DLC policy director Will Marshall.[36] As a result, Bush was able to overcome the considerable negative associations that moderate voters had for the Republican leadership by embracing a Centrist style. By appearing as the more Centrist candidate, Bush was able to close the gap and ultimately come out ahead.

Bush was careful to reiterate the campaign's Centrist themes in his first speech to the American public as president-elect, and chose a symbolic backdrop to reinforce his message. Early in his address on the night of December 13, Bush declared, "Tonight I chose to speak from the chamber of the Texas House of Representatives because it has been a home to bipartisan cooperation. Here in a place where Democrats have the majority, Republicans and Democrats have worked together to do what is right for the people we represent." He then spoke of his legislative priorities as president, beginning with education, Social Security, and Medicare—all issues traditionally identified with Democratic candidates—followed by the military and tax cuts. Then he summed up: "This is the essence of compassionate conservatism and it will be a foundation of my administration. These priorities are not merely Republican concerns or Democratic concerns; they are American responsibilities."[37]

Bush was calling for a new politics that transcended party labels, using common sense to achieve common, bipartisan goals. The Centrist playbook Bill Clinton had used to govern for eight years was again in effect, being used by the victorious candidate from the opposite party.

Bill Clinton was visiting British prime minister Tony Blair in England when the Supreme Court's decision was handed down. At a hastily arranged press conference outside the prime minister's country estate, one could almost hear a grudging hint of approval in Bill Clinton's voice. "I wish President-elect Bush well," he said. "Like him, I came to Washington as governor, eager to work with both Republicans and Democrats. And when we reached across party lines to forge a vital center, America was stronger at home and abroad. The American people, however divided they were in this election, overwhelmingly want us to build on that vital center."[38]

CONCLUSION

On the front cover of every American citizen's passport is the Great Seal of the United States: an American eagle holding an olive branch in one talon and a cluster of arrows in the other. The eagle faces the olive branch, symbolizing our nation's desire for peace, but the arrows are kept close at hand, indicating our determination to defend our freedom. Ideological purists such as pacifists might prefer that the eagle hold only olive branches, while militarists might wish that the eagle hold only arrows. But in an independent nation a responsible balance is required—the arrows and the olive branch, both realism and idealism.

Throughout the history of the United States, Centrists have stood for the responsible balance of the best ideas from both parties, transcending the false dichotomies of extreme partisanship and keeping faith with the characteristically American quest for independence.

In the story of the vital center since Theodore Roosevelt, common themes emerge that reinforce our nation's need for a bipartisan balance between the extremes.

- Theodore Roosevelt resolved to set himself "as resolutely against improper corporate influence on the one hand as against demagogy and mob rule on the other,[1] remarking that "I have to carefully guard myself against the extremists of both sides."[2]

- Woodrow Wilson cautioned that "government is not a warfare of interests,"[3] and warned that "the country will not tolerate a party of discontent or radical experiment, but it does need a party of conservative reform."[4]

- Harry Truman "disliked the terms 'progressive' and 'liberal.' What he wanted was a 'forward looking program,' "[5] and declared that political "partisanship must end at the water's edge."[6]

- Dwight D. Eisenhower believed that "extremes to the right and left of any political dispute are always wrong."[7]

- John F. Kennedy marveled that "extreme opposites resemble the other. Each believes that we have only two choices: appeasement or war, suicide or surrender, humiliation or holocaust, to be either Red or dead."[8]

- Richard Nixon reasoned, "Extremists on the left tend to be just as critical of pragmatism as extremists on the right."[9]

- Bill Clinton insisted that "when we put aside partisanship, embrace the best ideas regardless of where they come from and work for principled compromise, we can move America not left or right, but forward."[10]

- George W. Bush pledged to set out priorities that "are not merely Republican concerns or Democratic concerns; they are American responsibilities."[11]

These presidential perspectives each reflect an understanding that narrow partisanship is not in the best interest of the American people. And yet while the moderate majority of Americans increasingly reject partisan politics as usual by registering as Independent in record numbers and overwhelmingly favoring solutions that come from the center of the political spectrum, our elected representatives in Congress have grown more partisan over the past two decades—not less. The tone in Washington has changed—for the worse.

In the past, this was merely dispiriting; now it is dangerous. The attacks of September 11 marked the beginning of a new era. The geopolitical competition between communism and fascism that dominated so much of the twentieth century finally faded after millions of people were murdered in the name of rigid adherence to ideology, only to be replaced in the twenty-first century by a new conflict between freedom and fundamentalism, terrorists who use extremist ideology to excuse mass murder.

President George W. Bush quoted FDR when he spoke of the "warm courage of national unity" in the National Cathedral prayer service following the September 11 attacks. That moment of patriotic bipartisan purposefulness now threatens to be forgotten as we drift back toward the divisive politics that dominated so much of the past several decades. The harshly partisan us-against-them mentality of years past is wholly inappropriate for the times in which we are living.

Nonetheless, ideological extremists are manning the partisan ramparts with increasing fervor. Grover Norquist, a right-wing activist and the president of Americans for Tax Reform, used the occasion of a Republican Unity Breakfast on the morning of President George W. Bush's inauguration to declare that "the lefties, the takers, the coercive utopians are not stupid. They are evil. Evil!"[12] On the left, Democratic congresswoman Cynthia McKinney reflexively reached for the language of Watergate when she demanded, "What did this administration know and when did it know it about the events of September 11th?"[13] Encouraged by vastly expanded media coverage, the politics of personal destruction on both sides has become a cottage industry and a spectator sport.

Centrism is under attack in America. Both parties are disproportionately influenced by their most extreme wings. In this environment, Centrists need to stand up and be counted. Until now, the moderate majority has been slumbering, powerful in numbers but unaware of its own influence. It is time for Centrist leaders and citizens to assert themselves and proactively define the terms of the debate. Senator Margaret Chase Smith of Maine was ahead of her time—but on target—when she said, "It is time that the great center of our people, who reject the violence and unreasonableness of both the extreme right and the extreme left, searched their consciences, mustered their moral and physical courage, shed their intimidated silence, and declared their consciences."[14]

Rigid commitment to ideology has been used throughout history to excuse extremism. In contrast, Centrism promises civility. Critics sometimes call Centrists "fence-sitters," but that is like calling a wise man "dull." Building upon the belief that neither party has an inherent monopoly on good ideas, Centrists have a unique ability to search for the best solutions to persistent problems and emerging issues. Centrists are not beholden to special interest groups, and as a result they can serve as the honest brokers of politics, restoring a much-needed sense of perspective to our degraded national political discourse.

Our Founding Fathers understood that the inherent self-interest of pressure groups and political parties was not to be trusted, despite the fact that their existence was integral to open discussion and debate. In his farewell address, George Washington warned that because political parties were in "constant danger of excess, the effort ought to be by force of public opinion, to mitigate and assuage it. A fire not to be quenched, it demands a uniform vigilance to prevent its bursting into a flame, lest, instead of warming, it should consume."[15] Centrists have the potential to play an important role in getting us closer to the Founding Fathers' original vision by communicating and cooperating across party lines to prevent the passion of partisan debate from "bursting into a flame," as Washington feared.

CNN news anchor Aaron Brown once sympathetically admitted, "The fact is that it is easier to cover the extremes; they make the most noise."[16] The voices of the moderate majority are being drowned out by demagogues on both sides. To restore a sense of balance, Centrists need to become an increasingly recognized voice in our national discourse, filling the void between the contentious talking heads from the left and the right. This will help Centrism become even more of a trusted self-definition, used by voters and candidates alike to help move both parties away from the margins and back toward the center of the electorate.

In order to offer more than situational solutions and seven-second sound bites, Centrists need to agree on a core principle, a consistent lens through which to determine whether or not coordinated action across party lines needs to be taken. Bill Clinton's New Democrat mantra of "Opportunity and Responsibility" was embraced with equal enthusiasm by candidate George W. Bush. The balance between opportunity and responsibility is reminiscent of Thomas Jefferson's enduring motto "Equal Opportunity for All, Special Privilege for None," with the implicit understanding that equality of opportunity cannot guarantee equality of outcomes. This Centrist perspective can be used to analyze a broad range of issues and determine the bipartisan Centrist agenda: pro-business but determined to stand up to corporate corruption; resolutely opposed to individual discrimination but resisting the drift toward a culture of victimization; looking beyond the old "hawk versus dove" debate toward an eagle foreign policy that supports America's leadership role in the world with a strong military that is not asked to unilaterally overextend itself; backing domestic policies that are socially inclusive but fiscally responsible.

The bottom line, as the late senator Paul Tsongas said, is that "the core of America is not racist. It is not hostile to women. It is increasingly offended by gay bashing. Yet it abhors government waste. It believes strongly in fiscal responsibility such as balanced budgets. It is pro–economic growth. It is concerned about the environment. It is intolerant of people on welfare who disdain the notion of work. But it wants poor kids to have school lunches and it wants to spend money to have good schools. In sum, most Americans are sensible, good-hearted, and prudent. The issue, then, is whether there is a political party that can welcome them home."[17]

Centrists must build on this obvious but all-too-often politically isolated common ground. To this end, Centrists must become a more effective and coherent force in practical politics. The biographical sketches of Centrist leaders throughout *Independent Nation* can offer some practical lessons from recent American history on how to avoid common failures while steering toward greater success.

- *Inclusive Leadership.* Centrist leaders need to practice the politics of addition, not division. Inclusive leadership—in both style and substance—allows a leader to realign politics by reaching beyond a party's traditional base, bringing together a majority coalition that more accurately reflects the will of the people.

- *Momentum and Direction.* Many of the risks of Centrist leadership can be minimized by keeping up momentum, consistently directing actions toward a clearly defined set of commonsense reforms that cut across party lines. As a British prime minister once said, "If you rattle along at great speed everybody inside is too exhilarated or too seasick to cause any trouble. But if you stop, everybody gets out and argues about where to go next."[18] Motion must not be mistaken for progress, however, and clear legislative priorities need to be established, along with a good working relationship with the other branches of government, if the Centrist reformer is to be effective and respected.

- *Build a Lasting Legacy.* One classic mistake Centrist reform leaders tend to make is trying to organize a movement around the strength of their own personality and political insights, like Jimmy Carter or Nelson Rockefeller. A lasting realignment requires a larger sense of purpose that people can work toward, rather than investing all their hopes in a single imperfect human being. Centrist leaders need to remember that a messenger alone does not make a lasting movement.

- *Strategy Is Not a Sin.* Centrists need to choose their battles wisely. In the existing two-party system, at least a loose affiliation with an established political organization is necessary to rise to high elected office unless celebrity, considerable self-funding, or incumbent status permits a completely independent candidate to be taken seriously by voters. Centrists must be able to articulate the core values that they share with their party and then be consistent on these issues come hell or high water. Otherwise, they will find themselves cut adrift when they come under attack, with their support broad but not deep.

- *Politics Is Perception.* People enter the voting booth not knowing a candidate personally; instead, they have only an idea of who the individual is—a combination of policy, biography, imagery, and gut instinct. People need to go through the surface to get to the heart. Centrist candidates must establish a disciplined communications strategy from the outset to gain control of the terms of the debate, aggressively countering negative perceptions, remembering that the best defense is an honorable offense.

Candidates or political parties that associate themselves with the principles of individualism, moderation, common sense, and patriotism win elections. In contrast, association with extremists is kryptonite to a candidate or a broad-based movement because it alienates the majority of Americans and invites a lasting backlash.

For example, the expansive vision of social programs lost credibility when the Johnson administration—on the heels of LBJ's massive defeat of Barry Goldwater—went too far. When hardworking Americans began to feel they were being penalized to subsidize other people's lifestyles, the door to conservative populism swung wide open—the Republicans were able to run against the Great Society's excesses for thirty years. In addition, the extremism of the anti–Vietnam War protests ultimately alienated more people than it won over. A prime example is the evolution of Peggy Noonan from a middle-class Irish Catholic Kennedy supporter to Ronald Reagan's most eloquent speechwriter. As she recounted:

> I was a teenager in the 1960s. . . . I was swayed by JFK and Bobby, by their implicit sense of honor about being Americans, as if they thought to be an American was a great gift and yet had a price: You had to help your country, you had to have guts and an open mind, you had to care about people others forgot.
>
> But the antiwar movement startled me. I knew America was imperfect, but I also loved it. I had no illusion that other countries were perfect, or superior. I couldn't imagine an unelected dictator had more legitimacy than an American president. I will never forget a moment when on local television they showed one day an antiwar march meeting up with a bunch of New York hard hats near City Hall. They fought, and the hard hats tried to raise the American flag. I watched and realized I was pulling for the hard hats.[19]

The fallen currency of the word "liberal" in contemporary politics can be traced to this disastrous drift of the antiwar movement toward anti-Americanism, compounded by the more absurd excesses of the "politically correct" movement in recent years. As a result, alone in the voting booth, Americans are more inclined to take a chance on a conservative who might love America too much rather than a liberal who might love it too little.

The Republicans' Achilles' heel, however, remains the far-right wing and its association with bigotry and intolerance. When, in the wake of 9/11, Republicans recaptured the Senate, Majority Leader Trent Lott's wistful birthday tribute to Strom Thurmond's 1948 segregationist Dixiecrat campaign resurrected unwelcome old ghosts, bringing new attention to an interview he gave as a congressman to the neo-Confederate *Southern Partisan* magazine in 1984, in which he said, "I think a lot of the fundamental principles that [Confederate president] Jefferson Davis believed in are very important to people across the country and they apply to the Republican Party."[20] President Bush understood that Americans turned away from Newt Gingrich's 1994 Republican Revolution when it was perceived as too extreme, and took the uncharacteristic step of supporting the removal of Senator Lott from his leadership position and replacing him with a senator more evidently in line with the administration's "compassionate conservative" philosophy. Even in the first decade of the twenty-first century, Centrism was being played out on the grounds of civil rights and the unresolved split between the progressive and conservative wings of the Republican Party, as it had since the first decade of the twentieth century.

Centrism will remain at the vanguard of American politics in part because it represents an overdue realignment from a time when parochial local politics determined national policy. Until relatively recently, political party identification in the United States was handed down as an article of faith within families. For example, from the time of the Civil War until the civil rights struggles of the 1960s, white southerners voted straight down the Democratic line in large part because Abraham Lincoln had been the first Republican to be elected president. Those who lose wars have long memories. When LBJ, an old southern Democrat, signed the 1965 Voting Act, he murmured to his press secretary, Bill Moyers, "I just gave the South to the Republicans for your lifetime and mine."[21] His vision has come to pass; the white South is almost exclusively Republican in 2004.

Increasingly, however, the largely racial and class-oriented divisions that have determined political alignments in America are losing their validity. Improved equality of educational opportunity and a much higher standard of living have created a less-bifurcated American society. Regional identification is likewise more fluid, with Americans moving to different parts of the country at different points in their lives. Through it all, a truly national—as opposed to regional—culture is emerging through television, film, and the Internet. Hard-line political identification had its roots in a regional parochialism that has been steadily fading in America. A more national political perspective has taken its place.

Another sign of the overdue realignment in American politics is that moderates within the Democratic and Republican parties often have far more in common politically than they do with extremists in their own party. For example, the congressional voting record and political instincts of a Democratic moderate from a suburban district is much more likely to be in line with a Republican counterpart than with a fellow Democratic representative from an inner-city district who prides himself as a defender of the late-1960s liberal traditions. Ironically, the positions of those on the fringes of the political spectrum are beginning to blur as well, despite their diametrically opposed ideologies; therefore, the ideas held by Pat Buchanan and Ralph Nader about economic protectionism have much more in common with each other than with the broadly pro–free trade policies of moderates in the Democratic or Republican party leadership.

The perception that the Democratic and Republican parties are controlled by extremists who are out of touch with mainstream Americans is manifesting itself in the increasing appetite among the electorate for Independent Centrist reform candidates. The number of self-identified Independents has doubled in the past fifty years:[22] Forty-four percent of those aged eighteen to twenty-nine identify themselves as Independents.[23] The election of the Independent Centrist governors of the 1990s—Weicker, King, and Ventura—is evidence of an important shift from the days when independent movements in American represented the protest candidacies of the far left—Henry Wallace in 1948—or far right—George Wallace in 1968.

On the national stage, billionaire businessman Ross Perot's Independent 1992 candidacy centered on fiscal responsibility and government reform briefly propelled him into first place ahead of then-president George H. W. Bush and Democratic candidate Bill Clinton. When General Colin Powell explored a run for the presidency in 1996—declaring that "the time may be at hand for a third party to emerge from the sensible center of the American political spectrum"[24]—polls showed him winning a three-way race against Bill Clinton and Bob Dole.[25] In 2000, John McCain's reform Republican candidacy occupied this middle ground, infuriating establishment Republicans with his refusal to play ball with big business and the religious right, while capturing the imagination of Independents and reform Democrats to such an extent that polls showed that he would have beaten Al Gore decisively,[26] causing former Clinton pollster Dick Morris to imagine that "a President McCain, beholden to neither the union-dominated Democrats nor the Christian-Right Republicans, could reshape American politics."[27] But internal party mobilization against McCain showed that the progressive wing of the Republican Party first led into battle by Theodore Roosevelt had still not found a permanent home within the two-party system as the new century settled in. No third-party presidential candidate has been able to exceed TR's 27 percent of the popular vote in 1912.

In January 2001, in the aftermath of the closest election in American history—with the Senate evenly divided between Democrats and Republicans—many people assumed that George W. Bush would have to govern as he'd campaigned: as a Centrist. Journalist Joe Klein wrote, "Given the circumstances, there is only one possible governing strategy: a quiet, patient and persistent bipartisanship."[28] Having lost the popular vote, it stood to reason that Bush would reach out to moderate Gore voters in an effort to extend his base and build a majority coalition of support. But instead, ever mindful of the lessons stemming from his father's single term in the White House, George W. Bush acted quickly to solidify the support of the right wing of the Republican Party. "There isn't an us and them with this administration," breathlessly exclaimed Grover Norquist. "They is us. We is them."[29]

As Bush administration actions and appointments appeared to unite the party at the expense of dividing the nation, they alienated many moderate Democrats and even some moderate Republicans like Vermont senator Jim Jeffords, who suddenly threw control of the Senate to the Democrats in May 2001 by changing his party affiliation to Independent. Jeffords argued that the Republican Party was abandoning its founding principles of "moderation, tolerance, and fiscal responsibility."[30]

In the wake of Jeffords's declaration of independence, President Bush's approval rating fell more than 10 percent in a single month. The rest of the summer was mercifully quiet, as the Democrats took over the Senate and the Bush administration began to tack back toward the center. Then, with a rumble and shudder in the blue-sky morning of September 11, everything changed.

The attacks united the nation around President Bush, whose resolute leadership style proved well suited to wartime. When senators of both parties began singing "God Bless America" on the Capitol steps the night of the attack, partisan politics blessedly faded into the background. The nation's unity under fire caused memories of the political division surrounding the 2000 election to be swept away, replaced by a patriotism that transcended party labels, prompting a reassertion of Centrism well expressed by a young African-American author and Internet diarist named Oliver Willis three days after the attack in a posting titled "Liberal No More":

> For most of my life, I identified myself as a Centrist. More recently, especially after the election, I felt I identified with liberalism more. The idea was simple—equality and opportunity for all. Sure, I disagreed on some things, but I still felt I was "a liberal." In the past few months, I've felt liberals can be just as blind as conservatives. Illogic and stubbornness run rampant. This attack broke the camel's back. For people to somehow suggest the attack was somehow justified, or deserved is revolting. I want no association with a group of that ilk. Once again I see myself as a Centrist. Socially

moderate-liberal, fiscally moderate-conservative. I want nothing to do with liberalism, if America is last on their list. It's first on mine.[31]

Buoyed by popular support for his wartime leadership, President Bush was largely immune from the effects of a struggling economy and the rightward tilt of his administration. In the 2002 midterm elections, Bush was able to reestablish Republican control of Congress, a rare feat for an incumbent president. But as professional partisans on both sides beat the media drum about an increasingly polarized nation divided into Republican-leaning "red" states and Democrat-inclined "blue" states, the American people were sending a more Centrist message.

In fact, by 2003, seven of the so-called blue states that had voted by the widest margins for Al Gore in 2000—California, Connecticut, Hawaii, Maryland, Massachusetts, New York, and Rhode Island— had elected Republican governors. And Democrats had been elected to govern so-called red states such as Arizona, Kansas, North Carolina, and Virginia. These governors were all fiscally conservative and tough on crime but generally progressive on social issues—and therefore popular across party lines.

These results reinforced the conclusion of Stanford professor Morris Fiorina's book *Culture War? The Myth of a Polarized America*, which showed that voters in both red and blue states overwhelmingly see themselves in the center of the political spectrum, while they see the two parties as dominated by the extremes.[32] This presented a portrait of a nation that was closely divided between the parties, but not deeply divided on the underlying issues.

But the inside-the-beltway crowd still has blinders on when it comes to recognizing the country's clear message about the ability of strong Centrist leaders to bridge the divide, and the atmosphere in Congress continues to grow more harshly partisan. As the presidential elections of 2004 approached, the "us against them" attitude threatened to jump the curb from the war on terror to domestic political debate.

When Al Gore decided not to run again, the Democratic nomination in the post–Bill Clinton era was thrown wide open. For the first time, the Democratic field was dominated by Centrist senators such as John Kerry, John Edwards, Joe Lieberman, Bob Graham, and retired general Wesley Clark, with liberals taking comfort only in the fringe candidacies of Al Sharpton, Dennis Kucinich, and a tax-cutting, pro-gun Vermont governor named Howard Dean. Dean energized the Democratic troops with his unambiguous stand against the war in Iraq and claimed to represent "the Democratic wing of the Democratic party." But his candidacy peaked too early when Dean, flush with enthusiasm, allowed himself to be painted as the second coming of George McGovern, too liberal to be elected president of the United States. Pragmatic Democrats in Iowa and New Hampshire instead backed the candidacy of Massachusetts senator John Kerry, the first Vietnam War combat veteran nominated for president by either party.

The cerebral John Kerry understood that he would need to win over disaffected Centrists and Independents to win the presidency. On the campaign trail, he mentioned his friend and senate colleague John McCain at every stop, and even repeatedly tried to convince the Arizona Republican to run as his vice president—a move unprecedented in modern American politics. Talk of the possible bipartisan Kerry-McCain ticket caused the often-drifting campaign to briefly surge in the polls.

John McCain, however, was busy becoming a strong force in the Senate. As leader of what was sometimes dubbed the "Mod Squad"— a collection of Centrist Republicans that included Senators Susan Collins and Olympia Snowe of Maine—in the summer of 2004 McCain successfully stood up for fiscal responsibility, insisting that the president's $2.4 trillion budget needed provisions to cut spending and reduce the spiraling deficit. This same group provided the core of Senate support to stop the proposed constitutional ban on gay marriage. Working with Centrist Democratic senators such as Joe Lieberman and Evan Bayh, they moved forward toward enacting the bipartisan 9/11 Commission report recommendations. As a result, the center held against intense pressure in a divided Senate.

As the campaign built momentum, President Bush was staring down the gauntlet of a far tougher race than a Republican incumbent during wartime should have to face. His job approval numbers hovered around 50 percent, with lingering doubts about the economy, the deepening war in Iraq, and the direction of the country. The president was still beloved by the right, but columnist Tom Friedman captured the fervor of the "Anybody but Bush" movement when he wrote, "By exploiting the emotions around 9/11, Mr. Bush took a far-right agenda on taxes, the environment and social issues—for which he had no electoral mandate—and drove it into a 9/12 world. In doing so, Mr. Bush made himself the most divisive and polarizing president in modern history."[33]

In July, the Democrats arrived in Boston for their convention as a party unified in their heated dislike of President Bush and their desire to win back the White House. Even in the spiritual home of liberalism, they attempted to tack back toward the center with a convention that focused on addressing their perceived weaknesses on issues of military strength, fiscal responsibility, and foreign policy. Kerry selected the Centrist North Carolina senator John Edwards as his running mate to balance the ticket with a southern Democrat. The son of the recently deceased Ronald Reagan spoke in support of the stem-cell research restricted by the Bush administration. But there was also a retrospective tone to the convention, with a night devoted to honoring the career of Ted Kennedy. Only the keynote speech, by Illinois Senate candidate Barack Obama, sent a confident message about the future of the party. He brought the crowd to its feet with his admonition against the politics of division: "There is not a liberal America and a conservative America—there is the United States of America."[34]

While the Democrats went home for their convention, the Republicans reached out and held theirs in New York. This was not just a return to Ground Zero, it was an intentional reversal of the first President Bush's disastrous convention in Houston in 1992. While the Houston convention highlighted the party's extremists, the New York convention could have been called the revenge of the Centrists. The religious right was nowhere in sight—Pat Roberston and Jerry Falwell groused that they had not even been invited. In Houston, the opening-night speech had been a declaration of a culture war by Pat Buchanan that alienated moderates of both parties and solidified opposition. In New York the opening-night speakers were John McCain and Rudy Giuliani. The second night featured a speech by California governor Arnold Schwarzenegger—whose muscular Centrism had almost single-handedly revived the California Republican Party. The keynote address was even delivered by a Democrat, Georgia senator Zell Miller, who had delivered the keynote for Bill Clinton's convention in the same hall twelve years before, but now had broken ranks and written a book called *A National Party No More: The Conscience of a Conservative Democrat*.

Roaring out of New York with a double-digit bounce in the polls, George W. Bush never retreated from the conservative substance of his message, but as in 2000, he embraced the style of Centrism. In the final months of the campaign, the president campaigned constantly with Rudy Giuliani, John McCain, and Arnold Schwarzenegger—all of whom had been targets of right-wing attacks in the past but who now were acknowledged as the most broadly popular Republicans in the country. In contrast, conservative members of his cabinet such as Attorney General John Ashcroft almost never appeared at the president's side.

The Democrats countered with ads featuring testimonies from former Bush voters who now intended to pull the lever for Senator Kerry, including retired general Tony McPeak, who served as air force chief of staff in the Persian Gulf War under President Bush's father. The Republicans continued to hammer the Democrats as being representative of the far left, with the president confronting Senator Kerry in the debates by saying, "There's a mainstream in American politics and you sit right on the far left bank. As a matter of fact, your record is such that Ted Kennedy, your colleague, is the conservative senator from Massachusetts."[35] Bush also aggressively campaigned for Democratic votes in swing states, asserting that "the party of Franklin Roosevelt and Harry Truman and John Kennedy is rightly remembered for confidence and resolve in times of war and hours of crisis . . . today many Democrats in this country do not recognize their own party."[36]

In a close election marked by record voter turnout, President Bush proved victorious, increasing his support around the country. As in recent elections, there were considerably more self-identified moderate voters than either conservatives or liberals.[37] Moderate voters gave Senator Kerry a nine-point edge, while President Bush and Senator Kerry split Independent voters almost evenly.[38] Bush was able to remain competitive among moderates and Independents while rallying record numbers of conservatives to his side. President Bush's 51 percent of the popular vote made him the first majority president elected since his father, but the results fell far short of the landslides enjoyed by Presidents Nixon and Reagan. In fact, it was the lowest number of electoral votes that any winning incumbent president had received since Woodrow Wilson in 1916, and no victorious incumbent Republican president in American history had ever received a lower percentage of the popular vote. Significantly, the broadest popular mandate for a statewide candidate in 2004 was for John McCain, who won reelection to the Senate from Arizona with 77 percent support.

In the postelection coming together, Senator Kerry said, "I pledge to do my part to try to bridge the partisan divide,"[39] while President Bush greeted reelection by saying, "A new term is a new opportunity to reach out to the whole nation."[40]

Regardless of rhetoric, the center is likely to come under increased attack in the coming years, as both parties struggle to free themselves from the powerful but disproportionate influence of special interests. In this environment, Centrists need to unite across party lines to open up the process and the political dialogue. This includes fighting for election reforms such as open primaries and against polarizing practices like the congressional gerrymandering that blocks competitive elections and empowers the extremes. Independents and Centrists must send the message that it is patriotic to stand up to extreme partisanship.

As Democrats look to reclaim the White House, it is impossible to ignore the fact that every Democrat elected president in the past half a century has been a Centrist. Jack Kennedy, Jimmy Carter, and Bill Clinton all self-consciously ran against the liberal wing of their party to win the presidency, while onetime "Eisenhower Democrat" Lyndon Johnson's 1964 landslide was as much a rejection of Barry Goldwater's ideological defense of extremism as an endorsement of the Great Society in the wake of Kennedy's assassination.

American politics have shifted toward the center in part because cultural liberalism has become so extreme that people feel they need a check on its excesses. As Professor William B. Mayer explained in his book *The Changing American Mind,* "The major problem with liberalism is not that public opinion has grown more conservative, but that liberalism itself has moved too far left."[41] Some activists argue that liberals' recent problem getting elected stems from not being far enough to the left; but their argument is absurd, having already been overwhelmingly rejected by the American people—twice. In contrast to the successful candidacies of JFK, Johnson, Carter, and Clinton, when liberals have determined the Democratic Party nominee, they've gotten Barry Goldwater in reverse: losing forty-eight states with George McGovern in 1972 and forty-nine states with Walter Mondale in 1984.

It is important to appreciate that while moderates outnumber both liberals and conservatives across the nation, the number of self-identified conservatives in the nation considerably outweighs the number of self-described liberals. To an even greater extent than the Republican Party, Democrats depend on moderates to get elected: There are no longer enough liberals in the nation to form a stable base for a majority political party, while conservatives can currently claim the allegiance of nearly one-third of Americans. The upshot of this is that while hard-line conservative groups try to press moderates like John McCain and Colin Powell out of the Republican Party, moderate Democrats are more often welcomed into the Democratic Party leadership if only because Democrats need the moderates more. But in point of fact, candidates from both parties will need to appeal to the moderate majority. This is not a movement that either political party can afford to ignore. In the simplest terms, no candidate can be elected president unless he or she appeals to the growing number of Independent Centrist voters.

Centrism is the most effective means for winning elections and governing in the national interest; but there is also a higher purpose inherent in Centrist politics. Centrists try to transcend the pursuit of essentially self-interested politics, attempting to find a mutually beneficial balance of rights and responsibilities consistent with the creation of a more civil society. Centrism resonates because it stems from something even deeper than American history; it is rooted in centuries of accumulated wisdom passed on from generation to generation.

More than twenty-three hundred years ago, Aristotle wrote an essay on politics and ethics in which he described the basic Centrist dynamic: "The people at the extremes push the intermediate man each over to the other, and the brave man is called rash by the coward, cowardly by the rash man."[42] The Chinese philosopher Lao-tzu reflected that "to hold the center is to listen to the voice of the inner mind." In the Bible, the durable prophet Isaiah cautioned, "While from behind, a voice shall sound in your ears: 'This is the way; walk in it,' when you would turn to the right or to the left."[43] In *Titus Andronicus,* Shakespeare pleaded through one of his characters: "O brother, speak with possibilities/And do not break into these deep extremes."[44]

When the civic life of the state is overtaken by one ideological extreme or the other, it causes the pendulum of history to swing violently between the extremes, allowing resentments and backlashes to build. Centrism calms these violent passions, appealing to reason and the human desire for balance and harmony in our lives. Extreme partisanship is the problem; Centrism is the solution. It is admittedly far easier to divide than unite. But while dividers may win battles, uniters win wars. The most moral and durable ground on which to base a political movement is a realistic sense of generational responsibility. Decency is ultimately the most practical form of politics.

Centrism will remain the most effective means for achieving the classic mission of politics: the peaceful reconciliation of competing interests. By combining the best elements of both parties—the tough mind and the tender heart, the olive branch and the arrows—a new choice emerges that allows society to move not left or right but forward.

As you look back at the eagle on the Great Seal of the United States, above the olive branch and arrows is a banner on which is written our national motto, *E Pluribus Unum*—Out of Many, One. Our Founding Fathers' hope was that we would transcend narrow definitions of self-interest. The search for the common good is the motivating principle behind democracy. The common good is what Centrists are determined to articulate and defend.

There is a moderate majority in this independent nation: one-half of the electorate divided between two parties, underrepresented in the national political debate and the current composition of Congress. As a battle rages between freedom and fundamentalism at home and abroad, Americans need to hear the voice of the broad and vital center, restoring a sense of balance with backbone. Centrists must organize their efforts across party lines armed with a sense of history—looking beyond the partisan blinders built by power brokers, rising above racial and geographic lines, and reflecting the reality of life seen through the eyes of a new generation with a more global perspective. Flying across the United States, looking down at the earth, we quickly comprehend the artificiality of the borders that divide us, the man-made separations of the states themselves dwarfing the more petty but all-too-prominent historical divisions between Democrats and Republicans, black and white, North and South. But the day-to-day operations of our partisan political system still encourage these old divisions by imposing the corrosive conformity of an us-against-them ideology. By refusing to accept these divisions at face value, Centrists choose to view America not in terms of group affiliation, but as a diverse collection of individuals working in concert, restoring a sense of perspective, and recognizing that what we share as Americans is far greater than what divides us.

NOTES

EPIGRAPH

Cited in Theodore White's *Making of the President, 1964* (New York: Atheneum, 1965), p. 180.

INTRODUCTION

1. Washington's Farewell Address, September 19, 1796, full text available on the Avalon Project at Yale Law School website: www.yale.edu/lawweb/avalon/washing.htm.
2. Poll conducted by the Voter News Service and the *Los Angeles Times,* cited in Ted Halstead and Michael Lind, *The Radical Center: The Future of American Politics* (New York: Doubleday, 2001), p. 3.
3. *USA Today*/CNN/Gallup Poll, October 2002.
4. Ted Halstead, "A Politics for Generation X," *Atlantic Online,* August 1999, p. 3.
5. "Common Causes: Left and Right Are Crossing Paths," *New York Times,* July 11, 1999.
6. Robert Sobel, author of *Coolidge: An American Enigma,* interview on *Booknotes* with Brian Lamb, C-SPAN, August 30, 1998.
7. Alexis de Tocqueville, *Democracy in America* (New York: Harper Perennial, 1988), p. 173.
8. Quoted in Richard Hofstadter, *The Idea of a Party System* (Berkeley: University of California Press, 1969), p. 96.
9. Quoted in ibid., p. 38.
10. Quoted in ibid., p. 17.
11. Quoted in ibid., p. 46.
12. Quoted in ibid., pp. 122–123.
13. Quoted in ibid., p. 152.
14. William Safire, "On Language: What's an Extremist?" *New York Times,* January 14, 1996.
15. Ralph Waldo Emerson, "The Conservative," lecture, Boston, December 9, 1841.
16. Robert Donovan, "The Nixon Team: Decision-Making Will Be Different," *Los Angeles Times,* November 8, 1968.
17. Arthur Larson, *A Republican Looks at His Party* (New York: Harper & Row, 1956), p. 19.
18. James Reston, "The Decisive Political Center," *New York Times,* November 7, 1965.
19. Vaclav Havel, "The Power of the Powerless," in *Open Letters: Selected Writings, 1965–1990,* ed. Paul Wilson (New York: Random House, 1985), p. 133.
20. Steve Miller, "Black Leaders Rally in Racial Rhetoric, Sharpton Says 'America Owes Us,' " *New York Times,* November 3, 2001.

21. Ron Woodgeard, "You Decide What Falwell Meant to Say," *Macon Telegraph,* September 16, 2001.

22. Nancy Gibbs, "Fire and Brimstone," *Time,* March 13, 2000.

23. Eric Hoffer, *The True Believer: Thoughts on the Nature of Mass Movements* (New York: Harper & Row, 1951), pp. 85–86.

24. James Pool, *Hitler and His Secret Partners* (New York: Pocket Books, 1997), pp. 32–33.

25. Ibid., pp. 35–36.

26. Stephen Koch, *Double Lives: Soviet Espionage* (New York: Free Press, 2000), pp. 14–15.

27. Arthur Schlesinger Jr., *The Vital Center: The Politics of Freedom* New York: Da Capo, 1988), pp. xix–xx.

28. Claude Andrew Clegg III, *An Original Man: The Life and Times of Elijah Muhammad* (New York: St. Martin's, 1997), pp. 153–154.

29. Ibid., p. 318.

30. Hermann Rauschning, *The Voice of Destruction* (New York: Putnam, 1940), p. 131.

31. Quoted in Benjamin Gitlow, *I Confess!* (New York: Dutton, 1940), p. 561.

32. Schlesinger, *Vital Center,* p. 54.

33. Paul Berman, *Terror and Liberalism* (New York: Norton, 2003), pp. 119–121.

34. Franklin D. Roosevelt, *Public Papers and Addresses, 1940* (New York: n.p., 1941), p. 28.

35. Keith Poole and Howard Rosenthal, "D-Nominate, After 10 Years: An Update to Congress: A Political-Economic History of Roll Call Voting," *Legislative Studies Quarterly* 26:5–29, 2001.

36. George Will, "Ethics Debate Suited to Reign of Accuser," *St. Louis Post-Dispatch,* June 9, 1989.

37. Cited in "Let the Independents In," memo by Al From, published in *Blueprint,* September–October 2002.

38. Harvard University Kennedy School of Government, Vanishing Voter Project, December 1999 Poll, cited in Rob Ritchie and Steven Hill, "John McCain: Going Independent?" Knight Ridder/Tribune News Service, February 18, 2000.

39. Gordon S. Black and Benjamin D. Black, *The Politics of American Discontent: How a New Party Can Make Democracy Work Again* (New York: John Wiley & Sons, 1994), p. 150.

40. Halstead, "Politics for Generation X," p. 3.

41. Ibid.

42. Richard Berke, "From Not Quite Acceptable to Maybe Even Electable," *New York Times,* October 2, 1994.

43. Dwight D. Eisenhower, "The Future of the Republican Party," *Saturday Evening Post,* January 30, 1965.

44. Carl M. Cannon, "A Pox on Both Our Parties," *National Journal,* March 6, 1999.

45. DLC/Penn, Schoen & Berland Associates 2000 Poll.

46. Based on a chart originally published in DLC/Progressive Policy Institute's *New Democrat,* Summer 2000.

47. Halstead and Lind, *Radical Center,* p. 3.

48. Joe Klein, *The Natural: The Misunderstood Presidency of Bill Clinton* (New York: Doubleday, 2002), p. 30.

49. George F. Will, "Is the ACLU Being Reasonable?" *Newsweek,* January 31, 1983.

50. Alan Wolfe, *One Nation, After All* (New York: Viking, 1998), p. 72.

51. Roy Basler, ed., *The Collected Works of Abraham Lincoln,* vol. 2 (New Brunswick, N.J.: Rutgers University Press, 1959), pp. 220–221.

52. Winston Churchill, quoted in *New York Times,* July 5, 1954.

PART 1. THE INCUMBENT UNDER ATTACK FROM BOTH SIDES

1. W. B. Yeats, "The Second Coming" in *The Collected Poems of W. B. Yeats,* ed. Richard J. Finneran, 2nd rev. ed. (New York: Scribner, 1996), p. 187.

2. Mary T. Schmich, "Louisiana Dilemma Near an End," *Chicago Tribune,* November 15, 1991.

THEODORE ROOSEVELT—1904: THE ROUGH RIDER TAKES ON THE ROBBER BARONS

1. Theodore Roosevelt to T. C. Platt, Spring 1899, in *The Works of Theodore Roosevelt,* Memorial Edition, 24 vols. (New York: Scribner's, 1923–1926), vol. 23, p. 146.

2. Theodore Roosevelt, speech, "The Leader and the Cause," October 14, 1912, Milwaukee.

3. Theodore Roosevelt at Cairo, Ill., October 3, 1907, in *The Works of Theodore Roosevelt,* Memorial Edition, 24 vols. (New York: Scribner's, 1923–1926), vol. 18, p. 19.

4. Jacob K. Javits, *Order of Battle: A Republican's Call to Reason* (New York: Atheneum, 1964, p. 101.

5. John Morton Blum, *The Republican Roosevelt* (Cambridge, Mass.: Harvard University Press, 1977), p. 23.

6. Theodore Roosevelt to Arthur Hamilton Lee, December 26, 1907.

7. Francis E. Leupp, "Roosevelt the Politician," *Atlantic Monthly,* June 1912.

8. *Outlook,* March 29, 1913.

9. *The Works of Theodore Roosevelt,* Memorial Edition, 24 vols. (New York: Scribner's, 1923–1926), vol. 18.

10. "Letter from John Burroughs," in *Theodore Roosevelt: Memorial Addresses Delivered Before the Century Association* (New York: Century Association, 1919), pp. 55–60.

11. Blum, *Republican Roosevelt,* p. 60.

12. Edmund Morris, *Theodore Rex* (New York: Random House, 2001).

13. *Theodore Roosevelt: An Autobiography* (New York: Macmillan, 1913).

14. David H. Burton, *Theodore Roosevelt, American Politician: An Assessment* (Rutherford, N.J.: Fairleigh Dickinson University Press, 1997), p. 44.

15. *The Works of Theodore Roosevelt,* Memorial Edition, 24 vols. (New York: Scribner's, 1923–1926), vol. 21, p. 60.

16. Letter on display as part of permanent exhibit in the First Floor Gallery

in the Theodore Roosevelt Birthplace National Historic Site at 28 East Twentieth Street, New York City, operated by the National Park Service.

17. Ibid.
18. Edmund Morris, *The Rise of Theodore Roosevelt* (New York: Ballantine, 1980), p. 244.
19. Ibid., p. 248.
20. Theodore Roosevelt, *Ranch Life and the Hunting Trail* (1888; reprint, New York: Century, 1918), pp. 431–432.
21. Quoted in Morris, *Rise of Theodore Roosevelt,* p. 583.
22. Burton, *Theodore Roosevelt,* p. 34.
23. Speech given at the New York State Bar Association banquet, January 18, 1899.
24. On exhibit at the Theodore Roosevelt Birthplace, New York City.
25. John McCain, *Worth the Fighting For* (New York: Random House, 2002), p. 311.
26. Blum, *Republican Roosevelt,* p. 22.
27. Theodore Roosevelt to Henry Cabot Lodge, September 23, 1901.
28. Henry F. Pringle, *Theodore Roosevelt: A Biography* (New York: Harvest Books, 1956), p. 168.
29. *Forum,* February 1895.
30. Theodore Roosevelt, message to Congress, December 1901.
31. Theodore Roosevelt, *The Foes of Our Own Household* (New York: George H. Duran, 1917), p. 177.
32. Union League Club of Philadelphia, January 30, 1905, in *Works of Theodore Roosevelt,* vol. 23, p. 49.
33. Jean Strouse, quoted in "TR: The Story of Theodore Roosevelt," *The American Experience,* PBS, 2002, available at www.pbs.org.
34. Quote in permanent exhibit at Theodore Roosevelt Birthplace, New York City.
35. Morris, *Theodore Rex,* p. 151.
36. "TR: The Story of Theodore Roosevelt," *The American Experience,* PBS, 2002.
37. Morris, *Theodore Rex,* p. 157.
38. Ibid., p. 151.
39. Theodore Roosevelt, *Theodore Roosevelt's America* (New York: Devin-Adair, 1955), p. 8.
40. Javits, *Order of Battle,* p. 106.
41. Blum, *Republican Roosevelt,* p. 60.
42. Ibid., p. 104.
43. "The New Nationalism" speech, Osawatomie, Kansas, August 31, 1910.
44. Theodore Roosevelt, speech at Stanford University, May 12, 1903.
45. Kathleen Dalton, *Theodore Roosevelt: A Strenuous Life* (New York: Knopf, 2002), p. 216.
46. Morris, *Theodore Rex,* p. 58.
47. Dalton, *Theodore Roosevelt,* p. 261.

48. Morris, *Theodore Rex,* p. 303.

49. Ibid., p. 323.

50. Ibid., p. 310.

51. Ibid., p. 332.

52. Stefan Lorant, *The Glorious Burden: The American Presidency* (New York: Harper & Row, 1968), p. 523.

53. William H. Harbaugh, "Election of 1904," in Arthur M. Schlesinger Jr., ed., *A History of American Presidential Elections,* vol. 3 (New York: Chelsea House, 1976), p. 1976.

54. Morris, *Theodore Rex,* p. 342.

55. Dalton, *Theodore Roosevelt,* p. 263.

56. Ibid., p. 264.

57. Harbaugh, "Election of 1904," p. 1991.

58. Theodore Roosevelt, inaugural address, March 4, 1905, Washington, D.C.

59. John Milton Cooper Jr., *The Warrior and the Priest: Woodrow Wilson and Theodore Roosevelt* (Cambridge, Mass.: Belknap Press of Harvard University Press, 1983), p. 157.

60. Ibid., p. 161.

61. Ibid., p. 153.

62. Theodore Roosevelt, letter to Cecil Spring Rice, March 12, 1900, in *The Letters and Friendships of Sir Cecil Spring Rice* (Boston: Houghton Mifflin, 1929), pp. 1, 3, 7.

63. Burton, *Theodore Roosevelt,* p. 44.

64. John Mason Potter, *Plots Against the Presidents* (New York: Astor-Honor, 1968), p. 200.

65. Steve Tally, *Bland Ambition* (New York: Harcourt Brace Jovanovich, 1992), p. 207.

HARRY TRUMAN—1948: THE MAN FROM INDEPENDENCE FIGHTS A THREE-FRONT WAR

1. David McCullough, *Truman* (New York: Simon & Schuster, 1992), p. 633.

2. "Truman," *The American Experience,* PBS, David Grubin, producer, 1997.

3. Harry S. Truman, speech at the 1948 Democratic National Convention, July 15, 1948.

4. "Philadelphia 1948: When Conventions Really Mattered," *U.S. News & World Report,* August 7, 2000.

5. McCullough, *Truman,* p. 644.

6. Ibid., p. 663.

7. Harry S. Truman, speech at the 1948 Democratic National Convention, July 15, 1948.

8. Harry S. Truman, *Years of Trial and Hope, 1946–1952* (New York: Doubleday, 1956).

9. McCullough, *Truman,* p. 558.

10. Richard Norton Smith, *Thomas E. Dewey and His Times* (New York: Simon & Schuster, 1982), p. 26.

11. *New York Daily News,* October 15, 1948.

12. Truman, *Years of Trial and Hope,* p. 178.

13. Thomas Reynolds, "The West Sees a New Truman," *PM,* June 13, 1948.

14. Harry Truman, speech, Louisville, Kentucky, September 30, 1948.

15. William Leuchtenburg, "The Conversion of Harry Truman," *American Heritage,* November 1991.

16. Zachary Karabell, *The Last Campaign* (New York: Random House, 2000), p. 158.

17. Ibid., p. 164.

18. Strom Thurmond, Acceptance Speech for the Presidential Nomination of the States' Rights Party, August 11, 1948, reprinted in TheState.com, August 23, 2003.

19. Karabell, *Last Campaign,* pp. 167–168.

20. John Popham, "Thurmond, Candidate of Rebels, Decries White Supremacy Idea," *New York Times,* July 20, 1948.

21. William Safire, *Safire's New Political Dictionary* (New York: Random House, 1993), p. 422.

22. Irwin Ross, *The Loneliest Campaign* (New York: New American Library, 1968), p. 147.

23. Ibid., p. 162.

24. "Wallace Proposes Campaign Promise," *New York Times,* February 2, 1948.

25. Henry Wallace, speech at Madison Square Garden, May 11, 1948.

26. McCullough, *Truman,* p. 564.

27. Arthur Schlesinger Jr., *The Vital Center: The Politics of Freedom* (New York: Da Capo, 1988), p. 37.

28. David E. Lilienthal, *The Journals of David E. Lilienthal, 1945–1950* (New York: Praeger, 1998), vol. 2, pp. 378–379.

29. Clark Clifford, "The Clifford Memo," November 19, 1947, located in the Truman Library Files, Box 22, Independence, Missouri.

30. Harry S. Truman, speech at the 1948 Democratic National Convention, July 15, 1948.

31. Ibid.

32. Ibid.

33. Ibid.

34. "Clifford Memo."

35. Safire, *Safire's New Political Dictionary,* p. 194.

36. McCullough, *Truman,* pp. 660, 661.

37. "Truman," *The American Experience,* PBS, David Grubin, producer, 1997.

38. Karabell, *Last Campaign,* p. 218.

39. Godfrey Sperling, "When the Polls Got It Wrong," *Christian Science Monitor,* October 8, 1996.

40. Schlesinger, *Vital Center,* p. 32.

41. Harold F. Gosnell, *Truman's Crises: A Political Biography of Harry S. Truman* (Westport, Conn.: Greenwood Publishing Group, 1980), p. 412.

42. Truman, *Years of Trial and Hope,* pp. 221–222.

THE RISE AND FALL OF JIMMY CARTER: FACING RONALD REAGAN, JOHN ANDERSON, AND TED KENNEDY IN THE ELECTION OF 1980

1. Bill Adler, ed., *The Wit and Wisdom of Jimmy Carter* (Secaucus, N.J.: Citadel Press, 1977), p. 120.

2. Recounted in Edmund Morris, *Dutch: A Memoir of Ronald Reagan* (New York: Random House, 1999), p. 407.

3. Arthur Schlesinger Jr., *The Cycles of American History* (Boston: Mariner Books, 1986), p. 33.

4. "Man of the Year," *Time,* January 3, 1977.

5. Steven F. Hayward, *The Age of Reagan, 1964–1980: The Fall of the Old Liberal Order* (Roseville, Calif.: Prima, 2001), pp. 489–490.

6. Lou Cannon, "Dixie Whistles a Different Tune," *Time,* May 31, 1971.

7. Hayward, *Age of Reagan,* pp. 489–490.

8. Hunter S. Thompson, *The Great Shark Hunt: Strange Tales from a Strange Time,* in vol. I, *Gonzo Papers* (New York: Ballantine, 1979), p. 476.

9. Hayward, *Age of Reagan,* p. 488.

10. Thompson, *Great Shark Hunt,* pp. 476–477.

11. Hayward, *Age of Reagan,* p. 491.

12. Ibid., p. 515.

13. Adler, *Wit and Wisdom of Jimmy Carter,* p. 58.

14. Ibid., p. 120.

15. Hayward, *Age of Reagan,* p. 491.

16. Adler, *Wit and Wisdom of Jimmy Carter,* p. 106.

17. Ibid., p. 96.

18. Hayward, *Age of Reagan,* p. 496.

19. David S. Broder, "Reagan's Reverse Sales Pitch," *Washington Post,* September 16, 1986.

20. Hayward, *Age of Reagan,* p. 504.

21. Ibid., p. 496.

22. Ibid.

23. Ibid.

24. Ibid., p. 506.

25. "Man of the Year."

26. "Jimmy Carter," *The American Experience,* PBS, 2002.

27. Hayward, *Age of Reagan,* p. 512.

28. "Jimmy Carter," *The American Experience,* PBS, 2002.

29. William Doyle, *Inside the Oval Office* (New York: Kodansha, 1999), p. 232.

30. Ibid., p. 236.

31. Hayward, *Age of Reagan,* p. 513.

32. Tom Mathews, "Jimmy vs. the Liberals," *Newsweek,* May 16, 1977. p. 44.

33. Doyle, *Inside the Oval Office,* p. 229.

34. Ibid., p. 235.

35. Ibid., p. 236.

36. Merrill Sheils with Eleanor Clift, "Carter's Rx on Health," *Newsweek,* June 25, 1979.

37. Ibid.

38. Ibid.

39. Hayward, *Age of Reagan,* p. 514.

40. Theodore H. White, *America in Search of Itself: The Making of the President, 1956–1980* (New York: Harper & Row, 1982), p. 273.

41. Chris Matthews, *Hardball* (New York: Simon & Schuster, 1999), p. 198.

42. Paul Hendrickson, "Ronald Reagan: Rugged Runner in the Biggest Race; at 68, Easing into the Campaign Where Duty and Destiny Converge," *Washington Post,* November 13, 1979.

43. Harry F. Rosenthal, "Anderson Says He Won't Leave GOP Even if He Runs as Independent," Associated Press, April 10, 1980.

44. *Newsweek,* June 9, 1980.

45. White, *America in Search of Itself,* pp. 379–380.

46. Haynes Johnson, *In the Absence of Power: Governing America* (New York: Viking, 1980), p. 288.

47. "Not All His Fault," *Economist,* August 9, 1980, p. 11.

48. Quoted in Martin Amis, *The Moronic Inferno* (London: Penguin, 1986), p. 95.

49. Jimmy Carter, remarks accepting the presidential nomination at the 1980 Democratic National Convention, New York City, August 14, 1980.

50. Ronald Reagan, remarks accepting the presidential nomination at the 1980 Republican National Convention, Detroit, July 17, 1980

51. James Fallows, "The Passionless Presidency," *Atlantic Monthly,* May 1979.

GOVERNOR BUDDY ROEMER—1991: A REFORMER FALLS TO A CROOK AND THE KKK IN THE BIG EASY

1. John Maginnis, *Cross to Bear* (Baton Rouge, La.: Darkhorse Press, 1992), p. 41.

2. Ibid.

3. Ibid.

4. Ibid., p. 2.

5. Quoted in Elaine Davenport, "Sun-King Meets Ex-Klansman," *Independent* (London), November 15, 1991.

6. Maginnis, *Cross to Bear,* p. 12.

7. Ibid., p. 28.

8. Ibid., p. 29.

9. Ibid., p. 2.

10. Ibid., p. 5.

11. Ibid.

12. Ibid.

13. Ibid.

14. Ibid., p. 43.

15. Mathew Cooper, "Tense Times on the Bayou," *U.S. News & World Report,* July 30, 1990.

16. Maginnis, *Cross to Bear,* p. 43.

17. Ibid., p. 45.

18. Ibid., p. 44.

19. Ibid., p. 45.

20. Ibid., p. 46.

21. Cooper, "Tense Times on the Bayou."

22. Ibid.

23. Maginnis, *Cross to Bear,* p. 52.

24. Ibid., p. 138.

25. Ibid., p. 114.

26. Ibid., p. 116.

27. Peter Applebome, "Louisiana Politics Dances to Music of Rage," *New York Times,* November 25, 1991.

28. Ronald Brownstein, "Record Vote May Cap Louisiana Turmoil," *Los Angeles Times,* December 16, 1991.

29. Maginnis, *Cross to Bear,* p. 293.

30. Applebome, "Louisiana Politics Dances to Music of Rage."

31. Dan Quayle, interview, "Louisiana Governor: What's Next for David Duke?" *Hotline,* ABC, November 18, 1991.

32. Simon Tisdall, "Eyewitness: Two Repentant Sinners Vie for South's Votes," *Guardian* (London), November 16, 1991.

33. "Jackson Says Duke 'Helped' by Bush, Reagan," United Press International, December 1, 1991.

34. Maginnis, *Cross to Bear,* p. 56.

35. Ibid., p. 211.

36. Ibid., p. 7.

37. Ibid., p. 254.

38. Ibid., p. 236.

39. Ibid., p. 84.

40. Ibid., p. 266.

41. Davenport, "Sun-King Meets Ex-Klansman."

42. Maginnis, *Cross to Bear,* p. 289.

43. Ibid., p. 264.

44. Lynne Duke and Lou Cannon, "Meredith Makes Ad for Ex-Klansman," *Washington Post,* September 24, 1991.

45. Maginnis, *Cross to Bear,* p. 311.

46. Davenport, "Sun-King Meets Ex-Klansman."

47. Maginnis, *Cross to Bear,* p. 319.

48. Victory speech by Louisiana Democratic Governor-elect Edwin Edwards,

Federal Information Systems Corporation, Federal News Service, November 16, 1991.

49. Maginnis, *Cross to Bear*, p. 351.
50. Telephone interview by author with Buddy Roemer, June 2003.
51. Ibid.
52. Leslie Zganjar, "Exclusive Interview with Governor Buddy Roemer," *Baton Rouge Business Report*, December 3, 1991.

PART 2. THE OPPOSITION CANDIDATE REACHES OUT

1. Professor Erwin C. Hargrove, "The Better Angels of Our Nature: The Moral and Cultural Dimensions of Political Leadership," *Miller Center Journal*, vol. 2, Spring 1995.
2. Richard L. Berke, "Triangulation: New Geometry Is Old Math," *New York Times*, October 17, 1999.

WOODROW WILSON—1912: A PROGRESSIVE BEATS THE PARTY BOSSES

1. John Milton Cooper Jr., *The Warrior and the Priest: Woodrow Wilson and Theodore Roosevelt* (Cambridge, Mass.: Belknap Press of Harvard University Press, 1983), p. 192.
2. Special credit for finding this earliest of campaign commercials should go to Mark Benbow, resident historian at the Woodrow Wilson House, Washington, D.C.
3. Woodrow Wilson, *Division and Reunion* (New York, 1894), pp. 44–45, 127–129, 216; "From Wilson's Confidential Journal," p. 462.
4. Gary Wills, *Nixon Agonistes: The Crisis of the Self-Made Man* (Boston: Houghton Mifflin, 1970), p. 495.
5. Quoted in James M. McPherson, *To the Best of My Ability* (New York: Agincourt, 2000), p. 197.
6. John Morton Blum, *Woodrow Wilson and the Politics of Morality* (Boston: Little, Brown, 1956), p. 9.
7. Ibid., p. 15.
8. David Cronon, ed., *The Political Thought of Woodrow Wilson* (Indianapolis: Bobbs-Merrill, 1965), pp. 109–110.
9. Ibid., p. 140.
10. Woodrow Wilson, "The Ideals of Public Life," speech in Cleveland, Ohio, November 16, 1907, excerpted in ibid., p. 124.
11. Cronon, *Political Thought of Woodrow Wilson*, pp. 139–140.
12. Blum, *Woodrow Wilson*, p. 45.
13. Don Stancavish, "Wilson's 1910 Campaign Galvanized Public," *Record* (Bergen County, N.J.), August 15, 1999.
14. Cooper, *Warrior and the Priest*, p. 168.
15. Woodrow Wilson Papers, p. 173.
16. Cooper, *Warrior and the Priest*, p. 173.
17. Virginia Tyler Hudson, "Wilson to Attempt to Kill Lobby," *Newark Evening News*, January 17, 1911.

18. Reprinted in Ray Stannard Baker, *Woodrow Wilson: Life and Letters, Governor 1910–1913* (Garden City, N.Y.: Doubleday, Doran, 1931) pp. 146–147.

19. Notes for an address before the Kansas Society, repr. in ibid., p. 148.

20. Woodrow Wilson speech, Elizabeth, New Jersey, October 28, 1910, repr. in Cooper, *Warrior and the Priest,* p. 174.

21. Ibid., p. 174.

22. Ibid., p. 135.

23. Ibid., p. 144.

24. Ibid.

25. August Heckscher, *Woodrow Wilson* (New York: Scribner's, 1991), p. 233.

26. Cooper, *Warrior and the Priest,* p. 161.

27. Ibid., p. 160.

28. Ibid., p. 192.

29. William Allen White, *Woodrow Wilson* (Boston: Houghton Mifflin, 1924), p. 264.

30. Wills, *Nixon Agonistes,* p. 496.

31. Fred Siegel and Will Marshall, "The Lost Tradition of American Liberalism," *New Democrat,* September 1995.

32. Cronon, *Political Thought of Woodrow Wilson,* p. 181.

33. Ibid., p. 184.

34. "Wilson Ends Talks; Takes Time to Think," *New York Times,* November 7, 1912.

35. D. F. Houghton, *Eight Years with Wilson's Cabinet* (Garden City, N.Y.: Doubleday, Page, 1926), vol. 1, pp. 52–55.

36. Cooper, *Warrior and the Priest,* p. 167.

37. Ibid., p. 240.

38. Ibid., p. 248.

39. Address to the U.S. Chamber of Commerce, February 3, 1915, in Arthur S. Link, ed., *The Papers of Woodrow Wilson,* vol. 32, *January 1–April 16, 1915* (Princeton, N.J.: Princeton University Press, 1980), p. 179.

40. Woodrow Wilson to House, March 22, 1918, in Arthur S. Link, ed., *The Papers of Woodrow Wilson,* vol. 47, *March 13–May 12, 1918* (Princeton, N.J.: Princeton University Press, 1984), p. 105.

41. McPherson, *To the Best of My Ability,* p. 204.

42. Gene Smith, *When the Cheering Stopped: The Last Years of Woodrow Wilson* (New York: William Morrow, 1964), p. 232.

JOHN F. KENNEDY—1960: AN IDEALIST WITHOUT ILLUSIONS CHARTS A COLD-WARRIOR COURSE

1. John F. Kennedy, "Remarks to the Democratic State Committee," undelivered speech, released by the Office of the White House Press Secretary, November 22, 1963.

2. Chris Matthews, *Kennedy and Nixon* (New York: Simon & Schuster, 1996), p. 192.

3. Arthur Schlesinger Jr., "What If RFK Had Survived?" *Newsweek,* June 8, 1998, p. 55.

4. Arthur Schlesinger Jr., *A Thousand Days: John F. Kennedy in the White House* (Boston: Houghton Mifflin, 1965), p. xi.

5. Ibid., p. 95.

6. "Both Sides of the Political Coin," *Saturday Review,* October 29, 1960.

7. Richard Whalen, *Taking Sides: A Personal View of America from Kennedy to Nixon to Kennedy* (Boston: Houghton Mifflin, 1974), p. 24.

8. "Both Sides of the Political Coin."

9. Whalen, *Taking Sides,* p. 22.

10. John W. Douglas, "Robert Kennedy and the Qualities of Personal Leadership," speech, Loyola University, Chicago, October 31, 1968, Archives of the Kennedy Library, Boston.

11. John F. Kennedy, "Where Democrats Should Go from Here," *Life,* March 11, 1957, pp. 164–179.

12. "Senator Kennedy Is a Realist Who Fights Own Battles," *Tulsa World,* May 7, 1957.

13. "Kennedy Combines Tough Practicality and Egg-Headed Political Concepts," *Louisville Courier Journal,* March 10, 1957.

14. Russell Turner, "Senator Kennedy: The Perfect Politician," *American Mercury,* March 1957, p. 33.

15. Schlesinger, *Thousand Days,* 14.

16. Theodore H. White, *Making of the President, 1960* (New York: Atheneum, 1962), p. 105.

17. Schlesinger, *Thousand Days,* p. 66.

18. Ibid., p. 58.

19. Ibid.

20. James MacGregor Burns, "Candidate on the Eve: Liberalism Without Tears," *New Republic,* October 31, 1960.

21. John Chamberlain, "The Chameleon Image of John F. Kennedy," *National Review,* April 23, 1960, p. 261.

22. White, *Making of the President, 1960,* p. 279.

23. Ibid., p. 283.

24. Ibid., p. 285.

25. Quoted in Thomas A. Reeves, *A Question of Character: A Life of John F. Kennedy* (New York: Free Press, 1991), p. 194.

26. Ibid., p. 320.

27. Matthews, *Kennedy and Nixon,* p. 179.

28. Schlesinger, *Thousand Days,* p. xi.

29. Kenneth O'Donnell and Dave Powers, *Johnny We Hardly Knew Ye* (New York: Pocket Books, 1973), p. 275.

30. Matthews, *Kennedy and Nixon,* p. 209.

31. Ibid.

32. Arthur Schlesinger Jr., *The Cycles of American History* (Boston: Houghton Mifflin, 1986), p. 408.

33. Schlesinger, *Thousand Days,* p. 755.

34. Ernest R. May and Philip D. Zelikow, *The Kennedy Tapes: Inside the White House During the Cuban Missile Crisis* (Cambridge, Mass.: Harvard University Press, 1997), p. 178.

35. Schlesinger, *Thousand Days,* p. 817.

36. Ibid.

37. Richard Reeves, *President Kennedy: Profile of Power* (New York: Simon & Schuster, 1993), p. 427.

38. Quoted in Todd S. Purdum, "The World: At the Brink, Then and Now: The Missiles of 1962 Haunt the Iraq Debate," *New York Times,* October 13, 2002.

39. Reeves, *President Kennedy,* pp. 451–452.

40. Seymour Harris, "Kennedy and the Liberals," *New Republic,* June 1, 1963.

41. William Manchester, *Portrait of a President,* rev. ed. (Little, Brown, 1967), p. 190.

42. Sidney Hyman, "Why There's Trouble on the New Frontier," *Look,* July 2, 1963.

43. Reeves, *President Kennedy,* p. 656.

44. Report of the Select Committee on Assassination, U.S. House of Representatives, Findings in the Assassination of President John F. Kennedy in Dallas, p. 37, available at www.archives.gov.

45. John F. Kennedy, "Remarks to the Democratic State Committee," undelivered speech, released by the Office of the White House Press Secretary, November 22, 1963.

RICHARD NIXON—1968: A PROMISE TO "BRING US TOGETHER"

1. "Dole's Bond with Nixon," *Boston Globe,* October 19, 1996.

2. "Bush: The Battle to Come: US Presidential Election," *Times* (London), November 13, 1988.

3. Earl Mazo and Stephen Hess, *Nixon: A Political Portrait* (New York: Harper & Row, 1968), pp. 306–307.

4. Theodore H. White, *The Making of the President, 1968* (New York: Pocket Books, 1968), p. 158.

5. Jules Whitcover, *The Resurrection of Richard Nixon* (New York: Putnam, 1970), p. 358.

6. R. Emmett Tyrrell, *Public Nuisances* (New York: Basic Books, 1979), p. 137.

7. David Gergen, *Eyewitness to Power: The Essence of Leadership, Nixon to Clinton* (New York: Simon & Schuster, 2000), p. 29.

8. Alan L. Otten, "Nixon Watching: An Eye on Disraeli" *Wall Street Journal,* August 20, 1969.

9. Richard Nixon, *In The Arena: A Memoir of Victory, Defeat, and Renewal* (New York: Simon & Schuster, 1990), p. 286.

10. Gary Allen, *Richard Nixon: The Man Behind the Mask* (Boston: Western Islands, 1971), p. 51.

11. Earl Mazo, *Richard Nixon* (New York: Harper & Brothers, 1959).

12. Roger Morris, *Richard Milhous Nixon: The Rise of an American Politician* (New York: Henry Holt, 1990) p. 271.

13. Gary Wills, *Nixon Agonistes: The Crisis of the Self-Made Man* (Boston: Houghton Mifflin, 1970), p. 76.

14. "Nixon," *The American Experience,* PBS, Elizabeth Deane, executive producer, 1997.

15. Ibid.

16. Ibid.

17. Albert Cook, "Nixon's Strategy—Ike Hopes to Convert Failings into Strength, Woo Independents, and Show He Can Win," *Wall Street Journal,* April 27, 1959.

18. Gladin Hill, "Nixon Says G.O.P. Lacks Strength to Win 1956 Vote," *New York Times,* March 15, 1955.

19. Mazo and Hess, *Nixon,* back cover.

20. "The 'In' Party's Dramatic Triumph," *Newsweek,* November 19, 1962.

21. "California: Career's End," *Time,* November 19, 1962.

22. *Oakland Tribune,* November 10, 1964,

23. Mazo and Hess, *Nixon,* p. 300.

24. Ibid.

25. Dean J. Kotlowski, "Was Richard M. Nixon a Closet Liberal?" *Baltimore Sun,* June 9, 2002.

26. Ibid.

27. Stanley B. Greenberg, *Middle Class Dreams: The Politics and Power of the New American Majority* (New York: Times Books, 1995), p. 111.

28. Joe McGinniss, *The Selling of the President, 1968* (New York: Trident, 1969), p. 35.

29. Ralph McGill, "All Civilized Persons Are Indebted to Nixon," *Indianapolis Sunday Star,* August 18, 1968.

30. Mazo and Hess, *Nixon,* p. 301.

31. Robert J. Donovan, "Nixon Will Guard the Center from the Right and Left," *Los Angeles Times,* November 7, 1968.

32. White, *Making of the President, 1968,* p. 65.

33. Ibid., p. 71.

34. Ibid., p. 316.

35. Ibid.

36. Quoted in Richard Wilson, "Nixon's Big Gamble," *Look,* May 5, 1970.

37. Richard Nixon, "A New Alignment for American Unity," address on the CBS Radio Network, Thursday, May 16, 1968.

38. Ibid.

39. Ibid.

40. "Fouls in the Final Rounds," *Time,* November 1, 1968.

41. Gergen, *Eyewitness to Power,* p. 89.

42. Donovan, "Nixon Will Guard the Center from the Right and Left."

43. "The Nixon Administration: Color Is Green . . . ," *Washington Post,* December 12, 1968.

44. Richard M. Nixon's 1969 Inaugural Address, cited in James M. McPherson, *To the Best of My Ability* (New York: Agincourt, 2000), p. 436.

45. Gergen, *Eyewitness to Power,* p. 64.

46. Kotlowski, "Was Richard M. Nixon a Closet Liberal?"

47. Alonzo L. Hamby, *Liberalism and Its Challengers,* 2nd ed. (New York: Oxford University Press, 1992), p. 318.

48. *U.S. News & World Report,* February 2, 1970.

49. Pat Buchanan, memo to Richard Nixon, January 7, 1971, in Richard Reeves, *President Nixon Alone in the White House* (New York: Simon & Schuster, 2001), pp. 294–295.

50. Wilson, "Nixon's Big Gamble."

51. Christopher Hitchens, *For the Sake of Argument* (London: Verso, 1993), p. 246.

52. Allen, *Richard Nixon,* p. 325.

53. Fred Siegel, "The Nixon Realignment," *Reviews in American History,* December 1990, p. 559.

54. Nixon, *In the Arena,* p. 290.

BILL CLINTON—1992: LEADING THE DEMOCRATS OUT OF THE WILDERNESS AND INTO THE WHITE HOUSE

1. Governor Bill Clinton, "A New Covenant," acceptance address at the Democratic National Convention in New York City, July 16, 1992, repr. in Bill Clinton and Al Gore, *Putting People First: How We Can All Change America* (New York: Times Books, 1992), p. 217.

2. Samuel Popkin, *The Reasoning Voter* (Chicago: University of Chicago Press, 1994), p. 241.

3. Joe Klein, *The Natural: The Misunderstood Presidency of Bill Clinton* (New York: Doubleday, 2002), pp. 38–39.

4. Stanley B. Greenberg, *Middle Class Dreams: The Politics and Power of the New American Majority* (New York: Times Books, 1995), p. 141.

5. Ibid., p. 50.

6. Ibid., p. 42.

7. Al From, memo to Bill Clinton, January 1990, in ibid., p. 205.

8. The New Orleans Declaration, statement endorsed at the Fourth Annual DLC Conference, March 1, 1990, available at www.ndol.org.

9. Klein, *Natural,* p. 28.

10. Donald Baer, Matthew Cooper, and David Gergen, "Bill Clinton's Hidden Life," *U.S. News & World Report,* July 20, 1992.

11. Taylor Branch, "Clinton Without Apologies," *Esquire,* September 1996, p. 108.

12. Peter Applebome, "Bill Clinton's Uncertain Journey," *The New York Times Magazine,* March 8, 1992.

13. Greenberg, *Middle Class Dreams*, p. 189.

14. Ibid.

15. Ibid., p. 187.

16. David Maraniss, "A Look at What Clinton Should Do Next," *Washington Post*, October 8, 2000.

17. Timothy Clifford and Gaylord Shaw, "Clinton: Peacemaker, Until War," *Newsday*, July 12, 1992.

18. David Maraniss, *First in His Class: A Biography of Bill Clinton* (New York: Simon & Schuster, 1995), p. 407.

19. Clinton campaign announcement, repr. in Clinton and Gore, *Putting People First*, pp. 191–192.

20. Applebome, "Bill Clinton's Uncertain Journey."

21. "Spring Is in the Air—and in the Step of the Democrats," *Economist*, March 23, 1985.

22. George J. Church, "Is Bill Clinton for Real? The Pundits and Politicians Have Made Him Front-Runner. Who Knows, They Might Be Right," *Time*, January, 27, 1992.

23. Michael Marlow, "ICSC Hears a Chorus," *WWD*, May 31, 1995.

24. Applebome, "Bill Clinton's Uncertain Journey."

25. Dan Balz, "Protest Votes Cuts Bush's N.H Margin: Tsongas, Clinton Top Democratic Field: Kerry Is Third, Harkin Fourth," *Washington Post*, February 19, 1992.

26. Baer, Cooper, and Gergen, "Bill Clinton's Hidden Life."

27. Sam Fulwood III, "Clinton Chides Rap Singer, Stuns Jackson," *Los Angeles Times*, June 14, 1992.

28. Ibid.

29. Clifford and Shaw, "Clinton."

30. R. W. Apple Jr., "The 1992 Campaign: Democrats; Jackson Sees a 'Character Flaw' in Clinton's Remarks on Racism," *New York Times*, June 19, 1992.

31. Fulwood, "Clinton Chides Rap Singer."

32. Ibid.

33. "Clinton and Jackson: Sound and Fury Signifying . . . Something?" *Hotline*, June 22, 1992.

34. Apple, "The 1992 Campaign."

35. Reuters, May 2, 1990.

36. Herbert S. Parmet, *George Bush: The Life of a Lone Star Yankee* (New York: Scribner, 1997), p. 349.

37. Paul F. Boller Jr., *Presidential Campaigns* (New York: Oxford University Press, 1996), p. 396.

38. Clinton and Gore, *Putting People First*, p. 225.

39. Clinton, "A New Covenant," p. 217.

40. Ibid.

41. Ibid.

42. Ibid.

43. Norman Mailer, "By Heaven Inspired: Republican Convention Revisited; Houston, Texas, 1992 Republican National Convention," *New Republic,* October 12, 1992, p. 22.

44. Text of the speech delivered by Patrick J. Buchanan at the Republican National Convention, repr. by Associated Press, August 17, 1992.

45. Walter Goodman, "Republicans Play a Dissonant Tune," *New York Times,* August 18, 1992.

46. William DeGregorio, *The Complete Book of U.S. Presidents from FDR to Bush* (New York: Wings Books, 1992), p. 719.

47. Wayne King, "G.O.P. Defectors: Who and Why?" *New York Times,* November 1, 1992.

48. Kevin Phillips, "Pulpit Bullies: When the Big Tent Becomes a Revival Meeting," *Los Angeles Times,* September 6, 1992.

49. Howard Fineman, "Minus Perot: The New Math," *Newsweek,* July 27, 1992.

50. Ibid.

51. Baer, Cooper, and Gergen, "Bill Clinton's Hidden Life."

52. Chris Matthews, *Hardball* (New York: Simon & Schuster, 1999), p. 120.

53. Haynes Johnson, *Divided We Fall* (New York: Norton, 1995), p. 51.

54. "Time to Choose," *Economist,* October 31, 1992.

55. Peter Applebome, "Religious Right Intensifies Campaign for Bush," *New York Times,* October 31, 1992.

56. Klein, *Natural,* p. 45.

57. Recounted in Johnson, *Divided We Fall,* p. 61.

58. Dick Morris, *Behind the Oval Office* (New York: Random House, 1997), p. 80.

59. Robin Toner, "Revival Helps Mask a Party's Flaws," *New York Times,* December 27, 2000.

60. "Clinton Calls for Cooperation, Campaign Reform," AllPolitics.com, November 8, 1996.

PART 3. THE PRIMARY CHALLENGE: REFORMERS VS. THE OLD GUARD

1. Jack Newfield, "GOP May Pay for Sins of the Religious Right," *New York Post,* March 6, 2000.

2. Ed Cray, *Chief Justice: A Biography of Earl Warren* (New York: Simon & Schuster, 1997), p. 139.

3. Richard Norton Smith, *Thomas E. Dewey and His Times* (New York: Simon & Schuster, 1982), p. 442.

4. William Safire, *Safire's New Political Dictionary* (New York: Random House, 1993), p. 453.

5. George H. W. Bush, "The Republican Party and the Conservative Movement," *National Review,* December 1, 1964.

6. "Moynihan Accuses Rep. Abzug of 'Rule-or-Ruin' Stand," *New York Times,* August 30, 1976.

7. Sam Roberts, "Word for Word: A Moynihan Sampler," *New York Times,* March 30, 2003.

8. "Democrats Split on Moynihan," *New York Times,* September 16, 1976, p. 1.

9. Peter Perl, "Absolute Truth: Tom DeLay Is Certain That Christian Family Values Will Solve America's Problems. But He's Uncertain How to Face His Own Family," *Washington Post,* May 13, 2001.

CALIFORNIA GOVERNOR EARL WARREN—1946: THE KNIGHT OF NONPARTISANSHIP WINS BOTH PRIMARIES

1. Leo Katcher, *Earl Warren: A Political Biography* (New York: McGraw-Hill, 1967), pp. 196–197.
2. Irving Stone, *Earl Warren* (New York: Prentice-Hall, 1948), p. 3.
3. Ibid., p. 50.
4. Ibid., p. 63.
5. Ibid., p. 65.
6. Ibid., p. 62.
7. *The Memoirs of Chief Justice Earl Warren* (Garden City, N.Y.: Doubleday, 1977), pp. 171–172.
8. Stone, *Earl Warren,* p. 93.
9. Ibid.
10. Ed Cray, *Chief Justice: A Biography of Earl Warren* (New York: Simon & Schuster, 1997), p. 125.
11. Ibid., p. 128.
12. Ibid., p. 126.
13. *Memoirs of Earl Warren,* pp. 171–172.
14. Cray, *Chief Justice,* p. 127.
15. Ibid., p. 128.
16. Katcher, *Earl Warren,* p. 165.
17. Cray, *Chief Justice,* p. 129.
18. Katcher, *Earl Warren,* p. 164.
19. Ibid., p. 132.
20. Ibid., p. 173.
21. Cray, *Chief Justice,* p. 139.
22. Ibid.
23. Ibid., pp. 139–140.
24. Ibid., p. 139.
25. Katcher, *Earl Warren,* p. 168.
26. G. Edward White, *Earl Warren: A Public Life* (New York: Oxford University Press, 1982), p. 105.
27. Ibid.
28. Earl Warren, "What Is Liberalism?" *New York Times,* April 18, 1948.
29. Keynote address of Governor Earl Warren before the Republican National Convention, June 26, 1944.
30. Cray, *Chief Justice,* pp. 161–162.
31. Ibid., p. 163.
32. Ibid.
33. Katcher, *Earl Warren,* pp. 190–191.

34. Cray, *Chief Justice,* pp. 165–166.

35. Katcher, *Earl Warren,* p. 199.

36. Ibid., pp. 198–199.

37. Ibid., pp. 196–197.

38. Ibid., p. 201.

39. Ibid., p. 200.

40. "Significance of California Primary," *Los Angeles Times,* June 6, 1946.

41. Ibid.

42. Richard Nixon, *In the Arena: A Memoir of Victory, Defeat, and Renewal* (New York: Simon & Schuster, 1990), pp. 266–267.

43. Lawrence E. Davies, "Warren Sworn In, Asks Party Peace," *New York Times,* January 7, 1947.

44. Ibid.

45. Katcher, *Earl Warren,* p. 196.

EISENHOWER VS. TAFT—1952: THE INTERNATIONALIST VS. THE ISOLATIONIST

1. William Safire, *Safire's New Political Dictionary* (New York: Random House, 1993), p. 453.

2. Alonzo L. Hamby, *Liberalism and Its Challengers,* 2nd ed. (New York: Oxford University Press, 1992), p. 104.

3. Ibid., p. 113.

4. Eisenhower press conference, "Eisenhower," *The American Experience,* PBS, Adriana Bosch, producer, 1993.

5. Safire, *Safire's New Political Dictionary,* pp. 452–453.

6. Steve Neal, *Harry and Ike: The Partnership That Remade the Postwar World* (New York: Scribner, 2001), p. 159.

7. Ibid., p. 156.

8. Safire, *Safire's New Political Dictionary,* p. 554.

9. Neal, *Harry and Ike,* p. 226.

10. Ibid.

11. Dwight David Eisenhower, speech to the Canadian Club, Ottowa, Canada, January 10, 1946.

12. Neal, *Harry and Ike,* p. 231.

13. Ibid.

14. Ibid., p. 232.

15. Ibid.

16. Ibid., p. 233.

17. Ibid., p. 227.

18. Ibid., pp. 24–25.

19. Piers Brendon, *Ike: His Life and Times* (New York: Harper & Row,), p. 212.

20. Rick Montgomery, "It Sure Looks Like Ike's Strategy in 1952," *Kansas City Star,* September 30, 1995.

21. Stephen E. Ambrose, *Eisenhower: Soldier and President* (New York: Simon & Schuster, 1990), p. 266.

22. "Eisenhower," *The American Experience,* PBS, Adriana Bosch, producer, 1993.

23. Hamby, *Liberalism and Its Challengers,* p. 107.

24. Stephen Goode, "Is Voter Crossover 1952, Deja Vu?" *Insight on the News,* March 13, 2000.

25. Ambrose, *Eisenhower,* p. 272.

26. Brendon, *Ike,* p. 216.

27. Ambrose, *Eisenhower,* p. 274.

28. Ibid., p. 270.

29. James Reston, "The Two Candidates," *New York Times,* July 27, 1952, repr. in *Sketches in the Sand* (New York: Knopf, 1967).

30. Fred I. Greenstein, *The Presidential Difference: Leadership Style from FDR to Clinton* (Princeton, N.J.: Princeton University Press, 2000), p. 49.

31. Murray Kempton, "The Underestimation of Dwight D. Eisenhower," repr. in *Rebellions, Perversities and Main Events* (New York: Times Books, 1994), p. 446.

32. Richard Nixon, *Six Crises* (New York: Doubleday, 1962), p. 161.

33. Kempton, "Underestimation of Dwight D. Eisenhower," p. 438.

34. Ambrose, *Eisenhower,* p. 269.

35. Ibid., p. 276.

36. Martin J. Medhurst, "Text and Context in the 1952 Presidential Campaign: Eisenhower's 'I Shall Go to Korea' Speech," Center for the Study of the Presidency, *Presidential Studies Quarterly,* September 1, 2000.

37. Brendon, *Ike,* p. 214.

38. Robert A. Caro, *Master of the Senate* (New York: Knopf, 2002), p. 525.

39. Safire, *Safire's New Political Dictionary,* p. 453.

40. Paul G. Hoffman, "How Eisenhower Saved the Republican Party," *Collier's,* October 26, 1956, p. 44.

41. Roy Basler, ed., *The Collected Works of Abraham Lincoln,* vol. 2 (New Brunswick, N.J.: Rutgers University Press, 1959), pp. 220–221.

42. Dwight D. Eisenhower, address at Republican Precinct Day rally, Denver, October 8, 1954.

43. Quoted in Michael Barone, "Clinton Should Govern Like Ike," *U.S. News & World Report,* June 14, 1993.

44. Hoffman, "How Eisenhower Saved the Republican Party."

45. Dwight David Eisenhower, "Ike Takes a Look at the GOP," *Saturday Evening Post,* April 21, 1962, p. 19.

46. Safire, *Safire's New Political Dictionary,* p. 177.

47. Ibid., p. 606.

48. Greenstein, *Presidential Difference,* p. 49.

49. Michael R. Beschloss, *MAYDAY: Eisenhower, Khrushchev and the U-2 Affair* (New York: Harper & Row, 1986), p. 153.

50. Hoffman, "How Eisenhower Saved the Republican Party."

51. Beschloss, *MAYDAY,* p. 153.

52. Peter Lyon, *Eisenhower: Portrait of a Hero* (Boston: Little, Brown, 1974), p. 854.

53. Quoted in Jacob K. Javits, *Order of Battle: A Republican's Call to Reason* (New York: Atheneum, 1964), p. 116.

NELSON ROCKEFELLER VS. BARRY GOLDWATER—1964: THE LIBERAL REPUBLICAN VS. AN ADVOCATE OF "EXTREMISM"

1. Michael Kramer and Sam Roberts, *I Never Wanted to Be Vice-President of Anything: An Investigative Biography of Nelson Rockefeller* (New York: Basic Books, 1976), p 266.

2. Theodore H. White, *The Making of the President, 1964* (New York: Atheneum, 1965), p. 98.

3. Obituary of Nelson Rockefeller, *Washington Post,* January 28, 1979.

4. White, *Making of the President, 1964,* p. 74.

5. Joseph E. Persico, *The Imperial Rockefeller* (New York: Simon & Schuster, 1982), pp. 80–81.

6. Barry Goldwater, *The Conscience of a Conservative* (Shepardsville, Ky.: Victor Publishing, 1960).

7. Quoted in Harold Faber, *The Road to the White House* (New York: McGraw-Hill, 1965), p. 87.

8. Quoted in Jack Bell, *Mr. Conservative: Barry Goldwater* (Garden City, N.Y.: Doubleday, 1962), p. 222, Macfadden edition (1964).

9. *Chicago Tribune,* September 25, 1961, quoted in Arthur Frommer, *Goldwater from A to Z: A Critical Handbook* (New York: Frommer/Pasmantier, 1964), p. 62.

10. Senate speech, 1955, quoted in Bell, *Mr. Conservative: Barry Goldwater,* p. 83.

11. Remarks to a Republican breakfast meeting in Mississippi, April 17, 1959, reported in *Baltimore Sun,* April 18, 1959, in Frommer, *Goldwater from A to Z,* p. 86.

12. Quoted in *Chicago Tribune,* September 30, 1961, in Frommer, *Goldwater from A to Z,* p. 45.

13. Sam Tanenhaus, "The GOP, or Goldwater's Old Party," *New Republic,* June 11, 2001.

14. Quoted in Bell, *Mr. Conservative: Barry Goldwater,* p. 85, in Frommer, *Goldwater from A to Z,* p. 47.

15. Harry Overstreet and Bonaro Overstreet, *The Strange Tactics of Extremism* (New York: Norton, 1964), p. 234.

16. Kramer and Roberts, *I Never Wanted to Be Vice-President of Anything,* p. 266.

17. White, *Making of the President, 1964,* p. 74.

18. Ibid., p. 80.

19. Kramer and Roberts, *I Never Wanted to Be Vice-President of Anything,* p. 270.

20. Ibid., p. 272.

21. "Statement by Governor Rockefeller," State of New York, Executive Chamber, Albany, June 14, 1963.

22. Kramer and Roberts, *I Never Wanted to Be Vice-President of Anything*, p. 270.

23. Christopher Caldwell, "Goldwater the Refusenik: A Different Kind of Republican," *New York Observer,* March 19, 2001.

24. White, *Making of the President, 1964*, p. 93.

25. Tanenhaus, "GOP, or Goldwater's Old Party."

26. Michael J. Gerson and Mike Tharp, "Mr. Right," *U.S. News & World Report,* June 8, 1998.

27. Faber, *Road to the White House,* p. 16.

28. Barry Goldwater, *Why Not Victory?* (New York: McGraw-Hill, 1962) p. 85, Macfadden edition (1963).

29. "I would not use atomic weapons when conventional weapons will do the job. But I would leave it up to the commanders." Press conference in the offices of the *San Diego Union & Tribune* on May 26, 1964, as reported in *New Republic* on July 25, 1964.

30. Remarks made on the "American Forum of the Air," September 29, 1953, quoted in Frommer, *Goldwater from A to Z*, p. 61.

31. As quoted in the *Congressional Record,* September 3, 1963, p. 15360.

32. Frommer, *Goldwater from A to Z,* p. 83.

33. Interview with Eric Sevareid on *CBS Reports,* March 8, 1962, in Frommer, *Goldwater from A to Z,* p. 83.

34. David Broder, "A Sense of Incompleteness," *Washington Post,* January 28, 1979.

35. Faber, *Road to the White House,* p. 82.

36. Rick Perlstein, *Before the Storm* (New York: Hill & Wang, 2001), p. 333.

37. Matt Kelley, "Barry Goldwater, Outspoken Icon of Conservatism, Dies at 89," Associated Press, May 29, 1998.

38. Perlstein, *Before the Storm,* p. 337.

39. Allen J. Matusow, *The Unraveling of America: A History of Liberalism in the 1960s* (New York: Harper & Row, 1984), p. 136.

40. White, *Making of the President, 1964,* p. 121.

41. Ben Wattenberg and Richard Scammon, *The Real Majority* (New York: Coward-McCann, 1970), pp. 159–160.

42. Nadine Cohodas, *Strom Thurmond and the Politics of Southern Change* (New York: Simon & Schuster, 1993), p. 295.

43. Tanenhaus, "GOP, or Goldwater's Old Party."

44. Ibid.

45. Gerson and Tharp, "Mr. Right."

46. Overstreet and Overstreet, *Strange Tactics of Extremism,* p. 231.

47. Ibid.

48. Ibid., p. 232.

49. Kramer and Roberts, *I Never Wanted to Be Vice-President of Anything*, p. 284.

50. Robert D. Novak, *The Agony of the G.O.P., 1964* (New York: MacMillan, 1965), p. 452.

51. Stephen Ambrose, *To America* (New York: Simon & Schuster, 2002), p. 164.

52. Lee Edwards, *Goldwater: The Man Who Made a Revolution* (Washington, D.C.: Regnery, 1995), p. 276.

53. Cohodas, *Strom Thurmond*, p. 357.

54. Ibid., p. 361.

55. Tanenhaus, "GOP, or Goldwater's Old Party."

56. "The Threat to the Party System," *New York Herald Tribune*, October 25, 1964.

57. Kathleen Hall Jamieson, *Packaging the Presidency: A History and Criticism of Presidential Campaign Advertising* (New York: Oxford University Press, 1984), pp. 195–196.

58. Tom Wicker, "Johnson Sweeps Goldwater," *New York Times*, November 4, 1964.

59. Thomas Edsall Byrne, "Strom Thurmond and the Politics of Southern Change," *New Republic*, April 5, 1993.

60. Tanenhaus, "GOP, or Goldwater's Old Party."

61. Novak, *Agony of the G.O.P., 1964*, p. 469.

62. James Reston, "The Decisive Political Center," *New York Times*, November 7, 1965.

DANIEL PATRICK MOYNIHAN VS. BELLA ABZUG—1976: THE NEO-CON VS. THE NEW LEFT

1. "Where Are the Liberals?" *Time*, April 5, 1976.

2. Ibid.

3. Steven Rattner, "Upstart in the Senate," *New York Times*, January 7, 1979.

4. "Paddy, We Hardly Knew Ye; Daniel Patrick Moynihan Was Once the Great Neoconservative Hope," *Policy Review*, Spring 1984, p. 42.

5. Godfrey Hodgson, *The Gentleman from New York* (Boston: Houghton Mifflin, 2000), p. 37.

6. Theodore H. White, *The Making of the President, 1964* (New York: Atheneum, 1965), p. ix.

7. Hodgson, *Gentleman from New York*, p. 85.

8. Daniel Patrick Moynihan, "The Negro Family—a Case for National Action," in Mark Gerson, *The Essential Neoconservative Reader* (New York: Addison-Wesley, 1996).

9. Alonzo L. Hamby, *Liberalism and Its Challengers*, 2nd ed. (New York: Oxford University Press, 1992), p. 300.

10. Ibid., pp. 317–318.

11. Hodgson, *Gentleman from New York*, p. 142.

12. "Brawler at the U.N.," *The New York Times Sunday Magazine*, December 7, 1975.

13. Allan L. Otten, "Nixon Watching: An Eye on Disraeli," *Wall Street Journal*, August 20, 1969, p. 14.

14. Hamby, *Liberalism and Its Challengers,* p. 321.

15. Daniel Patrick Moynihan, memorandum to President Nixon, "General Assessment of the Position of Negroes," January 26, 1970.

16. Daniel Patrick Moynihan, "The United States in Opposition," *Commentary,* March 1975.

17. "Brawler at the U.N."

18. Ibid.

19. Hodgson, *Gentleman from New York,* p. 238.

20. Ibid., p. 240.

21. Obituary of Daniel Patrick Moynihan, *Economist,* March 23, 2003.

22. "Moynihan Is Open to a Senate Race," *New York Times,* February 3, 1976.

23. R. W. Apple Jr., "Moynihan Tests Political Winds," *New York Times,* April 5, 1976.

24. Ibid.

25. "Paddy, We Hardly Knew Ye," p. 42.

26. David E. Rosenbaum, "Democrats Put Moynihan on Platform Subcommittee," *New York Times,* May 18, 1976.

27. Maurice Carroll, "Moynihan Begins State Political Tour," *New York Times,* April 21, 1976.

28. "Moynihan Accuses Rep. Abzug of 'Rule-or-Ruin' Stand," *New York Times,* August 30, 1976.

29. James P. Gannon, "The Ghost in New York's Primary," *Wall Street Journal,* September 3, 1976.

30. Frank Lynn, "Senate Contenders in New York State Still Seek Issue," *New York Times,* September 2, 1976.

31. Bella Abzug, quoted in *Newsweek,* November 3, 1986.

32. Lynn, "Senate Contenders in New York State."

33. "Mrs. Abzug Says She Won't Back Moynihan If He Wins Primary," *New York Times,* August 29, 1976.

34. Ibid.

35. Ibid.

36. Gannon, "Ghost in New York's Primary."

37. Maurice Carroll, "Moynihan Rejects Isolation for U.S.; Hispanic Group Supports Mrs. Abzug," *New York Times,* August 26, 1976.

38. Ibid.

39. Gannon, "Ghost in New York's Primary."

40. Ibid.

41. "Mrs. Abzug Says She Won't Back Moynihan."

42. "Moynihan Accuses Rep. Abzug of 'Rule-or-Ruin' Stand."

43. "Excerpts from Debate of 5 Democratic Senate Candidates," *New York Times,* September 9, 1976.

44. Frank Lynn, "Campaign Ads Portraying Moynihan as a Moderate," *New York Times,* August 8, 1976.

45. "Moynihan Accuses Rep. Abzug of 'Rule-or-Ruin' Stand."

46. "Moynihan for the Senate," *New York Times,* September 10, 1976.

47. Ibid.

48. "Democrats Split on Moynihan," *New York Times,* September 16, 1976, p. 1.

49. "Mrs. Abzug Offers to Aid Winner; Buckley Calls Moynihan 'to the Left,'" *New York Times,* September 16, 1976.

50. "Just the Right Guy," *New York Daily News,* "Big Town Chronicles," September 28, 2001.

51. Ibid.

SENATOR MARGARET CHASE SMITH—1950: THE LADY FROM MAINE STANDS UP TO JOE MCCARTHY

1. Margaret Chase Smith, "Declaration of Conscience, Twenty Years Later," *Senate Journal,* June 1, 1970.

2. "A Chic Lady Who Fights—Margaret Chase Smith," *New York Times,* January 28, 1964.

3. Margaret Chase Smith, "Declaration of Conscience," *Senate Journal,* June 1, 1950.

4. Joe Rankin, "Conscience Was Her Guide," *Central Maine Morning Sentinel,* July 9, 2000.

5. Cabell Phillips, "G.O.P. Progressives Want 'Dynamic Conservatism,'" *New York Times,* June 11, 1950.

6. Margaret Chase Smith, *Declaration of Conscience* (Garden City, N.Y.: Doubleday, 1972), p. 4.

7. "Chic Lady Who Fights."

8. Janann Sherman, *No Place for a Woman: A Life of Senator Margaret Chase Smith* (Piscataway, N.J.: Rutgers University Press, 2000), p. 104.

9. Ibid.

10. Smith, *Declaration of Conscience,* p. 9.

11. Ibid.

12. Jack Thomas, "Eyewitness to a Century: Former Senator Margaret Chase Smith Looks Back on Her Outspoken Years on Capitol Hill," *Boston Globe,* April 9, 1991.

13. "Chic Lady Who Fights."

14. "Smith Beats Jones," *Time,* July 5, 1954.

15. "Margaret Chase Smith: Still Involved," *New York Times,* September 21, 1975.

16. Phillips, "G.O.P. Progressives."

17. Jack Anderson and Drew Pearson, *The Case Against Congress: A Compelling Indictment of Corruption on Capitol Hill* (New York: Simon & Schuster, 1968), p. 415.

18. Thomas, "Eyewitness to a Century."

19. Paul Greenberg, "My Kind of Feminist," *Arkansas Democrat Gazette,* July 4, 1995.

20. Margaret Chase Smith, Senate speech, September 21, 1961.

21. John Ripley, "Maine Legend Senator Smith Dies," *Bangor Daily News,* May 3, 1995.

22. "Chic Lady Who Fights."

23. Thomas, "Eyewitness to a Century."

24. Ibid.

25. Ibid.

26. Ibid.

27. Ibid.

28. Tom Long, "Margaret Chase Smith, Senator of 24 Years, Dies," *Boston Globe,* May 30, 1995.

29. Greenberg, "My Kind of Feminist."

30. Thomas, "Eyewitness to a Century."

31. "Excerpts from Speech by Senator Margaret Chase Smith," *New York Times,* January 28, 1964.

32. Ibid.

33. Smith, "Declaration of Conscience, Twenty Years Later."

34. "Mrs. Smith's Good Counsel," *New York Times,* June 3, 1970.

35. Thomas, "Eyewitness to a Century."

36. Ibid.

37. Cited on home page of Margaret Chase Smith Library (www.mcslibrary.org).

SENATOR EDWARD W. BROOKE—1973: STUCK IN THE MIDDLE OF THE CIVIL RIGHTS MOVEMENT

1. Senator Ed Brooke's speech at the Republican National Convention, "To Forge a New Unity," in *Vital Speeches of the Day,* vol. 34, no. 22, September 1, 1968, p. 691.

2. David Brock, *The Seduction of Hillary Rodham* (New York: Free Press, 1996), p. 21.

3. Ibid., p. 22.

4. Donnie Radcliffe, *Hillary Rodham Clinton: A First Lady for Our Time* (New York: Warner Books, 1993), pp. 82–83.

5. Telephone interview by author with Senator Edward Brooke, June 13, 2003.

6. "U.S. Senator Edward Brooke: An Individual Who Happens to Be a Negro," *Time,* February 17, 1967, p. 23.

7. John Henry Cutler, *Ed Brooke: Biography of a Senator* (Indianapolis: Bobbs-Merrill, 1972), p. 329.

8. E. J. Dionne, "The Party of Lincoln—or Lott?" *Washington Post,* December 12, 2002, p. A45.

9. Cutler, *Ed Brooke,* p. 49.

10. Ibid., p. 55.

11. Ibid., p. 59.

12. Ibid., p. 89.

13. Ibid., p. 91.

14. Ibid., p. 89.

15. Quoted in ibid., p. 90.

16. Ibid., p. 92.

17. Brooke interview.

18. Cutler, *Ed Brooke,* p. 117.

19. Ibid., p. 118.

20. Ibid., p. 120.

21. Ibid.

22. Quoted in ibid., p. 124.

23. Edward Brooke, *The Challenge of Change* (Boston: Little, Brown, 1966), p. 67.

24. Ibid., p. 76.

25. Ibid., p. 4.

26. Ibid., p. 17.

27. Ibid., p. 13.

28. Ibid., p. 15.

29. "U.S. Senator Edward Brooke," p. 21.

30. Brooke, *Challenge of Change,* p. 182.

31. Cutler, *Ed Brooke,* p. 175.

32. Ibid., p. 187.

33. Ibid., p. 164.

34. Ibid., p. 187.

35. Ibid., p. 191.

36. Ibid., p. 204.

37. Ibid., p. 2.

38. "U.S. Senator Edward Brooke," p. 22.

39. Ibid., p. 21.

40. Ibid., p. 21.

41. Ibid., p. 22.

42. Cutler, *Ed Brooke,* p. 5.

43. Senator Edward Brooke, excerpt from unpublished manuscript of his autobiography, chapter entitled "Member of the Club," faxed to author on June 14, 2003.

44. Ibid.

45. Ibid.

46. Ibid.

47. Interview with Hugh Pearson, author of *Shadow of the Panther* (New York: Perseus, 1994), for author's column, "Pictures with Panthers," *New York Sun,* July 31, 2003.

48. Brooke, "To Forge a New Unity," p. 691.

49. Quoted in Cutler, *Ed Brooke,* p. 322.

50. Ibid., p. 324

51. Quoted in the *New York Times,* March 17, 1970, anthologized in *The*

Macmillan Dictionary of Political Quotations, ed. Lewis D. Eigen and Jonathen P. Siegel (New York: MacMillan, 1993).

52. Cutler, *Ed Brooke,* p. 324.

53. Ibid.

54. Ibid., p. 326.

55. Ibid., p. 328.

56. Ibid., p. 331.

57. "The Brooke Scenario," *Time,* December 13, 1971, p. 13.

58. Ibid.

59. Richard L. Malden, "Brooke Appeals to Nixon to Resign for Nation's Sake," *New York Times,* November 5, 1973.

60. Michael Kenney, "Brooke Warns of 'Powerful Forces' Opposing Citizen Privacy," *Boston Globe,* May 2, 1974, p. 14.

61. "Blacks' Goal Now: Elect More Officeholders—in Both Parties," *U.S. News & World Report,* January 26, 1976, p. 45.

62. Brooke interview.

63. Dionne, "Party of Lincoln—or Lott?"

64. Brooke, *Challenge of Change,* p. 15.

RADICAL CENTRISTS: THE GOVERNORS OF THE 1990S

1. Author interview with Angus King, March 10, 2003.

2. Marsha Mercer, "Independent Governor Finds Smooth Going in Rocky Maine," *Tampa Tribune,* December 27, 1995.

3. Bruce Shapiro, "Third Party of One," *Nation,* February 6, 1995.

4. Lowell P. Weicker Jr. and Barry Sussman, *Maverick: A Life in Politics* (Boston: Little, Brown, 1995), p. 170.

5. Ibid., p. 186.

6. Shapiro, "Third Party of One."

7. Weicker and Sussman, *Maverick,* p. 186.

8. Ibid., p. 189.

9. Shapiro, "Third Party of One."

10. David Ellis Hartford, "The Gutsiest Governor in America," *Time,* April 13, 1992.

11. Shapiro, "Third Party of One."

12. "States Should Rethink Structural Reform," *Seattle Post-Intelligencer,* July 2, 2003.

13. Shapiro, "Third Party of One."

14. Paul Tsongas, Tim Penny, John Anderson, Lowell Weicker, Gary Hart, and Richard Lamm, "The Road to Generational Equity," paper given at the International Conference Foundation 1995 National Symposium, "Locating the New Political Center in America," Minneapolis, December 18, 1995.

15. "The Governor from 'Jurassic Park'?" editorial, *Hartford Courant,* October 1, 1993.

16. George Judson, "Connecticut Set to Change the Guard," *New York Times,* April 11, 1994.

17. Jesse Ventura, *I Ain't Got Time to Bleed* (New York: Signet, 2000), pp. 13–14.

18. Kenneth T. Walsh, "A New Governor Hellbent on Innovative Politics," *U.S News & World Report,* December 28, 1998.

19. David Hanners, "Nothing Ventura'd, Nothing Gained; Ex-Wrester Serious About Long-Shot Bid for Governor," *Saint Paul Pioneer Press,* July 19, 1998.

20. Matt Bai, "Wrestling for the Center," *Newsweek,* June 5, 2000.

21. Marc Fisher, "Perot's Party All Grown Up, Swaps Pie Charts for Pizzazz," *Washington Post,* July 25, 1999.

22. Richard Leiby, "Minnesota Showdown; Things Get a Mite Chilly as a State Wrestles with Its Image," *Washington Post,* March 5, 1999.

23. Jason Lewis, "Jesse Leaves the Ring; Minnesota's Tough-Guy Governor Bows Out," *Weekly Standard,* July 1, 2002/July 8, 2002, p. 19.

24. Ted Halstead, "A Politics for Generation X," *Atlantic Online,* August 1999, p. 10.

25. Helen Kennedy, "Governor Jesse Puts His Pal in Senate," *New York Daily News,* November 5, 2002.

26. Federal News Service, "Why Should We Get Only 2 Choices, 2 Major Choices? Ventura Shares No-Holds-Barred Perspective on Politics," *Washington Times,* February 24, 1999.

27. Ibid.

28. King interview.

29. Ibid.

30. Jay Davis, "The Political Wisdom of Angus King," *Maine Times,* January 15, 1998.

31. Ibid.

32. David Broder, "For Independents, Trying to Beat the System Is Often No Party," *Washington Post,* October 24, 1994.

33. Davis, "Political Wisdom of Angus King."

34. King interview.

35. Bob Von Sternberg, "The Maine Attraction Could Be a Primer for Minnesota," *Minneapolis Star Tribune,* November 22, 1998.

36. John Powers, "Declaration of Independence," *Boston Globe,* June 11, 1995.

37. Ibid.

38. Carey Goldberg, "Maine Democrats Fear Loss of Status," *New York Times,* May 25, 1998.

39. Ibid.

40. King interview.

41. Elizabeth Mehren, "A Man of Independent Means," *Los Angeles Times,* April 26, 1995.

RUDY GIULIANI—1997: AN INDEPENDENT REFORMER RESTORES THE GLORY TO GOTHAM

1. Rudolph W. Giuliani, "New Urban Agenda," address at Kennedy School of Government, September 29, 1997.

2. David Firestone, "Jaws Drop as Giuliani Steals Show in Heels," *New York Times,* March 3, 1997.

3. "Quality of Life: The Mayor Who Understood," *Daily News,* December 17, 1998.

4. Thomas Kessner, *Fiorello H. La Guardia and the Making of Modern New York* (New York: McGraw-Hill, 1989), p. 267.

5. *Economist,* March 22, 1997.

6. "Two Confident Fighters Ready to Take On a New Year," *New York Times,* December 30, 1994.

7. "Love and the Law," *Daily News,* in the series "Path to Power," May 13, 1997.

8. Rudolph W. Giuliani with Ken Kurson, *Leadership* (New York: Talk Miramax Books, 2002), p. 180.

9. "Gotcha! Nancy Collins Cross-Examines Crime Buster Rudolph Giuliani," *New York,* May 25, 1987, p. 36.

10. Ibid.

11. Giuliani and Kurson, *Leadership,* p. 181.

12. "Gotcha!" p. 36.

13. Wayne Barret and Jack Newfield, *City for Sale: Ed Koch and the Betrayal of New York* (New York: Harper & Row, 1988), p. 19.

14. Quoted in Fred Siegel, *The Future Once Happened Here* (New York: Free Press, 1997), p. 180.

15. Rudolph W. Giuliani, inaugural address, January 2, 1994.

16. Rudolph W. Giuliani, State of the City address, City Hall, New York, February 9, 1994.

17. Ibid.

18. Ibid.

19. Craig Horowitz, "The Suddenly Safer City," *New York,* August 14, 1995.

20. "Mr. Giuliani's Calming Message," editorial, *New York Times,* March 3, 1994.

21. James Rosen, "Rudolph Giuliani: A Donkey in Elephant's Clothing?" *City Magazine,* Fall–Winter 1994.

22. Ibid.

23. "Giuliani Sues Government over Benefits for Immigrants," *New York Times,* March 21, 1997.

24. Clyde Haberman, "NYC: Ellis Island Still Vexes Its Neighbors," *New York Times,* January 10, 1997.

25. Dale Russakoff, "New York Mayor Galls GOP by Becoming Champion of Immigrants," *Washington Post,* October 7, 1996, p. A-4.

26. Ibid.

27. Ibid.

28. "The Tolerant Bully," *Advocate,* June 28, 1993.

29. Ibid.

30. Rudolph W. Giuliani, opening remarks at the NARAL "Champions of Choice" Lunch, Yale Club, New York City, April 5, 2001.

31. Republican Pro-Choice Coalition/American Viewpoint Poll, January 2000.

32. Text of Al Sharpton remarks on WWRL radio, September 9, 1995.

33. Rudolph W. Giuliani, "Address on Tolerance," New York City, March 26, 1996.

34. Peter Beinart, "The New Progressives," *New Republic,* June 30, 1997.

35. Jim Sleeper, "Apple Juice," *New Republic,* May 9, 1994.

36. Ibid.

37. "Workfare for the Able-Bodied," *New York Post,* March 16, 1994.

38. Siegel, *Future Once Happened Here,* p. 211.

39. Ibid., p. 225.

40. Richard Brookhiser, "Big Apple Pie," *National Review,* November, 10, 1997.

41. "Ms. Messinger's Budget Blunder," editorial, *New York Times,* July 18, 1997.

42. "Louima Says His Attackers Did Not Yell 'Giuliani Time,' " *New York Times,* January 15, 1998.

43. Mark Jacobson, "How Far Can Rudy Go?" *New York,* November 10, 1997.

44. Rudolph W. Giuliani, victory speech, November 7, 1997.

45. "Our Finest Hour," editorial, *New York Observer,* September 24, 2001, p. 4.

ELECTION 2000: THE COMPASSIONATE CONSERVATIVE VS. A PRACTICAL IDEALIST AND THE STRAIGHT TALK EXPRESS

1. John Harwood, "G.O.P.'s New Campaign Themes Copied from Clinton Playbook," *Pittsburgh Post-Gazette,* October 18, 1998.

2. R. G. Ratcliffe, "Bush Leads Statewide GOP Blitz," *Houston Chronicle,* November 4, 1998.

3. Dan Balz, "Bush Takes Clinton Cue; Team Melds Policy, Politics in Drive to Center," *Washington Post,* June 6, 2000.

4. Ibid.

5. Stuart Stevens, *The Big Enchilada: Campaign Adventures with the Cockeyed Optimists from Texas Who Won the Biggest Prize in Politics* (New York: Free Press, 2001), p. 26.

6. Joe Klein, "The Fascinatin' John McCain," *The New Yorker,* February 14, 2000.

7. Pat Flannery and Michael Murphy, "McCain Runs Full Tilt," *Arizona Republic,* January 3, 1999.

8. John McCain with Mark Salter, *Worth the Fighting For* (New York: Random House, 2002).

9. "Bush: 'Leave No One Out' as Nation Prospers," *New York Times,* June 20, 1999.

10. "Caught in Clinton's Shadow," *Newsweek*, November 20, 2000.

11. *National Journal*, September 2, 2000.

12. Richard L. Berke, "Money and the Middle," *New York Times*, January 23, 2000.

13. Frank Bruni, *Ambling into History: The Unlikely Odyssey of George W. Bush* (New York: HarperCollins, 2002), p. 89.

14. Daniel Mills, "Sister Souljah's Call to Arms: The Rapper Says the Riots Were Payback. Are You Paying Attention?" *Washington Post*, May 13, 1992.

15. Michael Tackett, "Good Times Put Poverty Back in Political Fore," *Chicago Tribune*, October 22, 1999.

16. R. G. Ratcliffe and Greg McDonald, "Bush Scolds over Social Issues," *Houston Chronicle*, October 6, 1999.

17. George W. Bush, address at NAACP Annual Convention, July 10, 2000.

18. Howard Fineman, "Al and W's Balancing Act," *Newsweek*, October 18, 1999.

19. Ibid.

20. Klein, "Fascinatin' John McCain."

21. Edward Walsh, "John McCain; Arizona Insurgent Issues a Wake-Up Call," *Washington Post*, February 2, 2000.

22. Julie Mason, "Bush Takes Lott to Task," *Houston Chronicle*, December 13, 2002.

23. Joe Klein, "Go Negative, Act Positive: The Eddie Haskell Response," *The New Yorker*, March 6, 2000.

24. Transcript, *CNN Late Edition*, February 13, 2000.

25. Joe Klein, "Authentic Is Out," *The New Yorker*, March 20, 2000.

26. Klein, "Go Negative, Act Positive."

27. "The Rebirth of American Oratory: The Rough Rider Is Back," editorial, *Arkansas Democrat Gazette*, March 1, 2000.

28. Alan Wolfe, "Whose Body Politic?" *American Prospect*, Winter 1993.

29. George F. Will, "Bush Lite," *Washington Post*, August 11, 1999.

30. Dick Morris, *Power Plays* (New York: HarperCollins, 2002), p. 86.

31. Allison Stevens, "Lieberman Gives Gore a Ritual Cleansing," *Hill*, August 13, 2000.

32. Ibid.

33. Jordan Rau, "Clinton Applauds Gore's VP Choice / She and Lieberman Are Similar, Hillary Says," *Newsday*, August 9, 2000.

34. Hector Tobar and Bill Stall, "Green Party Nominates Nader for President," *Los Angeles Times*, August 20, 1996.

35. Penn, Schoen & Berland Associates, November 11–12, 2000.

36. Will Marshall, "Revitalizing the Party of Ideas," *Blueprint*, January 2001, p. 13.

37. "Bush Vows to Seek Unity," *Washington Post*, December 14, 2000.

38. Marc Lacey, "Clinton Praises Speeches That Ended Campaign," *New York Times*, December 15, 2000.

CONCLUSION

1. Theodore Roosevelt to T. C. Platt, Spring 1899, in *The Works of Theodore Roosevelt,* Memorial Edition, 24 vols. (New York: Scribner's, 1923–1926), vol. 23, p. 146.

2. Theodore Roosevelt, *Theodore Roosevelt's America* (New York: Devin-Adair, 1955), p. 8.

3. John Milton Cooper Jr., *The Warrior and the Priest: Woodrow Wilson and Theodore Roosevelt* (Cambridge, Mass.: Belknap Press of Harvard University Press, 1983), p. 167.

4. David Cronon, ed., *The Political Thought of Woodrow Wilson* (Indianapolis: Bobbs-Merrill, 1965), p. 140.

5. David McCullough, *Truman* (New York: Simon & Schuster, 1992), p. 558.

6. Harry Truman, speech at the 1948 Democratic National Convention, July 15, 1948.

7. Stephen Ambrose, *To America* (New York: Simon & Schuster, 2002), p. 164.

8. John F. Kennedy, speech at the University of Washington, November 16, 1961.

9. Richard Nixon, *In The Arena: A Memoir of Victory, Defeat, and Renewal* (New York: Simon & Schuster, 1990), p. 286.

10. "Clinton Calls for Cooperation, Campaign Reform," AllPolitics.com, November 8, 1996.

11. "Bush Vows to Seek Unity," *Washington Post,* December 14, 2000.

12. Hendrik Hertzberg, "Can You Forgive Him?" *The New Yorker,* March 11, 2002.

13. "McKinney Is Back with Yet Another Amazing Charge," *Times* (Gainesville, Ga.), April 13, 2002.

14. Margaret Chase Smith, "Declaration of Conscience, Twenty Years Later," *Senate Journal,* June 1, 1970.

15. Washington's farewell address, quoted in Richard Hofstadter, *The Idea of a Party System* (Berkeley: University of California Press, 1969), p. 97.

16. Aaron Brown, CNN *Newsnight,* March 18, 2003.

17. Paul Tsongas, *Journey of Purpose* (New Haven, Conn.: Yale University Press, 1995), pp. 90–91.

18. British prime minister Harold Wilson, quoted in Ian McIntyre, "Is Bambi Carnivorous? Review of The Modernizer," *Times* Newspapers (U.K.), February 9, 1995.

19. Peggy Noonan, "Dem Problems," WSJ.com *Opinion Journal,* March 3, 2003.

20. Peter Applebome, "Impeachment Republicans, 130 Years Later; Dueling with the Heirs of Jeff Davis," *New York Times,* December 27, 1998.

21. Nicholas Lemann, *The Promised Land* (New York: Knopf, 1991), p. 183.

22. Cited in "Let the Independents In," memo by Al From, published in *Blueprint,* September–October 2002.

23. Ted Halstead, "A Politics for Generation X," *Atlantic Online,* August 1999, p. 3.

24. Joe Klein, "Stalking the Radical Middle," *Newsweek,* September 25, 1995.

25. Louis Harris Poll, cited in Chuck Raasch, "Poll Shows Powell Winning 2-way or 3-way Race," *Chicago Sun Times,* October 31, 1995.

26. "Zogby: Gore Beats Bush by Two, but McCain Beats Gore," *Hotline,* February 8, 2000.

27. Dick Morris, "It's Time to Go Third Party," *New York Post,* February 22, 2000.

28. Joe Klein, "Winners and Losers: Talk of the Town," *The New Yorker,* November 20, 2000.

29. "Religious Right Achieves Top Access at White House," *Church and State,* May 1, 2001.

30. Transcript of Senator Jim Jeffords, "Balance of Power," *New York Times,* May 25, 2001.

31. Available at www.oliverwillis.com/2001_09_09_archives.php.

32. Morris Fiorina with Samuel J. Abrams and Jeremy C. Pope, *Culture War? The Myth of a Polarized America* (New York: Pearson Longman, 2004).

33. Thomas L. Friedman, "Addicted to 9/11," *New York Times*, October 14, 2004.

34. Barack Obama, Remarks to the Democratic National Convention, July 26, 2004.

35. Andrew Miga, "Left, Right Jabs in Nasty Third Round," Boston Herald.com, October 14, 2004.

36. David E. Sanger, "In Rural Tour, Bush Asks Democrats for their Vote," *New York Times*, October 27, 2004.

37. National Election Pool 2004, Edison Media Research and Mitofsky International.

38. Ibid.

39. Senator John F. Kerry, CNN.com transcript, November 4, 2004.

40. President George W. Bush, CNN.com transcript, November 4, 2004.

41. William B. Mayer, *The Changing American Mind* (New York: Norton), p. 318.

42. Aristotle, "Characteristics of the Extreme and Mean States: Practical Corollaries," in Aristotle, *Nicomachean Ethics,* trans. David Ross, World's Classics Paperbacks (New York: Oxford University Press, 1980), p. 44.

43. Isaiah 30:21, *New American Bible* (Washington, D.C.: Confraternity of Christian Doctrine, 1970).

44. William Shakespeare, *Titus Andronicus,* Act III, Scene I.

SELECTED CENTRIST BIBLIOGRAPHY

Acheson, Dean. *A Democrat Looks at His Party*. New York: Harper & Row, 1955.

Black, Gordon S., and Benjamin D. Black. *The Politics of American Discontent: How a New Party Can Make Democracy Work Again*. New York: John Wiley & Sons, 1994.

Broder, Davis S. *The Party's Over: The Failure of Politics in America*. New York: Harper & Row, 1971.

Brooke, Edward W. *The Challenge of Change*. Boston: Little, Brown, 1966.

Cooper, John Milton, Jr. *The Warrior and the Priest: Woodrow Wilson and Theodore Roosevelt*. Cambridge, Mass.: Belknap Press of Harvard University Press, 1983.

Fiorina, Morris P. *Culture War?: The Myth of a Polarized America*, New York: Pearson Longman, 2005.

Gergen, David. *Eyewitness to Power: The Essence of Leadership, Nixon to Clinton*. New York: Simon & Schuster, 2000.

Greenberg, Stanley B. *Middle Class Dreams: The Politics and Power of the New American Majority*. New York: Times Books, 1995.

Greenstein, Fred I. *The Presidential Difference: Leadership Style from FDR to Clinton*. Princeton, N.J.: Princeton University Press, 2000.

Giuliani, Rudolph W., with Ken Kurson. *Leadership*. New York: Talk Miramax, 2002.

Halstead, Ted, and Michael Lind. *The Radical Center: The Future of American Politics*. New York: Doubleday, 2001.

Hamby, Alonzo L. *Liberalism and Its Challengers*. 2nd ed. New York: Oxford University Press, 1992.

Hofstadter, Richard. *The Idea of a Party System*. Berkeley: University of California Press, 1969.

Javits, Jacob K. *Order of Battle: A Republican's Call to Reason*. New York: Atheneum, 1964.

Karabell, Zachary. *The Last Campaign*. New York: Random House, 2000.

Klein, Joe. *The Natural: The Misunderstood Presidency of Bill Clinton*. New York: Doubleday, 2002.

Larson, Arthur. *A Republican Looks at His Party*. New York: Harper & Row, 1956.

Lieberman, Joe. *In Praise of Public Life*. New York: Simon & Schuster, 2000.

Lubell, Samuel. *Revolt of the Moderates*. New York: Harper & Brothers, 1956.

Maginnis, John. *Cross to Bear*. Baton Rouge, La.: Darkhorse Press, 1992.

Matthews, Chris. *Kennedy and Nixon*. New York: Simon & Schuster, 1996.

Matusow, Allen J. *The Unraveling of America: A History of Liberalism in the 1960s*. New York: Harper & Row, 1984.

McCain, John, with Mark Salter. *Worth the Fighting For*. New York: Random House, 2002.

Morris, Dick. *Power Plays*. New York: HarperCollins, 2002.

Morris, Edmund. *The Rise of Theodore Roosevelt*. New York: Ballantine, 1980.

———. *Theodore Rex*. New York: Random House, 2001.

Neal, Steve. *Harry and Ike: The Partnership That Remade the Postwar World*. New York: Scribner, 2001.

Nixon, Richard. *In the Arena: A Memoir of Victory, Defeat, and Renewal*. New York: Simon & Schuster, 1990.

Olin, Spencer C., Jr. *California's Prodigal Sons*. Berkeley: University of California Press, 1968.

Overstreet, Harry, and Bonaro Overstreet. *The Strange Tactics of Extremism*. New York: Norton, 1964.

Reston, James. *Sketches in the Sand*. New York: Knopf, 1967.

Richardson, Elliot. *Reflections of a Radical Moderate*. New York: Pantheon, 1996.

Roosevelt, Theodore. *The Man in the Arena*. Ed. John Allen Gable. Oyster Bay, N.Y.: Theodore Roosevelt Association, 1987.

Safire, William. *Safire's New Political Dictionary*. New York: Random House, 1993.

Scammon, Richard, and Ben Wattenberg. *The Real Majority*. New York: Coward-McCann, 1970.

Schlesinger, Arthur, Jr. *The Cycles of American History*. Boston: Houghton Mifflin, 1986.

———. *The Vital Center: The Politics of Freedom*. New York: Da Capo, 1988.

Siegel, Fred. *The Future Once Happened Here*. New York: Free Press, 1997.

Tocqueville, Alexis de. *Democracy in America*. Ed. J. P. Mayer. Trans. George Lawrence. New York: Harper Perennial, 1988.

Tsongas, Paul. *Journey of Purpose*. New Haven, Conn.: Yale University Press, 1995.

Warren, Earl. *The Memoirs of Chief Justice Earl Warren*. Garden City, N.Y.: Doubleday, 1977.

White, Theodore H. *America in Search of Itself: The Making of the President, 1956–1980*. New York: Harper & Row, 1982.

———. *The Making of the President, 1964*. New York: Atheneum, 1965.

Wills, Garry. *Nixon Agonistes: The Crisis of the Self-Made Man*. Boston: Houghton Mifflin, 1970.

Wolfe, Alan. *One Nation, After All*. New York: Viking, 1998.

ACKNOWLEDGMENTS

First and foremost, I'd like to thank my parents, John and Dianne Avlon, whose love, support, wisdom, kindness, and good humor made everything possible.

The publication of this book would not have been possible without Jake Morrissey—who first believed in the book enough to convince Harmony Press to publish it—and my editor, Kim Kanner Meisner, who with grace and tact taught me how the process works in fact. I'd also like to thank Shaye Areheart for having faith in this project and Sibylle Kazeroid for all her essential work behind the scenes. Ian Klienert stayed with the project from its earliest days, and for that I am very grateful. Gary Pagano was an invaluable research assistant, who, along with Mikol Rudd and Suzie Geller, made it possible to finish the book in just under a year.

The people I am privileged to call my family and friends combine a good mind, a good heart, and good humor: my brother, Reynolds; cousin, Alexander; aunts Joan and Lexa; uncles Alex and David; godparents Elaine and Peter John; Karen; Stephen Palmer and Ruth Ayer; my godchildren Benjamin and Flora Damon and Alexandra Catlin; Whitney and Winn Jewett; Jay and Sandy Vanderzee; Leslie Vanderzee-Marvin; Laurel Boylen; Carlene and Ian Damon; George and Kim Catlin; Shawn Milnes; Christine and Pasco Alfaro; Rich and Margaret Wager; Mike Jackson; Amy Kindred; Jamie Schriebl; Brad Buchanan; Ali Guess; Jesse Angelo; Matt Pottinger; Eric Morrissey; Howard Gould and Ashliegh Banfield; Adam Silver; Mike Kopcha; Dimetri Martin; Ed Lintz; Jeremy Carl, Bronwyn Gerrity; Ted and Karen Flagg; Ben and Shannon Johnston; Max and Barbara Koltuv; Justine Stamen; Marcia Kebbon; Ted, Janet, Ashton, and Lavonne Phillips; Barbara and Conrad Zimmerman; Janice and Tom Waring; Kathleen and John Rivers; the Cleveland family; Ben Allston Moore Jr.; the Thomas and Carvelas families; the Ogdens and the McGraths; June and Robert Konopka; Diana Hambleton; Candice and John Olds; Reverend John and Marie Howard; David and Nicki Dunbar; and, rounding out the list, my grandparents Dr. Alexander and Toula Phillips (to whom this book is dedicated), and the memory of Mother Ayer, Linda Tepper Jewett, and John and Carol Avlon.

My colleagues in the Giuliani administration deserve special thanks because they are valued teachers, friends, and mentors who gave me extraordinary opportunities from the time I joined the team at twenty-four to the age of twenty-eight, when we left City Hall at the end of 2001: Mayor Rudy Giuliani and his wife, Judith; Denny Young, Larry Levy, Joe Lhota, Beth Petrone Hatton, Kate Anson, and Thomas Von Essen; John Odermatt and everyone at the Office of Emergency Management; Randy Mastro, Michael Hess, Geoff Hess, Eric Hatzimemos, Steve Fishner, Julie Mendik, Ryan

Medrano, Fred Cerullo, Rudy Washington, George Vellonakis, Tony and Carol Carbonetti, Tony Coles, Cristyne Nicholas, Coleen Roche, Bob Harding, Alan Dobrin, Brian Cohen, Richie Sheirer, Bernard Kerik, Vinny LaPadula, Nick Scoppetta, Anthony Crowell, Josh Greenman, Ken Kurson, Matt Mahoney, Jay Weinkam, Manny Papir, Calvin Drayton, John Huvane, Patti Varone, Shelia Gallagher, Janna Mancini, Greg and Deborah Miley, Sunny Mindel, Dwight Williams, and many others; fellow members of the Bilingual Education Reform Task Force; the City Hall Park Restoration committee; the 2001 Charter Revision Commission; and my brothers in arms on the speechwriting team after the attacks of 9/11—Owen Brennan Rounds, Mark Ribbing, and Matt Lockwood.

I would also like to thank my editors and colleagues at the *New York Sun*—especially Seth Lipsky (didn't miss a column, as promised), Ira Stoll, Jack Newfield, Robert Messenger, Ryan Sager, Harry Siegel, Ben Smith, and Errol Louis; my partners in Prides Crossing Executive Communication—Mal MacDougall, George Catlin, Steve Judson, Stu Gottlieb, and Peter Scoblic; the faculty of Milton Academy and Yale College; my students at Hunter College; Bronx Academy of Letters students and board; the Independent Party of the Yale Political Union; George Cahill, Anne De Simone, Kurt Thomas, and Leus Perlas; the Milton Paper; and my fellow band members in Blind Dog Whiskey and Angel Carver Blues. I would also like to thank Dr. Flo McAfee, my boss at the White House, and the late senator Paul Tsongas, whose 1995 lectures at Yale were hugely influential and formed the basis of his book *Journey of Purpose*. Some other prominent Centrist leaders who deserved to be included in this book if it could have been twice the size are Senator Henry "Scoop" Jackson, Senator Jacob Javits, Senator Mark Hatfield, Senator Gary Hart, Wendell Wilkie, Mayor Fiorello La Guardia, Mayor Michael White, Mayor Richard Riordan, Mayor John Norquist, Massachusetts governor William Weld, and the legendary California governor Hiram Johnson.

I am very grateful to the many people who gave their time and shared their expertise to improve *Independent Nation*. Chief among these are Dr. John Gable, president of the Theodore Roosevelt Association; Arthur Schlesinger Jr., whose conversations over lunch were an education and an honor and whose books—especially *The Vital Center* and *Robert Kennedy and His Times*—have been an inspiration; the late senator Daniel Patrick Moynihan—who took time just weeks before his death to edit and approve his chapter, as well as suggest the quote that begins it; Senator Edward Brooke, one of the pioneering public figures of our times; Ray Price—the only American to have written two inaugural addresses and a resignation speech, as well as the only person to have been on friendly terms with both Jack Kerouac and Richard Nixon; Leon Panetta, who generously shared his perspective on Centrist leaders from Earl Warren to Bill Clinton, as well as life on the Monterey Peninsula, one of my favorite places on earth; Earl Warren Jr.; Jody Powell, for writing a memo on the Carter chapter and delivering the wonderful line "The problem with moderates is that we are moderate"; Fred Siegel, a writer and thinker I admire who I am now honored to call a friend; Mark Benbow, the historian at Woodrow Wilson House, for reading over that chapter and copying a tape of the early campaign film *The Old Way and the New;* Angus King, for giving an interview while on vacation with his family; the director of the Margaret Chase Smith Library, Dr. Gregory P. Gallant; Goldwater Professor of History Robert Allan Goldberg; Professor William B. Pickett; Mike Janeway; Frank Luntz; James Humes; Peggy Noonan; the John F. Kennedy Library; and Edmund Morris, who offered valuable advice on how to write readable history as this process began.

I also need to mention the writers who have been, without knowing it, my greatest (and certainly most patient) teachers: David Remnick, Martin Amis, J. D. Salinger, John Updike, Jack Kerouac, Hunter S. Thompson, Ralph Ellison, and Jim Harrison among them. Music has meant enough to my life that I wouldn't be honest if I didn't thank U2, Lyle Lovett, Neil Young, Otis Redding, Aaron Copland, Van Morrison, REM, Uncle Tupelo, The Pogues, Johnny Cash, Bob Dylan, Randy Newman, Peter Gabriel, Miles Davis, and Louis Armstrong for always being dependable sources of inspiration. Finally, given that this is a work of biographical history, I should thank some of my very human heroes from history who never fail to help me find a little more courage: Thomas Jefferson, Abraham Lincoln, Theodore Roosevelt, Winston Churchill, Dr. Martin Luther King Jr., Vaclav Havel, and Robert F. Kennedy.

INDEX

Abzug, Bella, 24, 220, 221, 288, 303–309
Adams, Sherman, 255
African-Americans. *See* civil rights; race
Agnew, Spiro, 82, 176, 353
Aiken, George, 324, 328
Ailes, Roger, 177, 190
Aldrich, Nelson, 130
Allen, Gary, 165
Alsop, Stewart, 271
Ambro, Jerome, Jr., 302
American eagle, as symbol of Centrism, 4, 432
Americans for Democratic Action, 70, 85, 140, 146, 295, 337
Amin, Idi, 299
Anderson, John, 31, 76, 89, 92, 94, 364
anti-Semitism, 181, 299–300, 310, 395, 396
antiwar movement, 173, 175, 180, 303, 328, 344, 345, 439
Arizona, 266, 272, 341
Ashcroft, John, 446
Atwater, Lee, 190
Auletta, Ken, 385

Barkley, Dean, 368, 371
Baruch, Bernard, 325
Bauer, Gary, 416, 420
Bayh, Birch, 351
Bayh, Evan, 444
Beame, Abe, 294
Beasley, David, 421
Bell, Daniel, 294
Benhadj, Ali, 12–13
Berlin, Irving, 254
Berman, Paul, 12
Beverage, Albion, 320

bipartisanship, 6–7, 218–19, 223, 377, 416
Bush (G. W.) and, 430–31, 433, 436, 444
Eisenhower and, 242–43, 245, 254, 262
Giuliani and, 385–87, 391
Warren and, 225–36, 237–40
Black, Stephanie, 358
black militants, 11, 297, 312, 333, 334, 339, 344, 347, 348–49
Blaine, James G., 38, 39
Blair, Tony, 431
Blake, Robert, 296
Blum, John Morton, 35
Bob Jones University, 421
Bohlen, Charles, 260
Bolton, Josh, 410
Bork, Robert, 278
Boshwitz, Rudy, 371
Bozell, Brent, 265
Brademas, John, 86
Bradley, Bill, 364, 427
Branch, Taylor, 193
Brandeis, Louis, 132, 350
Brawley, Tawana, 10, 395
Breaux, John, 416, 427
Brennan, Joe, 374
Bricker, John, 233
Brooke, Edward, 24, 176, 312, 332–56
Brown, Aaron, 435
Brown, H. Rap, 348–49
Brown, Pat, 170
Brown, Robert, 208
Brownell, Herbert, 252, 263
Brown v. Board of Education, 223, 274, 278

Bryan, William Jennings, 50, 51, 52, 124, 131, 134
Buchanan, Pat, 3, 89, 183, 205, 393, 395, 396, 416, 428, 440
Republican National Convention speech, 208
Buckley, James, 220, 221, 300, 302, 304, 307, 308, 309
Buckley, William F., Jr., 171, 220, 265, 272, 294, 300, 360
Bullock, Bob, 410
Bundy, McGeorge, 153, 157
Burns, Arthur, 181
Burns, James MacGregor, 148
Burroughs, John, 35
Bush, George H. W., 3, 9, 31, 73, 188–90, 384, 421, 424, 425, 427
approval ratings, 100, 188, 205
Louisiana politics and, 98–99, 105, 111, 114
on militant conservatives, 219
1992 campaign, 204–11, 372, 407–408, 441
Reagan candidacy and, 89, 92
Bush, George P., 423
Bush, George W., 198, 407–31, 434, 439, 443, 446, 447
Centrist campaign, 6–7, 407–11, 415–17, 423–24, 430–31, 434, 436
right-wing appointments, 445
Bush, Prescott, 269

Caddell, Pat, 83, 90–91
California
  John Birch Society
    and, 267
  Johnson (Hiram) and,
    54, 222, 229, 231,
    234, 236, 276
  Nixon and, 166–69,
    170, 255
  Republican 1964 pri-
    mary, 275–76
  Warren and, 218,
    222–40, 276
Calley, William, 78
campaign finance re-
    form, 20–21, 22,
    126–27, 128, 368,
    412, 422
Cannon, Joseph, 47, 130
Carlson, Tucker, 422
Carmen, Daniel J., 345
Carmichael, Stokely,
    344, 349
Carney, David, 16
Carrillo, Leo, 228
Carson, Johnny, 191
Carswell, Harrold, 351–53
Carter, Jimmy, 7, 31,
    75–95, 189, 195,
    205, 309, 383, 437
  Centrist theme, 75,
    76–83, 94
Catholicism, 142,
    144–45, 149, 326,
    336, 340, 394, 421,
    426
Centrism, 1–27
  as American tradition,
    4–7, 286, 435
  arguments for, 2–4,
    117–18
  Clinton statement on,
    187
  common themes of,
    432–33
  core beliefs of, 22–23,
    436
  definition of, 2
  Independent gover-
    nors and, 357–78
  practical lessons of,
    436–39
  as voter majority,
    16–23, 429–30

Wilson statement on,
    122–23
Chamberlain, Wilt, 178
Chance, James, 121
Cheney, Dick, 423
China, 3, 117, 138, 163,
    164, 172, 185, 256,
    321
Chotiner, Murray, 166
Christian, Mike, 420
Christian Coalition, 421.
    See also religious
    right
Churchill, Winston, 26,
    59
civil rights, 175, 312
  Brooke and, 333,
    334–40, 344–53
  Carter and, 78, 80
  Dewey and, 59
  Johnson and, 171,
    277, 340, 418,
    439–40
  Kennedy (J. F.) and,
    143, 147, 155, 270,
    338–39
  Nixon and, 178, 182,
    351–53
  Republicans and,
    269–70, 273, 278,
    280, 336–37, 342,
    417–18, 439–40
  Truman and, 6, 30,
    58–62, 69, 73
Civil Rights Act (1964),
    277
Clark, Champ, 131
Clark, Edgar, 45
Clark, Ramsey, 303, 305
Clark, Wesley, 444
Clarke, Una, 397
Cleveland, Grover, 37,
    40, 76, 135
Clifford, Clark, 67
Clinton, Bill, 10, 24, 117,
    187–216, 352n, 363,
    387, 441
  Bush (G. W.) campaign
    co-options from,
    411, 417, 425, 431,
    436
  Centrist theme, 7,
    82–83, 118, 191–92,
    198, 213, 214–15,

366, 407, 418, 433,
    435
  political fervor
    against, 14
  sex scandal/impeach-
    ment of, 366, 409,
    412, 425, 426
  2000 presidential
    campaign and, 425,
    428, 429–30
  welfare reform, 3, 262,
    343, 391, 392, 397,
    415
Clinton, Hillary Rodham,
    10, 193, 195, 208,
    332–33, 404, 427
Coakley, Frank, 224
Cohen, William, 375
Cold War, 6, 241
  Carter and, 82–83
  Eisenhower and, 244,
    256, 262
  extremism and, 65,
    156–57, 267, 273,
    279
  Ford and, 82
  isolationism and, 218
  Kennedy (J. F.) and,
    116, 138–39, 148,
    151, 154, 156–59,
    292, 325
  liberal split on, 30, 57,
    58, 64–65, 70, 148,
    166, 167
  McCarthyism and. See
    McCarthy, Joseph
  Moynihan and, 289,
    290, 298–99, 304,
    309
  neoconservatives and,
    294
  Nixon and, 3, 117,
    165–69, 172, 185,
    253, 255, 323
  Reagan and, 82, 91–92
  Taft and, 242, 250
  Truman and, 30, 57,
    58, 64, 70, 73, 82,
    138
Coleman, Norm, 366,
    370
Collins, Susan, 331, 375
Commager, Henry
    Steele, 263

Communism, 10–12, 42, 138, 239. *See also* Cold War; Soviet Union

Congress
  Bush (G. H. W.) and, 73
  Carter and, 31, 76, 83–84, 86–87
  Eisenhower and, 258–59, 261
  increased partisanship in, 13–14, 434
  Nixon and, 163, 182
  Republican Revolution, 14, 215, 391, 409, 417, 439
  Roosevelt (T.) and, 47
  Truman and, 30, 58–59, 61, 69
  Wilson and, 121, 134
  See also Senate

Congress of Industrial Organizations, 236, 239

Connally, John, 89, 161

Connecticut, 313, 357, 358–65

Contract for America, 391

Cooper, John Milton, 132

Cortelyou, George, 50

Coupland, Douglas, 15

Courtney, Kent, 267, 278

Coyne, John, 82

Craig, May, 320

Crangle, Joseph, 300, 306

Crowe, William J., Jr., 210

Cuban missile crisis, 158, 273

culture wars, 100, 209–10, 417–18

Cuomo, Mario, 198, 203n, 390

Curley, James Michael, 336

Daley, Richard, 169

Danforth, John, 208

Daniels, Josephus, 134

Davies, Joseph, 244, 247

Davis, Henry G., 51

Davis, Jefferson, 121, 439

Dean, Howard, 444

Debs, Eugene, 120, 132, 133

DeLay, Tom, 221

Democratic Leadership Council
  Bush co-options from, 410
  Clinton and, 188, 191, 192
  From and, 22, 190, 191
  Gore and, 408–409, 414, 425, 430
  Lieberman and, 426
  founding and goals of, 188
  statement of principles, 191–192
  See also New Democrats

Dewey, Thomas, 56, 59–60, 67, 70, 71–72, 230, 232, 233, 235, 243, 245, 252, 253, 254

Dillon, Douglas, 153

Dinkins, David, 302, 385

Dionne, E. J., 356

Dirksen, Everett, 251

Disraeli, Benjamin, 164, 296

Dixiecrats, 57, 62, 67, 69, 73, 267, 356, 417, 439

Dole, Bob, 10, 216, 398, 428, 430, 441

Donovan, Robert, 156

Douglas, Helen Gahagan, 168

Douglas, John W., 140

Douglas, Paul, 243

Downey, Sheridan, 236

Dukakis, Michael, 106, 190, 199, 209, 400, 408

Duke, David, 3, 31–32, 98–99, 105, 106–14

Dulles, Allen, 153

Dulles, John Foster, 267

Dylan, Bob, 79–80

Eastland, James, 61

Eaton, Cornell, 339

Edelman, Marian Wright, 415

Edmunds, George F., 38–39

Edwards, Edwin, 31, 97–114

Edwards, John, 444, 445

Eisenhower, Dwight D., 16, 70, 139, 142, 154, 171, 175, 241–63
  Centrist theme, 6, 24, 118, 219, 242–60, 271, 280–81, 342, 433
  McCarthyism and, 256, 260
  Nixon vice presidency, 149, 151, 168, 176n, 182, 253, 255, 260
  presidential races, 248–59, 285, 325
  right-wing charges against, 267, 278

Eisenhower, John, 250

Eisenhower, Mamie, 246, 247, 249

Eizenstat, Stuart, 204

Emerson, Ralph Waldo, 5

Environmental Protection Agency, 117, 163, 182

Evans, Rowland, 293

Evers, Medgar, 339

extremism, 3, 8–13, 26, 217, 272, 279, 341, 435
  backlashes against, 438
  Brooke's statement against, 342
  campaign defeats of, 448
  danger of, 8–13, 15
  in Democratic Party, 302
  Eisenhower's distrust of, 244, 260–61
  growth in major parties, 22, 435

Independents' responses to, 313
Kennedy (J. F.) as victim of, 160
Kennedy (J. F.) speech on, 156, 161
Louisiana politics and, 96–114
Nixon on, 164, 171, 178–79
party apparatus control by, 217
political defeats for, 447
in Republican Party, 1, 7, 205, 276–79, 366, 421–23, 439
Rockefeller warning against, 279
Roosevelt (T.) warning against, 129
Smith warning against, 311, 315, 316–19, 324, 328–31

Fallows, James, 94–95
Falwell, Jerry, 8–9, 423
Family Assistance Plan, 183, 185, 293, 302
Farmer, James, 182
fascism, 10, 11, 251, 321
Feingold, Russ, 21, 412
feminism, 303, 329
Ferrer, Fernando, 398
Fineman, Howard, 419
Fitzgerald, John F. ("Honey Fitz"), 138
Flavin, Robert, 301
Fleeson, Doris, 230
Florida, 428, 430
Flowers, Gennifer, 199
Ford, Gerald, 82, 84, 220, 300, 309, 355
Fortas, Abe, 350
Founding Fathers, 2, 4–5, 27
Franklin, Benjamin, 26
Franks, Gary, 356
Frist, Bill, 416
From, Al, 22, 190, 191
Furcolo, Foster, 141

Galleghy, Elton, 392
Gang of 8, 364, 427

Gavin, William, 172
gay rights, 18, 213, 381, 386, 394, 400, 403
Georgia, 77
Gingrich, Newt, 14, 215, 391, 417, 439
Giuliani, Rudy, 24, 214, 313, 379–405
Gladstone, William, 121
Goebbels, Joseph, 12
Goldberg, Arthur, 154, 291
Golden, Harry, 266
Goldsmith, Steve, 397
Goldwater, Barry, 7, 24, 92, 117, 159–60, 170–71, 184, 211, 219–20, 264–86, 326, 340, 341, 438, 448
Goodell, Charles, 300
Goodwin, Dick, 150
Gore, Al, Jr., 83, 190, 204, 209
  2000 campaign and, 407–30, 441
Gore, Tipper, 408, 414
Gould, Jay, 37
governors, 15–16, 32, 40, 290–91
  Bush (G. W.) as, 408, 409
  Carter as, 78–79
  Clinton as, 194–96
  Cuomo-Pataki race, 390
  Independents of 1990s, 357–78, 441
  Rockefeller as, 265, 267–68, 291
  Roemer's 1991 race, 96–114
  Warren as, 222–40
  Wilson as, 124–29
Graham, Bob, 444
Graham, Michael, 421
Grasso, Ella, 361
Great Society, 117, 171, 181, 189, 292, 343, 438
Green Party, 427–28
Gulf War, 188, 204
Guthrie, Woody, 65

Haig, Alexander, 384
Halberstam, Ari, 390, 405
Haldeman, H. R., 164
Halstead, Ted, 370
Hamilton, Alexander, 4
Hammerschmidt, John, 193, 194
Hanna, Mark, 40, 49–50, 411
Hannegan, Robert, 63n
Hargrove, Erwin, 115
Harriman, Averell, 290–91
Hart, Gary, 190, 364
Hatfield, Mark, 176, 275, 346
Hathaway, William, 373
Havel, Vaclav, 8
Hawkins, Yusef, 385
Haynsworth, Clement F., 350
Hayward, Steven, 84
Hebert, Bobby, 111
Heckscher, August, 130
Herter Committee, 167n
Hewett, Chuck, 376
Hildreth, Horace, 320
Hirschfield, Abe, 303–304
Hiss, Alger, 167, 170, 253
Hitler, Adolf, 10–11, 12
Hoffer, Eric, 10
Hollings, Fritz, 351
Holloway, Clyde, 106, 110, 111
Hoover, Herbert, 143, 144, 152, 186, 224, 231, 246, 250
House Un-American Activities Committee, 167, 253
Hruska, Roman, 351
Hughes, Emmet John, 260
Humphrey, Hubert, 145, 146, 173, 179–80, 185, 193, 281, 296, 425
Humphrey, Hubert, III, 366
Hyman, Sidney, 159

immigrants, 381, 390, 391–94
Independent voices, 24–25, 31, 76, 90, 92, 94, 311–403, 440
Independent voters, 7, 30, 59, 212, 430
  Eisenhower and, 243, 244, 246–47
  Perot and, 209
  rising numbers of, 1, 13–16, 313, 433, 441
  Truman and, 67–68, 69, 71
India, 298
internationalism, 136, 218, 241, 243–63
Iranian hostage crisis, 75–76, 90
Ireland, Doug, 306
isolationism, 6, 218, 242–45, 246, 250–51, 253–254, 263, 267
Israel, 12, 91, 299–300, 305

Jackson, Henry, 78, 300, 301, 383
Jackson, Jesse, 98, 188, 190, 203, 205, 384, 418
Jefferson, Thomas, 5, 23, 35, 62, 140, 436
Jeffords, Jim, 442
John Birch Society, 265, 267, 279, 281
Johnson, Hiram, 54, 222, 229, 231, 234, 236, 276
Johnson, Lady Bird, 281
Johnson, Lyndon, 7, 87, 117, 146–47, 153, 170–74, 189, 211, 271, 277, 297, 340, 418, 438–40
  Moynihan report and, 292–93
  1964 campaign, 271, 281–85

Senate leadership, 259, 260
Vietnam War and, 171, 179, 180, 344
Jones, Robert L., 324

Katcher, Leo, 240
Katz, Hippo, 111
Kefauver, Estes, 142
Keller, Lanny, 97
Kelling, George, 389
Kelly, Earl Lee, 235, 238
Kelly, Frank, 337
Kemp, Jack, 384
Kempton, Murray, 255
Kennedy, Jacqueline Bouvier, 138, 143
Kennedy, John F., 6, 24, 87, 116–17, 137–61, 167, 169, 180, 265, 277, 325, 327, 338, 438
  assassination of, 161, 271, 292, 326, 382
  Centrist theme, 140, 143, 145, 152, 153–61, 220, 291–92, 309, 383, 433
  Rockefeller compared with, 267–68
Kennedy, Joseph P., 137, 138, 140
Kennedy, Robert F., 87, 140–41, 146, 155, 157, 175, 220, 293–96, 309, 333, 338, 382, 384
  disassociation from liberal label, 141
Kennedy, Ted, 31, 76, 85, 87–88, 158, 190, 338, 346
Kenny, Robert, 236, 237, 238, 239
Kent, Jack, 110
Kent State shootings (1970), 329
Kerry, John, 444–45, 446, 447
Khrushchev, Nikita, 149, 157, 158, 169, 325
King, Angus, 15, 313, 357, 358, 364, 371–78, 440

King, David C., 22
King, Martin Luther, Jr., 77, 89, 277, 333, 346, 373, 398
King, Rodney, 203, 208
Kissinger, Henry, 180, 298, 300, 309
Klein, Joe, 420, 441
Koch, Ed, 384, 385, 402
Korean War, 253, 255, 257–58, 321
Kristol, Irving, 294
Krueger, Liz, 398
Kuchel, Tom, 276
Kucinich, Dennis, 444
Ku Klux Klan, 31, 96, 98–100, 106, 107, 111, 113, 144, 265, 283

labor, 37, 43–46, 58, 64, 68, 72, 149, 155, 236, 239, 384
La Follette, Robert M., Jr., 321
La Guardia, Fiorello, 380, 384, 387
Lamm, Richard, 384
Lao-tzu, 449
Larson, Arthur, 7
Latinos, 21, 410, 423, 424
Leach, Buddy, 101
League of Nations, 136, 218
Lee, J. Bracken, 278
Lee, Robert E., 62, 121
LeMay, Curtis, 157
Lewinsky, Monica, 426
liberalism
  classical, 178–79
  J. F. and R. F. Kennedy Centrist theme vs., 140–41, 143, 145, 151, 153, 159, 220
  Moynihan on challenges for, 295, 304
  reasons for fallen currency of, 438
Lieberman, Joe, 359, 426–27, 444
Lilienthal, David, 67
Limbaugh, Rush, 419

Lincoln, Abraham, 23, 92, 151, 328
  Republican Party tradition and, 270, 336, 340, 342, 356, 419, 423, 439
  as Roosevelt (T.) hero, 36, 45, 51
Lindsay, John, 176, 280, 294, 391
Lippmann, Walter, 323
Lodge, Henry Cabot, 39, 45
Lodge, Henry Cabot, Jr., 74, 139, 149, 245, 246, 275, 276
Long, Huey, 97, 100, 107
Long, Russell, 87
Longley, James, 376
Los Angeles riots, 203, 208
Lott, Trent, 356, 421, 439
Louima, Abner, 401
Louisiana, 32, 96–114
Lowi, Ted, 24
Luce, Henry, 140
Luciano, Lucky, 59, 230
Luntz, Frank, 368
Lynn, Christopher, 386

MacArthur, Douglas, 250
Machiavelli, Niccolò, 214
Maddox, Lester, 77
Madison, James, 5, 140
Mafia, 100, 291, 383
Maginnis, John, 97
Maine, 313, 319–20, 324, 325, 328, 331, 357
  Independent governor, 357, 358, 371–78
Malcolm X, 11
Malone, Joe, 375
Manes, Donald, 384
Mankiewicz, Frank, 353
Mao Tse-tung, 138, 185, 256, 321
Maraniss, David, 195
Marcantonio, Vito, 168
Marshall, George, 66, 250, 256–57
Marshall, Thomas, 55

Marshall, Will, 410, 430
Marshall Plan, 66, 167n, 244, 256
Martin, Ricky, 424
Massachusetts, 133, 138, 142, 143, 149, 190, 199, 336
  Brooke and, 332–56
Mathias, Charles, 352
Mayer, William B., 448
mayors, 24, 39, 290, 294, 379–405
  third-way of 1990s, 313, 397–98
Mazo, Earl, 173
McCain, John, 10, 411–13, 419–20, 422, 441, 448
McCain-Feingold bill, 21, 412
McCarthy, Joseph, 70, 139, 219, 242, 244, 267, 273, 325, 330
  Eisenhower and, 256, 260
  Senate censure of, 260, 318, 322–23
  Smith's challenge to, 311, 315–31
McConnell, Mitch, 412
McCormack, John, 142
McCormick, Edward, 337
McCullough, David, 59
McGinniss, Joe, 176n
McGovern, George, 3, 7, 85, 163, 193, 302, 354, 382, 418n
McGrory, Mary, 292n
McKinley, William, 29, 40, 41, 49, 211, 411
McKinney, Cynthia, 434
McNamara, Robert, 153, 155, 157, 325
Medicare, 416, 430
Meredith, James, 112, 155–56
Merriam, Frank, 225
Messinger, Ruth, 398–403
Miller, William, 280
Miller, Zell, 446

Minnesota, 313, 357, 358, 365–71
Mitchell, John, 171
Molinari, Guy, 391
Mondale, Walter, 82, 190, 209, 373, 425
Monroe, James, 6
Morgan, J. P., 42, 43, 119
Morris, Dick, 117–18, 195, 200, 214, 441
Morris, Edmund, 36
Moss, Mitchell, 403
Moyers, Bill, 440
Moynihan, Daniel Patrick, 24, 83, 181, 183, 220, 287–310
Moynihan Report, 294, 297
Mudd, Roger, 88
Muhammad, Elijah, 11
Munch, Edvard, 205
Murrow, Edward R., 323
Muskie, Ed, 328

NAACP, 284, 336, 344, 419
Nader, Ralph, 3, 291, 427–28, 440
NAFTA, 214
NATO, 244, 246, 258, 260
Nazi Germany, 10–11, 12
neoconservatives, 285, 295–99, 304–306, 310
neo-Nazis, 99, 108, 111
Neville, Aaron, 111
New Deal, 30, 54, 61, 65, 68, 116, 139, 147, 165, 241, 261, 290
New Democrats, 117, 197, 213, 366, 407, 410, 416, 424, 425, 428
  mantra of, 436
Newfield, Jack, 156n, 217
New Jersey, 125–28
New Left, 179, 288, 303, 309
New Nationalism, 130, 132

New Orleans
Declaration, 191–92
New South, 78, 81, 96
New York City, 37,
39–40, 290, 294,
309
Giuliani mayoralty, 24,
313, 379–405
New York State, 265,
268, 291, 382, 390,
404
Democratic senatorial
primary, 24, 83, 220,
287–88, 300–10
Roosevelt (T.) political
career, 37–41
New York Yankees, 382,
397, 399
Niebuhr, Reinhold, 79,
147
Nixon, Richard M., 77,
80, 162–86, 220,
237, 280, 323, 329,
359
Centrist theme, 2, 6,
116–18, 144, 149,
163, 166, 171, 174,
180, 185, 239, 296,
433
"Checkers" speech,
256
China visit, 3, 117,
163, 164, 172,
185
as Eisenhower vice
president, 149, 152,
169, 176n, 181, 253,
255, 260
Kennedy similarities,
149, 167
Moynihan and, 288,
295–98, 303, 305
1972 landslide, 117,
164, 353, 382
1960 campaign,
147–50, 169–70,
267, 275
1968 campaign,
171–80, 349
resignation, 186, 312,
354
southern strategy, 182,
350–53
"Nixon in China," mean-

ing of, 3, 164, 172,
185, 262
Noonan, Peggy, 438
Norquist, Grover, 434,
442
Norquist, John, 397
Novak, Robert, 83, 280,
285, 293
Nungesser, Billy, 106

Oakes, John, 308
Obama, Barack, 445
O'Donnell, Kenny, 153
O'Dwyer, Paul, 303
Olson, Culbert, 226–27,
230
O'Neill, Thomas P.
("Tip"), 83–84, 101,
190, 306
O'Neill, William, 361
O'Reilly, Don Allejandro,
100
Otto, Lewis, 107

Pagan, Antonio, 400
Palmer, Kyle, 226, 236,
238
Panetta, Leon, 352
Parker, Alton, 51, 94
party politics, 1–5,
97–114
Centrist balance and,
22–25
moderate voter rejec-
tion of, 366, 433
opposition candidates,
115–36
outsider candidates,
77, 82, 84–85, 87,
106, 242–48
polarization trend,
13–16. See also ex-
tremism
realignments, 281,
439
Pataki, George, 391
Patterson, Ellis, 237
Payne, Dan, 374
Peabody, Endicott
("Chubb"), 344, 345
Penn, Mark, 429
Penny, Tim, 364
Percy, Charles, 346
Perot, H. Ross, 202, 206,

209, 211, 216, 358,
362, 364, 366, 372,
373, 441
Phillips, Kevin, 178,
209
Pinchot, Gifford, 129
Podhoretz, Norman, 301
populism, 49–52,
123–25, 147, 185,
194, 206
Gore campaign and,
428, 429
Louisiana and, 100,
107
Powell, Adam Clayton,
346
Powell, Colin, 16, 278,
423, 441, 448
Powell, Jody, 85
Price, Ray, 163
primaries, 24, 130,
145–46, 217–21
New York senatorial,
24, 83, 220, 287–88,
300–310
open vs. closed, 114,
217, 218, 222–23,
228, 235–36,
237–38
Republican (2000),
411–14, 417,
418–23, 441
Princeton University,
123, 133
Progressive Party (1912),
33, 39, 54, 90,
130–32, 135, 321
Wilson co-opts
from, 116, 121, 135
Progressive Party (1948),
16, 57, 62, 65, 73,
289, 312
progressivism
California and, 222,
224–25, 227, 231,
233, 234, 237, 275
electorate's endorse-
ment of in 1912,
133–34
Giuliani and the New
Progressives, 381
Nixon and, 165
as outside two-party
system, 441

Roosevelt (T.) on, 12, 129

Warren and, 225, 227, 228, 231, 233, 234, 237–38

Wilson definition of, 129

Quayle, Dan, 106, 108, 204, 205, 209, 213

Rabin, Yitzhak, 12

race

Brooke and, 312, 334, 342–56

Bush (G. W.) and, 410, 418, 419, 421, 423–24

Carter and, 77

Clinton and, 194, 203–204, 418

Democratic Party and, 68, 73, 285, 355

Giuliani and, 384–87, 401

Louisiana politics and, 109, 110, 113

Moynihan and, 288; 292–98, 302

Nixon and, 171, 177–78, 182

Roosevelt (T.) and, 48–49

school voucher support, 22n

Sharpton and, 395–96

Truman and, 61, 68

See also black militants; civil rights

racial violence, 203, 208, 348, 385, 390, 395, 396

racism, 48, 62, 99, 171, 194, 299–300, 334, 335, 337, 348

Duke and, 98–99, 107, 111–12

reverse, 203

radical, 26, 36, 128

Rangel, Charles, 87

reactionary, 128

Read, Ralph, 417

Reagan, Ronald, 3, 84, 188, 191, 195, 208,

278, 358, 381, 383, 384, 421, 423, 438

acceptance speech (1980), 93

"Big Tent" philosophy, 393, 425

Bush (G. W.) and, 442–43

Centrist presidential campaign strategy, 67, 73, 88–94

as conservative icon, 31, 76, 82, 87, 174, 175

as Democrat, 70, 82

Goldwater support by, 267, 276, 285

political polarization and, 13–14

Reagan Democrats, 31, 101, 189

Reform Party, 364, 366, 368, 372

Rehnquist, William, 278

Reinsch, J. Leonard, 150

religious right, 1, 8, 13, 201, 207–209, 212, 359, 366, 419

Bush (G. W.) and, 417, 420–23

as Carter supporters, 79, 82–83

Duke and, 112

as Reagan supporters, 89–90

Republican Revolution (1994), 14, 215, 391, 409, 417, 439

Reston, James, 7, 254, 286

Rhodes, James, 174

Rice, Condoleezza, 417

Richardson, Elliot, 337

RICO law, 384

Ridge, Tom, 423

Riis, Jacob, 123

Riordan, Richard, 397

Ripon Society, 342

Robertson, Pat, 8–9, 79, 208, 422

Robeson, Paul, 65

Robinson, Douglas, 41

Robinson, Jackie, 178

Rockefeller, Happy (Margaretta), 268, 269, 276–77

Rockefeller, Mary Todhunter Clark, 268

Rockefeller, Nelson, 24, 160, 174, 175, 180, 198, 264–86, 291, 354, 437

divorce/remarriage issue, 268–69, 271, 275, 276–77

as moderate, 219, 270–71, 279, 285–86

Rockwell, George Lincoln, 11, 345

Rodham, Hillary. See Clinton, Hillary Rodham

Roemer, Buddy, 31, 96–114

Roe v. Wade, 19, 416

Rogers, Will, Jr., 237

Romney, George, 174, 349

Roosevelt, Eleanor, 63n, 139

Roosevelt, Franklin Delano, 13, 31, 54, 58, 64, 68, 69, 93, 140, 148, 152, 156, 189, 242, 372

vice presidents, 30, 57, 63, 64

Warren and, 217–18, 226, 233

Wilson's legacy to, 116, 136

See also New Deal

Roosevelt, Franklin Delano, Jr., 146

Roosevelt, Kermit, 131

Roosevelt, Theodore, 24, 29–30, 33–55, 94, 123, 135, 149, 165, 252, 271n

Carter contrasted with, 75–76

Centrist themes, 35, 39, 45, 46, 47, 51, 54, 432–33

contemporary
Republican admirers
of, 381, 387, 411,
420, 423
Progressive candidacy,
33, 39, 53–54, 90,
121, 128, 129–34,
212, 441
on Wilson's success,
135
Roosevelt, Theodore, Sr.,
36, 37, 41
Root, Elihu, 49
Rose, James, 68
Ross, Leonora, 327
Rove, Karl, 198, 410–11
Royster, John, Jr.,
389–90
Rudman, Warren, 419
Rusk, Dean, 153
Russell, Bertrand, 157
Russell, Richard, 326

Sadat, Anwar, 12
Saltonstall, Leverett, 141,
320, 341, 346
Schlesinger, Arthur, Jr.,
11, 138, 145, 147,
149
school prayer, 20, 22,
340, 359
school vouchers, 22n
Schottland, Charles, 229
Schrank, John N., 55
Schwarzenegger, Arnold,
367, 446
Scot, Joe, 204
Scranton, William,
278–79, 280, 285
See It Now (television
program), 323
Senate, 441
Brooke's indepen-
dence in, 345–56
censure of McCarthy
by, 260, 318, 323
direct election of
members, 135
Jeffords's party switch
in, 442
Kennedy (J. F.) and,
139, 142, 143, 149
Kennedy (R. F.) and,
293–94, 309, 382

McCarthy's power in,
315–16, 322
Minnesota appointee,
371
Moynihan-Abzug pri-
mary, 288, 300–310
Nixon campaign vic-
tory for, 168
Smith's independence
in, 311, 315–31
September 11 attack,
442
extremism and, 8–9,
12, 434, 435, 438
Giuliani's response to,
313–14, 404–405
Sevareid, Eric, 274
Shakespeare, William,
398, 449
Sharpton, Al, 3, 8, 10,
395, 401, 402
Sheldon, Lou, 79
Sherry, Frank, 393
Siegel, Fred, 185
Siegel, Norman, 398,
401
"silent majority," 179,
297
Simon, Paul, 384
Sinatra, Frank, 146
Smith, Al, 144, 224
Smith, Bob, 416
Smith, Clyde, 319
Smith, Margaret Chase,
24, 311, 315–31,
378, 434
Declaration of
Conscience, 311,
316–19, 324,
329–31
Smith, "Sugar Jim," 125,
127
Snowe, Olympia, 331,
375
Social Security, 86, 182,
261, 415, 430
Sorensen, Ted, 141, 150
Souljah, Sister, 204, 418
South Carolina primary,
420–23
Soviet Union, 10, 12, 58,
65, 76, 383
arms race and, 148,
149, 321, 325

Cuban missile crisis
and, 158
fall of, 310
Ford's misstatement
on, 82
Wallace (H.) and,
64–65, 70
See also Cold War
Spanish-American War,
40
Stalin, Joseph, 6, 10, 12,
30, 58, 64, 65, 244,
289, 321
Stassen, Harold, 59, 248,
252
State Department, 139,
167, 242, 260, 311,
322
states' rights, 61, 219,
267, 277, 341
States' Rights Party. See
Dixiecrats
Stephanopoulos, George,
210
Stevens, Stuart, 410–11
Stevenson, Adlai, 6, 116,
139, 140, 145, 146,
153, 160, 254–58,
291, 325
Stone, Irving, 222
Sulzberger, Arthur
("Punch"), 308
Supreme Court, U.S.
antitrust ruling, 43n
church and state rul-
ings, 340
Goldwater's view of,
274, 278
Nixon nominees,
351–53
school vouchers rul-
ing, 22n
2000 election ruling,
430
Warren's chief justice-
ship, 223
Sutton, Percy, 302

Taft, Robert, 24, 59,
218, 241–58, 267,
323
Taft, William Howard,
52, 120, 128–32,
247, 250, 252

Tammany Hall, 37, 40, 290, 380–81
Teamsters, 384
Texas, 153, 252, 259
    Bush (G. W.) and, 407, 410, 430
    Kennedy (J. F.) threats in, 156, 160
third-way mayors, 313, 397
third world, 298, 299, 309
Thompson, Hunter S., 78–81
Thurmond, Strom, 57, 60, 62, 70, 72, 219, 267, 277, 281, 285, 356, 417, 439
Tillman, Benjamin ("Pitchfork"), 48
tolerance, 23
Tocqueville, Alexis de, 4
tort reform, 21
totalitarianism, 11
Treen, John, 99
"triangulation" strategy, 118, 154, 215
Truman, Bess, 56
Truman, Harry, 6, 24, 30, 56–74, 82, 136, 152, 189, 209, 220, 261, 289, 311, 320, 428
    Centrist theme, 433
    Eisenhower and, 242, 243, 245, 246, 247, 254, 257, 258
    "Give 'em Hell" persona, 57
    Kennedy (J. F.) distancing from, 140
    Korean War and, 253, 255, 257–58
    Marshall Plan and, 65, 167n
    McCarthy charges and, 311, 315, 321, 323
    National Convention speech, 63–69, 92
    upset victory, 73
Tsongas, Paul, 199–200, 355, 364, 373, 436

Tuchman, Barbara, 157, 158
Tuchman, Jessica, 158
Tyrrell, Emmett, 164
Tyson Foods, 195

United Nations, 136, 139, 153, 157, 163
    Moynihan and, 299–300, 304, 308
U.S. Steel, 43n, 155

Van Buren, Martin, 5
Vandenberg, Arthur, 74
Vardaman, James, 49
Ventura, Jesse, 16, 17, 313, 357, 358, 365–71, 440–41
Vermont, 442, 444
Vidal, Gore, 92
Vietnam War, 78, 199, 204, 273, 344, 345, 420–21, 424
    Democratic split over, 117, 172, 180
    McCain and, 411, 420–21
    Nixon and, 163, 173, 328
    Smith and, 325, 328
    See also antiwar movement
Volpe, John, 336, 337, 345
Voorhis, Jerry, 166, 167
voting age, 163, 182
Voting Rights Act, 171, 418, 439

Wagner, Robert, 290, 294
Wagner, Robert, Jr., 385
Walker, Jimmy, 381
Wallace, George, 3, 16, 81, 178, 180, 185, 194, 297, 312, 350, 358, 441
Wallace, Henry, 3, 16, 57, 62–65, 70, 73, 289, 312, 358, 441
Walters, Ronald, 203
Warren, Earl, 217, 222–40, 266, 276
Washington, Booker T., 48, 49

Washington, George, 1, 4, 243, 435
Watergate, 78, 177, 186, 300, 354, 359
Watsky, Steven, 99
Wattenberg, Ben, 300
Watts, J. C., 356, 417
Wayne, John, 276
Webb, U. S., 225
Webster, Daniel, 5
Wednesday Club, 352
Weicker, Lowell, 16, 313, 357, 359–65, 440
Welch, Robert, 267
welfare resentment, 107, 114
Wellesley College, 332–33
Wellstone, Paul, 370
West Virginia primary (1960), 145–46
Wherry, Kenneth, 244
Whitaker, John C., 171
White, Clifton, 272, 276
White, Kevin, 337
White, Michael, 397
White, Theodore, 176, 264, 268, 292, 341
White, William Allen, 38, 132
White Citizens Councils, 194
Whitman, Christie Todd, 423
Wicker, Tom, 266
Will, George, 14, 22, 381
Willis, Oliver, 442
Wilson, Ellen Axson, 122, 131
Wilson, James Q., 389
Wilson, Woodrow, 6, 54, 119–36, 140, 152, 165, 182, 218, 231, 350
    Centrist theme, 120–23, 129, 133, 135, 433
Wisconsin, 256
Wolf, Naomi, 414
Wolfe, Alan, 1, 23, 424
Woodworth, Roger, 339

workfare, 397
World War I, 136, 157
World War II, 11, 58,
    60–61, 136, 149,
    157, 166, 223, 241,
    334–35

bipartisanship and,
    226–31, 233
Eisenhower and, 242,
    250, 254–55
isolationists, 219, 242,
    250–51

Wright, Jim, 85

Yeats, W. B., 29, 32

Zionism, UN resolution
    on, 299

ABOUT THE AUTHOR

 **JOHN P. AVLON** is a columnist for the *New York Sun* and served as chief speechwriter and deputy communications director for Mayor Rudolph W. Giuliani. He is the president of Prides Crossing Executive Communication and worked on Bill Clinton's 1996 presidential campaign. His essay on the attacks of September 11—"The Resilient City," published in the anthology *Empire City: New York Through the Centuries*—won acclaim from Fred Siegel, author of *The Future Once Happened Here,* as "the single best essay written in the wake of 9/11." For further information or to contact the author, visit his website: www.IndependentNation.org.

973.9

BASEMENT